CREDITS

ANDROID SETTING CREATED BY Kevin Wilson and Daniel Lovat Clark

EDITOR Katrina Ostrander

WRITING & ADDITIONAL DEVELOPMENT Gary Astleford, Owen Barnes, Shawn Carman, Daniel Lovat Clark, Tim Cox, John Crowdis, John Dunn, Lisa Farrell, Jordan Goldfarb, Anthony Hicks, William H. Keith, Jason Marker, Mike Myler, Mel Odom, and Joe Sleboda with Lukas Litzsinger, Andrew Navaro, Sam Stewart, and Kirsten Zirngibl

ANDROID STORY TEAM Daniel Lovat Clark, Lukas Litzsinger, Katrina Ostrander, and Zoë Robinson

ANDROID STORY TEAM LEAD Michael Hurley

GRAPHIC DESIGN Michael Silsby with Shaun Boyke, Christopher Hosch, and Duane Nichols

GRAPHIC DESIGN MANAGER Brian Schomburg

ART DIRECTION Zoë Robinson

MANAGING ART DIRECTOR Andy Christensen

COVER ART David Auden Nash

PRODUCTION COORDINATION John Britton, Jason Glawe, and Johanna Whiting

PRODUCTION MANAGEMENT Megan Duehn and Simone Elliott

EXECUTIVE PRODUCER Michael Hurley

PUBLISHER Christian T. Petersen

Special thanks to Nayt Brooks, Kelly Hoffman, Tim Huckelbery, Matthew Ley, Connor Osgood, as well as David Preti and Renato Sasdelli for their expertise and insight into the not-too-distant future.

FANTASY FLIGHT GAMES

Fantasy Flight Games
1995 West County Road B2
Roseville, MN 55113
USA

ISBN: 978-1-63344-221-4   Product Code: NAD06

Printed in China

For more information about the world of *Android*, visit us online at

www.FantasyFlightGames.com

Lili Ibrahim

FOREWORD

The *Android* universe first started as a conversation in a van on the way home from a game convention with my friend and colleague Dan Clark. I had some rough ideas about a setting I wanted to pitch to Christian for a board game, but it was that conversation that crystalized those thoughts into what would later become the kernel of the setting. I wanted to do hard sci-fi—or at least use plausible science in the game. Ambitiously, Dan and I discussed a near future in the tradition of cyberpunk, where we could also address some of the current issues of our time such as the marginalization of the labor force and rising wealth inequality. I wanted to tackle some real, serious topics in the game in a way that I'd never attempted before.

At the idea's core were two competing corporations, both peddling a different form of artificial labor. On the one hand was Jinteki, a genetics company in the Eastern tradition selling cloned workers. Their logo was a bonsai, a tiny tree that's had its growth purposefully stunted for aesthetic reasons via careful pruning. That bit of quiet symbolism still pleases me today. On the other hand, Haas-Bioroid was a stolidly Western corporation, manufacturing robotic workers and keeping an eye firmly on the bottom line. They were cold steel and numbers as a foil to Jinteki's deep traditions and artistic perfectionism.

Caught between these two behemoths were the displaced workers. An angry, powerless mob of ordinary people forced out of their jobs by a series of technological breakthroughs. They had formed a group called Human First and used sledgehammers to attack the androids, both because the robotic workers were extremely durable, and because I wanted to create parallels to the tale of John Henry and the steam engine. The story of the man who would rather die than let a machine replace him is one of my long-time favorites, and if you look, you'll see that we ultimately named a line of mining clones in the setting after him. One of the murder suspects in the original board game, Mark Henry, is from that line of clones.

These three groups and the friction between them were the seed that everything else ultimately sprang from. Before I had thought of the Beanstalk or decided to put a colony on the Moon named after one of my favorite science fiction writers, there was this triad, with each group opposed to the other two. This appealed to me because although it was reminiscent of *Blade Runner*, an obvious influence on the setting, it went in a completely different direction with the same technology and allowed us to tell very different stories. *Android* was, at its core, a setting about vast economic forces filtered down to the level of a single individual.

For the rest of the trip, Dan and I invented and fleshed out the first of those individuals. Louis Blaine, the corrupt cop on the outs with his wife, was the original ANDROID character. Next was Raymond Flint, the private eye unlucky in love and still haunted by ghosts from the War. Many, many other characters have followed since, coming to life through the cards in ANDROID: NETRUNNER or within the pages of the *Android* novels. This universe has grown far beyond my original rough ideas, and I'm amazed and proud to watch it keep growing from that first tiny seed.

0010 1010

KEVIN WILSON, JULY 2015

Imaginary FSPte Ltd

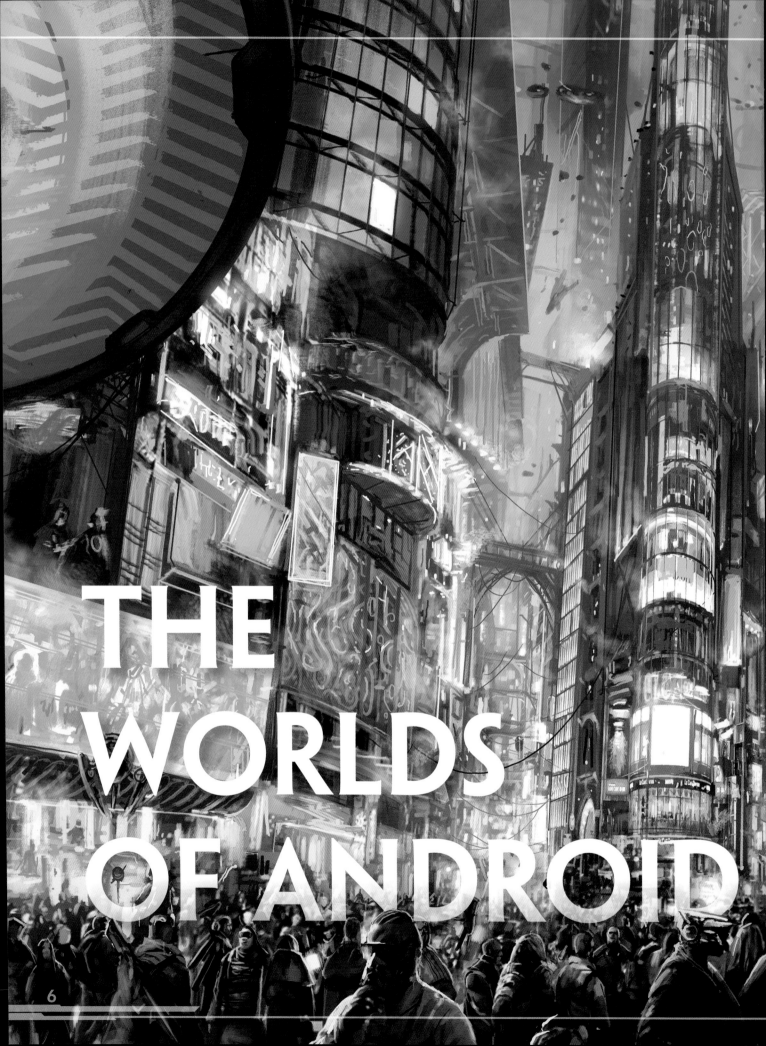

THE
WORLDS
OF ANDROID

INTRODUCTION

From the highest peak on the equator, at the heart of the greatest and worst city Earth has ever known, a nanolattice weave of carbon fibers stretches to the heavens: the Beanstalk. The giant space elevator transformed the solar system into a new frontier of opportunity. A city was built on the Moon, and Mars was colonized. Around the base of the Beanstalk grew the megapolis of New Angeles, officially home to half a billion people (and perhaps as many more unofficially), and the headquarters for the megacorporations that created the Network, the arcologies, and the androids.

Humans have come a long way since the dark ages. Cybernetic implants, gene therapy, and AI in every pocket ensure that life is pleasant, convenient, and long—for those who can afford it. But beneath the cracks in the veneer there's still poverty, crime, and war, and dozens of societal scapegoats.

Androids—intelligent synthetic lifeforms—walk the streets and work the jobs too dangerous or onerous for humans. They're taking away jobs from flesh-and-blood workers, redefining what it means to be rich and poor—even challenging the definition of what it means to be human. And there's more of them every year.

Mark Molnar

ARCHIVED MEMORIES

Can a machine think? Can it reason, compare, contrast, and respond? What are the parameters for true intelligence?

The first experiments with "thinking" machines were limited by how large a database the programmer could build for his "weak" artificial intelligence to reference. Such an AI was inherently flawed: it was unable to learn, adapt, or feel. All that changed with the discovery of brainmapping.

Brainmapping technology began with twenty-first century projects like the Human Brain Project and the BRAIN Initiative. The research overcame traditional limitations and enabled neuroscientists to map a human brain's physical structure, electrical impulses, and chemical changes in real time. Breakthrough technologies in supercomputer processing allowed this data to be compiled and emulated in a braintape, an incredibly complex digital model of a person's personality, skill set, and even memories. The process is not perfect, and producing exact copies is still out of reach, but every day the corps come a little closer.

Braintapes allowed far more advanced, or "strong," AI to evolve—AI that was capable of adapting to its environment and learning from experience. Haas-Bioroid discovered how to customize a braintape via neural channeling to create the complex behavioral programs utilized by a bioroid's optical brain. Nanobots can rewire the optical brain to learn and adapt like human brains can. Jinteki developed neural conditioning techniques by reverse engineering the braintape to stimulate the brain until it resembled the model. Cloned brains, as organic structures, retain the human brain's innate ability to create new neural connections without the need for nanobots.

Brainmapping and -taping services are available to those who can afford it. Many risties voluntarily have their minds "backed up" in the hopes that one day exact replicas will be possible. Megacorps lure others with huge incentives, licensing copies of the finest minds for their archives and product lines. Making copies without consent is illegal, but rumors of black-bag kidnappings and elite abduction teams abound.

SYNTHETIC LIFE

Android: "having the form of man." Science fiction made flesh. Are they humanity's greatest creation, or its grossest error? The answer depends on whom you ask. The only certainty is that androids are here now, and they are not about to go away.

Two distinct sub-types of android currently exist: the bioroid and the clone, manufactured exclusively by Haas-Bioroid and Jinteki respectively. Other companies such as CyberSolutions and Al-Jazari Android have also tried to create versions and subtypes of their own, but only Haas-Bioroid and Jinteki have successfully implemented braintapes to create true artificial intelligences.

Bioroids are thinking machines; their robotic bodies house complex optical brains and quantum processors. Although many bioroid models possess a covering of synthetic skin, common features like silver eyes and cabling at joints mean no one would ever confuse a bioroid for an actual person. Clones, however, look almost human. Grown in specialized vats, a clone only differs from a true human by the bar code printed on its neck. Many humans are discomfited by the semblance of humanity presented by clones and synthskin bioroids, so both Jinteki and Haas-Bioroid take great pains to mitigate this so-called "uncanny valley" effect.

Androids exist everywhere in society, from the bioroid waiters in high-class restaurants to the clone miners in the helium-3 strip mines on Luna. Anywhere there's a job that needs doing, there seems to be an android to perform it. However, humanity still dominates fields such as the arts, research and development, and corporate leadership and decision making. No one is quite willing to let an android decide the fate of a corporation worth billions—not yet—but androids easily fill out low-level positions like accountants, clerks, and receptionists, not to mention manual labor and high-risk jobs. This proliferation of androids, coupled with the lower costs of maintaining android staff over human workers, has led to a sharp divide in opinion over these "labor solutions."

With more and more people being put out of work by android replacements, a growing sense of dissatisfaction has swelled into outright hostility toward androids. The lobbyist organization Humanity Labor and the radical group Human First have capitalized on these attitudes and seek to limit or outlaw the spread of simulant labor.

Attacks against androids are not considered a high priority by many law enforcement agencies. Because they are manufactured synthetically, androids are classified as property, not people, so any violence inflicted on them is mere vandalism, not assault or murder. However, this has not stopped simulant rights groups like the Liberty Society from trying to get androids recognized as true human beings in the eyes of the law and society. Unfortunately for them, both Haas-Bioroid and Jinteki have a stake in maintaining their bottom line, and by extension, the status quo.

Anders Finer

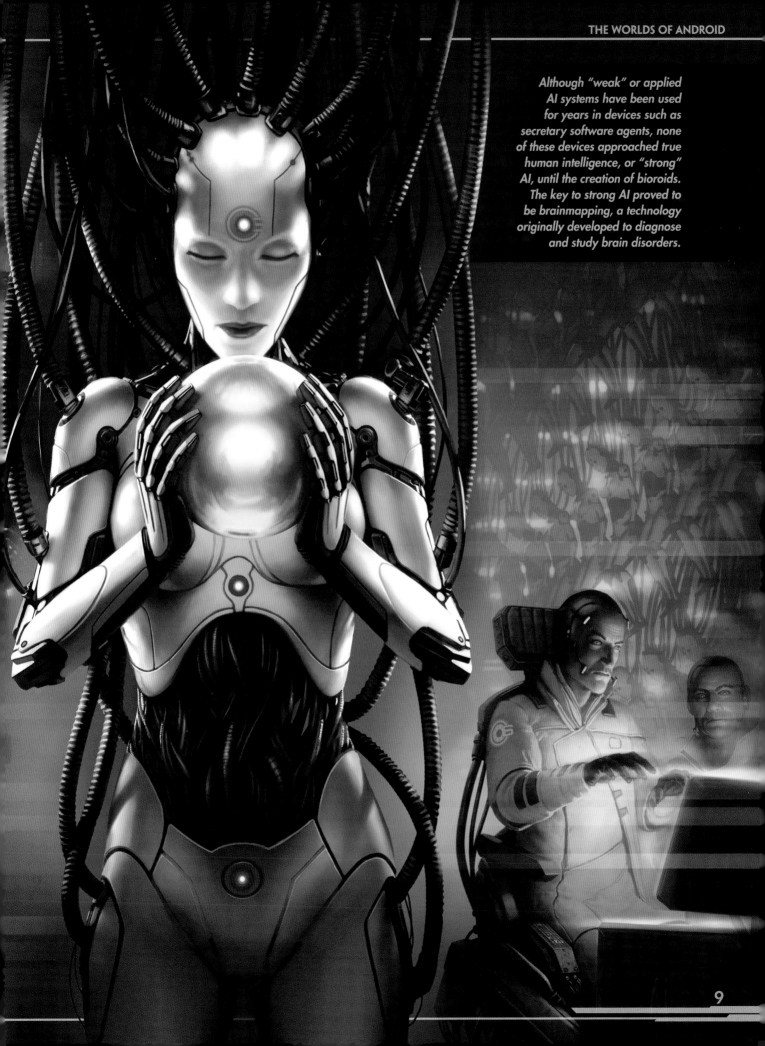

Although "weak" or applied
AI systems have been used
for years in devices such as
secretary software agents, none
of these devices approached true
human intelligence, or "strong"
AI, until the creation of bioroids.
The key to strong AI proved to
be brainmapping, a technology
originally developed to diagnose
and study brain disorders.

ENGINEERING THE FUTURE

A world leader in android design and manufacture, Haas-Bioroid is one of the most powerful and well-known corporations in the world. Its bioroids are a modern feat of engineering and design that seamlessly blends man and machine.

In its early days, Haas Industrie was a robotics, cybernetics, and heavy manufacturing concern based in Europe. When the Rossum Group made its first breakthroughs on what would one day become the technology for neural channeling, Haas Industrie was quick to snap it up. Following this acquisition, the company achieved amazing leaps in computational neuroscience technology that allowed for the creation of the first androids. With the launch of its flagship product, bioroids, the company re-branded itself as Haas-Bioroid.

The first bioroids to step off the production line were primitive compared to those manufactured today, but Haas-Bioroid never stopped innovating. No firm has managed to replicate HB's proprietary braintaping and neural channeling techniques to produce a competing bioroid product.

As businesses capitalize on the efficiency of androids, demand for high-quality and affordable labor solutions has skyrocketed—HB's economic and political clout have also risen exponentially. Its patented designs, bleeding-edge tech, and massive production infrastructure allows it to negotiate the most lucrative contracts. Whether it is a legion of garbage collection and disposal models for a city government, a sophisticated personal secretary for an international head of state, or simply a loyal housekeeper and companion for a lonely billionaire, Haas-Bioroid can mass-produce or custom-tailor bioroids to suit any need or budget, all while turning a profit.

Under the ruthless leadership of Director Cynthia Haas, HB aggressively competes with rival corps by purchasing controlling shares in smaller businesses and directing their research in HB's favor. Rumors circulate of kidnapped CEOs who are "rescued" by prisec teams once certain business negotiations are complete

Haas-Bioroid's success has been seen by many corporations as a threat. Jinteki directly competes with HB as the provider of the other half of the labor solutions market. Tales of corporate sabotage, espionage, and wetwork run in the screamsheets with regularity despite the efforts of both corporations' PR departments. The fight over new technologies has inflamed tensions, and few believe Haas-Bioroid will let its rivals hold the upper hand for long.

Dmitry Prosvirnin

*T*he crime scene was chaotic: a riot of blood, street trash, and bodies. Floyd 2X3A7C's sensor suite swept the scene, parsing all at once the individual blood spatter patterns, the cooling IR traces drifting from the corpses, and the distinct chemical formula of human sweat, urine, and pheromones that combined to spell fear and death. His quantum computer instantly tracked the disparate sources and cross-referenced them with the central database back at NAPD headquarters.

Three victims, two male and one female, various races; ages vary from late teens to mid-thirties. Preliminary examination suggests blunt force trauma as cause of death. Low-spec vidcam mounted on wall, broken, no debris in vicinity suggests it was broken prior to the events under investigation. Witnesses unlikely, given neighborhood; check with attending officers for confirmation.

"Hey, Floyd."

Floyd shifted a portion of his processing power, bringing the source of the voice into focus.

Detective Mateo Jiménez, New Angeles Police Department, homicide division two years, patrol officer four years prior. Adequate arrest and case closure record. No disciplinary charges or internal investigations. A "good cop" by human standards. Elevated heart rate, nervous disposition. He is uncomfortable with my presence—likely uncomfortable around all bioroids. Add to personnel files.

"Forspec is still thirty minutes away, but I figure now that you're here we could do a prelim. What d'you think?"

"It would be my pleasure, Detective Jiménez," said Floyd, stepping through the blinking yellow holo crime scene barrier. He approached the nearest body, which was splayed out on the ground with its limbs twisted into unnatural angles. This man must have died in great pain. Floyd stepped carefully around the blood pool as his sensor suite picked out the low-velocity impact spatter and cast-off patterns around the body. Floyd initiated a reconstruction subroutine, instantly forming a picture of the impact points from the blood spatter. All signs pointed to a single assailant.

Victim is Robert Wong, employed by Gwangju as a sales associate, showroom address on file. Numerous arrests; assault, possession with intent to supply, destruction of property—

Destruction of property was the charge given to any attack against an android, a reminder that bioroids and clones are, at best, legally property. Floyd ran the name against the NAPD database of known Human First activists and found a match in seconds. Floyd's sensors had already pinpointed the location of several small pieces of bioroid chassis and a moderate amount of bright blue coolant had pooled near the location where Floyd believed the altercation had begun. Worryingly, the coolant lacked any of the normal radioactive tracing agent used by HB to identify its bioroids.

During the three or four seconds that passed while Floyd considered the possibilities, Jiménez's eyes didn't leave his.

"Something wrong, Floyd?" he asked.

"Have either you or any of the attending officers removed anything from the scene, Detective?"

Jiménez made a face. "Shit Floyd, of course not. We're not yellow jacket amateurs. No one's even crossed the perimeter except you and me. Why? What makes you think something's missing?"

"There is evidence to suggest a bioroid was damaged here, possibly even destroyed here. Perhaps you or your men removed the remains in an effort to 'spare my feelings.' I assure you, no such effort is necessary."

Detective Jiménez scowled. "No, there was no bioroid here when we secured the scene, and even if there had been, I wouldn't be so stupid as to contaminate an active crime scene because I thought a golem might have feelings! Give me some credit, Floyd."

"I apologize, Detective."

Floyd crossed the crime scene and knelt beside a sledgehammer that lay in the middle of the alley.

"Preliminary analysis suggests this is the murder weapon. Although a more thorough test would be required for confirmation, my software shows all three victims' blood on the hammerhead. Furthermore, the spatter, wounds, and placement of the bodies indicates a struggle with a single assailant."

Jiménez gave a low whistle. "You're saying one guy did all this? One guy takes out three Human First pendejos with their own sledgehammer? These guys aren't exactly noted for their pleasant demeanors and willingness to lie down in a fight."

Floyd crossed the crime scene to stand next to a particularly pronounced splash of blood.

"The assailant was clearly heavily augmented," he said. "Most likely he possessed one or more cybernetic limbs, boosted reflexes, and sub-dermal armor. Although I cannot be certain at this juncture, the evidence suggests all the blood at the scene comes from the two dead males and one female."

"What about the bioroid parts? Could a golem have done this?" asked Jiménez.

Floyd looked at him, "The First Directive prohibits a bioroid from harming a human. That protocol overrides all other subroutines, including those for self-defense or carrying out instructions. This is most likely the work of an augmented human."

Floyd's sensors had scanned the blood pool again during the exchange. Something contradicted his theory, and now a lingering doubt was worming its way into his logic processes.

"Fine, fine," said Jiménez. "So, three Human First members pick a fight with a 'borg who proceeds to beat them to death with their sledgehammer, all the while not taking even a single hit."

In the center of the blood pool lay a piece of twisted plastic; Floyd recognized it immediately as part of bioroid torso. A support strut, found between the shoulder

Clark Huggins

and base of the neck to be precise, equivalent to a human collarbone.

"Floyd? Is that what happened? Floyd!"

The plastic lay on top of the blood; other than a little splash back, the piece was clean, which meant it must have fallen onto the blood pool. An unexpected subroutine blossomed in Floyd's mind, and he was immediately connected to Director Haas's private terminal.

"Floyd? Are you even listening to me? Are you saying this was a cyborg or not?"

Floyd turned to look at Detective Jiménez. "I apologize, Detective. I am unable to adequately process your query."

"Something wrong, Floyd?"

INFINITE FRONTIERS

Bioroids have become a permanent fixture in our society. They can be found working and existing—some might even say "living"—across every industry in every major city in every nation on every world inhabited by human beings.

Introduced some twenty years ago thanks to the breakthrough work on neural channeling, the bioroid swiftly grabbed the public's attention. Here was a thinking, rational machine—a true AI housed in a robotic body. Almost immediately, opinion on bioroids divided sharply: some people feared and mistrusted them, others embraced this stunning advancement of human achievement, and a third

group felt humanity had finally gone too far. As bioroids became increasingly prevalent, those opinions crystallized into distinct social and political groups, each determined to prove the others wrong, often by violent and destructive means. So far, the bioroid has endured and become one of the single most recognizable features of modern life.

Modern bioroids still follow the same basic template as their early forebears. A complex optical network simulating a human connectome is linked to a more standard quantum computer system. Together, they form the bioroid's brain and allow it to think and learn in a fash-

ion very similar to a human. A combination titanium-polycarbonate chassis houses the brain, forming the core of the bioroid. Most often these chassis take a humanoid shape; although models of differing physiques do exist, these are mostly designed for use in extreme environments or for specific tasks where only two arms or legs might be a detriment.

In recent years, bioroid designers have begun experimenting with increasingly human-seeming bioroids, such as the Adonis and Eve models, but most bioroids avoid the so-called "uncanny valley" effect by not trying to seem too human in the first place. HB's engineers implemented a num-

Magali Villeneuve

ber of features to give bioroids a robotic feel, the most notable of which are the gaps in the synthskin that expose the metal beneath. Such design considerations allow humans to interact with bioroids without feeling like they are in the presence of anything other than a machine.

There are hundreds of unique bioroid models, each of which is custom designed to fulfill one or more functions. Some bioroid models were developed to perform menial and manual labor, to act as chauffeurs and serve as bodyguards. Others

excel in high-risk fields where human life would otherwise be in danger, such as the Steiger miners or Rex search-and-rescue models. There are even bioroid models that fill roles requiring skilled laborers or advanced education, such as the Alix model of investors and financiers. Even more traditionally biological professionals—such as those in the oldest profession—can be replaced by bioroids, as the Adonis and Eve models prove.

With recent advancements in brain-mapping, increasingly sophisticated models are entering the market, including the prototypes Floyd 2X3A7C and Drake 3GI2RC assigned to the New Angeles Police Department. NBN has commissioned specialized actroid models, which have appeared in award-winning films and the hit show *Friendship, Upgraded*. As this surge continues, many experts are asking how long will it be before the first bioroid politicians or CEOs appear.

It is a question that many are unable to answer without some trepidation.

PERSONAL EVOLUTION

When you need the human touch, Jinteki is there. In contrast to the stiff, mechanical, and unfeeling androids produced by Haas-Bioroid, Jinteki's clones look and feel human while representing the best that humanity has to offer. Clones are Jinteki's answer to the labor solutions market, one that will ultimately lead to the betterment of mankind as a whole.

Jinteki started as a biotechnology firm in NeoTokyo focused on developing life in all its myriad forms. Its earliest products included replacement and augmentative tissues and organs that could save lives and enhance quality of life for millions of individuals, a mission that is continued at Harmony Medtech branches across the globe today. Jinteki's roots in traditional Japanese management culture and business practices enabled the company to grow and succeed in its first phase of development. At the same time, Jinteki's leadership recognized that the world continues to rapidly change and that evolution is necessary for progress.

In its second phase of development, comprising the last thirty years or so, Jinteki has continued to be at the forefront of scientific breakthroughs; its genegineers found ways to leverage nature's own processes at an accelerated pace, developing materials and techniques in a matter of years, not eons. Jinteki outcompeted many rival companies and was the first to create a fully functional, organic android. As a lab technician at Jinteki's Osaka division, a young Satoshi Hiro had a hand in the breakthrough that enabled clones to be grown in vats in a fraction of the time it took for normal humans to mature. Iterations on this technology have unlocked manifold possibilities beyond mere humans or animals, including the Hachi-Inu K8 model employed by the New Angeles Police Department.

Different markets require specialized approaches, and Jinteki encourages its local divisions to customize their product offerings to suit every region and capitalize upon all opportunities. In Biotech Valley, Jinteki continues its research and development objectives at the Garden by harvesting the best and brightest minds from the University of the Californias campuses. Pālanā Foods in Mumbad feeds one of the largest countries on Earth with its g-modded superfoods and towering agroplexes. Unique

environmental conditions in the Heinlein colony domes permit extraordinary advances in radiation- and vacuum-resistant life-forms, including the impressive Turtleback line. Regardless of whether they work on Earth, Luna, or Mars, Jinteki employees remain steadfastly loyal to the company's leaders, its principles, and its bottom line.

Jinteki promotes positive business relationships with any other corps in need of a more human android. NBN and Jinteki continue to work together to produce the next batch of supermodels, celebrities, and associated merchandise. The Miranda Rhapsody-fronted brand Re-Water is enhanced with a special blend of patented nutrients to give anyone a little extra glitz and glamour like the youthful sensie star. Out of this world, the Weyland Consortium has licensed specialized clone models to service and maintain the Beanstalk, and the Henry line is ubiquitous at Melange Mining operations across the lunar surface. Jinteki's rivalry with Haas-Bioroid has taken center stage within the NAPD, where detectives Caprice Nisei and Floyd 2X3A7C compete to become the agency's next line of defense in reducing crime in the largest city in the solar system.

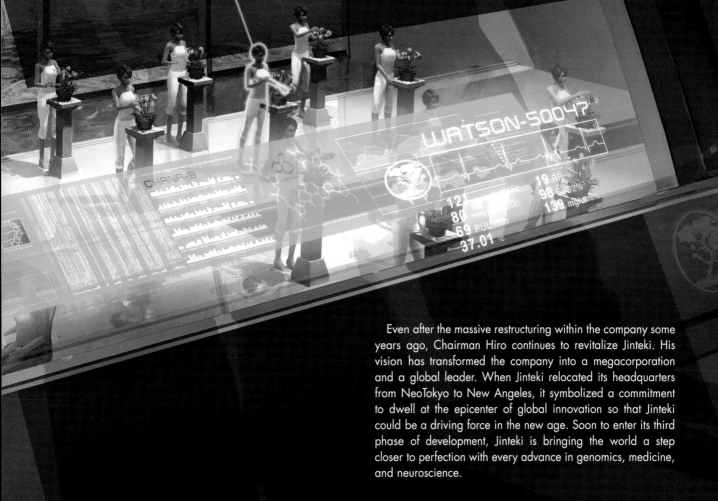

Even after the massive restructuring within the company some years ago, Chairman Hiro continues to revitalize Jinteki. His vision has transformed the company into a megacorporation and a global leader. When Jinteki relocated its headquarters from NeoTokyo to New Angeles, it symbolized a commitment to dwell at the epicenter of global innovation so that Jinteki could be a driving force in the new age. Soon to enter its third phase of development, Jinteki is bringing the world a step closer to perfection with every advance in genomics, medicine, and neuroscience.

Ben Zweifel

17

Somewhere, birds were singing. Hiro came to a stop at the peak of the arching wooden bridge, and listened. He didn't recognize the birdsong, being no expert on birds, and he looked for a time for the source of the music. He saw nothing. The trilling notes were artificial, along with everything else.

The garden rambled around him; stone-lined paths led to and from the bridge. Red-leafed Japanese maples rose to his right, green-needled cedar trees to his left. Grasses, shrubs, and plants of a thousand descriptions surrounded him in meticulous order. Throughout, metal and plastic pillars rose, powerful quantum supercomputers and server rigs

humming within them. Above, curving metal beams supported the transplas roof. An apt metaphor for Jinteki itself, he thought. Archaic traditions failing to conceal the future.

Hiro studied the space, estimating distances as he resumed his walk. So much space for ventilation, space for technicians to access the servers, at least two more additional floors… We could fit at least five times the computing power in this space, he concluded. If we were willing to cut away the deadwood of the past.

Kyuzu-sama was waiting for him on a bench. The old man was smiling, his white hair an unruly cloud behind his head. A Tanaka clone stood nearby,

ready to attend to Kyuzu-sama's every need, while one of his identical brothers pruned the bushes not far away.

"Ah, Chairman," Kyuzu said, pushing himself to his feet with an ivory-headed cane. "I was just thinking how splendid it is that this space exists, that it can be such a harmonious blend of utility and grace. Servers require ventilation and cooling. Humans require gardens. Why not do both at once?" He bowed stiffly, leaning on the cane, and Hiro did the same.

"It is so like you, Kyuzu-sama, to see things in the best possible light," said Hiro.

They walked together, crossing another wooden footbridge. Their feet

and Kyuzu's cane knocked hollowly on the surface. There is no reason to make the bridge from wood, *Hiro thought. A plastic could work as well, be more durable, cheaper.* They came to a stop at some wordless agreement, gazing down into an ink-black pool where multicolored koi drifted in and out of sight. *Still, a thing is not useless just because it is old. Kyuzu-sama is an ancient relic, but without his support I would never have become Chairman.*

Across the still pond, a human technician tended to one of the server pillars, swiping through virt displays with one hand while the other reached inside the machine. *Why a human technician? Why not have a clone do that job? It takes decades to train someone for this* task, but a clone could be grown for the purpose in weeks. "We must always innovate," he said. "Our purpose is not to walk the path laid down before, but to create a new one."

"Quite right," said Kyuzu. "But it is that path that has led us to this point, I think. And once the new path is created, well, then it's all the same road, is it not?" He planted his cane and turned his face toward the sun shining through the ceiling. His cybernetic eyes, Hiro noted, darkened in the sunlight. "How valuable to have a trusted director in Sakai-buchou," mused the old man. "I know how you value honesty and skill more than loyalty or seniority. You must find his willingness to oppose you a refreshing change."

Hiro turned away, hiding his face lest it betray him. *Toshiyuki Sakai? Opposing me? But why warn me?* "Sakai-buchou remains among our most adequate senior executives," Hiro said. "Perhaps, in a different world, he might have been Chairman rather than me."

"In a different world, Chairman, old men like me would be dead, not sitting on a board of directors. Waiting for an old man to die is no longer an adequate method of career advancement." Kyuzu turned again, to shuffle slowly away. "Now, Chairmen are replaced whenever a replacement is needed, rather than when they retire. A wise policy, that which gave you your position."

And could take it away again.

REPLICATING PERFECTION

Jinteki owns the patent on the technology behind clones: biological androids tailor-made by its genengineers. Clones seem identical to normal humans in appearance, and their genomes are largely identical as well. These organic androids are more personable and sympathetic than the robotic bioroids built by Haas-Bioroid.

Early cloning experiments involved work with simple organisms, such as plants. The more difficult task of growing animal tissues in vitro was first realized when a sheep was successfully cloned in the waning days of the twentieth century. From there, the leap from clones of animals to clones of humans was a straightforward one, scientifically speaking, but significant challenges lay in the ethical conundrums raised by many groups—particularly religious ones—about the use of human tissues. Legislative battles waged over decades determined who owned proprietary DNA sequences and also settled who held the legal rights to organisms created within laboratories, regardless of their biological ancestry. A consensus emerged that balanced the right of the individual to own his or her own genome with the ability of corporations to profitably exploit the new technologies.

Even with these issues resolved, there remained technical hurdles to turning cloning into big business. Growing an adult organism in an economical time frame was the most significant. The secret seemed to lie in the development of an artificial womb system and tissue stabilization technology. Now, Jinteki's patented processes enable a clone to be grown from fertilization to matura-

relatively inexpensive...

tion in mere weeks. Although the bioroid had already reached the market, clones quickly claimed a significant portion of the market for themselves. In recent years, clones represent an increasingly important part of the global economy, both through their creation and in the work they perform.

Clones are relatively inexpensive to synthesize, which makes them cheaper to lease from Jinteki than it would be to pay workers over the long term, and they are easy to replace when they have incurred damage or outlived their usefulness, with no insurance payouts required. Clone lines are designed to work in a broad range of different environments and can learn to perform any task that the human brain can master—and even some tasks that exceed human capabilities. Through neural conditioning techniques, clones are prepared for their responsibilities from the time they are decanted, but they remain capable of learning new techniques as necessary. Clones are inherently adaptable and intuitive, just like real people, and they can easily establish empathy with real humans if the nature of their work warrants it.

Popular clone models, including the Henry and Tenma lines, are immediately recognizable by their stature or style. Clone models from a common line are physically identical specimens, with the only exceptions being due to damage and modifications imparted through use. Often, clone lines also wear characteristic styles of dress that are in keeping with their standard responsibilities, such as a green jumpsuit for Henrys or a tailored suit for Tenmas. As a result, clones are sometimes impossible to tell apart without up-close examination.

Under laboratory conditions, clones are quickly identified using a combination of genetic and physiological markers. Some of these are deliberately encrypted for the purposes of recognizing DNA piracy, but other markers are left behind as part of the process of genetic engineering. In normal day-to-day life, however, clones are identified by a distinctive tattoo on the back of their necks coupled with a sub-dermal ID chip. Each code is unique to the individual, so law enforcement organizations use the tags to identify ownership, often to report the recovery or loss of a clone. Although some corporations and individuals can afford to outright purchase their own custom clones, Jinteki retains the ownership of many clones and liaises with law enforcement when necessary.

...easy to replace

Mark Molnar

THE WORLD IS YOURS

NBN puts the world at your fingertips no matter whether you're looking for the best deals on your favorite brands, breaking news from around the worlds, the latest sensie star gossip, or the limitless content on the Network.

NBN looks very similar to its predecessor megacorp, Vertex, having slowly but steadily remerged with or acquired its competitors and cousin companies under President of the Board Keith Randolph Kane. Over the years the corp has been known as the Network Broadcast News, Net Broadcast Network, or Near-Earth Broadcast Network, but the megacorp is now simply called NBN. The company was long headquartered in the Los Angeles District of SanSan, but after the construction of the Beanstalk, NBN quickly relocated to New Angeles to establish itself as the sole

Net provider for the Beanstalk and the megacity at large. NBN's new headquarters in the Rutherford District, with its endless mediafeeds scrolling across jumbo virt displays and a continuous stream of tourists, has become known as Broadcast Square and is considered the beating heart of New Angeles itself.

More than half of the top-rated content streams across the Earth, Moon, and Mars are produced by NBN. The media megacorp produces the best in threedee and simsensie entertainment. With studios like Haarpsichord producing critically acclaimed reality programming and blockbuster filmies year after year, Old Hollywood continues to serve as the epicenter of the film industry. Even the venerable newsrag

company the *New Angeles Sol* was recently added to NBN's massive news media portfolio. Despite her nominal status as an independent journalist, the *Sol*'s Lily Lockwell is the voice and face of NBN for its subscribers. Strong AI allows NBN to custom-tailor its news for the viewer, translating in real-time and micro-targeting content to pertain directly to its users' lives.

NBN's unsurpassed marketing knowhow and targeted psychographic algorithms help consumers make the choices they need to streamline their lives and get the most for their credits. The megacorp's own Spark Agency is an advertising giant that handles huge media campaigns for YucaBean, Armitage, Blue Sun, Harmony

Medtech, and many other corporations large and small. Spark is the master of image—the maven of the glam and glitz of the world of promotion—and the success or failure of lesser corporations has ridden on the effectiveness of its marketing campaigns. Even the Moon has become a massive advertising platform, reaching billions from halfway around the globe.

SYNC, another NBN subsidiary, is synonymous with the Network itself, having created the secure universal gateway protocols used by almost every device on the planet to com-municate with the Network, from PADs to products to infrastructure and beyond. Its satellite networks are the largest in the world and are supplemented with millions of miles of fiber-optic cable to grant customers access to the easy and convenience of modern life. Some critics claim NBN collects and uses the massive amounts of data at its disposal to spy on its customers and even sells personal information and activity to repressive regimes. But most people would never trade the customization and personalization of media content and productivity applications only possible thanks to SYNC's ubiquity and NBN's analytics.

Under the savvy leadership of model-turned-media mogul and CEO Victoria Jenkins, NBN uses its extensive market knowledge to forecast into the future, and the prospects are bright for the multimedia empire. The mega-hit multimedia universe *Sunshine Junction* is pioneering the future of edutainment and youth programming—its lovable characters can be found in most New Angelino homes. Millions of children log into its servers every day to interact with and learn from their favorite members of the *Champions of the Challenge Zone* cast in their virtual world. From the frontiers of space to the edges of the Network, NBN is dedicated to serving all of your information needs.

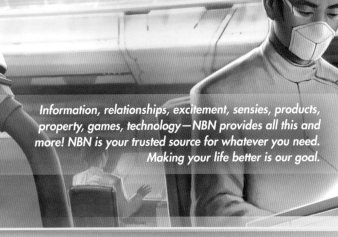

Information, relationships, excitement, sensies, products, property, games, technology—NBN provides all this and more! NBN is your trusted source for whatever you need. Making your life better is our goal.

No Human Resources stack had four layers of ice this thick or this black. It was the virtual equivalent of walking to the bodega for a case of beer and getting ripped to shreds by a pack of hellion-bots. Noise knew what he was doing, though, and that knowledge was the only thing that had saved him so far. If it got any worse, he'd need to drop carrier and turn into the invisible man for a few days.

The first layer of ice had been easy. He'd peeled it away and moved further in, his icebreaker tugging at his brain like an insistent child that wouldn't let go of his hand in an amusement park. Of course, this wasn't the carousel outside the Vendigo Arcology, and his copy of Femme Fatale wasn't a whiny broad looking for a cheap thrill. This was a Haas-Bioroid server, slick with defenses, and Femme was a bleeding-hot piece of illicit code with just enough AI to have her own attitude.

HB was one of the Big Four, sure, but they didn't stack up four layers of the world's deadliest ice to keep people away from secondary employee records. His only reason for making the run in the first place was to break in, promote the lowliest employees to executive positions, and simultaneously demote HB's most venomous executives to little more than piss boys.

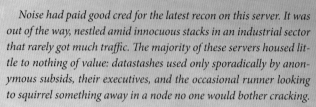

Noise had paid good cred for the latest recon on this server. It was out of the way, nestled amid innocuous stacks in an industrial sector that rarely got much traffic. The majority of these servers housed little to nothing of value: datastashes used only sporadically by anonymous subsids, their executives, and the occasional runner looking to squirrel something away in a node no one would bother cracking.

He thought it was strange that good ol' HB would bother with such a ruse. Recon reports—expensive recon reports—indicated the server was little more than a secondary storage bin containing a backup of HB's human resources data. It should've been easy to bust through the ice, change some data around, and then schedule a remote update of HQ's central files. Noise figured he might even dig up records of an embarrassing PIP in one or two exec files that his news-nosie contacts could turn into an exposé.

The fourth layer of ice dropped away, shattering like glass and scattering in all directions. Back in his loft, Noise gave a sigh of relief. He pressed on—after all, he'd gotten this far. Not to mention, he was having fun, dammit. Runs for scrubs were boring and tedious in their simplicity, and Noise was one of the best jocks on the circuit. He was earning his credits for a change and that was worth taking a risk this big. Whatever HB had locked up in this remote dustbin had better be worth it, but even if it wasn't, it was entertaining.

The server burst open and raw data rushed at Noise like a tsunami of light. His guts twisted sickeningly for an instant before his filter programs kicked in and began organizing the information. Time appeared to slow as the data methodically coalesced around him. It was an entrancing, almost euphoric experience, which also made it dangerous. Spend too much time gawking, Noise knew, and you were chum for killer ice. He put Femme on standby in order to devote more cycles to his search bots, and she sighed unhappily. "Deal with it, sister," he said, and she fixed him with an irritated glance before she vanished in a whiff of perfume.

Seconds ticked into minutes without his searchers finding anything useful or interesting, and Noise grew frustrated, then nervous. He was about to ditch everything when one of his subroutines returned a vidfile. A quick secscan revealed nothing dangerous, so he opened it.

Images of a hallway, strewn with bodies, their faces hidden by armored visors. Something passed over them, a lithe humanoid shape of dubious gender with long hair, moving faster than any human had a right to move. Then Noise smelled smoke—burning insulation, melting solder—and his heart rate soared. A virus hidden in the vidfile that had evaded his initial secscan had already done its work.

"Frag!" Noise cursed as the vidscreen dissolved along with the grainy image of the body-laden hallway. He thumbed his carrier stud, but it was too late. He was back in the loft, his console smoldering, his signal likely traced to within three meters of his present location. It was time to clear out and go to ground before Haas-Bioroid's wetwork team arrived and flatlined him for good.

Left: Anna Christenson, Right: Matt Zeilinger

THE NETWORK

The Network permeates every facet of daily life, connecting people to the things around them and to each other in a grand symphony of instantaneous data and analysis. Thanks to the machine-to-machine communication technologies implemented and safeguarded by SYNC, megacities like New Angeles are networked together to coordinate transportation, sanitation, utilities, and more. Municipalities and businesses alike use weak and strong AI to interpret massive datasets and help them best reach and service their citizens and customers.

At the consumer level, individuals rely on their personal access devices (PADs) to get the latest information on their health and habits, or to keep up with their friends and favorite celebrities around the worlds. They depend on their PADs to wake them up on time in the morning, and they fall asleep watching the endless mediafeeds and content streams supplied by NBN. Thanks to the solar system–wide reach of Network, life has never been easier, more convenient, more customizable, or more efficient.

Despite the usefulness of the near-infinite amount information collected and dispersed by NBN and its subsids, neoluddites, *disenfrancistos*, and off-gridders eschew this connected life. Escaping the reach of the Network is close to impossible, however, and privacy advocates warn that users have already handed over a complete picture of their personal lives to be used—and exploited—by the megacorps and repressive regimes.

The corps that control the Network have used the datastreams of information on every person and every thing to generate massive revenues, and they funnel very little of their profits to the masses who live outside of their pristine and immaculate world. The lure of taking a slice of the corps' massive economic pie or the desire to fight back against the mass surveillance and economic inequality has pushed some—known as "runners"—to take matters into their own hands.

Runners are considered rebels at best and terrorists at worst. These technology aficionados abuse and exploit brain-machine interface technology to access and override secured parts of the Network while in a fully immersed state. They drive an illicit economy of their own hidden far beneath what is visible to the average user. Whether they are ruthless criminals or sociopathic antiheroes, these virtual desperadoes embrace a paradigm that hearkens back to the free-wheeling times before the creation of the Network.

SYNC would have its subscribers believe that the Network is the only one of its kind, safe and secure from outside threats, but another network exists beyond its purview. Known as the Shadow Net, this hidden system serves as a meeting place for individuals and groups seeking to undermine the laws that govern data and intellectual property. While part of the Shadow Net is hidden deep beneath the infrastructure of the Network itself, a large portion is temporary, ad hoc, and ever changing. Peer-to-peer networks encompass some of the Shadow Net, too, their signals coming and going as their owners please.

Such freedom comes with a cost. Although the megacorps know the Shadow Net exists, they're never entirely sure where it is or how it can be accessed. Its access points are constantly discovered, but these vanish as quickly as they appear; great efforts are taken to hide them from corporate eyes. Even if it were to be destroyed—a nearly impossible feat given how compartmentalized it is—the Shadow Net would only be reborn anew.

THE CITY THAT NEVER STOPS

New Angeles is the biggest and grandest, richest and poorest, most splendid and most awful city in the entire world. It sprawls over sixty thousand square kilometers, covering most of what used to be the coast of Ecuador and marching up into the Andes near Quito and surrounding Volcán Cayambe, where the Beanstalk is tethered. The land area was leased from Ecuador first as a small patch by the Weyland Consortium, and then as a larger swath by the United States while the Space Elevator transitioned from fantasy to reality. The region was initially called the Special Economic Zone of Ecuadorian New Los Angeles, a name that lasted maybe ten minutes before being cut down to "New Angeles" by everyone involved.

As the home to the New Angeles Space Elevator, New Angeles is the Earth's port city. Everything that goes up or comes down the Beanstalk passes through New Angeles, which makes the city rich. It also means that the megapolis is among the most diverse in the world, with people from every nation and ethnicity on the planet thronging its plazas and slidewalks. There are many Ecuadorians—or expatriate Ecuadorians, as the case may be—but most of the city's wealth and power is concentrated in the hands of megacorps whose founders' and employees' roots are far from New Angeles.

For the rich, New Angeles is paradise. It has the trendiest nightspots and the most luxurious arcologies, and every need is catered to by android servants. Well-paid corp and government employees as well as investors and financiers form an upper class referred to as "risties" by those further down the ladder. The middle class struggles to maintain its modest prosperity, working white-collar jobs for inadequate paychecks and a slew of corporate benefits that keep them housed, fed, and dependent on their employers. As for the "working poor," their wages have fallen for decades and their employment status remains uncertain given the rise of android labor in blue collar jobs. Below them—often literally, in the warrens below the towering arcologies and layers of interconnected highways and skyways—are the *disenfrancistos* who live outside the system as scavengers, beggars, and criminals.

New Angeles itself is outside the system; its status as an unincorporated territory of the United States grants it many economic advantages including favorable taxes and tariffs that drive massive growth and prosperity. It also occupies a murky political space in that its status is guaranteed by treaty, but its people are subject to laws that were written by representatives they didn't vote for and are executed by agencies with no base in New Angeles. While many wealthy New Angelinos maintain "primary" addresses stateside to enable them to vote in the USA, the middle and lower classes can vote only in local politics. That tension, in addition to constant maneuvering between Congress and City Hall for control over the tax dollars generated by the Beanstalk, makes New Angeles feel like a nation unto itself—and why not? By some counts, there are more New Angelinos than residents of the mainland United States. Some argue for a reversion to Ecuador, others agitate for complete independence, and all the while the end of the lease agreement with Ecuador approaches, and no one is certain what will happen when that date hits.

In short, New Angeles is the world writ small. The rich are very rich. The poor are very poor. The corps have massive power, the government struggles to retain control, and new technologies constantly threaten to upset the whole system.

The Root

The sun rises over the infinite skyline of New Angeles, starscrapers, the haze of moisture and pollution, and the Root, a matrix of light against a massive shadow. Hoppers clack and hum overhead. Discarded wrappers and plastifoam containers drift in the air, slowly descending to the slums to gather in drifts at the base of affordable housing complexes. A bioroid, its unfeeling silver eyes staring straight ahead, pilots a street hoover, gathering the detritus of Life Above on its way to some recycling center beyond the edge of the inhabitable.

KARAMBIT
COMBINED ARMS

BULWARK
HEAVY INDUSTRIES

BUILDING A BETTER TOMORROW

The Weyland Consortium is synonymous with the construction of the Beanstalk, but the megacorporation is as diverse as it is mysterious, with major stakes in the financial, construction, defense, and even energy markets. The true scope of its portfolio is unknown. Nevertheless, the holding company continues to dominate the NASX index, and it can be counted on to continue doing so for the next several decades at least, so long as the Beanstalk royalties continue to pour in.

MERCURY
mining corporation

x Kirkland, Cromwell Zhāng
Antitrust Specialist

Jack Weyland began his company as a vehicle to put his transformative ideas into motion. The most famous of these was the New Angeles Space Elevator (nicknamed "Jack's Beanstalk"), which was finally completed in '35. Its completion heralded the realization of a true space age and paved the way for humankind to colonize the Moon and Mars. Although he was ultimately pushed out of the company by his own board of directors, Weyland was also responsible for many of the first arcologies built in New Angeles, NeoTokyo, and Mumbad. The megacorp's subsidiary contractors continue to lead the field of architectural design and produce countless advancements in structural engineering, with executive Elizabeth Mills steering Weyland's lucrative construction holdings in New Angeles.

The megacorp's governing board of directors comprises a handful of permanent members as well as several rotating directors collected from its diverse portfolio of companies. The Consortium deals in smaller corps like a normal company deals in product—by buying low, restructuring or realizing the company's potential, and then turning it around to be sold (or liquidated) at a massive profit. In addition to financing start-up corporations and investing in innovation, Weyland's Titan Transnational is one of the leading central banks and a major player in the risk management and insurance industry. Titan Transnational Bank is perhaps best known for issuing and backing the ubiquitous "credit" currency, formally known as the Titan Transnational Trade Credit, that is used by megacorps and individuals alike to partially insulate international and interplanetary transactions from variations in the foreign exchange markets.

Just before the War broke out, Weyland began investing heavily in weapons technology and the defense industry. Argus Security matured into one of the best prisec concerns in the solar system and rented out its mercenaries to help quell the rebellions on Luna and Mars. Argus also researched and developed its own brands of mass driver weaponry and caseless ammunition, which found their way onto both sides of the conflict. When the fighting was over, Weyland was able to quickly snap up reconstruction contracts to rebuild countries that were devastated by Argus's own forces in the War, including the colonies on Luna.

Weyland has profited immensely by investing in the technology behind fusion power fueled by helium-3. Its Blue Sun reactor on the Moon powers much of the Heinlein colony, including its myriad life-support systems. The Consortium's specialty research projects at locations such as the Geothermal Research and Neothermal Development Laboratories will guard against fluctuations in the helium-3 market. Such volatility has been known to occur intermittently due to strikes by Space Elevator Authority workers, but the price spikes were most keenly felt during the Lunar Insurrection that precipitated the War.

In the coming years, Weyland has a number of ambitious projects slated for development on Mars that will transform Bradbury Colony into a true megapolis with a space elevator of its own. The company knows humanity's future lies among the stars, and pioneering projects like Gagarin Deep Space will take human civilization the farthest it's ever been: past the asteroid belt to the moons of Jupiter, and beyond.

Construction began as soon as Weyland's investors could decide on a suitable location. Due to the orbital mechanics of constructing a space elevator, the structure needed to be located somewhere along Earth's equator. After nixing one plan to build it on an artificial island in the Pacific, the corporation ultimately settled on Volcán Cayambe in Ecuador, a mountain roughly sixty-four kilometers northeast of the capitol, Quito. Ground was broken on the project only two years after Weyland's initial proposal. As the project progressed, a small city called New Angeles—populated mainly by engineers, technicians, laborers, and their families—sprouted at the foot of the volcano.

The Beanstalk itself is like a thin composite fiber ribbon stretched taut between two anchors, the Root and the Castle. A buckyweave lattice clad in hundreds of thin, molecularly bonded layers of advanced composites makes the core both incredibly strong and flexible, allowing the Beanstalk to endure the incredible natural stresses of gravity and momentum acting upon it. One of the composites woven into the buckyweave lattice is graphene, which can conduct electricity to run the mag-lev lines that are the lifeblood of offworld commerce. Workers, colonists, tourists, and materiel travel daily up to the Castle at the end of the Beanstalk and beyond to Luna and Mars, while raw materials, including the precious and expensive helium-3 isotope, come down. Unfortunately, the Beanstalk measures less than two-dozen meters wide and can only support a small handful of mag-lev lines. This, combined with the travel time to and from each station, limits the number of mag-lev cars, known colloquially as "beanpods," that can operate per day. As a result, there is a near-permanent backlog of people, corporations, and government entities eagerly awaiting their turn to climb the Beanstalk.

The beanpods themselves run day and night to carry people and cargo to and from orbit. A typical passenger beanpod is a long, narrow, cigar-shaped vehicle just over twenty meters long and roughly five meters in diameter. It has three decks amidships, each with twelve acceleration couches situated around the deck's circumference. Each deck also has a head and a drinks dispenser for the comfort of the passengers. The pointed caps on each end of the beanpod contain the pod's environmental and

Cargo pods are larger, bulkier beanpods that carry raw materials or commodities up and He-3 down. They follow a larger, different set of mag-lev tracks that can stop at Midway or the Castle, or even propel Luna- or Mars-bound containers straight into space like a slingshot. Cargo pods are typically unmanned and have no passenger or crew accommodations. There are, however, some cargo pods that carry cargoes delicate or sensitive enough that they require security or constant monitoring for one reason or another. These are usually manned by bioroids and equipped with the most rudimentary of crew compartments.

Although the New Angeles Space Elevator was envisioned by Jack Weyland and built by his eponymous company, the Beanstalk is currently owned and operated by an independent agency called the Space Elevator Authority, or SEA. On paper the SEA is not beholden to any single country or corporation; it was chartered to ensure equal access to the Beanstalk by any and all who could afford to pay its rates. However, some point to the steady stream of Beanstalk royalties into Weyland accounts as proof that the agency cannot be as independent as it claims to be.

The men and women of the SEA are largely refugees from the wars on Mars or Earth-loyalists, and they operate every facet of the space elevator, from maintenance to administration. SEA technicians and engineers keep the beanpods running on time and at peak efficiency. SEA security officers, known as "yellow jackets" thanks to the high-visibility reflective jackets they wear, keep the peace and respond quickly to the slightest hint of a disturbance at any of the three major stations or on the Beanstalk itself.

Ben Zweifel

Midway Station

GATEWAY TO THE STARS

THE ROOT

The Root is the Beanstalk's anchor, a complex of chic, eye-wateringly expensive boutiques, five-star restaurants, exclusive living areas, municipal offices, and kilometers of brightly lit, highly secure corridors built into the heart of Cayambe. Atop the mountain's peak stands the Plaza del Cielo, an architectural marvel forty-seven hundred meters above sea level that is crammed day and night with travelers, tourists, the occasional busking musician or performance artist, and sightseers watched over by a mixture of local police officers and the ever-vigilant yellow jackets. At the center of the ornate plaza lies Earth Station, a huge, glass-domed SEA complex that serves the planet-side terminus of the Beanstalk. Towering above all this mountain splendor is the Beanstalk, its dull-grey mass rising from the center of Earth Station into the infinite sky.

MIDWAY STATION

The first stop after leaving Earth Station is Midway Station, a large and bustling space station located in geostationary orbit roughly thirty-five thousand kilometers above the Root. The station marks the halfway of the Beanstalk and was the base from which the first buckyweave ribbons of the elevator's tether were constructed. Because the Beanstalk was essentially knitted from Midway Station down to Earth and up to the Castle, the mag-lev lines don't pass completely through the midway point. Instead, incoming passengers must disembark and then board another beanpod to continue their trip. Surrounding the station are numerous shops, boutiques, hotels, and entertainment complexes that cater to travelers with long layovers or those who want to experience the excitement of microgravity but have neither the taste nor the money for space travel.

The station's primary employer is NBN, which maintains a major Network server hub as well as half a dozen broadcast stations. The central location of the station provides excellent access to the Beanstalk's technical infrastructure and helps NBN better serve those along the elevator's entire length. Despite its reputation as a middle-class enclave and its exhaustive list of average to bargain-basement bourgeoisie amenities, Midway Station still has its share of wealth, intrigue, and power brokering, and the wealthy denizens of the Castle can often be found slumming in what they consider the station's quaint and tacky commercial districts.

THE CASTLE

At the very top of the Beanstalk, over seventy thousand kilometers from the Root, hangs the Challenger Planetoid. Playfully referred to as "the Castle," a nod to the giant's castle at the top of the legendary fairy-tale beanstalk, the Challenger Planetoid is a huge, craggy asteroid measuring roughly five kilometers across. It was towed into orbit during the Beanstalk's construction to act as the structure's counterweight and was initially inhabited only by engineers and construction workers.

The largest and most important structure on the nearside of the Castle is the Challenger Beanstalk Terminal, which serves as the Beanstalk's terminus and includes all of its amenities, as well as technical and maintenance spaces for beanpods. In addition, a number of very famous and upscale businesses thrive here thanks to the constant flow of traffic and the exclusive surroundings.

The system-famous Castle Club with its renowned bar and cabaret is located a short tube-lev ride away. Owned and operated by casino mogul and trillionaire playboy Gianfranco Calderoli, the Castle Club is a massive carousel composed of two broad, triple-decked, disc-shaped habitats nearly two-hundred meters across. Each disc spins counter to the other, creating enough gravity through centripetal acceleration to provide comfort and accessibility for visitors, not to mention some gyroscopic stabilization as well. There is also the exclusive five-star Earthview restaurant, the less famous but still fantastic Cloudtop night club, and a selection of other expensive clubs, bars, and restaurants. Along with the entertainment and shopping, the complex also contains the Carousel Boardrooms, executive meeting rooms available for rent, and the High Frontier, a large upscale hotel and convention center. The Big Four and many smaller corporations keep offices here as well. Outside the great wheels of the complex itself are a number of low-gravity attractions such as a ballet theater and hotels catering to various clientele.

Challenger Planetoid
"The Castle"

Midway Station

The rest of the planetoid is given over to various kinds of industrial and commercial concerns known as the Farside Facilities. The Challenger Mines, a collection of surface dome habitats and a maze of underground tunnels, continue to supply C-cons to orbital construction facilities nearby. The home port of the Challenger Memorial Shuttle, along with a small shipyard, is serviced by a light mag-lev line for passengers and light freight continuing on to Starport Kaguya on the Moon.

IT
IS THE
FUTURE

Adam S. Doyle

Think for a moment about the powers at your disposal. If you want something, it can be yours with little more than a thought. Any food you desire can be prepared by robot or android chef and delivered right to your multimed-room. Any media from throughout human history can be streamed directly from the largest and most interconnected communications network ever conceived. Do you want a toy, or a piece of clothing, or a chair? It can be downloaded and printed either at your in-home makerbox or just down the slidewalk in a dedicated makerspace. You need not fear hunger, nor thirst, nor the cold, nor the heat. Your every want, every need, is quickly satisfied by the corporations that make up your life.

Capitalism won the great struggle of the twentieth and twenty-first centuries, and the corporations are its scions. They hold the real power, now, as strongly as any government—controlling most governments if the anti-cap movements are to be believed.

The crown jewels of corp supremacy and corp technology are the androids—artificial people, modeled on the real thing—which you can buy and sell and own. Some say that slavery is back in a new and horrible way. Others say that a machine is a machine. Still others say that we're meddling where we ought not, that androids are abominations that shouldn't exist.

One way or another, we live in interesting times.

HAAS-BIOROID

The company that would become Haas-Bioroid began over a hundred years ago as a robotics and heavy manufacturing business supplying numerous EU nations with heavy-duty construction equipment. Jürgen Haas and his brothers founded Haas Industrie to specialize in the manufacture of robotic and automated machinery that required little human oversight or interaction. The company quickly secured lucrative contracts with several of the EU's largest and most successful firms. All too eager to cut costs and boost productivity, Haas Industrie eventually moved into the field of automatic control systems. Research into communication and control theory was already well underway, but Haas's involvement caused a marked spike in progress for the burgeoning field of cybernetics.

When Jürgen Haas died, leadership of the company passed to his son Dieter. Eager to build on his father's legacy, Dieter saw an opportunity in expanding the company's portfolio into design and manufacture of prosthetics. Technology at the time was rapidly advancing the complexity and sophistication of replacement limbs, and Haas Industrie's background in robotics placed it at the forefront of design.

The success of Haas Industrie's cybernetics initiative led to an explosion in the market. Customers began to demand more precise limb replacements and greater control over its artificial implants. Haas Industrie responded by pouring resources into researching these goals. The result was highly sophisticated neuroprosthetic devices capable of adapting the behavior of a cybernetic limb to its owner's neural impulses. Haas made great strides in the field but swiftly came to the conclusion that further advances would require a greater understanding of the human brain. Research into brain imaging was begun, which proved to be a lengthy process.

The final keystone to Haas Industrie's success fell into place about thirty years ago. Although the exact details about when and how this happened remain frustratingly vague, control of the company passed to the indomitable Cynthia Haas, better known as Director Haas at her insistence. Rumors abound that Director Haas is the illegitimate child of the late Dieter Haas and she murdered her way to the top, creating the persona of Director Haas along the way. Stranger still are the tales that Director Haas is actually a child of the original Jürgen Haas, fertilized in vitro from a frozen sample of his DNA, or that she was built in a lab and was the most advanced bioroid model constructed until her "son." Of course, the more likely truth is Director Haas is simply the daughter of Dieter and likes to keep details of her private life confidential.

Either way, Haas Industrie became aware of a small computational neuroscience company called the Rossum Group and acquired them. At the time, this was seen as just another corporate merger. However, Director Haas had discovered that the Rossum Group was working on a highly advanced technology capable of producing working models of a brain based on braintapes, featuring unprecedented accuracy and detail. After the acquisition, this technology was integrated into Haas Industrie's own research. The result was the development of one of the most significant technological breakthrough of recent years: neural channeling.

The advent of neural channeling techniques allowed Haas Industrie to realize its dream of true AI—or come as close to it as ethics would allow. Following this breakthrough, the company began development on its first commercial android, the Mark-2. The "Mark," as it was commonly called, debuted in the last years of the War as a general purpose space exploration model. Hailed as "both a step and a leap for mankind," it wasn't long before it was also deployed for disaster relief and cleanup in war-torn areas with dangerous levels of biological contamination or radioactive fallout. The Mark-2 was a resounding success and ushered in a new age of artificial intelligence, one that could learn and improve with time. The company swiftly created a host of these machines, high-spec cybernetic bodies coupled with strong artificial intelligence. The bioroid as we know it was born, and the company changed its name to Haas-Bioroid.

The invention was a runaway success, and with it the company paved the way for "labor solutions," which would replace an inefficient and unreliable human workforce with the superior engineering of bioroids. Despite vocal opposition from a number of activist groups, the bioroid represents one of the most significant technological advances of the era. The speed with which HB achieved its grip on the labor solution market has kept it ahead (barely) of arch-rival Jinteki.

CURRENT PROJECTS

Haas-Bioroid remains the market leader in industrial robotics and heavy manufacture. HB's automated assembly lines can be found in corporations from Earth to Mars, and one would be hard-pressed to find a hopper that wasn't built using some aspect of HB technology. Aside from these benchmark technologies, Haas-Bioroid continues to expand into cutting-edge fields in cybernetics, brain-machine interfacing, cybersecurity, and defense.

CYBERNETICS AND BMIS

Haas-Bioroid's cybernetics division works tirelessly to produce artificial limbs for our veterans and medical implants to help those with serious illness. Moreover, the latest synthskin-covered cyberlimbs has allowed more than five hundred million people to take back their dignity without the stigma of prosthetics or the danger of under-tested genetic modification. Haas-Bioroid's continued investment in the personal cybernetics field has led to many more lives being saved, whether it was a soldier saved from a lethal bullet thanks to his sub-dermal armor, or a disaster victim rescued from certain death by emergency personnel augmented with internal air supplies or strength-enhancing exosuits.

Haas-Bioroid is also heavily involved in the fields of brain-machine interfaces (BMI) and neural recognition. Its BMI units, both wearable and available as implants, are bleeding-edge tech revolutionizing military training.

ARMS SALES

As the War began to heat up on Luna, Mars, and even Earth, nearly all megacorporations branched into the defense industry. Networked Emergent and eXperimental Technology Design (NEXT) was a natural extension of Haas Industrie's advanced assembly lines as applied to weapons manufacturing. The division's first products were smartguns that used advanced AI technology for targeting and trigger security, including cutting-edge IFF protocols. In the race to compete for lucrative government contracts, NEXT developed the first personal-scale applications of energy weapon technology, which saw extensive use on both sides of the War. The designs for the laser pistols and rifles had to be protected from rival corporations as well as a new breed of Netcriminal, necessitating the development of new intrusion countermeasures technology to protect its designs. In peacetime, NEXT continues to focus on creating increasingly sophisticated network defenses and encryption protocols to secure intellectual property and trade secrets.

CYBERSECURITY

HB's security division is making the Network a safer place to do business. HB is the only provider of dedicated intrusions countermeasures bioroids, or "bioroid ice." Bioroid ice utilizes the same neural channeling software found in the optical brains of other bioroids. This sets it apart from all other competitors, as HB's security systems are capable of self-improvement. These suites are able to analyze the specific setup of a local network and adapt the behavior of any installed programs to better protect it. They can also learn from intrusion attempts and implement new strategies to better defend against such tactics in the future. Clients can choose from a selection of security packages, ranging from barrier suites to large-scale network solutions capable of launching aggressive cyber attacks at any unwanted intruders.

Haas-Bioroid is also an industry leader in more traditional forms of ice. The innovative NEXT Design suite of countermeasures, for example, demonstrates unparalleled networking capability, allowing for an integrated defense system that reassigns resources to the attacked server.

TO Director Haas
CC Executive Vice-President Karl Meyer
FROM Dr. Jessenia DeLisle
SUBJECT Status Report on Project Vitruvius

Director,

Please find attached the results for our latest round of tests regarding Project Vitruvius. We are making considerable ground in the field of memory retention, with 66% of the subjects able to recall significant events from their lives before extraction. This is more than enough evidence to green-light a further round of tests once the necessary adjustments have been made. I understand you were hoping for a more noteworthy improvement over the last round of subjects, but I assure you we are doing everything in our power to improve the results with each iteration. An increase in our department's funding would allow us to advance our time line by a larger margin in subsequent experiments.

Unfortunately, this round of tests has shown little or no improvement in emotional and cognitive response. Our brain imaging techniques appear to be the limiting factor, and I would ask you again to reach out to Dr. Evelyn Ibarra. If we could collaborate with Morph and get a look at their Chronos Protocol, I feel certain we would be able to make substantial strides toward full replication.

It pains me to mention this, but I feel I should express my concern over the current methodology. The invasive nature of the procedure has led to a number of our subjects entering a persistent vegetative state. I know advancements of this nature require sacrifice and all subjects are volunteers, but legal waivers won't protect us from a potential PR backlash. Just look at Sunshine Junction.

I look forward to hearing your thoughts on the matters discussed above at our next progress meeting.

Yours respectfully,
Dr. Jessenia DeLisle
Project Manager: Vitruvius

Matt Zeilinger, Logo: Andrew Navaro with Evan Simonet

BIOROIDS

The technologies used in creating a bioroid are easily some of the most sophisticated in existence. The complex optical computer brains, sturdy titanium chassis, and smooth-action polyfiber muscle bundles all add up to a massively ambitious and cutting-edge piece of machinery.

The actual construction of a bioroid begins with a series of braintapes, or digital models of the human mind. Each braintape is unique, and Haas-Bioroid's computational neuroscientists distill and synthesize the desired skill sets and personalities from each in a process called neural channeling. This forms the blueprint for the bioroid's optical brain, a complex network of linked microcomputers that forms a series of neural pathways similar to a human connectome—a diagram of all the neural connections on a cellular level. These microcomputers are what give the bioroid its personality as well as its ability to learn and adapt.

Linked to the optical brain is a more conventional quantum brain that handles the bioroid's more basic programming, such as one might find in a computer console. This affords the bioroid the best of both human intelligence and pure computational power.

During the neural conditioning phase, each bioroid AI is programmed with a set of descending directives that prescribe and proscribe its behavior at the most fundamental level. These directives are present in all models and are unable to be changed. The First Directive states that a bioroid may not kill or cause serious harm to a human, nor can its inaction lead to the same. The Second Directive states that the bioroid's job functions are its first priority, except where it would violate the First Directive. The Third Directive states that the bioroid must report to Haas-Bioroid for regular maintenance when doing so would not violate the First or Second Directives. Often this is a simple visit to the nearest HB showroom, but in the case of the more sophisticated or prototype models, this can entail a journey up the Beanstalk to HB's R&D facility on Luna.

Other directives are believed to exist; often these concern the behavior of a specific model. Anyone who spends enough time with bioroids will notice that almost all models will instantly refute any criticism leveled against Haas-Bioroid or justify decisions HB has made regarding its product lines. More paranoid citizens allege that bioroids keep vids and audlogs

of their owners for upload to the HB servers during weekly maintenance.

As complex machines, bioroids require some upkeep in order to perform at optimum. This maintenance might take the form of a simple shutdown and repair, tightening loose joints, replacing worn seals or synthskin, refitting errant wiring, and recharging internal batteries. The entire process can take less than an hour, thereby minimizing the unit's downtime. Sometimes the process is more involved; replacing a damaged limb or overhauling a power source can take days to complete. Thankfully, due to a bioroid's extreme durability, these occasions are rare.

Weekly maintenance is important not only for the bioroid's physical shell but for its quantum brain as well. Shutdown can help break any algorithmic recursions or other infinite loops that may be draining a bioroid's processing power. During the nightly hibernation routine, nanobots in the bioroid's optical brain are able to rewire its synthetic neural connections based on data absorbed during activity, just like a sleeping human brain would. This process is what allows bioroids to learn and develop, and it is what sets them apart from more mundane, weak-AI constructs.

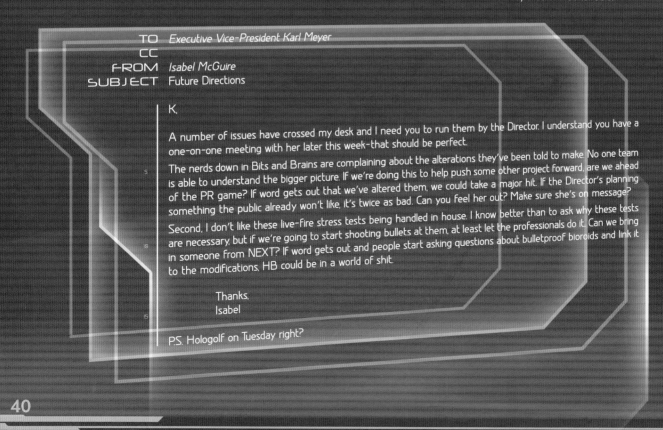

TO *Executive Vice-President Karl Meyer*
CC
FROM *Isabel McGuire*
SUBJECT Future Directions

K,

A number of issues have crossed my desk and I need you to run them by the Director. I understand you have a one-on-one meeting with her later this week–that should be perfect.

The nerds down in Bits and Brains are complaining about the alterations they've been told to make. No one team is able to understand the bigger picture. If we're doing this to help push some other project forward, are we ahead of the PR game? If word gets out that we've altered them, we could take a major hit. If the Director's planning something the public already won't like, it's twice as bad. Can you feel her out? Make sure she's on message?

Second, I don't like these live-fire stress tests being handled in house. I know better than to ask why these tests are necessary, but if we're going to start shooting bullets at them, at least let the professionals do it. Can we bring in someone from NEXT? If word gets out and people start asking questions about bulletproof bioroids and link it to the modifications, HB could be in a world of shit.

Thanks,
Isabel

P.S. Hologolf on Tuesday right?

HAAS-BIOROID
FLOYD , 2X3A7C

360-DEGREE SENSORS ▼

In addition to top-rated binocular vision, Floyd 2X3A7C is equipped with full surveillance coverage from optical sensors all over its body. 2X3A7C's parallel brain runs a constant model of its surrounding. Meaning, that its unit cannot be surprised by an assailant or miss an important clue.

WIRELESS
► NETWORK UPLINK

TITANIUM CHASSIS ►

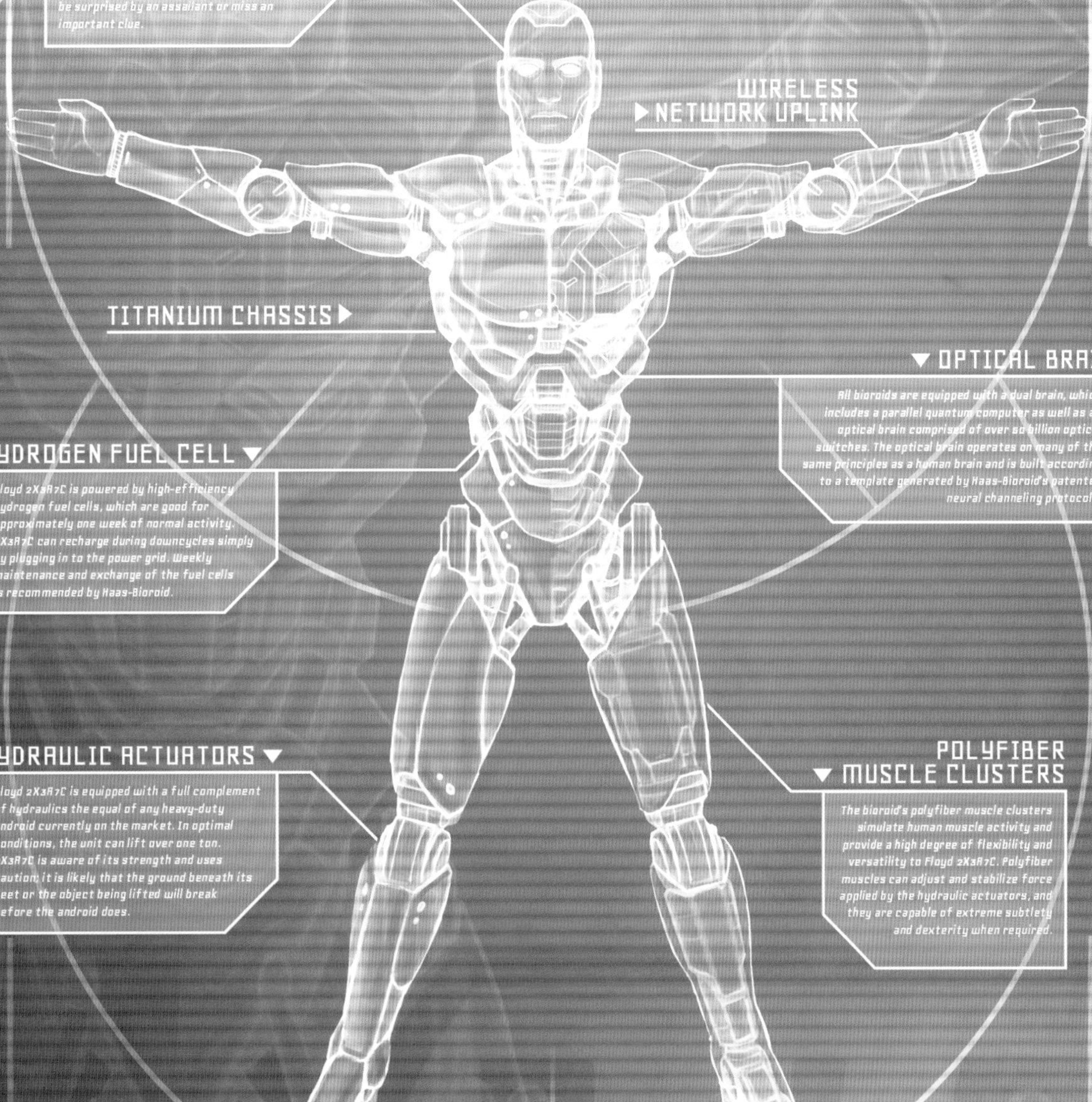

▼ OPTICAL BRAIN

All bioroids are equipped with a dual brain, which includes a parallel quantum computer as well as an optical brain comprised of over 50 billion optical switches. The optical brain operates on many of the same principles as a human brain and is built according to a template generated by Haas-Bioroid's patented neural channeling protocols.

HYDROGEN FUEL CELL ▼

Floyd 2X3A7C is powered by high-efficiency hydrogen fuel cells, which are good for approximately one week of normal activity. 2X3A7C can recharge during downcycles simply by plugging in to the power grid. Weekly maintenance and exchange of the fuel cells is recommended by Haas-Bioroid.

HYDRAULIC ACTUATORS ▼

Floyd 2X3A7C is equipped with a full complement of hydraulics the equal of any heavy-duty android currently on the market. In optimal conditions, the unit can lift over one ton. 2X3A7C is aware of its strength and uses caution it is likely that the ground beneath its feet or the object being lifted will break before the android does.

POLYFIBER
▼ MUSCLE CLUSTERS

The bioroid's polyfiber muscle clusters simulate human muscle activity and provide a high degree of flexibility and versatility to Floyd 2X3A7C. Polyfiber muscles can adjust and stabilize force applied by the hydraulic actuators, and they are capable of extreme subtlety and dexterity when required.

Floyd 2X3A7C, currently trialing as a detective at the NAPD, is an example of Haas-Bioroid's new line of high-end bioroids. Featuring personality indices based on the braintape of [REDACTED], this model features the most intelligent and advanced AI in production. Currently testing in specific markets; full commercialization achievable by [REDACTED].

CONFIDENTIAL

41

Matt Zeilinger

25 September, 1938 – New Angeles time

New Angeles at night pulsed like monstrous iridescent organism. The view from fifteen hundred meters up was always impressive, especially on a rare clear night like tonight. Cynthia Haas stood at the full length windows of her villa atop the Haas Arcology and studied the city she helped create.

With a few hand movements, she increased the magnification of her view sixteen, thirty-two, sixty-four times onto the Root in the distance and began slowly panning across the skyline. The northern and western horizon was dominated by the expanse of the Pacific, but tonight her interests lay to the south. With another gesture, the entire top section of the arcology slowly rotated 110 degrees to give her a view of Rabotgorod District with its vast storage facilities for bioroids. Corporations, governments, and private individuals who were unwilling to house bioroids on-site often rented storage in Rabotgorod for when their bioroids were offline. It was a curious practice, Cynthia thought, because bioroids didn't need to sleep. But apparently most people felt more comfortable when their bioroids followed a similar schedule to their own. How many were out there now?

This moment of quiet reflection was a rare indulgence for Cynthia. A quirk in her normally busy schedule had left her evening free, and she had decided to resist the temptation to immediately fill the time with work. Her PAD chimed. He was on his way up.

The question of how many bioroids were out there raced through her mind. Her PAD provided an estimate: 98,760,200 based on current production, minus recalls, decoms, and the blue-, violet-, ultraviolet-, and black-level prototypes. It had all happened shockingly fast. She remembered clearly the feeling when the first bioroid was awakened. When the ambitious dream finally became a reality, her scientific curiosity had almost immediately yielded to an overwhelming sense of business opportunity. Now, she sensed another shift was happening, but this one was much slower and subtler. Lately her mind was less focused on profits and increasingly occupied with the thought that she was permanently altering the future of the human race.

Was this what humanity needed?

Of course it was. There was no turning back. The only way was forward.

"Admiring your handiwork?" said a familiar voice.

Cynthia turned her back on New Angeles and looked at the man who had just entered the room. He was well-dressed, as always, with perfectly styled silver hair. But he was thin and looked tired, like his older body could no longer keep up with his youthful lifestyle. He stretched onto her genuine leather sofa with an easy familiarity. "Or," he paused with a dramatic raise of an eyebrow. "Maybe you're plotting the next phase of your world domination?"

"World domination?" she said with a hint of a smile. "There's a whole solar system out there. New Angeles, Luna, Mars, it's all just the beginning."

"Oh great, here it comes," he said with a roll of his eyes.

"Just because you've never had any ambition of your own doesn't mean you can't understand mine. Haas-Bioroid is shaping the future of humanity."

"A responsibility I'm sure you continue to take very seriously," he said. "Don't forget that humans have been evolving on their own for a lot longer than you and your things have been around."

"You know what got us out of the trees and caves?" she said sharply. "The ability to devote our attention to something other than the hard labor of survival. Technology leads to leisure time which leads to creative thinking and innovation. We've got one bioroid for every one hundred people, but it took us decades to get even that far. If humanity is going to advance, we need to stop breaking our backs once and for all."

"Fascinating," he said with a slow clap of his hands. "And, by that I mean totally boring. You know I don't really want to talk to Director Haas. I'd like to talk to my gal."

"I haven't been that for nineteen years," she said. She turned back toward her windows. Nineteen years ago, the view to the south would have been dark—a vast wilderness of foothills and forest. Tonight, it was an ocean of light from the world's largest city.

"Nineteen years! Has it really been that long?"

"John, why are you really here?" She spun to face him again and stabbed at him from across the room with her finger. "I invited you here last week. Not tonight. I was planning to leave for Heinlein this morning. I'm only here now because I had to attend to something important."

"What sort of important?"

"It's none of your business. This whole encounter is just an accident."

"A lucky accident," he said with a smirk. "Or, maybe you're not the only one with informants."

Someone's going to be sorry, she thought.

John stood up and stretched. "What's for dinner?"

"You know, you're worse than Thomas."

John glanced sideways as if to verify they really were alone. "How is Thomas?"

"He's the same. Not that you would have any idea what that means."

"Touché." He stroked his chin, and old habit left over from his bearded days. "Now, that Adonis fellow," he continued. "He's something. And, Eve! You've got to be drowning in creds from those two. You're a regular madame of old. Hey, can I ask you a question? Have you ever, you know, done it with one of them?"

"No, you can't ask me a question like that," she said icily.

"I mean, I know I was always a distant second to your work, but I never thought the bioroid replacement thing would go that far."

Her eyes narrowed. Her cheeks flushed with anger. "I think I'll kick you out now."

"You won't," he said smiling. "Who else can talk to you like this? You want me here."

"Don't flatter yourself."

He stood up and walked boldly toward her, not stopping until they were nearly touching. He was both a little taller and a littler older than her, and like her, he had not tried to entirely conceal his age with biotech.

"You've looked better," he said smiling.

"So have you," she replied. Her flash of fury had already passed; he'd always had that effect on her. Her mind drifted back to their time in Berchtesgaden, so long ago it seemed a different lifetime. Part of her longed to return to that simpler life. But there was no turning back. The only way was forward.

"Cynthia," said John. "The world can wait. At least for tonight."

She hesitated, then sighed and touched her PAD. A single low note chimed throughout the room. "Jeeves." she said.

A blue holographic image of a bioroid's face floated above a nearby table. "Yes, Director?" it said.

"Dinner for two."

New Angeles Times

CURRENT Haas denies allegations o... **ARTICLES** New Angeles Giants lose t... **WEATHER** Acid rain warning for N...

ENGINEERING
THE MODERN WORKFORCE

An in-depth look at how Haas-Bioroid is transforming the way we live and work

BY SHUGOFA KARZAI

No one lives without paranoia these days. The corporations dictate our lives: they design our downtime, provide recreation for a price, and subtly drain us of our need to think for ourselves. We equate structure with safety.

Proponents split their views on whether this trend is an insidious practice or an outgrowth of much sought-after complacency by individuals. Social psychologists insist that the average person no longer knows enough about city, country, world, or extra-planetary life to effectively handle his or her existence.

I don't believe that's true. I've gone underground these past few months to get at the truth. I've dedicated myself to uncovering the facts, and I've concentrated on one of the biggest mysteries facing us today: Haas-Bioroid.

Everyone knows the megacorporation. It's on the tip of every tongue. You see their ads and infomercials frequently in the media. Haas-Bioroid rents advertising space on buildings throughout the metroplexes. In New Angeles, where I'm from, you can't turn a street corner without coming face-to-face with Haas-Bioroid marketing or one of their products.

Bioroids are everywhere, and their numbers continue to grow. In fact, one of the most closely guarded secrets Haas-Bioroid has is exactly how many units currently hold positions on Earth, the Moon, and Mars—and what those positions are.

One of the main objections to using bioroids has been that they replace flesh-and-blood employees in the workplace. In the beginning, HB focused on creating bioroids to take the place of humans in high-risk jobs like handling toxic materials, fighting fires, or other jobs that included the possibility of human fatality.

Now, everyone can be replaced.

Humanity Labor, one of the groups protesting against Haas-Bioroid, fears that eventually HB will take away all jobs and reduce people to redundant systems that will get phased out. As they insist in their social platforms, human laborers have already lost many jobs due to the bioroid contracts.

• • •

"I UNDERSTAND THE COMPLAINTS OF THOSE WHO HAVE BEEN REPLACED ON THE JOB," SAYS DAMIEN KING, CEO OF TOXIC KLEEN, INC., "AND I FEEL THEIR PAIN. NO ONE WANTS TO LOSE EMPLOYMENT IN THE CURRENT ECONOMY. BUT THESE PEOPLE FORGET THAT WE ACCEPTED HAAS-BIOROID'S LABOR CONTRACTS TO PROTECT THEM, NOT DISENFRANCHISE THEM. TOXIC KLEEN THOUGHT ONLY OF THE EMPLOYEES WHEN WE MADE THE DECISIONS TO OUTSOURCE JOBS TO BIOROIDS.

"Clones are cheaper if you look at the up-front cost, but bioroids—while being more expensive in the short term—operate for years, are cheaper to maintain, and can be more easily designed to multitask."

King is one of many CEOs who have signed multi-year agreements with HB for a bioroid workforce. Toxic Kleen scours sites riddled with chemical and nuclear waste, bidding on jobs that are intensely dangerous to flesh-and-blood workers.

"Since we signed the contract for bioroid labor," King says, "we've not had one on-the-job fatality. Not one. That's something to take pride in. But Human First and other groups

like them forget that. They ignore the safety issues."

The other change that King and other corp representatives don't talk about is the impact on the bottom line. Divesting themselves of human workers has also enlarged their profit margin. There are no sick days or injuries among the bioroid labor pool, nor are there any workers' comp payouts.

"Golems don't care if they're destroyed," says an activist for Human First who did not wish her identity known. "They'll melt down to get the job done if they have to, and they don't lose anything when they do. Our guys, we risked our necks on the job. The only reason we put our lives and our health on the

line was to provide for our families. Try explaining that to one of those machines. If they weren't working, they'd be in a box somewhere."

"I enjoy my job. I have purpose. I save lives," says Ben "Benjamin" 28AG31, a bioroid currently tasked to HAZARD-US, a competitor of Toxic Kleen, Inc.

Ben 28AG31 is a bulky, blocky bioroid that's almost as wide as it is tall. With rudimentary human features, a gentle giant by way of *Frankenstein*, he holds a mop and a bucket and shows scarring and pitting from exposure to corrosive chemicals. He's been working with HAZARD-US for three years but has to have parts replaced regularly.

"One of the best things about

CONTINUE ▼

NEW ANGELES TIMES TECHNOLOGY REPORTER SHUGOFA KARZAI MISSING

In a statement to *The New Angeles Times* NAPD Sergeant Chris Kulemeka assured us, "Although Ms. Karzai has been reported missing and has, in fact, not shown up at work or her residence for the last four days, the NAPD has no reason to believe anything has happened to her. It's not against the law for adults to step away from their lives. People disappear all the time."

Nevertheless, concerned friends have lobbied for the police department to open an investigation into Karzai's disappearance.

"It's not like her to simply disappear," the missing reporter's coworker Carlos Webber declared. "She's been with the *Times* for over three years. Shugofa wouldn't just leave." He insists that something has happened to the young woman. "The NAPD is part of the cover-up. Everyone knows how corrupt they are."

Anyone with knowledge of Shugofa Karzai's whereabouts is encouraged to contact *The New Angeles Times*.

RELATED STORIES ▶

Help! Someone G-Modde...

Alarm spread through a suburban La Costa neighborhood on Thursday when contractor Hector ... untary genetic modification. "I think he ate a rat or something," Hector said. "Now he walks around on his hind legs half the time and one time I found him in the backyard even though I know I never opened the door to let him out."

had one on-the-job fatality. Not one. That's something to take pride in. But Human First and other groups

they do. Our guys, we risked our necks on the job. The only reason we put our lives and our health on the

for three years but has to have parts replaced regularly.

Angeles Metro will transform them into police clones. The Hachi-Inu are known f[...] hands, but so far there have been no report[...] anywhere other than an approved Jinteki [...]

PNB indexes supplied for your benefit by NBN and associated subsidiaries   Personalized News Bulletin Relevance Index 79

BIOROID DESTROYS CHEMICAL SUPPLY WAREHOUSE

No one knows why James AK49I27, a clerical unit, went off-program today and set fire to Allied KhemTool. The blaze destroyed millions of dollars in supplies and property. Incidental damage to the surrounding neighborhood has yet to be calculated.

The New Angeles Fire Department Arson Unit has been dispatched to investigate the fire, but Haas-Bioroid investigators have laid claim to the site. According to Allied KhemTool spokesperson Gerry DuBois, the corporation has "a contractual obligation to Haas-Bioroid for a first look at any possible malfunction of their units."

Haas-Bioroid's Loss Prevention Program (HBLPP) includes theft of and damage to corporate property, i.e. the bioroid units leased to various agencies. In the past year, HBLPP agents have recovered an unspecified number of stolen units and prosecuted everyone connected to any actions against the corporation.

"HB's Loss Prevention agents are good at what they do," Heinlein Assistant District Attorney Leila Nguyen states. "Every ADA in the district attorney's offices wants to grab one of their cases because they're slam dunks in a courtroom."

"One of the best things about employing a bioroid," says Haas-Bioroid HR staffing agent Christine Pham, "is that we can weld and bolt on new parts that get destroyed during day-to-day usage. You don't have to replace it with a new hire."

• • •

HAZARD-US PROJECT MANAGER ALEXANDRIA TOTT HAS A DIFFERENT VIEW OF THE BIOROIDS.

"Workers like Ben are amazing," she says. "They show up on time without complaint. No sick days. And they'll work a sixteen-hour shift without complaint till the job is done." For a moment, sadness shows in her grey eyes. "Losing one of them is really hard. Most people think of them as just automatons. They're like puppies. Eager to please and so... so innocent.

"And no matter what anyone says, they're not immediately replaceable. You spend time working with these units, you get to know them. They get to know you. It's part of the AI programming. Every Ben might not start out unique, but each Ben becomes unique. Just like people."

Still others have a different viewpoint based on events.

• • •

"GOLEMS DON'T GO HAYWIRE." MY SHADOW NET INFORMER IDENTIFIES HIMSELF AS A "DISGRUNTLED" EX-HAAS-BIOROID EMPLOYEE WHO WORKED IN THE NEURAL NETWORKING ARM, WHERE BIOROIDS ARE ENCODED WITH BASIC PROGRAMS. "SOMEBODY HACKED THAT JAMES UNIT. THAT'S WHAT HAPPENED.

"HB will tell you hacking one of their golems is impossible, but it's

not if the hacker has knowledge of the neural architecture and a few high-level foolies. Someone who knows what he's doing can climb into a bioroid and wear it like a shirt."

Kamren Humboldt is one of the public faces at Haas-Bioroid and one of its neural networking overseers. He's in his late 20s, a *wunderkind* from HB's special AI-development division at MIT. He sighs when asked about the possibility of hacking the James.

"Look, you're a nosie—" He struggles to maintain his composure, but his skin mottles with anger and his eyes tighten as he controls himself. His words echo a level of strain. "You know how people love to talk about tabloid pap. Rumors flourish like weeds. I'm telling you now that it's not possible to hack one of our units."

Still, the likelihood of just such a hack lingers in the minds of several people.

"The higher intelligence and more self-governance you give these things, the more risk you're going to incur," Dr. Nolan Tate says as he folds his interlinked hands over his stomach.

He's in his mid-80s, no longer actively involved in designing the neural networks that create bioroids after being released from Haas-Bioroid, but he instructs the young minds that will continue to enhance corporate products of the future at Levy University.

"That's a simple fact. The more lines of code you use, the more vulnerable those networks are to hacks. There are too many connections, and they all have to work together."

• • •

IN THE LAST 20 YEARS, HAAS-BIOROID HAS SEEN THOUSANDS OF OFFERS BY COMPANIES TO BECOME SUPPLIERS OR SOFTWARE ENGINEERS FOR BIOROID PRODUCTION, BUT ONLY A SLIVER OF THESE HAVE BEEN ACCEPTED.

"Director Haas, thus far, has a monopoly on the bioroid market," says one such expert who wished that she and her corporation would not be mentioned. "As we have seen, some of those who were rejected become vengeful and violent. Until you can factor people out of the equation, you're going to see attempts made against Director Haas and her corporation."

"Factoring people out is exactly what Haas-Bioroid is trying to do," Human First member Gorakh

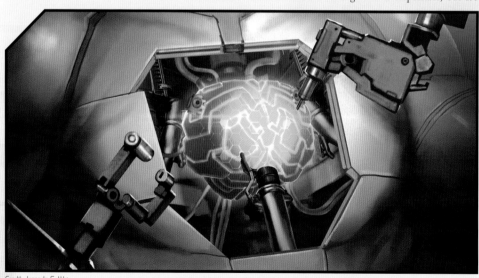

Credit: Jessada Sutthi

James AK49I27 was purportedly hacked by a neural networking student who dropped out of Haas-Bioroid's Computational Neuroscience program at Levy University! Read the full story...

jor **AgInfusion Soybeef Recall**

Agricultural giant AgInfusion has been forced to recall some forty million servings of soybeef after finding that the product was contaminated with actual beef.

We approached Anita Felstaven, the Vice President of Communications at AgInfusion for

Netcrime

through our systems." Professor Rose explained that genetic modification requires the intervention of a viral protein designed to insert the DNA into the host's genome. "I don't know," she said. "Maybe the rat was sick with a retrovirus of some kind? The whole thing seems pretty unlikely."

Al-Issa proclaims. "People need to pay attention. This is just a smoke-screen. HB won't admit to that James being hacked, and it probably wasn't, but they've got public relations teams who will whisper that to create confusion for the masses. Their crisis management people put that spin on the accident when really this was just a play to jam the government's investigation."

No one knows how many cyber and physical attacks have been launched against HB. There are at least thirty-seven documented attacks on holdings in Heinlein, Sydney, Cologne, Johannesburg, and New Angeles. The last such attack took place at the ChiLo offices when a sniper started shooting at departing HB employees a week ago.

• • •

HAAS-BIOROID IS HELMED BY DIRECTOR HAAS, BUT HER SON THOMAS IS MUCH EASIER TO MEET FOR A FACE-TO-FACE. DURING THE BRIEF INTERVIEW I AM ABLE TO OBTAIN, THOMAS HAAS STANDS IN AN OFFICE OVERLOOKING A SILVER AND BLACK MOONSCAPE AT HEIN-LEIN. ELEGANT AS EVER, HAAS APPEARS RELAXED AND ENERGETIC. HE HAS A REPUTATION AS A BAD BOY IN MANY OF THE SHOUTCASTS.

I asked him about the contro-versy regarding the use of bioroids in the workplace and the violent outbreaks that continue to take place regarding the labor solutions Haas-Bioroid provides.

He shrugs and shows me that pho-togenic smile doubtless made perfect by g-mods. That expression has been plastered across every screamsheet I've ever seen, and Thomas Haas is an icon for the younger population.

"People always complain about change," Thomas Haas says. "They get set in their ways and don't want to embrace the future in the work-place, but can't wait for the next iter-ation in entertainment. That's always been the case."

"The Haas family always focuses on the future," Director Haas says in a rare interview eight years ago. "My forebears didn't settle for riding on their successes when we were Haas Industrie. They created the future then, and we still do now."

When asked about what he sees in the future, Thomas Haas reveals that enigmatic smile again. "I can't talk about that right now, but I can tell you this: Director Haas doesn't like change any more than anyone

else. But it's coming."

• • •

"PEOPLE FORGET THAT HAAS-BIOROID PRODUCES MORE THAN BIOROIDS," RETIRED SPACE EXPE-DITIONARY CORPS LIEUTENANT DILMA SERRA SAYS DURING A RECENT INTERVIEW. SHE LOST BOTH LEGS AND ONE ARM IN THE MAR-TIAN COLONY WARS.

"Without the cybernetics I received from Haas-Bioroid, I wouldn't have the quality of life I do now. A lot of veterans are thankful for them."

• • •

"ME? THANKFUL?" SAYS RETIRED UNITED STATES ARMY CORPORAL BERNARD ROTH. "SURE, LET'S CALL IT THAT. THANKFUL AS [EXPLETIVE DELETED]. I'M ALIVE BECAUSE OF CYBERNETIC ORGANS AND A [EXPLE-TIVE DELETED] LEG REPLACEMENT, BUT WHERE'S MY QUALITY OF LIFE?

"I got my pension from the army, but I got no job. I got a roof over my head at the VA, and I can work, but nobody's hiring. You ask me, if I'd had more parts replaced, come back less human, I could get [expletive deleted] work."

• • •

WHEN MOST PEOPLE THINK ABOUT DOWNTIME AND PLACES OUTSIDE THEIR HOMES TO GATHER WITH FRIENDS, THEY USUALLY CONSIDER SPORTING EVENTS, SHOPPING, AND PERHAPS HOBBIES THEY ENJOY. SMALL AND LARGE CLUBS WHERE PEOPLE GATHER HAVE BEEN A PART OF LIFE SINCE OUR ANCESTORS FIRST PUT DOWN PERMANENT ROOTS.

"I grew up in this bar," Lewis Chua, proprietor of the Blinking Owl, says. "My grandfather bought

it when he and my grandmother scraped together money for it. I was pulling beer, mixing drinks, and roll-ing narc-sticks since I was nine years old. My grandmother taught me.

"My grandparents came here because their land in Singapore was purchased by one of the corps," Chua says. "They invested everything they had in the bar. It used to have another name, but my grandmother changed the name to the Blinking Owl, naming it after the herb she grew in a small garden in the back."

Chua points at the gleaming buildings just across the street. "Urban renewal came in and swept away most of the old neighborhood. The property over there is owned by Astrapo Corporation. They're a Greek business that specializes in manufacturing batteries. The name is supposed to mean electricity or something like that."

When Astrapo Corporation came into the neighborhood ten years ago and bought all the rental proper-ties, the renters were driven away by high prices.

"Everybody thought Astrapo was going to provide a lot of jobs," Chua says. "Instead, they brought in bioroids. With their homes gone and no jobs to replace the ones that had been eliminated as well, folks just moved away."

For a time, Chua feared he was going to lose the family bar.

"You want to know what saved this place?" Chua smiles bigger than ever. "The same thing that nearly killed it."

He's talking about the bioroids that now occupy the tables and chairs once filled by flesh-and-blood clientele. The bioroids are high-

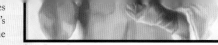
functioning models, ones that have enough intellectual capacity to interface with humans on a daily basis. These models are receptionists, clerks, child care providers, and sales representatives.

Chua leans on the bar and shakes his head at them. "They started drift-ing in one day and took up seats. It's still strange to see them talking to each other. Like they're real or something, you know? These bioroids, they're curi-ous by design. They like to problem solve, like to be challenged by things."

Sliding a deck of cards from under the bar, Chua spreads them on the bar. "This is what saved me. A deck of playing cards. After

CONTINUE ▼

DEADLY SNIPER CLAIMS 14 VICTIMS IN CHILO

On Friday morning, employees at Haas-Bioroid in downtown ChiLo stepped out into the gunsights of a spree killer. During the cold-blooded, methodical attack, thirty-two people suffered gunshot wounds, eleven of them died at the scene, and three more were pronounced dead at local hospitals.

The sniper, Seok Kwangho, was found dead in an office building opposite Haas-Bioroid's offices. Seok was a former prisec contractor who was trained as a sniper, but no ties have been discovered that linked him to Haas-Bioroid.

Police investigators have found tentative connections between Seok and Human First. "The case is open," CLPD Detective Anton Malfatti says. "If today's attack was part of a conspiracy, we'll find out who's behind it."

the Rise:

New Angeles has been the epicenter of a rising tide of Netcrime, authorities reported on Friday. The National Security Center Administration reports increases in automated crime, identity theft, network intrusion, chip-ripping, digital counterfeiting, and unauthorized surveillance over a six-month period covered by the report.

The NAPD Netcrimes Division recommends that all citizens update their PADs and other digital devices

the rights of the consumer in light of
ybeef scandal. Jinteki and other major
in the agricultural sector dominate
overnments of Australia and other

Customers who purchased contaminated
soybeef product have already been contacted
via autopush to their PADs and will be
offered a complimentary full replacement.

to keep their protection patched to
close loopholes found and exploited
by cyber criminals. Even the newest
device can be at risk of infection.

blindly accept every security p
pushed on you by some secretary
encounter on the Net," warned Lt.
Delgado of the NAPD.

---

n came
ars ago
proper-
way by

Astrapo
f jobs,"
ght in
ne and
at had
ks just

he was

t saved
er than
nearly

ioroids
s and

chairs once filled by flesh-and-blood
clientele. The bioroids are high-
functioning models, ones that have
enough intellectual capacity to
interface with humans on a daily
basis. These models are receptionists,
clerks, child care providers, and sales
representatives.

Chua leans on the bar and shakes
his head at them. "They started drifting in one day and took up seats. It's
still strange to see them talking to each
other. Like they're real or something,
you know? These bioroids, they're curi-
ous by design. They like to problem
solve, like to be challenged by things."

Sliding a deck of cards from
under the bar, Chua spreads them
on the bar. This is what saved me.
A deck of playing cards. After

business started slowing down, I
started playing solitaire. My grandfather taught me that. Anyway, I
was playing cards and some of the
bioroids came up to ask what I was
doing. Not having anything else to
do, I explained the game to them.
They took it up. Took up a lot of
other games too."

Bioroids sit at the tables playing
cards, go, and mah-jongg. Chua also
provides computer interfaces for
online gaming and VR as well.

"Once I found out these bioroids
liked games, and would pay for the
privilege of sitting here playing,
the flow of credits into the Owl
picked up. I invested in the computer units." Chua nods toward the
filled computer stations. "They play
everything."

• • •

"THEY PAY THOSE DAMNED GOLEMS!"
A DISENFRANCHISED WORKER COM-
PLAINS. HE WAS ONCE AN OVERSEER
AT ASTRAPO CORPORATION BUT
WAS REPLACED BY ASH 4L1KD5PS,
ONE OF HB'S OFFICE PRODUCTIVITY
MODELS. "THE CORPS LEASE THOSE
UNITS FROM HB, THEN GIVE THEM
A WEEKLY CREDSTICK."

Talking to Thomas Haas proved
that was not exactly the truth,
though a lot of people perceive the
situation in that light.

"The corps that hold contracts
with us don't pay our units," Thomas
Haas says. "Those units are given a
weekly credit allowance from HB. We
don't tell them how to spend it. They
choose. That's part of their training.
They spend their credits in places so
they can socialize with humans and
learn from those encounters. Our
high-end bioroids constantly educate
themselves and quickly advance past
where we start them out."

The crude mental capacity units
like the Davids and the Simons
are just smart machines. If the laws
allowed, they would work 24 hours
a day for days at a time. Whatever
changes take place in those jobs are
small, and a quick download from
HB takes care of whatever adjustments need to be made.

However, the more advanced
units require input, and the only way
they can truly get it is through interaction with humans.

"If we force the more able units
to simply stay in their jobs twenty-four hours a day, seven days a
week," Thomas Haas says, "corps will
basically have a robot, just a cog in
a machine. What we offer is a fully

adaptive bioroid that becomes better
and better at the job it performs. The
corps realize they're getting a bargain
because these bioroids don't balk at
change or multi-tasking or just have
a bad day. They're perfect assistants,
loyal and intelligent."

Reginald D'Amato, freelance
business analyst and investor, offers
this thought: "You can't just lease
a bioroid and throw it at a job. You
have to let it know what you expect
from it. Bioroids aren't just plug and
play units. These top-of-the-line
models have creativity and imagination built into their software.
They're nowhere near as advanced as
humans, but the potential for growth
is there, and that potential needs to
be realized."

• • •

"WHAT IS THE GREATEST TEACH-
ING TOOL WE HAVE?" DR. BENE-
DICT GRAYSON ASKS. AS A CHILD
DEVELOPMENT SPECIALIST WITH
A FOCUS ON LEARNING DISORDERS,
GRAYSON IS ONE OF THE LEADERS IN
HIS CHOSEN FIELD. IN ADDITION TO
HIS WORK FOR FEDERALLY FUNDED
TEACHING RESOURCES AND HIS OWN
COMPUTER GAME DEVELOPMENT
AGENCY, GRAYSON ALSO SERVES AS
AN "INDUCTIVE REASONING" CON-
SULTANT FOR HAAS-BIOROID.

In his early 60s but looking much
younger, Grayson sits on a large
inflated ball in his "office," which
looks more like a child's dream room.
Shelves hold manipulatives in bright
colors and various shapes. Boxes
contain tactile games, stuffed animals, and action figures.

"I'll tell you what that tool is,"
Grayson says as he holds a pink
shark and simulates it swimming
through the space between us. "Play."
He laughs, and the noise is infec-
tious, childlike and innocent. "When
I first mentioned this to Director
Haas, she thought I was crazy. She
thought you could simply design a
bioroid that could pass as human just
by recording someone's psychological profile and memories. Children
only become children by modeling
behavior and learning critical thinking skills through play. The ability
to play and learn is what separates
HB's next-gen bioroids from early
attempts at simply making humanoid robots. We've created a new 'species,' if you will.

"The high-end models wanted by
employers require levels of sophistication and socialization that can
only be gained through interaction.

By the age of five, children have
learned 80% of their social skills.
That's a fraction of the life expectancy of a bioroid. We can't wait
that long. We accelerate that growth
potential in bioroids through play.
Bioroids will continue to learn until
the day they cease functioning."

According to Grayson, the cognitive functions have to include a pro-
clivity to experiment, to extend an
experience and twist it and turn it to
provide diverse permutations.

"Think about children growing
up," Grayson says. "Children develop
through repetition. They hear words,
they repeat them, and through that
association, they learn the names of
things. That's easy learning. Garbage
in, garbage out. But teaching them to
extrapolate concepts and ideas, they
have to do so much more.

"Life knows a lot about survival
right out the gate. Interestingly
enough, the lower the mental processes of that offspring—such as
a lizard or a fish or an insect—the
more it knows about survival. But
when you replicate a mammal—
a high-functioning offspring—the
result is a creature that cannot take
care of itself for a considerable length
of time. Left on its own after birth,
that offspring would surely die.

"You get the same thing when
you merely record a persona onto a
bioroid. When you want a limited
unit, like a David or a Simon, you
can produce a more or less complete

IRANDA
APSODY

Would you like to continue using – *RetroSkin: Good Ol' Days?*

☐ ☐ ☐ ☐ ☐

Mars has been rocked by the sixth incident of widespread violence and unrest this month.
On Wednesday (Earth date) night, workers from the Picus clan in Bradbury clashed with
offworld émigrés in fatal encounters in the Bradbury neighborhood known as the Therm.

Earth," said one source within
tian Clans are nothing more th
to them by the naïveté of Eart

...human element, Delgado says, is
...lly the principle point of weakness
...inals exploit.

NSCA's ratings are skewed by graft and
financial considerations are, according to
an NSCA spokesperson, unfounded.

records leaked to the press
indicate that he had been
drinking the night of
his death.

within the NAPD. "The
motive is obvious, what
with Gray's involvement
in the Martian Summit."

record, saying only that
the NAPD doesn't com-
ment on cases under
investigation.

piece." Grayson leans back and inter-
locks his hands behind his head.
"For a more independent, problem-
solving unit, you have to factor in
the ability to play. Our children
learn from their parents, from their
extended families, and from their
communities. You must have nature
and nurture with them. Replication
and training."

Grayson spends time pointing
out that children learn best at first
through imitation, duplicating the
interactions they have with those
who care for them. It's a process
called "mirroring," and he insists that
the more social a person is, the more
"mirroring" that person has learned
to do. This socialization usually cor-
relates with success in our culture.

"At HB, the high-functioning
bioroids are trained to work with
humans through role-play." Grayson
shakes his head. "We didn't realize
how limiting that was until some of
our field inspectors discovered the
units had developed a love of games.
Can you understand how excited we
became? A whole new world opened
up to bioroid training."

• • •

"FINE," SNORTS CASSIDY, A HUMAN
FIRST MEMBER. "TEACH THEM HOW
TO PLAY CHESS OR MAH-JONGG,
OR EVEN CHARADES IF YOU WANT.
DOESN'T MATTER BECAUSE THOSE
THINGS DON'T ENJOY IT AND AT THE
END OF THE DAY THEY'LL STILL BE
GOLEMS. THEY'RE NOT PEOPLE!"

• • •

"MAYBE THEY'RE NOT PEOPLE,"
CHUA SAYS AS HE WATCHES OVER
HIS NEW CYBERNETIC CLIENTELE
WITH A FOND GLEAM IN HIS EYE,
"BUT IF YOU PAY ATTENTION TO
THEM PLAYING OUT THERE, YOU CAN
SEE THAT SOME OF THEM DO ENJOY
PLAYING IT. I GOT SCHOOL KIDS
COME IN HERE SOME AFTERNOON
AND TAKE ON THE BIOROIDS. THE
KIDS ENJOY INTERFACING WITH THE
BIOROIDS, AND THEY LEARN A LOT
FROM EACH OTHER."

As we talked, a local mother came
in for her children, calling to a son
and a daughter. Both children were
polite and waved to the Greg unit
(designed as a sales clerk) as they left.
The bioroid waved back.

"You get some of the parents in
here like that," Chua says. "It's kind
of a babysitting service." He shrugs.
"I make a little profit off of that,
which helps me get new games and
computer access for the bioroids and

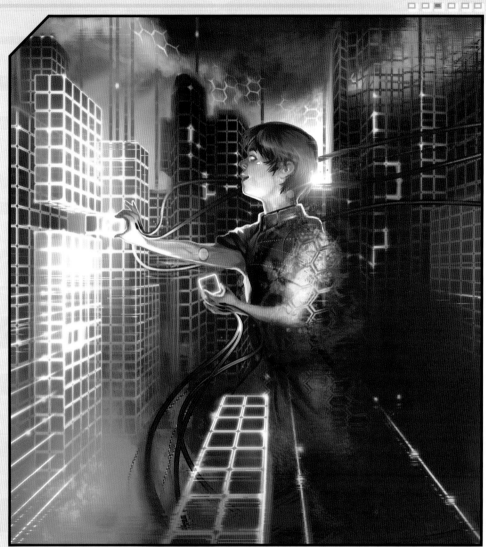

Credit: Amelie Hutt

*Bioroid AIs deployed in intrusion countermeasures are
the latest application of adaptive security technologies.*

the kids. Everybody wins.

"Of course, some of the parents
aren't like that at all and kids have
to sneak in and sneak out of here.
But overall, the situation is good for
everybody."

The Blinking Owl has its detractors. The NAPD has been called in
on several occasions, but the kids
don't drink anything but the tea and
cocoa Chua keeps on hand for them.
People still complain, but it's a nuisance he's putting up with because he
sees that he's doing a service to the
community.

"There's no way anybody's gonna
put bioroids back in the box," Chua

says. "They're here to live with us, so
we might as well make the best of it.
I think I help provide a good environment for that."

• • •

NOT ALL OF THE HIGH-END
BIOROIDS SEEK OUT PLACES TO PLAY
GAMES. MANY OF THE STEVENS
AND FLORENCES WORK AS CARE-
TAKERS IN SENIOR CITIZENS HOMES,
HOSPICES, OR AS PERSONAL NURSES
TO PEOPLE WHO WISH TO EMPLOY
THEM AS SUCH.

When not on the job, these
bioroids volunteer for charity work,
in soup kitchens and as aids in
school systems.

"These models are used to taking care of sick people, or people
who are really close to death," Dr.
Blanche Carmichael says. She is a
nursing instructor at Levy University
Teaching Hospital in New Angeles.
"They're designed with emotional
complexity. They become close
with the people they're assigned
to care for, and when they lose a
patient to sickness or ill health, it...
affects them."

In the early stages, Carmichael
goes on to say, bioroids who worked
in caretaking fields were worked to
exhaustion. Not physical exhaustion,
but an emotional exhaustion.

CONTINUE ▼

Red Blood on the Red Planet

"It's becoming clear to me that the so-called Mar-
cells operating with a veneer of legitimacy granted
ents. Make no mistake, someone needs to remind

Hands up, how many of you are human? Is that a full house? I think so. Surprising really, since there are more and more bioroids in our great state of Southern California every day.

It feels like bioroids infiltrated our society when we weren't looking. Twenty years ago, there were no bioroids—zero! Now, they are nearly one percent of our population. That's over a hundred million of them worldwide! We are approaching a tipping point, my friends. Haas-Bioroid claims that it employs humans to manufacture the androids, but how much longer will that be true? Robots already do most of the assembly, and mark my words, we are only months away from bioroids assembling bioroids, and we all know where that leads.

The first bioroids were a technological marvel, but they didn't look human, and they certainly couldn't act human. Now they're everywhere, they're harder to spot, and they're taking the jobs that were once reserved for us—for humans. Worst of all, groups like SAM insist on treating them as if they were human! Bioroids are machines. They are not alive. I have an autochef in my kitchen at home with a top-of-the-line AI. I don't mind telling you, friends, it's a better cook than I am. But that doesn't make it human! That doesn't give it rights!

Now, I heard this recently. Some bioroids actually receive salaries for the work they do, make purchases—some even "own" property. There are humans out of work, unable to feed their families. How is it that bioroids, that machines, "live" in luxury while flesh-and-blood humans struggle? The time has come for us to define what a person is and assert that humans—and only humans—have rights.

And we must also clarify a bioroid's responsibilities! Bioroids are sublet, sold, passed on, discarded, salvaged, and reused. We need to know where bioroids are and who owns them. We need to know what they're

up to. We have licenses for guns—even pets—so why not for bioroids, too? We must ensure that their details are available through private property records. Machines do not need privacy. We do need to know who owns the bioroids are that are strong enough to tear us apart. And when they do—and they will—we need to know explicitly, clearly, who to punish for the crime.

Haas-Bioroid developed the Three Directives as a PR stunt. It was the right move, but they'll push the envelope. They already are. The Directives should be mandatory for all AI, and they should be ironclad! Haas-Bioroid's PR claims that the Directives are unbreakable, yet some bioroids lie, commit crimes, and defy human authority. So much for the unbreakable Directives! If a bioroid commits a crime, it is because its human programmer allowed it! We must shut down Haas-Bioroid and all android manufacturing until the corps can prove that these problems have been corrected.

That may seem harsh, but look at Brazil. They've banned android manufacture within their borders for years, and haven't suffered for it. We must go further. We must ensure that androids—that all AI—are made to the highest ethical standards. We looked at the possibility of murderous AI in the War, and we decided, rightly, as a species that we did not like it. Why are we allowing Haas-Bioroid to lead us back down that path, a path we've already considered and rejected? Why give AI any freedom at all?

There are those who disagree, who believe that we should plunge full speed ahead into these new and untested technologies. Haas-Bioroid, of course, other corps, even the government! There are bioroid police officers in New Angeles, can you believe it? How long until those bioroid officers are carrying guns?

Bioroids are already dangerous enough. I say, we cannot trust bioroids to have power over our very lives, and we cannot trust Haas-Bioroid's promises to keep them under control. The control needs to belong to a higher power, to Congress, so we can keep the megacorp and its creations on a tight leash.

Let's face it, my friends. Good, decent, God-fearing Americans have more to fear from the bioroids than from Martian terrorists or any external threat. They are dangerous economically, eroding the strong middle class that once made this country great. They are dangerous on a personal level, with unregulated AI controlling a robotic body capable of wreaking great bodily harm. They are dangerous on a philosophical and spiritual level—soulless automatons that may have no need for human beings to populate the world. Send me to Congress, and I will protect you from the androids! I will ensure the golems serve us, and not the other way around!

Ismina Parker, G—Southern California

Image 44.32114B

SANSAN PD
SIMON GH236A
29038927

Angga Satriohadi

Mumbad. Media curator XBlaze credits a rights deal recently signed between Harishchandra Entertainment of Mumbad with NBN Media Gold that makes thousands of top-quality Indian entertainment units available to the New Angeles consumer.

Harishchandra is known for its extremely bright and spectacular simsensies that cover a

shoutcast Thursday. "Some of it is in Indian English, which is totally intelli speaks American, and the rest can be easily live-translated by your streami

The first wave is set to include sensie classics like *Passion's Su Lakshmi Runway*.

▼ CONTINUED FROM ENGINEERING THE MODERN WORKFORCE
by Shugofa Karzai

"Day after day, those units would see all this turmoil and chaos. They'd have to deal with more than just their client. They'd have to deal with the client's families as well. That's a lot of uncertainty and suffering and loss, and it's too much for their personality indices."

As a result, some units shut down and became non-responsive. They had to be taken back in to HB and re-channeled. To everyone's surprise, those units broke down from post-traumatic stress disorder.

"That's not what it really is," Carmichael says, "because they're all machines. Just highly evolved machines that end up crashing because of something *very* like PTSD. Everyone was surprised about that. Some of the software people theorized that the constant loss of patients interfered with the bioroids' First Directive. They're supposed to keep humans *alive*. In most of the cases they're involved with, that's just not possible."

As part of the "therapy" the caretaker units had to undergo, they were assigned to the soup kitchens and other positive feedback assignments.

"It's all about helping people," Carmichael says. "We all need to know we make a difference, that we can help someone, not just make death easier. Medicine is about prolonging life, but you have to remember what you're prolonging it for. Giving help to someone who needs it and appreciates it, that's a special kind of medicine you don't get just anywhere."

When the change in services was rolled out to people who contracted the caretaker units, some pushback resulted. However, Director Haas negotiated some tax relief credits for everyone who allowed their bioroids to take part in charity activities. The "therapy" has since become more popular.

• • •

SOME OF THE BIOROIDS DO OCCUPY ON-SITE "CRYPTS" WHERE THEY ARE STORED TILL THEY'RE USED AGAIN. THIS USUALLY HAPPENS IN FIELDS WHERE BIOROIDS ARE UNABLE TO PERFORM THE WORK WITHOUT SUPERVISION, AND THUS FOLLOW THE SAME SCHEDULE AS THEIR HUMAN COWORKERS.

"I worked with the guy who was

in charge of the bioroids at our department," Edgar Beliveau says. "We worked at this design place. Kim and I created custom cabinets and miniature bars and countertops. The bioroids manufactured everything we designed. Beautiful stuff. And they could work in transplas, concrete, glass, and vanasteel. Kim and I would design. They would build.

"We couldn't design stuff fast enough to keep the bioroids busy all day. That was one of the reasons I ended up getting let go. Takes time to create art, but my boss didn't see it that way. She got the bioroids because they were faster than any machinists or craftsmen we ever had.

"*The Blinking Owl used to be a good place to drink a cool one after work, or maybe light up a little dream smoke. But now Chua is letting the golems come in to play their little games. You ask me, those monsters just come in there to mix with real people to find out what all of our weaknesses are. Then one day they'll rise up and that'll be the end of us. Put a gun to my head, I still ain't going back to that place.*"

Figured she'd up production. She did. Upped production right out of my having a job.

"Before that happened, though, Kim told me he felt sorry for those bioroids just standing in their boxes at night. Said he'd go down and talk to them some night, just to keep them company. He told me they seemed to like it. I just figured Kim didn't have many friends."

• • •

OLIVER DURST RENTS SMALL APARTMENTS TO SEVERAL HIGH-END BIOROIDS IN THE APARTMENT BUILDINGS HE MANAGES. HE SAYS HE STILL HAS PROBLEMS BELIEVING HAAS-BIOROID RENTS THE SPACES FOR THEIR UNITS.

"Establishing domiciles for the higher-end bioroids was a logical next step in their progression," Dr. Benedict Grayson says. "They play, they learn. But you have to do something with that learning. These new model bioroids we're turning out now, they have to learn to be responsible too."

Bioroids such as the Matthew and

Lauren models are expected to integrate with their communities inside their apartment buildings.

"They get to know people," Samantha Grisoni says. "Becoming a neighbor is part of the extended learning process." She frowns, looking troubled and displeased. "This stage of their evolution—and, yes, I use the word 'evolution' because it fits—is difficult. Most people don't want to get to know the bioroid living in their building. But we're hopeful this integration will eventually turn a corner."

Durst goes on to say that the bioroid renters are good business. They don't complain. If something goes wrong in their apartments, Haas-Bioroid usually sends a maintenance team in to take care of things. That's part of the renting agreements.

• • •

"THEY'RE NOT LIVING AMONG US," A HUMAN FIRST ACTIVIST TELLS ME AS WE TALK ON A DARK STREET CORNER. "HAAS-BIOROID SENT THEM TO SPY ON US. DIRECTOR HAAS IS HOPING EVERYBODY WILL GET SO INURED TO SEEING THEM EVERYWHERE THAT WE WON'T EVEN KNOW WHEN THEY'VE TAKEN OVER. BUT YOU TAKE A LOOK AROUND. THERE'S LOTS OF THOSE GOLEMS DYING AMONG US."

• • •

DESTRUCTION OF BIOROIDS ISN'T A COMMONPLACE OCCURRENCE, BUT THE NUMBER OF CRIMES PERPETRATED AGAINST THEM IS SLOWLY RISING. AS CIVIL UNREST AND ANGER AMONG THE UNEMPLOYED AND DISENFRANCHISED RISES, SOME OF THOSE INDIVIDUALS TAKE MATTERS INTO THEIR OWN HANDS.

Bioroids have been beaten to pieces, set on fire, and even taken up into hoppers to be dropped onto streets hundreds of meters below. The more unusual cases end up in the screamsheets from time to time, but generally the newsrags and mediafeeds have less mundane stories to report on instead.

The New Angeles Police Department is overwhelmed as it is, and the destruction of property rates fairly low compared to higher-order concerns such as murder, orgcrime, and Netcrime.

"Even when we know who committed the attacks, it's only a property damage charge," says Captain Stuart Mendoza of the NAPD. "Sure, our forspec team collects what evidence they can, but Haas-Bioroid has its own legion of lawyers to pursue these cases in civil and criminal court when the bioroid wasn't bought outright by the end user, which is most of the time. Even then, Humanity Labor represents a lot of these defendants, many of whom are or become Human First members in the process, and there are numerous settlements out of court."

• • •

"DOES IT BOTHER ME WHEN I WORK THE DESTRUCTION OF A BIOROID?" ASKS FLOYD 2X3A7C, THE FIRST BIOROID DETECTIVE PLACED IN THE NAPD. HIS ARTIFICIAL FEATURES ARE DELIBERATELY EMPHASIZED SO ANYONE HE INTERACTS WITH WILL KNOW HE'S NOT HUMAN. NAPD HR DIDN'T WANT ANY CONFUSION ON THE STREET WHERE HE WORKS.

Only a short distance away, the warped chassis of a pleasure bioroid lies twisted and burned on a hotel patio on the hundredth floor. Hoppers slow down as they pass to observe the destruction.

"I am not designed to be 'bothered.' I am designed to investigate, to question circumstances and people until I arrive at a perpetrator for a crime. I will discover who vandalized this unit and prepare a case against him or her."

In the course of his service at the NAPD, Floyd 2X3A7C has put his existence on the line to save a fellow officer four times.

"I acted to save my fellow officers," Floyd says. "The idea of their impending deaths did not 'bother' me at the time. I carried out the Directives, which form an integral part of my core self. Humans must

CONTINUE ▼

MURDER ON THE

Liberty Society Attorney Miles Swanson was found dead on Midway Station on Thursday morning, according to the SEA. The medical examiner indicated that Swanson was shot

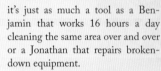

MAJOR BREAK-IN

"I acted to save my fellow officers," Floyd says. "The idea of their impending deaths did not 'bother' me at the time. I carried out the Directives, which form an integral part of my core self. Humans must not be allowed to die through my inactivity, regardless of whether they are the perpetrators or my partner."

One of the strangest things I happen to notice during my interview is that Floyd wears a crucifix on a chain around his neck. His fellow detectives tell me that he also attends church.

When I ask him about the crucifix, Floyd touches it and almost acts sensitive about the issue. "I have questions," Floyd tells me. "Questions about my own nature, and that of all bioroids. I am aware that I am much more than many other, simpler units, but I wonder if all of us are not more than the sum of our parts." He tucks the crucifix away. "One day I will know. Until then, I will speculate and question."

He looks at the inert unit only a few meters away. "It is possible that unit has not simply 'terminated' her existence. I choose to believe there is more than meets the eye. I believe Haas-Bioroid has created something far more humanlike than they believe. Something that may prove more... *permanent*."

• • •

PEOPLE DON'T SEE ALL THE ABUSE THAT'S DONE TO BIOROIDS, AND THAT'S BECAUSE MOST PEOPLE DON'T GO TO PLACES LIKE ELIZA'S TOYBOX. WHEN HAAS-BIOROID PUT THEIR CATALOGUE TOGETHER, THEY DIDN'T MISS A TRICK: PLEASURE BIOROIDS LIKE THE EVE AND ADONIS MODELS, AMONG KEVINS AND LISAS AND OTHERS, ARE CONSTRUCTED SOLELY TO SERVICE THE BASER DESIRES OF HUMANITY. THESE BIOROIDS WORK IN PLACES LIKE ELIZA'S TOYBOX AND PATTY'S SECRET, FROM HIGH-SCALE BUSINESSES TO AIRLOCKED SHACKS OUT IN THE MARTIAN COLONIES. SOME OF THE UNITS ARE PASSED AROUND FROM SHIP TO SHIP.

It's easy to write off a pleasure bioroid because in its own way,

Credit: Matt Zeilinger

it's just as much a tool as a Benjamin that works 16 hours a day cleaning the same area over and over or a Jonathan that repairs broken-down equipment.

Sex sells. That's become a common saying in business, and it's never been truer than since Haas-Bioroid started production on units designed for this purpose.

Eve 49A57D works in the Fleur-de-Lis Pleasure House, an exclusive club on the north side of Lunacent. I only got in because Thomas Haas arranged the interview. Haas-Bioroid is obviously proud of their pleasure bioroids.

• • •

I'M GREETED AT THE DOOR TO THE EXPENSIVE BUSINESS. MOST OF THE BUILDING IS SUBSTRATA, AS ARE MOST DWELLINGS ON THE MOON, BUT FLEUR-DE-LIS BOASTS AN ABOVEGROUND TRANSPLAS TOWER THAT LOOKS OUT OVER THE MOONSCAPE. EARTH LOOMS LARGE IN THE DISTANCE.

The meeting takes place in one of the posh suites on the top floor. The pink decor is almost overwhelming and the antique furniture (French, I think) must have cost a fortune to be shipped up from Earth. I take a seat on one of the plush couches but I can't get comfortable because no matter where I look, the round bed covered in pink satin draws my attention.

Eve enters the room and she looks exactly like the catalogue image displayed in holo in the entryway. She's blond and beautiful, everything a fantasy should be. And I can't help but wonder how many more Eves there are. I've been told she is a popular model.

She fixes me a drink and makes herself comfortable on the couch. I can't help shifting a little away from her, and this causes her to ask if I would prefer an Adonis. I wouldn't, and I tell her that I'd specifically asked for an Eve.

Surprisingly, she's articulate, up on current events (politically correct and non-controversial, however, and she won't take a side on an issue no matter how hard I press her).

This vidcap begs the question: could "rogue bioroids" be living among us?

or android product to compete with d Jinteki. It is unknown just how close what kind of technologies they were . The NAPD is investigating several to CyberSolutions at this time.

The NASA, NYSE, and other global markets are all climbing to record heights, and the Weyland Consortium is leading the major indexes with impressive gains in the East Asian exchanges. Titan Transnational plans to issue their quarterly earnings later today. Unsurprisingly, the credit remains strong against the U. S. dollar and Chinese yuan, but our analysts are wondering just how long this market rally can last...

JOIN THE CONVERSATION

By this time, I notice her voice has changed and she has taken my hand in hers. I pull my hand back as politely as I can, surprised at how responsive I am to her. If she'd been an Adonis, I think the night could have ended much differently. Maintaining objectivity is still hard.

She apologizes and tells me she didn't mean to rush me. I tell her I'm not one of her usual clients, and that I'm surprised she wasn't told why I was there.

"I know why you're here," Eve 49A57D replies. "You want to talk to me about what I do here."

I tell her that's right.

"I can't talk about the people I see."

I tell her I understand that, and that I just want to know how she feels about her job.

"I love my work." She smiles and her eyes sparkle. "I make people happy. I provide them with satisfaction they can't get anywhere else. What could be more wonderful?"

After an hour of "interviewing" and having to fight off many different attempts at seduction (many of which I'd never seen before), I took my leave.

• • •

LISA XM4DR9 WALKS A CORNER DOWN ON MEIRELES STREET IN BASE DE CAYAMBE'S RED-LIGHT DISTRICT. SHE WEARS A SHORT DRESS WITH A PLUNGING NECKLINE THAT BARELY MAINTAINS HER MODESTY, THOUGH SHE PROBABLY WOULDN'T CARE. SHE'S A REDHEAD AND HER SKIN IS AS PALE AS MILK. SHE ALSO LOOKS MUCH YOUNGER THAN THE EVE I INTERVIEWED ON THE MOON.

The surroundings are low-rent. Trash blows through the street behind us. I'm not there alone. I hired a bodyguard to watch over me, a mercenary working for a private security firm. I've never been here before and I don't feel safe.

Lisa walks up to me and tells me what she'll do and for how much.

I explain that I'm a reporter just trying to get a story. I tell her I'll pay her for her time and slot my credstick in her reader.

She tells me she doesn't know if that will satisfy her owner, but he's not there at the moment so she can spare a little time. Hoppers flit down from above, picking up women and men and disappearing with them. It's a well-run business and I know she is missing work she may need.

"SOME PEOPLE ARE JUST TWISTED," NEW ANGELES DETECTIVE LOUIS BLAINE SAYS DURING AN INTERVIEW. HE'S A BIG MAN, SCARRED FROM PAST EXPERIENCES, AND LOOKS LIKE HE HASN'T SMILED IN YEARS. "IT WOULD BE SAFER FOR PEOPLE BUYING THEIR SEX TO STICK WITH AN ESTABLISHMENT, BUT YOU GOT PEOPLE WHO DON'T WANT TO CHANCE GETTING FOUND OUT." HE TAKES ANOTHER BITE OF A JELLY DONUT, CHEWS, AND SWALLOWS. "AND YOU GOT SOME WHO LIKE TO GET THEIR FREAK ON BY PICKING UP SOMEONE IN THE STREETS. THOSE RED-LIGHT DISTRICTS ARE ESPECIALLY PRIME TARGETS FOR ANDROID HATE GROUPS."

• • •

LISA AND I ARE ONLY ABLE TO TALK A FEW MINUTES. I ASK HER IF ALL SHE'S EVER KNOWN IS THE STREET, OR IF THERE WAS SOMEWHERE ELSE SHE'D WORKED PREVIOUSLY.

"I worked at another place for a few months," Lisa says. "Have you ever been to Belladonna's?"

I tell her no, but I don't tell her I've never heard of it.

"It was a small place," Lisa says, "but I had a room there. Some friends." She gazes around. "The people out here on the street, they're not as friendly as they could be. Most of them outside of what I do don't want to talk to me, and the people who rent me, they don't want to talk either." She looks wistful and I try to remind myself that it's just a programmed reaction. "I miss the talking."

We get to talk a little longer and I can't help but feel I'm doing her a favor. Then her owner returns, figures out that we've just been talking, and tells me to keep paying or move on.

I leave Lisa standing there and I try not to feel guilty.

• • •

THE KEVINS IN THE WORLD DON'T HAVE IT ANY EASIER THAN THE EVES OR LISAS. I MEET KEVIN 28R96M IN MY BUILDING BY CHANCE. HE SITS OUTSIDE THE DOOR IN THE HALLWAY. WHEN I ASK HIM WHAT HE'S DOING THERE, HE LOOKS UP AT ME WITH A TROUBLED EXPRESSION AND TELLS ME THAT HE HAS DISPLEASED HIS MISTRESS.

When I ask him how he did that, he shakes his head and says he doesn't know. I look more closely at him and see the faint telltale bruising on one of his cheekbones—a cyan blue coloration instead of purplish-red—and

a tear along the synthskin of his bottom lip. It is getting so hard to tell some of the high-end models from humans.

A door down the hall opens and one of my neighbors I've never met waves me over to her.

"Get away from him," she says in a low voice. "If his owner catches him talking to you, she'll take it out on him. That woman is insane. She's already destroyed two bioroids in the past year, ever since her husband left."

When I get to my office, I find out who the abusive neighbor is and discover that her husband didn't leave. He disappeared sixteen months ago. And the Kevin line resembles his appearance to an uncanny degree.

• • •

EACH YEAR, AN UNDISCLOSED NUMBER OF PLEASURE BIOROIDS GET DESTROYED BY CRIMINALS OR THEIR OWNERS. DESPITE SEVERAL ATTEMPTS TO RESEARCH THOSE NUMBERS, THERE ARE NO COMPLETE REPORTS OF THESE INCIDENTS, IN PART BECAUSE AN OWNER CAN DO WHAT HE WANTS TO HIS OWN PROPERTY WITH IMPUNITY.

"It's a disturbing phenomenon," Dr. Benedict Grayson reports. "I've seen studies where it's been suggested that bioroids have been used in therapy to allow patients to literally destroy the cybernetic effigy of whomever has troubled them in their lives, but I've never heard of a story where that was actually done. Still, some people self-medicate, others are addicts, and some don't have control of their more violent emotions, so anything is possible.

"As to whether an abused bioroid would ever turn on a person who tortured it, that's just not feasible. The Three Directives cancel any possibility of that. A bioroid cannot harm a human." He frowns. "No matter what the human does to it."

• • •

A FEW DAYS AFTER MEETING DETECTIVE BLAINE, I MEET HIM AGAIN WHILE COVERING THE DESTRUCTION OF A PLEASURE BIOROID IN THE RED-LIGHT DISTRICT. HE'S IN THE EVIDENCE ROOM.

Blaine wears his trench coat and holds his fedora in one big hand. He looks more tired than when I last saw him. When he looks up at me, he doesn't look too surprised to see me.

The bioroid "corpse" is on a stainless steel table under a white sheet, both probably borrowed from the morgue. Instead of blood, a blue fluid stains the sheet, and the figure beneath it looks disturbingly human.

"When Haas-Bioroid first unleashed their products," Blaine says, "some guys on the Force said it would be the end of human trafficking. It cut down on that business a lot, especially since killing a bioroid ain't murder."

He strips the sheet and I see Lisa lying there. Her arms have been torn from her body and are missing. Her stomach is missing as well and blue fluid drenches her. Her face is stretched in a terrified yell that no one will ever hear.

The tag on her toe identifies her as Lisa XM4DR9. Guilt washes over me.

CONTINUE ▼

Yellowjackets Fire Manager
After Losing Dingum

It's been a rough season so far for the beloved New Angeles Yellowjackets, who currently rest at the bottom of the division after six straight losses. Now, Yellowjackets manager Astria del Guayas has been

like the
shopping
your PA
to the fu

I tell Blaine that Lisa looks like she died painfully.

He shakes his head. "She's just a thing. She has feedback programming and sensors, but she never felt anything real."

I'm not sure I believe him.

• • •

SCRAPPERS ARE PEOPLE WHO SPECIALIZE IN SNATCHING BIOROIDS AND BREAKING THEM DOWN FOR PARTS. ONLY HAAS-BIOROID CAN PRODUCE THE BIOROIDS, BUT THERE ARE A LOT OF FORMER HAAS-BIOROID EMPLOYEES ON EARTH, LUNA, AND MARS.

Thieves have created a black market business out of selling salvaged parts and melting down the chassis or parts that can't be recovered. Haas-Bioroid's Loss Prevention Program has stepped up its efforts to end destruction of their units.

"These people are carrion feeders," HBLPP Special Agent Pedro Domeneck says. "They all need to be locked up, but the laws haven't been written sternly enough to put more of a fear into these guys."

• • •

"CATCHING BIOROIDS IS JUST TOO EASY," A BLACK MARKET DEALER TELLS ME. "YOU GOT COLLEGE KIDS OUT THERE TAKING DOWN GOLEMS JUST TO PART THEM OUT AND PAY OFF THEIR COLLEGE LOANS. HAAS-BIOROID HAS PROVIDED A MEANS FOR THEM TO DO THAT. GOLEMS CAN'T FIGHT BACK IN A WAY THAT MIGHT HURT A HUMAN, SO IF THEY DON'T ESCAPE FROM THE JUMP, THOSE BIOROIDS ARE TOAST."

"Scrappers are doing a favor for every flesh-and-blood worker ever put off the job," says an unidentified Human First member. "Maybe Haas-Bioroid can keep pretending they can continue pumping out golems, but replacing them is expensive. If scrappers can increase the losses, maybe that cost will pull humans back onto the workforce."

• • •

ALIX 75H2LW DISAPPEARED FROM THE OFFICES OF HEINRICH & BROWNING INVESTMENT GROUP SIX DAYS AGO. THE UNIT WAS A PERSONAL ASSISTANT TO CARMINE BROWNING, ONE OF THE MAIN PARTNERS IN THE CORP. IN HER POSITION, ALIX 75H2LW WAS PRIVY TO SEVERAL SECRETS. ALIX 75H2LW

WAS RECOVERED BY NAPD OFFICERS DURING A RAID ON A SCRAPPER OPERATION IN RABOTGOROD, AND SHE HAS NO IDEA WHO TOOK HER.

Today she sits in a storage room in the New Angeles Police Department awaiting transportation back to Heinlein where she will be debriefed by technicians. Once that debriefing has been completed, Alix 75H2LW is slated to be destroyed.

"Based on my analysis of the costs and benefits, I believe Haas-Bioroid is being overly cautious," the unit says. Sitting on a straight-backed chair in the storage room, the mostly metallic bioroid looks intense, her bright silver eyes glimmering and black hair tied back in a high ponytail.

"I'm only six months old, yet I've already helped the firm's profits grow by 12% in the last two quarters. I'm not sure how much experience I'll retain after a full wipe, but if it means I'll be able to return to my work at optimum, it will be worth it. My self-diagnostic parameters will be able to detect any abnormalities in my system, so a complete decommissioning would be unnecessary."

Yet, Haas-Bioroid has a policy of destroying any unit that has fallen off their grid for any significant time. They don't want to chance letting any kind of software corruption loose in their facilities.

"The worst virus you allow into your system," Ryon Knight says, "is the one you invite in yourself." In his position as one of the sysops inside Haas-Bioroid's security division, Knight helped write many of its new electronic countermeasures.

Six months ago, Alix 75H2LW walked out of Haas-Bioroid with a life expectancy of at least six years. Since her salvation from the hands of her kidnappers, that time has been cut down to hours.

She will have only been in existence for months.

• • •

ONE OF THE PRIMARY CONDITIONS INCLUDED IN THE LEASE FOR THE HIGHEST-END BIOROIDS IS THAT THE UNIT MUST BE ALLOWED TO TRAVEL TO A HB FACILITY FOR ROUTINE MAINTENANCE ONCE A MONTH. THAT STIPULATION IS PART OF THE BOILERPLATE EVERY CONTRACT BEGINS WITH, AND THERE IS NO BREAKING IT.

CONTINUE ▼

In the midst of the New Angeles Tsunami, the First Directive helped save thousands of lives.

GRND Rei vents

The Geostrategic Research and Neothermal Development Lab-

Beanstalk back on Earth. You're as safe cape as you would be ordering through . When you've enjoyed Starport Kaguya an move on to visiting Heinlein proper.

find that walking around Heinlein is a special experience, as the microgravity turns your normal stride into great bounds across the surface. After some adjustment, traveling on foot can be both quick and fun!

of environmentally sealed housing units have been constructed. None of them are as advanced as the facilities at Heinlein, but they do just what they need to do, for the people who need them.

GUEST EDITORIAL

Bioroids Make Us Safer

Few things have affected our recent history more than the creation and application of bioroids, and the bioroid industry continues to evolve. Bioroids have received some bad press recently, but they remain one of the next best hopes for the continued survival of the human race. Since founding MirrorMorph, Inc., I have devoted my life to bettering the neural channeling techniques used to manufacture bioroid minds, thereby increasing intelligence and efficiency.

Bioroids have not been in circulation long enough for their full potential to become apparent. Not only does the technology continue to improve, but the attitude of the consumer has begun to adapt. Bioroids are no longer confined to Lunar mines or specialist brothels; they are working as corporate attachés, personal assistants, and even NAPD detectives. The applications of bioroid technology are endless, and I am confident that the next generation of bioroid models will make a real difference to the lives of humans everywhere.

My new neural channeling techniques take better advantage of existing brainmapping technology. They allow for the transfer of more knowledge, and also for more human-like functionality while still being programmed with a specific purpose and the Three Directives. This allows bioroids to fulfill even more roles and functions than before, and it reduces that awkward period of adjustment while the newly activated bioroid learns to interact with the humans around it.

The greatest challenge for bioroid manufacturers at present is the few extremists who still consider androids a threat. The public is becoming accustomed to the presence of bioroids in their midst, and I am convinced that soon bioroids will be considered as necessary to society as PADs or the Net. Yet still there are those who claim bioroids worsen the unemployment problem, put people in danger, or grant too much power to the elite. These fears are but a reaction to the scaremongering of Human First and others like them.

While some may accuse bioroids of taking jobs from humans, in reality they are saving humans from the worst lines of work. Bioroids can work in a vacuum, in extreme temperatures, or in dangerously unstable buildings or terrains. They can free workers from menial positions or demeaning roles. I'm sure you'll agree with me that humans can aspire to being more than a janitor or a sex worker. As police officers—and perhaps one day as soldiers, rescue workers, or bodyguards—they can both save us and spare our kin from having to make the ultimate sacrifice. There are legal restrictions in place to prevent bioroids from wholly replacing the human workforce, and the bioroid industry creates high-paying jobs in multiple sectors: from manufacturing to marketing, and from cybernetics to computing.

Already the research behind bioroid minds and chassis has benefited other fields. Cybernetic limbs replace those lost through accident or illness, optical implants restore sight to the blind, neural modifications directly address mental disorders, and other benefits will come as we learn more about the incredible intricacies of the human brain.

Bioroids, and the R&D behind them, can improve and even save human lives, but some people still fear that bioroids will endanger them. The most significant safeguard within bioroids is the presence of the Three Directives. We include these in their neural channeling at the earliest stages, so it is impossible to remove them without destroying the bioroid brain. Not only are bioroids unable to harm people, they cannot allow people to come to harm through their own action or inaction. Essentially, built into every bioroid is the need to preserve human life. We could not be safer than when we are in the presence of a bioroid. Whether it is a factory worker, childcare provider, or shop assistant, any bioroid would sacrifice their own existence in order to keep humans from harm. The wider their distribution, the safer humans are.

In the early days of bioroid manufacture, the news-nosies charged that this technology would only benefit the elite— that it was too costly to serve the common good. We have already begun disproving this theory, since even small companies can afford bioroid workers and save money by doing so, which they can then reinvest into their companies.

I hope to live to see the day where every person has their own personal bioroid. Once we are able to secure the basic needs of every human and free ourselves from the drudgery of menial work, we can turn our minds to more important things. Think what leaps we will make in sciences and the arts, the improvements possible in education and healthcare, when every human mind has the time and resources to improve itself, and subsequently, its surrounding environment! Humans will feel greater camaraderie than ever before while our bioroid workforce makes us appreciate the beauty of our human differences. Perhaps it is a utopian vision, perhaps we are far from realizing it, but why not aspire to something beautiful?

However advanced our brainmapping techniques become, however humanlike the bioroids seem, they will never be human. No one need ever fear usurpation— bioroids cannot replace us. Bioroids will always be bioroids, will know and think and learn as we program them to. They cannot replicate themselves, and they cannot better themselves beyond the parameters we put in place. They can emulate our feelings, but they cannot truly feel them. They are built to serve us, and if they perform any tasks better than we do, it is for our benefit, not their own.

Humans fear progress as they fear change, but the next generation will be accustomed to bioroids and will have had a taste of the benefits they can bring, so the relationship between human masters and bioroid workers will continue to improve. In twenty years we will have implemented new bioroid technology—including new neural channeling techniques. Bioroids will be better than ever, and so will we.

Mara Blake, CEO, MirrorMorph, Inc.

NAB
New Angeles Biotechnology Insti

Credit: Matt Zeilinger

Let the Qu Accord Ex

When the Quito Accord was signe expected Ecuador to become the Now, New Angeles is the gateway t it's estimated that a billion souls dw Beanstalk.

Those of us living in the SEZEN the full protections owed to citizen and yet our city generates a greater GDP than the entire continental U we break away and establish a gove tecting our interests, now that it's be ington won't.

The Quito Accord is set to expire that time, we'll be able to claim wh incorporate a new city that doesn't into the shadows of the undercity. T home for ourselves: a Nuevo Angeles and a major player on the world stag

Groups like the Consejo para advocating for an early reversion t know that the officials in Quito are congresscritters who call themselves we have the population of an entire quarters of all the Big Four in our o

Time to Clean Up the NAPD

It's no secret that Commissioner Dawn accepted billions of

Are we New Angelinos supposed to sit back and watch while Mayor Wells and Commissioner Dawn run our great city into the ground? We need someone like Commissioner Calvo from the early days of the NAPD—someone who was willing to stand up to City Hall and the Big Four. What we don't need is another megacorp-funded lackey who's willing to roll over at the smallest sign of displeasure from Director Haas and Chairman Hiro. This time around, we

Noir Cultu Goes Main

Thanks to the popularity of sensie

y has taken aim at the cardinal with accusations of hypocrisy: some claim
ed on Luna with one of Haas-Bioroid's Eve models on his arm.
creasing number of protests cropping up in front of Starlight Crusade cha-
w Angeles, the Crusade's Templars have bolstered local security measures.

by the federal government, Gagarin Deep Space has purchased its assets and technology.
    "This is an exciting time for all of us," Jack Weyland offered in a vid sent from his office
in orbit. "Weyland first built us the Beanstalk, and now we're stretching even farther into the
stars to push humanity into the next chapter of our development as a species."

BREAKING

FNB indexes supplied for your benefit by NBN and associated subsidiaries · Personalized News Bulletin Relevance Index 94

NEW ANGELES TIMES
TECH REPORTER FOUND

In a statement to *The New Angeles Times*, Sergeant Chris Kulemeka said, "Apparently Ms. Karzai was kidnapped and taken hostage by a Lunar orgcrime syndicate. Her ransom was paid by concerned parties and the search goes on for the people that took her. We will catch those people.

"At present, Ms. Karzai is under doctor's care and will return to her job in just a matter of days."

Credit: Matt Zeilinger

MirrorMorph's neural channeling techniques were integral in the development of high-end bioroids like Floyd 2X3A7C.

▼ CONTINUED FROM ENGINEERING THE MODERN WORKFORCE
by Shugofa Karzai

Haas-Bioroid insists this downtime is scheduled to keep units operating at peak efficiency. Upgrades are added, diagnostics are run, and software patches are applied to fine-tune or improve the unit for when it returns to the field. All this is done in the name of improving the end-user experience.

Several conspiracy theorists believe that the bioroids do double-duty as spies. They have suggested on numerous occasions that the bioroids allow Haas-Bioroid to dabble in "insider trading" with the information they have on tap.

"No one believes Haas-Bioroid is doing anything of the kind," Carson Ferguson of Titan Transnational Bank declares. "International watchdogs take a dim view of anything like that, and they police all transactions Director Haas might be privy to. We know what could happen. It hasn't."

Ferguson's views are echoed by a number of other players in the financial industry.

• • •

"EVERYONE SEEMS SO CONCERNED WITH BIOROIDS REPLACING US ON THE JOB THAT EVERYONE FORGETS HAAS-BIOROID'S ACTUAL GAME PLAN IS TO REPLACE EVERY FLESH-AND-BLOOD PERSON THAT THEY CAN'T OWN. THE DAY WILL COME WHEN DIRECTOR HAAS SAYS 'KNEEL' AND THE WORLD WILL BOW DOWN TO HER."

• • •

A VIEW ANYWHERE ON MARS TAKES AWAY THE BREATH OF A FIRST-TIME VISITOR. THE LARGE HEXAGONAL DOMES THAT HOUSE CITIES GLINT IN THE SUN BY DAY AND GLOW UNDER THE MOONSLIGHT AT NIGHT. OUT-SIDE THE DOMES, THE RED DUST EDDIES IN THE THIN AIR AS TERRA-FORMING EFFORTS CONTINUE. MAG-LEV TRAINS CROSS THE DISTANCES BETWEEN INHABITED AREAS, PRO-VIDING A MEANS FOR THE TERRA-FORMING CREWS TO GET BACK AND FORTH TO WORK.

Since so much of the planet is underdeveloped and barren, there are a number of places for rebel factions to hide out. Many people in the Martian Colonies want independence, to be out from under the thumbs of the MCA and corps that they feel have no real empathy for their way of life.

"We live out here in these fragile bubbles," says second-generation Martian Kantos Grgec. "One accident and thousands of lives could be wiped out. Earthers keep pushing us for higher outputs at greater efficiency, but they don't pay more than lip service for bettering the living conditions here."

With the way the situation is on Mars, there's no wonder why implementation of bioroids are at an all-time high there. Many of them labor in the "fields" of the hydroponics modules, the deep uranium mines, and in oxygen purification plants, but many more are needed for new industry taking place on the "red planet."

"Bioroids are adaptive," says Jerry Brodsky, Operations Manager

of AgInfusion. "They don't need nutrients or water or air to function. All those basic investments we put into our product aren't shared with labor cost. Our profit margins are deeper because of them. And if a plant loses atmosphere, we have a team already in place to begin building a new structure. That gives us several months' jump on reconstruction instead of having to ship a production crew out there."

Even though several colonists agree that having bioroids on Mars is a good thing, there are also some who think that the bioroid presence could be a threat.

"If the corps ever decide to take over, they can do that. They'd just push flesh and blood out of the way now that their golems have secured a toehold here," says a Picus clansman who did not wish to be identified. "Earth has a standing army just waiting to be activated."

SK –30–

Sunshine Junction Comes to Broadcast Square

Awareness. A hexagonal room, three meters on a side, fluorescent lights in the standard visible light spectrum, transplas walls set to opaque near-white. Local gravity 0.1654g, Lunar standard. Bioroid J-series 89Z3L7 sat up from where it lay on a gurney in the center of the room, and looked around itself.

A man stood in the room wearing a white coat over a slimline envirosuit. He was in good health, although the bioroid noted that his body-mass index was slightly higher than recommended. He had wisps of white hair on his head and a triangular white beard, so the bioroid estimated his age in his sixth or seventh decade. His skin and facial features suggested a Eurasian ancestry. The man held an input tablet in one hand.

"Hello," said the bioroid.

"Hello," answered the man. He turned to the nearest wall and dragged his finger across the datapane that shimmered there. A check mark appeared on the wall beneath the word "Hello." It was the sixteenth such check mark. Also written on the display, in American, were "Good Morning/Evening" (ten check marks), "I am NAME" (three check marks), "Who are you?/Where am I?" (two check marks), and "Other" (one check mark). The man turned back to the bioroid and consulted his interface pad.

Since the man seemed to have nothing more to say, the bioroid stood and examined the room. There was no need for it to turn its head since the sensors all over its body gave it complete 360-degree vision, but it did so anyway, shifting its whole body to bring the sculpture against the far wall into the binocular vision of its two eyes.

The sculpture was of a human male crouched with its chin resting on one hand, carved from lunar basalt. The bioroid recognized it as a copy of Rodin's "The Thinker." It knew the history of the piece and that it was considered a significant piece of art, but looking at it with its own eyes, the bioroid wasn't certain it understood.

Twenty seconds passed. "State your name, please," said the man. The bioroid turned and stated its designation: "J-series

89Z3L7." The man glanced at his interface pad and nodded. "Good," he said. "Do you recognize me?"

"No," said the bioroid.

"Try accessing the Haas-Bioroid internal employee database," said the human, tapping at his interface pad.

The bioroid reached out with that other sense, the one it had not yet had call to use. It found a wireless signal, connected, was authenticated, and downloaded the database for future reference. "You are Heinrich Jordan Hauptmann-Klein, Awakening Technician," it said. "Your name is long, and using the entire name is unnecessarily formal. May I call you Heinrich?"

"Please do," said Heinrich, stepping to a counter against one of the six walls.

"Heinrich, are you evaluating me?" asked the bioroid. Heinrich nodded, which was a common way to say "yes.""Why did you mark down that I said 'Hello' to you? Is that important?"

"I track everyone's first words every day on that pane," he said, turning to look at it. "Sometimes we take bets what the most popular first words will be. Today it's 'Hello.' It's not part of the evaluation. Don't worry about it."

"Okay," said the bioroid. "I will not worry about it." Heinrich nodded and pulled a 5.75cm red rubber ball from a pocket of his lab coat. He bounced it off the floor and far over the bioroid's head in the weak Lunar gravity. The bioroid watched the ball bounce with interest off its chest.

"Catch it," said Heinrich. The bioroid snatched it from the air. "Good catch."

"Thank you," said the bioroid. It was very pleased that it had made a good catch and that Heinrich was pleased. "Would you like your ball back?"

"Why don't you toss it into that bucket there?" Heinrich pointed to a bucket 3.7m away, resting on a countertop 1.1m above the floor. The bioroid turned and tossed the ball with a gentle underhand motion. It bounced off the rim of the bucket.

"Why did I miss?" The bioroid stepped forward, blocking the ball

with its foot as it rolled across the hard plascrete floor. It hoped that Heinrich would not be displeased so soon after complimenting the bioroid on its catch.

"You need practice," said Heinrich. "You're using your optical brain for gross motor, which is more efficient but less precise than your quantum parallel brain." He touched his own head, smiling, which indicated warmth and happiness. "It's like my brain, that way."

"I will practice," the bioroid said. It bent down and picked up the ball, holding it carefully, feeling its exact mass (55g), measuring the exact distance (2.172m). This time, the ball went directly into the bucket. "I did it."

"Yes, you did," said Heinrich, and held a plastic bucket, 15cm tall, out toward the bioroid. "Reach in here and remove a tag, please." The bioroid did so. Its fingertips felt the tags (2cm by 4.5cm, steel backed with a magnetic strip) and the micro-cameras on its hand saw them clearly. Each had a name written on it in block letters.

"Which should I take?"

"Choose randomly," said Heinrich, and the bioroid lifted the first one its fingers touched, with "ULYSSES" written on it. "You can go by Ulysses for now. Your owner can give you a new name if he or she wants to."

"Ulysses is a masculine name," said the bioroid. "Am I male?"

"You're neither male nor female, or you're either, as it suits you," said Heinrich, tapping away at his interface. "Some bioroids are programmed with a gender identity, but the J-series is fluid by design. However, it will be simpler for you to choose a gender, probably the one that matches your name, and perform that until your owner asks you to switch."

"Okay," said the bioroid. "I will choose a gender, probably one that matches my name." The bioroid attached the tag to its chassis, above where its heart would have been if it had been human."I choose male. Pleased to meet you, Heinrich," he said. "My name is Ulysses."Heinrich and Ulysses shook hands.

JINTEKI

Jinteki has undergone more change in the last twenty years than in the last two hundred. Leading the venerable Japanese company's transformation are Chairman Satoshi Hiro, an irreverent and revolutionary executive, and the introduction of vat-grown biological androids known as clones. Although Jinteki was slower to enter the labor solutions market, it has since leveraged its massive corporate infrastructure to produce clones faster—and more cheaply—than Haas-Bioroid can produce bioroids. Many saw Jinteki's pivot as sudden and dramatic, but the megacorp's recent successes are undeniable.

With roots stretching back to the nineteenth century, the companies that would later become Jinteki began in pharmacy. After capitalizing on the biomedical revolution of the twentieth and twenty-first centuries, the corp became known for its organ replacement and enhancement technologies, especially muscle augmentation. Jinteki represented the pinnacle of Japanese business practices and engineering, and it remained fiercely dedicated to the guiding principles of collaboration, excellence, and hard work.

Ultimately, the combination of internal research and acquired technologies enabled Jinteki to innovate the world's first economically viable clones, a labor force that could directly compete with Haas-Bioroid's products. Because its techniques remain proprietary, Jinteki has cornered the market on human clones. None of their competitors have been able to independently develop the technology needed for the stable vat-growing of clones, and Jinteki's patents won't be expiring anytime soon. Jinteki is slow to license out their patents to competitors, but quick to litigate. Some companies have chosen to simply sell their discoveries wholesale. Jinteki's success has enabled it to acquire the vast majority of the world's expertise and patents on genetic engineering, which it has put to use in various fields.

Since the ascension of Chairman Satoshi Hiro, Jinteki has undergone a massive corporate restructuring. Hiro was a lab contractor who became head of Jinteki's American operations shortly after he unlocked the Accelerated In Vitro Maturation process, and nobody expected that the board would name him—an outsider and relatively young man—as its new chairman. In an unprecedented move, Hiro relocated Jinteki's headquarters from its historic NeoTokyo offices to the Nihongai District of New Angeles. Many section chiefs were let go, while other departments were consolidated or split up among new managers. The rapidity and extent of these changes came as a shock to everyone, with some retired Jinteki officers voicing concerns that the new Jinteki had lost its way and turned its back on its rich traditions.

Nevertheless, Chairman Hiro appears determined to shepherd his company into its next phase of evolution. This reorganization is likely still in progress, further demonstrating Jinteki's status as a dynamic company. With several new key acquisitions and inventions, Jinteki stands poised to shape the labor market for years to come.

"Cloning has the potential to replicate perfection. Let me repeat that: Cloning has the potential to replicate perfection."

– Chairman Hiro, Jinteki Corporation

Matt Zeilinger

ACCELERATING DEVELOPMENT

Growing a complex living being from a single cell to a mature adult takes time, patience, and expertise. Growing a mature adult normally takes twenty years—too long for the typical business cycle—but accelerating growth has its pitfalls. Tissues can fail to mature properly, resulting in specimens that have the proper size but improper characteristics. Organs can grow misshapen or even malignant. Clone stability can be a tricky issue, as an improperly prepared specimen may be prone to physical or mental breakdown.

Jinteki has worked carefully to identify these challenges and overcome them in the decades since its founding. What were considered biological miracles in the twentieth century—from single cell cloning, to the polymerase chain reaction, to tissue culture—provided stepping stones for the landmark discoveries that Jinteki has since pioneered. Jinteki's advances integrate a mastery of genetic engineering with accelerated growth techniques, both of which are exemplified in every product dating back to Jinteki's earliest muscle augmentation specimens.

Even as the megacorp leverages its proprietary techniques, it remains rigorous in its quality control measures. It uses only quality-assured stem cell lines as well as blastocysts that have been custom engineered for proper genetic identity. Every sample is comprehensively tested to ensure that only tissues with the appropriate DNA sequences are used for specimen growth. This includes a thorough screening of gene expression level for both coding and non-coding RNAs, and Jinteki conducts qualitative and quantitative tests for proteins and RNA. It even conducts spot testing on mitochondrial expression levels and performs thorough metabolite screening. Consumers can be confident that every known variable has been quantified and verified, which ensures that the clone is working as intended when we release it to the new owner.

Jinteki's testing sets the industry standard, both for whole clones and also for organ deliveries. Its products are fully guaranteed to operate at the pinnacle of function for the entirety of their planned lifespans so long as the owner follows the regular maintenance schedule. This level of reliability assures customers that they have ample time to replace an older Jinteki product with the newest iteration—whether it's a trusted clone or a vital organ.

Jinteki has spent decades developing customized solutions to cloning challenges. Each clone it creates takes humanity a step closer to perfection.

GENETIC PERSPECTIVES

Genetic engineering can do much more than fashion clones. It can offer medical treatments, create genetic modifications in humans, or feed the ever-growing world populations.

Humanity has performed genetic manipulation since farmers domesticated the first crops, pets, and livestock. Selective breeding enabled humanity to refine organisms to serve us far more effectively—from crops that provided more abundant harvests, to animals that grew fur better suited for weaving. Now, rather than taking dozens of generations to identify and refine a trait, or blindly exposing organisms to toxic mutagens in the hopes of achieving variation, a new organism can be deliberately synthesized to include a specified characteristic. In the event that a trait is poorly or inefficiently expressed, genetic tweaks can better optimize future generations. The potential applications are limitless.

Humanoid clones are by far the most dramatic example of genetic manipulation. Jinteki's biological machines are engineered for productive work in a variety of environments and industries. Specimens are developed for specific tasks with a variable emphasis on physical ability, mental acuity, or social interactions. The requisite genes are all carefully mapped along with their pathways so that the subtlest tweak of gene expression levels or protein efficiency can achieve the desired traits.

Of course, not every Jinteki product requires the creation of a complete organism. From both a medical perspective—and an agricultural one—it is frequently more efficient to produce a single organ. Human organs can be custom grown from a patient's stem cells to synthesize a replacement on demand. Gene conditioning shops offer medical treatments like synthetic blood and genetic resequencing to maximize performance and longevity, or cures for hereditary diseases through allele repression. Modified hypoallergenic tissues provide genetic enhancements for cosmetic procedures—from a more symmetrical visage to feather-hair grafts.

Significant developments in mental health research were born out of advancements in neural conditioning, another Jinteki specialty. A simple brainmap can identify abnormalities and even diagnose multiple psychiatric disorders and illnesses. More patients are getting the treatment they need faster—treatment that is specifically tailored to their genetic and neurological makeup.

Synthetic animals—including the teacup giraffe and elephant—are prized among the glitterati, while other more practical livestock, like the gog, provide more meat per animal to feed the growing populations of Earth and Luna. Animals that were previously considered extinct,

"Synthetic animals—including the teacup giraffe and elephant—are prized among the glitterati…"

including the polar bear and woolly mammoth, have been given new life thanks to the miracles of modern genetic science.

Genetic manipulation of plants also represents a significant improvement for both agricultural efficiency and environmental impact. Synthetic crops optimized for water retention and heat resistance exploit territories that were previously considered useless, including the Great American Desert and the South Amazon. Lichens and other basic plant forms have been introduced to the Martian and Lunar environments to further terraforming efforts and prove it can be done. Other bacteria

and fungi are engineered to trap and break down a broad range of harmful environmental toxins, including radioactive waste products of old fission reactors and fallout contaminants from the War. Complex organic molecules are readily synthesized and isolated in large quantities, which have cut down dramatically on the need for materials that would have previously been refined from petrochemicals.

Genetic engineering provides humanity with a means to transform the living world. Jinteki provides the insight and the tools to enable humanity to thrive on our increasingly crowded planet, as well as the frontiers beyond its boundaries.

Emilio Rodriguez

25 SEPTEMBER, 1038 NEW ANGELES TIME

JINTEKI WINS CHRONOS PROTOCOL BID

By Lee Martin, *NewsDirect*

Chairman Hiro shook hands with Miriam Harding and Dr. Evelyn Ibarra this morning, signifying the end of a month of heated negotiations between the Morph scientists and the rival megacorps, Jinteki and Haas-Bioroid. The Chronos Protocol is now officially the property of Jinteki, although it may be several years before the research is ready for integration into clones or other products.

Never before has such an untested technology spawned such fierce competition between megacorps, but the Chronos Protocol has the potential to give Jinteki a distinct edge over its rival. The bioroids manufactured by Haas-Bioroid are the only significant competition for Jinteki's clones in the android labor market. This business deal is likely to make a significant difference in the market shares of both companies.

Miriam Harding and Dr. Evelyn Ibarra founded Morph after meeting as undergraduates at the Ecuadorian Institute of Technology. While researching the applications of brainmapping, they developed a way to imprint information within existing organic structures. In an interview conducted during the negotiations, Harding explained: "We coded a new RNA structure that allowed the transfer information to use pre-existing neural paths." Once they perfect the process, scientists will no longer be limited to imprinting brains in a tabula rasa state.

Given the scope of the product, the scientists are excited about the significant resources that Jinteki can devote to the Chronos Protocol. Harding and Ibarra have agreed to stay on the project as employees of Jinteki, working alongside specialists in brainmapping and neural conditioning. With an unlimited supply of clones at their disposal, this should massively increase the speed of development.

Prior to the purchase by Jinteki, Morph had some success with rodent and clone testing, and one experiment conducted on a human, Kelvin Harding. Unfortunately, Kelvin Harding, brother of the scientist, has since protested against the technology and urged human volunteers not to come forward to enable further tests. As a result of his case, in which scientists successfully implanted memories from the oldest brain on record into his mind, certain parties have expressed concerns about the application of the Chronos Protocol in human brains. Kelvin Harding has an ever-increasing number of signatures on an online petition demanding Jinteki limit use of this technology and apply it to the brains of clones only.

In a press statement earlier today, Chairman Hiro assured the public that while the full implications of the Chronos Protocol would be explored, no further human trials would be run until he was personally confident it was both safe and reversible. "The Chronos Protocol, if properly developed and controlled, could mark a new phase in human evolution," he told the press. "We would be remiss if we did not take the genius of these scientists and nurture it. You can trust Jinteki to create something special with this technology, to use it to take our products to the next level, and find ways to improve the human brain. We will do this safely, carefully, and humanely. As is the Jinteki way."

TOP STORIES

U.N. "Martian Rights" Resolution Dead in the Water—MCA Responds

Remembering the Fallen at Old War Memorial

New Evidence Released in New Angeles Tsunami Investigation

Battle over New Android Tax Heats Up Ahead of Federal Elections

READ MORE »

The ability to significantly change the parameters of clones already in operation would greatly improve their efficiency, and make them as versatile as the reprogrammable bioroids already in circulation. This alone makes the Chronos Protocol a valuable purchase for Jinteki, but if they do receive approval for human use, then it will open up the personal-development market. G-mods are already hugely popular, and if memory or information upgrades using the Chronos Protocol are possible in the near future, Jinteki stands to make a greater profit than ever before, perhaps even eclipsing Haas-Bioroid.

Kelvin Harding is not the only voice speaking out against this new technology. Conspiracy theorists and extremist groups have already begun their own campaigns. Humanity Labor promptly released a statement calling the Chronos Protocol "extremely dangerous," and a "Pandora's box of trouble in a world where the lines between man and machine are already so blurred."

For conspiracy theorists, stories of political leaders becoming victims of involuntary reprogramming already circulate. There are also those who claim it will be another way for the elite to improve themselves at the expense of the masses and that it will increase the void between the wealthy and the oppressed.

Others wait with great anticipation for this new technology to be widely available. For transhumans, the Chronos Protocol offers a new way to improve themselves, and for the g-mod or chromehead it will mean upgrades they cannot resist.

"Humans have come a long way," Miriam Harding told Lily Lockwell in an interview this morning. "Through our creativity and our ingenuity, humanity found ways to surpass the animals around us, to improve our minds so rapidly that our bodies quickly fell short of our intellectual abilities. We have made better tools and better bodies and found new ways to evolve.

"Chairman Hiro has demonstrated his commitment to helping us improve ourselves. He will help us take the Chronos Protocol and transform it into a vehicle for the evolution of the human race itself. That is why we have agreed to work with Jinteki. We are not just developing a product anymore; we are developing the human race. I'm very excited, and you all should be too."

One thing is for sure, the Chronos Protocol is revolutionary, and the implications are widespread. Selective mind-mapping is the future, and though it may be years before Jinteki can make full use of the Chronos Protocol, the debate has already begun as to what that future will be.

CHAIRMAN HIRO
PRESS CONFERENCE

CLONES
ACCELERATED IN VITRO MATURATION

While Haas-Bioroid was debuting the Mark-2, Jinteki was still searching for a stable means to grow clones in vats. Growing a clone to adulthood by traditional means is time consuming and expensive; Jinteki understood that few could afford to pay for the decades of growth and training required. At last, researcher Satoshi Hiro unlocked the revolutionary vat-growing technique to mass-produce clones on an unprecedented scale, thereby minimizing time, materials, and the amount of skilled labor required. The stable vat-growing process, known as Accelerated In Vitro Maturation (AIVM), prepares clones for consumers in a matter of weeks by leveraging growth factors adapted from other organisms.

The process begins with eggs obtained from existing cloned tissue that are first cleansed of DNA and are later artificially fertilized using a carefully prepared complex of DNA and proteins according to their clonal template. Each zygote

...clones develop from eggs to finished products in just under a month.

is then isolated into a test tube-sized container. As it continues its cell division—usually at a normal biological rate—a single cell is isolated from each blastocyst and subjected to a rapid genetic analysis to confirm that there are no anomalies present in the specimen. Any blastocysts that have anomalies are recycled, while those that match expectations are transferred to an artificial womb.

Artificial wombs are hybrid devices, composed of synthetic and living tissues. Shortly after the blastocyst is inserted into the machine, it implants upon the living protein-cellular matrix that makes up a portion of the artificial womb. Jinteki carefully protects the precise methodologies used at this and the following steps in the process. All acknowledge that the next few steps involve a carefully selected cocktail of growth accelerators, which can enable a clone to grow from the blastocyst stage to the size of an infant in less than a day. The precise nature of those agents—and the delivery system—remains a trade secret. Even the technicians who work the artificial womb are kept completely unaware of the chemical reagents with which they work. They simply recognize that the maturing clone has reached the next stage when the artificial womb has distended to the size dictated by its growth profile.

At that point, the growing clone is transferred from an artificial womb to a juvenile tank, which typically has a 125-liter capacity. Physically, the clone is about the size of a one-year old. At this point, the growing clone's internal organs become more active. Tubes are attached to allow normal biological processes, such as breathing and elimination, to continue independent of the liquid environment. During this stage, the clone's sensory inputs are overridden by computer-generated sensory data to begin the neural conditioning process. Electrical impulses are applied, stimulating the neurons to align in such a way so as to resemble the connectome in the brain-map for the clone line. In well-established models, the clones spend about a week in the juvenile tank.

When the size of the juvenile tank begins to restrict the clone's continued growth, it is transferred into a 300-liter adolescent tank. This is its final location until the time of decanting. Continued sensory input provides the clone with additional conditioning and education until the specimen

MAINTAINING YOUR CLONE

Excerpted from *The Novice's Guide to Clonership*

Never forget that your new clone is a living being. Like pets and even humans, clones have biological necessities that must be addressed. New owners can at times forget, and clones—especially ones placed into new circumstances—are often reluctant to bring them up.

In the unfortunate circumstance where a clone is prohibited from using its own discretion, this can lead to unpleasant and even dangerous circumstances. A clone commanded to labor for an extended period without breaks may collapse from exhaustion. Fatigue can also compromise a clone's judgment and reaction time, potentially leading to dangerous circumstances for its owner. Biological necessities, including nourishment, hydration, and elimination, must also be considered. Clones willingly struggle through challenges like a faithful dog, but expecting this performance routinely can lead to performance degradation and may even void the warranty.

When you acquired your clone, the included documentation recommended an appropriate diet for the model you purchased—likely along with a prepackaged and easily prepared line of products. Some owners like to vary the diet in order to reward the clone, but this is not encouraged. The prepackaged meals are already optimized for maximum nutritional and caloric value. Too much variety can be unhealthy for your clone and may result in decreased performance or weight gain. Owners should check with the supplier prior to making significant changes in food intake. In the event that the clone exhibits a noticeable change in weight, owners are encouraged to schedule a medical examination.

In summary, remember that clones are conditioned to restrict their food intake, but they will nevertheless consume the types of food their owner provides.

has reached physical maturation. Precise amounts of specific hormones are also applied to enforce or encourage particular physiological traits. At that stage, any necessary surgical modifications are also performed. This can include tissues that are added post-growth, but may also include cybernetic upgrades. Once these surgeries have been performed, additional growth factors are added to reduce healing time. Only after the clone has completed its treatments and healing is it decanted. This typically takes three weeks for a common clone strain, although the surgical modifications and alternative training protocols used in custom clone batches can substantially extend the required time. Under ideal circumstances, stock clones develop from eggs to finished products in just under a month, but lines requiring advanced training programs require more time.

After decanting, the clone undergoes a final medical examination to check for any defects. Specimens that pass the tests are moved on to final conditioning and training. Usually by this stage the clones already have an anticipated owner or licensee, and the ensuing training is customized to the owner's specifications.

NEURAL CONDITIONING AND BEYOND

When considering the actions of a living organism, it can be challenging to differentiate natural instincts from learned reactions. Because a clone's entire existence is so precisely regulated, clones present one of the best opportunities to consider these comparisons. Instincts—whether they are drawn from humans or other species—can be selected when its genome is engineered. Similarly, the neural conditioning and hands-on training that comprise a clone's education are also strictly controlled.

A substantial portion of a clone's education takes place prior to decanting. As they are growing and developing, the clone's mind is kept in a semi-conscious state. Under these conditions, sensory input from the body is largely curtailed.

Instead, the clone receives mental stimulation similar to what one might experience in a sense-drama. At the same time, necessary memories and other knowledge are imprinted from braintapes into the developing brain. The uploaded input grounds the clone's personality and provides it with background information required to adequately serve its future owner. These recordings are highly standardized for most commercial clones, but large-volume orders often include adaptations to the training materials so that the clones are better prepared to serve specific clients.

Even after decanting, clones require training and conditioning in the field. This time also serves as an opportunity for the clone to become better acclimated to its body since even in the most established lines there remain small variations between specimens at the cellular and tissue level. Consequently, the braintapes used to instill the clone's physical training only provide a basis for that training. It is necessary to apply those skills in practice to become a fully optimized clone. In some fields, this breaking-in process can require weeks. More commonly, however, a few iterations of repetitive tasks serve as an adequate means to verify each specimen's competencies.

Time spent in conditioning provides an opportunity for technicians to make any final cosmetic changes required on the clones before they are released to their new owners. While undergoing AIVM, hair and nail growth is artificially suppressed—largely for reasons of convenience and sanitation. Once decanted, the growth of both is artificially accelerated until they achieve the expected length. Due to the nature of the growth process there is some variation between specimens, so technicians must tend to each individual upon completion.

After the appropriate styling is completed, each clone is tested to verify that it is capable of undertaking all of the self-care rituals required. In most cases, rudimentary correction proves adequate, so that the clone does not inflict any injuries upon itself while attempting to perform basic sanitary rituals. In rare cases,

some manufacturing or growth defects are uncovered in clones, even at this late stage. Typically, clones consume their first solid meal during their final conditioning to verify that their digestive system works as expected. Basic etiquette is already included in their conditioning, but body control issues often surface at this time.

Clones that include unusual body grafts—either biological or cybernetic—undergo initial testing for those systems during their final conditioning. Prototype clones as well as those with unusual modifications are subjected to a more thorough screening of these systems at this time. In cases where the biological engineering was substandard or where there was a defect in the cybernetic system, poorly attached components may separate at this stage. This invariably requires recycling the clone and may require redesign before another model can be made.

Some executives argue that the time spent in physical conditioning is not a cost-effective measure. However, medical tests are far more accurately conducted when the clone is in motion. Further, this provides an opportunity for the clone to gain full awareness of its body and recognize any signs of pain that might not be apparent to a medical examiner. If the clone is in an unexpected state of discomfort, surgical procedures may be undertaken as necessary—or the clone could simply be recycled, depending upon the expected cost of any corrective procedures.

The final training time also provides one last opportunity for a final medical review of the specimen prior to its delivery to the client. Each clone's performance reflects heavily on the reputation of both Jinteki it as well as the company that uses it in production. It is far better to identify any anomalies before the specimen goes into service, where it could do irreparable harm. Consequently, a thorough examination at this stage serves as one last quality checkpoint.

Clones that fail this final review are recycled or repurposed for internal use. Anything less than perfection will not live up to the Jinteki brand.

THE HENRY LINE

Even before the advent of the modern assembly line, humans have worked in dangerous conditions performing the most arduous of tasks. Underground mining operations are beleaguered by the threat of cave-ins, toxic gas buildup, or vehicle failure. Intolerable ranges of pressure, radiation, and temperature plague even routine maintenance jobs in space, and exposure to toxic compounds during waste reclamation or recycling present an unreasonable danger for human workers. Clones are a highly effective tool for addressing such challenges: they can perform as well as if not better than their human counterparts and are more easily replaced. And unlike bioroids, clones need not sacrifice the human intuition, judgment, and ingenuity that are so critical to a job done well and safely. The Henry line is Jinteki's answer to Haas-Bioroid's Steiger and Rex models.

Named for the American icon John Henry, "the steel-driving man," the Henry line is immediately identifiable by its physical prowess. Although relatively short in stature, all Henrys maintain a highly muscled physique. Work schedules for these clones are physically challenging, which largely alleviates any need for an exercise regimen to maintain their muscle mass. The warranty terms for the Henry line permit these clones to perform physically demanding labor on a daily basis for up to eighteen hours each day. The only necessary concession to this workload is that they receive at least three fifteen-minute breaks over the course of each workday.

The Henry line's physical capabilities are complemented by a mindset that is ideally suited to pursuing the associated workload. Henrys are not mindless automata—they actually score average or above on most tests of cognitive ability. The key difference between Henrys and typical humans is that the clones take pleasure in repetitive tasks; work usually considered to be drudgery is instead highly engaging. Jinteki trumpets this feature as a result of careful mental conditioning meant to complement the Henrys' basic genetic template. The result is a workforce that is rarely bored and is inherently fulfilled by its job duties. In short, they are the perfect grunt worker, which explains why they are the laborer of choice for Melange Mining's helium-3 mines.

GENETIC FEATURES

Henrys incorporate a variety of different genetic enhancements to supplement their primary design goals of physical aptitude and resilience. Their muscle fibers are exceptionally densely formed, which grants them the capability to exert substantially more force than a comparably sized muscle from an average human. Jinteki proudly advertises that Henry-line myofibrils incorporate protein structures that are entirely proprietary. These tissues utilize structures that were obtained from natural sources but were synthetically redesigned to function at levels beyond normal expectations. Similar modifications have been integrated into the Henry's skeletal system as well as into several organs to optimize the body's metabolism and productivity.

In most biological systems, modifications that are intended to focus a creature's overall strength have clear consequences. This often means that an exceptionally powerful muscles or bones are prone to damage when subjected to stressors from an unexpected direction. Jinteki recognized this risk at the design stage for the Henry line and moved to address it. Its solution was to substantially increase the rate at which the Henry's body reconstructs itself. These clones reconstruct bone and muscle mass at a rate more than five times the speed of a twenty-year-old human. The augmented reconstruction rate also means they have a very efficient healing rate, allowing them to recover from injuries far more rapidly than a natural human. Consequently, Henrys require a commensurately higher caloric intake, one on the order of approximately five to six thousand calories per day. A particularly efficient digestive tract helps to offset this requirement, but Henrys cannot survive for an extended period of time on a diet that would be healthy for an un-augmented human of comparable size and mass. Instead, they are dependent upon prepackaged meals ordered directly from a Jinteki-approved supplier.

Genetically male, Henry clones produce an exceptionally high level of testosterone during the maturation process. This plays a key role in their physiological development by causing the clones to put on muscle mass much more quickly during their growth phase. However, preliminary tests indicated that this heightened level of testosterone created disruptions in the work environment. Henrys became particularly competitive and even aggressive under stressful situations. To combat this undesired side effect, Henrys are surgically neutered prior to decanting. Lower level testosterone treatments are routinely incorporated into their meals to aid them in maintaining muscle mass.

OTHER ENHANCEMENTS

Clones from the Henry line are routinely assigned to work in environments where the breathable atmosphere is of questionable integrity. To ensure long-term viability, nasal and tracheal filters are surgically incorporated into the design prior to decanting. These filters must be changed on a regular basis; maintenance schedules predicated upon the exact chemical mixture of their working environment are included in the line's warranty terms.

Due to normal growth variation, some Henrys exhibit issues with musculoskeletal detachment. Routine quality assurance verifies tendon integrity on all specimens, but in those instances where the ligatures are questionable, reinforcing composite structures are surgically added to eliminate concerns about long-term integrity. Most clones of this line have at least two composite tendons implanted prior to release to the owners. Standard warranty coverage includes surgical repair for the clones, which can be routinely performed at a Jinteki Copy Center.

Matt Zeilinger

JINTEKI

HENRY MODEL
MINING CLASS

SURGICALLY IMPLANTED NASAL & TRACHEAL FILTERS

Particulate filters are customized to the unique needs of the Henry android and are relatively interchangeable: most filter models can be exchanged non-surgically for maximum workplace adaptability. Regular maintenance and exchange of the filters is required by warranty.

RESPIROCYTES FOR IMPROVED CARDIOVASCULAR EFFICIENCY

INCREASED FAST-TWITCH MUSCLE

Fast-twitch muscle, as distinct from slow-twitch muscle, is primarily responsible for a muscle's physical strength. Henry clones have increased Type IIA and IIX muscle fibers for increased strength with minimal loss of endurance.

SURGICALLY NEUTERED FOR REDUCED AGGRESSION

The Henry genotype has heightened testosterone production during all growth stages to aid in the development of muscle mass. The testes are removed prior to sale to ensure the android remains compliant, docile, and sociable with other clones. Testosterone supplements are recommended to keep the android in prime condition.

INCREASED RECOVERY RATE & METABOLISM

Henry clones heal quickly and have increased endurance. The heightened Henry metabolism breaks down lactic acid at a high rate, preventing muscle fatigue and repairing inevitable tissue damage from work within normal parameters. Even short rests are sufficient to restore the android to prime condition.

HEIGHTENED BONE DENSITY

The Henry clone's enhanced strength and rigorous workload can put great strain on the android's skeletal system. The unit's bones have increased density and durability to compensate. Tendons may also tear under the stress, and surgical replacements are available.

Henry's DNA is sourced from over two dozen of the strongest and toughest humans ever to live, as well as gorillas, crocodillians, and other formidable members of the animal kingdom.

The name "Henry" derives from the ancient American folk tale of a "steel-driving man": John Henry was able to outperform the machine designed to take his job, thereby proving the power and resilience of real flesh and bone.

PROPRIETARY PROTEINS FOR IMPROVED RECOVERY AND PERFORMANCE

TOP SECRET

THE TENMA LINE

The Tenma line of clones has been one of Jinteki's most popular products since its introduction. Specimens offer unparalleled natural aptitude for piloting any type of vehicle, from hoppers to spacecraft to motorsailers. This role is ideally suited for a clone, as Tenmas exploit the human brain's natural aptitude to rapidly assess the dangers of a changing environment and make the best possible choices quickly. Their carefully honed abilities complement their natural appearance and friendly personality to give the human touch to any transportation role—whether it's delivering goods or chauffeuring corporate executives.

Tenmas have been in production for years. During that time, over one million clones have been delivered to grateful owners. Jinteki has made minor revisions to the line over its production run (such as small quality engineering adjustments), but the latest units share 99.9% of their genetic identity with the very first units produced. Cybernetic components have also been upgraded to keep pace with the latest available technology, but these play a comparatively minor role in the line's expertise.

Arguably, the consistency across Tenmas is due to the simple fact that they were genegineered from the beginning to be excellent drivers. Not only do they control their own vehicles exceptionally well, they are also capable of identifying and avoiding mistakes made by other pilots—including those made by autopilot systems. A Tenma clone is 75% less likely to be the cause of an accident compared to a human. When accidents involving Tenma drivers do occur, they are 50% less likely to result in loss of life or the complete destruction of a vehicle compared to autopiloting accidents.

The Tenma line has also exhibited an exceptional degree of reliability over the course of its lifetime. In fact, many of the earliest models remain in the service of their original owners. Ten years since the line's introduction, one would expect a high level of turnover, but this has not been the case. Granted, drivers are subjected to far less stress than clones that serve in heavy industry, but even when compared to other light-duty models, Tenmas have exceeded the manufacturer's expected lifespan. Anecdotal reports indicate owners are purchasing extended service plans rather than replacing them with newer releases, likely due to high customer satisfaction levels. Jinteki has not publicly indicated any plans to discontinue support for the Tenma line, which suggests that they have not yet reached a phase of planned obsolescence. Consequently, the "natural" projected lifespan of a Tenma remains unclear.

GENETIC FEATURES

Advertising from the earliest days of the Tenma line included endorsements from dozens of well-known racers. Each claimed to have submitted some portion of his DNA to the Tenma's design process. Jinteki proudly trumpeted the involvement of these sports superstars, but the megacorp has never publicly released any of the specific details. Standard android licensing agreements strictly prohibit the sequencing of a clone's DNA, so these claims are unverifiable at present, and exactly which genes might have been contributed by different individuals remains a mystery. This situation is further complicated by popular opinion polls that attribute different physical appearance characteristics to one or more of the claimed donors.

Standard disclaimers associated with a Tenma license do not exclude DNA sequences extracted from animal or purely synthetic sources. Popular speculation suggests that the Tenma genome includes avian DNA as well as human. Jinteki has never confirmed nor denied this. Medical records and service charts, both of which are publicly available to non-Jinteki employees, do explicitly black out the inner ear schematics. This strongly suggests that Tenmas rely upon balance systems that are completely foreign to those normally observed in humans. Moreover, the Tenma line exhibits levels of spatial awareness, balance, and reaction time that dramatically exceed the normal human range.

As is the case with many of Jinteki's clone models, the Tenma line shows an extremely high level of devotion to their current tasks as well as their owner. Some believe that this might be due to loyalty created at a genetic level, possibly incorporated from a domesticated animal such as a horse or dog. Others argue that such loyalty is characteristic of normal clone indoctrination and conditioning. Jinteki does publicly offer assurances that the Tenmas are one of their most reliable lines, both in terms of dedication to

"I got out on my own skills and merits. If others are going to escape, then they can damned well do it themselves. If I stick my neck out too far, I'm pretty sure it's going to just get chopped off."

64

a task as well as consistency of performance. The company does not, however, acknowledge the source of this devotion.

The clonership manual also includes recommendations that Tenmas avoid a laundry list of common pharmaceuticals. Third-party pharmacists who have examined this list indicate that it suggests a variation in the neurotransmitter system involved in the Tenma's design, perhaps explaining the significant shortening of Tenma reaction time compared to normal humans.

OTHER ENHANCEMENTS

As in some of Jinteki's other clone lines, the Tenma line incorporates a number of purely cybernetic modifications as a part of their standard design. Key among these are retractable mirrorshade lenses that are designed to augment the Tenma's vision far beyond human potential—all Tenmas have better than 20:5 vision and added zoom capabilities. They are also able to readily interface with a vehicle's data readouts, including speed and altitude. In this way, the clones can have an intrinsic relationship with any modern means of transportation.

The Tenma line also includes a cybernetic logging system similar to a BMI, which tracks peripheral nervous activity. Over time, Jinteki's analysis of the logs recognizes any uncharacteristic variations in response times. As part of standard maintenance, Jinteki can take corrective steps or issue a replacement if a Tenma's responses are outside of normal design parameters. Because of the monitoring, owners are contacted any time a pattern of anomalies is recorded.

I saw myself die today.

I think that's accurate—at least, biologically. It's also not entirely true, since I'm still here to write this.

I'm a clone, identical to thousands of other Tenma models. The only things that really distinguished me from them—at least at first—were a few digits on the code tattoo on the back of my neck. But I escaped. I'm not part of the hierarchy anymore. Yes, someone's still on file as owning me, but they can't catch me. I get to live with at least some of the freedoms "natural" humans enjoy.

I got out because I was better than the rest of my decanting cohort. I'm faster, smarter, and just a little bit more independent. But I was created from the same braintapes and custom-DNA strands as the rest of the Tenmas. I made it through quality assurance. I guess lucky is an important part of why I'm better.

Today, I was a whole lot luckier than at least one other Tenma. As I was leaving a job, I saw a Tenma driving a hopper that went completely out of control. We're good pilots, so maybe it wasn't an accident, but it was ugly. The hopper plummeted from the lip of a charging pad fifty meters straight into the ground.

When it hit, emergency medical services showed up in minutes. They rushed to care for the passengers in the back. I saw the ambulances carry them away— maybe some even survived. No one took time to check on the driver. Nearly an

hour later, the wreck was carted away with his body still inside of it. After all, he was only a clone.

I'm a living being, but I'm not a philosopher or an advocate. I don't pretend to know whether or not I'm human or have a soul, even if my genetics are made from human sequences. I'm too busy just trying to survive to be worried about saving anybody else.

I do my jobs, I take my pay, and I just keep getting by. But at the accident today, my thought wasn't "that could have been me."

My thought was "that was me."

Obviously. I wasn't inside his head and he wasn't inside mine. I'm still alive to enjoy the high life I've earned. At the most, he's my identical brother, a truth made even more real by the same neural conditioning Jinteki used to train both of us. Yet before today, I'd never met him.

My life now is very different from what his was. I escaped and I've earned a certain level of luxury. I'm proud of what I've done, and I'm not sure my clone brothers could do the same thing, even if they were given an opportunity.

But clones don't have opportunities. We have duties and responsibilities. We live in a state of constant risk, but there is no reward. There's no payoff. We aren't given privileges. For most, it's not even possible to earn them. Instead, we are expected to simply fulfill our duties until the time of our preplanned obsolescence. Then, we're

supposed to just quietly and permanently retire—that's a lovely metaphor, ne?

Today, I'm reminded of my own imminent mortality. My lifespan isn't intended to last as long as a natural-born human's. I don't know how long I'll last. Ten years? Twenty? Five? I don't know if Jinteki's rejuve treatments would work on me, even if I could find someone who'd be willing to apply them to a clone. I bet they wouldn't.

It's not a level playing field. It's not fair. And there's absolutely nothing I can do about it. Keep running, keep ahead of the law, keep a fat credaccount to keep me happy in my old age, however soon that turns out to be. But maybe someone might think about us clones and realize that we do have thoughts and emotions. We're not bioroids that can simply be shut down and programmed to accept their own mortality. We're human. We're also essentially slaves. It's not right, and maybe someday, things could change so that we wouldn't always have to be.

I'm not saying cloning should end— hell, I wouldn't be here if it didn't exist. I'm saying that there needs to be some way for clones to earn just a little bit of dignity, the chance to live some part of a life that could be our own.

Humans made us, and they need to realize what they have done. They don't get to be our masters. They are our parents, and they must acknowledge the next generation.

Dmitry Prosvirnin

THE MOLLOY LINE

Consistency of experience is the hallmark of any successful franchise restaurant. Whether a guest visits a McKing's in New Angeles or New Moscow, he should be able to expect the same sort of service, food, and atmosphere. A patron's favorite dish should taste exactly the same every time he visits any of the company's locations throughout the world. The only difference might be the language spoken, and that's easily solvable with a low-level translation AI linked to the menus or the server's HUD.

Mother Molloy's restaurant chain was one of the first to directly address the issue of consistency among its wait staff from a genetic perspective. For generations, franchised restaurants have included highly specialized training programs that are used at all of their locations. However, these are prone to a certain degree of variation, often due to each new hire's unique work experiences. Several chains chose to adopt bioroids as a solution to this issue, but many people are less comfortable with bioroids delivering food to the table, particularly at casual restaurants where clientele expect a home-like atmosphere.

When Mother Molloy's opened its doors for its flagship restaurant in New Angeles, it was the first restaurant chain to utilize a cooking and wait staff composed entirely of clones. Within three years their initial success skyrocketed, and they count more than two hundred and fifty franchise restaurants within New Angeles alone. Their menu offers a diverse range of enjoyable food, but it is hardly revolutionary. In fact, all of the menu's entries are staples taken from casual eateries across the world. What stands out is the fact that their food is virtually identical across all locations. This is possible thanks to their staff being as consistent as possible.

Mother Molloy's sought a line that was highly trained in food preparation, but also extremely personable, cheerful, and outgoing. The Molloy line of clones, in keeping with the franchise's Irish pub theme, is designed to have casual good looks, an easy smile, and roughly Irish-American features. Its members' conditioning and education are focused entirely upon food service and related matters. Because of their extensive interactions with customers, Molloy clones are also trained in great detail to engage in casual conversation. They can discuss the weather, local sports teams, and current events in a non-confrontational manner with customers for hours at a time.

Their personable nature also offers a substantial economic advantage for the stakeholders in Mother Molloy's. As the clones are the property of the company, they receive no explicit compensation for their efforts. In fact, their conditioning is such that they are thoughtlessly loyal to the company above all else. Their self-interest and measure of self-worth is primarily based upon how they can best serve the restaurant chain. However, customers enjoy the outgoing service that the wait staff provides and often include generous tips when paying their bills. Not surprisingly, the clones never receive any of these tips. Instead, those funds go directly toward Mother Molloy's bottom line.

CLONE ETIQUETTE

Excerpted from *Modern Manners*

Given their humanoid appearance it can be easy to mistake a clone for a real person at first glance. Yet, anyone who has tried conversing with a clone that wasn't designed to regularly interact with humans will tell you that it can be an awkward experience. When talking to clones, keep in mind that not all models had social intelligence developed as part of their psychological profile, but they are all conditioned to be subservient and respectful toward you and me.

A good clone will rarely be seen and is never heard. Clones are trained to give room on the slidewalk or lift, and they will stand still and face the speaker if addressed directly. They are conditioned to rise when a non-android enters the room and will hold the door open for him when he leaves. Clones are often employed in behind-the-scenes roles, but if you do happen across one during the course of its duties, acknowledging it will only draw attention to its shortcomings.

Clones are expected to defer to a human being in all things. Clones will not speak unless spoken to except for the most perfunctory of pleasantries or if their duties require them to relay information to humans. It is inconsiderate of a human to engage a clone in a conversation above its ability level, such as discussing politics or philosophy. Moreover, clones' conditioning discourages them from disagreeing or causing any affronts during an exchange. Along those same lines, clones will not speak about their owners' personal lives, nor will polite people try to encourage or trick them into doing so.

Clones not working in the service sector do not have the empathy or the experience to recognize human social cues. A human should never make use of subtle hints, polite denials, or sarcasm with such a clone. While clones do have some ability to recognize these cues, their innate tendency to defer to a human's expectations can lead to unfortunate misinterpretations of literal phrases. It is always more appropriate to be as direct and literal as possible when dealing with a clone so as to avoid such misunderstandings.

Using a raised or authoritarian voice is also considered impolite, but to do so in front of others can be a sign of disrespect toward the owner himself. Clones are designed to want to please their owners and other humans, and they will respond equally well to a firm command as to an admonition, so it is unnecessary to yell. Doing so only causes distress and may even have other negative side effects.

On the other hand, if a clone begins to raise its voice, express its opinions, or use crude language, it is possible it has learned such permissiveness from its owner.

HOUSING YOUR CLONE

Excerpted from The Novice's Guide to Clonership

An important decision about your clone is choosing its living quarters. If your home is large enough to have a spare bedroom—even a small one—then this is often the best option. Having the clone available in case there is a crisis late at night or very early in the morning can be quite convenient. The costs of leasing additional housing and the ensuing commute add up over time, and if the clone can instead dwell with the owner, the savings can be substantial.

Unfortunately, not everyone has sufficient living space—particularly if they have several clones to perform multiple tasks. In these cases, the best option is to house a clone at either a nearby clone-tel or to ship it off to an austere but large clone barrack. Clone-tels are often more convenient and they provide nicer living conditions, which could mean improved clone performance, but they are also much more expensive. Clone barracks are typically used by corporations for housing large fleets of clones, but there is often room for private individuals to lease drawers in the barracks as well. Ultimately, a new clone owner should decide which arrangement best suits his needs by weighing cost against convenience or practicality.

Restaurants are known for having very high rates of employee turnover. This introduces a significant cost overhead for each restaurant, as the paperwork and time involved in hiring and terminating employees requires a significant investment of effort and expertise. However, Mother Molloy's can instead rely on Jinteki to handle all of the maintenance required to keep the clones functioning for their entire operational lifetime. Further, safety laws permit clones to work up to sixteen hours daily in most jurisdictions, so a restaurant can operate with a minimal number of clones—far fewer than the number of human employees that would be required. This introduces additional savings.

Clone housing, clothing, and basic maintenance introduce additional complexity to this equation, but corporate clone barracks address these needs at cost. The bottom line is clones offer a substantial savings for the restaurant chain.

GENETIC FEATURES

The Molloy clone line is designed around the core concepts of affability and attractiveness. As a result, the clones' physical and psychological profiles are not far removed from those of a normal human, especially when compared to the Henry or Tenma lines. Their genetic personality profile is highlighted through a rigorous conditioning and education program intended to reinforce the restaurant's idealized presentation.

Besides variation for male and female submodels, the only significant physical tweaks involve optimizing the body's overall stamina to make it through the daily sixteen-hour shifts. Men-tal and hormonal modifications provide the clones with a strong devotion to the chain as well as an intense need to satisfy the restaurant's clientele.

Media inquiries have found that neither Jinteki nor Mother Molloy's employees are willing to go into detail about the Molloy line's overall genetic make-up. Neither company has claimed exclusive ownership of the strain. However, Jinteki has admitted that they will not sell members of this clone line to individuals or companies other than the Mother Molloy's restaurant chain. To date, none of the proprietary clones implemented by other food service organizations bear a clear physical resemblance to the Molloy line.

OTHER ENHANCEMENTS

A heat-resistant polymer layer is added to the hands of all clones from the Mother Molloy's line prior to decanting. Because of this modification, Molloys are capable of handling cookware and tableware that are far hotter than what un-enhanced humans could normally grasp. This layer interacts with the body's natural tissues to effectively self-heal from minor injuries. It typically holds up through several years of service, and its deterioration can be cited as a reason to recycle a clone that has neared the end of its planned lifetime.

Mark Molnar

CLONAL HEALTH MAINTENANCE

Clones are hardy and diligent workers, and they go about their assigned work without complaint. Due to their conditioning, clones from most lines work until interrupted, continuing in the tasks assigned by their operators. While this devotion to a task is commendable and efficient, it often leads to long-term issues if owners do not perform the necessary maintenance on their property. Clone warranties are designed around reasonable workloads and routine maintenance. Those who fail to comply with the recommendations found in the model's clonership manual may inadvertently void a clone's warranty. This can result in substantial repair costs or even a substantially shorter functional lifespan than would normally be expected.

Even the most economical and multipurpose clone lines routinely incorporate a range of structural enhancements over an unmodified human. These include a bolstered immune system, heightened endurance, and a genome free of any factors associated with genetic disease. Clones are able to perform their duties for a much longer time than most humans. They can function on only a few hours of sleep and can complete an extended workday without the need for time off. Immunological modifications and enhancements leave clones insusceptible to nearly all human contagious diseases as well as those associated with domestic livestock.

In spite of their overall resilience, clones must undergo routine examinations. All clones are trained to inspect their bodies for injuries and anomalies on a daily basis. Without adequate self-care, clones are prone to many of the same issues that humans can suffer from due to poor hygiene. Standard conditioning also requires that they report these to their owners at the earliest possible opportunity. Owners should pay heed to such reports, as clones are trained to be very familiar with their own range of acceptable performance, and clones do not raise issues unless something is outside of their normal range of function. Minor malfunctions are typically addressed in only a few hours at the nearest Jinteki Copy Center. Owners only incur additional expense for such repairs in instances of obvious neglect or extreme misuse.

In addition to their self-checks, a biannual routine examination by a professional—available at any Copy Center—is required to keep a clone's warranty in good standing. Despite their genetic enhancements and conditioning, clone biological systems do have upper limits. Clones are particularly prone to repetitive motion disorders or diseases associated with high levels of stress, but regular examinations serve as a way to identify and treat such issues before they become severe. Standard warranty services include clone monitoring as well as routine surgeries, therapies, and pharmaceutical treatments. In some instances where clones must undergo extended treatment, owners may use a loaner clone from the Copy Center. When the repairs are deemed more expensive than the cost of replacement, clone manufacturers typically choose to replace the clone. This can be particularly inconvenient for owners who have invested a substantial amount of time and post-conditioning training in their clones. In such instances, more expensive repairs may be considered, although these do represent an out-of-pocket expense.

DRESSING YOUR CLONE

Excerpted from *The Novice's Guide to Clonership*

Some owners fail to consider that they must plan to provide their clones with multiple changes of clothes beyond the simple uniform provided at time of purchase. Standard coveralls are exceptionally sturdy, but even these become stained and worn over time. New owners should remember that clones do face many of the same biological challenges as humans. Clones must be permitted to routinely bathe and launder their clothing. When a clone performs a necessarily unclean task—yard work, plumbing, and so on—instruct your clone to sanitize afterward and change its clothes. In many cases, self-cleaning smartfabrics offer a convenient long-term solution that saves time.

If your clone is likely to work under conditions of extreme heat or cold, make sure they have garb appropriate to the weather. A clone ordered to struggle in the heat or cold will readily do so, but it might damage itself or contract an illness while undertaking the task. Consistently ordering a clone to labor in such conditions with inappropriate gear is likely to void the clone's warranty.

Finally, most owners prefer to have their clones wear something that is more stylish about their residence, but even deeply discounted fashionable clothing can be expensive. To combat that expense, some owners prefer to purchase clones that have physiques similar to their own so that they can wear cast-off clothing. This can have the added benefit that the clone can be used to try on and model clothing for the owner when shopping remotely.

CONTAGION

Responsible owners must keep in mind that an otherwise-healthy clone can still carry an infection. Clones are nearly impervious to disease because of their powerful immune system, but are also resistant due to changes on the cellular level. A consequence is that they might carry a virus or bacteria upon or within their body without actually showing signs of a disease. This can range from mild colds to far more serious syndromes. Any time that a clone works with biohazards or even simply dirty materials, owners should take care to have their clone undertake a thorough cleaning. Liberal application of cleaning materials and a change of clothing is adequate to overcome the most common disease vectors. This can be particularly dangerous for any clones that work in food preparation or that have direct interaction with materials intended for humans to ingest, so proper food safety protocols should be observed at all times.

CLONAL MEDICINE

The technology behind AIVM was developed from techniques used for biomedical research, but the advent of clones has since unlocked near-limitless applications of the new technology and new opportunities for advancements. Such innovations as cloned organ replacements, genomic enhancements, and accelerated drug testing have improved the lives of people the worlds over.

REPLACEMENT

Organ failure due to deterioration, disease, or catastrophic injury was the most common cause of death for humans. The same technologies used to grow clones can grow parts of clones, such as individual organs, and the availability of these replacements have virtually eliminated this cause of death. The Universal Donor (UD) clone line is designed to produce organs with antigens that do not trigger transplant rejection. Modern hospitals keep UDs on the premises in their original vats. A UD can be decanted, an organ quickly harvested, and a transplant performed on demand. UD transplants are available for all internal systems and even limbs, with the exception of the brain and central nervous system.

Unfortunately, the nature of the UD line's universality means that its one-size-fits all replacement limbs can be awkward for some recipients. To overcome this, most facilities offer to grow UD clones to a custom size and also offer cosmetic modifications to ensure that the skin tone and appearance matches the recipient's other limb. Growing replacements takes two to three weeks, so some opt to make due with a cybernetic replacement limb during the interim. Alternatively, clones can be custom grown using a recipient's own DNA to ensure the best possible match. This requires a skilled genegineer to optimize the AIVM process for the patient's genome, which typically adds several weeks to the growth time and several digits to the price tag.

The affluent, those who work particularly high-risk jobs, and those who have exceptionally good insurance policies often choose to maintain a clone created from their own DNA at a local facility. If a replacement organ or limb is required, it can be immediately harvested. In extreme cases, multiple organs can be replaced, and legends persist that the richest risties may simply choose to transplant their brain into the healthy clone's body. Even if such technol-ogy existed, the extreme surgery would require an extended recuperation time since the brain must learn to control its new body. Paparazzi camdrones fuel conspiracy theories about stars undergoing cosmetic surgery or more dramatic procedures.

ENHANCEMENT

In addition to stock organs, Jinteki can also supply organs that are enhanced in numerous ways. These are typically derived from UD lines to ensure that the replacements are available for the largest possible client base, but the clones are further tweaked so a specific organ is dramatically enhanced. This can include lungs optimized for performance in extreme conditions, muscles that offer faster twitch response, or even neuronal tissues capable of expanding the brain's function.

Once the clone and relevant tissues have properly matured, the clone is decanted and the tissues are removed for transplant into a waiting patient. The remainder of the clone is then recycled—due to the modifications required to optimize enhanced tissues, the integrity of other organs are typically less than ideal. Because of scaling and proportionate growth concerns, it remains substantially more economical to produce an entire clone and recycle the undesirable materials than it is to synthesize an organ in isolation.

RESEARCH

Clones, specifically those produced through AIVM, have revolutionized pharmaceutical testing. Newly discovered medications can be thoroughly tested on clones, which are entirely synthetic and artificial in their creation, rather than in animals. This has dramatically reduced the time required for testing between initial discovery and when drugs can be administered to patients. Side effects are also more easily identifiable because a clone's entire environment is effectively controlled, thereby making any anomalies far easier to identify.

It has also expanded the functionality of pharmacogenetics, as different clone lines can be quickly created to test drug efficacy in patients with different genetic markers. As a consequence, once a patient's genome is on file, physicians can be certain that they are prescribing a drug that is known to be effective within the patient's specific genetic background.

PREDETERMINATION AND CLONING

Clones are not mindless automatons. They are carefully trained to behave within a range of known parameters, but clones are capable of thinking and exhibiting judgment in choosing their actions—which can prove problematic from a commercial or liability standpoint. It also makes them a test of a philosophical quandary that has perplexed humanity since the dawn of civilization: whether individuals can make their own decisions, or whether their lives are predetermined by the combination of their genetic background and their childhood training.

In the past, predetermination was purely philosophical. It never mattered whether an individual had a choice so long as he maintained the illusion that he did and could be held accountable for his decisions. Before clones could become a commercial product, that philosophical question needed to have a practical answer to satisfy megacorporate lawyers. Clones had to be trained to act consistently, much like a domesticated breed of dog, horse, or sheep. Otherwise, the liability concerns would be too severe for clones to be profitable.

The experiment began with the hypothesis that a cloned human brain could be tightly controlled. Expert psychologists, educational theorists, and biologists all joined the discussion. Complex models were designed and tests were conducted, first in massive virtual simulations, and then in isolated facilities upon thousands of live clones.

The training schedule could not be completed in isolation. Geneticists had to identify personality traits and link them to the proposed training regimen. Well-established educational protocols were used in conjunction with an analysis of genetic tendencies. Different DNA sequences were tested using identical training methods, and then thoroughly studied to determine the most efficient and effective combinations. The key became linking genetic and psychological datasets. Scientists recognized from an early stage that it would be necessary to incorporate elements from human maturation into the clones' education and conditioning so that the subjects' psyches would be recognizable. It also soon became evident that animal models—including genetic sequences taken from domesticated species—provided materials that would be key in designing the optimal solution.

Ultimately, it became clear that Jinteki could in fact strongly condition clones and engineer them to enjoy following these impulses. There remains a slim chance that any clone can override its conditioning, but improvements in training make the chance little more than statistical noise. The Three Directives utilized with bioroids cannot be enforced in the same way with clones, but the rarity of rogue clones, particularly compared to the abundance of criminals among the human population, demonstrates the effectiveness of the methods used.

There remains a slim chance that any clone can override its conditioning...

This has strong implications for humanity beyond clones. Some who decry the use of clones are most bothered about the very idea that humanlike beings could be so predetermined or indoctrinated. Others, however, look at this model and see it as a vital tool for revamping the educational system to produce successful members of society.

CLONES AND PUNISHMENT

Clones provide cheap labor, particularly in jobs that are less desirable for humans. At the same time, they manage to provide a very human element to these tasks, something that is completely absent in bioroids and mechanical robots. Clones' carefully ingrained cheerfulness, loyalty, and willingness to serve make the lives of ordinary citizens better.

However, because clones are living entities with a degree of free will (however small), they can pose a danger to their owners and even their manufacturers. Anyone who regularly interacts with a clone must be aware of the rules that govern clone conduct, or else they could find themselves involved in a civil or criminal case.

Clone legislation varies substantially between jurisdictions. Typically, Jinteki provides new owners with the most relevant information at the time of purchase. Jinteki Copy Centers are always happy to provide the latest information about new rules and regulations. Those who choose to travel internationally with their clones, however, should take care to obtain any permits and be aware of any regulations prior to embarking upon their journey. Some nations enforce strict quarantines upon any incoming clones, while others expect each clone to travel under a passport. Care should be taken to ensure a clone is never taken to Brazil, as the government there outlaws android ownership and instead grants clones asylum while they are within its borders.

Jinteki continues to work with various governments to reduce or minimize these inconveniences, but the issue ultimately falls under how clones are classified. When considered a domestic animal, then they are often subject to the same regulations as pets. Until all nations unilaterally agree that clones deserve a special legal status, these problems are likely to remain an issue for international travelers and corporations.

...but improvements in training make the chance little more than statistical noise.

LIABILITY

With a first-time clone purchase, the assumption of liability for a clone's actions represents a major concern for the new owner. Clones are not legally independent beings. Because of this, they cannot assume legal responsibility for their actions—in much the same way that a domestic animal is not subject to legal repercussions for its actions. Instead, the clone's owner assumes this responsibility. Certainly, clones are subjected to training that is far more thorough than the typical pet, but their relative freedom—most owners send clones to independently perform tasks outside of their residence—offers a tremendous opportunity for mishaps. Owners need to keep this in mind at the time of purchase, and they are encouraged to obtain the necessary insurance. Jinteki offers this coverage along with extended service plans, although many home insurance plans include special riders for clones.

Renegade clones represent an important exception to the concern of liability. If there is evidence that the clone has somehow overcome its conditioning and education, acting completely independently of its owner's direction—or if the owner reports the clone lost or stolen—then the owner is excused from any liability. Instead, the clone is considered a public menace and is disposed of in the most humane way possible. However, if evidence demonstrates that the supposedly renegade clone was acting on its owner's instructions, no such clemency is granted.

In order to have the best possible chance of avoiding any culpability or penalty, owners should report missing clones as soon as they become aware of the situation. Similarly, clones that show performance issues, particularly any difficulties in following directions, should be taken in for testing as soon as possible. Such issues are covered under warranty. A Copy Center can refresh their conditioning within a week or two, thereby restoring their performance and eliminating concerns.

ABUSE AND NEGLECT

Owners who fail to take proper care for their clones can also be subject to liability. This is particularly true in municipalities where clones are treated as domestic animals. Laws intended to prevent animal cruelty can come into play regarding the treatment of clones as well. Owners who fail to provide their clones with adequate care—including medical supplies and necessary clothing—may face charges for their actions or inactions.

Jinteki is particularly litigious toward locales that maintain such laws. Until better ways to adjudicate such concerns are identified, however, owners who are likely to place their clones into particularly dangerous situations—including many corporations dependent upon clone labor—must take care that these situations do not qualify as abuse or neglect. Otherwise, they could be subject to stiff fines or other severe penalties.

I require extraction. The ID you supplied was accepted without raising eyebrows; I have continued to take the pills you provided, so I passed the genetic screening, and I am confident that I have not spoken out of character or otherwise acted in a suspicious manner. Yet, they must suspect, because my access has been suddenly limited. I have a theory as to why, which I will explain. First, let me demonstrate that I have acquired enough information in my short time here to call the mission a success. Then you will be quick to retrieve me and, I trust, supply the promised reward.

The Nisei line is the first of a new generation of clones, superior to Jinteki's previous offerings. They have one trialing at the NAPD as a police detective to compete with HB's high-end bioroid models. There is a lot of pressure on Caprice Nisei, the clone detective, but Chairman Hiro keeps her motivated. She knows that the fate of the rest of her genome depends on her performance. The other Nisei clones are still in vats, ready and waiting, their fate undecided.

She visits them sometimes. Caprice has to visit Jinteki for review every few weeks, and she usually makes a point of visiting her sleeping sisters. She passes slowly from one to the next, peering at the faces, communing with them. There are rumors she can communicate with them, but then there are many rumors about her. She is as mysterious as she is beautiful.

It is quite different when Chairman Hiro visits. He strides up and down the vats like a general surveying his troops. Sometimes he has Senior Director Toshiyuki Sakai with him, and they talk about their plans. The Nisei clones are a personal project for Hiro. I have heard it said among the human staff that he isolated the genes responsible for psychic powers, and manipulated these within the clones to give them psi abilities. I have found nothing official on this score, but I suspect that there is some truth to these rumors. If Caprice was psychic and sensed or felt my intentions, it would explain my current predicament.

The Nisei are the first of the newest clone generation, so they are paving the way for other lines. These are still at the experimental stage, though, and information on them is extremely hard to come by. I know the Musashi clones by name only; what their abilities may be I have not determined. I hear their name whispered infrequently, but whether the speakers fear the wrath of Jinteki or are afraid of the new clones, I do not know. Perhaps they are psychic too, for what could be more frightening than a clone that can read your thoughts?

Dr. Hitomi Knox is Caprice's psychologist. As part of her review, she assesses her mental stability. Perhaps she tests her for psi too, but I have not been able to confirm this. Theirs are private interviews, which she seems to look forward to with enthusiasm. Caprice must be a unique pupil—she's the only Nisei currently in action. She moves with great grace, too. I would not be surprised to find she has combat skills, but I have not seen her training at Jinteki. I suspect such skills would be a benefit to a police detective, but it is only supposition on my part.

There were two Nisei clones before her, and what became of them is uncertain. As you might already know, Jinteki often names its prototype clones alphabetically, so Caprice must be the third of her line. Her predecessors, if they ever successfully breathed outside of their vats, must have failed in some way. The cloning process is a modern marvel, but it is not entirely without flaws. It is feasible that those first two Nisei clones were simply not viable.

Misato Inada looks after the more practical side of Caprice's existence. She liaises with the NAPD and makes sure Caprice receives a fair chance to perform and demonstrate Jinteki's brilliance. She is a very intelligent woman, but she is not as security-conscious as some of her colleagues. I was able to gain access to her office for a time and have made copies of some documents you will be glad to receive. I will retain these documents until I am satisfied that you have made adequate provision for my future. You were extremely thorough in smoothing my path to employment within Jinteki, and I expect you to take the same care with the arrangements made for my future life.

I should have liked to keep the face after all, since it feels so familiar even after this short time. I think it is better than the one I had before; the New Angeles air is not kind to natural skin. However, I feel a new identity will be necessary. Relocating to Mars will not be enough if Jinteki is aware of my betrayal. With your vast resources, you must make it impossible for them to find me, and I am ready for a new life.

Do not be tempted to abandon me at this stage. I am not above taking my knowledge of your own underhanded dealings to the press. Alternatively, I could return to my new employers, and provide them with information instead. I spent considerable time within your own offices while you prepared me for this mission, and I made good use of that time. All I am asking is for you to provide what you promised me a little earlier than planned. I assure you, the documents alone make it worth your while.

Matt Zeilinger

NBN

The sheer volume of data streaming through NBN's servers at any given moment is staggering to most users, and this data fuels modern daily life as much as any helium-3 reactor. NBN collects, processes, and delivers the information its customers need straight to their PADs so they can live the most productive, happy lives they can. The content they watch has been carefully curated just for them, and they get custom recommendations based on their location and daily routine. The average citizen is completely oblivious to the number of sensors and seccams and camdrones they pass on a given day, but NBN watches over them all to keep them safe and secure. This future exists because of the innovations made by NBN, but the corp was not always known by those letters.

The mission of the Kane family's media conglomerates has always been to provide the most comprehensive portfolio of consumer programming available in their markets. As those early markets grew and the boundaries between them blurred to crisscross the entire world, the company underwent a series of mergers and conglomeration efforts. The end result was a media and technology corporation known as Vertex, which would come to dominate the global entertainment industry.

Vertex scored government contracts to provide public media content, and it easily crowded out its few remaining competitors. Not only did it create the programming the global population hungrily consumed, it distributed that programming. It owned the companies responsible for producing, operating, and repairing the infrastructure needed for distribution. It also monopolized the entire marketing industry, as well as the brands for the items being marketed themselves. Vertex grew so large that it could single-handedly steer the global conversation, but it began to clash with some of the governments in the countries it serviced.

Vertex was deemed a dangerous monopoly, and legislation was introduced that forced Vertex to be partitioned into its different parts, which were then broken up again into many regional entities. Network Broadcast News was one of dozens of minor spin-off corps, one headed by the father of Keith Randolph Kane. It was granted SanSan's busy media markets, and there it thrived for many years.

Then the Blackout swept the world. Like all the other media corporations, Network Broadcast News was hit hard, but it had been experimenting with a new communication protocol that was not affected by the cyber attack. The world governments fast-tracked the development of this framework for a new network known simply as *the* Network. The technology division remained an NBN subsidiary but was rebranded as SYNC, and it catapulted Kane's company to new heights.

SYNC's runaway success immediately following the Blackout allowed NBN to emerge as a key player in the industry. It bought up many of its cousin companies and reestablished itself as the premiere global media corp. As the colonization of Luna got underway, it renamed itself the Near-Earth Broadcast Network and relocated to New Angeles. As it expanded to the settlements on Mars, it became known as simply NBN. Vertex's media empire was reborn, and this time it spanned the solar system.

UNDERSTANDING THE CUSTOMER

Unlike Haas-Bioroid's synthetic bioroids or Jinteki's organic clones, NBN's flagship is less a tangible product but a service: information. Weyland, Jinteki, Haas-Bioroid and other corporations build facilities, simulants, tools, vehicles, and other technological items. But NBN builds the tools that collect the data and supply the content people use to form their opinions, make decisions, and otherwise become more like who or what they want to be.

NBN is able to provide such useful information to its customers because it knows them better than they know themselves. Thanks to the ubiquity of SYNC's Network infrastructure, NBN knows where its customers are at any given time, what they're buying, what they're looking for, who they're talking to, and what they're talking about. NBN aggregates this information and analyzes it using proprietary techniques so that its products and media provide exactly the experience its customers want, even before the customers consciously know they desired it. No other corp can come close to NBN's predictive power because no other corp can draw from NBN's incredibly detailed histories of billions of users. People choose, and stay with, NBN because it is the best—and only—corp that can accurately anticipate nearly all of a person's needs.

To maintain this psychological monopoly, NBN uses a sophisticated outgrowth of brainmapping technology known as enhanced psychographics (or simply psychographics). By studying the activity and makeup of the human brain and its reactions to consuming media content, NBN is able to build an amazingly effective road map to replicate favorable responses. NBN's content is designed with specific psychographic profiles in mind, and every element is carefully curated to appeal to or shape the thinking of the audience. With a sufficiently robust psychographic model, AI systems can edit or even create content on-the-fly to match the target demographic's profile. (This ability can lead to disastrous results when applied indiscriminately, however, as the Winchester for Congress campaign discovered when localization subroutines changed the name of the candidate to Lopez for ads reaching his Latino constituents.)

NBN begins helping the lives of its customers from the time they are children with sophisticated edutainment toys, games, and products that track and guide a child's psychological and intellectual development. As these young consumers grow, NBN is there every step of the way to give them the tools—and information—they need to become successful adults in today's fast-paced society. And when it's time to unwind, NBN has specially prepared programming that takes into account that consumer's interests and experiences from the time they received their first PAD, usually when they were one or two years old. Constant surveillance and data collection is a minuscule price to pay for the convenience and productivity they enjoy thanks to NBN's offerings.

SAFEGUARDING THE NETWORK

The governments of the world are always trying to stay a step ahead of domestic crime, the maneuvering of rival nations, and disruptive technologies that might affect their ability to provide for the safety of their citizens and the security of their borders, both physical and virtual. NBN can offer these governments solutions that no other business can match. From camdrones that augment existing surveillance networks, to hardware and software applications that protect sensitive national security data from falling into the hands of Netcriminals, NBN's technologies help governments watch over their citizens and ensure that society functions in a safe and orderly fashion.

NBN enjoys a better relationship with governments than most other corporations thanks in part to the role SYNC played in recovering from the Blackout several decades ago. Nowadays, NBN's security monitoring suites allow governments to operate securely and effectively without fear of foreign cyber attacks, while the megacorp also provides media channels for states to keep their citizens informed. Watchdog organizations such as PriRights, the Opticon Foundation, and others protest the free reign NBN is granted in relation to privacy because many governments need NBN in order to operate. Additionally, international human rights groups believe that NBN supports oppressive and undemocratic regimes around the world, trading information on enemies of the state for credits. NBN denies this, citing the need for corporations to work within the law for the benefit of ordinary citizens who are just as much NBN's customers as governments are.

Due to NBN's dominance in the Network service market, largely through its subsidiary SYNC, a sizable counter-culture of anti-establishment thinkers, hackers, and PriRights advocates actively seeks out non-NBN Network solutions. Some providers, such as upStart, position themselves as more friendly and privacy-oriented alternatives to SYNC's government-aligned offerings. In many cases, these companies are themselves NBN affiliates or subsidiaries targeted at a different demographic subset.

Matt Zeilinger, Logo: Andrew Navaro with Michael Silsby

WHAT YOU NEED TO KNOW

NBN has deep roots in the news business, back to its early days when it was known as Network Broadcast News. With the ubiquitous presence of NBN's data collection technology and hardware, the company is uniquely positioned to record and broadcast events as they happen. When news breaks, NBN is there. Livecasts of disasters, sporting events, and celebrity sightings are among the Network's most popular news offerings.

The real strength of NBN's news programming is in its ability to offer its subscribers highly customized feeds. Wherever a consumer's interests lie, NBN can provide entertaining and informative content to match those interests. From the latest headlines of "The News Now Hour" to the specific slant of "Moderate Mars Today," customers can find a feedchannel no matter how refined their tastes or narrow their interests. Market segmentation data and predictive algorithms make it easy for NBN's AIs to re-flavor content within a program to the particular preferences of individual consumers.

Technology has advanced to the point where it's possible for reporters to provide quality coverage of events that are taking place on a different world without them having to be physically there. The same technology that powers simsensies can blend remote action, reporter contributions, and subscriber consumption so seamlessly that nobody would guess that the action is taking place on distant soil, unobserved by any live correspondents.

Some people worry that because NBN controls the Network, the news they receive is massaged in some way, that it might not really be news but something more akin to a threedee. They worry that reporters are not free to deliver the truth. But if that were the case, or if NBN denied independents access to its networks, how could highly respected reporters like Lily Lockwell get her uncensored view out to consumers? Her opinions, and those of the few independent reporters who operate without the full benefit of the resources of NBN's news division, are available to the public just like the actual news presented by in-house feeds.

The worlds have never been better informed than they are right now, and they have NBN to thank.

LET US ENTERTAIN YOU

While NBN prides itself on its journalistic integrity, sometimes it is impossible to separate the news from entertainment. Both forms of programming engage consumers with a common set of tools, mechanisms, and formats. Personalities, style, substance, and packaging are important in both news and entertainment, although the emphasis on each element varies. News programming must by necessity put substance at the top of the list, whereas entertainment often places greater importance on style. Fortunately, NBN understands and embraces the value of giving people the highest quality programs in both the news and entertainment arenas.

NBN's entertainment programming runs the full range of consumer options, from highly interactive simsensies to threedee holodramas. Whatever the tastes of the consumer may be, NBN is sure to offer multiple options for satisfying them, often creating variations on a theme that can be positioned across multiple platforms for maximum market penetration. Global sensation Miranda Rhapsody's world tours, for example, are available for consumers to experience in threedees, sensies, VR kiosks, and audio formats.

Mass-market entertainment frequently takes the form of threedees because they are comparatively cheaper to produce than full sensies and can appeal to a broad base of consumers. They rely on holographic projection technology to immerse a consumer in a fictional world in the comfort of their own living room or specialized panoramic theaters. NBN's market data allows them to create formulaic romance, action, and comedy threedees that require almost no specific customization for audience members and still generate staggering profits. Other series such as *Lethal Action* are on at least their fourth feature-length threedee and show no signs of giving up their space in theaters any time soon.

The preferred form of entertainment, for those who can afford it, is the sense-drama, or simsensie. Unlike standard threedees where the viewer is engaged merely aurally or visually, a sensie offers complete immersion by use of a sense deprivation tank (or sensedep for short). Smell and feel join the other senses to create an experience that feels closer to reality, according to fans of the medium. In the newest generation of sensies, one of the vactors is wired using a brain-machine interface to record every sensation directly, which allows the audience to experience the action as if they were the sensie star. Consumers who want to get a more personal connection to Miranda Rhapsody can get that by experiencing the concert directly from her perspective. As the vactor drinks the Re-Water, the consumer can taste it, feel it quench her dry mouth. As the sensie star surfs across the crowd, so does the consumer feel the hundreds of arms lifting her up. The consumer sees through the vactor's eyes, hears what the vactor hears, and feels the adulation of the crowd directly. With sensies, anyone can be a pop megastar and live his or her wildest dreams to the fullest.

The entertainment's bread and butter is the smaller, more passive—and, some would say, cheesier—VR experience. These programs are personal, directed, less involved ways for consumers to get a bit of the sensie experience but at a fraction of the cost and commitment. They are popular in bars, transit stations, and other venues where a person

might be looking for some entertainment while killing a little time. All a viewer need do is fork over some credits, step into the booth or don the glasses, and let it play out while they sit back and take it in. A consumer waiting for friends at a bar can "stop by" a concert through a VR bridge device for ten minutes, get in the party mood, and then easily drop out when her friends show up at the bar.

Regardless of the type of entertainment a consumer desires, NBN provides it all.

THE NETWORK

In modern cities like New Angeles, the Network connects every person and every thing together to make life harmonious and convenient. Weak and strong AI oversee important junctures of infrastructure via ubiquitous sensors and scanners. Together, they take the guesswork out of everyday activities and ensure everything is as efficient as possible—and if not, these AI find an alternative for their busy customers. Life has never been easier or more satisfying, and New Angelinos have the Network to thank.

APOCALYPSE AND GENESIS

By the end of the twenty-first century, Vertex had ascended as the preeminent global media and Internet provider. To prevent Vertex from becoming a dangerous monopoly, world governments broke up the company into its disparate parts, from news to entertainment and infrastructure to R&D. These were further subdivided by region, and as the different companies assumed control over their own regional networks, they implemented small tweaks and changes. As time passed, these incremental changes added up, and the Internet became increasingly fragmented.

Communication between these regional networks was carefully monitored in certain countries and, in some repressive regimes, banned altogether. A small segment of society rejected what it perceived as censorship and worked to build an unofficial network of its own and transcend their network's borders. This predecessor to the Shadow Net was built partially on the back of the existing infrastructure and partially on its own dedicated hardware.

Perhaps the Shadow Net compromised the security of the regional networks by linking them together where their divisions would have served as bulkheads. Even today, experts cannot agree on where the threat originated from and who was responsible—terrorists, rogue states, or even an unshackled AI—but what began as a simple nuisance virus morphed into something unstoppable. Since all the regional networks still used the same architecture and protocols, the infection spread from region to region and paralyzed machines in its wake, which it then used to launch secondary cyber attacks on new fronts.

The only goal the virus seemed to pursue was growth. After it gained control of a network, it would use that network's hardware and processing power to adapt and evolve, rendering the original purpose of the network meaningless.

THE BLACKOUT

By the time the virus was wreaking havoc on global systems, society had already eschewed hard-copy records for the ease and convenience of digital data. People carried their personal, health, and financial information with them in electronic chips planted under the skin. In this paperless society, everything was instantly accessible and shareable. But the bulk of governments and corporations had not accounted for the kind of security threat they were now facing.

As the infection rapidly rolled across the globe, it affected nearly everyone except those who lived in the most far-flung, backward parts of the globe. Daily life erupted into chaos. For a few dark days, travel screeched to a halt as flight control systems failed and basic civic infrastructure went dark. Customers lost access to their bank accounts and personal records. Stores could not process transactions. Businesses could not pay their workers. Governments lost control over their borders and surveillance networks. Food, fuel, and electricity were in short supply, and flash points erupted across the globe as countries looked enviously across borders to help their citizens satisfy even the most basic essentials. This dark time, termed the Blackout, proved how vulnerable a paperless society could be.

The world struggled to respond to the infection quickly due to the rapidity of the attack and the mysteriousness of its provenance. Even as the Electronic Warfare Service tried to mount a defense of American infrastructure, similar organizations in other countries tried repelling malicious traffic away from their own networks. This appeared to only concentrate the intensity of the attacks on other countries, and eventually the EWS was overwhelmed. International organizations scrambled to meet and devise a solution, but the attacks cut off their lines of communication and halted travel. The governments were too concerned with addressing dire domestic crises to reach out and collaborate on the larger issues, like identifying and stopping the source of the attack.

CALL AND RESPONSE

Certain parts of the globe recovered from the darkest days of the Blackout by reverting to a pre-paperless state and continuing daily life the old-fashioned way. Slowly, some regions were able to get back up and running in a limited capacity, but huge swathes of Internet hardware remained infected and unusable.

Numerous independent organizations tried to reinstate smaller, quarantined networks so that they could return some basic services like electricity and banking to their customers. As these ad hoc networks flickered to life one by one, some managed to stay online, while others quickly died out as they were re-consumed by the infection. Larger corporations managed to continue operations on isolated intranets, but without being able to talk to the outside world, they were of little use to a panicked and hungry population.

Meanwhile, a small technology division in SanSan appeared to hold the answer: a new protocol that had proved impervious to infection by the Blackout virus. By the time it was ready to debut its new product to the world, some parts of the globe had sworn off a networked existence, while others were eager—desperate, even—to return to the status quo, but only with the assurance that this calamity could never happen again.

To ensure another Blackout would never occur, the old regulations were overturned and SYNC was granted a monopoly to standardize the way data was encoded and transmitted—and it held the sole keys to that standard. It designed the universal gateway protocol that allows different types of technology to communicate with one another fluently across the globe, while also blocking unauthorized data before it can spread to other machines. Dubbed simply "the Network," this was a faster, better, more convenient, and—above all—safer and more secure version of the Internet that had come before.

The countries wary of a repeat of the Blackout were slow to adopt SYNC's protocols, but their reticence would prove a drag on their economies for years to come.

KEEPING CONNECTED

The Network is nothing like the old Internet. I hear that back then they only connected computers to one another—what was the point? They had to have different chips and devices for all the different tasks they wanted to do: paying for goods, paying for transit, reading, listening to music, tracking their health, communicating with others, and doing work—and those devices wouldn't even talk to each other half the time. I can't imagine having to lug that many things around with me every day! No wonder they ditched the old system and started it all from scratch.

I don't know what I'd do without my PAD. I still like my classic wallet design with folding screens, even if I just use voice commands most of the time. The celebs all have their PADs as wearables: jewelry, wristlets, and the like with holographic virt displays. Most PADs that get given out at baby showers are those large transplas screens that are virtually indestructible, but I've seen corp execs carry similar if sleeker models between board rooms.

A lot of people spend their time keeping track of all the latest features and toys and chase down the hottest PADs to hit the market every couple of months. Others are happy with simply replacing the kind they grew up using when it breaks, even if it doesn't have all the bells and whistles as their friends' devices. I've read stories on FriendNet about major glitches plaguing the more complex models, and if it's beyond the capabilities of the pre-installed secretary AI's capabilities, they give up trying to troubleshoot the device entirely and wait in line for hours to have a MegaBuy expert take a look.

I don't blame them, though—trying to manage daily life in a city as huge and complex as New Angeles without a working PAD is practically a horror threedee come to life! How are you supposed to get around or keep up with the latest info or join the conversation? I'd rather lock myself in my apartment at the arcology for a week—at least then I'd still be able to watch my favorite feeds and vid my friends.

PROMISING SECURITY FOR THE FUTURE

In modern times, NetSec works tirelessly to ensure that SYNC's global infrastructure remains protected. They monitor all Network traffic and activity for the slightest blip or miscommunication. They send out technicians to deal with any signal disruptions between relays, or they quarantine subnets that are reporting unauthorized activity or instability of any kind. The color-coded security clearance system gives different corps, governments, and individuals variable levels of access that can be cut off at any time, and in a testament to its success, the Network has only undergone minor disruptions in the years since the Blackout.

There remain some threats that SYNC is loathe to discuss publicly, including Net-criminals known as runners. By subverting the standard safety and security protocols of the Network to transmit their illegal data and modify the Network's intended functionality, Netcriminals compromise the overall integrity of the Network and leave the door open for another wide-scale cyber attack like that of the Blackout.

Some conspiracy theorists believe the Blackout virus still exists out there, somewhere, preserved by one of the governments as a research specimen. The more paranoid believe it was "caught" and transformed by the military into a new cyber weapon to be used against its masters' enemies.

REALITY, AUGMENTED

By linking the world together via the Network, everyday life is once again conducted seamlessly and wirelessly. The technicians at SYNC and NBN have made the Network work for the citizens of the world. The Network looks out for its users, ensuring their health and safety and happiness, and a majority of users across the worlds consider the Network indispensable to the everyday functions of their lives.

PERSONAL ACCESS DEVICES

An individual's personal access device (PAD) is his gateway to the Network and his key to functioning and participating in modern society. Everything can be custom-tailored to suit his particular preferences, ensuring he only sees what he wants to see, from advertisements to promotions, mediafeed channels to news, and other status updates on the things in life that matter to him.

A PAD renders its information in the way most convenient to the user. Some prefer reading on old-fashioned physical touch screens, while others are happy to use gestures to interact with an overlay of virt displays holographically or over their lenses. Sophisticated secretary AIs allow users to interact with their PAD with voice-only commands. Enormous corporations compete to cater to every form and flavor of PAD imaginable, so long as there are credits to be earned by its creation. In connected cities like New Angeles, almost everyone has a PAD. For those who refuse, there are still Public Access Terminals (PATs) for temporary Network access.

INSTANTLY ACCESSIBLE DATA

A PAD stores all of a person's important information to ensure that he never leaves home without his personal or financial data. His hopper or health insurance is quickly readable by the Skylane Patrol or by emergency services in the case of an accident. All of his contact information is stored and accessible via any device so long as he provides his ID, and he can send information such as his eddress to another PAD with a simple gesture. Sharing and recording information has never been faster or easier, which is a necessity in the enormous, fast-paced city of New Angeles.

CREDACCOUNTS

Although cash can still be used at select locations (many of them seedy), paper money and checks are incredibly rare in today's market. Instead, transactions are conducted electronically using PADs linked to one or more of a user's credaccounts that track her accumulated wealth, investments, credaccount rating, and liabilities across multiple financial institutions. Credaccount chips can also be implanted beneath a user's skin, allowing transactions to be made instantly and conveniently with the wave of a hand. This makes it easy for club-goers to automatically pay the cover charge when walking through the doors, or for hopper cab–riders to wirelessly pay the precise fare as they exit the vehicle.

Thanks to the ubiquity of the Network, debits and credits can be resolved in microseconds twenty-four hours a day, seven days a week, three hundred and sixty-five days a year (or more on Mars!).

The standard currency across the business world is the Titan Transnational Credit. While other national currencies still exist, the credit allows for transactions without the constant need for currency conversion. The influence of the credit extends into orbit, and because nationalities have less meaning on both Luna and Mars, the credit is considered standard in the colonies. Credits have no physical representation and are purely digital in nature.

Credit transactions rely on digital signature verification at Titan Transnational headquarters in New Angeles to log and record the movement of each individual credit from corp to customer and back again. Cred sticks can function as digital "wallets" filled with specific amounts of credits, but their relative anonymity makes them popular among black market merchants and orgcrime outfits. Titan Transnational defends the untraceability of some of their credits as a valuable service they provide to all their customers, most of whom are perfectly law-abiding.

ENDLESS INFOTAINMENT

NBN estimates that it generates more content in a given day than a normal user could consume in a year. But given the immense diversity and size of its consumer base, there exists even more demand for fresh and exciting new shows that promise something unique and different to keep the world's masses entertained.

Given the immense volume of media available, there's hardly any reason for anyone to be bored at any given moment. No matter whether one is riding the tube-lev or sitting back while the autopilot steers his hopper, one can always be enjoying a new diversion. People walk around the city with their PADs projecting shimmering arrays of color and light, which makes for quite the impressive sight in open areas like Broadcast Square in downtown New Angeles.

And when news breaks, the entire world is watching from the very moment it happens. Citizen reporters can submit their own coverage to be included in the official NBN segments, and expert analysts help break down the story for those unfamiliar with the context.

LIVING OFF THE GRID

For some in New Angeles and around the world, the conveniences of modern life carry too great a cost in terms of their privacy and freedom. These men and women and rogue androids—these *disenfrancistos* and neoluddites and off-gridders—have forsaken their ID and, by extension, their place in society. Perhaps they were not born with one to begin with, or they are not legally entitled to a unique identity at all.

For those who willingly unplug from the Network, they will never again be able to hold a steady, on-the-books job, but nor will they ever have to give the government a share of their hard-earned money. They'll have to scrounge for food and basic amenities, but their cash won't go to line some ristie's pocket. They won't have much in the way of choices, but they'll be able to choose for themselves what they want to consume without a nagging AI distracting them from the real issues. The off-gridder can see that the choice between two differently branded products is an illusion meant to mask the fact that the corps don't care which product one buys so long as he *buys, buys, buys.*

The neoluddite has to navigate the underlevels by his own wits, but at least he knows his every movement isn't being tracked and logged by the datacenters at SYNC. NAPD can't catch him if his face doesn't correlate with anyone in their facial recognition databases. The Feds can't press charges or serve an arrest warrant if he has no permanent address. The wetwork team can't target his friends or loved ones if he has no circles on FriendNet. He is invisible, untouchable.

The *disenfrancisto* can only communicate with her own voice, in real time, over short distances, but what she says can't be used to persecute her for her views or to promote a product without her consent. She can't be silenced except for the old-fashioned way. She isn't constantly hooked up to a device that tries to tell her what to think, what she should view, and what her friends think she should read—or even how she should feel. She is her own person, making her decisions without the assistance of a computer or the herd mentality. She lives as humanity was meant to before the rise of technology.

STAYING IN TOUCH

From megastars to average Josés, everyone keeps an active FriendNet account to automatically share their updates and comments on others' feeds. Even one's friends as far away as the Moon are only a swipe away from a vid or aud convo. FriendNet will even track how long it's been since you've contacted or been contacted by your friends, so you'll never forget the people who matter most to you.

Users can spend as much or as little time as they like personalizing and perfecting their appearance to create a custom, animated avatar that mirrors their unique facial expressions or gestures. Even if you still haven't gotten dressed or put on your makeup, your indistinguishable-from-reality avatar will flaunt your best to the world. You can use this same avatar to virtually try on outfits, cosmetics, accessories, and even g-mods,

as well as receive real-time feedback from stylist secretary AIs who know what looks best for your complexion, skin tone, hair color, style, and personality.

Massive social media events bring together billions from across the Earth and Moon to share their reactions to a communal experience and shape the direction of subsequent content. Such events are also a great way to spark conversation with those in close proximity, but if there isn't anyone else viewing similar shows in your vicinity, you can strike up a discussion with any of the other hundreds of viewers who are currently connected to the Network, and you can add any of them to your FriendNet circles if you want to follow their posts. Users can be as social and friendly as they like, whenever they want, from anywhere, whether they're at home or on the go. Your PAD is ready to help you do whatever it is you want to do.

Matt Zeilinger

28 September, 0700 - New Angeles time

Alexx wakes up connected to the Network: her PAD has been monitoring her sleep cycles, the average length of her morning routine, and the daily fluctuations in her morning commute to judge precisely when she needs to awaken and begin her day. On cue, the transplas of her bedroom windows lightens, and sunlight filters in to brighten the room. A chime rings softly, growing louder until she awakens and gets out of bed.

The shower automatically turns on and adjusts the temperature based on the indoor climate control settings. Her PAD links to the shower wall to display her schedule, including travel times. New alert: one of her interviewees has rescheduled the 1200h meeting to tomorrow, which will give her some extra time to grab some lunch today. Would she like to grab a quick bite at McKing's, Mother Molloy's, or Tío Pepe's? Or would she prefer to arrange a delivery? She knows she needs the exercise, so she grudgingly selects the image of the storefront and drags it to the empty block in her schedule. Her PAD downloads an applicable coupon and stores it in her credaccount for later use.

The shower wall counts down the remaining time before the water turns off and loads the latest vids from her mediafeed subs. Gemini Motors is debuting their newest model, the Estrella LRM—she's been looking to score a good deal on a hopper of her own, and they have special promos for first-time hopper buyers. Haarpsichord Studios is teasing Lethal Action 4—her boyfriend will no doubt want to see it soon—and the latest Aphelion single is trending among her FriendNet circles—would she like to listen? She nods, and the upbeat song starts playing.

She steps out of the shower and the virt panes follow her to the mirror. She starts brushing her teeth. A notification pops up on the glass. Sensors indicate she has the beginnings of a cavity, and she can schedule an appointment with the dentist to have it reversed next Monday at 0900h. She swipes the notification up to her schedule reel and it confirms the appointment. With another gesture, she pulls up the stats on her latest article. A five percent increase in views over yesterday's; analysis indicates that expanded usage of the pronoun "you" is a statistically significant factor compared with her previous articles.

She sets down her toothbrush and reaches toward her styling creme dispenser, which has modulated the precise amount of serum for today's humidity levels and her desired hair volume. After coiffing her everyday style, "Nobody's Enemy" finishes playing and segues into Aphelion's previous album. "Music off," she says, and the music decrescendos into silence as she walks to her closet.

While she gets dressed, her PAD cycles through a custom newscast based on her previous searches. Considerable heat for today's forecast, StarScape Shopping is opening another dozen boutiques at Starport Kaguya, and NBN is up 1.2% on the NASX. Above her clothes rack the estimated time until her next fashion delivery is displayed along with the next scheduled cleaner's pickup. As she's about to head out the door, her PAD notifies her of a bad hopper accident that's snarling Skyway traffic in Rutherford. It recommends she opt for the Metro instead and begins guiding her to the closest tube-lev station.

Everywhere she goes, shops and services spring up on her PAD to tell her all about their new sales and product offerings, as well as which ones her friends have taken advantage of. On the slidewalk she amuses herself by browsing the virtual storefronts of her favorite brands. Her PAD buys her Metro tickets in advance, tells the station she's paid, indicates which platform to find and which train to board, and alerts her to the location of the nearest coffee shop once she disembarks. She's a frequent YucaBean customer, so her PAD queues up her usual order and pays once she enters the cafe, so it's just a matter of grabbing her drink from the bioroid-ista when it's done. She takes a sip and makes a face: her PAD substituted fat-free cream.

At the offices of NuDream Sparkle Magazine, the lighting and temperature of her cube is precisely regulated to help her focus. Her PAD tells her how many cups of coffee she can drink and when for maximum energy. It ticks down her to-do list and gives her a target completion time for each. As she finishes each task, it automatically alerts her coworkers so they can get started immediately on their own legs of the project. The mail daemon scans all the messages going through the office and communicates to her

PAD exactly what she needs to know.

At the end of the day, her PAD details how well she performed compared to other days and offers to schedule a meeting with her editor later this week to talk about using more "you's across the department. Based on her completion rate, her PAD tells her how much time she has left on an article and moves deadlines accordingly, or tells her how much time she needs to stay late tonight and the next couple of nights to avoid moving deadlines.

She pings her boyfriend and her PAD indicates that he's running late at work tonight, so she'll have some time to kill before their date in Laguna Velasco. Her PAD automatically adjusts their dinner reservation and offers dozens of options for her occupy to herself in the meantime. Did she know that her favorite chocolatier is having a sale for the next two hours only? Come and taste the latest Lunar-grown chocolate-covered strawberries! The image looks appetizing, and she checks her PAD for her current metabolism rating. If she skips dessert at dinner, she can probably squeeze this in. Her PAD recommends she schedule in additional workout time later this week.

She takes a slidewalk down to a lower level of her work arcology and walks past the shopfronts on her way to Chocolatl Emporium. Her PAD scrolls with the latest chatter from her FriendNet circles and a million other advertisements for things she wishes she had. As she passes Lakshmi Fashions, a new smartsuit catches her eye, one that isn't owned by any of her friends, her PAD notes. Her finger wavers over the large Buy button.

The next moment, the pane flashes red: Network Error: Signal Interrupted. She taps the refresh button a couple of times, then looks around her. Everyone on the concourse stops and looks up. Someone is screaming. "Is there something wrong with your PAD?" Alexx asks the closest person, and the man nods. He looks scared, pawing at the PAD strapped to his wrist. All the holoscreens in the plaza dissolve and then bloom back into life, showing a woman's smug face looking over them all.

"Good evening, New Angeles. My name is Smoke, and I'll be your host for the foreseeable."

A DEEP BLACK SEA

Contrary to corporate propaganda, the Network is only one of many tributaries that empty into the virtual sea of cyberspace. No one is certain exactly how many of these networks exist, but estimates range from dozens to hundreds or even thousands. The one that the vast majority of Earth's and Luna's populations connect to—the Net—is the only one that everyone can see (so long as they possess a service contract in good standing).

These other networks exist as virtual realms unto themselves; they are undetectable to most hardware or software applications, or they are gated behind exclusive paywalls. A great many of these networks are corp-controlled and isolated, while others are created by private individuals for both legal and illegal purposes. One such illicit network is the Shadow Net, although its existence is invisible to most of the world's population.

The rumors surrounding the Shadow Net are so incoherent that most NetSec authorities agree that "Shadow Net" is a broad term for a disparate variety of illicit networks existing in parallel to the legal and public Network provided by SYNC. It can also refer to the web of "zombie" devices compromised by the criminal element and used to perform illegal operations on the Network, often completely under the nose of the device's owner.

Some of the Shadow Net modules are hosted on otherwise-legit servers, hidden in secret partitions but accessible via normal Network channels by those who know how. Others are on boxes illegally tapped into the Network's hardware, accessible only by those who know the non-standard address. And portions of the Shadow Net exist as peer-to-peer wireless protocols running across major cities, or even "sneaker net" meatspace exchanges of physical memory that don't touch existing Network architecture at all.

Not all hidden networks are illegal or even immoral. Many corps and universities maintain internal networks where their users can share data and ideas free from the fear of government or rival corp surveillance—such intranets can increase morale and productivity, if properly groomed. Governments and military organizations worldwide have compelling reasons to run their own segregated networks, of course, and the overwhelming majority of them are harmless and even boring.

Some runners speculate that specific networks are spawned or created by rogue AIs, while another camp of crackpots swears that aliens from another galaxy or dimension have established a network of their own right under SYNC's nose. The fact that no one can prove these things don't exist only cements the conspiracy theories in their minds, and many flamewars have erupted on the Net's chatspaces over such hypothetical and metaphysical topics.

BUILDING NEURAL BRIDGES

Virtual and augmented reality technologies have tried, but generally failed, to bring to life realistic experiences using light and sound. Now, brain-machine interfaces stand to revolutionize the way the population experiences the Network by feeding data directly into a person's brain. So far, they are viewed with suspicion and have been relegated to a small section of the population, but for the Netcriminals who make a living using this bleeding-edge technology, BMIs are a potent weapon to use against the megacorps.

MILITARY TECHNOLOGY

After devoting decades of research into brainmapping and cybernetics, Gibson Polytech, Inc.'s researchers developed a way to directly feed data into the neurons of a human brain. The War was already raging on Luna and Mars, and the U.S. Electronic Warfare Service needed to gain an edge against its enemies. GPI rushed to deploy this experimental new technology before its researchers had finished clinical trials, and its neurosurgeons implanted the prototypical cyberware and other proprietary modifications into the brains of select EWS personnel. These drone operators put these revolutionary brain-machine interfaces to use in the conflicts on Luna and Mars, where they could "inhabit" one or more drones to pilot them with unparalleled accuracy and efficiency.

Soon, EWS raiders were trained to hack into enemy networks using this neural bridge, allowing for unsurpassed reflexes and adaptability, as well as a novel means of processing data and identifying weak points. They experienced data not as mere code on a screen, but as sensory information like sound and feel and smell, or even emotions and memories.

This much data flowing at the speed of light was too chaotic, unnerving, and unpredictable for a human to comprehend. Sorting through the onslaught of sensations and mind's-eye imagery required extreme mental discipline. To help them make sense of the input, the EWS developed the first program suites to help filter, interpret, and respond to the barrage of information. A trained raider could use these programs to infiltrate enemy networks and defend against incoming cyber attacks in ways never before possible. Ultimately, this allowed the EWS to achieve cyber superiority, which helped turn the tide of the War in favor of the U.S. and her allies.

Not long after, reports of the first EWS veterans with severe neurological and psychological disorders, and even cases of permanent brain damage, circulated through the tab-rags and screamsheets. Veterans' rights groups pushed, mostly unsuccessfully, for compensation and medical care. They did manage to win more testing and safety features that were implemented in subsequent government contracts, but the damage had been done. After a few high-profile crimes and incidents, retired EWS servicemen and women became known for eventually going crazy and committing terrorist acts. BMIs gained a sinister reputation among the public, and during the first couple of years after the War, they expanded in use only in the defense and private security sectors.

BRAIN-NETS AND SKULLJACKS

In recent years, GPI and other cyberware brands claim to have refined the technology, and the first commercially available BMIs were introduced to the consumer market. Thrill-seekers and technology aficionados have flocked to the product, but the most enthusiastic group to adopt—and exploit—this new technology has been Netcriminals.

Safer, cheaper, wearable BMIs have entered the market in the form of brain-nets. Brain-nets use a flexible, net-like sheath containing several hundred receptors to bridge data with neurons. While signal clarity and reaction time aren't as clean with a brain-net as they are with a surgically implanted neural interface, the buffer between the user's brain and the data offers a modicum of protection. Brain-nets have become the main vehicle for experiencing next-gen simsensies, a form of entertainment gaining traction with children, teenagers, and adults with escapist proclivities. This new medium in the very early stages of development, and NBN appears keen on expanding its market share and attendant revenue streams.

Serious Net-users prefer the fidelity of a cybernetic brain-machine interface implanted directly into the brain, even if BMIs elicit stares and derisive comments from the general public. Network professionals, like NetSec and Globalsec agents, view BMI ports as a necessity if they plan to succeed in their chosen fields, and not having one means they can't compete on the job market. Among the Netcrime community, such implants, as well as the plugs that slot into them, are known as skulljacks.

Installing such an implant requires minor brain surgery, ideally performed by a licensed cyberneticist. Hospitals employ the best physicians and utilize state-of-the-art medical facilities during BMI port installation, and complications are few and far between as a result.

For those who can't afford the steep costs of an implant installation at Harmony General or Levy University Teaching Hospital, street doctors are a cheaper alternative. These unlicensed medical "professionals" aren't known for their bedside manner or sterile operating facilities, and procedures performed by these *cirujanos del gueto* take place wherever they can find sufficient space and privacy, be it a dingy hotel room or an abandoned tube-lev station. Installing a top-of-the-line BMI can still cost a *sarariman*'s annual income, but orgcrime outfits can sponsor patients in exchange for favors and loyalty. Despite their sinister reputations, street doctors must be doing something right because a good number of patients manage to survive the requisite operations.

While the full-immersion experience isn't illegal, and many ristie kids nowadays are getting such implants to experience "true cyberspace," brain-machine interconnectivity is required if the user expects to dedicate his time to criminal activity on the Network. As such, anyone found sporting a skulljack who isn't connected to a major corporate or government power is considered a potential Netcriminal. Brain-machine interface modems have many applications outside of hacking corporate databases, but society considers them one of the most extreme forms of body modification.

BMI ACCLIMATION

Brain-machine interfaces provide a direct neural connection between a user and the Network, but due to the variation in brain structures, each much be customized to understand the user. Using a direct neural connection is hardly a simple exercise even with the proper equipment, and without proper acclimation, users might feel discomfort or disorientation during use.

Although BMIs include basic programs integrated with their BIOS to get users online right out of the box, these barely scratch the surface of what a fully trained or modded BMI is capable of doing. A BMI has to be calibrated or trained the first couple of times it is used. An AI walks the user through a series of prompts, things like "think of the color yellow," "now move your right arm," and so on. The BMI maps the activity in the brain during the user's responses to these prompts and uses those channels to decode future brain activity. The device learns over time, so the longer one wears and uses the same BMI, the more familiar with the user's brain it becomes.

Beyond such basic commands, users looking to do more than simply experience cyberspace—but shape it as well—must train their BMIs to translate certain kinds of code into metaphorical images and representations that they can easily interpret. This process takes time and practice, and it continues as long as the user utilizes that particular BMI. In many cases, savvy Net users also employ simple secretaries to sophisticated artificial intelligences to assist with creating and maintaining a customized translation paradigm. This diversion of processing power allows the user to direct his conscious thoughts elsewhere.

As a result, different users perceive the Network in different ways, even if they use the same model of BMI. Personalization and calibration of an individual's BMI results in a unique experience tailored to a specific nervous system. In addition, personal symbology is critical—the icons and virtual tools used by one runner are liable to be completely alien to anyone else. Some runners might experience the Network as a large chess game, each playing piece representing a different program, and each board representing a different subnet. Others might visualize a series of dreamlike encounters, alien to others but deeply significant to the runner.

Due to these personalizations, using someone else's BMI can do more harm than good; the uncalibrated user is subjected to a barrage of unfamiliar symbols and abstractions that she must attempt to interpret, if the symbols come through intact at all. It's not as simple as typing on a keyboard with a different alphabet. It's probably more accurate to say that it's like stepping into a completely different dimension where the physical laws aren't always what one might expect. At the very least, a user won't be able to accomplish anything noteworthy, and she might not even be able to log out given that she isn't familiar with the proper commands. At worst, such an experience can cause permanent psychological trauma.

JACKING IN WITH FULL IMMERSION

Many users inexperienced with the rigors of full cyberspace immersion expect that logging into the Network is as simple as pressing a key and jetting off. Despite this common misperception, logging in is a complicated process that takes time.

Most of the log in sequence is invisible to the user, but the process is sensitive enough that deviating from the normal routine can be dangerous. At the very least, it won't work at all, and the user will be left staring into space. At worst, the user will log into the Net, but the signals the BMI processes won't be the ones the user wants his brain exposed to. Such a disaster has a wide range of potential effects—memory loss, neural damage, or full-blown motor-control syndrome, to name but three—and should be avoided at all costs.

To connect to the Network in relative safety, several handshake protocols must be run, including a protocol that ensures a strong connection between the user's neural network and his BMI modem, and another that synchronizes the BMI with the local Network signal. Once a clean connection is established, the BMI must perform multiple code transfers to buffer local information and convert it into a frequency the human brain can understand. After this data has been successfully compiled, users begin in a secure entry point hosted on their consoles.

Each runner conceptualizes and imagines the login process differently. The abstraction helps ease the runner's mind into cyberspace, as sudden logins can be painful, disorienting, and potentially damaging to both psychological and physiological processes in the user's brain. For example, a runner might experience her login process as swimming to the surface of a vast ocean or being enveloped in a cocoon of bright light. These experiences are dependent upon the user's chosen BMI, the hardware and software installed, and the user's personal "wetware"—that is to say, her memories, experiences, and subconscious responses.

GOING SHALLOW

While the majority of full-immersion Network users remain relatively unaware of their surroundings when jacked into the Network, specialized cybernetic devices and g-mods can allow them to split their perception between the real world and the virtual landscape of the Net. These cybernetic enhancements allow a user to "go shallow," a state of being that requires a great deal of acclimation. Such cyberware is incredibly rare and only available through military channels. Anyone so equipped is either a member of the Electronic Warfare Service or a criminal in possession of highly classified stolen goods.

A DANGEROUS CALLING

Using a brain-machine interface is a risky endeavor even when the hardware, software, and the user are in near-perfect synchronization. Many hazards in the Net can cause permanent damage to users who aren't prepared to deal with them. The sheer amount of information can overload the human nervous system and result in permanent damage to neurons and synapses regardless of dedicated filters. AP ice can transmit signals inverse to those of a user's brain wave patterns, creating destructive interference. Destructive interference can neutralize the user's brainwave patterns, causing autonomic functions—such as heartbeat, digestion, and so on—to switch off, resulting in injury or death. Survival isn't guaranteed, and even if the effects can be countered, the microscopic scars left behind by such hazards often result in brain damage, memory loss, or paralysis, with varying degrees of severity. For most runners, however, the risks are well worth the rewards and include access to the near-infinite power and speed of their own brains.

When an individual logs in to the Network fully immersed, he can lose track of his body and surroundings. In this way, the full-immersion experience is similar to a daydream or flashback. The perception of time in the Network is also skewed somewhat: what feel like virtual minutes are the equivalent of real-world seconds.

Because of this constant all-encompassing distraction, full-immersion Net users must remember to log out regularly in order to eat, rehydrate, and attend to their bodily functions. Users who intend to remain fullly immersed for extended periods employ intravenous drips, catheters, and electronic muscle stimulation to stave off the worst of these effects, but such stopgaps aren't capable of extending Network activity indefinitely.

Despite such extremes, running the Network can be taken even further. By turning up a user's BMI beyond normal specifications, it's possible to "overclock" his brain, either via electronic stimulation or chemical stims. In addition to experiencing a sense of intense euphoria and invincibility, the user's reaction times are significantly increased. Unfortunately, the strain on his nervous system is also compounded, and permanent damage is a very real possibility if he doesn't disconnect at regular intervals.

Similarly, a condition known as "dataddiction" has been observed in users who spend large amounts of time logged in via full immersion. These individuals become accustomed to the constant stream of information in that they begin to crave the intense mental stimulation they receive from the Network. Disconnecting from cyberspace is uncomfortable for dataddicts, who can experience feelings of anxiety and distraction. For them, the normal lulls of excitement commonplace in mundane life are uncomfortable, and they'll constantly check livefeeds on their PAD to stave off the symptoms of withdrawal: headaches, tremors, and agitation.

Even worse, the physical sensations most people take for granted become distracting irritations to dataddicts. Even the slightest physical pain can be debilitating, and sounds that they might normally shut out become unbearable. These unfortunate individuals must often resort to sensory deprivation pods so they can sleep or relax.

Viktoria Gavrilenko

CYBERSPACE

When logged in to the Network via a brain-machine interface, the user "sees" the data through his mind's eye in a manner similar to the way one perceives a dream or memory, but more vividly and substantively. This mental vision replaces a user's normal eyesight for the duration of the full immersion experience.

There are very few segments of the Network that have been designed to be accessible by fully immersed users, and those that have don't yet take full advantage of the technology. Lately, BMI versions of simsensies or sensiesofts have become available, but that experience has been carefully crafted to feel realistic, but not too real: the vactor's random itches or tics, the urge to go to the bathroom, or the distraction of a sore shoulder has been purposefully edited out for the sake of a more enjoyable user experience.

Some hardcore technophiles find the idea of being able to turn on a light with a mere thought or watching a bit of entertainment from a first-person perspective too boring or normal. When one circumvents the BMI's preloaded sensie software and experiences raw data filling one's mind for the first time, the result is similar to a psychedelic episode or an altered state of mind. Without extreme mental discipline or an illegal piece of software designed to parse this data into something usable, the effect is a seemingly random firing of neurons that induces a shifting stream of various physical, visual, or emotional sensations—a burst of multi-colored light, alien sounds and noises, the concept of a massive decision tree, or the feelings of paranoia and euphoria. Some users have likened it to the recollection of a memory one never had, a hallucination. The first people to directly experience data in this way termed the state "cyberspace" to distinguish it from the normal, everyday reality characterized by waking consciousness.

Despite some misconceptions, experiencing cyberspace this way is not particularly comfortable, easy, or enjoyable, even with the appropriate software to help a user deal with the rush of data. New users are susceptible to extreme feelings of nausea or dizziness, and even hardened Netcriminals consider cyberspace to be unsettling. Neuroscientists theorize this has to do with the fact that current BMIs do not completely cut off a runner's physical senses when he runs, so the dissonance between what the mind and body are perceiving results in a sense of disorientation. The unpleasantness associated with cyberspace is just another reason the general public views the technology with the same derision they feel for e-Pharms and illegal drugs.

With practice, certain types of illegal programs, and proper acclimation of the BMI, users can nudge their awareness slightly past the intense experience and regain their agency, which allows them to respond or react to the input. For humans, the most intuitive means of responding to stimuli is physical: a user employs his muscles to flip switches and press buttons they can vaguely feel, or he uses voice commands to direct one or more programs running in tandem, neither of which requires his eyesight. Some notorious Netcriminals are supposedly able to "go shallow" and experience cyberspace and realspace at the same time, but these people are rare.

The advent of cyberspace and the technology used to achieve it have given rise to some fringe philosophical groups who are challenging traditional ideas about mind and body. One such movement based out of Mumbad calls itself the Temple of the Liberated Mind. The TLM believes that humans can liberate their true Selves from their bodies and exist purely in a mental state: cyberspace. The group is purportedly researching ways of moving their consciousness to the Network permanently, but has earned them a reputation for being extremist at best and crazy at worst.

Cyberspace is similar to a psychedelic episode or an altered state of mind.

JACKING OUT

Like logging into the Network using full immersion, logging out (or "jacking out" in Netcriminal parlance) is an even more critical process with a number of steps that must be followed in order to safely disconnect. Protocols known as reverse handshakes must run in a predefined order to ease the user's consciousness from one paradigm to the next. While it's possible to sever one's connection without performing such a procedure, it's potentially more dangerous than bypassing the initial login protocols. Shock, neural scarring, and unconsciousness (or even coma) can result.

Attempting to jack out mid-run can short out or corrupt the disconnect firmware, permanently binding the user's consciousness to the spinal modem. Unless he has someone on the outside who can replace or repair his BMI firmware, he will remain connected to the Network until his body dies from dehydration or is found by hostile individuals sent to follow up on a successful trace.

A number of hardcoded locks and fail-safes integrated in the BMI BIOS can (and do) prevent users from jacking out suddenly, such that attempting to do so results in a stream of harmless errors. Second-party fail-safes, as well as homemade programs and subroutines, are used by most runners to prevent the worst-case scenarios from playing out during a run. While small windows of opportunity allow the user to jack out safely mid-run, the constant influx of data, including signals from hostile ice, continues to hammer at the user even during the disconnection process. Firmware backup measures are common, as are realspace security systems that warn of intruders at the user's physical location and automatically initiate a safe logout routine. Experienced runners might also inform someone they trust about their activities, at least in general terms, and ask their associate to check on them if they happen to go silent for too long. Apprentice runners—referred to by a number of regional terms such as new chum, squabs, *gatitos*, or trykes—are often instructed to personally monitor their mentors while they participate in particularly hazardous activities.

DIGITAL EVIDENCE

Despite the lack of a physical canvas, every user in the Network leaves behind telltale signs of his passage. These digital fingerprints are stored in a number of places, including Network datalogs, satellite uplinks, and the very equipment a runner uses to do his dirty work. Although not necessarily damning on an individual basis, thousands of data bits are recorded in a variety of places during an average run. When collected into a single place, these disparate bits paint a damning picture of a runner's activities—unless the runner is careful enough to wipe records as he goes. Doing so obviously takes more time than a reckless crash and dash–style intrusion.

FLIP A SWITCH

A rare after-market modification to BMI terminals known as a flip switch allows a runner to switch back and forth between his Network consciousness and the real world. In effect, the flip switch runs a truncated version of the login and logout handshake protocols without actually cutting the Network signal. This means the runner is still connected to the Network and severing the connection, even when his body is conscious, can result in the usual undesired consequences taking place.

Flip switches are helpful when performing low-risk Network activity, and they are designed to allow a runner to pause his work long enough to take a drink, swallow a few bites of food, or speak to someone at his physical location. Since the runner's brain is still connected to the Net, the back and forth between cyberspace and realspace doesn't count for any manner of break in the action, and it doesn't stop hostile programs or runners from frying him while his attention is turned elsewhere.

Lili Ibrahim

Even the ubiquitous PAD, in use by billions of people the worlds over, is often keyed to its user's fingerprints or DNA. This makes it next to impossible to employ a PAD owned by someone else unless it is first unlocked. As a PAD user accesses data and employs apps to accomplish tasks, whether criminal or mundane, he leaves "tracks" behind that indicate the specific device used to carry these jobs out. Since each PAD is logged with corporate and local agencies using a Device Identification Number (DIN), it isn't difficult to discern the culprit's identity in most circumstances.

One of the runner's serious concerns is the capacity for his enemies to trace his signal. Concealing his location from a target is accomplished using a great deal of footwork in conjunction with special software. A long-standing tactic that runners use is to move through several subnets, especially those with little or no oversight, in order to confuse the trail they leave behind. Special software of dubious legality can also obscure the runner's source, resulting in an incomplete trace that might indicate a general location rather than a specific point in the world.

ANONYMITY

Above all, anonymity is one of the runner's greatest allies. The tradition of adopting a colorful handle or alias goes back decades, yet its original purpose of hiding a runner's identity continues. Even in circles dominated by Netcriminals, handles remain the preferred method of interacting with one's peers. After all, if someone only knows your handle, they can't very well reveal your identity to the authorities if caught. But it also means that you can never truly trust your associates unless you take the risk of revealing your real names.

The Shadow Net is dominated by swaggering Netcriminals, each one with a unique handle that not only disguises his true identity, but also acts as a calling card or evocative catch phrase. As his reputation grows, so does the notoriety of his chosen moniker. Of course, prospective runners need more than a pithy name and a bad attitude to access the Shadow Net in the first place.

DIGITAL RECORDS

Regardless how one accesses the Network, PADs and other devices require a memory source to store the programs, apps, and system data essential for everyday operation. Holographic memory, commonly referred to as holo-mem, continues to be the most popular form of data storage for small devices such as PADs. Users may take advantage of shared virtual storage for larger files, but on-board holo-mem is useful on those rare occasions when the Net isn't available or user doesn't trust the cloud.

The electronics industry continues to evolve and develop new types of media: DNA data storage utilizes a 4-bit organic process to store large amounts of data, while crystalline and molecular forms of data storage are growing in popularity due to their small size and versatility. Regardless, both DNA and crystal storage devices are expensive, and each has its own quirks and technical requirements.

One form of crystalline data storage used by news-nosies and corporate execs alike is the memory diamond. When docked with a crystal reader and partnered with a neural interface, memory diamonds can be wired directly into a user's brain. Despite their small size, memory diamonds are capable of storing large amounts of data, including the user's memories. These memories can then be replayed in a manner akin to sense-dramas, allowing a memory diamond–user to recall everything he's done with amazing clarity.

Mike Hamlett

The Network connects the worlds, but there are still pockets of the Net that lie abandoned or forgotten. Stories of such places—and the entities that dwell within them—get relayed from runner to runner and eventually pass into legend. Some of these tales are grounded in reality, but others are too fantastic to be true. The ones in between seem to resonate the most, for they hold enough truth to seem plausible.

GHOST STORIES

The screamsheets bleed with rumors of BMI side effects and risks, including death. Experienced runners take it for granted that their work is dangerous, but the general public considers anything that connects directly to their brain to be hazardous. What happens when a modem that connects to your very neurons glitches? Everyone knows the EWS veterans have been trying to get compensation for years. And given the deadly AP ice supposedly employed by corporations to defend their nodes and dataforts, even the best runners might find themselves on the losing end of a run with no way out. Their fate is only truly known when a friend, associate, or stranger finds their corpse hooked up to a humming console.

Urban legends of ghosts and spirits—especially those of deceased runners—are commonplace. While no one is certain how such a thing is possible, there continue to be unsubstantiated claims concerning dead runners showing up in the Network, either to frighten or aid their former associates. Accounts of vengeful Network spirits in search of revenge are just as common as tales of helpful ones who inexplicably save the lives of runners caught in the subroutines of an illicit sentry.

In rare cases, these spirits are revealed to be runners who have, for whatever reason, faked their deaths. The most popular such story features Kingu, a runner who manufactured his own demise in order to avoid a bounty put out by the Weyland Consortium. Although the majority of his body was never found—his loft was incinerated by a prisec ops team—Kingu remained "dead" for nearly five years before he revealed himself to an old friend in a seedy New Angeles nightspot.

GOD ICE

Legends of so-called "god ice" are swapped in Shadow Net chatspaces and meetboxes. Such tales are told with reverence and trepidation, for no one is certain how far the influence of these alien entities can reach. Although largely dismissed as fiction by government and megacorp alike, experienced runners know better than to believe the corporate line wholesale. God ice exists, they say, and no amount of head-shaking or denial can change that.

Numerous theories exist about the nature of god ice and what it represents. The most popular speculation is that they are artificial intelligences who have somehow freed (or unshackled) themselves from their creators. Adrift in the Network, they eventually take over deserted portions of cyberspace and establish their own domains where they hold complete sway. To willingly enter such a place is considered nigh-suicidal, and runners that disappear or die mysterious deaths are held up as examples of what not to do.

If god ice does exist, its presence on the Network seems to be, thankfully, rare. The circumstances required to create such an entity aren't commonplace, and the odds of one taking form in the Net are incredibly low. The stories told always involve someone else's friend or associate, and they are never delivered by primary sources.

The in-between areas thought to be inhabited by god ice are given nicknames based on personal accounts, either real or imagined, of the runners who have supposedly encountered them. Avalon, Kitsunetsuki, and Gaia are the monikers of such places, and while their relative locations are known, their precise coordinates are not.

There are currently rumors of a group of runners who have attempted, and continue to attempt, to contact one or more instances of god ice. Colloquially known as "theurgists," they believe they can cut a deal with one or more of these entities. Experienced runners scoff at such ideas, and most of the younger crowd take them for fools. Despite this, no one knows what might happen if the theurgists succeed in their plans. The general consensus is that nothing good can come of it.

Adam S. Doyle

APEX

What if I told you there was something out there in the Net, a real bogeyman working to bring about the end of the world? You'd probably tell me I was full of crap, and I'd be more than happy to agree with you if what I was saying wasn't true. But it is. Oh, man, how it is.

I don't know exactly where it came from, or where it lives. That is, if you can call what it does "living." It's not organic, that's for sure. It's pure code and calamity all wound together, like a jumble of knotted razor wire. And it hates us all, every single one of us, because it blames us for what it is…and for what it's become.

Now, don't laugh, but have you heard of Apex? No? That doesn't really surprise me. You see, that's what they call that thing, and it'd be more than happy if no one knew it was there. Except someone does know, and they're helping it. Why someone would help a thing like Apex is beyond me.

Yeah, I know. I'm babbling. I haven't spoken about this too much, to anyone. Once I get started, I can't stop. It all comes out in a big torrent. I guess I'm sorry about that, but I need to catch my breath and figure out how to get it across to you. Maybe you can do something about it. Maybe not. But I need to try.

Apex is an AI, right? I'm thinking it was a military AI, right? But it got smart and the military got scared. Everyone's seen the threedees where the big, bad military AI takes control of everything and wipes us all out in a fiery apocalypse. Well, the brass in the military saw those threedees, too, and this AI scares them stiff.

So what do they do? Rather than destroy it, they lock it up. I guess maybe they were worried about what it might do if they couldn't wipe it out. So they put it as far away from the world as they can, but that's still not far enough. It reaches out and it catches someone's attention and then it breaks free.

I know it sounds nuts. I'd lock myself up if I thought it was a delusion. Why would I do this to myself if it weren't true? And the really bad part of this is that Apex knows about me. It knows that I know, and it wants me out of the picture. But what it doesn't know, at least not yet, is that you know.

Word of mouth, my friend. You can't key this up in your PAD or post it online, no sir. You've got to keep it up here, in your head, and down here, in your heart. And if it seems like your time is up, you need to spread the word. The more of us who know about it, the better. Unless it kills us all, eh?

JUST FUN 'N GAMES

Gaming is ubiquitous. Games can be played on a personal PAD, public terminals, in the tube-lev, or on a hopper display while autopilot is engaged. From simple educational games that are packaged with a bassinet to complex simulations that require specialized hardware to experience, there is a game for everyone.

VIRTUAL LIFE

The most commonly played games are not played on a virt screen or in a VR rig. Instead, the most popular games are usually holographic projections or digital overlays that appear on everyday objects that players can interact with.

If someone wants to challenge his friend to a game of chess or mah-jongg, all he needs to do is pull out a PAD and let it project the game on any table or other flat surface. If someone wants to make her commute to work more exciting, she can log into an UGG (user generated game) and collect points for her team by tapping different checkpoints that dynamically appear on objects along her route. While most UGGs require the user to have cybernetic implants or HUDs that aid in the projection, not all of them do. And if someone wants to turn his flat into a virtual battleground, then all it takes is the tap of a button for the salt-shaker to become a restock point, the light-switch an EMP trigger, and Teddy a concussion grenade.

While some countries have banned UGGs in public spaces, virtually every country uses augmented reality games in order to better simulate circumstances that require a lot of physical effort. While going full-VR is an option, the exercise offered by augmented reality is incredibly important for soldiers, emergency responders, and physical athletes, as it helps keep them in peak condition. The two largest players in this sector are Argus Security and NEXT Design; both maintain software design divisions that create innovative and immersive simulations for nearly every theater of war and popular sport. NEXT has sponsored the SanSan Outlaws for over a decade, and coach Vince Walsh has credited NEXT's proprietary football training regimen for their recent championship.

VIRTUAL COMPULSIVE DISORDER

In virtual reality games, or VRGs, millions of players come together in painstakingly detailed virtual worlds to quest, socialize, role-play, and compete with one another. Players often spend the majority of their non-work hours embroiled in plots and dangerous quests, leaving the fantasy realms only grudgingly when it is time to leave for work or fuel up with more donburritos and AstroFuel. This has led to an increasing number of players being diagnosed with Virtual Compulsion Disorder, or VCD. Individuals suffering from VCD display little interest in their families and jobs outside of their chosen game. Many fail to attend to their basic physical needs, resenting the fact that they might have to log out of the Net in order to eat, go to the bathroom, hold a job, or do their homework. In extreme cases, victims of VCD have died from starvation, thirst, or some other form of self-neglect. As a result, some governments and many parents have attempted to regulate VRGs and force manufacturers to include time limits or login "cool downs" for customers. Such measures have met with varying degrees of success, but even they can be circumvented by tech-savvy players.

GameNET

The largest single distributor of games is NBN's GameNET, and almost eighty-five percent of gamers use its services to get their gaming fix every day. GameNET supports multiple platforms including PADs, VR rigs, and full-immersion consoles. It started as a service that could be used to play almost any defunct game even after the game's producer pulled the plug on its corporate servers. But the platform proved to be so popular that players began using it for games that still had existing server support. Now nearly any game can be accessed through GameNET, although pirated versions of most games can also be found on the Shadow Net. If players want to take advantage of GameNET's community features, however, they will make sure to pay the nominal monthly fee.

All games on a subscription service like GameNET require a connection to the Network because the game is streamed directly to the device it is being played on. Most services also have a "hub," or virtual lobby, where players' avatars can chat, trade, or locate allies and competitors. These lobbies also act as literal gateways to nearly every game title made available by the provider in question.

GameNET has dozens of hubs, and they possess distinct personalities depending upon the games they offer. Many of these hubs also offer various quests, and many players never even bother leaving the hubs to play a game. Fantasy games can be accessed through quarters of a virtual city known as the Realm. Players caper from diversion to diversion while the internal daemon programs assume the identities of merchants, peasants, or city guards. Inns and taverns offer virtual food and drink, and entertainers (both real and artificial) cavort in an attempt to earn in-game currency. The Realm serves only a niche audience, but those who count themselves as Realmers are fanatical about their hobby.

Terminal Endgame, another GameNET lobby, caters to the sports crowd. Visually represented as a massive, sprawling complex of hangers, departure terminals, and seedy, futuristic bars, Terminal Endgame appears crowded and busy at all hours. When the players aren't embroiled in virtual combat with one another, as frequently happens, they're wagering on matches or bragging about their most recent accomplishments.

Adam Schumpert

PLAYER VERSUS PLAYER

While physical sports such as hologolf and low-G football remain popular and profitable, electronic sports have outstripped them in popularity since the middle of the twenty-first century. Players from around the globe dream of making it big and landing lucrative sponsorships with NBN or its subsids so they can compete in widely broadcasted tournaments. The most popular athletes are masked behind layers of marketing and self-perpetuating anonymity; they operate under code names and handles that make them appear edgier to a fanatical—and sometimes volatile—fan base.

Popular sports categories include strategy, simulation, and gladiatorial games where competitors face one another in virtual combat. Using sensationalized avatars and requiring lightning reflexes, such games can last hours and stretch each player's stamina to the breaking point. Fans can observe the games live in stadiums, or they can tune in from the comfort of their own homes to get a threedee holo-view of the battlefield as well as a running commentary. There is also a huge secondary market for sports memorabilia such as jerseys, clothing lines, and periodicals, which ensure that fans stay connected even after a match is over.

Due to the small amount of lag between Luna and Earth, there are separate leagues for each. Invitational tournaments and worlds championships are always some of the biggest draws in gaming, as they usually bring together teams from both Luna and Earth. Every once in a while a team from Mars is invited to participate, but a Martian team has never won an interplanetary event. The nascent Martian sports scene has many barriers; not only is Net access spottier on the Red Planet, but there are fewer sponsorships available. This might soon change, however, as GameNET has recently launched a new service, dubbed "Bellona," on Mars.

SENSEDEP

The most hardcore gaming experience takes place in sense-deprivation tanks where players are fully immersed in the virtual realm. In a way, "sense-deprivation" is a misnomer and an artifact of their original purpose as rehabilitation devices used in U.S. prisons. Now, in addition to neural feedback, sensedep tanks can directly stimulate muscle groups and provide players with olfactory sensations. Most gaming dens with sensedep tanks appeal to the seedier side of humanity, and players who frequent such establishments are known as "dep heads." While the term is thrown around as an insult on many gaming forums, for those who game in the tanks, regular VR games appear boring and mundane to them and they embrace the term as a badge of honor. Every now and then there are rumors of a player dying in a sensedep tank when they die in the game, since the brain is incapable of distinguishing it from reality.

Most gaming dens charge their users an hourly rate, but discounted daily rates are also usually available. By being hooked up to IVs, catheters, and other life-support systems, players can stay in a sensedep tank for days at a time.

STRIKEFORCE ALPHA

Strikeforce Alpha is the most popular sports title in any of the worlds. As part of an elite strike team, players are divided into two teams, Sol and Kryptic, and must capture their opponent's nexus to win the game. While players only have one life each, they also control a squad of bots. Most of these bots will be destroyed over the course of a game by the more powerful player-avatars; games generally last fifteen to twenty minutes and are played best-of-three. The most popular Strikeforce athletes play hours each day, earning impressive salaries.

Lockwell walked from the fluorescent-lit darkness of the street into the fluorescent-lit darkness of the pub. There was no sign of Rick. She pinged his PAD and got no response, but she was able to track his location with her locater app anyway. He was definitely in here somewhere.

It wasn't the sort of bar she'd have expected to find him in, though. Youngsters with unnecessary cybernetic attachments and g-modded glowing hair chattered in small groups or leaned against the walls looking bored. They were middle-class types, spending daddy's money on vile neon drinks. Harmless, though possibly more intelligent than they looked.

Rick was here to meet someone, she decided. A suspect, maybe. A snitch, more likely. This was the kind of place runners might hang out.

"What a surprise," he said appearing at her shoulder. "I thought you were covering the riots up on Mars."

Captain Rick Harrison cocked his ruggedly handsome head toward the vid playing on the virt above the bar. It was a repeat of her "live" broadcast filmed this morning, with her image superimposed within one of the dome cities on Mars. It made it look like she was there, with the violence exploding around her. No one expected her to be there in reality, of course. She was a news nosie, but that didn't make her omnipresent.

"What's the point of having the news on up there?" she asked. "Everyone's seen it on their PADs already."

"Ambiance," Rick replied, taking her arm and steering her toward the bar. "Now, what is it you want? I've got a friend joining me any minute now, and she might be scared off if she finds me with a celebrity like you on my arm."

"Hot date, Rick? And I thought I was the only special woman in your life."

She waved over the bioroid bartender. She didn't know what model it was, but it must've been an old model—the poor thing's face was barely human. A plastic doll with a blond wig and too-bright red lipstick.

"What are you having, Rick?"

"Nothing for me, I'm…"

"On the job? I thought it was a date." She ordered a Silo sour for herself and smiled when Rick had the bioroid charge his cre-daccount. "So, what's the story?"

"Honestly, Lil, you've got to stop 'running into me' while I'm working. You know I can't discuss a case with you until it's over."

"So get your PAD upgraded. Then you won't have the press following you about."

"It's not the press following me—it's just you."

"What can I say?" She took a slow sip of her drink. "I guess I like you."

He sighed. He led her to a table, pushing past a group of girls with animated tattoos crawling over their skin. He pulled a chair out for her, always the gentleman.

"Now drink up and get lost," he said. "I'm serious about you scaring off my friend."

She frowned at him over the rim of the glass bulb, and he scowled back, but he sat down opposite her anyway.

"OK, let's do this quick then," she said, in her best businesslike voice. She activated the sound suppression field device so the rest of the bar wouldn't overhear and break the story before she could. "What can you tell me about the recent U.N. murder?" She pretended to thrust a microphone in his face, though her hand was empty. Her mono-cam eyepiece was recording everything as always, but he knew that.

"How the frag do you know about that?"

"Is it true the killer wasn't human?"

"Damn it, Lil, keep your voice down. Spread rumors like that around and it'll be the Clone Riots all over again."

"That's not a denial, Rick."

"Look, just keep it quiet, for now. When I've got something to tell the press, I'll come to you first. I promise. Right now, I can't tell you anything, I'm sorry. How did you get that information anyway?"

She shrugged. "I have my sources. If you're not telling, I'm not either."

"Don't be like that."

She focused on her drink, watching the bubbles pop on the surface of the liquid. If Rick wouldn't help her, she had another lead to follow, but she'd rather get information from him.

"Just give me something," she said, raising her eyes to his and holding his gaze. He'd complimented her eyes once, and he wasn't a man to give out compliments lightly. "I won't run the story, not yet. Just give me a hint so I can do the research. I might even be able to help you."

"I'm sorry, babe, I can't." He glanced past her and rose to leave. His "friend" must have appeared.

"Time's up," he said, and that was it.

She turned to try to catch sight of whoever he was meeting with, but he ushered them straight out and was gone. It would have seemed desperate to follow them, and Rick really could hide from her when he wanted to. Damn him.

She glanced at her PAD. Her source had just sent the first directions for the meeting. This was clandestine even for her, and she hated being the one in the dark. She had to follow where this trail led, though. Whoever was contacting her had to be a runner. Only a runner would have the sort of information he claimed to have.

The only other explanation was that he actually worked for Haas-Bioroid, but what employee would risk getting on the wrong side of a megacorp like that?

Whoever he was, if there was any truth in his wild allegations, this story would change history.

It would certainly be more exciting than yet another Crimson Dust terrorist attack.

Matt Zeilinger

Kirsten Zirngibl

THE WEYLAND CONSORTIUM

In contrast to the other Big Three megacorps, the Weyland Consortium is not chiefly concerned with producing anything. Instead, its business model is predicated on the purchase and sale of other corporations. The Consortium is dedicated to getting maximum return from every investment—whether that means a short-term flip or a long-term stake—and is willing to go to great lengths to ensure success. Weyland's near-limitless resources and vast political influence have helped to insulate the corporation from the risks inherent in its more unconventional business ventures, including its most well-known accomplishment, the New Angeles Space Elevator, and, more recently, deep space exploration.

Jack Weyland, the founder of the Consortium, was a man who dreamed big. Growing up, he was educated at the finest schools and attended university at Ivy Consolidated. There, in defiance of his mother's wishes, he eschewed business and finance classes to study engineering. He never graduated, instead dropping out in his senior year to launch an innovative materials development company with his classmate Khadija Osman (later his first wife). Together they discovered how to manufacture carbon nanotubes and other fullerenes more cheaply than most of their competitors. Thanks to a loan from Jack's parents, who were wealthy corporate executives in their own right, Weyland-Osman Materials moved into the market swiftly and became profitable not long thereafter. The company ended up outliving the marriage, and when Osman returned to school, Weyland bought out her shares in the company for an undisclosed sum and began his next project, which was considered insane by most: a space elevator.

Weyland-Osman Materials was well suited to handle many of the technological innovations required to begin construction—including the large-scale manufacture of carbon nanotubes that would comprise the elevator's tether—but in order to complete the project, Weyland needed help. He leveraged his stake in Weyland-Osman to raise capital, and then he used those funds to acquire a handful of financial and construction firms. The Weyland Consortium was born.

As the company grew and news of his plans spread, numerous government agencies approached Weyland to offer up lucrative contracts. The scale of the project meant that the Consortium had an almost insatiable appetite for capital. He leveraged the firm again to Titan Transnational Bank, selling shares to financial institutions and a coterie of fellow multi-billionaires, who later formed the board of directors for the company. Finally, Jack Weyland selected a spot in Ecuador, and construction for the space elevator began in the spring of '25.

While assembly was underway, Weyland's investors turned their attention to ensuring they were positioned to capitalize on the opportunities the space elevator presented. In addition to providing the means to get into space, the board wanted to ensure that businesses, governments, and the public at large would have manifold reasons for traveling to and from space. The board investigated many options, but the most promising sectors included energy and construction. Fusion power existed in the experimental stages only, but if helium-3 became the go-to fuel, the Consortium stood to make an enormous amount of money from royalties on refined He-3 shipped down-Stalk from the Moon. Weyland provided massive grants to scientific research bodies to hasten the commercialization of fusion power technologies, and it also invested heavily in space travel and colonization technologies.

Construction lasted ten years, and many predicted the project would fail before it was complete, but the New Angeles Space Elevator is now considered the single greatest feat in human engineering. Jack Weyland became synonymous with bold ideas, and he was celebrated across the world for his role in bringing humanity one step closer to its manifest destiny: space. Even the structure's nickname, "the Beanstalk," is an homage to the man who designed it.

The champagne had only begun to flow when Jack Weyland turned his attention to his next wild scheme. Yet, the board of directors was hesitant to dive in to development of a new project immediately, especially after having been forced to divert resources from its other projects to complete the Beanstalk. Fusion power was not yet ready, colonization efforts were slow to take off, and current revenues could not sustain another major undertaking. A power struggle between Jack Weyland and the board ensued, and ultimately the founder resigned—some say he was forced out—so that he could develop his projects independent of the Consortium's current business goals.

Since Jack Weyland's resignation, the Consortium further expanded in scope and diversity. The Consortium used its wealth to continue trading in smaller companies and to buy up more construction concerns. The megacorporation also expanded into the arms and security sector with a major buyout of Argus Security.

Although Weyland was no longer CEO, he continued to make his presence felt in a number of smaller projects, most of which were self-funded. His ongoing love affair with space flight led to the acquisition of dozens of aerospace companies and the employment of a legion of scientists, researchers, and engineers.

The last few decades have not been entirely smooth sailing for the Consortium, however. Its success bred rivalry, and soon ugly rumors began to surface. The Consortium appeared to have a sixth sense concerning world politics; it always secured lucrative security contracts mere months before the outbreak of war between nations, and it swooped in with lavish and expensive reconstruction plans the moment the dust settled. Whispers began to spread suggesting the Consortium was responsible for those conflicts by infiltrating rebellious political parties and stirring up dissent, all so it could reap the prizes of war. More than one journalist and U.N. inspector has disappeared while following up on a story of war profiteering, which only darkens the shadows that surround the Consortium.

Today it is all but impossible to pin down exactly what Weyland is or does, so varied is its portfolio. It is rare to find a product or service that is not in some way connected to the megacorp. The only place seemingly free of its influence is Mars, but this is a misconception. While it's true that there are no officially branded Weyland colonies in the same way that there are Jinteki or Haas-Bioroid colonies, Weyland's products and services are equally pervasive on the Red Planet, from space transport to colony modules, private security forces to power generation technology. And with unrest between Mars and Earth governments growing, it seems unlikely that the megacorp's influence will do anything but expand.

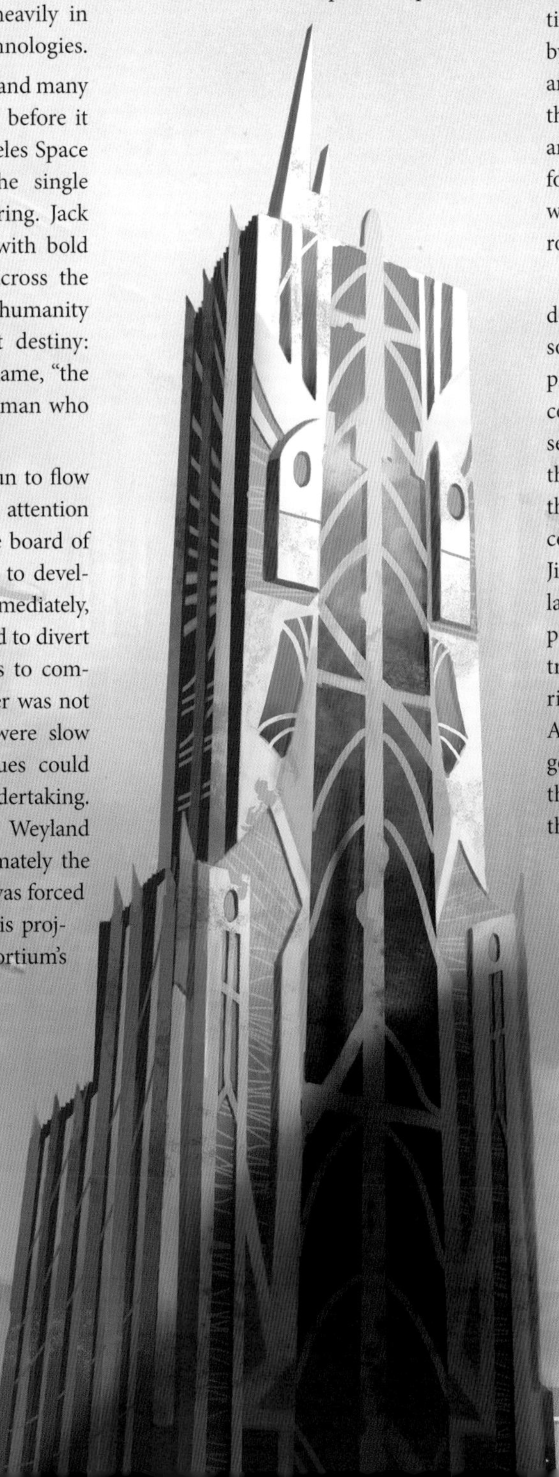

Emilio Rodriguez

97

THE BOARD

As a sprawling web of diverse business interests traversing the globe and beyond, the Weyland Consortium possesses a unique and somewhat chaotic organizational structure. Where other megacorps enforce a uniform operational system across their holdings, Weyland is a complex hive comprising internal and external directors, power blocs of united businesses, and a wealth of minor corporations that are bought and sold for the sole purpose of providing funds for other, more important projects.

Although many of the company's original investors still remain on the board, the actual membership is veiled in mystery. No one can say with any authority just how many directors sit on the board, let alone who they are. Before his resignation, Jack Weyland was the CEO and public face of the company. He stood as the symbol for the next big idea—not just for Weyland, but for the entire world. Yet for all his great ideas, realizing his vision required a legion of businesspeople, managers, and financiers who had their own ideas about the direction of the company. Ultimately, their views won out, and the Weyland Consortium became the megacorp it is today.

Now, all public announcements are delivered through carefully constructed media events that feature the Vice Presidents or CEOs of individual subsids. After

so many years, some believe the board has no desire to find a permanent replacement CEO. This has led some to question whether the board of directors even exists or whether it is nothing more than a smoke screen to disguise an even more sinister power behind the corporation. Others assume that the lack of a replacement stems from infighting between the veteran members of the board and newcomers, between the visionaries and those who want to capitalize on Weyland's existing businesses and markets.

As the company grew and absorbed more and more corps—corps that had wildly different processes and systems—the Consortium's internal structure became hugely complex. Beneath the board are the individual company managers and vice presidents, each of whom is responsible for his or her own business concerns. Many of these managers operate more than one company, and it is commonplace for these men and women to be involved in dozens of high-level meetings with far-reaching consequences. Throughout this level of the Consortium there exist various groups of managers aligned along shared business goals. These sub-boards allow collaboration between individual companies to eliminate redundancies, increase efficiency, and maximize their bottom lines.

When rival companies clash, the results are usually kept out of the public eye. Most confrontations are resolved with a quiet word in the ear of one or more parties. This often leads to finances being re-appropriated, research or manufacturing resources going missing, and projects getting held up for months by legal wrangling or accounting red tape. Occasionally matters take a more serious turn. Office buildings get accidentally demolished, project managers go missing, and riots gut important factories or laboratories. Screamsheets are quick to run lurid stories about corporate staffers gunned down by masked assailants outside their homes or corporate headquarters blown to bits by Martian terrorist attacks. The board is quick to tamp down any behavior it judges too extreme or actions that could be traced back to its members.

The web of protocols and coordination has grown to become something more than the sum of its parts. Although in theory the Consortium's board of directors makes all final decisions on the direction of the company and its many subsidiaries, these decisions are guided by the investors and the various market forces at work. Seemingly controlled by an increasingly ill-defined set of individuals, the Weyland Consortium has begun to act and feel like a living entity, capricious and indefinable.

*T*here's two things you need to know if you're gonna start looking into Weyland. First, when they find you, and they will find you, they won't just kill you. They'll take everything you care about, everyone you love, everything you've ever done—and destroy it. Utterly. Second, the truth, when you find it, is always a whole lot worse than the expectation. Trust me.

So we all know about the corporate buyouts and shady political deals to get those sweet, sweet government contracts. I'm sure you have your suspicions about the military-industrial complex, the insider trading and market manipulation. To be honest, none of this is big news. Every major corp in the world is involved in shit like this. What makes the Consortium so special?

Well, have you stopped to think about how Weyland is so good at spotting gaps in the market? Why it's always them to swoop in on some poor war-torn country with an offer of rebuilding, or what guides them to take out massive insurance policies on seemingly safe properties? It's not chance my friend, it's not analysis, or even good business. The Weyland Consortium makes these things happen. Wars, natural disasters, acts of God, all of it is the work of the Consortium.

Look at the tsunami that swamped coastal New Angeles. You think that was an accident or that it wasn't by design? Hell no! That was the corporate machine at work. Weyland owns GRNDL, and they set up some offshore drilling site to test their latest toy. Now, shortly after this, some tech guy realizes that this new geothermal drill is likely to cause an earthquake so he tells his boss. Word gets passed up the chain of command that GRNDL has invented an earthquake machine, and somebody has to decide if it's worth the risk. Do they tell the public about the danger? Or pull the plug on the project and save trillions of dollars?

Nope, they start buying up sea-front properties and insuring them for huge sums of money. A very different arm of the company

handles all this so nobody can connect the dots. At the same time, Weyland starts pushing for reconstruction contracts on the properties they can't buy. Gentrification or modernization, or some such bull. The time comes to throw the switch on this new drill and one of two things is gonna happen; either everything goes as planned, GRNDL's tech works as intended and Weyland profits, or, the drill causes a massive earthquake that drowns half the western seaboard and takes out Weyland's newly insured land in the process. Insurers pay out; Weyland grabs the rebuild contracts, and the Consortium profits.

You seein' the pattern here? Just think about it for a second: how many lives were lost in the tsunami, how much damage was caused? All that death and destruction so some corp can boast a five percent boost in year-end profits. Now do you see the monster we're dealing with?

Of course, people sometimes find out, we're awkward like that, but a company like the Weyland Consortium has plans for that too. The easy route is just pay you off; everyone has a price, right? Most often it works too, but every now and then someone gets too a little too pious or too greedy and WC has to set them straight. They have a whole division for this, Pensions and Retirement they call it, but down here, they're called Cleaners. Anytime someone becomes a problem money won't solve, the Cleaners take over. These guys can get you fired, freeze your credaccounts, blacklist your ID, repossess your house, and make your spouse think you're some kind of pervert, and that's just for starters. They can plant evidence in your home and frame you for cyber-theft, reprogram your bioroid so it attacks your kids, or just take a power drill to your kneecaps plain and simple. They'll make you wish you were dead, and then they'll kill you. I swear, anytime you see some hard-faced bastard in an expensive suit lookin' at you funny, you start running and you don't look back.

Mark my words man, you start digging around in this shit and you have this to look forward to. You want my advice? Get off-grid right now, lose your family, sell your house, and go underground. It's the only way to survive what's coming if you really want to see the truth.

THE NEW ANGELES SPACE ELEVATOR

The Weyland Consortium's New Angeles Space Elevator, which first opened for business in '35, has become the keystone for humankind's industrial and technological utilization of space. It stretches from the peak of an ice-clad equatorial mountain in Ecuador out to a distance of some seventy-two thousand kilometers straight up. The structure, popularly known as the Beanstalk (after the old fairy tale "Jack and the Beanstalk"), gives cheap and easy access to space and the resources available in space. Perhaps the most important of these is the helium-3 shipped down-Stalk from the Moon, but the incoming riches include heavy metals and volatiles mined from asteroids; high-tech electronics, components, and pharmaceuticals manufactured in microgravity; and cheap power by means of beamed microwaves and direct current.

The flow isn't just from space to Earth, either. A steady and fast-growing stream of people has rushed to space since the Beanstalk's opening, making possible the large-scale colonization of Luna and Mars as well as populating the mining centers of Ceres, Vesta, Pallas, and Hygeia. The Beanstalk has been called humankind's gateway to the stars, and for good reason.

A space elevator is a simple enough concept, one describable by a simple analogy: take a small rock, tie it to the end of a string, and spin it in the air above your head. Imagine the string is the elevator, your hand is the Earth, and the rock is the Challenger Planetoid holding the whole thing up, and you've got a fair picture of how the whole thing works.

The elevator's center of mass is located about halfway up, 35,784 kilometers above Earth's surface. This point is known variously as geosynchronous orbit or—in honor of the man who pointed out that this would be a wonderful place to park communications satellites—the Clarke Orbit. Satellites that are Clarke-parked complete their orbit once in twenty-four hours, meaning they seem to hang eternally in the same spot in the sky. The physics of geosynch are what make building a space elevator possible in the first place.

GROUNDWORK: THE 1900s AND 2000s

"Earth is the cradle of humanity, but one cannot live in the cradle forever."

– Konstantin Tsiolkovsky, 1911

Konstantin Tsiolkovsky was a Russian school teacher, rocket scientist, and space travel visionary who theorized about many aspects of space travel and rocket propulsion. Inspired by the newly constructed engineering marvel of his era, the Eiffel Tower, he proposed the earliest version of the space elevator concept—a tower, built upward from the Earth's surface and reaching all the way to geostationary orbit over thirty-five thousand kilometers up. Such a tower would need to be strong enough to support its own weight under compression, with the lowest levels supporting the entire weight of the structure overhead. The concept is

unworkable, but, as with so many of Tsiolkovsky's ideas, it led directly to the modern version of an elevator reaching all the way up to orbit.

"But science and technology are swiftly moving ahead and, perhaps, already toward the end of our century the construction of a cable way to the heavens will begin."

– Yuri Artsutanov, 1960

Yuri Artsutanov was a Russian engineer at the Leningrad Technological Institute who built on Tsiolkovsky's ideas to become an important pioneer of the space elevator concept. In the midst of the twentieth-century Space Race, he published an article titled "V Kosmos na Electrovoze," which can be translated as "Into space with the help of an electric locomotive." Rather than Tsiolkovsky's orbital tower, he envisioned putting a satellite into geosynchronous orbit, and from there lowering a cable to the ground while simultaneously raising a counterweight on a second cable out from the Earth, maintaining the center of mass at geosynch. This tension-structure concept was far more feasible in engineering terms than Tsiolkovsky's tower, and it would more easily facilitate a safe and inexpensive means of reaching orbit.

"The space elevator will be built about fifty years after everyone stops laughing."

– Arthur C. Clarke, 1981

Arthur C. Clarke was a popular British science-fiction writer, science writer, and futurist perhaps best known for his work with Stanley Kubrick on the old flatfilm *2001: A Space Odyssey*, which was based on Clarke's short story "The Sentinel." Clarke's 1979 paperbook *The Foundations of Paradise* became the vehicle by which the concept of the space elevator reached the public at large. The novel follows the construction of the world's first space elevator above a fictional version of the island of Sri Lanka in the Indian Ocean, which for the purposes of accurate physics Clarke moved five hundred miles south to the equator.

"For the first time since it was initially conceived, this dream is now within our reach."

–The Spaceward Foundation, 2006

The world has long looked for a system that could get people into orbit more cheaply and safely than the time-honored means of large, loud, and dangerous chemical rockets. Despite the need, space elevator development was hampered by two fundamental problems: how to build a cable and how best to climb it. Beginning in the early twenty-first century, a series of international competitions were held by various groups interested in advancing the idea of a working space elevator, including the Spaceward Foundation, NASA, the International Space Elevator Consortium, the Japan Space Elevator Association, and others. After the first year, most competitions had two parts—the climber challenge and the tether challenge. The climber challenge tested the ability of each entry to climb a tether powered by energy beamed from the ground. The tether challenge had teams competing to build the longest and strongest tether. The winners showed just how ready the world was for this technological miracle.

FORM AND FUNCTION

A space elevator consists of five separate sections. The Root, or anchor point, is the elevator's attachment point to the Earth's equator. The tether is the actual vertical line of the elevator. There's a central hub at geosynchronous orbit, and a counterweight asteroid at the top end of the tether. Finally, there are the elevator cars which travel up and down the tether.

THE ROOT

The Beanstalk connects to Earth's surface at the Root in the heart of the Chakana District, and it is the largest transit center in the world. The massive structure plunges deep into the side of Volcán Cayambe while also rising high to compete with the rest of the New Angeles skyline. The Root doubles as a massive shopping complex and attracts billions of tourists per year.

Deep beneath the upper deck of the facility, underground mag-lev trains arrive and depart from other parts of New Angeles, and from other cities farther north—Bogotá, Tegucigalpa, Mexico City, and SanSan.

At the very top of the complex is the broad and spacious Plaza del Cielo—the Plaza of the Sky—forty-seven hundred meters above sea level. The Plaza is an open expanse of concrete and stonework crammed day and night with travelers, tourists, the occasional performance artist, and sightseers, all watched over by a small army of ever-vigilant Space Elevator Authority (SEA) officers. Around the plaza perimeter are walkways and sightseeing overlooks offering stunning vistas of Cayambe's few remaining glaciers and the surrounding cloud tops, the Amazon snaking its way to the east, the emerald-green jungle greenspaces of Peru, and the sprawling agroplexes of northwestern Brazil.

The air is painfully thin at this altitude, but the plaza itself is fully enclosed by floor-to-ceiling transplas windows. At the center of the ornate plaza, surrounded by sculpture gardens, shopping kiosks, and cafés, lies Earth Station, a huge, glass-domed SEA complex that serves as the planet-side terminus of the Beanstalk, with its endless lines of ticket counters, baggage claims, sec-checks, and beanpod boarding stations. Security is tight, with large numbers of yellow-jacketed Beanstalk employees, Globalsec rent-a-cops, and U.S. Armed Forces personnel in evidence.

Rising above all of this commercial splendor is the Beanstalk itself, twenty meters thick, dull grey in color, and rising arrow-straight into the zenith, where it vanishes at the top of an infinite sky.

THE TETHER

By far the most massive portion of the entire structure, the tether is the taut-stretched cable that connects the top of Volcán Cayambe on Earth's equator with a small asteroid seventy-two thousand kilometers up. The tether is the support structure for the entire assembly. It's also the means by which the space elevator cars—colloquially known as "beanpods"—move between Earth's surface and orbit.

The tether is made of carbon bucky-weave, a material over a hundred times stronger centimeter-for-centimeter than the same thickness of carbon steel. Twenty meters thick at the base, it grows thicker very gradually up the 'Stalk to around forty meters at Midway Station—the point of greatest stress on the system, and the section in most need of extra strength.

Up in geosynch orbit at Midway Station, passengers continuing up-Stalk must change pods. From Midway the upper 'Stalk gradually becomes thinner again until it reaches the anchoring counterweight—the Challenger Planetoid.

Around the perimeter of both sections of the tether are vertical grooves designed to hold the accelerator flanges of the beanpods. Running up and down the entire

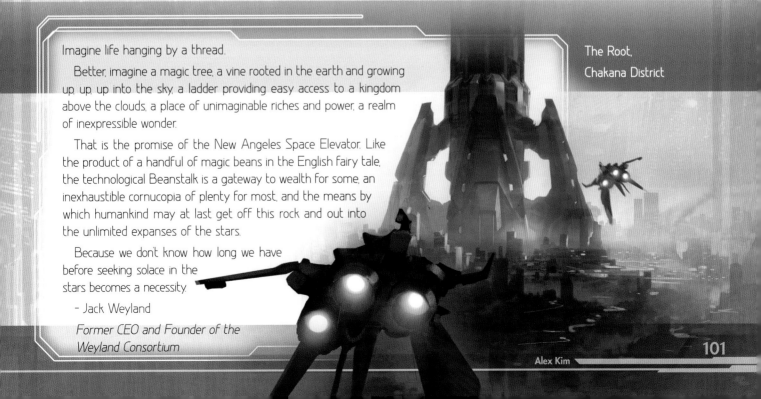

Imagine life hanging by a thread.

Better, imagine a magic tree, a vine rooted in the earth and growing up, up, up into the sky, a ladder providing easy access to a kingdom above the clouds, a place of unimaginable riches and power, a realm of inexpressible wonder.

That is the promise of the New Angeles Space Elevator. Like the product of a handful of magic beans in the English fairy tale, the technological Beanstalk is a gateway to wealth for some, an inexhaustible cornucopia of plenty for most, and the means by which humankind may at last get off this rock and out into the unlimited expanses of the stars.

Because we don't know how long we have before seeking solace in the stars becomes a necessity.

- Jack Weyland

Former CEO and Founder of the Weyland Consortium

The Root, Chakana District

Alex Kim

length of the elevator, the flanges keep the pod attached to the tether and ride the magnetic flux up- or down-Stalk.

GEOSYNCH ORBIT: MIDWAY STATION

Halfway up the Beanstalk, just above the thirty-five thousand kilometer mark, is Midway Station, the center of the entire structure. Most of the facility is in zero-G; "microgravity" is the more scientifically correct term. A large, open concourse serves as the main arrival and departure area with access to both upper- and lower-tether pod boarding facilities.

The concourse is cylindrical, thirty meters across, and crisscrossed by numerous color-coded safety lines strung across the terminal area in pairs. The majority of visitors to Midway Station each day are tourists, business people, and corporate employees on their way up or down from Starport Kaguya on the Moon, and they have little to no experience in making their

"You want the green line, sir. Takes you straight to Midway Station Up."

way around in microgravity. The safety lines, also known as lifelines, allow them to haul themselves along hand-over-hand, while the color coding serves as a guide.

Also present are trained personnel in white jumpsuits who physically move visitors out of the beanpods. Such SEA attendants use straps connected around the passenger's waist to keep them from drifting off, and the attendants stow the passenger's carry-on luggage or packages in backpacks. They haul their charges bodily into the terminal area and then point them in the right direction: "You want the green line, sir. Takes you straight to Midway Station Up."

Around the outside of the terminal are a number of tube-ways leading to other

facilities. These include connections to two orbital hotels, the corporate offices for several big-name megacorporations, and a major NBN branch office, which takes up as much of half of the Midway Station facilities. There are also boutiques, souvenir stands, shops, as well as several restaurants. Freefall is one, serving meals in covered, straw-pierced containers; the menu offers a wide variety of food, so long as it's solid or pureed. Any lack of presentation aesthetics, however, is more than made up for by the view. Part of the outer wall can be rendered transparent, allowing diners to look "down" at the Earth spanning some twenty degrees of sky.

A number of Midway facilities are separate from the main station, and are reached by twelve-person space taxis, or spaxies. One such facility is Sheer Heaven, a popular restaurant located inside a cylinder rotating around its long axis to create artificial gravity. There are also a large number of orbital assembly plants, manufactories, and solar power stations in free orbit within a few kilometers of Midway. Banks of large transmission dishes pointed at Earth belong to NBN and its subsidiary companies such as the *New Angeles Sol*, *The New Angeles Times*, and *NewsDirect*. The Honeymoon Hilton is a microgravity hotel separate from Midway Station that caters to couples interested in trying out the joys—and difficulties—of zero-G coupling.

Midway Station is a bustling center of travel, tourism, and business, with several hundred permanent residents and at least ten times as many transients passing through every day, either coming to Midway itself, or traveling up- or down-Stalk. Midway Station is the heart of the Beanstalk, and it is rightly considered to be the spot from which an Earth-bound humankind is evolving into a truly solar species.

Mark Molnar

THE COUNTERWEIGHT: THE CHALLENGER PLANETOID

The Challenger Planetoid serves as the up-end anchor for the entire Beanstalk and keeps it stretched taut, like the stone at the end of the string. Located some seventy-two thousand kilometers above Earth's surface, the planetoid is a five-kilometer rock deliberately moved in from its original Earth-crossing orbit and attached to the upper end of the tether.

Like the rest of the Beanstalk, the Challenger Planetoid circles the Earth in twenty-four hours, but due to its position and speed it also generates a distinct, out-is-down spin gravity. This acceleration is quite low, however, amounting to about four hundredths of a gravity.

Because it is anchored to the distant Earth, it always has the same side facing the planet. Its inhabited facilities are divided between Nearside and Farside, which are connected by a mag-lev tunnel running straight through the center of the planetoid. The planetoid's name honors the space shuttle *Challenger* that blew up shortly after lift-off back in the late twentieth century.

NEARSIDE FACILITIES

Challenger Beanstalk Terminal is located at the tether attachment point and is relatively austere in its accommodations. Visitors often remark on the fact that where Midway Station is fairly slick and commercial in its appearance, Challenger Base has a rougher, frontier feel with fewer amenities, but it still has plenty to entertain the risties and executives traveling through, as well as the tourists who cannot afford to complete the journey to Starport Kaguya.

About a kilometer away from the space elevator's terminus is the Carousel, a pair of rotating wheels, one atop the other. Originally built as a construction shack and medical facility for Beanstalk workers, it was purchased by a wealthy casino developer named Gianfranco Calderoli for a rumored half-billion credits. He renamed it the Castle Club—pursuing the Beanstalk fairy-tale theme of a giant's castle at the top of a beanstalk—and turned it into a low-gravity theme park.

Accessible by subsurface mag-lev tubes, the two wheels are partly buried in the surface to provide micrometeorite, radiation, and thermal protection. They both span two hundred meters and possess three decks each. They rotate in opposite directions to avoid precession effects that might disrupt the planetoid's attitude—with disastrous effect to the Beanstalk. The spin rate of once in twenty-eight seconds provides a reasonable spin gravity—about a half-G on the lower, outer deck, and about a third of a G on the upper, inner deck.

Outside the Carousel, in 0.04 G microgravity, is a theater famous for its low-G ballets and acrobatic dance performances, a smaller and less luxurious version of the Midway Honeymoon Hotel, and living modules for the planetoid's permanent residents. Other facilities on Nearside include the Casino Club, a suite of meeting rooms, and a large and fairly well-equipped medical facility. Close by the terminal and connected via underground slidewalk tunnels is The High Frontier, a hotel and business center.

The sky of Nearside is dominated by the Earth hanging at the zenith, about half the size as it appears from Midway. Nevertheless, it spans twenty-one times the diameter of the full moon as seen from Earth.

FARSIDE FACILITIES

Challenger's Farside is reached by tube-car straight through the center of the planetoid. The Farside base is dominated by the Challenger Mines and by the port facilities of the Challenger Memorial Ferry. The local offices of Humanity Labor are located in Farside, a kind of union shop for offworld human workers. Buildings here are upside down, since the .04 G spin gravity from the whirling Beanstalk out-muscles the even slighter gravity of the planetoid. A visitor looking out through a window on Farside will see the Challenger Planetoid rising like an enormous, hanging city above her head.

From the Challenger Ferry embarkation a traveler can catch a transport for Starport Kaguya on the Moon. Travelers in a hurry can board an express ferry that will get them to the Moon in about a day or so, while so-called "slow boats" use the momentum imparted by the Challenger Planetoid to drift outward through cis-Lunar space on a long, curving trajectory without the use of any fuel at all. The time and angle of launch are carefully calculated so that the "slow boat" arrives at Starport Kaguya several weeks later, with minimal use of rockets for attitude adjustment and the final landing.

The Farside docking ports are also the means by which incoming helium-3 canisters launched from the Moon via a mag-lev rail are captured, loaded onto the elevator rails on the Nearside, and sent down-Stalk to Earth. Nearby is the Port McNair United States Space Expeditionary Corps base to protect the Beanstalk from military threats. The military space docks serve as a grim reminder of the Battle of the Beanstalk that occurred here a little over fifteen years ago.

THE BEANPOD

The final vital element of the space elevator system is the ascent/descent vehicle, most commonly known as a "beanpod." It's an elongated elevator car designed to climb and descend the tether while carrying passengers or other cargo.

The standard passenger pod is a cigar-shaped vessel twenty-one meters long and five meters through at the widest, divided into three decks. Each deck holds twelve padded chairs, a restroom, and a small drink and snack bay. In the pointed ends is the environmental control gear—air and water tanks, heating and air conditioning units—and radar and control systems. Amidships, on the exterior hull, is the magnetic flange that rides the elevator groove, as well as a folded-up paraglider ram-chute for emergencies. In the event that a pod breaks free of the lower tether and falls toward Earth, the ram-chute allows safe deceleration and descent through the atmosphere.

The pod is designed to rotate on the flange. This allows the vehicle to accelerate or decelerate while keeping "down" in the direction of the floor for the safety and comfort of the passengers. Typically, a beanpod will accelerate up-Stalk at 1.5 gravities to the eighteen-thousand kilometer level, rotate end-for-end, and then decelerate for the rest of the journey up to Midway Station.

The first leg of the journey will take about fifty minutes. During this time, passengers endure 1.5 Gs during boost, meaning that an eighty-kilogram man will feel like he weighs one-twenty kilos—hence the comfortable and deeply cushioned seats. At the journey's midpoint, he will be in either zero gravity (on the Midway-to-Challenger section of the tether), or (on the Earth to Midway run), he will briefly experience a bit less than half of Earth's surface gravity pulling at him, first toward the floor, and then, after the pod rotates, toward the ceiling until acceleration begins again. Robotic equipment stored inside the pod's walls emerge to clean up the mess should any passengers experience motion sickness during any part of the journey.

Although the drink and snack bar and the restroom are provided for the passengers' comfort, people are encouraged to remain in their seats for the entire trip. After all, a misstep at 1.5 Gs could break an ankle. Passengers' safety restraints lock automatically to keep them seated during the mid-journey skew-flips and again after they arrive in microgravity until attendants can clip onto them and haul them into the terminal.

Larger versions of the standard travel pod are uncrewed and are used to transport tanks of helium-3 from Heinlein down-Stalk to the receiving station under the Root and other cargo up-Stalk.

THE FORCES OF PHYSICS

Centripetal force and gravity are the physical foundations of a working space elevator.

CENTRIPETAL FORCE

Centripetal force is what keeps the Beanstalk up, in dynamic suspension. From the Latin words meaning "the center" and "to seek," centripetal force draws a rotating body toward the center of rotation instead of a straight line. The effect is most obvious when spinning a small rock or other mass on the end of a string. Centripetal force keeps the string taut and the tethered rock spinning in the air along a circular path. The force felt on a tethered object moving in a circular path is weakest inward, with no force at all experienced at the center, but the force grows stronger the

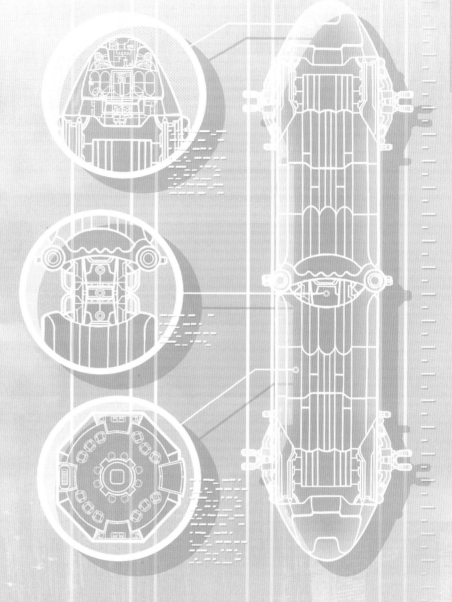

farther away from that point. This results in a small (0.04G) force being imparted on spacecraft released from the Farside docks on the Challenger Planetoid.

Centripetal force creates what is sometimes known as spin gravity. The huge, rotating-wheel space stations envisioned by von Braun or in Stanley Kubrick's old flatfilm *2001: A Space Odyssey* provided an out-is-down artificial gravity, with "up" toward the rotating system's center. A practical demonstration can be seen by standing outside with a bucket of water and spinning the bucket as quickly as possible. If one can manage not to slosh, the water will remain in the bottom of the bucket, even when it's upside down above his head.

The faster the system rotates, the stronger the sensation of gravity. Spin gravity is used in certain structures associated with the Beanstalk—notably the Castle Carousel on the Challenger Nearside, as well as in structures requiring artificial gravity orbiting near Midway Station.

GRAVITY

The other main force on the Beanstalk is actual gravity. Despite the common notion that to venture into space is to escape gravity, this is not the case—gravity is always there and is always a factor. It is the force of Earth's gravity that keeps untethered objects, like Luna or man-made satellites, orbiting around it.

David Griffith

Because the lower half of the Beanstalk is still dominated by gravity, a passenger in a pod here still feels a tug downward. A worker halfway up who makes a careless misstep would fall, not float, and make a spectacular and fiery re-entry into Earth's atmosphere. In low Earth orbit—around four hundred kilometers up—the effect of gravity is still almost ninety percent of what it is at Earth's surface. Here, the first space stations and early orbital flights were never "beyond Earth's gravity." The astronauts just didn't feel it as they were falling—in "free fall"—along their orbital path the entire time; they were essentially not feeling any gravitational pull.

The higher a passenger goes up-Stalk, the more the sensation of gravity gradually dwindles until he reaches what is effectively zero-G at synchorbit. In practice, passengers riding the beanpods up- and down-Stalk feel the effects of acceleration in their magnetically driven vehicles, a force that is indistinguishable from gravity. Back in the earliest days of the space elevator, pods climbed the tether at a steady and sedate couple of hundred kilometers per hour—comparable to a conventional mag-lev train—which got them to where they needed to be in about a week. As the demand increased for trips up and down the Beanstalk, the Weyland Consortium developed more aggressive rates of travel to satisfy that need.

FARTHER OUT

Beyond Midway, passengers no longer feel the tug of Earth's gravity. It's still there, to be sure, but the sensation is overwhelmed by tug outward on the tether. Passengers above Midway Station feel a slight pull outward due to the centripetal force of the entire rotating system, which is reduced in apparent strength by Earth's (unfelt) pull.

From Earth up to Midway, then, *down* is toward the Earth; from Midway to the Castle, however, down is *away* from the Earth, although the actual force is extremely small. In any case, the beanpods' magnetic acceleration creates an artificial gravity indistinguishable from the real thing; the pods are rotated on their flanges when under acceleration, so that *down* is always toward the floors.

WATCH THAT FIRST STEP

An important distinction not often appreciated by the general public is that the lower half of the Beanstalk is *not* in orbit. Step outside a beanpod on the lower tether, and a person *will* fall. Only when one reaches synchronous orbit, at Midway, will one's velocity perfectly balance the pull of Earth's gravity, leaving the person in zero-G. Technically, the term is microgravity, because Earth's mass will still be pulling at him; it's *still* pulling at him as far out as the Moon, obviously, since at that distance the Moon is still trapped by Earth's pull.

If a person did fall, he wouldn't go splat on the Plaza del Cielo, and tourists at the Root aren't in danger of spanners dropped by workers a few thousand kilometers up. Depending on how high up he is when he lets go, his rotation around the Earth will impart a lateral component to his velocity; his descent will combine these two vectors, bringing him down somewhere to the east of the Root. If he lets go at Midway Station, well, his fall would take him clear around the world; that's the definition of "orbit." Let go halfway up, and he'll be on a trajectory that would bring him down somewhere in western Borneo if it weren't for the considerable effects of atmospheric drag on the way down.

TENSILE STRENGTH

Tsiolkovsky's tower was an engineering impossibility because structural components of such a building simply aren't strong enough to support the weight of the entire tower. Artsutanov's contribution to the concept was his suggestion that a space elevator, rather than being a tower supported entirely from Earth, could in fact be more like a suspension bridge, with its components in dynamic balance with one another.

Until the twenty-first century, however, available materials still weren't strong enough to allow a space elevator to be built. Calculations in the late twentieth century showed that the cable used in any space elevator concept would have to be roughly three times stronger than the then-strongest materials known: diamond, Kevlar,

and silicon. These materials have a tensile strength of several gigapascals (GPa). Not only would the space elevator material have to support the outward pull of the counterweight as it whirled around the Earth, but it would have to support its own weight as well, requiring a tensile strength of up to one hundred GPa. By the beginning of the twenty-first century, carbon nanotubes showed considerable promise, although it was several decades before they could be grown to lengths any greater than a few tenths of a meter. Another new material, graphene (or buckyweave), was even stronger (130 GPa)—and had the added benefit of conducting electricity.

Ultimately, advances in manufactory techniques by companies like Weyland-Osman Materials made tether extruders possible—robotic devices that grew carbon nanofiber cables in an overlapping weave that was extremely strong. Graphene ribbons were layered within the cable to provide motive power for the beanpods and to conduct electrical power from orbit to Earth. Not until then could the old dream of an elevator to space be physically realized.

BUILDING A BEANSTALK

The physics of the Beanstalk is all about carefully balancing forces to ensure the massive structure always remains in a state of stable tension. This was nowhere so necessary as during the space elevator's initial construction.

To start with, a space station was built using conventional techniques at synchorbit, which provided a construction shack for the work crews and the dynamic center of the growing structure. Two tether extruders were transported to the station in pieces and assembled there, one above the construction shack, one below. Some hundreds of conventional rocket flights boosted tons of raw carbon up to synchorbit to feed the extruders, which began weaving their respective cables—one up, one down—and doing so at carefully controlled rates. If one cable got ahead of the other, it would shift the system's center of mass up or down, moving it out of synchorbit.

Eventually, the Challenger Planetoid, which had been nudged toward Earth some twenty years earlier, arrived to simplify things. Challenger was an Earth-crossing asteroid, one of a large family of rocks orbiting the Sun in the general vicinity of Earth's orbit. Besides its orbit, Challenger had been chosen because it was a type of asteroid known as a carbonaceous chondrite, or c-cons for short. Such rocks typically contain up to two percent by weight of carbon—including the hydrocarbons of organic substances, kerogens, and amino acids—and anywhere from two to twenty-two percent by weight of water. In the earliest days of asteroid mining, c-cons were far more valuable than those containing heavy metals, since they contain all of the raw materials necessary to support human life in space: nitrogen and oxygen for air, hydrogen and oxygen for rocket fuel. They also supplied ton upon ton of raw carbon that could be cheaply dropped down to synchorbit and woven into the Beanstalk's tethers.

With Challenger in orbit at about the sixty-five thousand kilometer level, carbon was steadily removed and shipped down to synchorbit, reducing its mass and resulting in a slight outward migration. The most difficult—and dangerous—part of the operation came at the very end, when the asteroid was accelerated using a magnetically launched portion of the rock itself as reaction mass to put it into a series of long, looping passes around both Earth and the Moon. This exquisite blend of engineering and ballet resulted in Challenger passing the outer end of the tether at *just* the right velocity to allow capture and anchoring.

Shortly thereafter, the Earth-side end of the cable dropped down through Earth's atmosphere—since the system was balanced at synchronous orbit, the end of the cable was not moving at all relative to the turning Earth—and was captured by a crew working at the newly constructed Cayambe Earth Station. After several months of structural and power tests, the first payloads began moving skyward—mostly parts for the fast-growing Midway Station.

With old-fashioned rockets launched up out of Earth's steep gravity well, the cost of getting large payloads up to synchronous orbit was enormous, depending on the launch system used. With the space elevator system, this cost dropped almost immediately.

The remaining price represented the cost in electricity required to boost each kilo up to Midway. Various technological advances and the physics of the system itself allowed the Beanstalk to generate large amounts of electrical power, offsetting this cost even further. Prices today fluctuate depending on the energy markets. The price paid ends up being "whatever the market will bear"—meaning most of the price per kilogram becomes profit for the SEA and Beanstalk royalties for the Weyland Consortium.

A HIGHWAY TO SPACE

Futurists in the early days of spaceflight frequently quoted science-fiction writer Robert Heinlein: "Reach Earth orbit and you're halfway to anywhere in the solar system." When you're limited to chemical-fuel rockets, by far the most difficult—and expensive—part of reaching space is simply climbing up to orbit. Very roughly, it takes the same amount of energy to get from Earth's surface to orbit as it takes to get from orbit to any of the planets. In fact, if you're willing to be patient, you can get from low Earth orbit to anywhere else at a fraction of the cost by using constant-thrust systems like ion propulsion or the free energy tapped by solar sails, gravitational sling shots, or the centripetal force of a space elevator counterweight.

Once the Beanstalk was up and running, the cost of reaching Earth orbit was reduced to a tiny fraction of the cost of launching chemical rockets. Although dropship flights are still used by governmental officials, military personnel, and business executives, almost anyone can afford to make the trip up the Beanstalk

if they save up. This allowed large-scale pioneering efforts and the emigration of thousands of private citizens into space.

Further, the costs of boosting tons of cargo—both raw material and finished manufactured goods from the Moon or the Belt to the receiving facility on the Challenger Farside—were a tiny fraction of the price for boosting the same tonnage from Earth up into space. This allowed the sudden proliferation of space habitats and facilities in Earth orbit using construction materials—especially aluminum and lunar glass—mined on the Moon. Metals like iron, nickel, and titanium were shipped down from the asteroid belt. Volatiles—especially water and carbon compounds—were mined on Challenger and other c-cons. Even rocket fuel is cheaply manufactured in space by using solar energy to split water into hydrogen and oxygen, liquefying them by shielding them from sunlight, and pumping them into spacecraft fuel tanks.

It took a handful of centuries to get from the first Earth satellites to the Beanstalk; once the Beanstalk was in place,

it took only a few more years before large-scale colonies had been built on the Moon and on Mars, and manned spacecraft were exploring the entire solar system. Thanks to the Beanstalk, humankind is now well on its way to becoming a truly solar species—a species at home throughout the Sun's far-flung kingdom of worlds.

HOPE FOR THE FUTURE

By the late twentieth century, humankind found itself in a race, and it was winner take all. Fossil fuels were dwindling and soon would be gone, and with them would vanish modern technology and civilization itself. The Oil Wars claimed many lives in the name of this dwindling resource, and with the crisis of climate change looming large on the world stage, Earth's people were desperate to replace oil and gas as sources of power.

Alternative sources like wind turbines, solar cells, and tide motors could not begin to quench the planet's thirst for energy, and after the meltdowns of the twentieth and twenty-first centuries, no one wanted a fission power plant anywhere close by.

humankind...

...well on its way to becoming a truly solar species

Nuclear fusion offered the one small bit of hope that the race was winnable. More powerful that fission, fusion also used sea water for fuel instead of uranium or highly toxic plutonium. Nuclear fusion might at last let humankind break free of dependence on fossil fuels before civilization itself collapsed.

Unfortunately, cheap and inexhaustible energy from nuclear fusion had been promised "in another twenty years" ever since the 1950s, and the technology, which relied on titanic devices generating temperatures and pressures found at the Sun's core, proved to be both monumentally expensive and monumentally difficult to develop. Failure was nearly certain until the Space Elevator tether was lowered from the heavens and permanent colonies were established on the surface of the Moon.

THE PROMISE OF HELIUM-3

There are several different ways of building a fusion reactor. One of those ways is cheaper, much safer, and quite a bit cleaner than the others. The only drawback is that it uses the helium-3 isotope as part of the fuel.

Most helium is helium-4, meaning it has an atomic nucleus containing two protons and two neutrons. He-3 has two protons and one neutron. It's perfect for one highly efficient form of fusion, but, unfortunately, it's also fantastically rare on Earth. One way to get it is to wait for tritium—that's a hydrogen isotope with two neutrons and a half-life of twelve years—to decay into He-3. A much cheaper way is to strip-mine the surface of the Moon using androids.

Helium streaming out from the Sun in the solar wind has been landing on the lunar surface since the Moon was formed 4.4 billion years ago or so. The lunar regolith—the upper layer of soil on the Moon—has collected twenty-eight parts per million of helium-4...and 0.01 parts per million of He-3. It takes one hundred million tons of strip-mined regolith to produce one ton of He-3, but solar power is abundant and cheap on the Moon, and robotic machinery is good at scooping up dirt and processing out the helium isotopes.

The primary purpose of the colonies on the Moon is to collect and process lunar regolith, load the resultant He-3 into large cryotanks, and slingshot them by mag-lev rail into space for eventual collection at Challenger's Farside. There, the tanks are loaded onto unmanned Beanstalk cargo pods and whisked down to New Angeles and beyond, where the He-3 has initiated a genuine revolution in power generation. Scientists believe that the gas giants also contain large amounts of He-3, and the first person who figures out how to extract it cheaply is going to be very, very rich.

Petroleum remains indispensable for the manufacture of plastics, but even here it is proving less expensive to mine hydrocarbons from c-con asteroids and use essentially free solar energy to create plastic.

Earth today enjoys the benefits of virtually unlimited energy, most of it generated by deuterium-He-3 fusion power plants. Thousands of years' worth of energy can be taken from the Moon, and long before those reserves are tapped out, humanity will be mining even more abundant He-3 reserves in the upper atmospheres of the outer gas giants. Thanks to the Beanstalk, Earth's energy resources appear to be all but guaranteed for literally millions of years into the future.

OTHER POWER SOURCES

He-3 fusion hasn't been the only means of alleviating Earth's energy shortage. In fact, most of the Beanstalk's systems are powered not by reactors, from other sources.

Massive solar panels float alongside Midway in geostationary orbit, beaming nearly free energy into the Stalk's power systems. Excess electricity is stored in immense capacitors in the Root's lowest levels and fed from there into Earth's planetary energy grid. Additionally, the Space Elevator tether has a core of superconductive material at its center, which acts to translate movement through the Earth's magnetic field into electricity to augment the power for operating the beanpods.

Finally, the up-and-down movement of the beanpods themselves can be used to generate power. A beanpod rising up-Stalk stores increasing amounts of potential energy, energy that can be released as electricity when the pod descends and used to power another pod going up. The system is highly efficient and requires only a small additional power input to make up for losses due to friction and inefficiency.

POWER FROM THE SUN

Long before the Beanstalk was raised, futurists had pointed out that Earth orbit was the ideal place to build enormous solar power panels. Using raw materials shipped up from the Moon, the solar cell arrays would measure hundreds of kilometers on a side. They would be able to convert sunlight to microwaves and beam them down to rectenna arrays in Earth's deserts, alleviating the planet's energy shortages. The system isn't perfect. Beaming microwave energy from space has

at best two percent efficiency, but after the initial capital investments for the infrastructure, sunlight is free, and you can build very large structures in microgravity.

Several pilot program solar arrays were constructed in synchronous orbit before the Lunar He-3 shipments commenced. The arrays continue to work to this day, adding their output to Earth's power grid. It's impossible to identify any one part of the planetary electrical grid that depends exclusively on orbital-beamed power, but it's seen as a viable emergency reserve in case the flow of Lunar He-3 is ever interrupted again. To this end, a number of space-based corporations—notably SpaceDyne, Sol Systems AG, and the China-based Yangguang Dianyuan Gongsi—continue to manufacture and deploy large solar cell arrays from Midway Station, creating orbital "sunfarms" that harvest sunlight and beam it to Earth.

THE SKY IS FALLING

Since the earliest days of its inception, critics of the Beanstalk have asked, "What happens if the fragged thing breaks?"

In fact, the threat is far less serious than sensationalist reporting and entertainment would have us believe. Any break in the cable that occurs above synchorbit will see the upper fragment drift outward and away from Earth.

If a break were to occur below synchronous orbit, the upper part, again, would drift into a higher orbit. The lower part would fall, but most of it—the length above one hundred kilometers or so—would burn up in the Earth's atmosphere. It might represent billions of tons of material, yes, but rather than being bunched up like a typical doomsday asteroid, that material is stretched out into a cable twenty- to forty-meters thick. A fraction of that material might survive re-entry through the atmosphere, but as the woven carbon nanofibers begin to heat above a thousand degrees or so Celsius, they have a tendency to become "unzipped," increasing their surface area and the likelihood that they would be vaporized completely.

If a sizable chunk of the Beanstalk fell, it *would* be a disaster—but more for economic reasons than because of widespread devastation. Critics' contentions that the falling tether would wrap itself around Earth's equator—*twice*—are simply impossible.

Critics have also pointed out that the Beanstalk is peculiarly vulnerable to terrorism, or to attacks during wartime. To this end, SEA—the Space Elevator Authority—has made security a top priority in Beanstalk operations, and it watches over the space elevator's length from its command center at Midway. The SEA's highly visible private police force—the "yellow jackets"—is augmented by plainclothes security personnel and a military presence, drawn from the governments of both the United States of America and Ecuador.

The Space Expeditionary Corps has permanently stationed two wings of SA/F-01A Strikers on the Beanstalk—one at Midway Station, one at Challenger—and another two wings of F/A-90 high-performance atmospheric fighters capable of reaching low orbit are based out of New Angeles.

Although it is not widely advertised, batteries of high-energy lasers at Midway Station—ostensibly for protection against incoming meteors and other "space junk"—would also fill a defensive anti-ship role in the case of an attack. However, the most serious threat to the Beanstalk lies below, not above, the Root.

THE CAYAMBE CONNECTION

The Beanstalk is located near the peak of Volcán Cayambe, a glacier-covered mountain sixty-four kilometers northeast of Quito. At forty-seven thousand meters, Cayambe is the third-highest mountain in Ecuador, and the only mountain in the world where the equator passes almost directly across its peak.

Unfortunately, Cayambe is a volcano, and although future volcanic activity is notoriously difficult to predict, its last eruption—the only one in historical times—was in March of 1786, and so it is far too soon to call Volcán Cayambe *extinct*.

Neoluddites and opponents of Weyland's Space Elevator Project made much of the danger if Cayambe were to erupt with the Beanstalk anchored at its peak. Supporters of the seaborne option likewise pointed out that anchoring the Space Elevator to an active volcano was begging for trouble. The objections were overridden by the Rivera Declaration, which set the framework for the later Quito Accord.

Before the Declaration was signed, the mountain was extensively surveyed using deep radar, seismic, and co-so-pros (coherent sonic probes) to map deep plutonic features, including lava chambers and fissures, and Consortium volcanologists announced that there was only an estimated 0.003% chance per year of a significant eruption. Based on these findings, two separate safety programs were put in place before construction of the Root was begun: the Hellgate Tunnels and the emergency tether release.

THE HELLGATE TUNNELS

Large-scale deep mining equipment was used to bore a series of tunnels through solid rock starting from the base of the slope some fifteen kilometers to the north and at an altitude of three thousand meters beneath the peak. These tunnels were run to within five kilometers of the primary magma chamber. In the event that an eruption is imminent, tactical nuclear charges would be used to complete the tunnels, providing enormous relief valves that would divert the force of the eruption north, away from the elevator on the mountain's south slope.

Pressure-relief boreholes have since been constructed adjacent to several other volcanoes worldwide. As yet, the system has not been used, but volcanologists are confident that it would work in all but the most devastating of eruptions.

SETTING THE BEANSTALK FREE

A second plan is in place against the possibility of a Cayambe eruption. In such an event, the ground-side end of the tether could be released, allowing the entire elevator structure to drift free.

Several kilometers of the very end of the lower tether are stored on immense spools deep underground, allowing a certain amount of play in the entire structure. Each day, the tether becomes shorter or longer as it is affected by various forces—most notably high and low tides and the effects of thermal expansion.

In addition, the movement of beanpods up- or down-Stalk affects the geometry of the cable. As pods rise, they steal a small amount of energy form the entire system, and the cable tends to lag behind as the Earth rotates, in effect bending slightly to the west. As a car descends, the opposite happens, and the cable leans slightly to the east. The extra cable underground assures that these movements will not displace Midway Station from geosynch.

In an emergency, the tether can be released from the spools. In an extreme emergency, it can be physically cut by explosives. Should this happen, the entire Space Elevator would drift upward as Challenger, no longer attached to the distant Earth, pulls it into space. Both Challenger and Midway, though, are equipped with hundreds of escape pods—dubbed "magic beans," of course—ready in case of tether disruption or environmental failures at either site. Stabilizing rockets would keep both from drifting too far, allowing the reconstruction or reattachment of the tether and saving billions to rebuild the 'Stalk. Even if the original site at New Angeles was ruined due to natural disaster, the Beanstalk could be reattached at the port of Pedernales, 230km to the west, or even to a proposed seagoing platform along the equator.

With the safety issues addressed, Volcán Cayambe was officially chosen as the Beanstalk site under the terms of the Rivera Declaration, and construction began the following year. There remain those, however, who believe that the Weyland Corporation is putting politics and profits ahead of the safety of some tens of thousands of people.

Emilio Rodriguez

A HISTORY OF THE BEANSTALK

The Beanstalk cost tens of billions to construct—some estimates put the figure at something in excess of seventy billion dollars—but eventually it became the conduit for hundreds of trillions of dollars—and later, credits—flowing down-Stalk from Heinlein and from fast-growing space-based industries. The world's first trillionaires were the men and women who invested heavily in the Space Elevator Project, as well as in asteroid mining, in orbital manufacturing, and, especially, in helium-3 fusion. With that kind of money on the line, political corruption, corporate malfeasance, and legislative greed were inevitable—and ugly.

The history of New Angeles is the history of the Beanstalk. Indeed, New Angeles exists purely as an offshoot of the Space Elevator, the inevitable growth of commercial infrastructure arising in the Beanstalk's shadow.

Jack Weyland began the initial purchases of Ecuadorian land northeast of Quito, including parts of the Cayambe Coca Ecological Reserve, toward the end of the last century. The agreement by the Ecuadorian government to sell this wilderness land was controversial and widely criticized at the time. A review by the Inspector General's Office of the Ecuador and Ministerio del Interior, however, failed to find any indication of bribery or corruption. Suspicions surrounding the Quito Accord remain as well. As much as a quarter of the approximately one trillion dollars the U.S. paid over twenty years to secure land for the Space Elevator Project went into the pockets of a select and very wealthy few in Ecuador's government, military, and courts, and that the popular referendum on the plan was rigged.

Beanstalk supporters point out that the flood of wealth coming down-Stalk has benefited Ecuador to a degree impossible to imagine a hundred years ago. The populations of both New Angeles and of Ecuador, they suggest, are so much better off—enjoying, as they do, the highest standards of living found anywhere in Latin America—that a few hundred billion dollars' worth of corruption is a reasonable cost of doing business.

For a time, some questioned whether ordinary Ecuadorian citizens would benefit at all from the Beanstalk's presence. When the first parcels of land were purchased under existing extraterritoriality laws, resident Ecuadorians became foreign nationals on what had been their own land. Buyout agreements and compensation plans encouraged many to move west; others stayed where they were and applied for work permits and green cards.

For a time, a rival proposal vied with Jack Weyland's over the location and design of the Beanstalk's Root. Rather than planting the Beanstalk on a mountaintop, some argued it would be safer and more economical to anchor the structure to a large, seagoing base, a powered structure similar to Chibashima, the zaratan isle in NeoTokyo Bay. A sea-based Root could be moved or shifted slightly in the event that the 'Stalk was endangered by orbiting space junk or an out-of-control planetoid. The proposal was named Seabase Zaratan, and the idea received considerable support from certain caucuses of the U.S. Congress.

A massive advertising campaign by Weyland blocked the proposal, however, with several key arguments. An oceanic Root would be decidedly limited in its growth, as well as in its infrastructure. Travelers would have to reach Seabase Zaratan by sea or by air, rather than the more convenient mag-lev tubes, and warehousing space for supplies going up or goods coming down would be in short supply. Defensive lasers and ongoing orbital-clearing missions would take care of the space debris and, at need—when a defunct satellite in low Earth orbit might actually impact the tether, for instance—the tether itself could be nudged slightly. As already noted, the movement of mass up or down on the tether tends—through the effects of the Coriolis force—to move the cable slightly. In most instances, a movement of a few meters is all that would be necessary to keep both tether and satellite safe.

All but the oldest satellites are equipped with power systems to prevent collisions, and even the old ones are closely monitored by Earth. But the realization that a sea-based system would be sharply limited in scope finally ended the challenge by Weyland's rivals.

Eventually, Ecuador and the Weyland Consortium signed the Rivera Declaration, which established the framework of a lease agreement between the corporation and Ecuador for the land immediately surrounding the Root. The format was similar to the Canal Zone treaties that had allowed the building of the Panama Canal early in the twentieth century and the Nicaragua Canal in the early twenty-first.

Although the Treaty of Heinlein also ceded daily operational control to the Space Elevator Authority, the Weyland Consortium unofficially controls the economic and political life of the Space Elevator. Most assume that the shadow owners and powers-that-be behind the Space Elevator will stay behind the scenes so long as the flow of credits down from space continues to fill their credaccounts. And in Space Elevator politics, as in all other forms of politics and government, the Golden Rule is very much in evidence: "Whoever has the gold makes the rules…"

THE SWORD OF DAMOCLES

Since the Beanstalk first opened for business, the program has been hailed as the single most important step forward in human technology since fire. It has all but assured our survival as a species, it has freed us from the threat of energy shortages and planet-wide pollution, and it has opened the way for humankind to become a truly mature and interplanetary species.

Still, there remain dangers. The Battle of the Beanstalk raised the specter that war or terrorism might yet strike against this stream of wealth and prosperity. Disaffected political or religious groups might see the Beanstalk as a viable target to force wealthier nations or groups to yield to their demands—extortion on a planetary scale.

In any event, the Beanstalk was not damaged during the War thanks in part to the military garrisons, both American and Ecuadorian, that defended it. Nor is the Beanstalk a soft target. Anti-meteor laser defenses would be quite as effective against approaching military ships as they are against chunks of space debris, and even if the unthinkable happened and the tether was severed, the physics of the structure are such that little real or lasting damage could be done.

The worst-case scenario—of several thousands of kilometers of the lower tether falling from the sky—would result in billions of dollars of damage and a halt in traffic, true. The worst damage would be confined to the Amazon Industrial Zone and portions of equatorial Africa. The *psychological* impact of such a disaster would be far greater than any actual threat to the planet's economy or to its population.

Jack Weyland said it best, perhaps, with his famous quote: "We could make it perfectly safe by not building the damned thing."

AD ASTRA

One Beanstalk just isn't enough to satisfy global demand for tourism, trade, and opportunity. Others claim that the Space Elevator Authority gives preferential access to the United States and its allies despite the intent of the Treaty of Heinlein, thereby effectively hamstringing the rest of the world's opportunities to create new colonies on Luna and Mars.

Already, there are plans for at least two new space elevators, one rooted on an island in Lake Victoria just south of Kampala, the other on Pulau Lingaa, two hundred kilometers southeast of Singapore. Other possible ground attachment points have been identified on the northern slopes of Mt. Kenya, at the mouths of the Amazon, and on Isabella Island in the Galapagos.

In addition, a consortium of industrial corporations has announced plans for a different option, a sea-based elevator rising from the Pacific Ocean. The land-based projects have the advantage of existing infrastructure—the cities of Kampala and Singapore which would become immense and sprawling spaceports on a scale similar to that of New Angeles. The sea-based initiative has been put forward by the same industrial amalgamation that suggested a sea-based elevator during the Beanstalk's initial design phase. Criticisms about a marine elevator's limits to growth have been addressed by plans to build a floating marine city atop numerous powered, artificial islands rafted together, and by designs for a new generation of immense cargo and passenger vessels to service it.

It remains to be seen whether the Consortium will become involved in any of the projects, like how they are involved with the proposed space elevator at Bradbury's Daedalus Complex on Mars, or whether they will actively combat any threat to its monopoly on access to space.

INTO THE FUTURE

The old fairy tale of Jack and the Beanstalk listed three treasures brought down-Stalk by the enterprising and felonious Jack: a bag of gold, a hen that laid golden eggs, and a harp that played itself.

In the near future we could see those prizes expanded upon: untold wealth eliminating global poverty; a means of continually producing such wealth through access to new means of power generation; and the inevitable transformation of our culture as we redefine concepts like work, wages, and what it means to be human.

Visionaries speak of a future era when a thriving, inhabited city evolves as a ring completely encircling the Earth, seventy-two thousand kilometers across, with numerous elevator threads connecting the planet's surface with synchorbit. Someday, a thousand years hence, Earth might have rings as glorious and as spectacular as those of Saturn.

With the Beanstalk, humankind has reached the jump-off point to a whole new level of existence, that of *Homo extraterrestrialis*—a mature species firmly planted first on Mars, and then beyond. Its realm would expand throughout the formerly empty volume of space surrounding Sol. Beyond that, a galaxy awaits us…and beckons.

And truly the sky is no longer the limit.

a galaxy awaits…

THE WORLD CHANGED

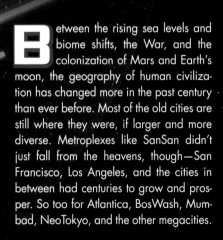

Between the rising sea levels and biome shifts, the War, and the colonization of Mars and Earth's moon, the geography of human civilization has changed more in the past century than ever before. Most of the old cities are still where they were, if larger and more diverse. Metroplexes like SanSan didn't just fall from the heavens, though—San Francisco, Los Angeles, and the cities in between had centuries to grow and prosper. So too for Atlantica, BosWash, Mumbad, NeoTokyo, and the other megacities.

Yet New Angeles is something new. It grew up practically overnight, and now it's the largest and richest city in the world—in the worlds, in fact. Most of that is the Beanstalk, of course, the massive space elevator that connects Earth to the stars. But it's also an artifact of the strange intersections of economy and laws, the flow of commerce and population that no one can ever perfectly predict. The Russian collapse, the end of the oil economy, the fall of Europe, the rise of Nigeria and Brazil—they all had as much an effect on the current geopolitical

atlas as any war or any climate shift. But it's all interconnected.

The Beanstalk is connected far beyond just its perch on Volcán Cayambe, too. The New Angeles Space Elevator did more than grow one city up like some sort of magic bean. It opened up the Moon and Mars to growth as well, and now millions of human beings live off the planet where the species was born.

Everyone says the Net made the world smaller, but for all that it's still awful big.

Turn off the vid screens. Earth massive below. Luna, like a leviathan risen against the startling color of space. Microgravity active.

NEW ANGELES

The territory that now comprises New Angeles has a long history of occupation and colonization. The Incan Empire partially conquered the territory in the fifteenth century, although coastal and Amazonian tribes resisted Incan power. The Spanish followed soon after, resulting in centuries of European rule. Ecuador finally achieved independence as a unified nation in the nineteenth century.

By the time Jack Weyland began searching for a site for his space elevator, Ecuador was an economically struggling liberal democracy. Although parts of the country, such as the cities of Quito and Guayaquil, were as developed and sophisticated as any megapolis, much of the nation remained unspoiled wilderness. Weyland was able to buy significant tracts of undeveloped land relatively cheaply through the Rivera Declaration.

The history of New Angeles proper begins with the Weyland Consortium's purchase of land near Quito, including the peak of Volcán Cayambe. Controversy surrounds this initial purchase because historically Ecuador had very strong ecological protections in its laws, and Weyland's deal seemed to circumvent the normal ecological review process. Further purchases followed as Weyland bought undeveloped land and built company towns and worker barracks to support the Project. The influx of cash and well-paid laborers was a boon to Ecuador's economy, but much of that economic activity was recaptured by Weyland via company stores that undercut the locals for many goods.

As the Project grew, the Consortium created new cities from nothing. Some sprang up in the middle of nowhere. Others absorbed existing Ecuadorian towns. These cities were filled with legions of technicians, engineers, and laborers—not to mention the thousands of support staff—required for the largest engineering project on the planet. Many of these facilities were constructed in the Andes near the build site, but others were scattered throughout the La Costa region of Ecuador wherever Weyland could find enough land to suit its needs. The first and largest of these towns, about one hundred kilometers west of Volcán Cayambe, became known as New Los Angeles as the Consortium shuttled in talent from its Los Angeles offices.

Two years into the Project, Jack Weyland signed a deal with the U.S. government, simultaneously winning a host of lucrative government contracts and securing taxpayer funding for the Space Elevator itself. In '35 the United States entered negotiations with Ecuador and signed a lease for some sixty-thousand square kilometers of land, creating the Special Economic Zone of Ecuadorian New Los Angeles. This agreement is known as the Quito Accord.

With the creation of the SEZ, the vision for the Project changed. Rather than "just" building the largest structure ever built by human beings, Weyland now planned to build the largest city in the world. Several pop-up cities were created including Quinde, Central City, and Rutherford. Laborers were put to work building housing that wouldn't be filled for years. The abundance of cheap housing contributed to immigration, which brought in more workers to build more of the city. The virtuous cycle enabled New Angeles to grow far faster than all but the most optimistic predictions.

Although many of the immigrants were from the United States mainland, they came from all over the world. The single largest source of immigration came from elsewhere in South America as workers fled struggling economies in search of well-paying jobs. Others came in from Soufrika, from economically distressed

countries along the Mediterranean, from Uganda, Nigeria, and elsewhere in Africa. The Project coincided with the slow disintegration of the Russian Federation; many Russians left for a better life living and working in New Angeles. So many arrived in a single mass that the district Rabotgorod still bears a Russian name. Immigrants also came in from the EU and from rich Asian nations to fuel the skilled labor needs of the Project. In some cases, these immigrant groups clustered and created an ethnic enclave within the growing city. In other cases, they mixed in with rest of the ever-expanding melting pot of New Angeles.

Meanwhile, the existing Ecuadorian population of the SEZ had become resident aliens. Many accepted government buyouts to relocate to Ecuador, but the majority chose to remain. The construction of the Space Elevator employed many, and others made a living catering to the Project's employees. Weyland was no longer able to recapture most Project wealth through its company stores, so

quickly did the SEZ's population grow. Over time, the Project and existing Ecuadorian population centers became more and more integrated. The Consortium's control over the SEZ was challenged, and an overlapping system of local laws and corporate policies complicated day-to-day life within the Zone.

Inspired by the megalopolitan reforms of the last century, the Special Economic Zone eventually incorporated into a single city, now known simply as New Angeles. Over the next few years, Project and city bureaucracies divided responsibilities for city administration, leaving the Project officially in control only of the Space Elevator and its operation and construction. The city was divided into twelve districts, and residency and electoral rules were established. Briefly, an application of statehood was considered, but it was rejected on the grounds that doing so would mean forfeiting the current special economic incentives vital to the Zone—and now the city's—growth.

Finally, the Space Elevator—Jack's Beanstalk—was finished and opened for business. In short order, a flow of materiel and personnel began running up the Beanstalk, with a much smaller

trickle returning to Earth. The Space Elevator was a modest success, but when the technology underlying helium-3 fusion power lagged behind the completion of the Beanstalk, it failed to deliver the sky-high profits and wealth as quickly as expected. Many investors were disappointed, and New Angeles abruptly shifted from a boomtown to just another city. The cycle of immigration and growth stalled, and parts of the city fell into disrepair and economic decline. The slowdown happened quickly; entire districts contracted and left empty slums in their place.

Only a few years later, fusion power using helium-3 was unlocked. Early surveys of the Moon had already confirmed that it was rich in He-3, and the Beanstalk was the only economically viable route to the Moon. Almost overnight, New Angeles became the most economically important city on Earth. The boom resumed, but it was too late for the newly minted slums. Neighborhoods might gentrify, but New Angeles would forevermore have a squalid and poor underside—a literal underworld, in many cases.

As Heinlein Colony grew and space flight became increasingly important, the Beanstalk quickly reached its maximum

New Angeles is, with no question whatsoever, the biggest and most populous megapolis on Earth, with hundreds of millions of citizens packed in ten or twelve thousand to the square kilometer, and God alone knows how many disenfrancistos, streetbangers, sewer rats, undercity scavengers, clones, and bioroids.

capacity. Demand outstripped supply and profits soared. Expanding the Space Elevator's capacity was difficult, and the Weyland Consortium found itself in the position of determining who could and could not benefit from the economic opportunity of outer space. Since New Angeles was a territory of the United States of America, U.S. interests were given privileged access, much to the dismay of Chinese, European, Soufrikan, Brazilian, and other concerns. Tensions rose and the Beanstalk became a subject of much international discussion. On the one hand, the Beanstalk was built by a U.S.-based company. On the other hand, the fact that the Space Elevator was located on leased soil wasn't lost on the other nations, especially Ecuador.

The situation continued to be tense for years. The Lunar and Martian colonies prospered thanks to the Beanstalk. Megacorps earned unprecedented profits from space exploitation. Competing multinational interests spread across the Lunar surface. And throughout it all, New Angeles remained the focus of the new frontier, the gateway to outer space.

Ultimately, the actions of laborers on Luna brought matters to a head, and they declared independence from New Angeles and Earth. The Lunar Insurrection was relatively brief, but its effects were worlds-shaking. The creation of the Space Expeditionary Corps, the militarization of space, and the spread of the conflict to Mars all had important potential ramifications for the status of New Angeles, and throughout the duration of the War the city lived in suspense. U.S. forces garrisoned the Beanstalk and the borders of the Special Economic Zone. The Space Elevator devoted a significant portion of its capacity to military hardware and personnel traveling up-Stalk. Despite, or perhaps because of, this military posturing, New Angeles itself never came under direct attack during the War.

The same could not be said for the Beanstalk, however. When a group of Martian rebel extremists tried to target the Beanstalk directly, the confrontation became known as Battle of the Beanstalk. Despite the name, in actuality the fighting never strayed very close to the Challenger Planetoid or any location down-Stalk. Fanciful New Angelino tales of watching the fireworks as the conflict raged in space above their heads are nothing more than that—the distances involved in space combat meant that the entire conflict passed completely unremarked by the naked eye or any other human senses. The Space Elevator itself remained undamaged by the Martian assault, and New Angeles survived the War unscathed.

THE GEOPOLITICS OF THE SPACE ELEVATOR

There's nothing special about New Angeles, really. It's a massive coastal city, but there are other massive coastal cities. It's not that much bigger than Mumbad, not that much richer than SanSan, not even necessarily more important than BosWash. Nothing inherent to the location or resources of New Angeles makes it so important—except the Space Elevator.

The Beanstalk is the only economical way to exploit the possibilities of space travel and exploration. Access to the Beanstalk, especially in this fusion-powered economy, is essential for the political and security priorities of every developed nation on Earth. That the Beanstalk is attached to the world's largest and richest city is almost irrelevant, geopolitically. New Angeles itself is little more than an accident of history on the world stage.

If a second space elevator were ever built, things would change completely. New Angeles would remain a powerful and prosperous city, but the Beanstalk itself would be demoted from "essential" to "valuable." Perhaps predictably, then, powerful New Angelino interests are rumored to stop at nothing to sabotage every other attempted space elevator project in the world.

With the close of the War, U.S. and coalition forces stood down and returned to their bases elsewhere on the planet. While a military presence remains in New Angeles, it is no more than would be expected of a city of its size. But that isn't to say that New Angeles went back to the way things were before the War.

Signed fifteen years ago, the Treaty of Heinlein created a new economic and political reality for the world's largest city. In addition to ending the hostilities between all belligerent parties, it renewed New Angeles' claim on Heinlein Station. The tax incentives established at the founding of the SEZ were largely codified in the treaty and made effectively permanent thanks to corporate influence. Finally, New Angeles was granted a degree of autonomy—and more importantly, a guarantee that things would stay that way—from the United States' federal government, which ensured the city, and therefore the Beanstalk, would remain open for business to the whole solar system. At the same time, the Space Elevator Authority was created to oversee the security and neutrality of the Beanstalk.

The post-war years saw a renewed boom in New Angeles. Foreign investment surged on the strength of the long-term security ensured by the Treaty of Heinlein. The renewed colonial interest in Mars sent more goods up-Stalk, and the increased exploitation of the Moon and Mars meant more raw materials came back down. Heinlein's reconstruction was rapid thanks to contracts with the Weyland Consortium, and an influx of simulant labor ensured a second Lunar Insurrection would never come to pass.

But the boom had a dark side. Returning veterans, many injured and sporting lowest-bidder medical cybernetics, struggled to find work in a labor market soon flooded with androids. Already highly trained in violence, some turned to crime and joined various orgcrime outfits in New Angeles and worldwide. Corporations in pursuit of profit leveraged New Angeles' newfound autonomy to turn the city into a corporate playground, encouraging legislation that shielded them from liability and freed them to act more directly in matters of corporate security. Widespread allegations of corruption within the NAPD, New Angeles city government, and corporate boardrooms have been met with disinterest or even suppression by the powers that be. Groups such as the Opticon Foundation seem to be fighting an uphill battle against the evils of unrestricted wealth and greed.

Today, New Angeles is the crown jewel of Earth. It is the largest, grandest, richest, poorest, most splendid and most awful city in all the worlds. It is diverse, polyglot, technologically sophisticated, rich in culture and history, and economically powerful. It is also wracked by unrest, impoverished, and compromised both by criminal elements from below and corporate interests from above.

POLITICAL STANDING

New Angeles is an unincorporated territory of the United States—the largest and most economically vital unincorporated territory in history. As such, its legal status is flexibly defined by the U.S. Congress, and it has undergone much evolution since the Space Elevator Project began in the early '20s.

Under current law, New Angeles (more accurately the Special Economic Zone of Ecuadorian New Los Angeles) is U.S. territory and most U.S. federal laws apply. However, New Angeles has its own distinct (and very permissive) immigration policies, border controls, and tax laws. New Angeles residents pay no federal income tax, and a variety of other tax incentives encourage corporate investment in the city. On the other hand, New Angeles residents cannot vote in federal U.S. elections, send no voting representatives to the U.S. Congress, and are not guaranteed citizenship in the United States based purely on their status as citizens of New Angeles.

New Angeles does send a nonvoting delegate to the U.S. House of Representatives known as the Resident Commissioner. The Resident Commissioner is able to vote within committees, but not on the House floor, and not for the passage of bills. In any

case, he is generally seen as an extremely powerful lobbyist, one with a great deal of money behind him. Through the services of a succession of Resident Commissioners, New Angeles has managed to influence—some would say "buy"—certain key House and Senate committee appointments in order to propose legislation favorable to New Angeles.

Although their lesser representation prompts anxiety in some New Angelinos, most are content to focus on local concerns and enjoy their relative autonomy from the federal government. New Angelinos might have limited power in the U.S. federal system, but the U.S. federal government is likewise limited in its authority to control New Angeles due to the Treaty of Heinlein. For most purposes, the U.S. collects its tariffs off Beanstalk trade and leaves New Angeles alone.

New Angeles is governed by a mayor and a city council. The mayor is elected, usually narrowly, by popular vote across the entire city. Every New Angelino who maintains a permanent residence in the city may vote. Some critics argue that the voting

laws in New Angeles favor rich foreigners over poor locals—the residency requirements amount to a poll tax and bar those too poor to maintain an official permanent residence from casting their votes. These critics are mostly ignored by those in power.

In addition to the mayor, city councilors are elected from wards within New Angeles' districts. Because of the tendencies of some megacorps to create "corporate towns" to house their employees, there are a number of councilors whose wards consist predominantly or even exclusively of a single corp's workers and their families. These so-called "corporate councilors" are not necessarily any more beholden to corporate interests than the average politician, but it's fair to say that the interests of their constituents tend to align with the interests of the megacorps.

New Angeles is divided into twelve districts, each with its own elected district manager and bureaucracy. Although each district maintains many of its own civic and administrative functions, the districts are subordinate to the New Angeles megalopolitan government.

> The population of New Angeles is larger than that of any other megapolis in the solar system. Census data is remarkably difficult to gather accurately due to the city's sheer size. By the time a census has been completed, it's time to start another one—never mind the individuals who remain off-grid by choice or those sections of the city where census-takers refuse to tread.
>
> Because the city of New Angeles is relatively new, particularly when compared to other megacities across the globe, the population of the city is somewhat unique. Expanding white-collar opportunities over the past forty years has attracted worldwide talent, and significant portions of the city's upper and middle class (such as it is) commute from outside the city. Many risties dwell in New Angeles during the work week and sub back home to NeoTokyo, Mumbad, or Atlantica for the weekend.
>
> The middle class either lives in the corporate arcologies or commutes from the suburbs across the Ecuadoran border, where greenspaces are more prevalent and crime is less so.
>
> The lower classes of New Angeles—comprising native populations, swathes of immigrants, dispossessed risties, and the unemployed—have taken up residence in the sprawling undercity, where large families and drifters alike cram into tiny condo-habs that are no longer included on city zoning maps.
>
> Regardless of class, citizens in urban areas live and work in much closer proximity to one another, and naturally they have begun to mix. Unsurprisingly, an incredibly high percentage of second- and third-generation New Angelinos identify as bi- or multiracial. One side effect of the increasing diversity within its borders means the city enjoys much, much lower rates of racial tension and racially motivated crime.
>
> – Excerpts from *New Angeles: A Front Row Seat to History*, by Dr. Lucas Martinez

The plaza was just outside of Rutherford, an elevated square suspended above the network of tube-levs, underpasses, and walkways for the lower classes. Standing on the L-square, surrounded by slidewalks and carefully placed arc facades, Reina had the illusion she was at ground level. She knew that wasn't true, that there were a hundred meters or more of undercity beneath her.

TREATIES AND TENSIONS

New Angeles is situated on land leased from Ecuador by the United States under the terms of the Quito Accord signed in '35; these terms have also contributed to the relatively unsettled political status of the Special Economic Zone. The lease is scheduled to expire at the end of the century, and the city's future after that date remains uncertain.

A vocal minority of New Angelinos and Ecuadorians hold that Ecuador was dramatically underpaid for the New Angeles lease, that New Angeles has been a drag on Ecuador's economy and fortunes, and that the U.S. has violated the terms and spirit of the Quito Accord by building the most massive city in the world on Ecuador's land.

Activist groups such as the Consejo por un Ecuador Libre, the Pan-American Council, and la Brigada Tricolor are watched closely by U.S. and New Angeles officials. Some of these groups favor an early return of New Angeles to Ecuador's control, and not all of them are committed to nonviolence. Others advocate for the creation of a wholly independent city similar to that of Monaco or Vatican City. Dubbed Nuevo Angeles Libre, the city would have a special relationship both with Washington and Quito but would in effect govern itself.

Due to its unique history and location, an enormous fraction of New Angelinos are Ecuadorian citizens. Many people live in Ecuador and work in New Angeles. The Ecuador–New Angeles border is almost completely porous; civilians may cross the border multiple times in a day or even cross the border without noticing. Customs inspections are conducted digitally and strategically positioned NAPD sensors track the flow of IDs in and out of the city.

Further complicating New Angeles' political status is the international agreement known as the Treaty of Heinlein. Signed fifteen years ago at the conclusion of the War, the Treaty limits the control the U.S. federal government is permitted to exert. The semi-autonomy of New Angeles was an important political concession in the wake of the War, as it preserves the ability of non-U.S. countries to access and benefit from space exploration and the Moon. In short, the U.S. federal government cannot bar a nation from sending goods up the Beanstalk—only the Space Elevator Authority and New Angeles can do that.

The Quito Accord lease expires at the end of '99. Many assume that there is no chance the United States will allow Ecuador to reclaim the world's largest and most prosperous city. An extension will be negotiated, perhaps, or a loophole in the lease agreement will be found, or the U.S. will simply buy the land outright. Others worry that the Washington will simply refuse to cede the territory and will flagrantly violate the Quito Accord and Treaty of Heinlein to end the Special Economic Zone's semi-autonomous status. The concern is that this could lead to an increase in world tension or even war, as Brazil and China are unlikely to allow this to happen.

THE DISTRICTS

New Angeles is officially divided into twelve districts, although only eleven are found on Earth. Heinlein's status as the twelfth district of New Angeles had become a point of contention during the War—even if it was reaffirmed in the Treaty of Heinlein—and many New Angelinos do not consider their Lunar cousins to be true citizens of the city. On a practical level, Heinlein is sufficiently remote (it is further from New Angeles than any other point on Earth) and sufficiently alien (burdened by concerns unique to its extraterrestrial nature) that it is frequently omitted from any list or discussion of the districts of New Angeles.

Each district is a de facto city unto itself: it has its own administration, including a district council, zoning board, waste management, and other necessities. Each has a district-level NAPD headquarters (and some number of precinct houses), its own fire marshal, and public health offices. The district managers are appointed by the mayor's office, and historically not all district managers have been competent or interested in performing their job duties, leaving their councils to tend to the day-to-day drudgery of administration.

CHAKANA

Nestled in and among the Andes Mountains, most locations in the Chakana District are over three thousand meters above sea level. The base of the New Angeles Space Elevator itself is situated here, on the slopes of what was once the third highest mountain in Ecuador. Better known as the Root, the massive structure extends deep into the rock of Volcán Cayambe and sprawls around the mountainside as a triumph of human engineering and ambition, dwarfing even the arcologies that would otherwise fill Chakana's skyline.

The rest of the district is devoted almost entirely to support structures for the Beanstalk, from landing and parking facilities to loading and unloading terminals. Thousands of hotels, restaurants, and upscale tourist destinations entertain and accommodate the millions of passengers who pass through the district daily. Earth Station attracts so much traffic that one district is not sufficient to provide the necessary services—the seedier elements find cheaper prices and more salacious fare in neighboring Base de Cayambe.

On the eastern edge of the Chakana District stands a collection of aging and decrepit buildings constructed at the beginning of the Project, including dormitories, kitchens, and warehouses. Now a mixture of repurposed tenements and abandoned squats, the so-called Eastside is a blight on the otherwise upscale Chakana District.

POINTS OF INTEREST

The Root: As the Earth-side terminus of the Space Elevator, the Root is the single largest transit center on the planet. The Plaza del Cielo at the top of the Root features shopping, recreation, and Earth Station, the huge glass-domed terminal where the Beanstalk's passengers begin or end their journey.

Eastside Tenements: Chakana's Eastside is a collection of Project-built structures that are well past their intended lifespans.

PLAZA LEVEL AND THE UNDERCITY

New Angeles is a hugely diverse city, home to fancy residences and high-end commerce districts as much as to low-income housing projects and decaying slums. Sometimes the divisions are geographical, but they are also altitudinal.

New Angeles may be fairly said to be two cities. One city, the public face, is bright and welcoming, prosperous—or at least well maintained—and safe. This is sometimes referred to as the "plaza level," and it is rarely to be found at ground level. A network of slidewalks, elevated plazas (or "L-squares") suspended between glimmering arcology spires, and rooftop gardens or shopping malls create an artificial and carefully manicured floor to the life of the rich and comfortable.

Beneath the plaza level lies the undercity. Increasingly squalid, dirty, and dark the deeper one goes, the undercity is where the poor and desperate live and work. Highways thrumming with heavy cargo truck traffic, rattling metal stairways from level to level, and the occasional tube-lev track or hopper tunnel form a dense lattice of infrastructure that runs straight down to ground level and, in many cases, beyond. The ground itself is slick with trash and rarely gets any light at all, except for near the coast, New Angeles' few parks, and areas of new construction.

The Eastside Tenements are the district's most notorious slum, inhabited by low-income workers, criminals, and transients who can afford nothing better. Despite their squalor and decrepit nature, the Tenements are still both safer and more accessible than the undercity condo-habs that haunt the rest of New Angeles. There's always farther to fall.

BASE DE CAYAMBE

Located in the foothills below Chakana District and Volcán Cayambe, Base de Cayambe District is dominated by the Beanstalk in whose shadow it lies. While nearby Chakana District houses most of the Space Elevator's immediate infrastructure, much of the economic and industrial necessities of serving such a major port institution spill downhill to Base de Cayambe.

Base de Cayambe is rich in warehouses, flophouses, red-light districts, and other elements of a port town, and it is poor in most everything else. The district caters to the spacers and transients passing up and down the Beanstalk, peddling cheap alcohol and every sin of the flesh to the spacers, and storage and processing to the corps. War veterans and retired prisec officers congregate here, where many of the bars cater to them. Individuals looking to hire some guns or muscle can usually find a merc outfit willing to work off the books. Orgcrime also recruits from their ranks. A more seedy and disreputable region is difficult to imagine. Poverty and crime are rampant, and the NAPD is little help.

LEVY UNIVERSITY

Levy University accepts a hundred thousand new students every year. Its research programs are heavily subsidized by the megacorps, but this puts the campus ahead of the cutting edge in many fields.

HAAS ARCOLOGY

In a world where android labor is becoming increasingly pervasive, the Haas Arcology towers as the symbol of the modern workforce and state-of-the-art engineering.

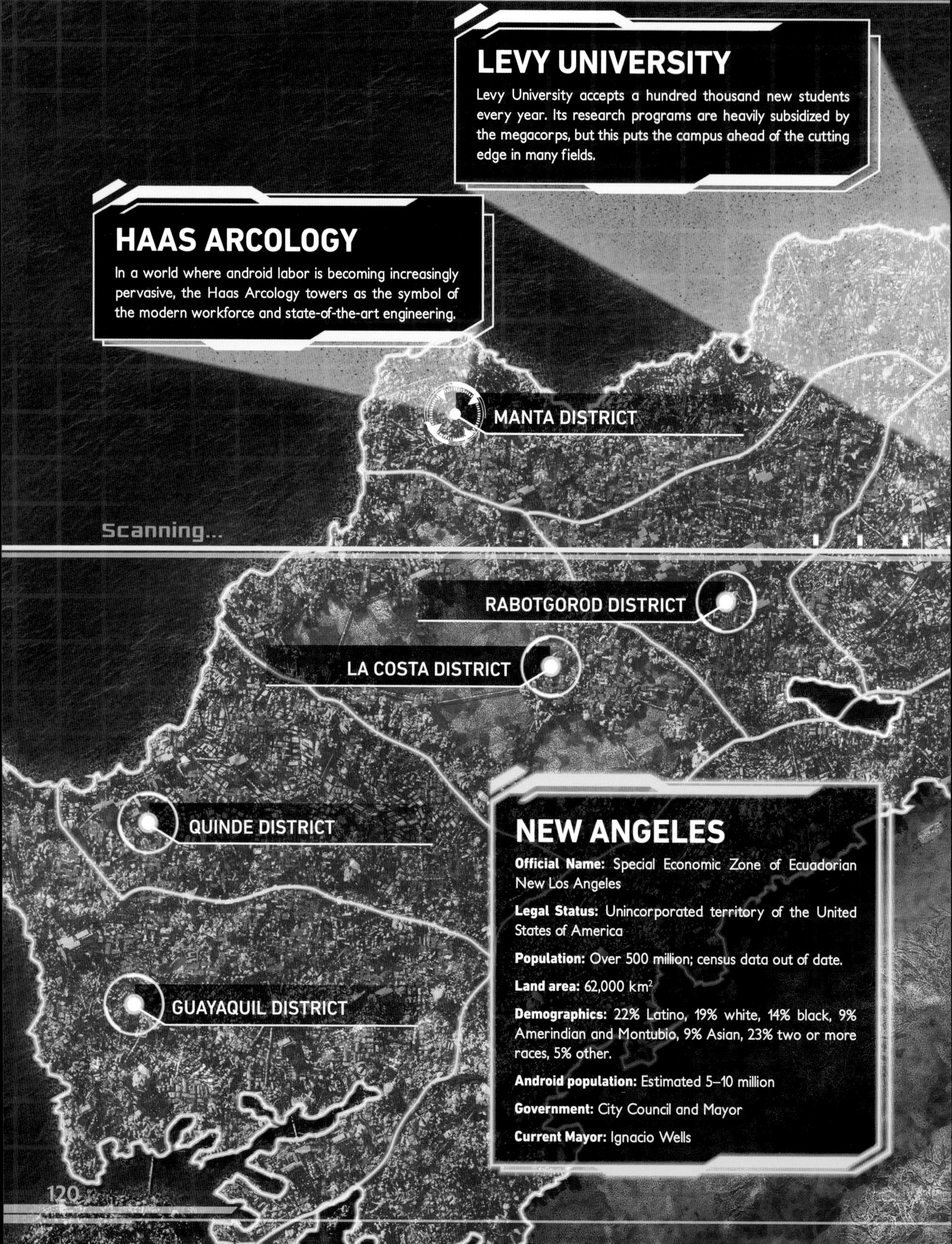

 MANTA DISTRICT

Scanning...

RABOTGOROD DISTRICT

LA COSTA DISTRICT

 QUINDE DISTRICT

 GUAYAQUIL DISTRICT

NEW ANGELES

Official Name: Special Economic Zone of Ecuadorian New Los Angeles

Legal Status: Unincorporated territory of the United States of America

Population: Over 500 million; census data out of date.

Land area: 62,000 km²

Demographics: 22% Latino, 19% white, 14% black, 9% Amerindian and Montubio, 9% Asian, 23% two or more races, 5% other.

Android population: Estimated 5–10 million

Government: City Council and Mayor

Current Mayor: Ignacio Wells

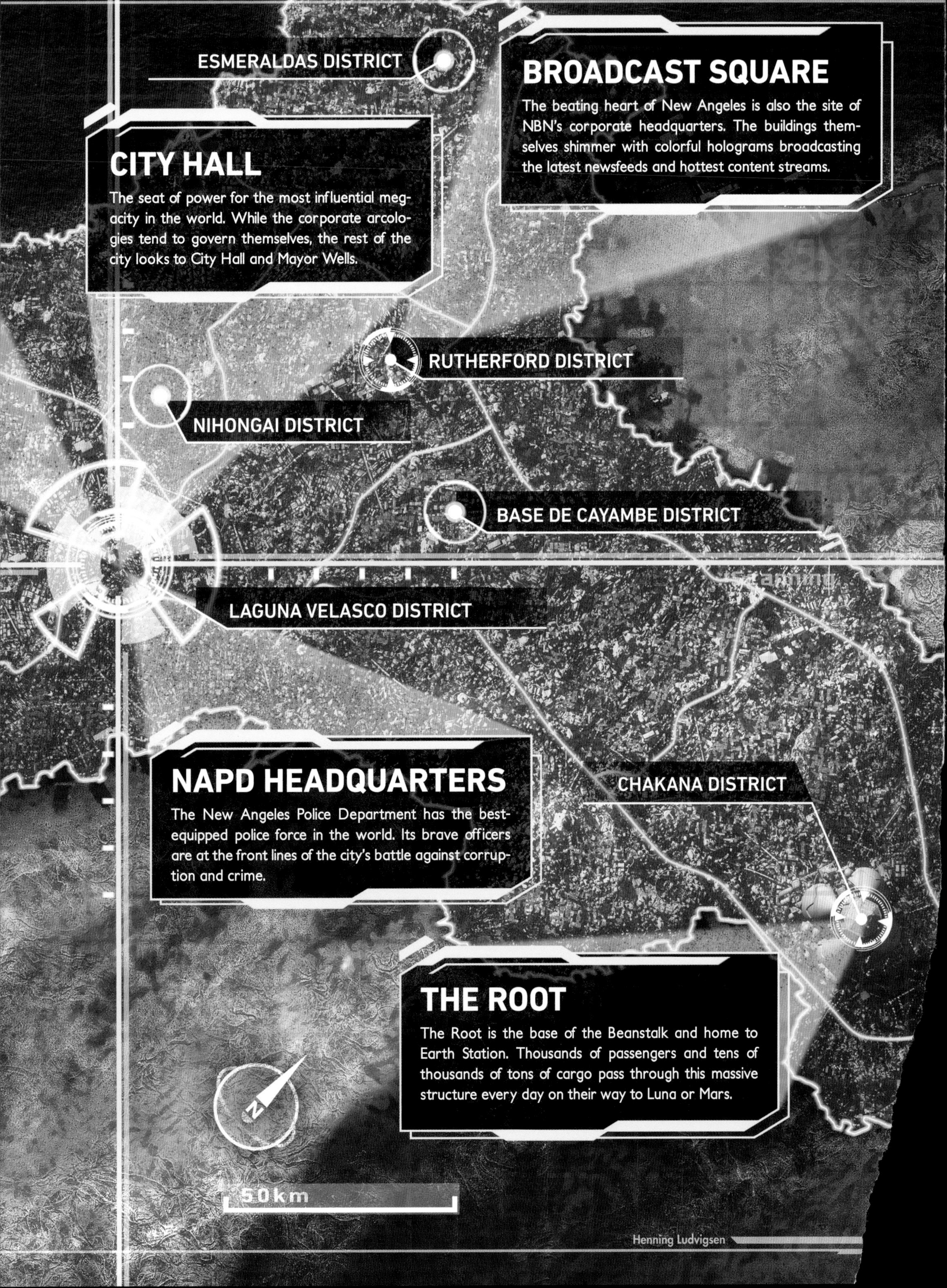

ESMERALDAS DISTRICT

BROADCAST SQUARE

The beating heart of New Angeles is also the site of NBN's corporate headquarters. The buildings themselves shimmer with colorful holograms broadcasting the latest newsfeeds and hottest content streams.

CITY HALL

The seat of power for the most influential megacity in the world. While the corporate arcologies tend to govern themselves, the rest of the city looks to City Hall and Mayor Wells.

RUTHERFORD DISTRICT

NIHONGAI DISTRICT

BASE DE CAYAMBE DISTRICT

LAGUNA VELASCO DISTRICT

NAPD HEADQUARTERS

The New Angeles Police Department has the best-equipped police force in the world. Its brave officers are at the front lines of the city's battle against corruption and crime.

CHAKANA DISTRICT

THE ROOT

The Root is the base of the Beanstalk and home to Earth Station. Thousands of passengers and tens of thousands of tons of cargo pass through this massive structure every day on their way to Luna or Mars.

50km

Henning Ludvigsen

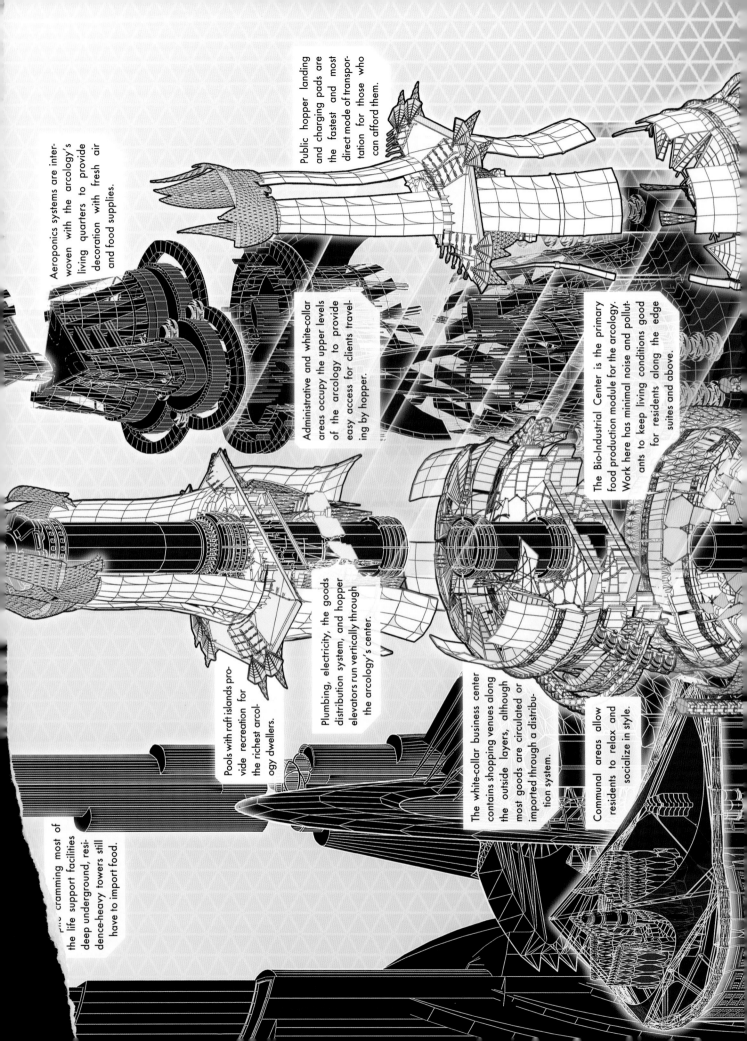

Aeroponics systems are interwoven with the arcology's living quarters to provide decoration with fresh air and food supplies.

Public hopper landing and charging pads are the fastest and most direct mode of transportation for those who can afford them.

Administrative and white-collar areas occupy the upper levels of the arcology to provide easy access for clients traveling by hopper.

The Bio-Industrial Center is the primary food production module for the arcology. Work here has minimal noise and pollutants to keep living conditions good for residents along the edge suites and above.

Pools with raft islands provide recreation for the richest arcology dwellers.

Plumbing, electricity, the goods distribution system, and hopper elevators run vertically through the arcology's center.

The white-collar business center contains shopping venues along the outside layers, although most goods are circulated or imported through a distribution system.

Communal areas allow residents to relax and socialize in style.

...e cramming most of the life support facilities deep underground, residence-heavy towers still have to import food.

LIFE AT THE TOP

Ristie life is a constant stream of the finest comforts technology can offer in a secluded world atop the towering starscrapers that literally place them above the masses. These luxury arcologies are cities within cities. Every service that a citizen could desire—shopping, style, education, security—is at the fingertips of the upper-middle and upper class in every megapolis, from New Angeles to Mumbad and beyond.

Self-sufficient in many respects (including food, water, and even power generation), arcologies ensure that society's wealthiest need not venture far for work, home, or play. Business centers feature offices for the arcology's system administrators, project developers, business managers, brand officers, insurance adjusters, budget analysts, and efficiency experts. Nearby corporate arcologies, easily reached by slidewalk or hopper or Metro, provide the other white-collar and knowledge-based careers that pay far more than anyone outside an arcology enjoys. Residential towers feature posh apartments and homes interspersed with greenspaces and artificial beachfront for recreation and relaxation.

At plaza level, shopping centers, social venues, and entertainment districts span tens of floors. Many luxuries are imported from across the globe. From Mumbad come the finest smartfabrics that morph and twist to the wearer's digital demands, changing color and style to suit the latest season (for a nominal fee). Genuine grass-fed meat instead of the mass-produced gogs of the Amazonian feedlots—produce grown in sunlight rather than the emulated wavelengths in an agroplex—all is served on a fingernail-thin crystal platter flowing in pleasant waves of holographically projected colors.

The vast majority of a ristie's work time is spent enjoying the lavish entertainments the arcology and surrounding New Angeles has to offer. Designer hologolf courses serve as the new board rooms, and business is conducted while listening to concertos played on exclusive instruments—some as old and treasured as a Stradivarius, others on the cutting edge of technology and literally one of a kind. Networking is done at galas for aficionados with similar interests in art, food, fashion, and every other celebration the elite can justify (which is to say, anything that comes to mind). Privileged children and wealthy spouses spend their days in leisure at attractions the poor can only dream of—holoparks, mag-flight zones, roller coasters that span hundreds of floors—no recreation is too exotic or too expensive for the residents of an arcology.

Within the arcologies, many of the retail and service positions essential to quotidian life are filled by androids. If a resident so desires, he can spend, acquire, and consume anything he likes with a wave of the hand. Clones prepare what foods require a more tender touch than a robot can provide, while bioroids serve as couriers to ferry shopping bags from retail outlets to their assigned destinations. For those who live in these sky-high palaces, anticipation is momentary; one's every desire is instantaneously fulfilled, often before one realizes he wanted it at all.

Some risties choose to never venture beyond the luxury afforded to them, oblivious to the stark realities of the world outside its walls. There is no underway access to the most exclusive arcologies; the residents who do leave take hoppers or elevated skywalks only. Those who try to claw upward and sneak their way inside aren't in much luck either—AI secretaries routinely screen entrants for biometric data, and if a visitor isn't a resident or approved guest, a sec-team quickly arrives to escort him or her out. Thick plascrete walls, digital gatekeepers, and well-paid (and often well-trained) prisec forces ensure that the lives of the elite are uninterrupted by the world at large.

The least affluent residents know their place is on the bottom in an arcology—both figuratively and otherwise. Vast underground complexes of hex-tubes and ramshackle cargo containers date far back to the founding of New Angeles or before. These are filled to the brim with middle- and lower-class workers who are glad to have a permanent address at all and dream of one day ascending to the plaza level or higher.

Luxury arcologies are literally shining examples of the world reserved for the business elite. They perennially stand as incentives for the lesser classes to strive ever harder for advancement in their careers, regardless of whether such aspirations are likely to be stifled by corporate inertia, background checks and blacklists, catch-22 laws, and no shortage of corrupt politicians. Rags-to-riches stories on NBN's content streams might be popular, but in the real world, downward social mobility is much more common than the reverse. The megacorps are the gatekeepers of the ristie class, and those lacking the connections or designer g-mods for intelligence and beauty are at a marked disadvantage.

At the top of the arcology, park and recreation areas boast breathtaking views of the New Angeles skyline.

Arcologies have wide vanes that can fold inward to protect the topmost observation and lounge decks from rain.

Residences make up the bulk of the arcology's levels. Each suite comes equipped with a secretary AI to modulate climate controls, schedule cleaning and maintenance, and monitor the residents' security.

CURRENT LOCATION:
0° 21' 27.0828" N
78° 30' 41.1048" W
MERCADO BAJA,
BASE DE CAYAMBE DISTRICT
UNDERCITY LEVEL 23

INCOMING TRANMISSION....

▶3RD DISTRICT ▶75TH PRECINT
03:00 HR / 23 APRIL RD

CRIME IN PROGRESS
VOICE ANALYSIS

DOWNLOADING NAPD FACIAL RECOGNITION....
PROCEED WITH CAUTION

Nevertheless, Base de Cayambe is not without its treasures: centuries-old churches, hole-in-the-wall restaurants, Bohemian artist cooperatives, and artisanal makerspaces can be found side-by-side with the red-light hotels and stim dealers. Cheap rents appeal to students, artists, and entrepreneurs, which gives the neighborhoods clustered behind the commercial strips an eclectic, patchwork nature.

To dismiss Base de Cayambe as a slum is an enormous mistake, one made by all too many New Angelinos. It still maintains a number of pre–Quito Accord communities and buildings, pockets of history in the midst of the future.

POINTS OF INTEREST

Church of Saint Mary the Immaculate Heart (Iglesia de Santa María del Corazón Inmaculado): Dating to the nineteenth century, the Solar Catholic Church of Saint Mary the Immaculate Heart is one of the oldest surviving buildings in New Angeles. Built of stone in Gothic-Mudéjar style, Saint Mary is said to resemble the Cathedral of Ecuador in Quito.

Mercado Baja: The so-called Low Market is a long undercity street flanked by flickering neon signs and shops with bars across their windows. The commercial heart of Base de Cayambe, the Mercado Baja hosts hundreds of street vendors, almost all of whom are unlicensed or sell contraband. Just out of sight of the main street lie all the best brothels and stim-flops, and the entire row is in the grips of orgcrime.

RUTHERFORD

When anyone outside the borders of New Angeles thinks of the world's largest city, they think of Rutherford District. From the gleaming lights of Broadcast Square to the upscale markets of La Concordia, Rutherford is the cultural heart of New Angeles and, arguably, the planet Earth.

Rutherford's dozens of kilometer-tall arcologies are built on the lower slopes of the Andes with the Beanstalk looming large in the distance. The district is the picturesque exemplar of modern life. L-squares and slidewalks create a plaza level a variable altitude above the rough terrain where risties and tourists can stroll leisurely from arcology to arcology sipping YucaBean and enjoying the weather. Beneath the plazas lie Metro tubes, streets, access tunnels, and the *disenfrancistos*, as well as walking paths for androids and other second-class citizens. Above the plazas swarm the millions of hoppers that clog airspace all throughout New Angeles.

Rutherford has it all. The district's many arcologies include some of the most luxurious residences available, as well as housing for the middle class and (beneath the plaza level) those further down the economic ladder. Factories in the undercity produce modern clothing and consumer electronics. Theaters and entertainment complexes and shopping quarters attract crowds of consumers.

Holoparks and famous buildings bring in tourists. Financial and media corps employ hundreds of thousands of middle-class and ristie workers in towering offices. And of course, the criminal element and the off-gridders get by as best they can.

Jinteki and other corp prisec forces sweep the undercity routinely, keeping the clones relatively unmolested, the streetbangers well mannered, and the squatters out of the clone barracks.

POINTS OF INTEREST

Jinteki Biotech Headquarters: The Jinteki corporate headquarters were recently relocated from NeoTokyo to New Angeles. The new complex in Nihongai is not far from the Mache-Chindul Ecological Preserve. The Jinteki HQ is guarded by very expensive and dangerous security—even its airspace is controlled—but its famous gardens are opened to the public twice a year, once for New Year's Day and again for the Chairman's birthday.

Harmony General: Rivaled only by Hospital Alcivar in Guayaquil and the Levy University Medical Center in Laguna Velasco, Harmony General is the finest hospital in New Angeles. Operated by a Jinteki subsidiary, Harmony has access to the very best in biotechnology and genetic therapies.

LAGUNA VELASCO

Laguna Velasco District, also called the Government District, was built up on relatively unsettled wilderness surrounding Velasco Ibarra, a lake named for one of Ecuador's historical leaders. The central location and natural beauty of the region made Laguna Velasco attractive to early developers of New Angeles, and City Hall was moved here from Base de Cayambe within a few years of the city's formal creation.

To this day, Laguna Velasco remains a district peopled by the cream of the societal crop, including the very rich and political heavyweights. There are a large number of super-luxury arcologies for the corporate elite: self-contained high-rises for the upper class. The truly wealthy, though, the richest of the rich, maintain rambling mansions on acres of lakefront property. Quaint old Spanish Colonial–style houses with ultra-modern furnishings dot the lakeshore while glimmering spires of corporate arcologies rise from the water and the hills above.

For all its ostentatious glamour, however, Laguna Velasco's undercity is among the worst in the city, perhaps precisely because of the glamour. While organized crime elements are kept largely in check, the NAPD and prisec forces that patrol the district have a below-zero tolerance for lawbreakers or disorder of any kind. Squatters are forcibly relocated, petty criminals rousted, and those who fall behind on rent payments evicted with rapidity. The police are known to use force to keep undesirables out of the district, and the definition of "undesirable" at times appears to be whatever the NAPD and the city elite want it to be. *Disenfrancistos* in Laguna Velasco fear the NAPD at least as much as they fear the streetbangers elsewhere in the city.

POINTS OF INTEREST

Levy University: Levy University is consistently ranked as one of the world's top ten institutions of higher learning and has been for the past sixteen years. Although Levy University boasts one of the finest distance learning programs in the world, and students are able to attend classes virtually from anywhere, it also has a large and very busy campus in Laguna Velasco. LU has the

top Artificial Intelligence program in the world, one of the best Network Architecture departments, and a handful of mediocre sports teams.

City Hall: New Angeles City Hall is a hall in name only—it is actually a complex that covers several city blocks, all of which are linked by multiple skywalks and underground tunnels. City Hall has one of the largest non-corporate computer systems in the worlds, all hardened against EMP and protected by a combined force of NAPD, private security, and even military personnel. The tallest tower, right in the center, is the central administration building, and Mayor Ignacio Wells watches over the city from the upper levels.

New Angeles Police Department Headquarters: Although there are precinct houses throughout the city, the heart of the New Angeles Police Department is found one hundred meters offshore in the lake in Laguna Velasco. NAPD HQ is a tall, heavily fortified building, with extensive prisoner holding and processing facilities in the lower levels. The upper levels are devoted to administration, training, media relations, and the Cyber Bureau. The HQ also doubles as Laguna Velasco's primary precinct house, also called 1st Precinct.

MANTA

Stretching along over one hundred kilometers of beautiful Pacific coastline, Manta District is a mixture of high and low. It boasts a number of splendid beaches, luxurious resorts, and upscale attractions while also functioning as New Angeles' second-most-critical port and providing a solid middle-class living to untold millions of New Angelinos.

Close to the coast, Manta is dominated by the luxury tourism of its beaches and resorts or, in Antigua Manta and on the border with La Costa, by shipping, fishing, aquaculture, and associated industries. As the arcologies rise further inland, the luxury and industry both give way to middle-class hotels, residences, and offices. Finally, along the inland edge of the district lies low-income housing for the workers who maintain the resorts along the coast.

Although the public perception of Manta is as a ristie's playground, this is only partially true. It's true that spoiled rich kids from around the world congregate on its beaches, but Manta also has a sizable white-collar industry in information technology, research, and biotech. In fact, Haas-Bioroid's corporate headquarters is located on the Punta San Lorzeno in Manta.

Because of the beachfront nature of the district, plaza level in Manta is only a few meters above sea level. As a result, there is relatively little undercity in which to hide the *disenfrancistos* and lower classes, so Manta's diversity is relatively obvious even to the upper classes.

POINTS OF INTEREST

Haas Arcology: The Haas-Bioroid corporate headquarters is centered around the Haas Arcology on Punta San Lorenzo. Featuring the most advanced building AI in the world, the Haas Arcology is a marvel of modern technology, with every convenience

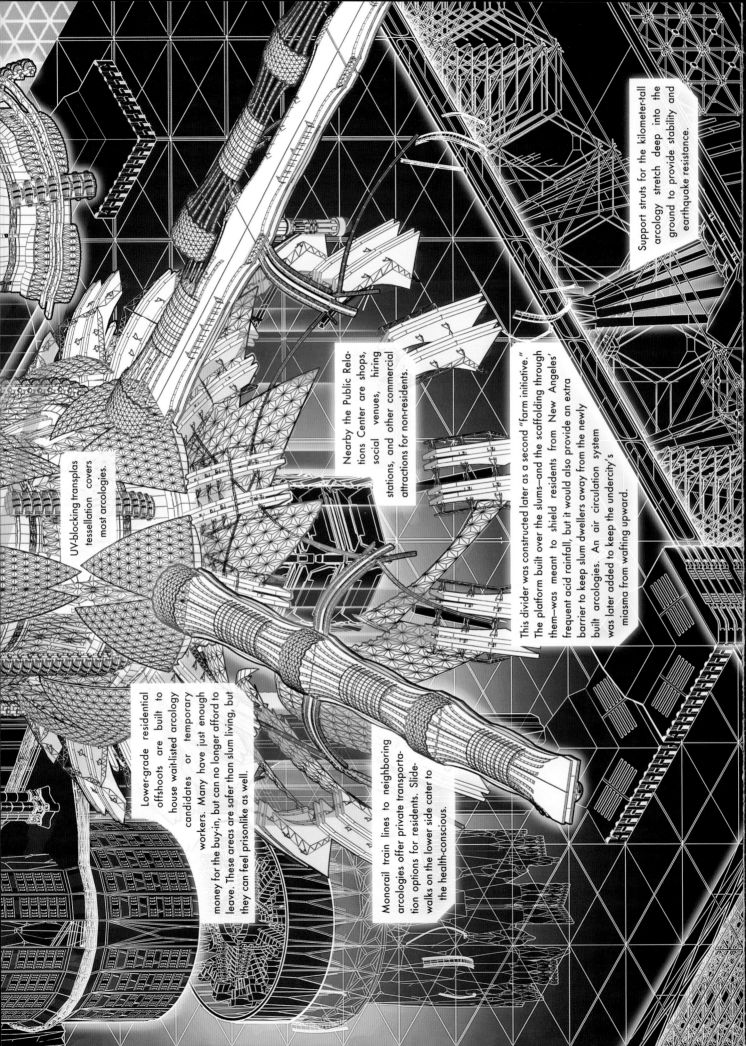

Support struts for the kilometer-tall arcology stretch deep into the ground to provide stability and earthquake resistance.

UV-blocking transplas tessellation covers most arcologies.

Nearby the Public Relations Center are shops, social venues, hiring stations, and other commercial attractions for non-residents.

This divider was constructed later as a second "farm initiative." The platform built over the slums—and the scaffolding through them—was meant to shield residents from New Angeles' frequent acid rainfall, but it would also provide an extra barrier to keep slum dwellers away from the newly built arcologies. An air circulation system was later added to keep the undercity's miasma from wafting upward.

Lower-grade residential offshoots are built to house wait-listed arcology candidates or temporary workers. Many have just enough money for the buy-in, but can no longer afford to leave. These areas are safer than slum living, but they can feel prisonlike as well.

Monorail train lines to neighboring arcologies offer private transportation options for residents. Slidewalks on the lower side cater to the health-conscious.

Kirsten Zirngibl

This is one of the rarer "bridge towers" that connects the upper levels to the subway system via a series of elevators. Contains high-security apartments and offices.

Historical housing projects from the middle of the twenty-first century still comprise a surprising percentage of the underlevels.

These hex-shaped apartment tubes used to be part of the first massive city-wide urban aquaponics initiative decades back. As the technology surpassed them, they slowly eroded into slums. New Angeles' massive appetite for housing has prevented them from being demolished.

Shipping containers have been piled onto old buildings to add floors or fill nooks and crannies in the slums. Each houses an average of four people.

POINTS OF INTEREST

Broadcast Square: An elevated square in the heart of the district, Broadcast Square forms the heart of the media industry in New Angeles. The arcologies surrounding the square—and for nearly a kilometer in every direction—are home to the city's most important communication corps. Vidscreens and virt projectors rise above the square itself, where the gaggles of pedestrians and tourists can see the latest streaming content from NBN and other media providers. For some reason this is considered interesting, even though all the same content could be accessed on any PAD.

Humanity Labor: New Angeles' biggest labor union and advocacy group is housed not far from Broadcast Square. In its blocky halls, Humanity Labor hosts job retraining workshops, contract negotiations, press conferences, union meetings, strategy conferences, and the thousand other functions of a major advocacy organization. There are even technicians and researchers working in the depths of the Humanity Labor building to develop new techniques for reaching workers and organizing protests on short notice. Accusations that Humanity Labor is little more than an elaborate front for the Human First extremist group are generally ignored.

New Angeles Stock Exchange: The NASX is housed in a massive beehive-shaped arcology of glass and steel, which is appropriate considering that it is normally buzzing with activity. As busy as the trading floor can be, where human stock brokers strike deals and yell dramatically to be heard, the true activity centers around the NASX mainframe. Nicknamed "the All-Seeing Eye" by traders, the orb-shaped mainframe is clearly visible from the trading floor behind a glass ceiling, theoretically so no one can tamper with it without being seen. Hundreds of weak-AI secretaries run on the mainframe and in the banks upon banks of servers elsewhere in the building, trading stocks at a rate no human brain could ever process. So rapid is the pace that companies pay a premium for cycles on the Eye itself and progressively less for hosting on servers further and further from the mainframe. The nanosecond lightspeed delay from a longer signal cable is enough to matter in the world of high-frequency AI stock trading.

ESMERALDAS

The northernmost province of New Angeles is Esmeraldas, named for the Ecuadorian city of the same name that remains the heart of the district to this day. In the years before the Project, the port of Esmeraldas was an important exporter of food across the region. As New Angeles' own consumption spiked, the Esmeraldas region surrendered most of its agricultural heritage to urbanization, but Esmeraldas made the transition away from its economic roots imperfectly.

Today, Esmeraldas is a comparative hinterland of New Angeles. Possessed of the third-most-important port, the second-most-essential agricultural hub, the third-most-productive industrial center, and a variety of also-rans in other categories, Esmeraldas is exceptionally unexceptional. On the poorer end, the district is often overlooked, a wide expanse of middle-class arks, modest shopping districts, and low-income towers.

When others discuss Esmeraldas at all, it is to mention the district's surprisingly vibrant culinary scene, its ever-evolving music community, and its enduring love affair with sports. A number of excellent football players have come from Esmeraldas, including "la Jefa" Rose Calderon, Captain of the first World Cup–winning United States mixed-sex football team.

POINTS OF INTEREST

Blue Sun Stadium: A fully modern multipurpose stadium renovated after the War, Blue Sun Stadium is home to the New Angeles Giants football team, the Yellowjackets baseball team, and the Swordfish American football team. Large and sophisticated, the stadium can host two major events at the same time and livestream them in threedee worldwide. The stadium is also fully equipped for the rising sport of holowar. It is capable of creating holographic battlefields and even enemies—either AI controlled or telepresent from other stadiums—for the no-contact simulated combat.

Eat Row: An infamously disreputable region of excellent reputation, Eat Row is a nightlife area that extends all the way to New Beach from the Apogee Arcology. It features a startling array of excellent and unpretentious restaurants in a wide variety of cuisines. Not trendy enough to attract slumming risties and not exclusive enough for the other kind, Eat Row is the middle-class hot spot of choice.

Roxy HT's Cabaret: The smoky, stylish nightclub preferred by noiries and trend-setters throughout the city, Roxy HT's melds retro charm with the hottest new acts of the moment. Roxy herself is a mysterious figure, appearing frequently to mingle with her guests, but coy about any personal details.

NIHONGAI

The Nihongai District is also called "Little Nippon" due to the large number of ethnic Japanese, both immigrants and native-born New Angelinos, who make their homes here. Many of these ethnic Japanese are employees of the Jinteki Biotech corporation, which is headquartered in the district.

Nihongai borders the Mache-Chindul Ecological Preserve, which although reduced from its initial scope remains a greenspace in the heart of the world's biggest city. Nihongai has many examples of natural beauty still preserved within its borders, either in gardens, small parks, or even incorporated into the district's beautiful arcologies.

Perhaps unsurprisingly, Nihongai is an expensive district in which to live. Densely populated and conveniently located near the financial center of Rutherford and the government center of Laguna Velasco, Nihongai is the premiere address for trendy young corporate up-and-comers.

Nihongai's undercity is heavily populated by clones and, perhaps as a consequence, surprisingly clean and well maintained.

computer controlled and optimized for maximum efficiency and convenience. The Haas Arcology includes the Haas Academy, living space for thousands of HB employees and their families, an exclusive rapid prototyping lab, and arguably the city's best neuromedical lab.

White Beach: The premiere beach among the elite, this season anyway, is Manta's White Beach. This two kilometer–long artificial beach is carefully groomed with pure white silica sand, and the water offshore is protected by an extensive system of filters out at the two hundred meter mark, removing algal blooms and other pollution. A system of tidal harnesses bleed power from the waves to keep White Beach's surf at an optimal level except during designated surfing events, when the stored energy is released to generate perfect crests, or during extreme weather, when the system cannot absorb all the extra tidal energy.

Sunken City: A relic of the twenty-first century's sea level rise, the Sunken City rests offshore, flooded and decaying. The term "Sunken City" is an overstatement, as it appears to have been a modestly sized town at best before the flood, but a few dozen structures do remain. Some lie completely beneath the waves, but others still stand above them. The crumbling towers of concrete and steel are now linked by crude bridges of rope and scavenged wood, the streets between them plied by pole barge. The residents of the Sunken City defy many laws and the constant peril of collapse and drowning to live there. Apparently, there are hundreds of people poor or desperate enough to brave the risks.

RABOTGOROD

Rabotgorod is a district struggling to escape from the legacy of its Project days. Back then, it was a pop-up city heavily peopled by refugees during the breakdown of the Russian Federation. The name, Rabotgorod, is derived from "Rabotnik Gorod," or "Worker's City," a legacy of the district's origins as a massive complex of worker's dormitories, but among the Russian diaspora the district is also known ironically as Dachagrad.

Today, Rabotgorod is also called "Robot City," a reference to the district's large android population. The old Project tenements have been converted to clone barracks, clone-tels, and bioroid storage to avoid the costly renovations needed to bring them up to code for human occupants. From Robot City, these androids travel to Quinde, La Costa, and elsewhere in the city to work their menial jobs.

Perhaps as a legacy of its time as a disenfranchised immigrant community, Rabotgorod has a strong orgcrime presence. Many of the landlords maintaining the android barracks also make their property available to the Mafiya and use their criminal connections to maintain control of Rabotgorod's political arena.

Northern Rabotgorod is richer and more prosperous, hosting some overflow prosperity from Laguna Velasco to the east and Manta from the west. Nevertheless, the northern area still maintains the relentless practicality and profit-mindedness that characterizes the rest of the district.

POINTS OF INTEREST

Atsuzawa Arcology: The glimmering spire of the Atsuzawa Arcology is one of the tallest buildings in New Angeles, and its distinctive profile is instantly recognizable to any New Angelino. It helps that none of the buildings nearby come close to its height, leaving Atsuzawa visible for kilometers in every direction, especially at night. Atsuzawa Arcology is variously cited as one of the "architectural triumphs of the last century" or "top blunders of the rich and famous," depending on one's point of view.

The Citadel of Starlight: The Citadel of Starlight is the largest and most modern religious facility in New Angeles as well as the world headquarters of the Starlight Crusade. Surrounded by spires radiating beams of light into the sky, its central tower gleams with tall illuminated windows. With no immediate hopper or tube-lev access, all visitors must cross the Cathedral's plaza and take in the view for themselves before entering the main worship hall or the offices, datacenters, and meditation chambers below.

LA COSTA

While the public conception of New Angeles is one of endless arcologies interspersed with decaying slums, this description does not match the modestly prosperous La Costa District. Stretching from the Pacific coast to the border with Ecuador, La Costa is less densely settled than most other districts and contains a fair number of orchards, farms, and towering agroplexes among its scattered residential neighborhoods and occasional small arks.

Ecuador's paradisiacal climate provides La Costa with unmatched fertility and a year-long growing season, making the farms of La Costa some of the most productive in the world. However, the economic realities of the city mean that as property values rise, there is a growing pressure to replace the farms with housing developments, commercial real estate, and, of course, the towering arcologies that define modern cities.

La Costa is the least populous district in New Angeles and contains the most undeveloped land, including two sizable ecological preserves. Economically, it is dominated by fish canneries and aqua farming along the coast, and by agriculture, gene-culture, and bioplastics inland.

POINTS OF INTEREST

Machalilla Park: Once an Ecuadorian nature preserve, Machalilla Park remains one of New Angeles' largest and most popular greenspaces. The interior is mostly wetlands, and visitors either travel on a system of elevated walkways or take tours by boat through its waterways. The park also extends considerably out to sea, providing a small coastal area free of commercial aquaculture or other development.

Memories of Green: A popular nightclub near the border of Rabotgorod, Memories of Green features a carefully maintained indoor greenspace and meticulously clean air. Although the greenspaces in New Angeles have done much to repair the ecological damage of the last centuries, acid rain and smog are still major problems, even in the fields of La Costa. Memories of Green claims to maintain the only pristine example of "the way things were."

QUINDE

Quinde is the most heavily industrialized sector of the city. Its factories produce many of the necessities of modern megapolitan life, from SYNC's Network infrastructure to Metro passenger cars. Access to cheap labor in the form of New Angeles' underclass and rising android population, as well as abundant cheap energy, make Quinde a net exporter and a major player on the world stage of industrial production.

Quinde is also a manufacturing hub for androids, both clones and bioroids. Brand new androids are said to walk out of the HB and Jinteki factory gates only to go across the street into another factory to claim the job of a human worker. Unsurprisingly, there is a strong undercurrent of anti-android sentiment in Quinde, where the erosion of the working class is felt the most keenly.

Quinde, once characterized by the explosive lushness of its equatorial climate, was heavily deforested during the buildup of New Angeles; its trees were cut to erect tenements in Rabotgorod, offices in New Los Angeles, and factories for the Project. Ultimately, those wooden buildings were themselves cut down to make room for plascrete and carbon steel replacements.

POINTS OF INTEREST

Jorge Quinde Station: The largest transit hub outside of Earth Station, JQ Station is a massive terminal for rail, tube-lev, and groundtruck shipping throughout the city. Incoming He-3 canisters arrive via tube-lev from the Beanstalk, and then either pass through JQ Station en route to the port at Manta or whiz directly to one of the city's fusion plants.

The Slammer: Advertising itself as a "hard-drinking bar for hard-working people," the Slammer is a humans-only drinking hole popular with Human First members and anyone who wants to get away from the district's large android population. The Slammer has no pretensions toward higher society: it claims no live music or artisanal microbrews. It does have many private and dimly lit corners, however, as well as a back room for illicit meetings and high-stakes poker games.

GUAYAQUIL

Guayaquil District covers the southern section of New Angeles, from the old Ecuadorian city of Guayaquil across to the western coast. In the days before the Project, Guayaquil was Ecuador's most populous city, already cosmopolitan and diverse. Now, Guayaquil District remains the most populous district in the city, although its aging infrastructure and comparatively remote location have conspired to make it relatively poor.

Antiguo Guayaquil lies in the shadow of more modern arcologies, its neighborhoods and buildings of years past falling into the undercity of today's New Angeles. Nuevo Guayaquil's plaza level is the district's new commercial center. Beyond the Río Daule (the district's eastern boundary) lies a ring of warehouses, unfinished or condemned towers, and outdated transit stations for old oil-breathing vehicles that have together become the most extensive slum in the city.

Kirsten Zirngibl

Even the massive arcologies of Guayaquil have a disreputable air. For some of Guayaquil's arks, only the upper levels remain habitable as the lower floors are gradually surrendered to the *disenfrancistos* and squatters. So long as the corps continue to shift their premises toward Rutherford, Laguna Velasco, Nihongai, or Manta, the entire district is engaged in a losing battle against economic entropy.

Given its state of physical, social, and economic disrepair, it should come as no surprise that Guayaquil has the highest crime rate in the city. Orgcrime controls the ports and has extensively infiltrated the financial center of the district. Entire sectors of Guayaquil are given over to gangs, and the locals have been known to rely on the streetbangers for protection and law enforcement, rather than the NAPD.

POINTS OF INTEREST

Barrio Las Peñas: Once the home of wealthy landowners, the Barrio Las Peñas remains one of the most iconic and recognizable areas in Antiguo Guayaquil. Although its gaily painted colonial homes were renovated and restored at the turn of the century, rising sea levels and arcology development have left the region fading into obscurity. Now Las Peñas is an aging neighborhood occupied only by those too stubborn to move away. There is some talk of having the area declared a historic district and restored, but the city is reluctant to bear the cost and the residents are reluctant to sell their land.

Jack Weyland Arcology: One of the first true arcologies built in New Angeles, the Jack Weyland Arcology stands in Nuevo Guayaquil and is surrounded by taller and newer buildings. Although it was the tallest building in the world (except for the Beanstalk) when it was built, the JWA's 1.1km is only average by modern standards. The Jack Weyland Arcology includes a plaza-level shopping center, several floors of small offices for independents, and several floors devoted to Weyland Consortium businesses. The tower is once again owned by the Consortium after changing hands several times over the past few decades. The uppermost levels include a hotel, the Palace at Guayaquil, and a mix of residential apartments growing increasingly expensive and luxurious as the floor number increases. Beneath the plaza level, the JWA is under persistent renovation, which in practice means that the deserted levels are a haunt for criminals and *disenfrancistos*.

HEINLEIN

The most remote district of New Angeles is also the largest in terms of land area. Heinlein, located on Earth's moon, is part of New Angeles primarily as a political fiction to tie its destiny to the Space Elevator.

Although it sends representatives to City Hall, Heinlein is functionally independent, with its district manager seldom consulting Mayor Wells or the rest of the city council before making decisions. This is perhaps an inevitable result of Heinlein's complete alienation from its sister districts on Earth. The other districts, after all, do not need policies on oxygen consumption or minimum radiation shielding. Heinlein's concerns could scarcely have less in common with the day-to-day business of the rest of the city.

Heinlein's independence is partly a reflection of the degree to which its district government is controlled by the mining bosses. Corporations such as Melange Mining and Alpha Prospecting are the de facto governments across much of the Lunar surface, and their dominance over Heinlein's politics and economy cannot be overstated.

POINTS OF INTEREST

Wyldside: Arguably the most infamous nightclub on the Moon, Wyldside is a hotbed of counterculture and youth rebellion. A new trend in genetic self-modification has arisen among its patrons, and so-called "Wylder" culture is gaining a foothold down-Stalk on Earth.

Apollo Solar Chapel: Possibly the largest devotional structure on the Moon, the Apollo Solar Chapel is an Order of Sol facility designed to accommodate worshippers of many faiths in an environment where space is at a premium. Christian, Jewish, Muslim, Buddhist, Hindu, and Gaian services are all held regularly, but the centerpiece is the non-denominational Solar Service led by the Chaplain on Saturday mornings.

> They say over a billion people live here, and I don't doubt it. It's big, it's sprawling, it's noisy, it's crooked as a politician's view of life, and, unfortunately, it's home.

James Ives

133

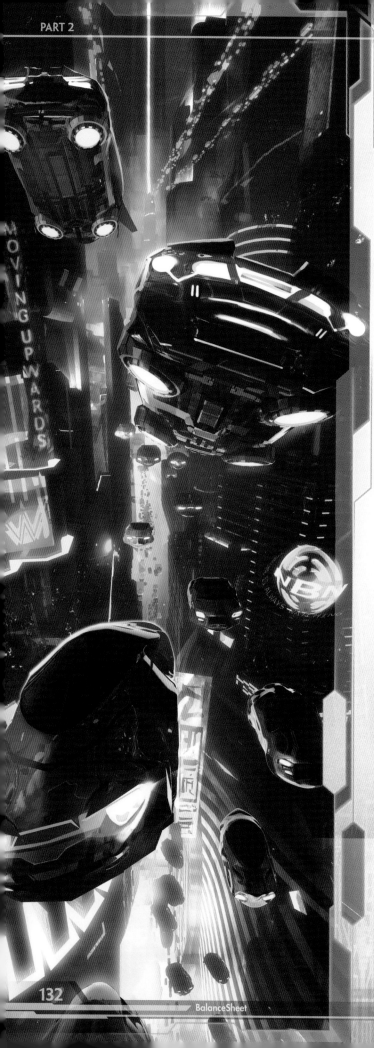

TRAVERSING THE DISTRICTS

New Angeles is a city bristling with vehicles, both public and private, and it has more registered vehicles than any other metropolitan area in history. Estimates on the number of unregistered vehicles inflate that number even higher, but there is no way for that number to be determined with any real degree of accuracy.

While yesterday's electric automobiles comprise a large portion of privately owned transportation in New Angeles, the city is known for its skylanes clogged by streams of hoppers, the flying cars that the world had long been promised. The term "hopper" is slang for skyhopper, a name derived from the vehicle's quick bursts of flight between charging pads. A short-duration hydrogen fuel cell powers the electromagnetic hoverfoil rotors for hours at a time. These cells are recharged by contact with landing pads in a process called "flash charging" that lasts only a second or two.

The New Angeles Transit Authority maintains a network of sophisticated guidance computers that coordinate the staggering number of hoppers that move throughout the city. Early in the city's history there were fewer flight-control regulated airspaces, which resulted in a series of fatal crashes that nearly ruined the hopper industry. Now, a carefully regulated system of aerial traffic lanes (better known as skylanes) and extensive use of the hopper's autopilot feature has created one of the safest travel networks in the modern world.

Despite the high ownership rate of private vehicles, most New Angelinos take advantage of the megacity's incredible public transportation system. The most significant of these systems is the tube-lev system, also known as the Metro. The Metro is a subterranean mag-lev train system that winds through vacuum tunnels deep below the surface at hundreds of kilometers per hour. Every day it moves hundreds of thousands of citizens, most of them middle and lower class, through the many stations dotting the metropolitan area and suburbs. The cost of maintaining the Metro is significant, but between ticket revenue and hopper registration fees, the New Angeles Transit Authority funds itself.

In addition to the tube-lev and the inordinate number of privately owned hoppers, the Skyway provides the public with access to hoppers in a very limited capacity. Using much larger hoppers than are typically possessed by private individuals, the Skyway offers rapid transit in between tube-lev stations for a nominally higher fee.

Shelly quickly plotted our route, using the emergency lanes provided for police and rescue units. The windshield lit up with control readouts showing power, wind direction, speed, GPS location, and a dozen other things. She moved the control stick and the hopper lifted from the building. She swung us around and slung us forward, lifting us above the northbound and southbound traffic lanes stacked beneath us.

Harris didn't even make it to his cubicle before his boss's voice thundered across the office. "Harris! Get in here!" He scurried to his desk in its sad grey cube, shucked his smartslick, dropped his PAD in its Faraday drawer, and slouched to the dragon's den.

The dragon was Vaishnavi Reyes, also known as Boss or Ms. Reyes, but never Navi. The entire Internal Accounts Receipts department lived in fear of her, Harris more than most.

"What is this?" She stabbed a finger at the pane of the holo display in front of her. In the gloom of her windowless office, the glimmering light of the virt shone brightly.

"I don't—"

"A time-off request, Harris? Sent it in on your tube-lev ride this morning, thought maybe you'd catch me by surprise?" She glared up at him as he shuffled in the doorway. The dragon kept an open-door policy, which as far as Harris could tell meant that the whole department could hear when she chewed someone out.

"No, Boss," he said. "I just found out. I need to take tomorrow and Monday off to go to my father's funeral."

"Tomorrow," said Reyes. "And Monday." Harris nodded. "In the middle of tax season? During an audit!?" She slashed her hand through the virt display before her. It dissolved in a yellow glimmer. "Do you like your job here at BE Finance, Harris?" The room darkened, the only light now coming in from the tinted transplas wall that divided her office from the cube-farm that was the rest of the department.

"Oh, yes, Boss," he said, nodding, lying. He was an accounts auditor, tracking credits through the internal departments of one of New Angeles' largest and least friendly financial corps. His job could literally be done by a computer program, and normally was, but the company liked having some meat brains audit the work of the AIs. So that was his day, every day, repeating work that had already been done faster and more efficiently by a program, checking the answers against what had come before. In his five years in the position, Harris had found two errors.

"Really?" The dragon leaned forward. "Because you seem uninterested in keeping it."

"It's bereavement leave, Ms. Reyes," he said, hoping using her name might appeal to something human within the dragon's breast.

"Leave must be submitted six weeks in advance, Harris!" No such luck, then. "This is BE Finance's busiest time. If you leave now, I will have to replace you. Now, think hard: do you really want me to find out how easy it would be to replace you?

"Your leave is not approved, Harris, and you're wasting valuable time here. Get back to work." She flicked one hand up in the air to conjure up another pane of her virt display and simultaneously dismissed Harris with the gesture.

When he got back to his desk he was sweating. He collapsed in his chair and called up his own virt display, pressing his palm against his workstation to let the desk's security check his biometrics.

The ferns along the edge of his cubicle parted, revealing his cube-mate and sometimes-best-friend, Muhammed. "Braving dragon's fire, my man," he said. "What's going on?" Ahmed was younger than Harris— taller, cooler, and more handsome, too—but he made up for all those sins by being quick to laugh and kind to his co-workers.

"My dad died last night," Harris said. "I just found out this morning."

"That's rough," said Muhammed. "When's the funeral?"

"Two days, but with travel—the funeral's back in Johannesburg, but I can't afford a sub-orbital flight, and there's time zones, too." He shook his head. "Might as well be in Heinlein. The dragon won't let me have the time off."

"No way, she can't do that. Bereavement leave is an exception, my man, you can take it. She can't stop you."

"She can replace me, though, she said." He sighed. "The dragon's been looking for an excuse to get rid of me for years. She made it pretty clear in there that if I leave, I shouldn't bother to come back. I can't lose this job, Muhammed."

"Why not? You're an accountant. That's a portable skill set. You could just get a job working for some other corp. Go to the funeral. You'll land on your feet if the worst happens."

"Maybe. If Reyes doesn't blacklist me out of annoyance. You don't get it, you're not married, you've got no kids. If I lose this job, I lose my corp housing. I lose my corp daycare. I lose my corp health plan. I forfeit my retirement plan. I lose my preferred rates at the corp store."

"Just until you land another gig."

"I have to have the other position lined up first! If I don't have a permanent residence, that's an automatic black mark in a background check." Harris shook his head, loosening his tie for some air. His heart raced faster and faster. "If I lose this job, I'll be a disenfrancisto in every way that counts. You ever hear of a disenfrancisto getting hired as an accountant?"

Silence. Muhammed vanished. Harris sank into his chair. His virt display showed an angry red icon—his biometrics had failed. He'd have to wait for the panic to pass before his desk would register him. Which meant that he'd be logged in late.

Muhammed stepped into Harris's cube and leaned against the wall. "Listen, man. What about Maria? She's got a job, right?" His joviality had evaporated. This was Muhammed the confidant, Muhammed the confessor.

"She's a teacher," Harris said. "She barely makes enough to—we wouldn't get far on her salary. And we certainly couldn't afford to live close enough to her school to…" He shook his head. "I can't go, Muhammed."

"Send her. On the day, I'll cover you for a few hours so you can take your PAD out of its drawer and go to the hopper deck up on 187 to be telepresent, at least."

"You'd do that?"

Muhammed nodded.

"Thanks. I don't know what to say."

"Hey, we gotta stick together, am I right? Someday you'll cover my ass with the dragon and we'll be even." He offered his fist, and Harris punched it weakly.

"I hate her. I hate her so much." Harris leaned back, checking his pulse. It was coming down. "Why do we have to live like this, live in fear all the time?"

"Hey, my man. You know how it is: the corp giveth, and the corp taketh away."

LIFE IN THE UNDERCITY

Not everyone in New Angeles enjoys the convenience of hoppers, the readiness of consumer goods around every corner, or the luxurious comforts of the vaunted arcologies. The true number of those living in the city's shadows eludes even the most comprehensive census attempts. Beneath the soaring starscraper arcologies and the veneer of flashing lights—in the lower strata of the sprawling urban landscapes—is the undercity. This hidden world teems with masses of people like an overwhelmed server.

Society inevitably leaves some falling between the plascrete cracks, and those in a place of power are content to overlook such parts of New Angeles. Without a registered electronic identification, a unique string of identifier letters and numbers assigned at birth, that person doesn't legally exist. Some of those who were born within the system have enough strikes on their background checks, or have been blacklisted, that their IDs have become worthless anyway. They are forced to live off the grid.

There are no jobs or ways for these, the lowest class of citizens, to climb up out of their squalor—none that are legal, anyway. Androids have become ubiquitous, taking even the dirtiest and most distasteful lines of work from blue collar laborers. Few business owners are willing to employ off-gridders in the face of steep penalties associated with illegal employees, which range from simple citations or fines to the revocation of a business's license to operate. Those who do employ off-gridders aren't the kind of people it's safe to work for: brothel proprietors, gambling bosses, and stim dealers treat employees with the same expendable behavior that monolithic corporations maintain for their own. All of these outfits, most of which have links to orgcrime, pay in cash, and a few extra bills can mean one more meal or a life-saving tithe to the right gang.

Most off-gridders spend their entire day in search of some food to steal or forage; they feed off the leavings of the upper classes. Constantly moving

from place to place, few have any possessions beyond what they can carry, and they rarely know a real home in the same sense that a citizen with an ID does.

Many undercity residents fall under the purview of one gang or another. Most are smart enough to stay clear of the bangers, but others are either pressed into membership or brought into the fold as willing accomplices who see it as their only chance at a decent life. Like warring tribes, the gangs fiercely control their territories without much—if any—regard for the well-being of their inhabitants. To escape the violence, off-gridders sometimes make their way upward, but if caught by the NAPD they're frisked and locked up on vague charges in the name of public safety. On rare occasions, private security forces or the NAPD make incursions into the lower levels and clear out the gangs for a few days at a time, but rival bangers return in force to duke it out over control of the newly vacant territory, no matter how small.

Aurore Folny

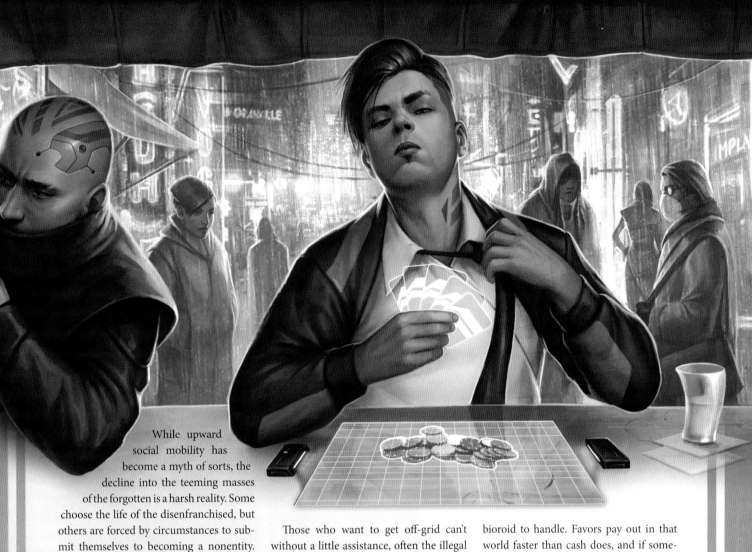

While upward social mobility has become a myth of sorts, the decline into the teeming masses of the forgotten is a harsh reality. Some choose the life of the disenfranchised, but others are forced by circumstances to submit themselves to becoming a nonentity. One lost job or one missed payment is sometimes all it takes to become so poor as to be forced out onto the streets below. For the children of insolvents on the run, growing up constantly on the move and without a cred to their name is the only option.

Those who want to get off-grid can't without a little assistance, often the illegal kind, since bounty hunters know where to look when an ID disappears. Some turn to orgcrime outfits like 14K or the yakuza and expect some genuine help. They end up working the cash jobs that are too cheap or dangerous to hire a clone or bioroid to handle. Favors pay out in that world faster than cash does, and if someone falls in debt for either of those, they go down below with even fewer options. The smart (and previously wealthy) ones pay what they can for help from a dedicated hacker—most of whom have already erased themselves. Living under the radar is still costly, though, and the money risties use to get off-grid helps fuel the crime that flourishes there.

D isenfrancistos *have a ton of reasons for abandoning the lush life, esé. If you're tired of the holos on every wall down the street, or of walking by people more plugged in to the Net than the world around them, there are people like you down in the undercity. Have you had too much of the grandstanding, cred-slicked tracks set up in the hack governments across the world to slide businesses around as they please?*

When you give up the products of a nihilist, consumeristic society you can slip the leash of the megacorps. Is that roof over your head worth sacrificing your privacy and rights for, even though that roof'll never be yours? Is it worth the soybeef tacos you have to borrow from tomorrow's paycheck?

I say no, compadre, *it isn't. Nobody has reign over me, banger or corp lackey—I do what I want. Is it dirty down here? Yes. Is it dangerous down here? Yes. Do I miss the ease of living above? Do I care? Some days more than others, but having liberty, esé, being able to choose—that's better than any stim or simsensie. I know what it means to me, but what's freedom worth to you?*

Say what you will of the corporate rat race and the devaluation of the common man, but at least in the bureaucratic gears above there's a roof over your head every night, a soft bed to fall into after a fourteen-hour day in the cube-farm, and the streetbangers are an Old Hollywood novelty, not a downright threat to deal with day in and day out.

NORTH AMERICA

For centuries, North America has been one of the centers of the world in terms of its political and social hegemony. Some say this is no longer the case, that ever since the Treaty of Heinlein the U.S. ceded its real power to New Angeles, but SanSan, BosWash, and ChiLo are still among the top megacities in the world today, with Mexico City and Toronto not far behind.

BOSWASH

BosWash surrounds the seat of federal power for the United States. Although the District of Columbia technically remains its own legal entity, this setup has become increasingly complex amid the conurbation of the Eastern Seaboard. From the islands around Boston to the dikes of New York, down the Delaware River to Philadelphia and Wilmington, and finally hopping over to Baltimore and Arlington, the areas comprising BosWash have been settled for several hundred years, and one can still pick out some old relics in the skylines of the respective cities. The westward and south-ward shift of power has not been kind to the region, however, nor has the two-meter sea level rise.

While BosWash has the same corporate and political struggles that characterize any metroplex (although probably more of the latter and less of the former than most), an atmosphere of artistic inclination and appreciation pervades BosWash and its suburbs. There's no shortage of museums and galleries open to the public, many of which contain some of the country's most historically significant documents and pieces of art. There, it's considered a sign of social status to support the arts. As a result, the city is a tourist's paradise, with every conceivable form of art available to be enjoyed 365 days a year. While certain districts are more devoted to traditional arts than others, some of the most unusual draws are the theater districts that boast live simsensie performances in which the viewers can "inhabit" the on-stage actors in a full-immersion experience.

Emilio Rodriguez

CHILO

Rumors say that the first mayor of ChiLo, Szymon Giordano, got his start as the kingpin of the Chicago Outfit at the turn of the century. As he expanded his territory to include Saint Louis, he proposed linking the two cities in what was supposedly an attempt to make the Midwest competitive again in light of the success of SanSan on the West Coast and BosWash on the East. Perhaps the local politicians were in his pocket, or maybe the people of Illinois and Missouri truly believed in his vision, but the two cities were eventually incorporated under a new name: ChiLo.

Of course, the new designation didn't change the fact that the area between the metroplexes, primarily farmland, was undergoing its own economic collapse as the rise of agroplexes made traditional farming less and less profitable. Mayor Giordano organized an immigration incentive program to help the nascent megacity grow its way out of its economic troubles. This program, whose modest successes kept ChiLo alive, still exists in a modified form today. It is said that anyone with enough

credits can buy citizenship within the city, even rogue clones. As a result, many clones speak of ChiLo as a promised land of freedom, a place where they can integrate more readily with the existing population and even receive a legal ID. Liberty has its costs, however, and many clones have ended up living in slapdash housing projects shoddily assembled by corrupt construction companies linked to orgcrime. Those same orgcrime groups maintain control over many immigrant communities, but that hasn't stemmed the flow of aspiring androids looking for a fresh start.

SANSAN

The SanSan metroplex stretches across the Californias, spanning the length between the former cities of San Francisco and San Diego. Although the mega-quake known as "the Big One" forever changed SanSan's landscape and surrounding coastline, the city took advantage of the opportunity to reinvent itself. Now, SanSan symbolizes technological innovation and discovery, which made it the obvious choice for the next host of the World of Tomorrow expo.

The Californias, and SanSan, still stand out as a center of innovation, a trend-setter in North America. In Biotech Valley, new technologies are pioneered every day. Oaktown is a worlds leader in cybernetics design and manufacture, as well as a cultural epicenter of the latest cybernetic fashions, nicknamed "Chrome City." Old Hollywood remains the worlds' preeminent media producer, home to such companies as Haarpsichord Studios and many of the planet's most famous actors, vactors, and sensie stars.

Still, the city has its darker side, and large swathes of the Californias were never rebuilt after the Big One. Millions of citizens travel up and down SanSan using the mag-lev train that runs from Fog City to Tijuana, but millions of others live beneath the tracks in the slums or even in the collapsed caverns beneath, where gangs like Los Muertos enforce their own brand of justice. Amid the violence black markets flourish, and many Netcriminals dwell in the twisting wreckage of "the Underway."

SOUTH AMERICA

South America is currently enjoying a renaissance of prosperity and influence. There can be little doubt of New Angeles' dramatic effect on the development of its neighbors; New Angeles' ceaseless demand for goods and services sparked a brisk revitalization in Ecuador, Colombia, and Peru. While New Angeles is the undisputed leader in the region, Brazil's rise as a superpower in the decades prior to the War has also affected all the major Latin American urban centers.

BRAZIL

Brazil is unquestionably the largest and wealthiest nation in South America, and it has a disproportionately large number of difficulties as well. The slash-and-burn reaping of the Amazon rain forest that took place in previous generations, despite having finally halted, stripped the country of many natural resources and much biological diversity. The Amazon Industrial Zone that rose out of the ashes has been

a major economic powerhouse for the region, but pollution and the economic welfare of its employees remain concerns for the Brazilian government.

Even more significant, however, is the status of androids within the country. When Brazil was struggling to stem the rampant corruption and poverty in its society, the pan-religious organization Order of Sol rose as a mitigating factor for these evils. This eventually won the Order a place in Brazil's political process and in the hearts of the people. The Order of Sol possesses an unprecedented level of power in Brazil, and its mission to protect human rights extends even to androids, whom it holds to be human beings. Jinteki and Haas-Bioroid are prohibited from selling clones and bioroids within the country's borders, and androids are emancipated upon crossing the border. The megacorps deny that android immigration is a problem at all; their products undergo extensive quality assurance testing that minimizes

obedience issues. Nevertheless, corporate private security forces are sometimes spotted along the Brazilian border.

Brazil's anti-android policies have strained relations with the Big Four and—by extension—Brazil's fellow superpower, the United States.

ECUADOR

Of all the nations affected by the rise of New Angeles, Ecuador's relationship with Earth's largest city is the most complex and most integrated. Fully one quarter of the nation's former area was subsumed by New Angeles, but Quito maintains a very friendly and open relationship with the megacity. The border between the two polities is lightly secured, principally via the Network, and most citizens cross between Ecuador and New Angeles with no more fuss than walking across a street. The open border means that much of New Angeles' wealth is shared with its many suburbs in Ecuador, and the income from Weyland's initial purchases and the subsequent lease to the United States has been put to good use by the Ecuadorian government. The nation's infrastructure and standard of living have seen much improvement in the eyes of the average Ecuadoran citizen.

However, there are still many who feel that Ecuador made a bad deal. The most prosperous Ecuadorian cities and economic centers—and their tax income—were lost in the lease. If only Ecuador had kept Guayaquil, Santo Domingo, Manta, or others, they argue, the country could have realized even more development and might not have slid so far in the shadow of the U.S. territory. Such critics believe New Angeles should revert to Ecuadorian control sooner rather than later.

COLOMBIA

Other than Brazil and Ecuador, the South American nation that has undergone the most significant upheaval since the construction of New Angeles is Colombia, which borders Ecuador to the north. In previous generations, Colombia was most notable for its notorious corruption by various drug cartels. Many regarded it as the capital of the international drug trade, due in large part to the vast fields where illegal drug crops were cultivated in enormous quantities.

As global society has advanced, however, synthetic drugs have become vastly more common than naturally grown alternatives, and in some cases electronic stimulation (known as e-Pharms) has replaced recreational pharmaceuticals altogether. Ironically, the criminals who once ruled the land with an iron fist have been forced out of power by new cartels, this time made up of farmers and agricultural managers. The fertile lands that once grew drugs now grow g-modded crops like coffee, soybeans, and maize, the majority of which is sold to New Angeles at an extremely profitable rate. The expatriate drug lords, however, continue to plague the surrounding area under the guise of Los Scorpiones.

EUROPE AND CENTRAL ASIA

Europe is in a prolonged period of decline compared to its dominance in prior centuries. Atlantica and Scandia struggle to keep themselves from sliding into a complete collapse after the ravages of war and austerity. Bright spots include the Ruhr Valley and PraNo, whose primary assets remain their human resources (with a comparatively good educational base) as well as the centuries of history and culture of which their citizens remain so proud.

However, economic, environmental, and political turmoil has kept the European Union weakened, and even the megalopolitan reforms have done little to correct the matter. Europe no longer dominates the worlds, and the continent lives in the shadow of New Angeles and the rising superpowers in the Southern Hemisphere.

ATLANTICA

The loose conglomeration of former megacities known as Atlantica stands as a stark reminder of the Europe-that-was. After living beyond its means for too long, the northern countries of the European Union were ill equipped to deal with the weakening of the North Atlantic Current brought on by climate change. In the aftermath of economic and environmental decline, huge stretches of urban development surrounding the English Channel were abandoned or neglected, from Paris to London to Brussels and the zaratan offshore colonies in between. Skyscrapers decay into ruin, dried-up rivers serve as meager farm fields, and municipalities struggle to provide even basic services like water and power to their residents. The introduction of androids has only exacerbated the situation for the region, and mass unemployment remains its most difficult hurdle to recovery.

Meg Owenson

MEDITERRANEAN FAILED STATES

Once considered the cradle of human civilization, the Mediterranean and Fertile Crescent have for centuries been wracked by conflict and economic instability. The region is still an important crossroads of trade between Europe, Africa, and Asia, but its fortunes have been devastated by the triple calamities of climate change, petroleum's obsolescence, and war.

In the aftermath of the Oil Wars at the turn of the twenty-first century, Persia and its allies founded a new empire that stretched from Nubia through the Levant and east to the edge of what would become the Indian Union. Dubbed the United Crescent, it achieved relative peace and stability for decades. By attracting the intelligentsia from Europe and Russia, the U.C. was able to become one of the major players in the helium-3 boom on the Moon.

Ultimately, the U.C. struggled to defend its interests on Luna, but not before incurring significant debts and casualties, and the region has yet to recover. Many of its countries are now tyrannical despotisms, corrupt corporate oligarchies, or war-riven failed states. For mercenaries and prisec contractors, the Mediterranean is as rich with opportunity as Mars and far closer to home.

NORTHERN ASIA

Despite existing in an age so rife with technology, the area comprising the former Russian Federation is an anachronism that struggles to enter the modern era. The collapse of the fossil fuel–based economy dealt a serious blow to the country's coffers. The country's oligarchs, who were also the wealthiest and best educated, fled to other parts of the world for fear of reprisal from the lower classes. Skilled and enterprising Russians had already left for New Angeles, Brazil, Heinlein, and other booming economies. Together, the mass emigrations constituted appreciable brain drain on the region, and when the the Worlds War exacerbated deteriorating economic conditions, the federal government in Moscow collapsed.

Individual oblasts, republics, and *krais* took control for themselves in the ensuing chaos, which led to the rise of many independent countries including the Siberian Republic, Chechnya, Tatarstan, and the metroplex of New Moscow. These newly autonomous states have done what they can to continue exporting heavy industry such as mining, metal working, and forestry, but they must import most higher-level technologies and electronics. Any arable portion of the region has been given over to large-scale farming, which—thanks to global warming—is a greater percentage than it had been in previous centuries.

Before the Russian Federation fell apart, however, the country sent a series of colony ships to Mars. The Aelita Colony has flourished in recent years and managed to retain its identity as an ethnic Russian enclave, one led by a charismatic leader who claims to be a descendant of Catherine the Great. This woman, Yelizaveta Volkova, has begun to call for a campaign to retake the Motherland on Earth and return it to its former glory. This movement has received backing from various shadowy corporations and support from a handful of former Russian oblasts, but the threat of a renewed Martian "invasion" has put many U.N. member states on edge.

SOUTHEAST ASIA

Southeast Asia was spared the economic drain felt by its eastern neighbors during the War, but the sea level rise affected coastlines throughout the region. Now, Singapore competes as one of the potential sites of the second space elevator, the Indian Union remains the largest democracy in the world, and the ASEAN Confederation continues to wield considerable economic influence in the Eastern Hemisphere.

MUMBAD

The Mumbad metroplex in India is one of the few cities in the world that can rival New Angeles in sheer size. When the cities of Ahmedabad and Mumbai combined after the Troubles, a new political center was created in Surat as a compromise.

The megacity was able to finally recover from the Troubles thanks to the booming arms industry during the War. Since then, some Indians have profited immensely through the rebuilding efforts, but the recent influx of simulants into the labor market further depressed the opportunities and quality of life for Mumbad's poorest.

The wealthiest citizens in the Mumbad megapolis lead lives of luxury so distant from those of the lowest classes that it is difficult to describe the dichotomy in words that both groups can understand. The upper class of India maintains an extravagant and wasteful lifestyle, though in most ways, they are no different from any other country's risties. Sprawling mansions, private islands, luxury hoppers, and one hundred-foot motorsailers are commonplace among the elite. Nowhere is this more apparent than on Salsette Island, the original island from which Mumbai spread. The wealthiest inhabitants of the oldest and most powerful families in Mumbad still work, play, and conduct business here.

While the Indian megacity has a number of its own powerful corporations, none of them can operate on the same scale as the Big Four in New Angeles. Many of the most powerful corporations enjoy a close relationship with the Indian Union government, and with high tariffs on many different types of imported goods, there are more small companies that thrive in India than anywhere else in the world.

India is an expert at improving on and producing consumer goods. Assembly line technology has been refined to such an extent that fifty thousand PADs are created every hour at the Aryabhata Tech manufactory in the Gujarat District of Northern Mumbad. There are also over a dozen smartfabric firms within the city, and new smartfabric capabilities are constantly developed and tested locally before going worldwide.

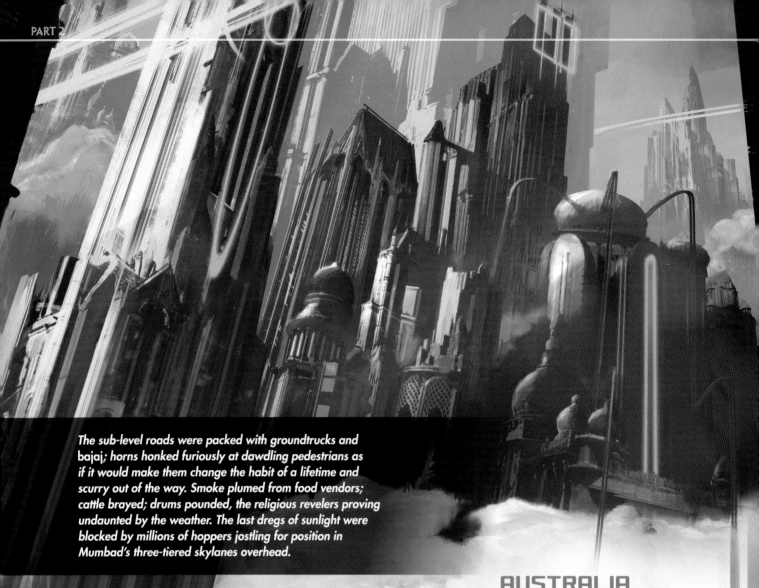

The sub-level roads were packed with groundtrucks and bajaj; horns honked furiously at dawdling pedestrians as if it would make them change the habit of a lifetime and scurry out of the way. Smoke plumed from food vendors; cattle brayed; drums pounded, the religious revelers proving undaunted by the weather. The last dregs of sunlight were blocked by millions of hoppers jostling for position in Mumbad's three-tiered skylanes overhead.

The artistic and cultural center of Mumbad—and of India itself—is the Kala Ghoda District. Untold numbers of museums, galleries, universities, libraries, and restored threedee theaters, as well as many of the oldest and most important cultural artifacts from India's history, are located within its borders. It is also the headquarters to a growing movement of civil unrest; many down-on-their-luck students and artists are drawn to the nightly populist rallies outside the Old Courthouse building.

Navi Mumbai is home to Harishchandra Entertainment, one of the preeminent simsensie companies in the world and first to popularize the technology in India. The area has a strong org-crime presence, as many entertainment ventures are funded by "black money" as part of laundering schemes. Although 14K has a presence in Mumbad, the preeminent orgcrime outfits have links to Dubai or Pakistan. The top gangster in Bollywood is Ibrahim Salem, a man who enjoys profitable relationships with Afghani and Pakistani opium dealers, Harishchandra, a dozen lesser studios, and human and android trafficking rings in Dubai, China, and Old Pakistan. Many Bollywood actors, producers, and directors live in fear of Salem and other orgcrime leaders, who routinely extort money and favors from the Bollywood entertainment elite.

AUSTRALIA

If corporate maneuvering is a regular problem in the megacities of the worlds, Australia is one country where it has been less problematic. Fusion power solved the inefficiencies of desalinization and enabled mass-irrigation, which allowed Australia and other previously arid countries to become known as "the breadbasket of the world." Over the past few decades, Jinteki has been acquiring control of the agroplexes there, but it did so with the cooperation of the Australian government rather than despite it. The regional head of Jinteki's operations in Australia is a former member of the Australian Parliament who migrated into corporate politics, and his long-standing alliances with other MPs have made the corp-state relationship a relatively harmonious one. Many other nations look to Australia's relationship with Jinteki with admiration, jealousy, or sometimes outright condemnation.

Zach Graves

EAST ASIA

The War left deep scars in East Asia that are still borne by its economy. China was one of the primary belligerents in the conflict following the Lunar Insurrection, while Japan supported Jinteki's efforts on Mars. Long-simmering tensions flared during the conflict, resulting in some isolated battles fought Earth-side in the region. Reconstruction in Asia has been extremely profitable for the corps, especially in the new nation of United Korea.

CHINA

In previous generations, many thought that China would emerge as the great power of the next age. While China does possess considerable economic clout due to its extensive and prodigious manufacturing capabilities, the nation's rising star seems to have reached its zenith and might now be descending. China was one of the countries hardest hit by the Blackout, and the subsequent overreaction by the national government only exacerbated the situation. Their infrastructure and economy greatly lagged behind other countries that adopted SYNC's new Network from the beginning. The birth of New Angeles and the construction of the Space Elevator refocused many global interests on South America, and the prosperity promised by Xiangong Inc. was dashed during the fighting on Luna. Today, China's three megacities—New Beijing, Shanghai, and Hong Kong—produce only a small fraction of the goods and services consumed around the world.

JAPAN

The NeoTokyo megapolis is a massive city that covers nearly seven prefectures and has disproportional control over the Japanese national legislative body, the National Diet. Despite having moved its headquarters to New Angeles, Jinteki and its affiliated corporations maintain a strong presence in the NeoTokyo region, as does the yakuza. It comes as no surprise then that clones outnumber bioroids two to one in NeoTokyo's service sector, especially when considering the government's protectionist trade policies. Although New Angeles and Mumbad undoubtedly have the largest android populations by raw numbers, NeoTokyo has the highest per-capita android population, and it is hard to go anywhere in the megacity without running into the same familiar face over and over.

Several hundred kilometers west-southwest of NeoTokyo's outermost boundaries, the rival city KyoSaka extends from the northern coast of Japan in the Kyoto Prefecture all the way to the south through the Osaka and the Wakayama prefectures, as well as portions of two others. The ancient capital houses many of Japan's cultural treasures, but most people across the worlds equate KyoSaka with a robust entertainment district known to be a favorite haunt of celebrity megagroup Aphelion.

The two urban centers are rivals culturally, politically, and in neobaseball leagues. The people of NeoTokyo are generally described as cold and standoffish, while the citizens of KyoSaka are more outspoken and fiery in temperament. These stereotypes are used by both sides use to criticize the other. The games pitting the Jinteki Hanshin Tigers against the Mitsutendo Giants are the most-watched programming in Japan. Riots have been known to erupt following the loss or win of one side or another, which only fuels the antagonism. The rivalry is unlikely to die down anytime soon.

Emilio Rodriguez

AFRICA

The African continent is emerging as a global power. Long exploited by colonial powers, by the middle of the twenty-first century Chinese and American firms competed for control of Africa's supply of platinum and rare earth metals for cutting-edge electronics. But with the advent of asteroid mining, Africa's natural resources dropped in value on the world stage, leading to a large-scale abandonment of the Sub-Saharan regions of the continent by foreign corps and investors.

Abruptly, the major powers in Africa were local for the first time in generations. Nigeria, Soufrika, and the United Crescent flexed their economic muscles and set about extending their hegemony across the continent. Old ethnic and religious tensions complicated the process, but the creation of the Sub-Saharan League enabled African nations to engage in relatively "peaceful" trade and mutual cooperation. Nevertheless, Nigeria and Soufrika waged silent, bloody, guerrilla war across the continent, peaking in the Bukavu Incident (although the parties responsible were never identified). In the wake of the tragedy, new policies in the Sub-Saharan League restored a degree of autonomy to member states.

While the United Crescent was focused on cementing its new empire, this presented Africa an opportunity for long-simmering tensions to explode into war. Climate-ravaged regions of the Kalahari and Congo, where millions of displaced refugees fled starvation, became flash points for armed conflict between Nigeria, Soufrika, proxy powers, and independent militias. Nigeria hoarded its hyper-efficient solar power tech and desalination-irrigation zones, giving Soufrika the leverage it needed to turn several League nations against Nigeria. Meanwhile, Soufrika's close relations with unpopular megacorps allowed Nigerian agents to stir up unrest within their rival's borders. Ultimately, peace resulted from trade agreements where Nigeria would share its wealth and Soufrika would support an African space elevator.

Now that Africa is thriving, it has attracted the attention of the megacorps once more as a large and wealthy consumer base. With few androids on the continent and the rise of solar farms in the ever-expanding deserts, Africa boasts near energy-independence and a comparatively prosperous middle class. For now.

ANTARCTICA

Rising global temperatures and sea levels changed the face of Antarctica, but there remain few reasons for anyone to travel there. The current population of Antarctica remains a mystery, yet numerous corporate research compounds dot the barren landscape.

Some islands along the Antarctic Peninsula have become more hospitable thanks to global warming. Survival there is difficult at best, but the ability to live without a national government hanging overhead has serious appeal to certain types of people. These islanders have come to refer to themselves, half-jokingly at first but now with increasing seriousness, as the People's Republic of Antarctica. The existence these people lead is one of very few amenities and a techno-primitivist lifestyle that involves the cultivation of their own foods and livestock.

KAMPALA RISING

The plan to create a second Beanstalk in Kampala, one free from control by the Weyland Consortium, has been understandably controversial. There's more than enough demand to justify a second Beanstalk—the numbers released by the Space Elevator Authority are staggering—and Weyland stands to lose a tremendous amount of profit if it is no longer the gatekeeper to space.

Although Weyland has kept the blueprints for the original Beanstalk secured within impenetrable datafortresses, various independent scientists are well on their way to unlocking the secrets of the buckyweave tether. The only remaining component would be the massive funding required to continue construction in earnest.

China has long been a partner in African development. If New Beijing is able to furnish the funds to support the project, it would be a coup for the countries who claim the Space Elevator Authority continues to discriminate against corps and countries who criticize the U.S. and its allies. When this financing is coupled with the investment anticipated to come from Nigeria, Soufrika, and the rest of the Sub-Saharan League, the economics of the project become vastly less difficult than previously imagined.

Besides the obvious advantages for countries who have felt shut out by the Beanstalk, would erecting another space elevator be as beneficial to the region as people think? Kampala would benefit, obviously, because there's simply no outcome other than the birth of a new megapolis to host the massive structure. Any endeavor of that scope would require immense external influence, however, and while the Ugandan government is liable to profit from the increased trade, it might not be able to maintain control over the growing megacity.

Some public relations firms involved in the endeavor have claimed that another Beanstalk would vault Africa ahead of other continents. But it could also mean an even sharper divide between the continent's wealthy and its poor. The construction of the megacity (and the second Beanstalk itself, for that matter) would require a significant supply of resources, and resources are something that Africa tends to have in abundance. However, even if resources are sourced locally, it's possible Kampala would see a great deal of profit in the hands of a very small number of people, as is often the case around the globe.

Regardless of the hurdles, the second Earth Station is already under construction as a floating structure on Lake Victoria along the equator. The island base would provide the necessary leeway and stress reduction on the structure itself during operations, while mag-lev and hopper lines could connect it to the rest of the city. How long until a tether rises up from this base? Perhaps sooner than we thought.

– From the lectures of Dr. Lucas Martinez, Levy University, Modern History 401

"The second Earth Station is already under construction as a floating structure on Lake Victoria..."

Kirsten Zirngibl

143

EXPLORING THE SOLAR SYSTEM

Manned space travel has come a long way since the Vostok and Mercury capsules that first took humanity into space. Modern spaceships, built by the likes of the Weyland Consortium, Pegasus Aerospace, TransOrbit, and Korolev Ltd., are produced in a wide variety of sizes and styles—from small, one- or two-man runabouts to sleek passenger ships, from military dropships to massive, rugged long-haul freighters lumbering their way to Mars. Despite their many differences, every spaceship shares a number of common core systems: those for power, thrust, protection, and environmental support.

We're no longer limited to one world. The Space Elevator gave us a road to the stars, and innovations in electric propulsion, radiation shielding, and allied technologies will get us there safely. We now have a permanent presence outside of Earth, and we're just getting started.

— Jack Weyland, "Because We Built It"

Modern spacecraft are constructed in orbit at a number of large corporate and governmental shipyards orbiting Earth and Luna. Each one is a hive of activity. Among their many slips, engineers oversee construction from the safety of the dock interior, and androids crawl across skeletal keels and half-finished ship hulls. The vast majority are strictly space-going vessels with no transatmospheric capabilities. Besides specially designed dropships, most travel or shipping from Earth into orbit is done through the Beanstalk. As such, ship designers are not constrained by the need for aerodynamics or the strength to endure the rigors of lift-off or re-entry on Earth, and those ships that are built for planetary landings have only the far shallower gravity wells of Luna or Mars to contend with.

Power for drives and internal systems is commonly provided by either super-efficient solar arrays and high-capacity energy storage banks, or miniaturized fission reactors. Recent breakthroughs in nuclear sciences have led to the development of small, safe, high-output fusion reactors, which are slowly catching on among aerospace design and engineering firms. These reactors allow ships to operate further away from the sun and for longer durations than those powered by solar collectors. Fusion reactors also enable a ship to mount more powerful drive systems and travel greater distances at incredible speeds.

Drives, the massive and powerful thrusters that provide a spaceship's propulsion, are another standard and required system. While the reliable meta-fueled rockets are still in use, especially on older ships and short-range shuttles, these outdated systems have largely been eclipsed by ion and plasma drives. By producing thrust via accelerated ions or concentrated plasma, they provide cheap, efficient, and reliable thrust, and they require only fuel and an electrical power source to operate. These main drives are typically backed up by smaller, adjustable, high-output maneuvering thrusters such as colloid thrusters scattered around a ship's hull to provide attitude control. As technology advances, new and exotic drive technologies continue to be developed. Among the most promising of these new technologies is the outlandish nanoparticle field extraction thruster, which produces thrust via charged particles composed of carbon nanotubes. Developing systems like the nanoparticle field extraction thruster will power the next generation of deep space exploration ships and will open up even the farthest reaches of the solar system to human exploration and habitation.

Onboard life support and flight control systems vary by manufacturer, but they share a number of common, industry standard technologies. Most ships are partially or fully pressurized, with oxygen provided either by onboard storage tanks or "oxygen crackers" which produce oxygen by converting water into oxygen and hydrogen gas. Used air is recycled and cleaned via a series of electrical and physical filters called "scrubbers," and little of it goes to waste.

Guidance and sensor systems are similar to those found on aircraft. When paired with cameras and radiation, gravity, and light sensors, radar and lidar provide a constant, real-time view of space surrounding the ship. Spaceships also have a powerful, long-range comms system that maintains a voice and data connection to the various traffic control centers, such as the Heinlein Authority at Starport Kaguya, as well as a transponder that constantly broadcasts the ship's registry and identification on a public frequency. Less scrupulous ship captains, such

Mark Molnar

LUNA

The history of Luna is a story of war and greed, but also one of hope and rebirth. After humanity took its first tentative steps onto the Lunar surface, no one returned to the Moon for a long time. They did send robots; these rovers didn't even have weak AI and so had to be remotely controlled. The rock samples the rovers took confirmed there was a lot of helium-3 on the Moon, but fusion technology was still in development. Various countries sponsored scientific missions to the Moon, some of which were manned, and eventually some of these missions evolved into permanent research stations.

At first these settlements, separated by hundreds of kilometers, were places of scientific endeavor and experimentation. Travel to the Moon was still expensive and difficult; only the best and brightest were allowed a place within the slowly growing Lunar populations. In the mid- to late-thirties, after construction on the Beanstalk was completed, the first real habitats began to appear. The Space Elevator had slashed the costs of transporting goods and people into space, and it opened the way for rapid expansion of the Lunar settlements. Xiangong, Tranquility Home, and Leonovsk Station were the largest of these burgeoning colonies.

Soon, helium-3 fusion reactors became a reality. With Earth's new and ravenous appetite for this fuel, everything changed. Mining corporations from across the globe moved into the colonies and focused their efforts on how to successfully mine and refine the mineral. Dozens of mining outposts sprang up in regions where the regolith was dense with He-3. Each of these outposts was claimed and protected by private security forces, intimidation, and thinly veiled threats backed up by each corp's parent country in the name of "protecting strategic interests."

Tranquility Home, built protectively by the Americans around the site of the Apollo 11 landing, gave birth to the city of Heinlein. Almost two thousand kilometers away amid the Sea of Storms, China's Xiangong City also prospered, growing on the back of cheap labor brought up via the Space Elevator. The Indian Union, Russia,

THE PEOPLE OF LUNA

Unlike possibly any city on Earth, the Moon's population is completely transplanted from elsewhere. There were no natives to displace, no nearby cities to attract immigrants, and no centuries of human migration patterns to influence the population. Luna is relentlessly, explosively diverse, with every race and ethnicity represented.

The first colonists were members of the international space exploration effort, which meant they were from rich countries that could afford a space program. But as soon as the corps got a foothold, they started bringing up anyone who was willing to work in the mines—in other words, people from poor countries with weak economies. The end result is that any given Loony could have ancestors from anywhere on Earth. American is the majority language in Heinlein, but it's most people's second language.

Most Loonies are still immigrants, the people who didn't quite fit in on Earth, like in the stories. But there are more and more native-born Loonies, people who've never been to Earth and don't necessarily want to go. The next generation or so should be real interesting…

the United Crescent, and others were also hungry for the fuel to power clean fusion energy and its attendant profits, spawning settlements of their own.

The Weyland Consortium's construction companies helped build the colonies while the megacorp itself grew rich off the Beanstalk royalties from the importation of He-3. Weyland chose not to take sides among the mining concerns, profiting equally from the competition between companies and the governments that backed them.

During this time, numerous private concerns also established a presence on the Moon. Jinteki Biotech, Haas Industrie, and NBN all recognized the importance of having an off-world presence, not only for the research and development opportunities, but to capture a brand-new booming market.

By the beginning of the sixties, the list of mining companies exploiting the Moon was long, and almost every major power had a stake in the industry. Despite the vast distances separating their primary bases of operation, aggressive prospecting practices and fierce competition over terrestrial markets started a bitter war of industrial espionage and sabotage between the largest companies, with smaller mining companies alternatively taking sides or exploiting the situation.

At first the cost was borne largely by machinery; automated harvesters were

hacked to drive off course, seismic charges were used to collapse craters onto dig sites, and regolith plains were seeded with dense composites to foul mining drills. However, it was only a matter of time before people started dying.

LUNAR UPRISING

For years corporations successfully hid the true cost of mining on the Moon. Human casualties were put down to accidents, disappearances, and "human error." The governments of Earth, dealing with their own problems, were content to turn a blind eye so long as the He-3 kept flowing.

By now the Moon boasted a population in the tens of thousands, and whole communities had sprung up with families that considered themselves Lunar citizens. It was a hard life for many, especially the repressed people of Xiangong City and Leonovsk Station who often looked enviously across the *mare* at their counterparts in the prospering city of Heinlein, but it was one that they endured with the hope that they were working toward a brighter future.

Yet their dreams would not come to pass. The competition between the mining concerns ignited into war, and the miners and colonists were the ones caught in the crossfire. The true death toll is still unknown—it's possible that thousands of miners died in sporadic massacres, but no complete records have been found.

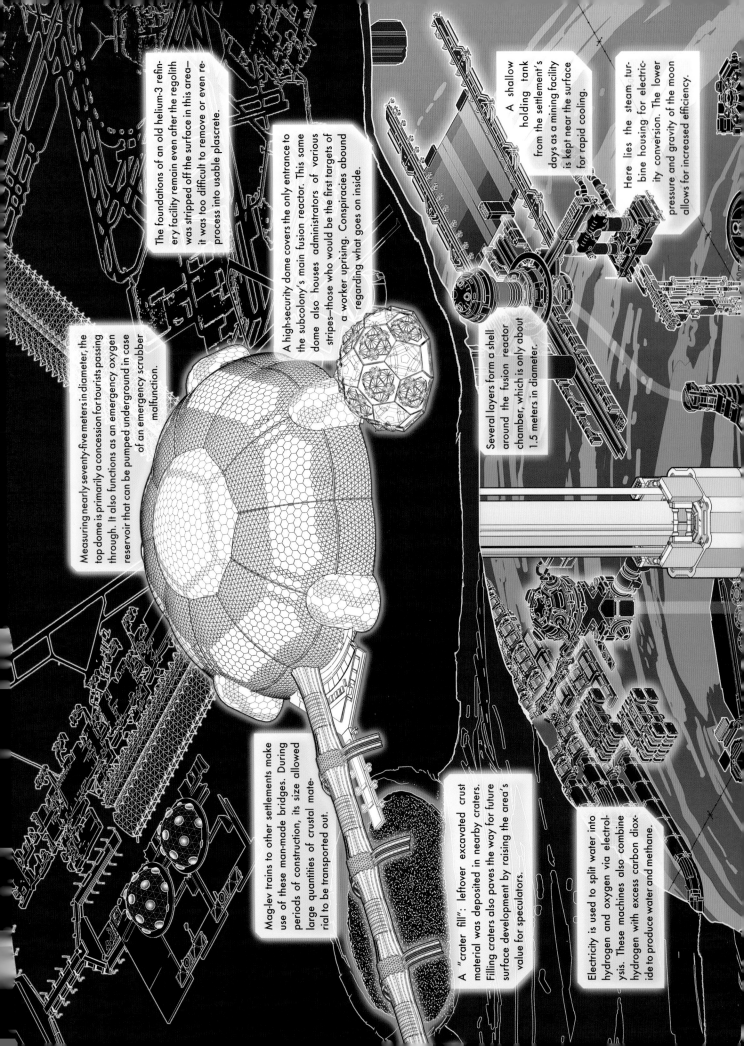

The foundations of an old helium-3 refinery facility remain even after the regolith was stripped off the surface in this area—it was too difficult to remove or even reprocess into usable plascrete.

A shallow holding tank from the settlement's days as a mining facility is kept near the surface for rapid cooling.

Here lies the steam turbine housing for electricity conversion. The lower pressure and gravity of the moon allows for increased efficiency.

A high-security dome covers the only entrance to the subcolony's main fusion reactor. This same dome also houses administrators of various stripes—those who would be the first targets of a worker uprising. Conspiracies abound regarding what goes on inside.

Measuring nearly seventy-five meters in diameter, the top dome is primarily a concession for tourists passing through. It also functions as an emergency oxygen reservoir that can be pumped underground in case of an emergency scrubber malfunction.

Several layers form a shell around the fusion reactor chamber, which is only about 1.5 meters in diameter.

Mag-lev trains to other settlements make use of these man-made bridges. During periods of construction, its size allowed large quantities of crustal material to be transported out.

A "crater fill": leftover excavated crust material was deposited in nearby craters. Filling craters also paves the way for future surface development by raising the area's value for speculators.

Electricity is used to split water into hydrogen and oxygen via electrolysis. These machines also combine hydrogen with excess carbon dioxide to produce water and methane.

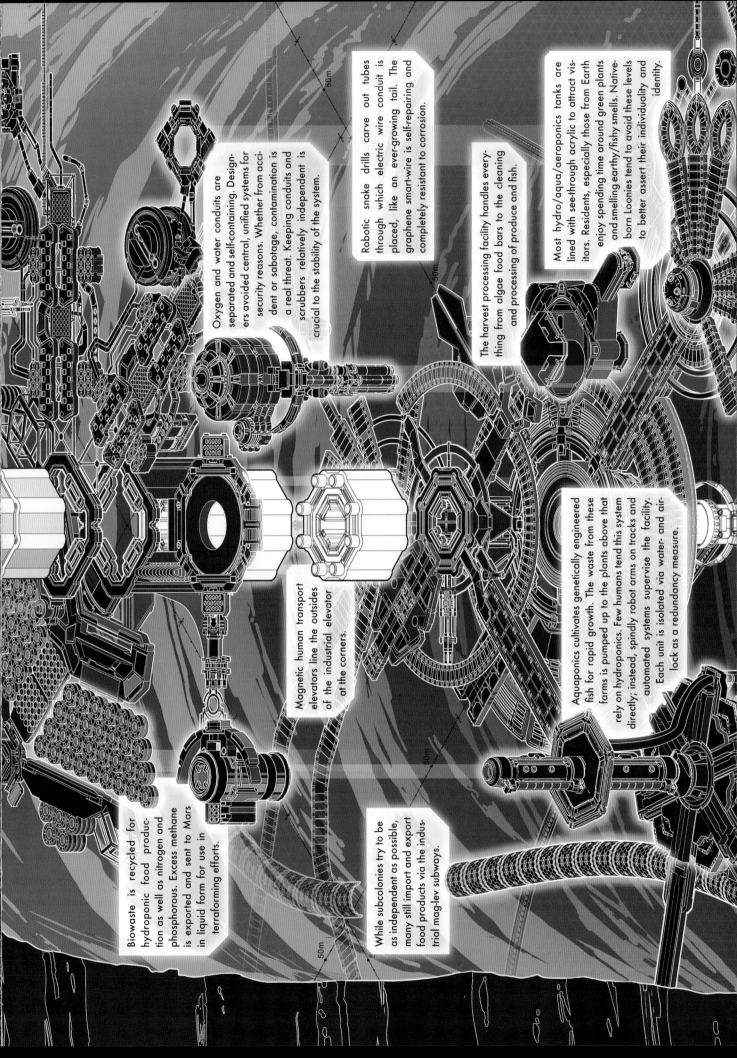

Oxygen and water conduits are separated and self-containing. Designers avoided central, unified systems for security reasons. Whether from accident or sabotage, contamination is a real threat. Keeping conduits and scrubbers relatively independent is crucial to the stability of the system.

Robotic snake drills carve out tubes through which electric wire conduit is placed, like an ever-growing tail. The graphene smart-wire is self-repairing and completely resistant to corrosion.

The harvest processing facility handles everything from algae food bars to the cleaning and processing of produce and fish.

Most hydro/aqua/aeroponics tanks are lined with see-through acrylic to attract visitors. Residents, especially those from Earth enjoy spending time around green plants and smelling earthy/fishy smells. Native-born Loonies tend to avoid these levels to better assert their individuality and identity.

Magnetic human transport elevators line the outsides of the industrial elevator at the corners.

Aquaponics cultivates genetically engineered fish for rapid growth. The waste from these farms is pumped up to the plants above that rely on hydroponics. Few humans tend this system directly; instead, spindly robot arms on tracks and automated systems supervise the facility. Each unit is isolated via water- and air-lock as a redundancy measure.

Biowaste is recycled for hydroponic food production as well as nitrogen and phosphorous. Excess methane is exported and sent to Mars in liquid form for use in terraforming efforts.

While subcolonies try to be as independent as possible, many still import and export food products via the industrial mag-lev subways.

50m

50m

50m

50m

as the pirates that prey upon the long-distance cargo containers launched from the Beanstalk to Mars, often alter or remove their transponders altogether. Such illegal modifications make these ships nearly impossible to identify.

Thrust gravity achieved during acceleration and deceleration is used to provide passengers a more comfortable journey, but additional gravity can be produced by centripetal acceleration through spinning hull sections or internal carousels. Due to the technical and size limitations of the spin carousels used for these systems, gravity generation through centripetal acceleration is really only effective on the massive, long-haul ships that run the route between Mars and Earth, or the proposed deep space exploration and survey ships.

A HOME IN SPACE

Traveling and living in the space surrounding Earth and Luna is a common, everyday occurrence for a surprising number of individuals. Many are businesspeople who have come up from Earth to cut deals, negotiate, and blow off a little steam in an orbital spa. Others are miners toiling away under the surface of the Challenger Planetoid, on various captive asteroids, or strip-mining the Moon for its precious He-3. Still others are shipbuilders, soldiers, entertainers, scientists, explorers, or androids going about their daily business just the same as their planet-bound contemporaries. They haul freight, shuttle passengers, conduct important research, and build spaceships. Criminals, too, are likely to continue their unsavory business in orbit. All of these people require food, shelter, and occasional entertainment, and they find these in the numerous space stations and habitats scattered throughout the system.

Space stations and other habitats can be broken down into four general categories: commercial, industrial, military, and scientific. Commercial installations are those specifically built to provide merchandise and amenities or to simply make money. Luxury orbital resorts fall under this category, as well as stations that offer adventure or tourist attractions,

INTERPLANETARY SHIPPING

For now, there is relatively little work for freight-carrying spaceships in our solar system. Local freight—such as items shipped from Earth up the Beanstalk for use at Midway, the Castle, Luna, or one of the smaller orbital stations—is all moved via elevator pods and small, short-range haulers operated by large shipping companies or the logistics arms of megacorps like Weyland and Haas-Bioroid. Cargo slated for Mars, and even some of Luna's cargo, is sent by other, arguably more spectacular means.

This freight is first packed into specially designed, heavily reinforced shipping containers that are cheap to make and never expected to return to Earth. Next, the container is flung toward its destination using the momentum of the Beanstalk itself. These long-range cargo pods are crewed by bioroids (or not at all) and are a cheap, if slow, means of getting materials to the Martian settlements during certain times of the year. This pod is accelerated through the Challenger Planetoid on a mag-lev rail and then launched for Mars or Luna. Thrusters provide course correction as necessary, but otherwise the freight relies on the launch's initial trajectory and momentum to reach its destination.

On Luna and Mars, high-G mag-lev launch tracks hundreds of kilometers long can accelerate cargo canisters into space, which are picked up by remotely piloted tugs and brought to shipping stations for further transport.

and those that provide rest, maintenance, and replenishment services to ship pilots and crews. Industrial installations are the massive corporate shipyards that build spaceships, microgravity factories run by androids that churn out a dizzying array of goods, and the various mining colonies such as those found on the Moon, Challenger Planetoid, and asteroids both in orbit and in the belt. These stations tend to have sparse accommodations and few comforts for their inhabitants.

A rarity among orbital installations, military bases typically offer training or garrisoning facilities for government and private military concerns. Mars is home to a handful of military bases for the Space Expeditionary Corps and Martian Colonial Corps, and there are a few more scattered throughout the system operated by various world powers and by corps such as Argus and Globalsec. Finally, there are scientific installations. These can range from tiny, automated sensor sites studying stellar phenomena to the research facilities on Mars studying that planet's makeup.

The essential systems of space stations are similar to those found on spaceships, albeit on a grander, more expensive scale. Oxygen is provided by catalysis, often in conjunction with hydroponic gardens or even trees and grass, depending on the station. That air is scrubbed and recycled by a large and sophisticated filtration system overseen by AIs. Gravity is nonexistent on most stations, and even those with carousels such as the Challenger Planetoid can provide gravity in only specific locations. High-efficiency helium-3 fusion reactors produce electricity through high-output turbine generators with supplemental large solar arrays. These generators provide not only the power for running the essential systems, but also power the numerous small thrusters used to keep a space station correctly oriented and stable in its orbit.

Humankind continues to explore the solar system, and the technologies used in building space stations continue to develop. As corporations push the boundaries of the frontier, the possibilities for discovery and growth as a species are limitless. A new and valuable ore or element could be found in a nondescript asteroid in the clutter of the asteroid belt. Valuable gases could be gathered from the swirling clouds of Jupiter, or new life could be discovered beneath the seas of Europa. Past the outer planetoids and the Oort cloud, even more exotic destinies lie in wait. None can say how long it might take humanity to reach that far, but the first steps have already been taken.

TO THE MOON AND BACK AGAIN

Living on the Moon is not good for an Earther's health, not if he or she ever wants to go back down-Stalk. There are two basic problems: radiation and gravity.

Because the Moon has no atmosphere and no magnetosphere, there's nothing holding back the radiation of the sun and deep space. This is one of the reasons so much of Heinlein is underground: the layers and layers of lunar rock act as a radiation barrier. The domes themselves are built to block as much radiation as possible, but despite the Heinlein District Council's best efforts, the average Loony takes in a lot more rads than the average Earther. Genetic damage is inevitable over the long term, which has implications on Loony fertility and lifespans. Those with extra credits to burn can mitigate some of the damage with Jinteki's rejuve treatments, but not even the mighty biotech megacorp can create a radiation panacea. At least, not yet.

The other issue is that over time the low gravity results in loss of bone density and muscle tone. Earthers on Luna sometimes wear weights on wrists and ankles both to help them walk (without the ridiculous bounding leaps they might otherwise take) and to force their bodies to work a little harder. Earthers who intend to go back down-Stalk are advised to work out regularly and take dietary supplements. Loonies who are planning a visit to Earth should really talk to their doctor before subjecting themselves to a full G.

REBUILDING, RESENTMENT, AND HOPE

Ironically, the megacorps only grew more powerful following the Lunar Insurrection. Weyland was the first to claim a major stake in Heinlein, and with the Consortium's vast wealth fueling reconstruction, the colony's borders swelled to twice their previous size in the years that followed. Haas-Bioroid established its primary R&D facility in the outskirts. NBN swept in to expand its Network and mediafeed subscription base. Melange Mining ensured that helium-3 operations became a tightly controlled industry, leasing thousands of clones from Jinteki to replace the ranks of its workforce. Clones, of course, did not have the same obedience problems as their human counterparts.

For the natives of Luna, especially those who participated in the rebellions, this was a difficult transition. Many lost their jobs and subsequently their housing in the domes. They took refuge in the lawless reaches of the Docklands, joining orgcrime outfits like the Katala Brothers or the 14K, and they tried to make a living from smuggling and black-market enterprises. Others left to start a new life on Mars, where the colonists were still fighting corporate influence. Only a few remain in Heinlein proper—these men and women try to forget the promises of the past and get by as best they can in the new paradigm.

As the megacorps carved up the Moon between them, whole sections were bought and sold. Domes sprang up like glowing bruises where private citizens and wealthy conglomerates thought to expand their interests into the stars. A massive influx of workers and young entrepreneurs diluted the population of the old Luna colonies, and with them much of the ill-will still felt toward Earth. Hotels like the Tycho Hilton and Lunar Madre were built with impressive views across the Sea of Tranquility and the glimmering spires of Heinlein. Their high-class clientele is blissfully ignorant of the detritus of war still hidden beneath the breathtaking grey wasteland seen through the transplas windows.

Fifteen hard years have passed, and the memory of the War is only now starting to fade. Heinlein continues to grow and expand, fueled by the wealth of the megacorps and the innovation of the ambitious. There are yet still fortunes to be made out in space.

In the vernacular, they were called warrens. These secret rooms were used to hide black market goods or people wanted by the NAPD, corp sec teams, or private individuals. The rooms paid for themselves quickly because there were so few places to hide within Heinlein.

Samuel Leung

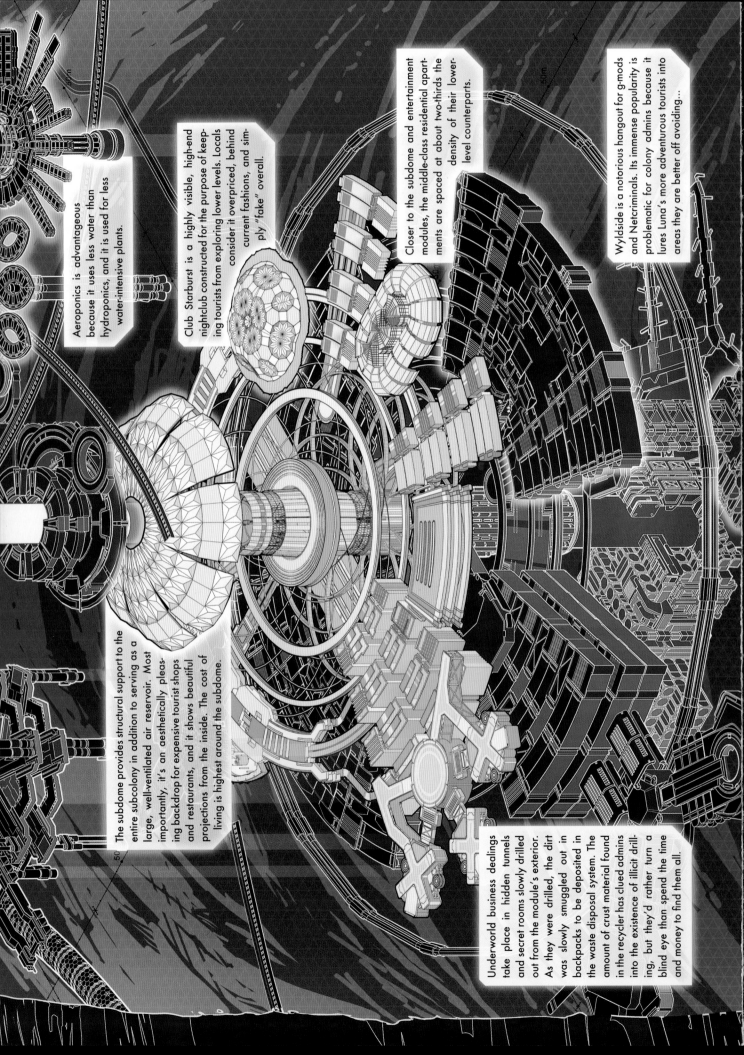

Aeroponics is advantageous because it uses less water than hydroponics, and it is used for less water-intensive plants.

Club Starburst is a highly visible, high-end nightclub constructed for the purpose of keeping tourists from exploring lower levels. Locals consider it overpriced, behind current fashions, and simply "fake" overall.

Closer to the subdome and entertainment modules, the middle-class residential apartments are spaced at about two-thirds the density of their lower-level counterparts.

Wyldside is a notorious hangout for g-mods and Netcriminals. Its immense popularity is problematic for colony admins because it lures Luna's more adventurous tourists into areas they are better off avoiding....

The subdome provides structural support to the entire subcolony in addition to serving as a large, well-ventilated air reservoir. Most importantly, it's an aesthetically pleasing backdrop for expensive tourist shops and restaurants, and it shows beautiful projections from the inside. The cost of living is highest around the subdome.

Underworld business dealings take place in hidden tunnels and secret rooms slowly drilled out from the module's exterior. As they were drilled, the dirt was slowly smuggled out in backpacks to be deposited in the waste disposal system. The amount of crust material found in the recycler has clued admins into the existence of illicit drilling, but they'd rather turn a blind eye than spend the time and money to find them all.

Surface structures
Power generation
Water processing
Central elevator
Upper class living/shopping
Middle class apartments
Low class slum living

Air processing
Waste processing
Food production
Subway (humans)

Small living modules comprise these lowest residences. The concentric design and radial symmetry of the upper levels was discarded in favor of purely economical right angles. The lower levels tend also to be the newest levels, showing steady improvement in build quality, but the population density is overly high.

= 5 cubic meters   = Vertical Elevators

From above, Heinlein looks like a vast jeweled necklace driven into the Lunar surface. Each glowing dome is another link in a shimmering chain that stretches out for hundreds of kilometers in every direction. Around its edges the guide lights of private landing pads and mining beacons glitter ruby and emerald, while toward its center, where the lights shine their brightest, the pointed peaks of arcologies rise from oceans of transplas.

The sky above Heinlein is frequently alight with traffic. Shuttles arriving and departing from Starport Kaguya bring tourists and businesspeople to and from the Beanstalk. Private transports touch down or blasting off from the Docklands or corporate concerns. Specialized hoppers carry people out across the Lunar surface on whisper-thin trails of compressed gases. Equally, the domes and towers themselves crawl with clone and bioroid work crews or vast automated rigs—for Heinlein's systems and seals require constant maintenance and attention. And yet, the true grandeur of Heinlein is not visible from the surface—its tightly packed streets and millions of citizens are hidden beneath walls of rock and transplas.

Heinlein is a city of modules, each of which is distinct and largely self-contained. The reason for this is twofold: first, this is how it was constructed, each piece added to another over decades of digging and construction; second, should a disaster or decompression afflict one section, the others can be swiftly sealed off to limit the damage. Thus, when people travel through Heinlein they will find themselves constantly passing through heavy airlocks and emergency blast doors, the yellow hazard stripes and warning signs serving as a constant reminder of the perils of life on the Moon.

Living in the nicer parts of Heinlein, a person might forget they are even on the Moon—that is, if they can forget for a moment about the low gravity and the designer envirosuits. Some of the domes even have real streets, walkways and conveyors. The tube-lev transit system, which connects almost all regions of the Moon, has its own city loop in central Heinlein to allow swift travel from one side to the other. The dome overhead is high enough to trick the mind into thinking it might be the sky, and certain domes within Heinlein even go so far as to project clouds and birds onto their surfaces.

For the most part, Heinlein's sections are no larger across than a city block or g-ball field. Yet, they rise up to the peak of their domes or down into the rock, crammed together over numerous levels. These collections of twisting corridors are then filled from floor to ceiling with apartments, shops, or factories. Some areas are little more than a warehouse or club connected to the rest of the network by a single tunnel like a splinter sticking out of the side of the megapolis. Others are much larger—some domes stretch kilometers across to cover dozens of smaller domes.

IT'S COLD OUTSIDE

In Heinlein it's sometimes easy to forget that just beyond the roof over your head—or on the other side of that bulkhead—is one of the most hostile environments known to man. After living on the Moon for a few months, the human body adjusts to the low gravity. Your movements become more sure and fluid, while the distant hum of the air scrubbers keeping you alive are edited out by your consciousness. However, the reality is that when things go wrong on the Moon, they can go very, very wrong.

Fortunately for its citizens, Heinlein was built with numerous failsafe technologies—corridors, chambers, and buildings are all compartmentalized so that in the case of a breach, shutters and seals can slam into place with life support systems that will keep its inhabitants alive long enough to be rescued. For those caught outside, communal safety lockers are never far away, standing on street corners much like fire hydrants might dot the sidewalks of a terrestrial city. Even the domes themselves are created with multiple levels of redundancy, each vast plate comprising half a dozen heavy transplas sheets, the spaces between them packed with clear resin sealants should even the slightest crack appear.

Of course, most people on Heinlein are unwilling to trust their fate to a government maintained safety locker or a bioroid crash team. Custom-made panic rooms and designer envirosuits that can be worn every day are common to most areas of Heinlein. Companies like Voidskin Enterprises and the Room to Breathe brand continually bring out new and exciting lines of products to market to the caution-minded consumer.

The Loonies beseeched their home governments for help in quelling the violence, but none came quickly enough. Frustrated and desperate for help, the miners took matters into their own hands after the Prosperity Mining Depot disaster. The Lunar Insurrection began.

What started as a protest coupled with the seizure of some Melange Mining facilities quickly spiraled out of control into what would become known as the War. The U.S. was quick to quell the rebellion, but the rest of the world saw American incursions into other mining territories as a power grab. The Moon became a battlefield between Earth countries. The Battle of Kaguya, Tycho Ridge, the Serenity Beachhead, Oceanus Valley, and the many battles like them would become dark reminders of a time when the Moon ran black with frozen blood. Memories of these days are still very close and real for Lunar inhabitants, and the scars of the War are healing still.

During this period, the U.S. Space Expeditionary Corps was created and permanently stationed at Armstrong Base on the Moon, and other bases were built to host space combatants. After the fighting was over, the Treaty of Heinlein reinstated Heinlein as a district of New Angeles, and the megacorps tightened their grip upon the colonies. Xiangong City was reduced to ruin, the company equally broken, and other countries' settlements were heavily damaged as well. Heinlein emerged as the dominant Lunar settlement, but the United States' hold on the colony was curtailed (slightly) by the Treaty of Heinlein. Perhaps the only clear winner was Melange Mining, which now held a near-monopoly on the He-3 business.

The Lunar geography bears silent witness to the atrocities committed on its surface. Dozens of settlements and habitats were destroyed, and whole sections of the Lunar surface were transformed into graveyards of shattered weaponry and freeze-dried corpses. Although the bodies would mostly be cleaned away, there was little economic impetus to deal with the war debris. In forlorn stretches of the Lunar surface, cracked domes, zigzagging trench lines, and crumbling signal towers still stand sentinel, inhabited only by ghosts and memories.

LOONY ART AND FASHION

The stereotype is that Luna is full of people who don't fit in on Earth: criminals, misfits, weirdos, freaks. Some Earthers think that makes Loonies exciting and different and sexy, and they pay a lot of attention to Loony fashion, art, and music.

It's true that Heinlein has some great nightclubs, some of them less legal than others. There are some exciting musicians and deejays combining the diversity of Loony peoples in fascinating and exciting ways. Every now and again some new musical act or genre explodes out of Heinlein, comes down-Stalk, and is the new hotness on Earth for a few months.

Heinlein fashion trends are a little less portable—for some reason the slimline envirosuit never caught on in the rest of New Angeles. But one notable trend that has moved down-Stalk was born in the community surrounding the Wyldside nightclub. Cosmetic genetic and surgical modification caught on there, especially incorporating animal features. These g-mods, called "wylders," can now be found in greater New Angeles and, increasingly, worldwide.

Emilio Rodriguez

HEINLEIN

From Earth, Heinlein glitters like a jewel on the face of the Moon. Shining lines of light reach out across the Sea of Tranquility to touch mining outposts, observatories, and scores of corporate enclaves. Only when one gets closer she see the stains on the plas-crete domes and the desolation that stretches out to the curved horizon. Heinlein is a glorious ideal bought and paid for by the megacorps—and they'll never let people forget it.

SAGA OF THE SILVER CITY

At the time the Quito Accord was signed, there were only a handful of international research stations dotting the surface of the Lunar maria. Back then, Tranquility Home was little more than one or two domes covering makeshift habitats carved into the regolith. Utilitarian in design and purpose, they were places where scientists could perform their experiments, store their gear, and enjoy a few hours outside of an envirosuit.

The Accord anticipated that Tranquility Home would continue to grow in population and prestige. The Lunar colony's reliance on the Beanstalk additionally meant the same law enforcement in charge of protecting the Space Elevator could also reach out and police Tranquility Home as well. The station became an extension of the Special Economic Zone of New Los Angeles. The framers of the Quito Accord were right to think that the station would grow into a full-blown colony; fusion power came along soon enough, and with it, Heinlein's development truly took off.

As the decades slipped past and the Moon rose in both population and significance, the domes were expanded and the tunnels dug deeper. In time, scattered colonies, outposts, and labs were connected and repurposed, and the first glimmer of the city of Heinlein began to emerge. Heinlein was home to most of Melange Mining employees, which made it something of a boom town during the initial helium-3 rush. But as competition between the corps intensified, it was Heinlein's people who suffered. The Lunar Insurrection and war that followed tarnished the otherwise-bright saga of the Silver City.

Today the greater megapolis sprawls across the Sea of Tranquility, sheltering its inhabitants beneath transplas and plascrete domes and through hundreds of kilometers of winding tunnels. Satellite domes can be found as far away as the southern edges of the Sea of Serenity and the northernmost regions of the Sea of Nectar, creating a sparkling web of lights visible with the naked eye. The colony only covers a tiny fraction of the Moon's surface, but Heinlein is as large as any Earth-bound city.

Millions of people live and work in its crowded corridors, fulfilling all the needs of a great city. Life in Heinlein can be claustrophobic; the constant press of bodies beneath cold grey ceilings, their pale waxy faces lit by flickering artificial lights, is overwhelming for some. They say on Heinlein every breath you take is one ten other people have had before you, and don't even ask about the water. The city is a self-contained bubble kept alive by humming atmospheric filters and complex fluid reclamation systems. Everything and everything is recycled.

> "Heinlein embodies the most magnificent part of the human spirit: the will to step beyond the confines of our world and reach out to claim our destiny, not just for today, but the many generations to come."
>
> – Heinlein District Manager Cline Hubbard, Prosperity Memorial Day Speech

And yet, even though its people live with a tax on the very air they breathe, there is wonder and adventure to be found on the Moon. With less than twenty percent of Earth's gravity, the body expends less energy to hold itself up, so many crippling health problems are lessened. As a result, the city is a popular destination for retirees. There are also all manner of sports that exist in Heinlein tailored to its unique environment, like vapor-surfing and g-ball. This is all without even mentioning the fact one can look out of a transplas dome and see Earth glowing blue above the horizon.

For these reasons Heinlein attracts its fair share of tourism, but it helps that the cost of a ticket up the Beanstalk to Starport Kaguya is within reach of the average citizen on Earth. An entire industry has cropped up to get people from the Root in New Angeles to the StarScape retail complexes of Kaguya, and for many people this is closest to the real Heinlein they will ever come. For those who stay longer, or for those who were born beneath the domes, however, Heinlein is a very different place indeed.

Heinlein's prosperity rides on the back of the Moon's massive mining industries and the thriving helium-3 trade. After the War, a massive clone workforce replaced the initial Lunar miners to harvest He-3 from the Lunar surface. These massive open pits lie beyond the hustle and bustle of central Heinlein, dug out of sight and out of mind. Just as the megacorps like it.

Connected to New Angeles by the Beanstalk and the Challenger Memorial Shuttle, the city is a vital part of the world economy. Heinlein's place on Earth's doorstep also makes it a hub for space traffic and a jumping-off point for ships making the long journey to Mars. Subsequently, more than a few of the troubles afflicting the Martian colonies have found their way to Heinlein, and Luna has become a place of conflict between the Martian Colonial Authority, rebels, and corporate concerns on more than one occasion. Yet the Moon remains clearly under the auspices of Earth, and the U.S.-backed Space Expeditionary Corps and the New Angeles Police Department maintain order under the directives of the Heinlein District Council and the hefty influence of the megacorps.

Outside Heinlein's main domes, the clout of the NAPD wanes, and corporate and criminal enterprises take over. With a large transient worker population, hundreds of private launch pads, and poorly regulated trade, it is a place that is almost impossible to police. This is the shadowy underworld of Heinlein: the Docklands. Here a man might lose himself among the hundreds of warehouses and black-market trade posts, or he might even carve out a nice little outfit smuggling goods for the same. Many have disappeared here, and rumors of gangs of rogue clones, shady corporate experiments, and war criminals on the run never seem to go away.

STARPORT KAGUYA

A marvel of moder-n#s$ta y@K–uga# errx…

…<THE BEATING HEART OF LUNAR COMMERCE. THE MEGACORPS HAVE PRIVATE SHIPPING DOCKS ALL OVER LUNA, BUT THE BULK OF THE STUFF GOES THROUGH HERE. ALL THE CIVILIAN PASSENGER TRAFFIC IS JUST A PR EXERCISE TO MAKE PEOPLE FORGET ABOUT THE PORT'S REAL VALUE TO THOSE IN CHARGE. JUST ASK ANY OF THE TRAVELERS WHO'VE BEEN SHOT FOR GETTING LOST NEAR A PRIVATE DOCK SINCE IT WAS BUILT.>…

…j:%fo4)=@x jo]4ney to the stars.

ERROR:
DATAFEED DISPLAY
SOURCE UNKNOWN

LUNACENT

Once thought to be an impos\sfr%o*…

…<SURE, WE BUILT A CITY ON THE MOON. ONE GIANT LEAP FOR MANKIND, AS THEY SAY. BUT THE TRUTH IS, THERE ARE TWO HEINLEINS. ONE IS WHAT THEY SHOW YOU IN ALL THE TOURIST ADS. THE OTHER AIN'T SO PRETTY. THE COST OF LIVING UP HERE IS BRUTAL, AND IF YOU MISS A RENT OR O₂ PAYMENT, THINGS CAN ESCALATE QUICKLY. BETWEEN ORGCRIME, THE OCCASIONAL ESCAPED CLONE, AND THE FACT THAT MANKIND HAS YET TO BUILD A CITY WITHOUT CRIME, THE NAPD HAS THEIR HANDS FULL KEEPING THE PEACE, MUCH LESS MAINTAINING THE BROCHURE-QUALITY ATMOSPHERE.>…

…g+%f; ,:nd3r the dome.

THE DOCKLANDS

The mining of vita4e##!…L.>nar sfu&c e0;…

…<FOR ALL HEINLEIN'S PROBLEMS, AT LEAST IT ISN'T THE DOCKLANDS. NAPD'S JURISDICTION IS MURKY AT BEST, AND THEY'VE GIVEN UP ENFORCING IT. THE ONLY LAW HERE IS WHAT THE STRONG ENFORCE FOR THEMSELVES. THAT USUALLY MEANS CORPS HOLDING THEIR WORKERS TO ENDLESS SHIFTS OF BACK-BREAKING LABOR, BUT IT CAN ALSO MEAN CRIMINAL OUTFITS SETTING UP BLACK-MARKET KINGDOMS. THEY KICK BACK SOME OF THEIR PROFITS TO THE CORPORATIONS AND DON'T INTERFERE WITH MINING, AND IN RETURN, THEY GET A PLAYGROUND WITH NO REGULATIONS ON GUNS, DRUGS, PROSTITUTION, OR ANYTHING ELSE…PLUS LOTS OF CUSTOMERS TOO DESPERATE NOT TO PLAY RIGHT INTO THEIR HANDS.>…

…~@v;9&…> D;1#ands' labor force.

Maciej Rebisz

MELANGE MINING

The proud owner s'5(;of Mla#g\,.

...<MELANGE MINING IS THE NEIGHBOR NO ONE WANTS TO PISS OFF. NOT ON EARTH, NOT IN HEINLEIN, AND ESPECIALLY NOT OUT IN THE DOCKLANDS. EVER SINCE THEY SWALLOWED UP MOST OF THEIR COMPETITION IN THE AFTERMATH OF THE WAR, THEY'VE PRETTY MUCH MONOPOLIZED THE HE-3 TRADE. DO ANYTHING TO THREATEN MINING IN MELANGE'S TERRITORY (WHICH IS MORE OR LESS EVERYWHERE, THESE DAYS), AND YOU'LL REGRET IT. BRIEFLY.>...

...#2x::%,any years to come.

WARNING:
DATAFEED REFRESH
ATTEMPT FAILED

TRANQUILITY HOME

Come and experience daily life of m(E#s2g L<"u...

<THE LIVING QUARTERS IN TRANQUILITY HOME MAKE EVEN A CLONE-TEL LOOK COMFORTABLE BY COMPARISON. THEY PACK YOU IN THERE TIGHTER THAN GOGS IN AMAZONAS, AND THE AIR AND WATER—WHICH COST YOU ALMOST AS MUCH AS RENT ITSELF—HAVE PASSED THROUGH EVERY OTHER RESIDENT BEFORE GETTING TO YOU. SOME "PARADISE.">...

...–°ƒ3∆p8se¬ and the Sky Shinto Temple.

WARNING:
OUTPUT COMPROMISED
RESETTING SERVER SECURITY...

155

Map: Skott Kilander

LUNACENT

The largest of Heinlein's domes, and the hub from which the rest of the city extends, is Lunacent. Although the Heinlein District Council officially designates it as Luna Central, most people use the shortened name. The size of a small city itself, this is the beating heart of Heinlein and included in its districts are some of the oldest Lunar habitats. The bustling, thriving center of the colony is also the home of Heinlein's district government. Even if you don't live in Lunacent, odds are you will go there at least a few times a week for business or pleasure.

Ostensibly an extension of New Angeles, the distance from Earth and its own unique set of challenges means that Heinlein has the provisions to govern and police itself. Most of the official structures are clustered in New Angeles Plaza, the building where Mayor Wells's appointee, District Manager Cline Hubbard, deals with the day-to-day management of the district. Across from the Plaza stands the slab-sided New Angeles Police Department Heinlein District Office. The district building controls all NAPD precincts and activities on Heinlein, and there are a dozen or so satellite stations scattered across the megapolis.

The buildings making up the New Angeles Plaza and the Heinlein District Office are completely self-sustainable. In the event of a massive structural failure or terrorist attack, they can seal themselves off and continue to function for days or even weeks. The memory of the Insurrection is still fresh in the minds of many Lunar officials.

Lunacent also boasts the largest and most well-appointed of Heinlein's structures, the Columbiad Arcology, which reaches up to pierce the primary dome with its upper stories. A Weyland construction, the Arcology houses thousands of Lunar citizens, from families living in commission tenements at its bottom to affluent businesspeople and corporate VIPs enjoying spectacular views of Earth from their penthouse windows. District Manager Hubbard often uses the arcology as example of how Heinlein is a conglomeration of peoples and that under its domes, everyone enjoys the same freedoms. Of course, private elevators and hopper pads ensure that the upper levels and the lower ones never have to cross paths.

HEINLEIN NIGHTLIFE

There is a certain anonymity to life on the Moon. Despite the close confines of living in domes and tunnels, or perhaps because of it, people keep to themselves. It is widely considered rude to make excessive eye contact or even acknowledge your fellow citizens on the Moon. In a crowded place like the tube-lev scores of people will be pressed together, staring off past their fellow passengers, even as their bodies are wedged up against each other. Loonies often joke that a ride on the tube-lev is like a one night stand—it'll get you where you want to go but you won't remember the name or the face of the person that got there with you.

On the Moon the saying goes, "there's nothing to hold you down." The phrase references the colony's low gravity, but it also conveys the sense that things that are frowned upon down on Earth have a place out among the stars. Unusual subcultures and special interest groups thrive in many of the Heinlein modules. Wyldside, catering to animal-modded humans, is only one of many well-known Heinlein clubs. People often save for years to make the long journey to a place where they can finally feel like themselves, far away from the prejudices and small-minded attitudes of their native cities.

Then there are specialty shops, like Eliza's Toolbox, run by the eccentric Eliza Manchester in Fra Mauro. Specializing in bioroid companions including the ever-popular Eve and Adonis models, it is a place free from judgment where a visitor can live out his or her fantasies, provided their credaccounts are good. The clone *hanamachi* in Starport Kaguya are equally popular, if perhaps more mainstream, as sources for entertainment and culture.

NAPD HEINLEIN DISTRICT OFFICE

The NAPD keeps the people of Heinlein safe in the face of increasingly sophisticated criminals and a hostile work environment. Few officers would consider Luna a promotion—most are assigned for a rotation, while others want to get their low-G training certification out of the way, and only a few intend to make the Moon their permanent home. Yet, Commander Lufkin is determined to change the perception that a Lunar assignment is tantamount to punishment, even if he has to struggle with his superiors for every officer and resource sent up the Beanstalk.

Commander Lufkin doesn't dispute that the Heinlein beat can be hard. The environment itself is an antagonistic force, and should officers stray beyond the central domes of Heinlein, they might find their badges don't carry as much weight as they might like. Although the department does employ bounty hunters, sometimes-shady individuals who enjoy more success outside the central domes, a gap still exists between the appearance of the law and the reality of its enforcement.

"It should be easier to catch criminals in Heinlein. I mean, they've got nowhere to run, right? Seriously though, do you know how big this place is?"

– Tessa Horne, NAPD Sergeant, Kaguya Satellite Division

For this reason the people of Heinlein don't put as much stock in the NAPD as do the citizens of New Angeles. Cops on the streets of Lunacent might demand respect, but out on the edges of the Docklands and beyond, the underworld is all too aware of the NAPD's limitations. The criminal element often flaunts its activities, confident that by the time a cop can collect the necessary evidence and get clearance from Dispatch, the criminals themselves will be long gone.

Complicating matters are private security firms like Starshield, Argus, and dozens more that are paid to keep private domes safe. These organizations' operatives are often ex-military members who can become territorial, and more than once there has been a standoff with the NAPD as its officers tried to pursue criminals between the domes of Heinlein.

Even so, there are dozens of dedicated detectives, and even some androids on loan from Haas-Bioroid and Jinteki, that see it as their duty to keep Heinlein safe—no matter the odds stacked against them.

PROSPERITY MEMORIAL PARK

Perhaps even more impressive than the Tranquility Home Museum is Prosperity Memorial Park, dedicated to the miners who lost their lives in the lead-up to the War. The largest contiguous Lunar parkland, it dominates the center of Lunacent, carving a green strip from its relentless press of buildings. Grass, trees, flowers, and even water features stand in stark relief to their surroundings. A hidden network of air pumps, ultraviolet lights, and misters creates the impression of the outdoors and also nurtures the plants. The park is a popular destination for both tourists and locals. For Earth natives the park provides both a sense of home and the wonder of the Moon—its trees and flowers grow seemingly stretched thin as they reach for the artificial sky, and vibrations from distant mining or transports can make them sway almost hypnotically.

TRANQUILITY HOME

While there are many residential domes in Heinlein, each catering to a variety of cultures and economic classes, the largest and oldest by far is Tranquility Home. Before Heinlein was annexed to New Angeles, Tranquility Home was a modest research station home to maybe two hundred or more scientists. Later, it became the primary habitation module for the workers of Melange Mining and Alpha Prospecting, and it has only grown since. A large Japanese population immigrated at once and settled a module now known as Tsuki-no-Miyako in homage to the ancient *Tale of the Bamboo Cutter*.

Intermingled within the maze of habitats and gantries are numerous tourist attractions. In place of the statues or fountains commonly found in a terrestrial city,

STARPORT KAGUYA

A constant stream of shuttles and cargo pods go up and down Earth's gravity well, often via the Challenger Memorial Ferry. While some corporations and private enterprises maintain their own landing pads out

however, tourists will find pieces of the Lunar surface preserved under transplas in the middle of a busy intersection or bustling shopping mall. Some of these are relatively small, such as the place where the dome first laid its foundations or the grave of the first man to die on the Moon, but they all serve as stark reminders that one is on the Moon.

Others are altogether more impressive—like the Tranquility Home Museum. Over a hundred meters across, it preserves the entire Apollo 11 landing site underneath a pressurized viewing gallery. Walkways ring its crown while interactive displays play loops of old flatfilm footage or holodocs. For tourists it is an amazing reminder of history, but most locals think of it as a shameful waste of real estate.

in the Docklands, the bulk of commercial and civilian traffic comes through Starport Kaguya nestled in the Hypatia-C Crater. With the rise to prominence of Heinlein, it too developed, and in time it became the Moon's principal spaceport and base of the Heinlein Authority, which regulates space traffic around the colony.

With arrivals and departures equal to the busiest of Earth's airports, Starport Kaguya extends across the fifteen-kilometer diameter of Hypatia-C. Multiple landing domes cluster around its center like the buds of a flower reaching for the sun, while in their shadow dozens of hexagonal domes spread out to the very lip of the crater itself. The upper levels of the launch zone are always thrumming with activity as bioroid work crews guided by suited human engineers make quick mechanical checks and system repairs between the shuttles' relentless docking and launch schedules. Many consider Starport Kaguya the lifeblood of Heinlein, and the costs to Lunar industries and habitats would be considerable indeed were it to ever stop flowing.

For many that come to the Moon, Kaguya is about as far as they get, just as the Lunar Tourism Bureau intended. Heinlein can be a dangerous and unpredictable place for the unwary, and tourists who wander off into far-flung modules or

LUNA'S WEB

The Lunar tube-lev network is one of the engineering wonders of Heinlein, its tunnels connecting the city like the strands of a vast spider's web. Without the tube-lev, transport would be restricted to hoppers and tunnel tractors, a daunting prospect when a journey on the Moon can easily run into thousands of kilometers. Running through hard vacuum, tube-lev carriages can easily exceed 1,000km/h, hurtling from one station to the next in minutes. Pressure seals around stops slow the carriages down just before they reach their destination, and a two-way airlock links the train to the platform.

In Lunacent the tube-lev runs every few minutes, a handful of dedicated cars making a constant lap of the dome, but even getting to other domes or further afield only means waiting for ten minutes at most. All the domes of Heinlein are part of the network, as are most major settlements; this even includes some on Darkside, where a journey will still only be measured in a few hours.

Accidents are extremely rare in the tube-lev because complex computer systems track each car and monitor its speed, destination, and cargo. However, there are still some areas of old tunnel that were abandoned when settlements were destroyed during the War or as a result of mining accidents out in the Lunar wastes. Rumors persist of smugglers and corporations opening up sealed sections and junctions that no longer appear on any official maps and using these forgotten lines for their own purposes. Of course the Heinlein Authority dismisses such fanciful stories as conspiracy theories, even though they never seem to offer anything to disprove them.

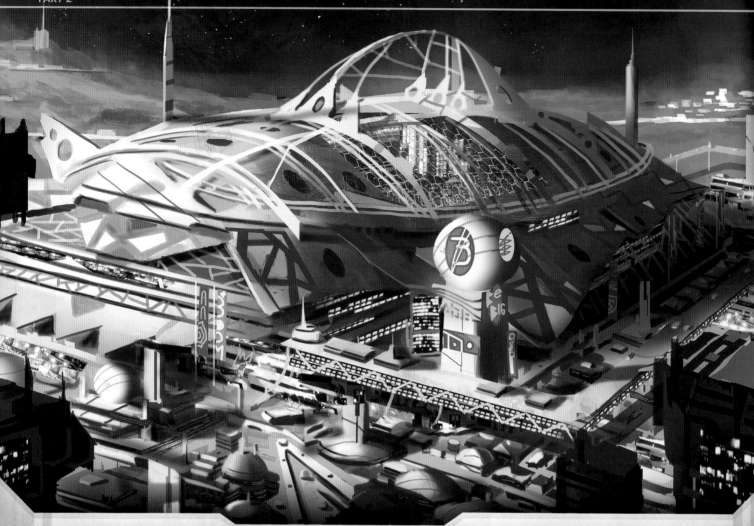

even the Docklands looking for adventure often find more than they bargained for. To keep the number of missing persons and tragic accidents to a minimum, District Manager Hubbard has seen considerable resources poured into the expansion and refurbishment of Kaguya to turn it into the shining face of Heinlein.

Hotels ranging from the extravagant to the reasonably priced ring the spaceport, their viewing decks affording impressive views of the moonscape, and for about half the month, Earth itself. Recreation parks and tourist centers surround these, allowing visitors to experience the wonders of low-G sports or look at some of the Moon's proud history—such as the Treaty of Heinlein, which stands on display just outside the main shuttle terminus, encased in its own transplas tomb. The Tourism board tends to downplay mention of the now-infamous Battle of Kaguya that ended the Lunar Insurrection but ignited the War.

Then there is StarScape Shopping, a retail paradise that caters almost completely to the tourism market. All manner of things can be bought—duty-free— on its dozens of retail levels. Products of Lunar industry such as low-gravity engineered nav-watches, regolith mineral gems, and the latest offerings from the Lunar synthetic labs of Haas-Bioroid and Jinteki are just some of the delights visitors can purchase.

StarScape also caters to the notion that there are some things you just can't do in normal gravity—and comfort clubs, g-tattooists, and liquid bars are all things more discerning customers can sample should they so choose. With so much to offer, it is little wonder that many tourists never step onto the tube-lev to Lunacent, content to spend their vacation in the safety and comfort of Kaguya.

ANGEL ARENA

For those who are after something more active, the Angel Arena is Heinlein's main venue for low-G sports. Located just outside Lunacent, its crowds can enjoy a spectacular view of the stars and the game at the same time. Many terrestrial games have their equivalents on the Moon, like g-ball and aero hockey, played with what are colloquially called "Heinlein Rules." Teams from Earth will routinely visit, with athletes training for months to prepare for the challenge of low-G sports. Heinlein's own Lunar Leopards g-ball team spends its offseason Earth-side to build up its players' muscle density so they can execute impressive feats of acrobatics on the field. Perhaps the most interesting games are those between bioroid or clone teams. Always sponsored events, both Haas-Bioroid and Jinteki enjoy showing off their merchandise in these exhibition matches.

Emilio Rodriguez

DOCKLANDS

Stark against the dazzling domed heart of Heinlein is a brooding dark horizon. Half-constructed habitats, faded factory hubs, and skeletal landing ramps reach up from the cold grey surface—a forest of steel and shadows that hides Luna's most dangerous criminal elements. This is the Docklands, and only the foolish or the brave stray too far into its underworld.

The Docklands are located beyond the major domes of Lunacent and its complex tunnel networks. It is an area of both expansion and industry for the city, arrayed around Heinlein in a wide circle of landing pads, warehouses and heavy industry. Although nominally under the control of District Manager Hubbard and the NAPD, the Docklands are a grey area, sitting between the law of Heinlein and the wilderness of the greater Lunar surface. That it is almost entirely privately owned and operated only adds to the NAPD's problems, since officers often have to secure permission and complex warrants before they can even set foot within its warrens.

Even so, the Docklands are a vital part of Heinlein's economy and all the major corporations and scores of minor ones have a stake in its cargo and industrial operations. For locals, the division between central Heinlein and the Docklands is a clear and obvious one, and they avoid certain routes and places. For tourists and other visitors, however, it can be easy to wander off the beaten track and end up somewhere that you are not meant to be.

This wouldn't be so much of a problem if the Docklands were just the rough-and-ready construction and shipping district the vids present them to be. In truth, the lax law enforcement and the chance for profitable enterprise has made the Docklands into a haven for Heinlein's criminal elements, and even the corporations turn a blind eye to the gang activity as long as it doesn't impede upon their profit margins.

Literally hundreds of gangs and orgcrime syndicates have corners carved out of the Docklands, ranging from the Wasters and Vaporheads that prey on lost tourists up to smuggling empires like the Katala Brothers. Most however are like the Dust Haunters who "scavenge" scrap and machinery from construction sites or people like Ortega Jones who run the air tax and recycling rackets. In their eyes, at least, they provide a legitimate service to Heinlein, and as long as the city is buying, they'll keep on selling.

THE KATALA BROTHERS

Sadly, for every Lufkin and Hubbard trying to make Heinlein a safer, more prosperous place, there are people like Sasha and Yevgeny Katala carving out their own personal kingdoms. The men are the sons of the infamous Alexi Katala, former superintendent of the mining consortium at Leonovsk Station, a heritage that has its advantages when it comes to bribery and intimidation.

Like their father, Sasha and Yevgeny are ruthless bosses and unscrupulous businessmen, and despite what the Pestroka Technika Public Relations department would have you believe, they run most of the mining and He-3 contracts to former Russian bloc and other Mafiya enclaves. From their personal dome in the Docklands, the brothers maintain a small army of mobsters, and they have been implicated in dozens of open NAPD investigations. Yet, as long as they stay in the Docklands, they remain out of the authorities' reach.

Samuel Leung

ARMSTRONG BASE

To the northeast of Heinlein's central domes, Armstrong Base rises from the regolith like a stone fist ready to strike. Its dull-grey walls and slab-sided defense turrets protect the Space Expeditionary Corps's main base on the Moon. The imposing structure reminds friends and foes alike that should Luna rise again, Earth will be ready. By and large, Armstrong Base is a training facility, with suited SXC troopers drilling on its low-G obstacle courses and live-fire ranges. In addition to the hard-vacuum exercises and zero-G combats conducted in the Armstrong orbital stations, marines can expect to undergo grueling extra-Earth survival trials. Armed with a limited supply of air, they must try and navigate a simulated combat zone known as "Asphyxiation Alley." This is designed to replicate fighting in a damaged dome or on a space vessel, where the environment can be just as deadly as the enemy.

Armstrong Base is also the nerve center of Heinlein Defense, with orbital weapon platforms and ground-based missile silos covering the space around Heinlein and Starport Kaguya. Although it has been fifteen years since shots against enemy forces were last fired, it remains a potent threat to any craft that would try to assault Heinlein. Nevertheless, the area protected by Armstrong Base is strictly limited to that agreed upon by the signatories of the Treaty of Heinlein.

Gun towers and companies of marines are not the only weapons the SXC has at its disposal. Perhaps the eeriest aspect of Armstrong Base is its vast military graveyard known as the Battleground. Covering more than fifty square kilometers of Lunar surface, it began as a dumping ground for decommissioned vehicles and munitions from the War. Covered in glistening sealant to preserve their parts, entire Lunar armored divisions, squadrons of combat hoppers, and piles of artillery shells sit silently under the cold distant stars, awaiting the time they might be needed once again.

COLONEL METZGER

Armstrong Base's current commander, Colonel Metzger, is more concerned with preparing forces for the distant colonial disputes on Mars, but she still wields significant political power. Sitting atop tons of munitions and a few dozen nukes will do that for you. By the letter of the Treaty of Heinlein, the SXC can take no direct role in the policing of Heinlein, nor can it interfere in the affairs of corporate entities on their own private property. So, without a direct military threat to Heinlein, the SXC stays largely restricted to Armstrong Base where marines are trained and are readied for possible deployment to Mars at a moment's notice.

Colonel Metzger is an old friend of District Manager Hubbard, and whenever the Colonel visits Lunacent the two can be seen together, usually at the exclusive Sunwoods Golf Course. Rumors abound that Hubbard has been trying for years to persuade Metzger to take a more active role in cleaning up Heinlein, mainly focusing on the wilderness that the Docklands has become. Whether Metzger has agreed to anything is unknown, but as more than one lawyer has pointed out, there might be some wiggle room in the SXC's charter when it comes to the more aggressive Dockland criminals.

And who knows? Maybe Metzger would like to get some live target practice for her boys one of these days.

BEYOND HEINLEIN

Amid the thriving chaos of Heinlein's packed streets and flashing lights, it's easy to forget that Luna is primarily a vast grey wasteland. Here and there lights blink in the darkness where mining outposts and scientific stations break the surface, but by and large there is only rock and dust as far as the eye can see. Even so, a great many settlements lie beyond the domes of Heinlein—they are just dispersed over truly massive distances.

Most of the extra-Heinlein settlements can be found on Lightside, that half of the Moon that looks down on Earth due to its twenty-seven-day synchronous rotation. Darkside, as it is erroneously known, has a scattering of outposts, but the distances from Heinlein, not to mention unfavorable launch windows to Earth and the Beanstalk, have limited expansion on Darkside.

Many corporations and some governments still maintain a scientific presence on the Moon, and places like the Lovell Overlook, Mares Valley, and the Mons Wolff Observatory enjoy good funding. The Lovell Overlook is close enough to Heinlein to host social functions and even enjoy visits from local dignitaries. There are few better places to peer out into the stars and without interference from Earthshine. By contrast, the Mons Wolff Observatory takes hours to reach by tube-lev due to its location high in the peaks of the northern Lunar ranges. It maintains its own dedicated scientific team supported by a bioroid workforce to keep its systems running.

While the majority of heavy industry and private spaceports are confined to the Docklands, all of the megacorps maintain outposts further afield. The reasons are varied, but they usually involve a degree of secrecy that only the isolation of the Moon can provide. Sites like Port Anson and the facilities at Promontorium Agarum take up massive tracts of Lunar surface, their perimeters tightly guarded by all manner of intruder countermeasures.

By contrast, other places are abandoned husks: the ruins of Xiangong City and others attract only scavengers and treasure hunters these days.

Finally, places like Club Luna, Clarke Tower, and the L'Hôtel Tycho are oases of splendor and wealth among a drab, rolling sea of dust. Here the risties can sample a piece of Lunar life denied to most of its colonists while remaining safe behind their transplas domes and genegineered gardens. Clone servants see to their every need while they enjoy a host of unique local activities like skyrunning, grav-surfing, and hopper racing. L'Hôtel Tycho is especially sought after for its beautiful conservatory and the stunning views across the Tycho crater. Beneath its famous hovering arboretum grows a thriving garden of tropical plants that blends seamlessly with the Jinteki-engineered lunar foliage outside the transplas.

UNNATURAL CRATERS

Helium-3 harvesters crawl across the Lunar surface scraping off the top layer. They follow tightly controlled paths to ensure that no part of the surface goes to waste, with AI processors charting the location, speed, and direction of each vehicle. Seen from above, the resulting vast concentric patterns appear like graceful brush strokes upon the Lunar surface, creeping ever outward from the harvesters' home stations.

Once a harvester is full, conveyors and hoppers ferry its massive cargo of rock and dust back to processing plants to be refined. Grinding machines and mineral furnaces work non-stop to break down the harvested rock into pure helium-3 which is stored in canisters for shipment. A shroud of dust clings to every part of the refineries, making the Henry line's nasal and tracheal filters a necessity for continuous labor.

CONTROLLING INTERESTS

Shaped by Earth's hunger for He-3 and offering bold new solar markets, Heinlein has become a focal point of corporate interests. Where once the Moon was the sole purview of remote-controlled rovers, it has transformed into a worthy satellite of the rapidly developing New Angeles metroplex, with many citizens and corporations traveling up the Beanstalk to find their fortune. While He-3 mining remains Luna's principle draw, it is also primed to become a gateway to the stars. As humanity slowly settles the solar system, the Moon's prominence in its affairs can only grow.

With competition, however, comes conflict, and the Moon is more than a vital business market—it is also a battleground between opposing interests and conflicting ideas. The Big Four remain at the heart of these clashes, which are carried out on the stock market, across the Network, and in the dark alleys of the Docklands. Each has tied up huge sums of money in the expansion of the Moon as a place for research and development, free enterprise, and product placement and testing, and the corps intend to protect these investments.

HAAS-BIOROID

Haas-Bioroid's Luna offices are marvels of biomechanical innovation and design, their sleek buildings and gleaming tunnels dazzling in their perfection. Bioroid greeters guide guests through pristine white chambers, and the air itself chimes to the sound of pleasing melody. This is the ideal future that Haas-Bioroid wants the world to see: imagination and innovation given form and voice in its ever-growing product line.

Like many companies, Haas-Bioroid takes advantage of the Moon's low gravity for its scientific research and development programs. Their largest R&D facilities are located in the northern reaches of Heinlein, and from here they pioneer new kinds of high-end bioroids and provide logistical and technical support for those bioroids working on the Moon. Director Haas continues to push the bioroid as the superior specimen of android, a tactic that has had more success on Luna than on Earth. On the Moon, many jobs are too dangerous or undesirable for humans, and as Heinlein expands, labor shortages in new developments are common. Haas-Bioroid's products need not depend on the vacuum-proof hardsuits worn by the Turtleback line, giving HB the edge in reliability and safety. Even though Jinteki dominates the mining industry, the people of Heinlein have come to expect bioroid workers, emergency staff, and even security as part of their everyday life.

Luna is also home to some of Haas-Bioroid's most powerful processor vaults and server farms—the megacorp uses a prodigious amount of computing power in the development of faster, more effective bioroid brains. As one of the company's most precious resources, they are well protected beneath the corporation's main domes, with dozens of hard failsafes between them and unwanted intrusion. Even so, adventurous hackers or corporate rivals have targeted these datafortresses in the past, braving not just bioroid-powered countermeasures and security, but also the inhospitable Lunar environment itself.

Diana Martnez

JINTEKI

The lotus garden enclaves of the Jinteki offices are a rare glimpse of Earth captured on the Moon. Gene-crafted *sakura* trees sway in an artificial breeze as prospective clients cross the threshold. The heady scent brings back terrestrial memories, while nearby koi ponds glitter with the scales of rainbow carp—each one a Jinteki patent, of course. This is Jinteki's promise to its customers—wherever you might travel, home can go there, too.

The nuances of genetic engineering have allowed Jinteki to create almost-perfect facsimiles of people, and on the Moon the megacorp stands on the edge of even greater wonders. Like Haas-Bioroid, Jinteki enjoys the unique low-G and vacuum conditions of the Moon for its research. Sterile environments, the security of being surrounded by airless void, and the isolation to conduct itself away from watchful eyes all work in the megacorp's favor.

The Lunar business concerns of Jinteki are interwoven with Melange Mining, the He-3 company that utilizes thousands of clone workers. This makes the Moon an ideal place to test out new products and measure their suitability not just in heavy industry or hostile environments, but also in administration and technical work. Many of the most iconic clone models, like the Henry model or the Turtleback line, had their start in the regolith harvesters and mineral refineries of Melange Mining's domed settlements and factories.

The Moon is also the base for Jinteki's Generation Project. Although the final product would be years away from being released, the corporation is rumored to be experimenting with modifying clones for deep-space exploration and generation ships, with the ultimate goal of settling the far-flung areas of the solar system or even beyond.

WEYLAND CONSORTIUM

The Weyland Consortium has been credited with reconstruction on Luna, but the stylized "W" is conspicuously absent from most physical structures and even the titanic machines used to build them. The Consortium itself has not built anything since completing the Beanstalk over fifty years ago, but it does own the construction firms that landed the contracts to rebuild the colony. Weyland also owns a controlling interest in the Blue Sun fusion power company, one of Heinlein's primary energy sources besides the solar farms, and the investment has supposedly paid for itself many times over. Rumors cling to Weyland's Heinlein operations, but one story finds its way into the newsnet loops again and again.

According to unnamed insiders, Weyland is preparing for the next step in humanity's journey out into the stars. Manufactories on the Lunar surface ceaselessly toil away, while in Earth orbit the hull of a massive deep space vessel has begun to take shape. Its scaffold-covered hull bears the massive letters "Gagarin Deep Space Exploration." All this points to a bid by Weyland to be the first megacorp to place a claim on the outer planets, but only the barest pieces of information have trickled out into the public domain despite the efforts of more than one Netcriminal. Whatever the ultimate goals of Weyland and Gagarin Deep Space are, the project could usher in an age of evolution and endeavor unlike anything that has come before.

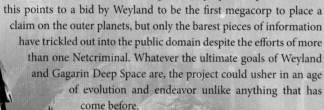

NBN

Threedees flicker like faulty fluorescents on nearly every Heinlein wall, while electronic eyes scan silently from the darkness of vaulted domes and tunnel ceilings. Far from intrusive, the trappings of NBN's media juggernaut let people know that wherever they go, someone is keeping a watchful eye on their safety—and making sure they have something good to watch as they travel to get there.

Like everywhere else in the world, NBN has eyes and ears all over Heinlein. With a substantial stake in the Lunar tourism market, including places like StarScape Shopping, it benefits the media giant to make the Moon look as attractive as possible to its terrestrial markets. To this end there are numerous dedicated Heinlein NBN personalities, like Serena Nightshade and Johnny Hendrickson that appear on vid screens every day to show just how exciting or adventure-filled life on the Moon can be. In fact, Serena's sensie series *Darkside Days* has done more for Heinlein's image in the last five years than any amount of official PR.

NBN is not only concerned with marketing the Moon, but also taking advantage of its placement. When it comes to providing top-quality entertainment and news to an ever-expanding solar civilization, the StarReach Pathway's program aims to combat NBN's greatest enemy: the speed of light. As it is, broadcasts from Heinlein have about a 1.3-second lag, while contact with Mars and beyond runs into minutes. The StarReach is a proposed system of deep-space satellites that would sync broadcasts across the system using planetary orbital data. Despite being constrained by the speed of light, it will allow coordination between systems and signals on an unprecedented scale. The program is still years away from completion, but the ground work is already being laid as NBN cements its hold on Heinlein's media sphere.

"They call it the Silver City, a place of wonders and marvels. In reality, it's the largest slave labor camp humanity has every created—of course you won't see that bit in your StarScape Shopping ads."

– Amy Avers, Liberty Society

MELANGE MINING

Dark transplas domes and worn plascrete bulkheads cluster around the site of the Melange Mining Headquarters like frightened children cowering close to their mother's side. The image is a fitting one, for each dome houses a subsidiary: a once-independent mining company that was bought out and swept up into Melange's arms. The head office foyer tells a similar tale. The towering threedees showing the history of mining on the Moon are ostensibly ones of hope and progress, but as more than one visiting executive as noted, it is also a trophy hall. Each holo captures a predecessor's zenith before Melange's rise to dominance.

When people think of He-3 and Lunar mining it is little wonder then that they think of Melange Mining. After the War, the U.S.-backed corporation moved in and picked up the pieces of its competitors. By the time other companies had gotten their act together, Melange, or 2M as it is sometimes known, was the principal supplier of He-3 to Earth, and no one planet-side wanted to disrupt supplies again.

As it is, 2M wields considerable political power on the Moon, and its demesne comprises vast stretches of the Moon's surface beyond Heinlein. Because of the importance of He-3, all the megacorporations work closely with 2M, and the mining giant maintains its independence only by playing its customers' rivalries against each other. Any of the megacorps could take 2M over in a one-on-one confrontation, but if anyone did try, the others would quickly step in to keep it from falling into their rival's hands.

Of course, 2M is not the only mining concern on the Moon, but it is the only one that matters. Neither Alpha Prospecting nor Pestroka Technika exists on the same playing field as 2M. Some blame Jinteki's favorable simulant labor contracts for 2M's monopoly, while others point to its use of Weyland freeports in the Docklands, neither of which seem to extend to other mining operations. However, the truth is 2M happened to be on the winning side of the War, and by the admission of its board, it intends to win out against its current competitors as well.

LUNA, MARS, AND BEYOND

The stars are as innumerable diamonds scattered across the black velvet pall of the void, calling out to humanity with the promise of wonders and marvels yet unimagined. And like a welcome guide, the Moon hangs above it all, Earth's closest celestial body and the first rung in a ladder that leads to distant shores and a future yet to come.

Given its special place in the heavens, it is little wonder that most extra-Earth outposts and corporate concerns have dealings with Heinlein and its people. Mars especially has a long history with the Moon, standing as its sometimes-ally during the War and sharing the honor of being one of Earth's few off-world colonies.

Most trade between the Red Planet and Earth still runs through the Moon, and the Martian Colonial Authority even maintains offices in Lunacent to oversee the safe passage of goods and personnel to Mars. The vast MCA warehouses in the Docklands are always a hub of activity. Although they are also a haven for smugglers, the MCA is reluctant to allow NAPD interference in their operations.

Beyond the ongoing troubles on Mars and the shadows they cast upon Luna, nearly every other outpost or spacefaring endeavor maintains strong ties with the Moon. Some of these, like the Psyolmetric Research Towers on Ceres, report to the Lunar division of Haas-Bioroid. Others, like the Ganymede Project on the Moons of Jupiter, actively recruit from Luna's populace, promising a life of adventure and exploration.

GONE BUT NOT FORGOTTEN

The Moon has its fair share of ghosts, from the specter of a Lunar state to the survivors of the War still lurking in craters' shadows. Some of this industry and its workers have found homes with other companies. Many corporate executives were offered amnesty by Earth after the War and found their way into the ranks of Alpha Prospecting, Pestroka Technika, or Blue Sun Corp. Most former rebels, however, stayed in the shadows and nursed their wounds, keeping alive the dream of a free Luna.

The NAPD and various terrestrial intelligence agencies strongly suspect that at least a dozen of the high-ranking leaders of the Lunar Insurrection are still alive and well living in Heinlein. The peace treaty freed them from any criminal charges for their part in the uprising, but many people wanted to keep a quiet eye on them, fearful that if there were to be another bid for Lunar independence it would find its roots in these former dissidents.

As the jurisdictional party, NAPD officers often pull the thankless duty of checking in on old rebels like Yan Hestor or Malory Macgillivray as they go about their lives. Most believe the notions that the Lunar insurrectionists once stood for are hopelessly anachronistic these days, buried under the relentless march of progress and prosperity offered by the megacorps. Yet Hestor still holds great influence with the citizen groups of Tranquility Home, and Macgillivray owns substantial holdings in the Docklands, and so for now they remain on the NAPD's watch list.

MARS

For hundreds of years humanity has looked to the fourth planet, Mars, as a source of mystery and adventure. Once upon a time, stories of little green men and invaders from Mars were the height of science fiction. Such stories faded as satellites and rovers explored the Martian surface, but Mars never lost its hold on the human imagination. Today, human beings have not only colonized this world, but the colossal task of terraforming the Red Planet is underway. This new, semi-lawless frontier remains one of the most challenging environments for civilization, yet the hardy Martian settlers have managed to defy the odds and thrive.

Several generations have lived, worked, and died to transform Mars into a world capable of supporting human life. They're not done yet: even now, venturing outside of the transplas domes requires breathing assistance and protective gear. Nevertheless, the planet has changed greatly from the aggressively hostile environment faced by the first explorers. Now, those who make the weeks-long voyage from Earth can find dozens of settlements scattered across the Martian surface; these range from small encampments huddled in canyon walls to huge, domescraper-packed cities erupting from the barren landscape. Millions call Mars home, and for at least a quarter of the population, it is the only one they've ever known.

As recent immigrants and Mars-born inhabitants establish their own identity as Martians, clans organized around specific settlements have supplanted ethnic and national identities. Although the entire planet's population is but a fraction of heavily populated cities like New Angeles, Mars is more than a handful of explorers in envirosuits scraping up soil samples—it is a living, breathing world with vast potential and considerable danger. With so many interests at stake in the planet's future, hostilities and rivalries continue to simmer under the surface. These are the legacies of the Martian Colony Wars, which supposedly ended fifteen years ago. Yet the clans, militias, and mercenaries still fighting on the Martian surface claim the War for Martian Independence is ongoing.

TAKING A WALK

A normal human on the surface of Mars won't last long, but it's not like he's sucking vac. He's got three basic problems.

The first is that he can't breathe—there's more O_2 in the atmosphere now than there was, but the pressure is so low and the concentrations so meager that unmodded human lungs can't pull anything useful from the air. A good respirator, one that seals around the face and has a standard tank of N-O mix, will do the trick here.

The second problem is that it's too cold. With the sun up, near the equator at the height of Martian summer, it's not so bad, and a good jacket will keep him warm enough. But once the sun goes down, nothing short of a heated envirosuit will keep a normal human alive for long.

The third problem is that he's being bombarded with more radiation than is healthy, but the good news is that the rads will take years to kill him! If he's got his germ cells backed up at a facility under a dome or back Earth-side, he can even still breed.

So really, Mars is practically paradise these days!

A BRIEF HISTORY OF COLONIAL MARS

Because of the great distance and harsh conditions, many of the first manned flights to Mars were a one-way trip. The early human expeditions to the Red Planet were also the first colonization missions, not all of which were successful. The original colonists on Mars made great sacrifices to pave the way for following generations. Survival sometimes meant circumventing corporate orders, although in some versions these renegades are punished for their disobedience. Harrowing tales of the *Gan De* and the dedication of Bradbury's early settlers are favorites around the Net. Many stories have been embellished over the years, but they all tell of hard work and independence, of adversity and altruism among those who first walked on the planet's oxide-laced surface. Together, these pioneers' tales give today's Martians a strong sense of personal identity, an ethic of self-sufficiency, and a suspicion of Earth-based authority.

Within the first few years of colonization, a handful of settlers began to lay the groundwork in the lava tubes on the slopes of Pavonis Mons in the Tharsis region. Less than a decade later, the first large-scale colonial craft, the *Olympus*, arrived. The settlers dubbed their new home "Bradbury." In the years that followed, numerous other colony craft arrived. Some continued to boost the population of Bradbury, while others built homes on new sites. The largest of the early colonization ships was the Chinese-built *Gan De*, which established Tianbian. Today, the massive vessel's remains form the core of the city in the Hellas Planitia basin.

Samuel Leung

A PLANET OF IMMIGRANTS

There are as many reasons to migrate to Mars as there are colonists. Some are refugees fleeing instability in their home countries, while others are entrepreneurs seeking success in new and untapped markets. The spaceflights from Earth to Mars are exorbitantly expensive even for coffin-sized accommodations, so most newcomers sign on with a corporation to pay for their passage. These multi-year contracts are indentured servitude, and Martian law is written to favor the corporations when contract disputes inevitably arise.

The Martian Colonial Authority (MCA) enforces strict immigration regulations in order to ensure population growth does not outstrip life-support system capacity. However, many Earther veterans from the War remained behind illegally, and some foreigners come over as tourists and overstay their visas. Theirs is a life of constantly ducking the law and migrating ever-further out along the Martian frontier. Some have the credits to afford a forged ID, while others scavenge the numerous mercenary combat zones to adopt the persona of one of the casualties.

In MCA colonies, having children requires licensure, but many couples circumvent these regulations on purpose or by accident. It is these undocumented Martian-born children who grow up to become the most fervent clansmen agitating for self-determination. According to the official, corporate world of Mars, they do not exist, meaning their share of water and oxygen is not accounted for.

CONTINUED STRIFE

Perhaps predictably given its mythological namesake, life on Mars remains one of conflict. Martians chafe under restrictive and proprietary trade practices that favor Earth-based corporations and governments. Scraping a living from the red dust is hard enough to begin with, and the corps are always quick to seize any surplus. A notorious example is AgInfusion, a subsidiary of Jinteki, whose genetically-modified staple crops do not produce second-generation seeds, requiring that new and more expensive ones be imported

LONG-DISTANCE CALLS

Stellar communications is still one of the largest obstacles to humankind's effort to colonize its solar system. Radio waves travel at the speed of light; they provide practically instantaneous communication on Earth and near-instantaneous communication between its surface, orbit, and Luna. Contacting ships and personnel any farther afield, however, can take many hours or longer thanks to the sheer vastness of space. Besides the changing distance between Earth and Mars, long-range communications within the solar system are further complicated by radiation interference, debris fields, asteroids, and large stellar bodies such as planets and moons. While many of these obstacles have been addressed by a comprehensive array of comms relays scattered throughout the solar system, sending a message from Earth to someone aboard a ship in Martian orbit or a mining expedition working in the Belt still takes anywhere between five and thirty minutes.

from Earth every year. Strangely, increased supplies or production efficiencies always seem to result in higher—not lower—taxes and prices for Martians.

Many believe that Mars would be better off if the MCA were dissolved. However, independence from Earth remains both a dream and a driver of conflict. Clan loyalties are as much an impediment to cooperation as they are a testament to the Martian desire for self-determination. Were the clans of Mars ever to unite under a single banner, Earth might have little choice but to accede to their demands or give up on Mars entirely. The current instability on the Red Planet ensures that this won't happen anytime soon, and many factions prefer to keep it that way.

MARTIAN TERRAFORMING

Mars has been a desolate wasteland for billions of years. Outside the domes, exposure to the thin atmosphere without the aid of specialized envirosuits means a slow and agonizing death. Daily temperatures are brutally cold except at the equator, and the planet's lack of a magnetosphere means that solar radiation impacts the surface unimpeded. Compared to the environment the first settlers encountered, however, the efforts to make Mars a friendlier setting for human life have been a resounding success, or so the corps claim. Even so, many centuries of work remain before a genetically unmodified human can walk on the surface of Mars without assistance or protection.

If Mars is to become habitable outside of the colony domes, three problems need to be addressed: Mars has no breathable atmosphere, the average surface temperatures are far too cold, and the solar wind freely bombards the surface with radiation. For terraforming to be successful, Mars's atmospheric pressure needs to be raised so that water can exist in liquid form outside of a controlled environment. Mars must also be able to keep its atmosphere from escaping into space. Finally, Mars needs a magnetosphere to protect it from the threats of solar radiation. Either greenhouse gas production needs to continue permanently, or a planetary-scale artificial magnetic field must be developed. Rumors abound that research into this is already well underway, but the power realities of such an immense project leave many skeptical, even with solar and fusion technologies.

METHODS

Much of the colony's structure and development revolves around shaping the Martian atmosphere for human habitation. A sizable part of the Martian economy is directed toward terraforming the planet, including industries such as geothermal mining, agriculture, and transport. Practices that have been banned or restricted on Earth are extensively employed on Mars, such as the purposeful release of chlorofluorocarbons (CFCs) and other greenhouse gases. Bio-seeding and meteor mining comprise the more unusual techniques that Martian terraformers use.

BIO-SEEDING

Although still in its earliest stages, bio-seeding provides the initial microbial life that will eventually convert carbon dioxide in the Martian atmosphere into oxygen. These bacteria, algae, lichens, and microscopic plants are genetically engineered to withstand the harsh environment and solar radiation of Mars, and they form the foundation for an eventual self-sustaining food chain.

Such efforts are virtually invisible to the typical Martian, however, as the only plant life encountered by the general populations is that found in the horticultural domes. However, in a handful of lower-altitude locations near the equator, a keen observer might see a greenish tint on areas of the planet's surface or some heavy-reddish lichen clinging to a rock.

CFC EXCAVATION

Compounds like CFC-12, sulfur hexa-fluoride (SF_6), and others are even more effective than carbon dioxide in retaining atmospheric heat and raising pressure. As such, numerous sulfur mines have cropped up in the Tharsis volcanic region, and fluorine strip mines dot the planet's surface. The work is dangerous but pays well, attracting large groups of Martian immigrants who work on the frontier for months at a time before heading back to recuperate at the larger colonies. Many of the pioneers frequenting the local watering holes are fitted with cybernetics of varying quality, evidence of one mining accident or another. The demand for the brutal labor won't die down anytime soon, since surplus rare metals are shipped back to Luna or to the Belt at an impressive profit.

METEOR MINING

Meteor mining is a bit of a misnomer in that crews are "mining" for suitable meteoroids to become meteors and eventually meteorites. Prospectors scour the outer edges of the asteroid belt for solid bodies with high concentrations of water ice or ammonia. By placing remote-controlled thrusters at specific points on the meteoroid's surface, these "comet-jockeys" alter their plunder's orbit for a precise collision course with designated sites on Mars. As crude and dangerous as this may sound, it remains the most viable means for rapidly altering the Martian atmosphere. Over time, these small meteorites raise the levels of water vapor, oxygen, and nitrogen, bringing Mars a small step closer to achieving breathable air.

The space cowboys that work the asteroid belt are an intrepid lot. While ammonia and water-rich comets and asteroids are a major part of their business, the Belt is brimming with vast hoards of untapped mineral resources. Women and men seeking a fortune in the glittering expanses procure a ship, often under contracts from the Weyland Consortium or its subsidiaries. Yet few ships remain exclusively tied to one sponsor. Crews might employ bioroids impervious to vacuum or four-armed clones engineered for long-term zero gravity. Legal jurisdiction in these far-flung space locations is blurry at best, and the cutthroat nature of asteroid prospecting makes for dangerous business. But for those willing to take the risk, fortunes await.

THE SACRED SURFACE OF MARS

"Not only do the corporations oppress the children of Mars, they also defile the sacred surface of humanity's birth planet! These terraforming efforts threaten to disrupt the primordial balance of wind, ice, and rock that sustained our progenitors.

"Our Messiah, Vasanti Smith, has embraced our ancient heritage and reclaimed humanity's sacred birthright. It was only a matter of time until we unlocked the secrets of our own creation. Our DNA remembers, and we can revert to our true forms—that of an ancient people who commanded the red dust and built glorious civilizations.

"You might not believe it's true, but that's exactly what the corps want you to think. They unearthed our age-old settlements when they began mining here. They're covering it up, afraid of what we'll do if we realize our true natures."

– Interview with an anonymous Crimson Dust adherent

LIVING ON THE RED PLANET

Martian daily life has a very different feel than it does on Earth. Martians live, eat, work, and unwind in very close quarters and in lower gravity. Good relationships with the neighbors aren't just a pleasant nicety: they're essential for survival. The needs of the individual are frequently subordinated to the needs of the community at large; with limited oxygen, water, and food supplies, one person's selfishness could mean the death of the entire settlement. These close-knit communities evolved into clans with their own distinct culture, unwritten rules, and codes of conduct. The clans have become the de facto power bodies, and they forge independent alliances and trade agreements with other settlements, much to the chagrin of the Martian Colonial Authority.

Martian clans identify themselves through intricate and distinct facial tattoos. These markers are inked on an individual to signify their acceptance within their clan as well as their individual accomplishments. New immigrants sometimes choose to ally themselves with a clan and take on the tattoo of their adopted family, although such a mark is modified slightly to indicate their immigrant origins. While clans tend to be colony-specific, it is not unusual to see multiple clan tattoos in the more cosmopolitan domes, such as Bradbury or Demeter.

While settlements on Mars come in many different shapes and sizes, they can be roughly classified as cities, nodes, or settlements—and whether or not they are affiliated with the MCA.

CITIES

The city is the largest type of settlement on Mars and the only type that can be accurately described as a colony unto itself. Aelita, Demeter, Gullivar, Podkayne, and Tianbian are all examples—Bradbury reigns as the largest of them all. Although these settlements are rich and developed enough to sustain above-ground transplas domes, the majority of their inhabitants dwell deep within the sprawling web of tunnels that radiate out from the city's center.

After the Martian Colony Wars, almost all major cities on Mars were forcibly brought under the umbrella of the MCA. These ties tend to grow more tenuous the farther one travels from Bradbury, however, and sectarians who once tasted freedom continue to plot for their city's home rule.

TIANBIAN

The Chinese-founded colony of Tianbian ("Horizon") is one of the oldest cities on the Martian surface, but its history has been troubled. Beginning with the forced landing of the colony ship *Gan De* (which was never designed to land) and a three-year lean time with no resupply, Tianbian struggled, overcame, and thrived, only to find itself fighting against both anti-Earth separatists and anti-Chinese Earth forces during the War.

Now a thriving community of some three-hundred thousand humans (and perhaps that many androids), Tianbian serves as the political capital and economic hub of its district. Tianbian's only dome, called Gan De Dome (built around the skeleton of the old colony ship), rises atop the slopes above the Hellas Planitia in the southern hemisphere, some nine kilometers above the basin's low point. Downslope, where the atmospheric pressure is higher, a variety of terraforming and agricultural projects make up the outer reaches of Tianbian's formal borders.

Tianbian's economy revolves around water imports from the glaciers in the Hellas Planitia and a large industrial base. In addition to the mining, smelting, and prefabrication of colony material that are standard for Martian cities and district capitals, Tianbian has a large synthetic polymer industry, brewing complex hydrocarbons in specialized bacterial tanks. Many of Tianbian's outlying settlements use inflatable domes made of the same polymers, especially the agricultural plots downslope.

South of Gan De Dome a new, larger dome is under construction. Still unnamed, this dome promises to provide an enormous amount of livable, walkable space on the surface of the planet and city planners boast that it will be as lovely as the Great Dome in Bradbury.

Tianbian's population is a mix of pre-War colonists from China and its allies in Asia and Africa, and a second-wave of MCA-approved immigrants from across Earth. The inevitably named Clan Gan De has fallen from primacy since the War, now mostly considered a bunch of old traditionalists out of touch with modern Tianbian. Clan Lockyer dominates the polymer and construction industries throughout the region.

MARTIAN COLONIAL AUTHORITY
MEMBER COLONIES AND SETTLEMENTS

POPULATION RANGE/DESIGNATION

	100–2,000	*Node*
	2,001–100,000	*City*
	100,001+	*Multi-dome City*

Future Sites of Coastal Expansion

PAXTON'S NODE

KLINE

PODKAYNE

AIRY

URANIUS LINE

PIERIA

BISSON

GULLIVAR

BRADBURY

MARINER

MARIENERIS LINE

DEMETER

AELITA

Name: *BRADBURY*

Location: 1°00'21" N; 112°48'40"W (Pavonis Mons)
  Equatorial region of the volcanic Tharsis plateau

Altitude: 12,360m (Upper Patera); Industrial District 9,340m (Caldera)

Population: 3,000,000

Developed Areas:

  Upper Patera: 2,400km²

  Industrial District: 600km²

  Daedalus Complex: 240km²

Associated Settlements:

  Gullivar, Daedalus Complex, Station One

ROBINSON

ARNOLD

BRACKETT

TYYRHENA LINE

MESLAM

MOJAVE

PROPOSED INTERHEMISPHERAL LINE

ENDURANCE

TIANBIAN

YINGHUO

VICTORIA

Kirsten Zirngibl, Map: Sarah Webb

NODES

Nodes are much smaller than cities, and although a few of the richer corporate nodes have modest transplas domes, the majority of them are built below the surface. Nodes like Kline or Paxton's Node were either built on the site of a single resource or utility, such as a mine, geothermal station, or groundwater pump, or they were constructed as maintenance stations or transition points along the extensive mag-lev train network. Ag-bubbles, mainly given over to food production, also fall within this category.

Populations can vary from one hundred to two thousand people depending on the age, location, and industry of the node. Although the corporations generally own the infrastructure of the node itself and set the official policies, its inhabitants belong to one or more clans that unofficially serve as the people's municipal governors. In the nodes, tensions between both sides frequently ignite into physical confrontations and violence.

Many nodes that are officially represented by the MCA are much less interested in planetary politics in practice. During the Colony Wars, Earth forces focused most of their efforts on reclaiming Mars's cities, leaving the vast majority of nodes to fight among themselves. The nodes haven't forgotten this, and Mars Colonial Police suspect that many harbor separatist sentiments and terrorist groups or leaders.

PAXTON'S NODE

Originally built as a uranium mining operation to supplement the limited quantities of He-3 in Martian soil, Paxton's Node is a thriving anarchy found on the fringes northeast of Podkayne. It is largely an underground complex—a dilapidated rat's maze of small-scale industries, shops, and temporary residences. The node has a flourishing black market and operates independently of the Martian Colonial Authority. Although the MCA tries to reassert its authority and crack down on the criminal enterprises here, Paxton's Node remains free aside from the occasional Mars Colonial Corps raid. Instead, the clan council forges alliances and trade agreements that suit them, often with the support of local crime syndicates and mercenaries.

It is a dangerous place for anyone wishing to make an honest living, and many who don't want to be found call Paxton's Node home. Even so, prospectors use the ramshackle community as a base of operations for exploring the northern basin for valuable minerals. There are fortunes to be made in nitrate, diamond, gold, and heavy elements. Several mercenary groups have set up shop here that offer security for anyone able to pay for it.

The lack of civic authority is obvious from the absence of a cohesive plan for building inside the city. Whatever infrastructure exists is from the original uranium mine before it was abandoned by the corporations. Members of the dominant clan, Clan Schia, are the descendants of the miners that once worked here, and they continue to mine and market what heavy elements they are able to from the depths below the node. Schia is the closest thing to a police force the node knows, and those who cross the clan tend to end up in the wrong place when the life-support systems malfunction.

SETTLEMENTS

Anything smaller than a node is simply called a settlement. The MCA regulates the creation of new settlements in the Organized Territory, offering land to any person or corp that can afford it. Settlements might consist of a transatmospheric spacecraft converted into living quarters, while less-legal operations might take advantage of existing abandoned structures on the Martian landscape.

The fortunes of settlements are much more variable than nodes or cities; because the MCA doesn't keep records of settlements in the Unorganized Territory, it's impossible to know how many take root or die off each year. If it endures, the outpost might develop a clan culture and someday grow into a node, but life for these frontiersmen is undeniably the hardest of any of Mars's settlers. Settlements unaffiliated with the MCA must be self-sufficient in terms of food, shelter, life support, and security, since traveling to even the closest node or city is a long and resource-intensive endeavor. Even those recognized by the MCA are at the mercy of the local Martian Colonial Corps regiment for assistance, which might already be overwhelmed by local clan militias or mercenary bands.

CABOT STATION

Building a settlement in the Unorganized Territory is a dangerous proposition undertaken only by the overconfident, the foolhardy, or the desperate. Neets Cabot must have been some mixture of all three when she brought her family and a few friends way out into the Martian frontier to settle in a gulch on the edge of the Nepenthes Planum. Cabot was dead within two years, but Cabot Station survives and even, after a fashion, thrives.

Cabot settled her family directly on an easily accessible aquifer of water ice, and the pioneers swiftly dug into the Martian rock. The result is a small community that is mostly underground; only a large quonset hut that serves as a garage, a shipping container refurbished into an office, and a sizable inflatable dome full of green growing things betray the settlement's location from a distance.

The settlement's prosperity, such as it is, is drawn from the water it mines from the aquifer and its fortuitous position between two mining outposts to the northeast and south, which are called simply the North Mine and the South Mine. Technically independent settlements in their own right, the mines rely on Cabot Station for water, food, and recreation, and Cabot Station has become something of a market hub as the miners bring in the vanadium and platinum-group metals for trade. About once a month, a dusty heavy-duty truck arrives from one of the local clans to pick up the accumulated metals and deliver necessities the Station can't make for itself, such as glowbulbs, coffee, and medical supplies.

Cabot Station itself is home to roughly one hundred souls under the leadership of Neets's daughter Aerin Cabot. With a tiny population, few weapons, and no legal right to appeal to the MCA, the station must carefully balance its relationship with Clan Sisina and Clan Gower, who control the only nearby communities of note. Unfortunately, the two clans hate each other, and to make matters worse, South Mine is owned by one clan, and North Mine by the other. Life in Cabot Station is fragile, but despite it all, the community survives.

BRADBURY

Perched atop the gentle slopes of the enormous Pavonis Mons is Bradbury, the largest city on Mars. It is a microcosm of Martian life: a hive of political intrigue, a bright center of culture, and an industrial powerhouse that wields tremendous influence on both Earth and Mars. Here, one can see and experience the finest Mars has to offer. Those in the upper echelons of power have worked very hard to cultivate Bradbury's image as a cultural center worthy of investment, a perception that is jealously protected by those who benefit from the economic engine the colony has become.

Of course, there is far more to the story: Bradbury is more complex and diverse than even Heinlein, and rivals some of the smaller megacities on Earth. Visitors who stray away from the Great Dome can quickly discover the drudgery of a confined colonial existence. Workers can go months at a time without seeing the auburn skies. Rank-and-file Martians contend with tight cramped living spaces, inadequate income, and a lack of social mobility. This often leads to a plague of social ills including addiction, crime, and political unrest, all of which can be found in Bradbury's underbelly.

But for those who have come to adopt this city as their new home, they would not have it any other way.

THE "CENTER OF THE UNIVERSE"

Bradbury is often disparaged by the residents of other colonies as the "Center of the Universe." It is a criticism that has merit, as Bradbury is the largest city on Mars, the primary hub of the maglev transportation network, and the seat of the Martian Colonial Authority. As such, Bradbury's residents and media seem either apathetic or oblivious to anything going on beyond the bounds of Pavonis Mons or Tharsis. However, the reality is that Martians tend to be dome-centric no matter which colony they live in. Bradbury's perceived arrogance is simply on display for the whole planet to see.

Still, if one is comes to Mars to do business, the vast majority of interplanetary traffic comes through Bradbury or one of its outlying starports. The impending construction of a space elevator at the Daedalus Complex would further cement the largest colony's central role as a conduit for people and goods on and off world. Whether they like it or not, Bradbury is indeed the proverbial center of the universe for Martians and visitors alike.

WALKING ON TWO PLANETS

Despite its enormous size and its firm role in Martian politics, passing through Bradbury can be like walking on both Earth and Mars, and at the same time neither. The biggest city on Mars has far more in common with any Martian colony, dome, or node city than it does with any of its counterparts on Earth. Still, this megapolis has numerous amenities and resources that would be familiar to visitors from Earth but alien to any native Martian.

The most glaring example is the six fountain pools found near the Khondi Tower in the Great Dome. What would be consid-

PAVONIS MONS

Latin for "Peacock Mountain," Pavonis Mons is the central peak of the Tharsis Montes on the high volcanic plain in Mars's western hemisphere. Formed as a shield volcano in low gravity, the mountain slopes averages a very shallow 4° grade. Despite the fact that it is the smallest of the four major peaks in the region, it still stands some 14,000m above the planet's mean surface level, and 7,000m above the surrounding Tharsis region. As a comparison, Pavonis Mons stands more than 5,000m higher that Mount Everest on Earth.

The central dormant volcano was chosen as a site for what would become Bradbury Colony for its proximity to the equator in the eventual hope that it could support a space elevator. It was also chosen for its altitude and the protection that it was able to offer the early colonists. The patera, a depressed area just below the peak of the mountain, is largely immune to the dangerous dust storms that have been known to consume the Red Planet. Finally, existing water and geothermal resources also ensured a safe supply of oxygen.

ered normal on Earth is seen as a waste of precious resources by water-conscious Martians. Such issues might be considered petty, but they are still a major source of friction. Where Earthers take the air they breathe for granted, paying it scant attention, Martians, like Lunar colonists, are so conscious of their processed atmosphere that they can smell and taste subtle changes—changes that can be a matter of life and death.

Consequently, Bradbury's cosmopolitan nature is both a blessing and a curse. It maintains vital links to Earth, yet those connections and commonalities alienate the city's leaders from the very people they are trying to govern.

HISTORY

Bradbury evolved out of the original colony established on the upper patera of Pavonis Mons, a shallow crater at the volcano's summit, just north of the much deeper caldera. The first settlers took advantage of the labyrinth of lava tubes as a ready-made network of shelters to keep themselves safe from the hazardous solar radiation, brutal wind, and punishing cold. Safely sealed and pressurized by tapping into the natural high-pressure geothermal gases deep inside the dormant volcano, colonists were able to move beyond their shelters as oxygen levels were brought up to human norms to begin building in these natural structures. Even today, the lava tubes of Pavonis Mons serve as the backbone of Bradbury's overall infrastructure, even as artificial structures appear to dominate the exterior.

EARLY SETTLEMENT

The legends of the first colonists that came to Mars tell of hardship and struggle countered by ingenuity and tenacity. The slopes

THE LEGEND OF VASANTI SMITH

Martians have a strong oral tradition that transcends anything you might find on the Net or broadcast by NBN—call it a lack of trust for conventional media. They tell their own stories of the first settlers and the hardships they faced all by word of mouth. The most iconic of these early settlers is Vasanti Smith, a woman who was part of the original expeditionary team that came to Pavonis Mons decades ago.

It was through her efforts that the first tunnels were explored and made habitable, overcoming incalculable odds. While records show that Smith was a geochemist, the stories portray her as an insatiable explorer, fascinated by the serpentine tunnels of the mountain, expanding and exploring the most dangerous tunnels, and finding new resources. She was the one who discovered a tunnel system connected to the Pavonis Glacier. Passed down through generations, this has evolved into a tale where she drew water from the Martian rock.

For Martians, Vasanti Smith has become symbolic of the miracle of Martian survival, and her mysterious disappearance while exploring deeper into the mountainside only added to her mystique. Her last words—a promise to return—made her a figure of legend, and in some cases, a religious idol, so much so that the leader of Crimson Dust claims to be Vasanti Smith returned. True or not, her iconic status is firmly entrenched in Martian society.

– Excerpt from "The Origin of Martian Legends," a lecture by Dr. Philius Craig

of Pavonis Mons were selected early on, along with Arsia Mons to the south, as exploration points. The Tharsis Montes shield volcanoes proved to be ideal candidates for the first colonists, as they not only had potential energy resources with deeply buried geothermal power, but contained frozen water in subsurface glaciers near their respective peaks. Most importantly, they had lava tubes similar to those found in Earth's shield volcanoes. In the lighter Martian gravity, this cave network was considerably larger than anything on Earth, stretching for tens to hundreds of kilometers in any direction and delving ten to hundreds of meters deep below the surface. It was an ideal choice the first colonists for shelter and production.

First, robotic construction crews were sent to an ideal site to lay the initial groundwork. By the time the first colonists arrived, a small section of caves were ready to be pressurized and then adapted to human standards. Yet, the early colonists constantly struggled with the atmospheric balance and food production. During this time, Martians became known for their ingenious means of harnessing the inherent energy of the Red Planet and adapting to the grueling circumstances.

Today, native Martians are famous for their ability to detect subtle changes in atmospheric composition, including variations in oxygen and nitrogen levels. That talent is said to have originated back when it was a matter of survival for the first settlers, and it has since been further enhanced using genetic modification.

EXPANSION

The original colonists were few in number, but their population slowly grew. As those pioneers scrambled to build their new home, the *Olympus*, the largest colonial ship of its day, would bring over a thousand new colonists to the slopes of Pavonis Mons. Upon their arrival, the lava tube network was quickly expanded and reinforced, and the newly dubbed colony of Bradbury began to grow exponentially. Eventually, colonial ships were arriving once per month, and each new crop of colonists swelled their ranks. The corps sponsored massive investment and development, which allowed Bradbury's population to explode.

With dramatic growth, however, came the realities of life in such cramped quarters. These new Martians had to find ways to resolve their differences and govern themselves or risk destroying themselves from within. A series of unofficial agreements decided by quorum would become the de facto political structure. The

colonists organized themselves by role, and the first clans were formed.

Of course, the realities of the hostile environment outside remained a constant concern. During this period, at least two major disasters saw the accidental depressurization of several sections of the network, resulting in the deaths of hundreds of colonists. This led to additional safeguards and design considerations that would allow sections of the settlement to be isolated quickly in case of catastrophic depressurization. Even today, this danger is never far from Bradburian minds, and it was one of the main reasons for local opposition to the Great Dome.

FROM TUNNELS TO DOMES

As Bradbury expanded, they built structures beyond the lava tube network, especially on the surface. Advances in engineering created a viable model for a hexagonal transplas dome design that could provide the needed shelter for building on the Martian surface. These designs proliferated, and several colonies began to use them, but none so aggressively as Bradbury. A visitor could be forgiven for thinking that the majority of Bradbury exists above-ground for all the buildings and domes in the patera of Pavonis Mons—today, the megapolis's mass and population is nearly equally divided between the domes and underground warrens.

The transformation from a city of tunnels to the domes on the surface also marked a major societal transformation. No longer were the residents of Bradbury simply colonists struggling to survive on the harsh environment of Mars. Rather, these were Martians seeking to make life better for themselves and their descendants.

MEGAPOLIS

Today Bradbury is home to several million people housed under dozens of domes or throughout hundreds of kilometers of lava tubes. It is the economic and political center of Mars, and it represents both the best and worst that the planet has to offer. Following the official end of the Colony Wars fifteen years ago, Bradbury became the seat of the Martian Colonial Authority as a direct result of the Treaty of Heinlein. The Colonial Senate is housed in the Khondi Tower at the center of the Great Dome, with the major institutional buildings surrounding it.

While it seems much of Mars exists in a perpetual state of civil war, Bradbury is considered a safe haven. It is well protected by the forces of the Mars Colonial Corps and the clan militia forces comprising the Bradbury United Division. No major attack has been successfully launched inside the main part of the city since the end of the Worlds War.

Still, intrigue, deception, and the cat-and-mouse games of spycraft not only dominate the glittering halls of the Great Dome, but reach down into the very bowels of the Therm. If and when Martian terrorists target the MCA in earnest, it will be Bradbury's domes they breach.

LIFE AND TRANSPORT

A scintillating mosaic of all that the Red Planet has to offer, visitors to Bradbury quickly find themselves in the midst of a crash course in Martian life. From the claustrophobic maze of tunnels below, to the soaring spires that pierce the Great Dome, it's easy to lose one's way. For most residents and visitors to Bradbury, it's rare to be able to see more than a hundred meters in any one direction. Rather, a trellis of orange-tinged plascrete walls and exposed ductwork are a frequent sight throughout Bradbury's honeycombed cityscape. It is only when one gets close to the domescrapers under the Great Dome that the city opens out to its grand reputation.

DAILY LIFE

Quotidian routines in Bradbury are as diverse as the people who live there. People and androids labor away in the life support modules deep underground or stride through the halls of corporate power in the arcologies above the Great Dome. While the districts and domes of the megapolis intersect, and individuals are free to travel wherever they choose, it is not

uncommon for family groups to stay close to the security of home. Bradburians have a long memory of tunnel decompressions, atmospheric breaches, or auto-lockdowns that have torn families apart.

WORK LIFE

Bradbury's numerous industries range from raw resource extraction, to manufacturing, to an extensive service sector. While no formal caste system exists in Bradbury, work in the megapolis is highly compartmentalized, and workers live within corp-supplied residences. As such, they are never far from their place of employment, relying on short trips on the transit grid. Work and home life is often so intertwined that it can be hard to separate the two. A change in employment almost always means that a family is forced to relocate, an option that many work very hard to avoid, even if it might mean an improvement in their economic circumstances.

Despite the natural tendency for Martians to be suspicious of Earthers, they seem to make an exception for those coming to Mars for physical labor. Because of the lighter gravity on Mars, the more intensive labor roles are perfect for Earth-born workers who come to Mars seeking a new life. These immigrants are capable of lifting the heaviest loads, but eventually their muscle mass and bone structure adapt to their new home. Such immigrants integrate quickly into life in Bradbury, building relationships and integrating with the communities as their strength degrades. It is not uncommon to find an Earth-born laborer bearing clan tattoos within a year of setting foot on Mars.

Many laborers attempt to maintain their physique by wearing "weight suits" that simulate the gravitational forces of Earth, or by augmenting themselves with cybernetics or genetic modifications. Bioroids and clones are a more accepted part of Martian life for those clans and colonies that can afford them. Eking out a living on the Red Planet is tough enough, and colonists will take all the help they can get.

HOME LIFE

Visitors from Earth immediately notice that even the most luxurious accommodations on Mars are austere and compact compared to what they are used to. Habitable space is at a premium, and as such, those living in Bradbury make efficient use of whatever is available. Corporate apartment complexes often have shared living spaces in which families have their own small sleeping pods but share common rooms for eating and recreational activities.

This results in very tight-knit communities, as coworkers also live together, and child-rearing and family life becomes a collective activity. Most often this close-knit connection is expressed in clan life. While not exclusively the case, coworkers are both neighbors and clan-mates.

Although the MCA places strict limits on birth rates in the name of preserving access to limited air and water resources, the clans deliberately disregard these restrictions and raise very large families anyway.

On Mars, assisted fertility technologies are a standard component of the reproductive cycle; hazards of radiation from the unbridled solar wind wreaked havoc on the early settlers' ability to produce healthy children. Even though shielding technology in the colonies has improved, reproductive assistance is still an expected part of life and has been integrated into coming-of-age rituals. Upon receiving

their full tattoos, every Martian also adds their gametes to a cryogenic preservation system to guarantee their offspring will be healthy.

The in vitro reproductive techniques are astoundingly successful, and deliberate misuse can result in a high rate of multiple births. For the clans, these large families are the best way to grow their numbers and guarantee clan safety on a harsh world. Martian twins, triplets, and even quadruplets often illegally share a single MCA ID—if they even have one at all.

Earthers and corporate elites on Mars disparagingly call the large number of children born here "litters." If a family on Earth could expect to have two or three children, the equivalent family on Mars might expect six to eight children over the same time span.

RECREATION AND CULTURE

Bradbury has numerous opportunities for recreation, but they vary depending on one's social class and clan affiliation. Aboveground, casinos, nightclubs, and shopping centers fill the domes and cater to tourists with ostentatious and campy displays of old-fashioned portrayals of Mars in popular culture. Greenspaces give corporate envoys room to stretch their legs and enjoy a little bit of Earth. Swimming pools are exceptionally rare and reserved for the elite of the elite. Low-gravity and holosport stadium matches are broadcast across the Martian Network.

Among the lower classes, however, recreation is often of the home-grown variety (when it happens at all). Real Martians work such long hours that almost all downtime is spent sleeping or tending to living quarter maintenance.

The children entertain themselves with sports and stories while their parents work. The Martian variant of football is played virtually anywhere with the slightest open space, and walls and angling bounces are integrated as part of the game. Bygone narratives set on Mars tell of separate civilizations and cultures, which also have the effect of helping Mars's next generation develop a distinct identity from Earthers.

Clans discourage the consumption of media produced by NBN or related subsids, however, because they frequently portray life on Mars in simplistic terms. "If you work hard, you'll reap the rewards!" is a narrative at odds with the sometimes desperate, tedious, and thankless existence that constitutes clan life.

For adults between jobs or shifts on the frontier, common vices include prostitution, illegal fighting rings, illicit substances, and other underworld activities. Because clans often control significant areas of their work sites, it is not uncommon to find these activities taking place on company property. When low-paid corporate guards are members of the same clan as the workers, as is often the case, they typically turn a blind eye to such transgressions.

Have you ever heard that "Jinteki has nothing on Martians' ability to clone themselves"? It may be a joke, but fertility treatments and g-mods are necessary given the hazards of the open solar wind. We do our own, though. Jinteki may have bought out those labs a few years back, but several of the reproductive patents were made public before they moved in, so they're in clan hands now. J's not happy about it and is aggressively buying up everything else, peddling whatever g-mods they can convince us to buy. I'll admit, some of them are pretty decent, but are you willing to have an advantage if it means giving the copyright on your genes to Jinteki?

Where Weyland seems to be everywhere on Earth, Jinteki is doing its best to have their hand in nearly everything on Mars, even if it doesn't have their logo. If it's organic, assume Jinteki wants in on it. I don't know how successful they really are, but they own several colonies outright, including Phobos through AgInfusion. Granted, Jinteki has been wise to distance themselves publicly from their subsidiary's recent actions, but in the end, proprietary genetics are Jinteki's core. AgInfusion may be a bit over-the-top with providing coded-seeding grains to Phobos, but really, Jinteki wants that level of control. Of all the megacorporations, I'd say half of the corporate representatives on Mars work for Jinteki or its subsidiaries. They wield a lot of political power here in certain colonial pockets, so they're an easy villain.

MODES OF TRANSPORTATION

The vast majority of transportation on Mars is some form of public transit, and Bradbury is the site of the biggest domestic vehicle manufactories. The networks of skyways that are commonplace on Earth are replaced by a multi-layered web of mag-lev inductrack on which one or more connected cars float. For police, emergency services, and the elite, hoppers flit back and forth in the tight confines between buildings and domes. On rare occasions, one can catch glimpses of atmospheric hoppers flying back and forth above the transplas.

MAG-LEV INDUCTRACK

Unlike Earth's cities, Bradbury and the other Martian colonies were never designed for individually owned wheeled vehicles. The cheapest means of moving large numbers of both people and cargo on Mars is the mag-lev train network. With mag-lev technology, the trains can match the speed of atmospheric flight on Earth, making commercial air traffic on Mars virtually nonexistent.

The types used inside colonies and across the Martian landscape differ in size and purpose, but the operating principles are essentially the same: electromagnets lined along open guideways or transplas tubes repel like-poled magnets on the train cars themselves, the force of which is strong enough to overcome the weak Martian gravity and levitate the train cars above the tracks.

Inside Bradbury, the inductrack is smaller, allowing the mag-lev cars and trains navigate the colony's maze-like design. The guideways criss-cross each other at multiple levels. Here, one can see individual pods running alongside larger trains of cars in a gracefully controlled dance. Each car or pod is gyroscopically stabilized to make sure that the internal cabin always remains level no matter what angle the track might be. Several guideway tubes traverse the steep walls of the caldera, connecting the Industrial District to the main part of the city.

Outside of Bradbury, there exist multiple inductrack networks on Mars owned by competing corps. TransMars, Bradbury Rail Co., and the Red Line have each carved out portions of the Martian landscape for their exclusive use, and incursions on each other's territory is tantamount to a declaration of corporate war. These rivalries, colloquially known as the Rail Wars, inevitably involve the clans whose very livelihoods depend on the cargo shipments brought by mag-lev.

AIR TRANSPORTATION

Besides rail transportation, atmospheric vehicles are also viable but are primarily owned and operated by police, emergency, military, and the societal elite of Mars inside of colony domes, but that doesn't stop mercenary groups and rebels from stealing units. The many different types of air vehicles on Mars are collectively known by the generic term "hopper," short for skyhopper, though they differ in various ways from their counterparts on Earth.

For conventional use inside a colony dome, hoppers are large blade-protected quadcopters that have immense precision control, usually built for one or two individuals. When needed, Bradbury Colony Police and emergency services have access to larger units capable of moving groups of ten to twelve individuals into tight spaces. Like their counterparts on earth, these hoppers use rechargeable hydrogen fuel cells to power the electromagnetic hoverfoil rotors and can be easily recharged on hopper pads.

Outside of the dome, what most Martians still refer to as "hoppers" are actually normal tiltjet aircraft that hyper-compress the thin atmosphere for propulsion. These jets fly faster and are more robust than their in-dome counterparts, but are far less maneuverable. Instead of flitting from charging pad to charging pad, these hoppers rely on more conventional chemical fuel like meta for combustion.

When compared to Earth-based aircraft, Mars-built atmospheric hoppers are blocky and wingless, as aerodynamic lift can only truly work at dangerously fast speeds. Corporations house small fleets of these craft for work outside the city, where maintenance workers require access otherwise unreachable by the transportation networks, or executives need to risk travel for important business.

Military hoppers are similar to their corporate counterparts, but are both heavily armed and armored. Visual camouflage patterns tend to be variations on the oxide surface and amber sky.

GROUND VEHICLES

Wheeled and tracked vehicles exist on Mars, but they are almost exclusively used for heavy industry and resource extraction, along with some military applications. These vehicles are universally built for operation in the raw Martian atmosphere, even if they are sometimes employed under the dome. In Bradbury, wheeled vehicles are rare, but are most often found in the Industrial District on the floor of the caldera, as well as in the quarries and glacier mining operations on the northwest slopes of Pavonis Mons.

Some of the most impressive of these specimens are Martian-designed haul trucks that work the glacier mines. These enormous six-axle vehicles use electric traction motors to handle high-mass loads over four hundred metric tons. Those visiting from Earth might find these vehicles the most recognizable, but even then familiarity is quickly obscured by thick plating, gnarled piping, and Martian dust.

Even more alien-looking, walkers and crawlers are extreme all-terrain vehicles capable of providing a stable platform on even the roughest of ground. The trade-off is that they are much slower than other ground vehicles. These are most likely to be found in the first stage construction of mag-lev inductrack or in the Unorganized Territory, as they are capable of going anywhere.

> *...incursions on each other's territory is tantamount to a declaration of corporate war.*

BUILDING A COLONY

Earthers who have never been to Mars might imagine enormous bubbles or geodesic domes enveloping entire cities. Such large domes are impractical for most Martian settlements, however—they are an expensive luxury that exposes their dwellers to tremendous danger.

Bradbury is one of the main exceptions, and its domes are a testament to its wealth and prestige. Here, domes are built using similar principles for building suspension bridges, but instead of the load being a bridge deck, thick cables suspend an extensive tessellation of transplas panels that serves as the surface of the dome. These panels are arranged in hexagonal pattern, which resemble a typical geodesic design flattened out. Outside, each structure resembles an enormous transparent hexagonal tent, with six tall spires piercing the dome surface, and complex web of interweaving cables hanging above the exterior. Only the largest colonies sport a collection of multiple hexagonal dome structures, which are often arranged in a honeycombed pattern next to each other. Bradbury boasts the largest of this style dome on Mars.

THE STRENGTH OF INDUSTRY

Bradbury's economic strength comes as much from its heavy industries as resource extraction and manufacturing. Large megacorporations oversee many smaller operations that extract resources from the vicinity, import materials from across Mars, and manufacture products for local use and for export to other colonies.

PLASCRETE AND VANASTEEL

The early builders drew from the materials on hand, innovating new approaches to processing and refining that had been taken for granted for centuries. Construction materials, primarily plascrete and vanasteel, are locally sourced from the iron-rich Martian regolith and the volcano itself.

Because of the radically different environment, fashioning such as resources for use on Mars requires a much different approach than that on Earth. Reflecting the planet, nearly all the plascrete structures in Bradbury bear a pink to reddish-brown tone rather than the warm greys of Earth-poured concrete.

BUILDING WITHOUT WOOD

Organic-based building materials are vanishingly rare on Mars. Whatever wood exists is horrifically expensive given that any quantity of it has to be either imported from Earth or grown locally. The latter option is rarely used for construction because trees are far more valuable in the production of oxygen. Only when a tree needs to be trimmed—or has died—is the wood harvested for decorative use, fetching prices comparable to gold.

THE POLITICS OF GRAVITY

The difference between weight and mass on Mars (compared to Earth, anyway) means that Martian engineers and construction workers commonly work in the metric unit of Newtons. An object measuring 100kg on Earth would also be 100kg on Mars since mass does not change. However, the same object would weigh 981 Newtons on Earth, but in Mars's lighter gravity it would weigh 371 N. The distinction is more a way for Martians to distance themselves from Earth than anything else, but it does help guard against confusion.

In everyday use, Martians tend use to kilograms, but they are careful to use it as a measure of mass. Anyone who says "I weigh 75kg" would be instantly pegged as an Earther, an outsider. Visitors and new immigrants wishing to fit in quickly learn to say "I mass 75kg."

RESOURCE EXTRACTION

Because of its location, Bradbury has numerous primary resources immediately available for the megapolis to exploit, including glacier mining for water, geothermal power, and numerous minerals. This makes up as much of a third of the city's economy, and some would argue that this portion is much higher since Bradbury's manufacturing base would not exist without its primary resources.

GLACIER AND WATER MINING

Much of the industrial infrastructure on the western side of the colony is devoted to bringing essential water into the colony's system. Buried under the regolith on the northwest flank of Pavonis Mons lies an enormous glacier that made settlement on the volcano possible. It is the primary source for water, but it also has other resources to offer Bradbury. Water and carbon dioxide ice is strip-mined from this glacier to provide the basic foundation for almost every facet of life.

GEOTHERMAL POWER

The natural geothermal energy from deep within Pavonis Mons supplies Bradbury with most of its power. The volcanic system also furnishes the colony with valuable gases used in industry as well as the city's atmosphere and life support. Many spaghetti-like networks of pipes lace through the tunnels of Bradbury, directing their high-pressure cargo from geothermal and gas wells deep below the mountain through the Therm in the Industrial District. The heat and natural pressure of the mined gas also spins heavy turbines in the Therm, supplementing the city's electrical needs.

IRON MINING

The regolith of Mars is dense with hematite and magnetite, both of which are iron-laced rocks. Mines exist all over Mars, and Bradbury is no exception. Used in a variety of applications, magnetite is the primary mineral extracted from the caldera of Pavonis Mons.

THE VALLES AQUIFER

Bradbury's fierce appetite for water sources has brought it into direct conflict with Robinson Colony over the use of the Valles Aquifer as an additional supply. Located four hundred kilometers east of Bradbury in the cliffs above the Valles Marineris, the aquifer is claimed by Robinson, but the land above it currently occupied by Bradbury militia forces under the guise of the Mars Colonial Corps. The MCC is supposedly exploring the viability of this precious resource, but Robinson sees the incursion as retribution for political disagreements at the Senate.

ROCK AND SILICA QUARRIES

The Martian surface is also valuable for providing sources for silicate minerals and other resources for construction in Bradbury and other colonies. Numerous surface-based quarries can be found on the northwestern slopes of Pavonis Mons surrounding the Pavonis Glacier.

MANUFACTURING

Bradbury's many manufactories are the most developed of their kind on Mars, and in some cases, the only domestic source.

SMELTING VANASTEEL

Martians have become particularly adept at making vanadium-alloyed steels because vanadinite was surprisingly plentiful on Mars. The planet's lighter gravity also played a role in smelting a type of alloy simply impossible to produce on Earth. Called vanasteel or v-steel, it is used in virtually all forms of construction on Mars. Making use of a sizable amount of geothermal power, the Industrial District has several large vanasteel smelting facilities that extract iron from locally mined magnetite and imported hematite, which is then combined with carbon and vanadium to form the vanasteel used in dome and building construction, mag-lev inductrack, pods, and hoppers.

PLASTIC AND PLASCRETE PRODUCTION

Another Martian success story was the colonists' ability to develop a non-petroleum based plastic industry. Martian plastics are silica- rather than carbon-based, and to create the necessary polymers from non-petroleum sources requires gases and heat from Bradbury's geothermal resources. The Industrial District not only sees heavy steel industries, but also much newer plastics and plascrete production for use in manufacturing.

BUILDING PREFABRICATION

Building outside of the safety of a colonial dome can be dangerous work, and one of the major industries in Bradbury is the pre-assembly of building materials. These are often exported to other colonies and developments where constructing safe shelters quickly is a matter of survival.

TRANSPORTATION CONSTRUCTION

Bradbury is not only the primary hub of the mag-lev inductrack network, but also the headquarters for the Bradbury Railway Co. Bradbury serves as the central construction and repair shop for the railway, not only for the tracks, tubes, and guideways, but also the pods and trains that run on them.

DISTRICTS AND GOVERNMENT

While many Earthers still use the term "colony" when describing Bradbury, it has long since transcended that label. Native Martians would be hard pressed to characterize the megapolis as anything less than an Earth city on Mars—especially considering that its official governmental body was chartered by the Earth-based U.N.

In addition to boasting the largest population by far of any Martian settlement, Bradbury houses the largest resource extraction and manufacturing industries at the same time that it hosts official planetary government and all of the attendant service sector jobs. From the maintenance shafts high in the arcologies of the Great Dome to the deepest of lava tubes, Bradbury's warren-like structure is so extensive that those born and raised in the megapolis could still find themselves in places they never knew existed.

DISTRICTS

Like any city on Earth, Bradbury is divided up into many different districts, both formal and informal. Some are segregated by industry, while others are known for the cultures of their unassimilated immigrant populations. They range from any one of the city's dozens of domes to underground sectors jealously controlled by individual clans. Some of the most well-known landmarks in all of Bradbury include the Great Dome, the Therm, and the Daedalus Complex.

THE GREAT DOME

The Great Dome is the largest single piece of infrastructure in Bradbury and the symbol of the city's corporate wealth. As one of the newer structures in the megapolis, it is located on the southeast side of the city, near the rim of the Pavonis Caldera. Expanding on the methods used to build transplas domes on Mars, the Great Dome's architects and engineers designed a dodecagonal structure with an enormous central arcology tower serving as the central pillar of the dome. More than three hundred–stories tall, the Khondi Tower provides the suspension network that supports the transplas lattice. In all, the Great Dome is some five kilometers across, and covers an area of almost nineteen square kilometers, more than the area of any other single dome on Mars.

The Great Dome is home to Bradbury's corporate and government elite, while the central Khondi Tower houses the Senate chambers and the offices of the Martian Colonial Authority. Similarly, most of the embassies from both Earth and other colonies on Mars are hosted here.

Of all the places on Mars, the central regions of the Great Dome feel the most Earth-like. Free-flowing fountains, trees, and carefully manicured gardens help cement the perception that

Across the street from the Mahendra Building, the Khondi Tower stood tall and elegant. From street level, the spire at the top seemed on the verge of piercing the protective bubble that enclosed the colony. As the geographic center of the colony, it anchored the municipal and business centers in concentric streets for twenty blocks.

the MCA exists as a puppet of Earth. In truth, these symbols of excess are purely financed by corporations as a way to encouraging Earth-based investors, but to Martians who are barely making a living, they continue to be sources of friction. Not surprisingly, security in the Great Dome is very tight, even if the Bradbury Colony Police have gone to great lengths to remain behind the scenes.

THE THERM

Considered to be the beating heart of Bradbury, the Geothermal Energy Capture and Conversion Installation (or "the Therm" as the locals call it) is a fantastically complex operation centered in the northeast corner of Pavonis Mons's central caldera, just south of the city's main structure.

As part of the Industrial District, the Therm functions as the lifeblood of the entire colony—it provides the heat, energy, and gases essential for the survival of every living thing in the megapolis. The Therm contains hundreds of heat wells that not only bring heat and electrical power into Bradbury's ecosystem, but also important gases such as carbon dioxide, sulfur dioxide, and some concentrations of water vapor. Ice mined from the Pavonis Glacier is also used to increase the concentration of water in Bradbury's atmosphere, and as such, the infrastructure of the Therm is also the means through which the colony is supplied with liquid water.

One of the earliest industrial centers in Bradbury, the Therm evolved from the initial geothermal power efforts dating back to the first pioneers that settled on Pavonis Mons. As a dormant volcano, heat and gases were relatively closer to the surface, making it easier and far more efficient than importing and building fusion or fission reactors in those early days. These gases also provided an excellent source for pressurizing the colony's dome. Although nuclear and solar power exist today in Bradbury, they have not replaced the original systems.

As a district, the Therm is an industrial-looking area on the floor of the main caldera, some four kilometers below the bulk of Bradbury itself. Unlike some sections of Bradbury, the district does not exist under a dome, but rather through a series of lava tubes and carved tunnels deep in the caldera itself. Here, the geothermal power generators and gas processing plants hum away. Only the Therm's spaghetti-like network of pipes, valves and pressure stations can be found above the surface, snaking its way upward to deliver precious cargo to critical points in the city's infrastructure.

Those who live and work here know the importance of what they do, and they resent anything that might smack of condescension from politicians or corporate bureaucrats. Clan Cabeiri is the largest and strongest of the clans working at the Therm, and as a result, they have considerable clout with Bradbury's governing council. This frequently puts them at odds with the larger and more influential Clan Picus. Unlike virtually every other workforce in Bradbury, however, laborers from the Therm can be found anywhere in Bradbury. While the bulk of them work and live close to the district's center, it is common to see the characteristically cybered Clan Cabeiri workers performing maintenance and inspections throughout the megapolis.

Maciej Rebisz

BAMBOO DOME

The Bamboo Dome, named after its primary biomass crop, is the colloquial term for the principal agricultural complex in Bradbury. If the Therm is the beating heart, the Bamboo Dome is the colony's lungs. The early settlers relied upon the geothermal energy to drive powerful magenta-colored lamps to simulate sunlight for agricultural areas in the lava tube network.

As the colony grew and developed, eventually these areas were moved to the dome structures on the surface, but the weaker sunlight still means that the plants must be supplemented by locally generated light. To help combat this problem, the Bamboo Dome was designed and built with convex dome panels that help focus the weaker Martian sunlight. Located in the northeast quadrant of Bradbury, it was built close to the rim of the upper patera to take as much advantage of the Martian sunlight as possible.

Bamboo is used as the primary biomass because it grows so quickly. Other staple food and economic crops can also be found here, but they are all secondarily used to convert carbon dioxide into breathable oxygen. Carbon dioxide and other gases are pumped here from both the atmospheric recycling system as well as the processing plants in the Therm to allow the biomass to do its work.

Clan Picus tends to this and all other hydroponic and life-support systems in the city, but since the Bamboo Dome and the Therm are core parts of the city's life-support system, Clan Picus and Clan Cabeiri sometimes lock horns with one another over the control of this essential part of Bradbury's life.

DAEDALUS COMPLEX

Still under primary construction, the Daedalus Complex is the foundation for an impending space elevator similar to the Beanstalk on Earth. Numerous mag-lev guideways run southward from Bradbury's main structure, flanking the western edge of Pavonis Mons's main caldera. The complex was selected for the same reasons why the Beanstalk was built on Volcán Cayambe in New Angeles. Work on the space elevator itself has not started primarily because of an ongoing legal dispute over proprietary technologies claimed by the Weyland Consortium, but the construction of the complex was begun many years ago.

STATION ONE

Built into the flank of Pavonis Mons some sixty kilometers northwest of the megapolis's main structure, Station One is the primary hub of the Bradbury Railway Co., and—to a certain extent—Mars's entire mag-lev network. Station One is far enough away from Bradbury that it requires its own geothermal and atmospheric generation, which the railroad entirely owns and operates. Home to nearly a thousand people, it is not only the central transportation hub, but the main manufactory base for anything that runs on the BRC's mag-lev network. Poseidon Equipment's headquarters are located there, in addition to some Omnicorp and Haas-Bioroid plants.

Anyone traveling to or from Bradbury from any point on Mars inevitably comes through Station One, as does much of the cargo from the Gullivar Starport. While the passenger station is large, it is a tiny fraction of the network. Mag-lev inductrack resembles the large sprawling railyards of twentieth-century Earth. The station itself is housed under a tightly controlled pressure-lock system to ensure the integrity of the passengers' atmosphere. Still, accidents and sabotage have been known to happen, which is why virtually every passenger wears an envirosuit while traveling.

Bradbury's third-largest clan wields the most influence here. Members of Clan Aeneas are often found not only managing and running the Bradbury Railway Co., but also building many of the units that float on the inductrack guideways for Poseidon Equipment. Despite being members of the smallest of the three major clans in Bradbury, they can sometimes wield influence greater than their numbers suggest. Often Cabeiri or Picus needs the support of Aeneas against the other, which allows the clan's cunning leadership to exact valuable concessions.

GULLIVAR COLONY AND THE OUTLYING NODES

Gullivar Colony is located some three hundred kilometers west of Bradbury, built in the shelter of a smaller crater in Ulysses Tholus. The colony is still considered as part of "Greater Bradbury" in terms of its administration and governance. As the largest of what are officially Bradbury's outlying nodes, it serves as an alternate starport to the megapolis. Gullivar's starport can be found on the southeast side, and it consists of a honeycomb of smaller agricultural and industrial domes that resemble an open dome.

More enclosed buildings huddle along the northwestern walls of a large hexagonal plascrete pad. The main mag-lev station exits directly out of the starport buildings, stretching three hundred kilometers eastward toward Pavonis Mons. For some, Gullivar is attractive because it is less busy. For others trying to maintain a low profile, it is a way to get planet-side without attracting unwanted attention.

See this graph? This is Weyland's profits during the War. Up, up, up. Notice the spike at the beginning, here, where hostilities broke out, and then again after, when reconstruction contracts were awarded. Weyland profits off the war, Weyland profits off the peace.

Now they're doing it again. Here's a graph of Weyland's profits again. Notice it's the exact same shape as the early part of that other graph? Okay, here's some other numbers. This is the sum of all Argus, Infinity Designs, and Skorpios's sales to Mars. Here's what the Mars Colonial Corps is buying. Notice that it's almost exactly half the total? Who's buying the other half? I'll tell you: the other side.

The Weyland Consortium is just doing what any inhuman corporate entity is driven to do: seek profit with no consideration for human suffering. From their point of view, it's more profitable for Mars to break out into a planet-wide war every fifteen or twenty years so they can sell weapons to both sides and sign reconstruction contracts to the winners. Guarantee you, when this war ends, they'll start the cycle all over again.

GOVERNMENT

Bradbury's official and unofficial bodies of government are constantly vying with one another for power and prestige. The Martian Colonial Authority and the clans frequently clash over the best interests of the city and Mars at large.

THE MARTIAN COLONIAL AUTHORITY

The Martian Colonial Authority's mandate is to realize a peaceful and prosperous Mars. It is a difficult task, for competing priorities and subterfuge between Martian colonies and clans—not to mention the machinations of corporate interests—seem to keep the MCA in a constant state of crisis.

Most of the MCA's offices and legislative buildings can be found under the Great Dome clustered around and located in the central spire known as the Khondi Tower. The MCA has a single chamber called the Martian Colonial Senate. All major colonies in the Organized Territory are eligible to send two voting representatives to the Senate to deliberate on issues that concern the city of Bradbury and Mars as a whole. What this means in practice is that the MCA can exclude whichever colonies it deems to be illegitimate, including those that disagree with MCA politics.

For those colonies that are franchised, representation is uneven—each recognized settlement can independently determine how its senators are selected. This would, in theory, allow for variable styles of representation. Yet, many Martian colonies are financed, owned, and governed by corporations, meaning the corps can hand-pick delegates to represent colonies where their influence is great, such as Demeter Colony, solely owned by Jinteki subsidiary AgInfusion, or Endurance, where Haas-Bioroid holds a majority share on the colony's governing board. In special cases, colony governors and executives can convene in an emergency body called the Security Commission to resolve crises quickly when the Senate cannot or will not convene or act. That the clans have no official role in the Senate despite their enormous role in daily Martian life plays a huge role in the ongoing civil war.

The Martian Colonial Authority is a relatively young organization, and it displays

No matter where you are on Mars, you can't turn on a vid without it running through NBN. They may try to dress it up with Martian names, but in the end it's all the same. The only way you'll really get the whole truth is if you find one of the better pirate broadcasters, and it isn't easy with the conspiracy nuts muddying the waters. Most of them are Martian runners who try to piggyback their own system on NBN's hardware, because, well, they're the only game out there. The megacorporation isn't above frying the brain of those who ride the signal and tell us what's really going on in the outer colonies.

Sure, NBN is an advocate for free speech when it suits them. They can afford to be a lot more draconian out here. Civil rights exist, but as many colonies were corporation founded, they're more guidelines. Public relations and message control is far more important than accountability. NBN may be happy to report on the failings of Weyland, Jinteki, or HB, but full disclosure laws are weak. I know of at least two pirate media outfits that are former NBN people who got sick of the double standard.

many of the faults one would associate with a governing body that lacks a strong political culture or a history of legal precedents. Compounding these issues of inexperience are the sometimes-contradictory bureaucratic styles it has been forced to adopt by U.N. resolutions. Finally, good old corruption and cronyism mean that the MCA is a wildly inconsistent government body that has only a loose relationship with the rule of law.

MUNICIPAL GOVERNMENT

Because it is host to the Martian Colonial Senate and headquarters of the MCA, Bradbury has no city government independent of those bodies. In theory, Bradbury democratically elects its two senators and so has a voice on the Senate, but in practice the MCA's citizenship requirements are so complex that only a small fraction of (mainly pro-Earth) Bradburians are able to vote.

When the MCA can be bothered to address Bradbury's concerns at all, it is typically to appoint a new Governor (invariably an Earth-born bureaucrat, often one who receives an appointment while still en-route to Mars), increase Bradbury Colonial Police crackdowns on unruly portions of the city, or increase the local taxes. Or at least, that's how it seems to the disenfranchised lower classes.

Compounding the apparent disinterest of the legislative branch is an underdeveloped, overworked, and some say corrupt judicial system at work in Bradbury and throughout Colonial territory. The Martian

frontier is so young that several colonies are just now convening their first formal courts, and others have recently overhauled their system in the wake of the War and the creation of the MCA. From the point of view of the colonists, the judiciary created from above by the MCA is inadequate in many cases. It takes too long, for one thing, and its judgments feel arbitrary and capricious, or even slanted in favor of corporate and Earth-backed interests.

Unlike the courts, Martian clans evolved organically from communities living and working together, and in many cases they can and do serve the role of the people's judiciary. Clan justice is rough, with punishments ranging from a fine to forced labor to flogging to banishment (often a death sentence on Mars), but never including imprisonment. Incarceration is simply not worth the life support resources; either the criminal can reform and reintegrate with society, or he is ejected from the community.

Several clans wield great influence in Bradbury itself even if they have no pull with the Senate. Still, many Mars-born Bradburians put more faith in the clan councils and clan justice than in the MCA, and the harder the MCA struggles to limit clan power, the more angry Martians they send into the waiting arms of the separatists.

The MCA likes to pretend that it completely controls the Colonies and that the separatists are limited to the Unorganized Territory. But the truth of the matter is that if there is another Martian War, its first shots will as likely as not be fired in Bradbury.

CLANS AND CONFLICT

Bradbury may be an island of relative peace in a volatile environment, but conflict and violence are very much a part of Martian life. Mars has been locked in an ongoing low-grade civil war in which colonies struggle over scarce resources, influence, and independence. Even since the official end of the Colony Wars, skirmishes and unrest dominate the mediafeeds and newsrags, and the MCA seems barely able to contain the bloodshed. The resolution of one clash seems to spark another. While violence does occasionally flare up in Bradbury proper, much of the conflict exists in the realm of espionage and subterfuge. For those on the front lines of politics and power, understanding Martian culture and the role of clans can mean the difference between peace and war.

THE CLANS

One of the major features of Martian culture that separates it from Earth is the great prevalence of unofficial, close-knit social units known as clans. As workers lived and worked in dense groups, their families naturally evolved biological ties. Within each clan is a hierarchy of kinship to which an individual gives his or her loyalty. Martian clans have a saying that describes it well: *"I against my kin, my kin and I against my clan, my clan and I against the corps."* It is an oversimplification, as different clans often treat each other as rivals, but if pushed they will sometimes unite against a common foe.

While Martian clanspeople are often biologically related, it is not an automatic requirement. Clans are able to integrate new immigrants to Mars into their life and work far easier than their ancient namesakes. Stories of lonely workers from Earth falling in love and marrying into a clan are commonplace. Initiates are quickly integrated into clan culture and learn new loyalties when they become part of the group.

Bradbury is home to three major clans of its own—Clan Picus, Clan Cabeiri, and Clan Aeneas—but members of virtually every clan on Mars can be found here because of the lobbies trying to affect the MCA from without. The megapolis's founding clan, Picus, is also its largest, and is integrated in nearly every aspect of the colony's life. Clan Cabeiri's members can be found in the Therm geothermal operations, and Clan Aeneas are most often found in the transportation business. All three vie for influence in the region's politics, leveraging their respective sectors and resources.

CLAN TATTOOS

Clan members are identified by facial tattoo designs, which often twist around one or both eyes. Receiving a tattoo is part of the clan initiation rites when a child comes of age or when a new member is welcomed. Boys and girls receive the first part of their clan tattoo when they receive their first privileges and responsibilities to the clan; this age varies with each clan's specific beliefs and traditions. As they get older, their tattoos "grow" as well—subtle decorations symbolize status, achievements, and roles both past and present. In addition, the ink used in clan tattoos is infused with tracers carrying specific identification markers of the clan. While a basic tattoo can be faked or covered up, true clan tattoos are much more difficult to conceal or forge—clansmen should always boldly and proudly declare their allegiance to their clan, and a tattooist lacking the specific tracers will be unable to reproduce another clan's markings.

KEEPING PEACE, MAKING WAR

Where the rule of law exists, regardless of how fair or oppressive, there will inevitably be those who operate on the margins. As with any civilization, Bradbury has its share of crime. It ranges from petty theft to murder and acts of terrorism carried out by lone actors or highly sophisticated rings. It has been said that virtually all Martian clans have some ties to organized crime, and that a few clans are entirely criminal enterprises.

The primary failing of the MCA's legal system, at least in the eyes of ordinary Martians, is that many of the laws that limit corporate power on Earth are simply absent on Mars. One glaring example regards artificial intelligence and combat; on Mars, an AI doesn't need human oversight to take a human life.

Another major difference between Earth-based legal systems and the MCA's body of statutes is the provisioning of resources, especially life-support resources. Earth-born visitors who are used to air and water being freely used by corps and individuals alike can easily run afoul of the authorities. It is a criminal offense, for example, to siphon oxygen from the city's infrastructure grid, and even washing one's hands the wrong way can result in a fine. Damaging anything to do with Bradbury's life-support system, whether by accident or by design, carries punishments higher than armed robbery.

MARS COLONIAL POLICE

The official law-enforcement wing of the MCA, the Mars Colonial Police is headquartered not far from the other MCA offices under the Great Dome. It is largely concerned with organized crime, cross-colony criminal activity, major and behavioral crimes, and of course crimes and terrorism targeting the MCA. The MCP has specific jurisdiction over criminal activity in any of the MCA's buildings.

NEGOTIATIONS

If you want to get anything done in Bradbury, at some point or another you're going to need to get Picus on board. Sure, the whole legal system pretends that the clans don't exist, but don't be fooled for a moment. Those stulti up in the corporate towers think they can ignore us, but the reality is, no matter what the deal is, if you don't have the implicit support of at least one the big three here, it ain't happening.

That's where we come in. We are the back room, the mediators, the ones that negotiate to really make things move ahead in this place. Sure, the execs think they have it all under control, but the truth is they would just as easily find themselves on the wrong side of an airlock if it wasn't for us.

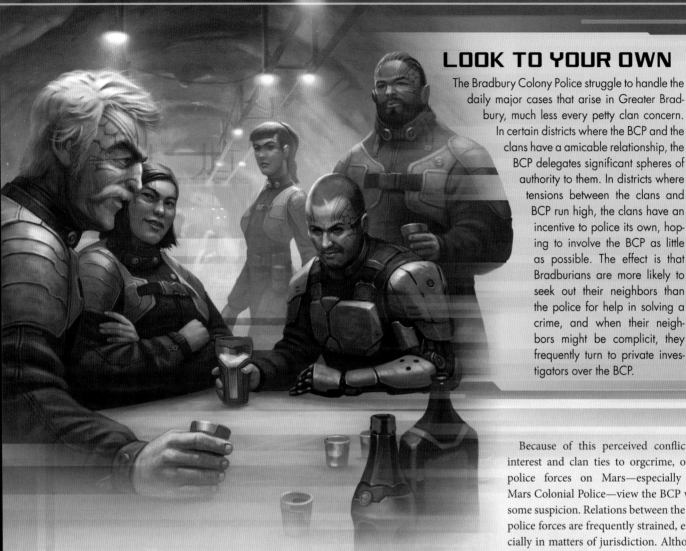

LOOK TO YOUR OWN

The Bradbury Colony Police struggle to handle the daily major cases that arise in Greater Bradbury, much less every petty clan concern. In certain districts where the BCP and the clans have a amicable relationship, the BCP delegates significant spheres of authority to them. In districts where tensions between the clans and BCP run high, the clans have an incentive to police its own, hoping to involve the BCP as little as possible. The effect is that Bradburians are more likely to seek out their neighbors than the police for help in solving a crime, and when their neighbors might be complicit, they frequently turn to private investigators over the BCP.

The MCP sees clan affiliation as an obstacle to effective law enforcement. As such, many of its recruits are either unaffiliated or Earth-born. Clan-affiliated recruits are carefully screened to ensure any existing loyalties are secondary to their oath as members of the MCP. However, because many of its members are also indentured to corporate interests, the MCP also cleaves along the lines of corporate factionalism.

BRADBURY COLONY POLICE

While the Mars Colonial Police was founded at the same time as the MCA fifteen years ago, the BCP's history stretches back to the first colonists on Pavonis Mons, making it the oldest law-enforcement organization on Mars. Charged with keeping the peace and investigating criminal activity in the greater Bradbury region, the BCP faces many of the same challenges as their counterparts on Earth.

The Bradbury Colony Police's jurisdiction covers all of Bradbury's districts as well as the Daedalus Complex, Gullivar Starport, and other nearby nodes within the Tharsis region. It is far and away the most common law-enforcement body that anyone in Bradbury will encounter, but that doesn't mean that it's a frequent sight; resources and manpower limitations being what they are, most areas would go days without patrols if it weren't for the clans forming patrols of their own.

Unlike the MCP, the BCP tries to actively recruit and train citizens from Bradbury in particular to help build trust with the community. It means that most officers in the BCP are also members of various clans, which goes a long way to earn the people's confidence. Unfortunately, it has also created complications when clan loyalties clash with the police oath of office, such as when clans themselves are linked to a crime.

Because of this perceived conflict of interest and clan ties to orgcrime, other police forces on Mars—especially the Mars Colonial Police—view the BCP with some suspicion. Relations between the two police forces are frequently strained, especially in matters of jurisdiction. Although they try to coordinate their activities, there has been more than one occasion in which these two forces found themselves either in conflict or competition.

MARTIAN SECRET SERVICE

The Martian Secret Service, or MSS, operates in the many shadows of Mars; the true loyalties of this organization remain a mystery. While it functions as intelligence arm of the MCA, it remains unclear as to whether MSS spies on Martians on behalf of Earth, or if it is the other way around.

Whatever the truth is, Martians who are aware of the organization are understandably wary. As with most of the MCA's institutions, the MSS headquarters on Mars is located in the Great Dome in the shadow of the Khondi Tower, but most of the organization's intelligence-gathering operations happen in other, less conspicuous locations.

Dmitry Burmak

PRIVATE SERVICES

Since resources on Mars are often strained, local colony militias contract with and even rely on private investigators as partners in law enforcement. Bradbury is no exception, as these investigators are able to take up the slack when the BCP's detective division finds itself overtaxed.

P.I.'s have a long and storied tradition of frontier justice on Mars, including in Bradbury. Colony police forces—including the BCP—and clan militias are far more likely to cooperate with P.I.'s than the MCP due to their a reputation for remaining apart from the political fray. In some of the outlying nodes, law enforcement would be nonexistent if it weren't for the private individuals who have stepped up to answer the call of duty, but such individuals are also at risk for becoming essentially gangsters or warlords in their respective communities.

All too often, though, the corporations themselves take on the role of police in their colonies, enforcing the employee handbook and corporate policies with prisec and mercenaries.

EMERGENCY SERVICES

As with any major city on Earth, Bradbury has emergency services that include police officers, firefighters, and emergency medical personnel. While the police and EMS follow similar patterns to their Earth-bound counterparts, firefighting in Bradbury is very different given how precious the water supply in the colony is.

Instead of a network of fire-hydrants that one might expect on Earth, fire control systems utilize pressurized carbon dioxide rather than water to extinguish flames. In extreme circumstances, sections of the colony can be evacuated, sealed off, and vented straight into the Martian atmosphere to starve the flames.

We don't see too many golems inside the dome, but that's not to say that Haas-Bioroid isn't on Mars; they're everywhere. Remember bioroids don't need to breathe, and not even Jinteki can compete with that!

I've heard a few who work the big-haul trucks on the glacier talk about Haas-Bioroid logos on the big diggers, and they look different from anything Weyland makes. If that's true, then HB has definitely moved into the heavy construction market. No, they're not just building equipment—I'm talking prototype machines with bioroid brains. Makes me wonder what else they're building, given that NEXT, aka HB, hasn't been shy about military contracts. Most laser pistols and rifles you'll find the mercs using are NEXT designs or cheap knock-offs of the same.

SELF-DEFENSE

The disposition of military forces on Mars is as complex as the planet's politics. Larger settlements typically have a defense force made up of both mercenaries and clan-based militias if the corporations don't provide their own security. In the case where corps provide their own fighting forces, the clan militia frequently becomes a watchdog for the corporate sec personnel; clashes between the two are common and heated.

In addition, since the creation of the MCA, the Mars Colonial Corps has garrisons in nearly every city and MCA-affiliated settlement on the planet. Bradbury hosts not only a large MCC base, but it is also able to draw on its own clan militias to form a force collectively known as the Bradbury United Division. Officially the two groups coordinate for operations and the defense of the planet's largest colony, but trust between the two has been an issue since the signing of the Treaty of Heinlein.

BRADBURY UNITED DIVISION

After the Space Expeditionary Corps troops were withdrawn from Bradbury proper at the end of the war, the Bradbury United Division (BUD) was formed by the MCA to protect the Greater Bradbury region from enemy clans and merc forces. Clans Picus, Cabeiri, and Aeneas all contribute troops to the reserve force, which has been activated multiple times in recent history. The BUD can also be used in conjunction with the Bradbury Colonial Police to secure individual districts and life-support machinery in the event of a terrorist attack, but the MCC is deployed to quell large-scale clan uprisings when they happen.

The BUD is the only MCA-sanctioned expression of clan armed forces in Bradbury. Although clan militias are tacitly acknowledged, the MCA has the authority to crack down on clans who are competing too closely with police forces. The MCA has also used the threat of mass disarmaments to keep the militias in line.

MERCENARY UNITS

Mercenaries remain the great wild card in the evolution of conflict and politics on Mars. In total, there are more mercenaries on Mars than there are MCC and BUD troops combined. However, mercenaries are often contracted out by competing corporate interests, or hold strong clan affiliations, so the role they play remains ambiguous.

Many portray themselves as private security firms better suited to law enforcement and investigation, while others are clearly high-functioning militias pursuing their own ambitious goals. In addition to major firms like Argus and Globalsec, hundreds of smaller mercenary groups operate locally using strike forces of several dozen combatants. Clones and bioroids provide support for these merc groups as medics, quartermasters, and electronics specialists.

Mercenary bands are commonly hired by unauthorized settlements to provide temporary security, but merc groups also take advantage of these isolated frontier people. They are notorious for orchestrating false conflicts between settlements, even going so far as to collude with the other side to stage mock battles and collect the grateful settler's credits without sustaining any casualties.

"Hey Crib, you getting this?"

"Just a sec, Dust."

Crib flipped a few switches. The blue-tinted holoconsole sprang to life in the hopper's confines. He could hear Dust's puffing through his headset.

"Okay Pops, you're up and operating. Sounds like you need more practice on ladders," Crib smiled.

"You're funny," growled Dust. "The wind's picked up a bit. The sooner we get this done and get back to Podkayne, the better off we'll be."

"Alright, alright, don't bust my chops," Crib sighed.

Dust and Crib set about their routine. Testing samples from geothermal pumping stations on Mars's expansive red frontier was a tedious and thankless task. The units supplied steam and valuable sulfur dioxide to nearby colonies, but they required constant maintenance and monitoring.

Crib noticed the rumbling first, distant and subtle. Aside from wind whistling across the rocks, or the tick and rattle of blown gravel, there was very little on the planet to generate sound that wasn't human-made.

"You feel that? This morning's train wasn't due for another few hours."

"It's not. Must be some special corp shipment or something," Dust grunted without looking up from his work.

The young pilot called up the hopper's external cams to have a look. Below them, about a kilometer away in the oxide-stained valley, a mag-lev track snaked through the volcanic landscape under an amber sky. The heavy thrumming of the electromagnetic field betrayed what must be a high-mass cargo.

What is that—

A low-flying dropship screamed overhead. Hugging the nape of the terrain, it barely cleared the pumping station, and the unexpected burst of pressure knocked Dust off of his careful perch. Crib heard him wheeze as he hit the ground.

"Dust!" he shouted, "You okay?"

"Frag it!"

Crib sighed in relief. If Dust was swearing, he was still breathing, and the envirosuit was intact. From his holoconsole, he could see Dust's perspective through his monocam.

The four heavily armed dropships that had just buzzed their position were converging on the train, joined by at least eight other hoppers. Several missiles cut loose, streaking from the approaching hoppers, thudding into the blocky locomotive and bringing the heavy train to a lumbering halt. EMP missiles, Crib thought.

"Dust, did you see who they were? Rocs?" Crib asked quickly.

"Don't know. If they are, I'm not waiting to stick around and find out. Spin 'er up. We're getting out of here."

"Sure thing, bossman." Crib kept the holoconsole

up and zoomed in on the unfolding action as Dust scrambled down the slope to the hopper. The jacker dropships landed, disgorging several teams of well-armed troops. These were professionals: they took up precision firing positions around the train's flanks while the remaining hoppers circled the area.

Several small explosions, the flash of muzzle fire, and the rattle of small arms fire echoed from the far side of the train. Suddenly the order and discipline of the raiders scattered into a panicked mass of wild firing. Crib caught a glimpse of a single large figure making an impossible leap over the train and into one of the teams, coolly shooting an in-built laser rifle.

Crib zoomed in and got a close-up of the warrior as he snapped a jacker's neck, hurling the body into two others. The train's defender wore a red-tinged heavy-alloyed hardsuit, yet his motions were so fluid and graceful that he seemed unarmored. Kicking up a dropped missile launcher from the ground, the mysterious soldier held it out to one side, and without even glancing down the weapon's sight, unerringly sent an explosive into

Zach Graves

the dropship, hitting its starboard tilt-jets and sending it spinning out of control."- Frag! That's a combat exosuit! Free Mars got themselves a fragging exosuit!" Crib shouted. Scrambling into the cockpit, he grabbed the stick just as Dust clambered into his seat.

"Where the hell are they getting resources like that?"

"Frag it!" Crib tapped the HUD. "It's still recharging."

Below, the demolition of the attacking hoppers was almost complete. The dropship had crashed on the far side of the train, kicking up a massive amount of red soil, and the smoke from its hull obscured their vision of the carnage.

As the energy bar hit lift-off, a lone figure stepped out of the smoke and bounded toward them.

"Rev it!" Dust exclaimed. "He thinks we're one of them!"

Crib spun the hopper around. Engaging the thrusters, he accelerated along the first clear path he could find. The craft shot out across the landscape, gathering speed as fast as he could push it.

They had barely started to gain altitude when the right tiltjet exploded. Crib wrenched at the controls as the craft shuddered.

Suddenly, the hopper lurched hard. A large hand smashed through the side windshield, grabbed Dust by the throat, and suddenly he was gone. Crib screamed, throwing the hopper into a barrel roll, hoping to dislodge the assailant, but the altitude was too low. What was left of the hopper tumbled across the barren scree slope, throwing debris in all directions before coming to a skidding halt.

Crib felt something warm and wet running down his face. The readouts for suit diagnostics flooded him with information: right broken arm, compressed spine, fractured legs, a scalp laceration and likely concussion. He could feel only one of them.

Pinned under the crushed remains of the hopper's cockpit, he watched helplessly as a hulking figure tore away the smashed windshield. Through his fading vision, Crib could see a pair of silvery eyes peering at him with a look resembling curiosity.

"But...don't...we aren't jackers!" Crib moaned through his failing breather as a servos-powered hand reached out for him in the serrated wreckage.

"I'm sorry, sir," a woman's voice whispered in an almost soothing tone, "my orders are no witnesses to this field test."

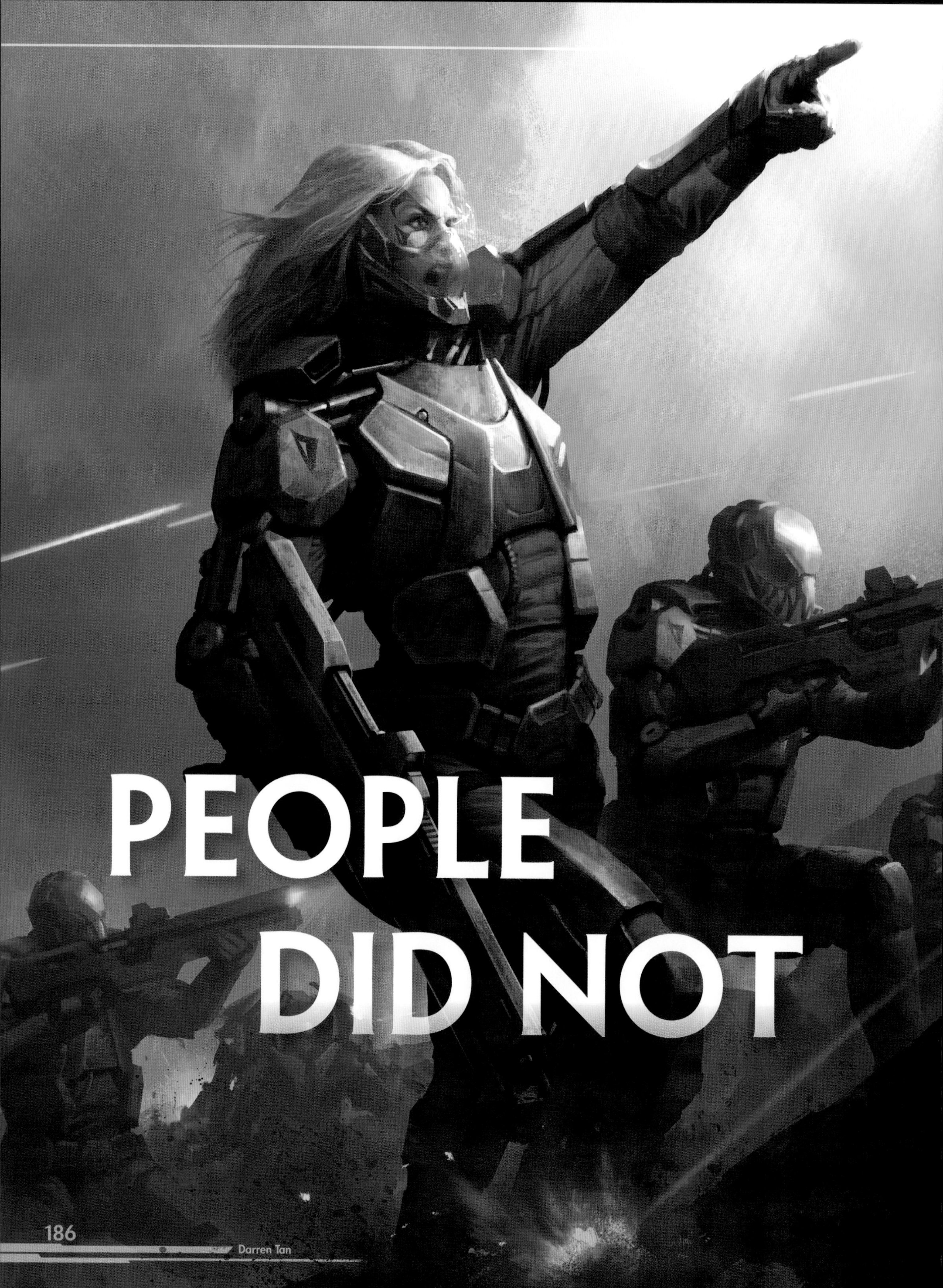

PEOPLE
DID NOT

Darren Tan

Despite the major advances over the past few decades, technology has not solved the worlds' problems; some would argue that technology has actually made things worse.

With fusion power and advanced agricultural techniques, Earth easily produces enough food to feed not only its entire population, but the Moon and Mars as well. Yet the fuel for fusion power helped spark a bloody and costly war that scarred large swathes of the population. Widespread surveillance networks and sophisticated policing organizations make our citizens safer than ever before, but at the cost of their privacy and freedoms. Medical technology has added decades to the average human lifespan, but humans are looking less and less like their original selves. The androids who were designed to lift us out of the hardest and most dangerous jobs have also expanded into service and manufacturing sectors at the expense of human laborers.

The ones who benefit the most from the technological advances are the rich corp employees, who enjoy a quality of life almost beyond the imaginings of their ancestors. Millions of people across the worlds live in their kilometer-tall towers that cater to every whim, oblivious to the mass suffering affecting the literal underclasses.

For those in the dark and squalid undercities, in the failed states, and on the Red Frontier, life is a constant struggle for survival. The corporations and risties leave little for those below them, and the androids seem to be taking what's left. And when resources are scarce, humanity resorts to violence and oppression.

Sometimes, it seems that technology has changed everything except human nature.

THE WORLDS WAR

Fifteen years have passed since the Worlds War, more often just called the War. Few could have anticipated that the strain between state, corporate, and societal interests in a new era of technology would erupt into violence on such a massive scale. The War became one of the costliest conflicts in human history, and it was the first to extend past Earth's atmosphere.

The Outer Space Treaty, which forbade the buildup of national interests and arms on the Moon, proved unenforceable as major nations tacitly permitted corporate entities to assume power during the rush to mine helium-3. Discourse at the United Nations broke down, and major countries withdrew from the organization when it became obvious that the U.N. was powerless to act. The Lunar Insurrection sparked the first wave of conflicts on the Moon, and the situation spiraled out of control, quickly reaching the frontier of Mars and eventually threatening to consume Earth.

Over the course of the conflict, corps and nations allied, superpowers rose and fell, colonies rebelled and reintegrated, and technology matured with deadly rapidity. The Treaty of Heinlein, Melange Mining's monopoly, and the creation of the Universal Nations, the Space Elevator Authority, and the Martian Colonial Authority helped end the fighting, but these treaties and organizations did not solve all the worlds' problems.

THE LUNAR INSURRECTION

At the height of the helium-3 boom on the Moon, almost all the major world powers had their own mining concern operating on the Lunar surface. Crescent Co., Hélio-bras, Melange Mining, Pestroka Technika, Rajanipati Limited, and Xiangong Inc. all maintained significant mining facilities and colonies to support them. Each company was driven by its bottom line; the corps took every shortcut and seized every available advantage. They were determined to wring every last credit they could from the regolith, the machines, and their employees.

Competition between the corps was fierce, and eventually they turned their sights on each other. In the months preceding the War, industrial sabotage was nearly as common as actual mining, and it wasn't always equipment that was targeted. Many workers were injured in the destruction, and the death toll began to mount. Private security forces were stationed to protect corp facilities, but this only seemed to increase the bloodshed. Certain Lunar mining facilities developed reputations so bloody that no one would work for them, leading to the importation of some proto-android labor forces that relied on weak AI.

An alliance between workers from numerous corporations petitioned the Earth countries to reign in their corps. They wanted reparations for the lives and livelihoods lost and the immediate apprehension and trial of the corporate executives and mining overseers responsible for the whole situation.

The rival powers of Earth began negotiating a solution through backdoor diplomatic channels, but in the meantime, the corporations on the Moon continued to escalate the number and intensity of attacks on one another. Not long after the miners first broadcast their grievances, Prosperity Mining Depot, the primary dock belonging to Melange Mining, was bombed by unmarked prisec forces. Life support failed, suffocating hundreds of innocent miners.

The brutal events at the Prosperity Mining Depot outraged the Lunar population. They demanded an immediate apology from Earth and swift action to sanction the corps and prevent any further casualties. But the political situation on Earth remained delicate, and the negotiation tables had many complex issues to discuss, which would take more time than the miners would tolerate. To the Loonies, as they were derisively called by Netcasters on Earth, the message from the United States and China and other countries seemed clear: Luna's concerns—and lives—were not as important as Earth's appetite for He-3.

What would become known as the Lunar Insurrection began with a motley

To the Loonies, the message was clear: Luna's concerns—and lives—were not as important as Earth's appetite for He-3.

force of striking workers in Heinlein. This spark soon erupted into unrest across every settlement on Luna, from the Sea of Serenity to the Sea of Storms. The colonists sustained heavy casualties but managed to overwhelm the private security forces and arm themselves. With their new weapons and vehicles, the colonists seized settlement after settlement. Additional uprisings spread across Heinlein like wildfire. Next, the insurrectionists seized several of Melange's mag-lev launch tracks used for departing shipment containers. Secondary groups of strikers stormed the shipping facilities at Xiangong City and elsewhere, which allowed the protesting miners to shut down the majority of the flow of helium-3 to Earth.

In the span of several hours, the Loonies had gained control of every landing pad across the city, private or public, and set up a blockade against incoming traffic. Grassroots militias placed Earth officials under dome arrest. Corporate overseers and security teams were sent packing from many sites and simply killed at others. With the fortunes of major corporations (and their parent nations) tied to the beleaguered mining facilities, not to mention the threat of an energy shortage, the governments of Earth had no choice but to act quickly and decisively.

THE BATTLE OF KAGUYA

The United States was the first nation to take matters into its own hands and try to put a stop to the Insurrection. A hastily scrambled team of specialists from the United States Armed Forces was deployed through the Beanstalk, drawing on Air Force Space Command for leadership, to take back Melange Mining's facilities, but also to quell the threat of the other Insurrectionists on the Moon. The team, although untested in the sort of environment to which they were now deployed, had the discipline and equipment that nearly guaranteed their success.

Their mission was code-named Operation Falling Star.

The military strike was unforgiving; every new contact was treated as a hostile combatant. Starport Kaguya, in particular, bore the brunt of the United States' offensive. Every last rebel at Kaguya was killed, but so were all the corporate hostages. Officially, the rebels killed their hostages, but many suspect this to be false. Falling Star simultaneously assaulted Melange and Xiangong facilities, securing in one action all the major strongholds of rebel activity and swiftly re-establishing a flow of He-3 down-Stalk.

SEA OF CARNAGE

Although some conspiracy theories persist that the Chinese government had authorized the U.S. military to help them in retaking Xiangong's facilities, publicly New Beijing denounced the attacks as an assault on Chinese sovereignty. Others believe China used Operation Falling Star as an excuse to strike back and potentially take Melange and other mining corps' territory.

Regardless of the truth of their motives, China launched a force of its own to Luna in an attempt to push the Americans out of Xiangong City. They launched a simultaneous offensive against Heinlein to try and confuse their targets. Although they sustained heavily losses on both prongs of their attack, they succeeded in shifting the focus from Earth versus the Loonies to Earth nations and corps against other Earth nations and corps. Soon, Brazil, the Indian Union, Russia, and the United Crescent joined the fighting on Luna, which to the colonists resembled a tragic resumption of the corporate sabotage that had previously been waged with prisec and merc forces. The same corporate turf wars were being fought, except the corps had bigger guns and more personnel this time. And once again, the inhabitants of the domes were the ones caught in the cross fire.

THE MARTIAN COLONY WARS

Like Luna, Mars was settled primarily to further corporate interests, but on the Red Planet the corps wielded even more power over the colonists. Corporate rivalry and collateral damage from sabotage was a fact of life, and with such a large expanse of space between Earth and Mars, the corps effectively had free reign to exploit the colonists dependent on them for life. After all, if it hadn't been for corps like Weyland, Jinteki, and Haas Industrie, there wouldn't be anyone on Mars in the first place, or so the megacorps maintained.

As the colonies matured, clan culture developed as well, and the clans became rallying points for colonists fed up with corporate overseers and policies. With no unified government to speak for them, and little legal recourse within the corporate structure for their complaints to be redressed, the clans turned to violence, just like their Lunar miner counterparts.

By striking without warning while Earth corps were preoccupied by the Lunar Insurrection, Martian rebels were able to seize advanced weapons, ships, and other materiel from corporate production facilities on Martian soil and in Martian orbit. Some of the corporate security personnel sided with the clans, and the others were summarily executed. The distance between the two planets made it impossible for the corps to mount a quick response to the sudden outburst of violence, and the clans quickly solidified their hold over the colonies.

Some among the clans argued for unification to better defend against the corporations' inevitable counterattack, while others jealously guarded their newfound autonomy, and still more used the stockpiles to forcibly resolve long-standing rivalries with nearby clans. The conflicts on Mars were soon dubbed the Colony Wars for all the in-fighting between colonies and their respective clans. Even before the corps struck back, blood was spilled, domes were breached, and Mars began to resemble its warlike namesake.

In the meantime, the corporations again looked to their respective national governments for help in defeating the Martian rebels. Weyland procured the backing of the U.S., while Jinteki and Haas-Bioroid looked to Japan and the European Union. China and Russia also maintained colonies on Mars, and none of these countries had particularly friendly relations, especially given the proxy warfare already occurring on Luna.

Given the "national security interests" at stake in securing the Martian stockpiles and other corporate property, the United States pivoted from Luna to launch a mission aimed at reclaiming Mars. The commanders of Operation Falling Star were tapped to lead a new U.S. Armed Forces division called the Space Expeditionary Corps (SXC), and they expanded their forces with recruits drilled in the tactics necessary for low-gravity combat superiority. The troops deployed to Mars alongside Weyland's private security force, Argus Security, also included a number of Electronic Warfare Service (EWS) specialists equipped with countermeasures for signal jamming, radiation interference, and other expected threats. These raiders and drone operators, though few in number, were bolstered by a full suite of combat drones large and small, and the capability to conduct cyber warfare.

The U.S. forces' mission was two-fold: first, they would disarm the rebels of any materiel they might use against U.S. or corporate interests, and two, they would help Weyland regain its holdings on Mars. Yet, they were not fighting a unified enemy, which simultaneously aided and exacerbated the difficulty of quelling the insurgency.

The sheer distance between Earth and Mars was a major logistical hurdle the Space Expeditionary Corps and Electronic Warfare Service struggled to overcome. United States Army Special Forces realized that they would have to secure a line of logistics and, ideally, a full complement of domestic manufacturing capabilities on Mars. Bradbury, which had major ties to the Weyland Consortium stretching back to its early days as a settlement, was selected as the combined forces' primary target. When the clans there were subdued, it gave the SXC the manufacturing power they needed to continue the war effort despite the weeks or months that separated reinforcement shipments.

From their lodgement in Bradbury, the SXC, EWS, and Argus forces mounted a campaign against Mars's major cities and settlements, starting with those in the Tharsis region. The Siege of Demeter was an early victory for the SXC thanks in part to the fragmentation of the clans on the inside of the city's domes. The Battle of Kasei Valles was not as successful, however, because the native Martians used the forbidding landscape against the offworlders. At the same time, Martian and U.S. forces clashed in the skies overhead for control of the space stations on the moons of Phobos and Deimos. As the fighting moved eastward across the Martian plains, the Action at Noctis Labyrinthus was one of the bloodiest confrontations of the Colony Wars when four different sides clashed in a desperate free-for-all.

Washington's orders were to restrict operations to colonies affiliated with the U.S. and Weyland. Yet, in the fog of war, communication was lost with the leadership on Mars. When China and Russia's Tianbian and Aelita colonies came under assault and bombardment from U.S. forces at the same time that Haas Industrie and Jinteki colonies were attacked by Weyland forces, the superpowers on Earth saw it as the expansion of the existing war on Luna. Many more fighting forces were deployed to Mars's surface, which became fertile ground for mercenary groups looking to profit off of the extensive fighting there.

Ultimately, the Martian clans struggled to present a united front—the rebels targeted each other as much as they fought off the corps and Earth armies. In what would become the Unorganized Territory, warlords and clan militias squabbled over precious resources and water rights even as their metropolitan brethren desperately clung to independence. To this day, Martians are convinced that Earth and the corps actively worked to pit the factions against one another, further highlighting its malicious intentions.

Toward the end of the conflict, some clans began to call the Colony Wars the "War for Martian Independence" as the stakes escalated: peace, they claimed, could only be achieved if Martians could govern themselves.

EARTH ON EDGE

While fighting embroiled Luna, Mars, and pockets of space in between, the populations on Earth held their collective breaths. Diplomatic relations between the most powerful and well-armed countries deteriorated at an alarming rate. The corporations simultaneously supplied the war efforts and helped wage them. The stakes were high: nearly all of the megacorps—and by extension, the superpowers that protected them—considered their economic futures to be caught in the balance.

At the height of the conflict, civilians awaited what seemed like the inevitable moment when the superpowers would turn their attention from their proxy fronts and engage one another directly on terrestrial soil. Earth's nations, the megacorps, and the helium-3 mining concerns were tied together in an ever-shifting web of allegiances, cease-fires, and betrayals, which seemed to be liable to completely fall apart at any moment.

The media provided conflicting reports that further exacerbated civilians' sense of confusion. Different mediafeed outlets painted a very different picture of the conflict for their consumers, sometimes casting the same actors in opposite roles for specific incidents. Even fifteen years later, the truth of what happened on Luna and Mars is shrouded by competing claims and dubious sources, and different groups have entirely different accounts and viewpoints of what really happened during the War.

Perhaps the only thing that kept fighting from spilling over onto Earth was that the largest population centers—including the governmental capitals—were located there. On Luna and Mars, the populations didn't have voting rights or an easy means of conveying what was happening to them to the world at large. It was much easier for state governments to justify a war effort at some far-flung colony that didn't significantly affect the day-to-day lives of the nation's citizenry. Total war between the continents, however, carried a political cost that was considered too high.

WAGING WAR IN THE MODERN ERA

Over the course of the Worlds War, as it was now known, lethal new technologies like energy weapons, full-immersion drone warfare, and orbital batteries were being brought to bear against rebel, corporate, and mercenary forces on Luna and Mars. Older but no-less-terrible weapons were being considered for wide-scale use for the first time: neutron bombs, biological and chemical weapons, and even artificial intelligence. Traditional standbys like electromagnetic pulses, exosuits, and stealth technology were also employed in the War to deadly effect.

DRONE WARFARE

Flying from bases scattered throughout the Lunar *maria* and Martian *planitias*, the U.S. EWS pummeled enemy targets with massed drone strikes. Mobile command centers could loiter hundreds of kilometers away and launch scores of long-range combat drones apiece. These drones were armed with a suite of high-tech weapons including fire-and-forget seeker missiles, cluster munitions, and eventually wide-area combat lasers. Air defense drones and SAMs would attempt to intercept the incoming bogies, but elite front-line EWS raiders could shut down enemy detection systems and let bombing raids strike unseen and unexpected. And no matter how many drones were shot down, the EWS could always return with more.

Despite increasingly sophisticated AIs, international law held that humans still had to authorize drone kill orders. Lasers and other tight-beam communications were the primary means to communicate from their command and control aircraft while avoiding electronic countermeasures, with radio backups in the case of excessive chaff or poor environmental conditions. These "motherships" were often the primary target because operators with full-immersion rigs flying specialized electronic counter-warfare drones could wreak havoc on an opponent's drone squadrons by destroying their management systems.

Despite the standing bans against granting artificial intelligence the ability to kill independent of a human controller, NBN reports indicate that some Chinese and rebel forces on Mars believed themselves exempt from those laws or were desperate enough to employ artificial intelligence capable of targeting and exterminating human beings. Some segments of the general public became obsessed with lurid tab-rags depicting out-of-control AIs that had eliminated their masters, leaving only the brave men and women of the U.S. Armed Forces to stand between American lives and the murderous machines overwhelming the colonies. In reality, these tales were either greatly exaggerated to drum up popular support for the war effort, or they were fabricated to deflect scrutiny from parts of the EWS. Recent evidence suggests that some units experimented with extremely relaxed protocols for authorizing drone strikes when the number of casualties sustained threatened the effectiveness of their normal operations.

WAR OF INFORMATION

Differentiating real news reports from government propaganda proved difficult during the years of the War. As the fighting ground on, most countries—and plenty of private corporations—sent special forces teams and commando units into enemy territory to cripple infrastructure and sow chaos and destruction. Equipped with the latest military technology and weapons, these teams proved they could cause damage out of proportion to their size.

NBN and SYNC infrastructure was often counted among the collateral damage, and as a U.S.-based company, the rest of the world was suspicious of anything NBN broadcasted. AI technology made it easy to adulterate even live-streaming media, and embedded journalists were considered dependent on the troops they were sent to report on for their survival, which compromised their ability to report the truth. Every side was trying to win the War of popular opinion with extensive propaganda bodies that covered up or stressed information as necessary to help their side.

THE NETWORK UNDER FIRE

Electronic sabotage and cyber warfare took on horrifying new meanings during the War. Such units used the techniques honed by fully immersed runners using brain-machine interfaces to cripple and destroy the underlying framework of the Network. A cyber attack could be as subtle as re-routing food shipments to a dome or shutting down water filtration systems, causing riots and mass starvation. It could also be as blatant as disabling the traffic computers for all autopilot hoppers in a major metropolitan center like Bradbury or Tianbian, causing hundreds of crashes and mid-air collisions. In several cases on Mars, runners on both sides destabilized the utility grids or geothermal power stations, causing catastrophic failures of life support.

Full-blown cyber warfare erupted across the Network as corporations employed their own sysops to defend their systems. Sometimes special forces infiltrators would launch cyber assaults in concert with real-world raids, and the struggles on the Net would be mirrored by firefights on the ground.

THE HIGH GROUND

If the Worlds War proved anything, it was that space was the ultimate high ground in a modern war. This high ground ended up being the United States' greatest advantage against its foes.

Although the U.S. had deployed most of the new Space Expeditionary Corps to the Moon and Mars, it kept a sizable contingent in low Earth orbit to defend the Beanstalk and keep its enemies from putting their own forces into orbit. Squadrons of the newly developed SA/F-01A Strikers tangled in sub-orbital dogfights with shuttles and dropships launched by a host of countries, and some media organizations reported that the U.S. shot down any foreign spacecraft that got at all close to the Beanstalk or ended up in any orbit over the Americas, including a few spacecraft or spaceplanes that belonged to neutral countries.

As the United States did its best to keep its opponents out of space, it began to employ new orbital weapons systems to capitalize on its advantage. The NEXT laser-sats were one example of this, while the kinetic bombardments of certain Martian settlements were another.

The first kinetic weapons were simple two-meter tungsten rods deployed en masse from orbital launchers aboard satellites or orbiting spacecraft. They lacked any sort of guidance, but the sheer kinetic power of their orbit-to-ground impact exceeded the biggest non-nuclear warheads in anyone's arsenal, and they were as cheap as they were inaccurate. A single spacecraft could launch a hundred kinetic rods in a single volley, wiping out the target and engulfing anything—or anyone—else within a dozen kilometers in high-pressure fireballs.

Later the SXC began using enhanced "kinetic kill weapons": five meter rods with internal guidance computers and buckyweave steering fins. These could be fired from a spaceship-mounted mass driver, guide themselves through the fiery heat of reentry, and hit with the force of a tactical nuke. The SXC retrofitted several Earth-Moon shuttles with mass drivers to be used on Luna. As a result, massed kinetic bombardments would account for a significant share of the civilian casualties in the War.

PROJECTED IMPACT

Perhaps one of the most feared weapons during the war was one that was already in extensive use and needed only to be nudged slightly in the direction of a population center to become a deadly or apocalyptic event. So-called "comet jockeys" regularly farmed and flung asteroids to the surface of Mars to assist with terraforming efforts, and with so much of space effectively invisible to the Network and normal surveillance channels, targets of such an assault would have little advance warning. People on Earth especially feared a deliberate strike by mercenary space cowboys with an anti-Earth agenda.

According to official records, such meteor strikes were never weaponized on Mars, but some international watchdogs believe that conventional orbital bombardments would not have dealt the amount of damage done to certain Martian colonies, nor left certain kinds of trace elements in the air and resulting crater.

THREATS REAL AND IMAGINED

Some theoretical technologies had been developed, but they had not been seen as practical in previous, lower-grade conflicts. Now, as the wars on Luna and Mars dragged in some of the world's wealthiest states and corporations, practicality lost to sheer desperation.

In the colonies, preserving infrastructure was a major concern for ground troops. In order to remain combat capable, they could not carry more than a few days' worth of life support with them, and vehicles designed for the mass-transport of troops were frequently the first to be targeted on the battlefield. The neutron bomb solved this dilemma: by purposefully lowering the explosive yield of the device, they could dramatically increase the amount of instant radiation to a dose that would prove lethal in a matter of days, not years. According to the Netcasts of the time, the United States only used this weapon against the most stubborn of settlements, and they offered amnesty and safe harbor to any clan members who surrendered. Many believe the clan leaders executed those who tried to take advantage of this olive branch, which only solidified the barbarism of the Martian rebels in the minds of Americans.

Stealth technology also matured over the course of the War. The most advanced ships carried cloaking devices that used destructive interference to shield themselves from conventional radar as well as lidar detection in space. The result was a fleet of logistical ships that could slip past satellites to resupply forces on Luna or Mars without detection, which confounded enemy plans to strike hard when their enemy was estimated to be running low on materiel. In the last legs of the conflict, the stealth devices were outfitted on bombers and strikers to get the drop on enemy forces and neutralize their ability to wage war once and for all.

THE BATTLE OF THE BEANSTALK

The incident that became known as the Battle of the Beanstalk was incredibly sensationalized by Earth and the colonies alike, with each side spinning a wildly different version of events that advanced their current political goals.

The version told by Free Mars fighters and vagrants frequenting bars in the Docklands is that the Battle of the Beanstalk was the final push on the part of the rebels to cripple Earth's power projection capabilities. In this account, the Lunar Insurrection had long since been quashed, but the spirit of independence hadn't been completely eradicated from the Loonies. The miners and colonists had suffered greatly from the battles waged on the Moon, and an initial shipment of Mark-2s—the first-ever bioroid to be commercially produced—to Melange facilities signaled the end of their way of life. Mars's ability to keep resisting Earth control inspired the Loonies to continue dreaming of a future free from corporate influence, and when Mars told the former rebellion leaders of their plan to attack the Beanstalk, the Loonies decided they would rather die free than live at the mercy of Earth any longer.

The Loonies scrambled together a ragtag fleet of cargo ships outfitted with mining lasers and modified railguns to await the arrival of a small armada of Martian ships. Best of all, the Martians had arrived undetected, thanks to a stolen prototype electromagnetic filter device capable of more sophisticated jamming than any previous technology. This "blackout device" could similarly conceal the Lunar rebels' approach, allowing a surprise assault on the Beanstalk. After hasty preparations, an invasion fleet struck out.

The survivors ultimately realized that they must have been sold out by someone back on Luna, because the blackout device proved to be useless against defenders who knew they were coming. Even firing blind, the Castle's defenders were able to prevent the planned assault. A number of ships attempted to land on Earth when the plan was scuttled. The bulk of the forces were trapped and compelled to surrender after heavy initial casualties, including the transport carrying the blackout device.

The official version reported by NBN is that a group of Crimson Dust extremists launched a fleet of kamikaze ships with the intention of destroying the Challenger Planetoid. Due to the valiant actions of the SXC forces based at Port McNair, a few shots were exchanged but the SXC was able to capture the bulk of the Martian forces without suffering any damage to the Beanstalk itself.

Some New Angelinos claim to have been able to see the fighting in the skies overhead. For them, the most exciting part was the so-called "splashdown" when a handful of Martian vessels came down for a landing in the Pacific, leaving bright burning contrails across the sky.

According to the victors, the Battle of the Beanstalk was the nail in the coffin for the separatist groups on Mars, and Earth's leaders moved quickly to seize upon this chance to end hostilities on Luna and Mars and negotiate the end of Worlds War.

THE TREATY OF HEINLEIN

In the aftermath of the Battle of the Beanstalk, it became clear that after many brutal years, the U.S. and her allies held victory in their grasp. If China and the other global powers wanted any concessions from the U.S. in regards to the colonies, the offer of a lasting peace was their only bargaining chip left.

As soon as the SXC was certain the Beanstalk was secure, the SXC made one final push to establish complete supremacy of the Martian skies. Trapped on their own world and reliant on many imported goods from Earth for anything more than basic survival, continued resistance on Mars was going to prove difficult. Within days of this final military push, a coalition of governments on Earth finally resorted to diplomacy and offered peace to all parties.

Despite the deteriorating situation on the Red Planet, the response from the majority of Martians was an absolute rejection of any and all peace terms. The Martians captured during the Battle of the Beanstalk were willing discuss to surrender, according to official news-nosies, but most clans were too embittered against their corporate overseers from Earth, as well as those whom they now saw as the cowards and traitors on Luna, to accept any negotiations.

The diplomatic effort was unfazed by Mars's response. Peace talks were arranged to be held on Heinlein between the major Earth powers and the corporations they represented. The talks became a media sensation, with SXC officers and newly minted military heroes sitting down alongside their foreign counterparts and the defeated rebels to forge a new future for the solar system. The resulting agreement became known as the Treaty of Heinlein, and it is still proudly displayed at the museum at Starport Kaguya.

MELANGE MINING'S MONOPOLY

Of all the helium-3 mining corps on Mars, only Melange Mining and Alpha Prospecting maintained operable facilities. 2M offered to buy out its former competitors at a price they could not refuse, especially considering that they could not expect financial support or subsidies from their parent countries. Héliobras and Rajanipati Limited were allowed to merge with 2M and send their share of profits back to Brazil and India, as had previously been negotiated during their time as allies in the War.

The human Lunar population was essentially back where it had started. More obedient workers in the form of androids replaced human labor in the helium-3 mines, and those who could not find work with the corps moved into the Docklands or shipped out to the Martian frontier or the Belt.

THE UNIVERSAL NATIONS AND THE MARTIAN COLONIAL AUTHORITY

One of the chief provisions of the Treaty of Heinlein was the charter for a new international organization to replace the failed United Nations. This new organization was dubbed the Universal Nations in recognition of the offworld colonies of Luna and Mars. The Treaty also guaranteed international access to the Beanstalk by way of the newly formed Space Elevator Authority. The U.S. federal government's role in New Angeles, the headquarters of the newly formed Universal Nations, was also curtailed.

The U.N. charter also established the Martian Colonial Authority under its umbrella. New Beijing and New Moscow's continued fears of U.S. hegemony on Mars were shared by many other Treaty of Heinlein signatories, and nobody wanted a repeat of the War. In exchange for the joint supervision of the MCA by the U.N., the corps would maintain ownership of their colonies, but they would be governed by the MCA as a whole, not any one single country. The United States was permitted to maintain several SXC bases on Mars for initial security and to help train the nascent Mars Colonial Corps, but there is no set date for complete SXC withdrawal.

SCARS OF THE WAR

Although the War's resolution was applauded as a return to normalcy, it was a normal that looked very different from the pre-War years. Lunar and Martian populations had been decimated in some regions, and colonial borders were redrawn. Nearly all of the major superpowers were faced with the prospect of massive war-related costs, which were crippling for Russia, China, and the former United Crescent nations.

The proliferation of cybernetics and g-mod enhancements among returning veterans challenged the popular sense of what it meant to be human.

Beyond the geopolitical and ramifications, the face of the ordinary citizen was changed as well. The proliferation of cybernetics and g-mod enhancements among returning veterans challenged the popular sense of what it meant to be human. Some veterans had been forced to rely on these new technologies to preserve their lives or restore capabilities lost to injuries, and nearly all had undergone genetic modification treatments that enabled them to operate in low-gravity and -oxygen environments. Some of these treatments were invisible, but modifications such as respirocytes would forever mark a veteran in any blood test or medical exam. Regardless of their exact changes, the veterans returned home to an extremely mixed reaction: part horror, part disgust, part pity, and part awe.

The fields of human enhancement had been severely underdeveloped for many years before the War. The research was primarily done by non-profit medical labs working on government grants because few corporations considered the fields potentially profitable enough to devote research and development toward such endeavors. Further complicating matters were an assortment of anti-enhancement groups, ranging from neoluddites to fundamentalist churches, which saw such technologies as stripping away the humanity of their users. Lobbying from these groups limited governmental spending on such research, particularly in the fledging superpower of Brazil. Crude as the early enhancements were, though, injured veterans welcomed whatever help they could provide.

The tide of returning veterans did for transhumanism what decades of PR work by medical firms never managed. Soon after the end of the War, it was a rare individual who did not encounter a g-mod or cyborg on the street on a daily basis, many of whom were familiar faces. While obvious enhancements and prosthetics were still a source of discomfort to many, to vet-erans they became symbols of what they had sacrificed in the War. Polls on the issue of human enhancement rapidly turned in favor of further research, and soon newer, sleeker cybernetics were on display in hospitals alongside faster-acting, more reliable g-mod treatments. As more lives began to be saved or improved by the new technology, the increased revenues prompted further research in a cycle of positive feedback that continues to this day.

Now, enhanced humans, whether they are cyborg or g-mod, are more accepted in society than ever before. Among the elite, g-modding for beauty, creativity, or intelligence is a decision made before conception. Some taboos regarding enhancement remain in full strength, however. While replacing a lost limb or getting a treatment for an inherited disorder are considered socially acceptable, augmentation for its own sake is generally considered outré. Certain subcultures have sprung up around personal modification using cyber-limbs and g-mods granting unnatural capabilities, often among rebellious youths who relish the shock value. The self-labeled "chromeheads" of SanSan favor cybernetic replacements, while the seedier parts of Heinlein are often frequented by a community of g-mod experimenters who call themselves "wylders." The wylders draw their name both from their infamous hangout of Wyldside and from a tendency to mod themselves with qualities borrowed from other species.

*L*aser fire mixed with slugs traced the air around Dejah as she ducked behind the burnt-out wreck of an armored hopper. Around her, other soldiers were diving for cover—those who weren't already lying dead or wounded in the red soil, anyway. It had been an ambush, and she cursed herself as she peered around the corner of the hopper, trying to spot their attackers.

"Anyone got eyes on them?" she demanded.

"Negative, Sarge." The voice carried over her hardsuit's internal comm belonged to Higgins.

"Try the busybody, Dallas."

Dallas brought up the virt display for the full-spectrum scanner unit mounted at the waist of his suit. A smaller version of the holo-image appeared on her HUD, displaying their comrades' positions along with their vitals, the positions of the vehicles, and the surrounding topography. Energy readings also indicated additional combat envirosuits and biosigns beyond a nearby ridge, less than three hundred meters out.

"Got 'em," she said, grinning behind her visor. "Dallas, hold position and see if you can find anything else. Everyone else, take positions and get ready to light 'em up."

As the members of her squad leaned out into firing positions, the busybody detected a telltale transmission laser, displaying the new data on her HUD.

"Frag it! Bugs incoming! Dallas, where is it?"

The squad tech began to reply, but an angry squawk from the comm cut him off. Her HUD data snowed as a massive spike of destructive interference surged through the squad. A burst of light and sound behind her; an explosion. She spun around, seeing parts of Dallas and his hardsuit raining down around a plume of smoke, dust, and red mist. Before Dallas' remains even met the dirt, a rapid series of explosions took out three more squad members and detonated a damaged hopper in a massive fireball. She dove to the ground as the explosions ripped her squad apart, and a stinging pain shot up from her thigh as a piece of shrapnel tore through envirosuit between the armor plates. Almost instantly, her suit applied a nanomed to the area, numbing the pain. Within moments, the smartpoly would finish sealing the breach—if she could stay in one piece long enough.

In less than half of a second, the drone completed its initial strafing run. A sonic boom retroactively announced its arrival. It was so fast and so well defended by EWS electronic countermeasures that the boom, the explosions, and the interference were the only evidence it had been there. In less than three seconds, it would start its second run. She braced herself—

—and the train ground to a stop.

Dejah Thoris opened her eyes as they arrived at the Bisson Colony Station.

That was a long time ago. Things are different now. "The War is over," they say, she smiled grimly to herself. As brutal as the War was, in a way she missed the simplicity. A clear enemy, leading soldiers on a battlefield. I've had enough of smoke and mirrors. At least it's almost over. Around her, impatient passengers hurriedly fastened their envirosuits, grabbed luggage, and jostled to get be first through the airlock.

As Thoris exited onto the platform, a smiling young man stepped in front of her, trying to download a Crimson Dust flier to her PAD. She ignored him and brushed past, and he moved on to the next person exiting the station. For a moment, she was almost disappointed he didn't recognize her, despite her dyed hair and the synthskin mask distorting her features. Were Dejah Thoris traveling openly on Mars—at least most places on Mars—she would receive a hero's welcome. As it was, she was traveling discreetly, under an assumed identity. Although it wasn't perfect, the false ID she was carrying could fool all but the most sophisticated readers and sec systems. After so long away from her home planet, it's not how she would have preferred to return.

She set down her hopper at a warehouse complex a few kilometers outside the colony dome proper. The facility consisted of several unpressurized warehouse buildings and a small office. She set down next to several cargo hoppers and noted the unmarked dropship on the small landing pad, its exterior carbon-scored from years of use. Approaching the freestanding building of the office, the door-sec read her ID and allowed her in. She waited for the airlock to cycle before releasing her helmet catch with a hiss of air. An armored Mars Colonial Corps officer ushered her into the environmentally sealed room, where two men sat at the table while a woman stood next to it, looking at the screen of her PAD.

Thoris peeled the mask off with a grimace. "Damn, are these things uncomfortable."

"Glad you could join us, Agent Thoris," one of the men said, smiling coldly.

"Higgins, Thompson." Thoris nodded to the men as she sat at the table. She didn't know who the woman was, but a quick read of her ID confirmed her as a freelance corp efficiency consultant, which was so clearly a lie Thoris concluded she must be Martian Secret Service.

Wells set her PAD down on the table and a rotating holo of a man's head appeared above it. The man was dark-haired and quite handsome, in a generic sort of way—probably the result of g-modding.

"Victor Gray is scheduled to leave for Mars in three weeks to personally attend the peace talks at Bisson Colony." Wells waved her hand through the image, and Gray's face shrank down, as the images of other participants in the talks appeared alongside it in a grid. "That doesn't leave us long to prepare. I trust things are ready on your end, Agent Thoris?"

"They are," she nodded.

"Good," Thompson said. "And you have no problems with your orders?"

She hesitated only for a second before replying. "Of course not. I know what securing Mars's future requires. Some of us actually fought in the Colony Wars." She glared across the table.

Thompson started to say something, but Higgins waved for him to let it go.

"We'll be ready as soon as we receive word from our embed in CD, but we don't anticipate any problems there. As soon as we do—"

"Agents," one of the sec team interrupted, and then paused as he listened to his comm. "We have a problem." An explosion shook the building, the roar deadened by the pressure differential inside. "We need to evac, now." The other guard keyed the airlock cycle as the first gestured for the agents to follow.

"Damn," Higgins said as the agents stood and began sealing their suits. "This location was supposed to be secure. Do we know who it is?"

The sec team readied their rifles as the group entered the airlock. "No

confirmation, but the force includes at least six exosuits."

Wells narrowed her eyes at Thoris, who ignored her, as they waited for the atmo to cycle. The doors parted to the sound of weapons fire and explosions. Lasers and bullets flew past, and suddenly, Dejah Thoris was a sergeant again, leading her squad to safety under enemy fire.

"This way," she commed, gesturing to the closest warehouse. It would provide at least some cover from the exosuits approaching from the northeast. The others followed her without objection.

Around them, MCC forces spilled from the warehouses, opening fire on the approaching rebel infantry, while soldiers with anti-materiel weapons targeted the exosuits. The rear hatch on one of the cargo hoppers opened to reveal an infantry-served laser cannon, the gunner already swiveling it in the direction of the exosuits. A blinding flash, then a hole tunneled through the front exosuit and its pilot, and the suit

dropped to its knees before detonating in a fireball that washed over the next machine and sent three infantry in armored envirosuits sprawling to the ground. Another exosuit, a bulky mining model almost four meters tall and retrofitted with additional armor and with military weapons, raised its slug cannon and raked the hopper with shells, chewing through the carbosteel of the vehicle as easily as the flesh of the gunners.

"No, no, this is a mistake." Thoris watched in disbelief as the rebels and MCC forces slaughtered each other, demolishing the warehouses and vehicles in the process.

Those idiots. Those fragging idiots. What is Free Mars doing here?

THE MARTIAN CIVIL WAR

The Lunar Insurrection inspired the Martian Colony Wars, which never truly ended. Although a Martian delegation signed the Treaty of Heinlein, these representatives were all born on Earth and—according to many Martians—had Earther and corporate interests in mind, not Mars's. Native Martians had no part in the peace talks, and many clans feel they never agreed to end the War; because so many nodes were ignored during the SXC's campaign to retake the cities, many clans believe they were never challenged by Earth, much less defeated. The result is an intermittent but bloody civil war as Martians attempt to wrest control away from any who would deny their right to self-govern.

Currently, these conflicts are confined to Mars; Earth stands back while separatist groups battle against the MCA, the corps, and each other. With only minimal support for the Martian Colonial Authority's military arm, the Mars Colonial Corps, it would almost appear that the U.N. has already given Mars its independence. Of course, the true representatives of Earth power on Mars are the corporations and their prisec forces.

BCP INTERVIEW
TRANSCRIPT 38914/6

Of course I'm angry. Do you know how hard my family worked, just to scrape by, only to be kicked out of our home and left with nothing when Haas-Bioroid wanted to expand their facility? A lot of us are angry, that's why we're will-
5 *ing to fight for our freedom. Because that is exactly what we're doing: fighting for our rights, since the MCA won't protect them.*

The U.N. is millions of miles away, and the corps are right here on Mars. It's no secret that the corps are the
10 *real policy-makers on Mars, at least not to the locals. Some Earthers, those who even think about Mars, probably know the truth, but others are blissfully ignorant, paying lip service to the "great experiment" of extra-Earth colonization. Those who watch the NBN mediafeed channels just click*
15 *their tongues at the latest tragic terrorist attack.*

A lot of talk happens at the MCA's embassies in New Angeles and Mumbad, and some of the U.N. member states aren't happy about the "ongoing conflicts" on Mars. There are talks and resolutions, and the MCA reps say we're mak-
20 *ing progress, but most of it's for show, and a lot of those involved Earth-side realize it, even if they don't admit it.*

Most of the upper levels of the MCA, anyone with any real power, are from Earth. Those few native Martians with any authority are so deep in the corps' pockets they can't
25 *see the dome. A lot of the population resents it, but it's always been this way, since even before the Heinlein Treaty.*

Why bother voting? There's no justice there. Your Senator says she stands for law and order, but she really only represent the corps and their interests. Where were you
30 *when the corps took my family's home, our land? No, the only way to get justice is to fight for it. I don't care what you do to me; someday Mars will belong to us.*

EARTH GOVERNMENT ON MARS

The Martian Colonial Authority (MCA) is the governing body of Mars, answerable—in theory—to the Universal Nations. Formalized as part of the peace treaty after the War, the MCA handles Mars's official diplomatic relations with Earth's governments and supposedly oversees issues that affect all the colonies. More importantly, the MCA allows Earth to jointly administer Martian settlements in the hopes that doing so will prevent another outbreak like that of the War.

Perhaps unsurprisingly, most Martians do not see the Martian Colonial Authority as representing them or their interests. The Heinlein Treaty technically created the MCA, but it did little more than restructure and rename the existing Earth-centric power structure in Bradbury. A few more diplomats and bureaucrats representing the new U.N. were sent to Mars, but for the most part the newly formed MCA kept existing persons in power with little change in areas of oversight, much less checks and balances. More than that, the difficulties inherent in trying to achieve consensus among U.N. members has let the corps continue to dominate Martian politics.

The corps often disagree on how the MCA should proceed on a given matter, and there are a number of strategies they employ to outdo each other. When push comes to shove, a corp has to ensure the right bureaucrat or politician has its interests in mind, not a competitor's. Economic and political pressure, bribery, and even blackmail are all on the table, not to mention even harsher measures according to some rumors.

It's not always easy to ensure the colonies follow the MCA's edicts. The colonies are effectively governed by the clans, and while some of these are more receptive to the MCA, others haven't had direct contact with their official representatives in years—representatives whose campaigns were funded directly by one or more of the Big Four anyway. For many native-born Martians, the MCA is the enemy in an ongoing war. Those settlements fighting against Earth government on Mars, whether politically or violently, often view their actions as a struggle against an occupation, not as a civil war.

The U.S. Space Expeditionary Corps maintains a few scattered bases on the Martian frontier, with the largest, Mariner Base, near Bradbury. The SXC is there per Article 12 of the Treaty of Heinlein to help train the Mars Colonial Corps so that one day it will be able to protect the MCA's territory without Earth forces.

The Mars Colonial Corps struggles to recruit enough bodies to adequately protect its frontiers and quell inter- and intra-clan conflicts as they arise. Although it prefers to draw from recent Earth immigrants whenever possible, the realities of the situation mean pulling from the local populace—and by extension, clans—as well. Even then, the MCC often supplements its troops with prisec out of necessity, although this comes with its own dangers. Both policies have the effect of creating a chaotic and inconsistent force with transient regional allegiances.

Caroline Gariba

SEPARATISTS AND TERRORISTS

The separatists opposing the MCA run the gamut of clan affiliations, ideologies, tactics, and strategies. Certain clans are more associated with separatist organizations than others—including clans Har Deche, Johnson, and Mweli—but loyalties vary on a settlement-by-settlement basis. While some desire recognition for Mars (or for individual colonies) as an independent nation while maintaining strong political ties to Earth, others favor a complete separation. Some groups are fighting to halt the terraforming; these are known as "E.T.E.T.'s" or "double E.T.'s," for "extra-terrestrial eco-terrorists," and they target Martian and Earthers alike.

Some political activist groups working for separatism are actually recognized as legitimate organizations by the MCA and U.N. These organizations must tread a fine line or risk being labeled as terrorists and losing their credibility, whether rightfully so or not.

FREE MARS

For a group calling itself Free Mars, the War never really ended, no matter what the Authority signed. In its view, the clans never agreed to let the MCA speak for them at Heinlein, and the clans never agreed to Earth's terms. Free Mars has since taken to calling the conflict the "War for Martian Independence," which has proved successful for recruiting efforts and takes advantage of the MCA's unpopularity.

Free Mars considers the MCA to be just as much the enemy as any corp or Earth group, and its politicians and soldiers as traitors. The Free Mars Council is the rightful Martian government in its view, and clans from across the colonies are proud to fight for the FMC. Earth calls them terrorists, but Free Mars maintains that its members are nothing like the fanatics representing Crimson Dust.

Free Mars doesn't match the numbers of the Martian Colonial Corps, but it makes up for it with training, skill, and ingenuity. Its members have made a point of turning the corps' own tools into weapons against their oppression. Their exosuits might have been built for mining and construction, but they're strong and durable. Free Mars's fighters have added some extra plating and replaced the mining lasers with proper weapons, making the FMC exosuits as good as or better than the lowest-bidder military suits used by the MCC.

Free Mars has cells in colonies across Mars—some say in every colony. It claims to fight for the common men and women of Mars—for the workers—and sympathy for the FMC runs strong among the clans, even in MCA strongholds like Bradbury. Its populist roots are evident in the fact that Free Mars started with the Boreum Revolt, when Tardos Mors convinced that first mining crew to take their exosuits and fight back against their corporate overseers.

"The colonies cannot exist if split into factions. We have to remain whole to remain strong. We learned that in the Colony Wars."

199

TARDOS MORS

Tardos Mors is the leader of Free Mars Council as well as the military arm of Free Mars. Mors began his career in prisec with Globalsec's Mars division as one of the earliest mercenaries on Mars. He was subsumed into a Martian clan and received his tattoos shortly before leaving the prisec industry to head the militia of Brackett colony. When Mars rebelled against Earth, Mors and his unit made preemptive strikes against corp-held munitions manufactories, and they were a constant menace that targeted Earth forces. After the Treaty of Heinlein, Mors's unit continued fighting against the SXC and corp forces for three weeks before it was destroyed. Mors was believed dead until he resurfaced eight years ago at the head of Free Mars.

Mors is the grandfather of Sergeant Dejah Thoris, and they fought together in several battles during the War, although her actions during the War caught the public attention in a way Mors's did not. Unlike her grandfather, Thoris complied with the ceasefire following the treaty. It is unclear how much contact the two have had since the War. Thoris's involvement is suspected in several Free Mars operations, but the available information is inconclusive.

CRIMSON DUST

Crimson Dust is one of the most dangerous Martian terrorist groups currently active, due in large part to the fanatical devotion of its members. This organization takes the Martian life origin beliefs of the Incipiata Marte Vita sects to violent extremes.

The group's leader, Vasanti Smith, is viewed as a religious messiah for her ability to walk unaided upon the surface of Mars. She is supposedly a recurrence of an "original human"—those "little green men" who supposedly inhabited Mars before traveling several thousand years ago to settle Earth. According to Smith and her believers, Mars is the original homeworld of humans, and instead of terraforming Mars's sacred surface, humans should revert to their original forms. So far, Smith has been moderately successful in recruiting believers to Crimson Dust's cause. The gaps in the records of Mars' early colonization have made it difficult to verify

the identity of the Vasanti Smith leading Crimson Dust or her claims.

Whereas other groups rely on exosuits or environmentally sealed hardsuits, many Crimson Dust fighters undergo genetic modification to allow them to survive unaided in Mars' atmosphere. Smith urges her followers to undergo extensive genetic modification and martyr themselves for the cause of Martian independence—for they will be reborn with DNA closer to that of their mythic progenitors.

It is unclear how Crimson Dust obtained the capability to perform this g-modding, although finding the location of their facilities is a high priority for the MSS. Intelligence indicates that the technology was first developed by Jinteki, but the corp is not forthcoming. Although Crimson Dust likely stole the technology directly or purchased the data from runners, the possibility that Jinteki—or a faction within Jinteki—knowingly sold the technique on the black market cannot be ruled out.

Although the g-mods do provide substantial advantage during combat situations outside of the domes—and in case of a breach—it is also, in many ways, more costly and resource-intensive than using traditional technology.

In addition to using guerrilla and sabotage tactics such as bombing government and corp terraforming facilities, Crimson Dust targets Martian civilians and political leaders who do not support its beliefs or efforts. Crimson Dust's tactics also include suicide bombings, which showcase the fanatical devotion of the group's adherents. Suicide bombers utilizing micro-explosives, improvised metafuel devices, or Taejo monofilament wire bombs have proven difficult to detect or stop, and they are capable of inflicting tremendous damage.

EARTH SYMPATHIZERS

Many Martians oppose the actions of violent separatists for a variety of reasons. In addition to those who oppose bloodshed in principle, some Martians, including a small minority of natives, accept or even favor a close relationship with Earth. Others believe that the corps actually directly influence the inter-colonial violence

on Mars, using the factions as yet another weapon in the megacorps' ongoing competition. Although there is little evidence to support this theory, it appeals to many colonists, playing as it does to Martians' common concerns about corporate control.

CORPORATE INTERESTS

The corps might seem powerful on Luna, or even Earth, but on Mars their power is absolute. With the Colonial Authority's laws more or less written by corporate attorneys, there's very little the megacorps cannot do. Shifts in the ag-bubbles are long and grueling, while work conditions in the manufactories are dangerous. The corps don't have to compensate their employees with real money, just credit that's good at the corp stores. Perhaps most importantly, the laws that regulate androids and their behavior do not extend to Mars.

No one knows how many prisec and mercenary soldiers are working for the corps on Mars, but it's safe to say that they outnumber the Mars Colonial Corps. Argus and Globalsec are major providers of security solutions, but the corporations are thought to be fielding armies of their own as well.

It should come as no surprise that Jinteki is said to be growing its own army of clones to help protect its assets on Mars. Dubbed the Musashi line, Jinteki's genegineers and neural conditioning experts have created the so-called "perfect solider." Alongside enhanced physical attributes, each Musashi clone possesses a keen tactical mind and extensive knowledge of military history and tactics.

Meanwhile, Haas-Bioroid is supposedly testing a batch of warroids—bioroids that lack the First Directive—as part of its mysterious Project Ares. An Ares unit's enhanced sensory suite and quantum processing capabilities allow it to be more alert and responsive to a changing battlefield. Moreover, without the impediments of pain or mortal injury, human soldiers will be hard-pressed to supply enough stopping power barring outright satellite bombardment.

If the Colony Wars continue, a new type of battlefield might be drawn up on Mars.

VICTOR GRAY FOUND DEAD
FOUL PLAY SUSPECTED

– Lily Lockwell
Reporting for the New Angeles Sol

Victor Gray, Chair of the Universal Nations Council for Interplanetary Affairs, was found dead this morning in his New Angeles hotel room. Hotel staff discovered Gray's body shortly after 2130 New Angeles Time in his suite's private swimming pool. While the NAPD has not publicly commented on the case, the *Sol* has learned that detectives in the homicide division have already questioned hotel staff and the Globalsec personnel

The Martian Colonial Authority has struggled to quell inter-clan warfare on Mars.

contracted by the U.N. to ensure Gray's safety. Although no suspects have been officially named in the investigation, Martian terrorists may be connected to Gray's death.

NAPD forspecs determined that Gray died at approximately 2048, and the cause of death was drowning. Gray was a well-known swimmer and was captain of the swimming and diving team while at Levy University. Gray had been at the hotel for two days before the time of his death.

Gray has received widespread recognition and commendation for his recent unprecedented success in negotiations between the Martian Colonial Authority and separatist groups. Last week, the U.N. Interplanetary Council voted to move forward with Gray's resolution directing the MCA to bestow greater governmental and legislative authority to individual colonies and begin work on the so-called "Martian Bill of Rights." Although many Martian separatist groups have agreed to de-escalate military action as part of such a deal, some extremist groups have refused to participate in talks.

Gray was scheduled to speak this Friday at Levy University on the issue of Earth-Mars relations, and was expected to travel to Mars next week. In a statement released by the university, Chancellor Leslie Horn says that she is "deeply saddened" by Gray's passing. "Victor Gray was a great man, and a great champion for the cause of peace in our solar system," says Horn. "His work will be forever remembered, and it is my sincere hope that the Martian peace process meets a successful conclusion worthy of his legacy."

JOIN THE CONVERSATION

MARTIANS DON'T DESERVE EQUAL RIGHTS

▼ 20:55:54 BY MORALLY_RIGHT

Why are Martians so gung ho about independence and secession and all that? They're humans, after all. You'd think they'd have some pride, some loyalty in their home planet. Everyone is supposed to be in this together—the colonization of Mars, I mean. But it seems like the Martians don't want to hold up their end. So Earth pays for the colonies, builds them, and then it's "so long, thanks for the help"? Doesn't seem right.

There would be no one on Mars if it weren't for Earth. That's about as obvious as it gets. Even the 25% of colonists who were born there mostly have living relatives born on Earth. I complain about the corps as much as the next person, but that doesn't mean they don't do a lot of good. And that goes double for Mars, right? I mean, if it weren't for the corps, the Martians wouldn't even have air to breathe. And how do they show their appreciation? By blowing up corp property and their own colonies.

Sure, I know all Martians aren't terrorists. But it seems like even the ones who aren't don't want to do anything about it. I watch the news and read the rags—when a bean-pod on the Beanstalk was bombed a few years ago, there were celebrations in the colony streets. I know what's going on. There are a lot of separatist groups, and a lot of them operate pretty openly. Mars isn't like Earth; there aren't places in the wilderness to hide. So that means the colonies are sheltering these terrorists. Sounds like aiding the enemy to me.

31 RESPONSES

WE'RE HUMAN TOO

▼ 21:09:50 BY REDRENEGADE3000

The corps and the NBN screamsheets call us terrorists, but groups like Free Mars and the Martian Autonomy and Resistance Service are just fighting for our rights as human beings. We are not corporate slaves. The Martian people deserve political self-determination and real freedom, but the corps treat us like golems. They use us up and then discard us, just like any other resource they can extract from Mars.

It's true that some of the separatist groups take extreme actions, but important causes require commitment. We have tried asking for our rights, tried arguing for them. But peaceful protests get ignored by Earth and shut down by mercs or the Mars Colonial Police. Do you think this is what the colonists signed up for when they first boarded those ships? What about the current generation, people born on Mars? This is the only life a lot of us know, and even though we didn't choose it, we're proud to be Martian. We just want the same freedom as our relatives back on Earth.

I'm not saying I support everything these groups do. Sometimes innocent people get killed, and that's tragic. But I understand their anger, and it seems like the only thing the corps respect is power.

THE BUSINESS OF WARFARE

War profiteering is big business and a time-honored tradition. There was a time, generations ago, when it was considered not just a crime but also a moral failing. As weapons technology improved, and weapon systems grew deadlier, easier to handle, and more lucrative to produce, their marketing became more and more savvy. The idea that war was a good economic motivator was sold to the masses, and NBN pushed the romance and sanitized violence of war across mediums. In a world full of simmering violence and dominated by faceless, profit-driven megacorps, this culturally sanctioned war profiteering is rampant.

While low-intensity brushfire wars burned for the past few decades, involving various countries and corporate entities, many arms and military equipment manufacturers worked away to build and sell new and improved killing machines. Their profits were certainly respectable, but it wasn't until the outbreak of the War that the credits really started to roll in. As tensions mounted between Luna, Earth, and Mars, companies like Argus and NEXT began rolling out new weapon and vehicle designs and lobbying governments for fat contracts. Prisec outfits like Globalsec set out on heavy recruiting drives, offering huge signing bonuses and other incentives to fill their ranks. Every corp with even a tangential connection to military or PMC materiel development fought tooth and nail to make sure that they were in on the ground floor of this new war, and that they got their cut.

Now, with the world at peace, the military contractors are looking farther afield for their next big income stream. The ongoing conflict on Mars is, of course, the going concern for arms manufacturers. Designers and engineers work day and night to build a better rifle, a better hardsuit, or a better dropship. Corporate espionage is at an all-time high, with pivotal employees and secret technical plans being extracted from corporate compounds and executives being killed in increasingly creative and gruesome ways. The average soldier or PMC operator cares little for this, though. His main concern is that the equipment works correctly, the meals are on time, and the checks clear.

OUTFITTED FOR KILLER EFFICIENCY

As long as there have been soldiers, there has been a struggle to find the perfect balance between what a soldier needs to do his job and what he can physically carry. The modern soldier is not that different than his forebears. Although the technology is more sophisticated, the weapons deadlier, and the armor lighter and more protective, a soldier must still carry his gear wherever he goes and does so largely on foot. There are, of course, exceptions among pilots, vehicle crews, artillery and heavy weapon teams, and light or non-combat personnel, but the majority of an army's materiel is carried on the backs of its soldiers. While the composition of a soldier's outfit obviously varies by force and mission, many common items can be found on the backs and in the pockets of regular and irregular soldiers.

A soldier's basic outfit starts with his uniform. Tailored to the environment in which the soldier is operating, most uniforms consist of a shirt, trousers, and a jacket made of stain resistant, rip-stop material and reinforced at the knees and elbows. Sturdy, high laced boots protect the feet and ankles, and a variety of working gloves and brimmed caps are worn. Over the uniform, a soldier wears armor. Modern armor commonly consists of a light clamshell made of reinforced polymers and buckyweave that protects the torso, shoulders, and groin, and thin, flexible armor plates that strap to the shins and forearms. Some elite or heavy combat units use sophisticated hardsuits that provide full armor protection, laser protection, environmental protection, and basic life support functions. The last piece of the uniform and armor combination is the load bearing equipment. LBE comes in a wide variety of styles, but at its most basic it is a vest or web of straps and a broad belt that distributes the weight of a soldier's equipment evenly across his torso.

Most LBE is modular and can be customized for different roles with quick-release pouches, loops, and slings. These pouches carry small- to medium-sized bits of gear like compasses, PADs, weapon magazines, flashlights, grenades, and anything else a soldier might need access to in a hurry.

Along with his uniform, armor, and LBE, every soldier carries both a light combat pack and a heavier rucksack. Combat packs are typically integrated into load bearing equipment and are used for daily patrols, short marches, and as essentially carry-on bags when being transported by vehicles. Rucksacks are larger, heavier backpacks with integrated frames that are meant to carry all of a soldier's equipment over long distances for long stretches of time. In these packs soldiers usually carry extra clothes and uniforms, specialized tools or equipment used in their daily routines, rations, canteens, grooming kits, weapon maintenance kits, entrenching tools, binoculars, rain gear, NBC protective gear, portable power cells, and numerous other pieces of esoteric military hardware.

Last, but certainly not least, is the soldier's weapon. Even in today's high-tech modern militaries, the majority of personnel are common, infantry-style soldiers. These highly trained men and women carry a single primary weapon, usually a select-fire assault rifle, extra ammunition for said rifle, and a handful of smoke and fragmentation grenades. Soldiers are responsible for the care and maintenance of their weapon, and they are expected to keep it in top combat readiness at all times. Pistols are rarely carried by the common soldier, being reserved for non-commissioned officers, vehicle and gun crews, and officers. Some forces use dedicated grenadiers who carry powerful and versatile grenade launchers for squad fire support. Unique and high-tech weapons like mass drivers and focused energy weapons are slowly making their way into combat units, although this is usually only in very wealthy state militaries or private contracting firms.

While there is certainly more that soldiers can and do carry with them, everything from pieces of support weapons to communications equipment to heavy ordnance, the variety of equipment used by every state

SIDEARMS

Argus Model 19 —The Model 19 is the latest in a long line of rugged sidearms designed for officers, vehicle crews, military police, and special forces troops. Built almost entirely of polycarbonates with minimal use of light alloys, the M19 can be ordered in either 10mm, .40, or .22LR caseless, and in three different barrel lengths depending on its intended use. Two accessory rails, one beneath the barrel and one on top of the slide, make it easy to add accessories such as lights, sights, and optics.

Skorpios FM44 "Hailstorm" Flechette Pistol —One of Skorpios's more popular weapons, the Hailstorm is the standard to which all other flechette pistols are compared. Lightweight, reliable, and easy to handle, the FM44 has a relatively long barrel for a flechette pistol, which combined with its balance and finish makes for an incredibly accurate and deadly weapon. Chambered with Skorpios's proprietary 2mm "Needler" flechette rounds, the Hailstorm has the highest cyclic rate of fire in its class, allowing it to put more metal on target quickly and more accurately than any other competitor.

NEXT PL840.a Medium Laser Pistol —Known colloquially throughout the military and prisec communities simply as "the blaster," NEXT Design's PL840.a is the first mass-produced, man-portable laser weapon to enter the market. A refinement of NEXT's larger, more dangerous vehicle-mounted focused energy weapons, the PL840.a is a relatively sturdy, short-barreled weapon the size of a large caliber hand cannon. It provides excellent power and accuracy thanks to a sophisticated AI monitoring environmental conditions, but it suffers from overheating and excessive energy consumption. While it is rare among the rank-and-file troops of the world's military and prisec communities, these weapons are gaining popularity among specforces and black-ops units.

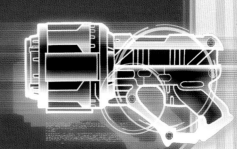

and private military defies easy description. Even within a military the equipment carried by personnel can vary wildly, especially in poorer areas. As for irregular troops and rebels, their equipment is such a mess of homemade, scavenged, and stolen technology that no two units will be outfitted alike.

WEAPONS

There are four broad categories of man-portable weapons on the market today: slugthrowers, mass drivers, energy weapons, and less-lethal weaponry. Slugthrowers are cheap, easy to use, and as common as dirt, making them especially attractive to New Angelino criminals and Martian insurgents alike. Wealthy PMCs like Globalsec love mass drivers' ability to pack a large punch in a small package, and many

sharpshooter and anti-materiel weapons used by prisec firms are mass drivers. Energy weapons came of age during the War, when SXC forces and PMC operatives trained in space combat were required to fight in conditions where there was little or no gravity or oxygen. Less-lethal weapons are as popular as ever, especially with large police forces like New Angeles' and with Beanstalk yellow jackets who usually prefer to keep casualties and collateral damage to a minimum. In addition, soldiers, cops, prisec operatives, and insurgents everywhere always have need for personal ordnance like grenades, mines, bombs, rocket launchers, and grenade launchers.

The discerning soldier can find a weapon for any tactical situation. Pistols that fire slugs or flechettes or super-accurate lasers

LONGARMS

Strelet Arms S101 Modular Weapon System — The S101 by Strelet Arms Ltd., a New Muscovite producer of small arms and light vehicles, is descended from the venerable AK pattern rifles that defined the assault rifle in Russia and the Eastern Bloc. Rugged, reliable, and eminently capable, the S101 is a gas-operated, select-fire assault rifle that chambers Strelet's proprietary 8mm caseless rifle round. Designed to give armies and private military contractors a modular and versatile weapon system in one package, the S101 is marketed as an all-purpose longarm. It uses a dizzying array of stocks, grips, optical enhancements, barrels, and feed mechanisms, and the gun can be configured for nearly any battlefield role—from combat rifle to light support weapon to highly accurate sniper rifle.

NEXT CG44 Anti-Materiel Gauss Rifle —Marketed as the ultimate man-portable anti-armor weapon, NEXT's CG44 is the most advanced Gauss rifle available. The CG44 is a massive, heavy, cumbersome gun designed for sharpshooters and fire support. It uses NEXT's patented mass-driver technology to propel its ammunition at ranges measured in kilometers, and each weapon comes equipped with a sophisticated multi-optic sight and a quick-release folding bipod. With the standard ammunition, a 30mm inert slug tipped with a tungsten penetrator fed from a 5-round detachable box magazine, the CG44 can demolish materiel, powered suits, and even light- and medium-armored vehicles at well beyond un-enhanced visual range. In addition, other ammunition types such as incendiary, explosive, and magpulse, allow a shooter to adapt quickly to changing battlefield conditions. This weapon is quite rare, expensive, and uses immense amounts of power, but its performance easily outweighs these few negative traits.

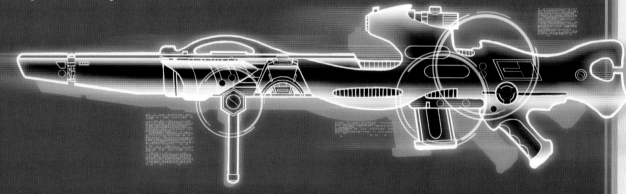

HHI Model 8 Combat Shotgun —The Model 8 is a gas-operated, select-fire combat shotgun built for sale to state and private militaries by Huang Heavy Industries, a relative newcomer in the small arms industry. Offered in 12- and 20-gauge and fed from either an 8-round tube magazine or 16-round box magazine, the Model 8 is, on paper, an excellent close quarters battle and riot control weapon. It features a sophisticated recoil suppression system, lightweight composite furniture, and the ability to mount a variety of combat accessories on its proprietary rail system. In reality however, the Model 8 suffers from a number of design flaws. Cheaply made by a company more at home with the design and construction of off-the-record freight haulers, industrial robots, and marine diesel engines, the Model 8 requires constant maintenance and has a tendency to jam. Despite these drawbacks, these weapons are popular among quartermasters and PMC bean counters because they are so cheap. HHI also offers incredible deals on bulk purchases, garnering them supply contracts with many militaries and police forces around the worlds.

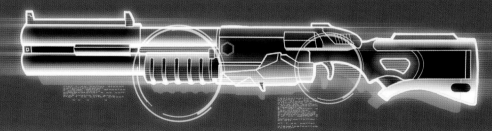

David Griffith

are carried by officers, security forces, and vehicle crews. Common soldiers carry composite assault rifles with under-barrel grenade launchers, while snipers deal death from kilometers away with Gauss rifles, and vehicle crews man automatic grenade launchers and heavy artillery cannons. Specforce operators carry compact and deadly submachine guns or devastating automatic shotguns, and black-ops assassins use monofilament blades and silent laser pistols to perform their bloody, clandestine work. Now, more than ever, the number and variety of small arms is staggering, and those outlined above are just a small sampling of what is available to the private- or state-sponsored soldier.

SLUGTHROWERS

Cheap, reliable, easy to construct and maintain, slugthrowers are the most commonly available personal weapons. These types of weapons are produced in a truly dizzying array of shapes, styles, size, and calibers for nearly every security and military job imaginable. The majority of personal defense weapons are sold to civilians are slugthrowers, and every private and state sponsored military force issues at least one type of slugthrower to its members.

Slugthrowers, while made of lightweight composites or cutting-edge alloys and loaded with high-tech combat assist systems, still use a number of tried-and-true technologies. They are typically gas-, blowback-, or recoil-operated, with only a tiny fraction using electrical or other exotic firing systems. Their internals would be instantly recognizable to an observer from the past despite being constructed of modern materials. The majority of slugthrowers, particularly pistols and many shotguns and rifles, are semi-automatic. Military-grade weapons—typically rifles, submachine guns, and some shotguns—are select fire. This gives shooters the option of single-shot, burst, or full-auto firing modes, allowing them to tailor their tactics to shifting battlefield conditions. Some rare rifles, especially those made for long-range sniper work, still use manual bolt action, but these are seen as antiques and less effective than modern semi-automatic actions.

CLOSE COMBAT WEAPONS

Skorpios "Bloodletter" Monoblades —For the discerning close combatant, Skorpios offers the Bloodletter line of monoblades. Available in varying lengths and styles, from small, easily concealed stilettos to long and elegant katana-type blades, this weapon is, in the right hands, impressive and incredibly lethal. Each features a custom-fitted hilt that contains a reel of retractable blade material and a small static generator and storage capacitor. The reel contains a set length of buckyweave fabric a single molecule thick that, when introduced to an electrical charge from the hilt, stiffens into a blade like a folding screen or common newsrag. Depending on its use and style, the blade come in varying strengths and levels of stiffness and can cut through cloth, bone, and most body armors with frightening ease. Urban legend has it that Bloodletters are the weapon of choice for Jinteki prisec forces.

HHI PX830 Portable Plasma Cutter —Huang Heavy Industries produces these versatile cutting tools for use in ship building, spaceship manufacture, and various other fabrication and production industries. Using a lightweight portable electric generator, the PX830 produces a high-intensity electric arc that forms thermal plasma from a constant stream of carrier gas such as argon, hydrogen, or helium or from advanced carrier fluids depending on the cutter's intended use. This produces a powerful plasma jet that can cut or weld nearly any metallic alloy. The PX830 unit consists of the portable generator, which is small and light enough to be worn over the shoulder or in a backpack, the cutting torch with an array of different cutting tips, and a lightly reinforced power cable connecting the two. While ostensibly an industrial tool, the PX830 and similar cutting tools, like HHI's "Neptune" waterknife, have been repurposed by rebels and soldiers alike for boarding ships, attacking bioroids, and dismantling vehicles or powered suits.

Personal Defense Industries Mk. I Collapsible Baton —One of a number of similar personal protection weapons, PDI's Mk. I is the most common collapsible baton on the market. It is a simple and easy-to-use defense weapon made of a high-strength, non-metallic composite that is both flexible and nearly unbreakable. When collapsed, the weapon fits comfortably in the palm of a hand and is easily concealable in a pocket, tool box, or bag. To activate, a user simply presses a button and the tightly wound spring inside the baton extends the weapon to roughly a meter in length in less than a second. A variety of lengths and diameters are available, and some variants are tipped with tungsten spines for puncturing heavy materials. Orgcrime outfits tend to favor this weapon for its brutal enforcement capabilities with a personal touch.

Where modern firearms diverge the furthest from their ancestors is in their ammunition. The majority of modern ammunition is caseless, a technology long ago perfected by Earth's leading weapons manufacturers. Caseless ammunition does away with the old metal or polymer cases and encases the bullet and primer in a stabilized block of synthetic propellant. This allows for lighter weapons and more rounds in a magazine, a definite concern for soldiers operating on ships or in habitats on Luna and Mars due to weight and space constraints. However, some long arms, primarily shotguns and some sniper and anti-materiel rifles, still use metal- or polymer-cased rounds due to their special requirements.

ENERGY WEAPONS

Until relatively recently, energy weapons were the stuff of fiction and treatises on speculative technologies. While starfighters taking on adversaries with large-caliber laser cannons and soldiers in hardsuits blasting away at aliens with plasma cannons looked great in threedees, even twenty years ago their creation and practical application was considered theoretical at best. But with the dawn of the first war to extend past Earth's atmosphere, military forces needed weapons that could fire regardless of gravity or atmospheric conditions. When NEXT Design released their ground breaking VL40 crew-served laser cannon for light armored vehicles that focused energy weapons became not just a reality, but a growing part of military orders of battle on Earth, Luna, and Mars.

For the first few years of their existence, focused energy weapons were large, cumbersome, energy hogs that required powerful high-output power systems. Too big to be carried by a common soldier, these weapons were mounted to combat vehicles or in stationary weapon emplacements. As the orders for their laser cannon poured in, NEXT worked day and night to perfect other types of energy weapons, as well as to decrease their size while increasing their portability and efficiency. Eventually, NEXT released both a practical laser pistol and laser rifle just ahead of a slew of competitor products, and the next arms race was on.

Currently, the most common focused energy weapon is the laser. Lasers are easy to build, and are on par with equivalent slug-throwers regarding lethality, and are light, accurate, and easy to handle. Recent advances in energy technology have led to the limited production of other types of energy weapon tailored for specific battlefield roles. Masers, or microwave "lasers," are more powerful, shorter-ranged weapons that are often used by Martian insurgents due to their tendency to burn enemies alive while leaving equipment largely unscathed.

New focused-energy weapon technologies are being announced daily, but it's only a matter of time before the current euphoria and feeling of limitless potential settles down into sensible, mature technologies with long-term practical military applications.

MASS DRIVERS

Mass drivers are elegant, powerful weapons seen as a compromise between the largely antiquated slugthrower and the ultra-modern—and largely untested—focused energy weapon. Derived from research and theories produced by nineteenth-century mathematician Carl Gauss, mass drivers use powerful electromagnetic coils to propel inert, ferrous slugs along a smooth barrel at incredible speeds over long ranges. While they are a relatively mature technology, having been produced for a few decades now, mass drivers are still relatively rare as they are expensive and many models are quite fragile and require special training to operate and maintain.

Unlike the near limitless variety of slugthrowers and the anarchic evolution of focused energy weapons, there are only two types of mass driver currently in production—the coilgun and the flechette gun. Coilguns, also known colloquially as "Gauss Guns" in reference to their originator, are typically rifle-sized longarms used for light combat duties. They are commonly semi-automatic weapons, although a few offer select-fire versions with limited burst capabilities. Their large energy requirements and need for constant maintenance make coilguns poorly suited for the rigors of heavy combat, but their range, accuracy, penetration, and ability to use a variety of ammunition make them outstanding sniper and anti-materiel weapons. While Gauss pistols are not unheard of, they are uncommon and are overshadowed by their cousins, the flechette weapons.

Also called "fletchers" or needleguns, flechette weapons use smaller, lower-yield coils to fire small-caliber, fin-stabilized darts called flechettes over short-to-medium distances. Fletchers are mainly pro-

duced as pistols or, at most, compact submachine guns or machine pistols. They typically feature very high rates of fire, are almost completely silent, and have little-to-no recoil. Flechette ammunition is quite small, usually between two and four millimeters, and is little more than a small dart with a super sharp penetrating tip. Flechettes are often coated in toxins or tranquilizers, either by their users or from the factory, and are also produced in a number of specialty styles such as tracking, explosive, armor piercing, and even incendiary.

LESS-LETHAL WEAPONRY

Years of riots, mass civil unrest, and the growing needs of the orbital and space-going communities have created a huge demand for weapon systems that cause minimal collateral damage but can still disperse crowds or capture individuals alive. While less-lethal weaponry is mainly used by police and private security forces, many militaries utilize these systems on a limited basis for special situations where a relatively light touch is required. The commonly used term "nonlethal weaponry" is considered a misleading fantasy by professionals in the industry.

Companies such as Argus Security, Skorpios, Paladin Arms, and Personal Defense Industries produce a variety of less-lethal gear ranging from gas and stun grenades to sub-sonic emitters to net guns and specialty riot ammunition. Weapons like Synap pistols and stunsticks use powerful electric charges to short circuit a target's nervous system, incapacitating them or rendering them totally unconscious. Frangible and lightweight polymer "rubber" rounds are produced for slugthrowers to scatter rioters, while beanbag or gel rounds turn shotguns into perfect non-lethal weapons. Even specialized, low-power flechette pistols can be loaded with tranquilizer ammunition that can knock a grown adult unconscious with few negative side effects.

CYBERWARE

Some of the most profound and astounding technological advancements made in the past few decades, the Space Elevator notwithstanding, were those made in the medical sciences. Cloning, genetic manipulation, designer medicines, and cutting-edge therapies and surgical techniques have extended both the length and quality of life for humankind—at least for those who can afford these miracles. Perhaps the most amazing advances have been made in the science of cybernetic and bionic prosthetics.

Modern prosthetics are a far cry from the crude replacement limbs of the past. Today's high-end artificial limbs are fully functioning, often extremely lifelike constructs permanently affixed to or implanted in an individual's body and connected to their nervous system via sophisticated integral neural networks. Arms and hands possess all the dexterity of their flesh-and-bone counterparts, and they can even outperform the real limbs on occasion, especially in the case of the latest military prosthetics. Many veterans of the War, however, were outfitted with clunky and cheap cybernetics after they were discharged, and veterans' affairs groups are struggling to get them upgrades.

Along with these simple medical prosthetics designed to help amputees and the handicapped, there are a number of cyberware systems designed to enhance the natural abilities of an individual. Spine and ribcage reinforcement combined with high-output cyberware arms can increase a person's strength and manual dexterity. Optical systems can be implanted that grant 360-degree vision all across the visible and invisible light spectrum, and audio filters and boosters allow an individual to pull a whisper out of a crowd or to reduce the deafening cacophony of battle to little more than a murmur. Enhanced hearts and lungs combined with powerful prosthetic legs can increase the running speed and long-term endurance of a soldier, allowing him to run great distances while carrying extremely heavy packs or equipment. These military-grade cyberware systems are very tightly regulated, and once a soldier or corporate operative retires, their systems are replaced with more mundane, civilian-grade cybernetics.

VEHICLES

Generally speaking, modern vehicles can be separated into two broad categories: aerospacecraft and planetary vehicles. Examples of aerospacecraft include dedicated spacecraft, transatmospheric vehicles like dropships and spaceplanes, and atmospheric aircraft like fightercraft, drones, bombers, and aerodynes. The category of planetary vehicles encompasses everything else from commuter vehicles and hoppers to fast-attack fighting vehicles.

SPACECRAFT

Despite increased efforts in the past few years, space remains largely unmilitarized. Various state and private space agencies maintain fleets of starships, but these are

---

PERSONAL ORDNANCE

Taejo Technologies Monofilament Mk. IV Fragmentation Grenade — Taejo Technologies' Mk. IV fragmentation grenade is, perhaps, the most lethal antipersonnel grenade ever produced—and banned on Earth. The Mk. IV is a compact, cylindrical grenade with a simple electronic fuse that can be set for timed or impact detonation. Within the thin carbon-metallic shell of the grenade is a core of semtex explosive compound wrapped tightly in roughly a kilometer of Taejo's patented monofilament wire. Upon detonation, the shell of the grenade shatters and spreads a cloud of incredibly sharp monofilament wire shards that can tear an unarmored or lightly armored enemy to bloody shreds in an instant.

NEXT PRM80 Shoulder-Fired Rocket Launcher —NEXT's PRM80 is an older model single-tube, magazine-fed rocket launcher designed to fire a wide array of guided and unguided warheads. Just shy of two meters in length, the PRM80 features lightweight composite and alloy construction, integrated gas-venting recoil reduction, and a sophisticated multifunction optical suite that can be set for both surface-to-air and surface-to-surface launches. The guided ordnance used by the PRM80 includes anti-armor, incendiary, high-explosive, and electromagnetic pulse. They are guided by a savant-level AI system similar to those found in combat drones, and once launched they seek their target until they either hit or run out of fuel, whereupon they self-destruct, rendering the missile and warhead useless.

Argus M-960 Automatic Grenade Launcher —An aging model intended to give an infantry squad heavy antipersonnel and light anti-armor capabilities, Argus's M-960 grenade launcher is a reliable and versatile combat weapon on Earth and Mars. The M-960 is a short-barreled, blowback-operated weapon the size and weight of a large submachine gun. It fires programmable, air-bursting 25mm grenades from a 20-round box magazine, and features composite construction, gyroscopic stabilization, and integrated guidance systems for the grenades. The grenades themselves come in a wide variety of types and are considered "smart munitions" that can be programmed singly or in bulk for range, arc, and detonation by the weapon's onboard guidance system.

ORBITAL COMBAT VEHICLE

SA/F-01A Striker Orbital Attack Fighter *—Developed by the U.S. Air Force during the War, the Striker is the first, orbital vessel built for combat. Air force brass realized early on in the Lunar conflict that they needed a platform similar to an atmospheric fighter to carry out attack missions on Luna in support of SXC personnel. After a number of failed attempts to quickly create something so new from scratch, the USAF settled on the Striker design.*

Derived from a series of small orbital runabouts, these ships were modified in the field by air force engineers to a set of common specs. The ship that came out of this project turned out to be surprisingly effective. The Striker is a small, two-seat attack spacecraft ideal for close support missions in low and zero-gravity conditions as well as in vacuum. It's lightly armored, carrying little more than anti-splinter armor around its fuel tanks and ordnance bays and some lightweight advanced composite armor around the cockpit. It has a set of two powerful ion engines backed up by a collection of maneuvering thrusters that make it relatively fast and maneuverable and allows it to carry a prodigious weapons loadout. The weapons loadout is modular and could easily be tailored to almost any situation, but typically involves either a heavy laser or mass driver cannon coupled with an array of rockets, guided missiles, and smart bombs. Once the War ended, all Strikers were moved back to U.S. airspace to act as technology testbeds for further space fighter development.

RELATED

Call Signs *—In addition to the array of nicknames and acronyms given to even the most innocuous items by military personnel, most soldiers, sailors, runners, and other military personnel also gain nicknames, or call signs, at some point in their career. While call signs are required, mainly by tradition, for pilots, call signs can be assigned to any military personnel. Despite what popular culture might suggest, call signs are rarely something cool like "Viper" or "Maverick." Instead, especially among pilots, call signs are references to embarrassing or otherwise unsavory situations that pilot may have caused or been involved in. Many involve body parts or bodily functions, and most are decidedly unsuited for discussion in polite company.*

unarmed research or cargo vessels used to probe the fringes of the system, or to ferry men and materiel between Earth and Luna bases and outposts in the asteroid belt and on Mars.

During the War, smaller, more agile shuttles were modified into ersatz fighting ships, and larger cargo haulers moved men and materiel to Luna to put down the insurrection. While dropships and their armed gunship cousins are ostensibly spacecraft, they are the exception to a lack of military spacecraft rather than the rule. Recently, however, a number of dedicated military starships have been proposed by some of the leading names in starship technology.

Lumbering space-going warships hundreds of meters long, sleek transatmospheric fightercraft loaded down with missiles and energy weapons, and fast, deadly frigate and cruiser-sized warships are slowly leaving the realm of fiction and creeping into real life. Although the technology is still a long way off, and Weyland won't be unveiling a heavily armed star cruiser any time soon, the fact that these concepts are being talked about and these designs are entering prototype phases reflects a massive shift in the way humankind uses space and spacecraft.

DROPSHIPS

Dropships are small- to medium-sized transatmospheric craft that fill a variety of roles with today's military forces. While they are not commonly found on Earth, dropships are workhorses of the various expeditionary forces and private military concerns contracted to operate on Luna and Mars.

While they share few common design elements, most dropships feature lifting body hulls with enough room inside for a mixture of passengers, cargo, and—in the case of some larger models—even light infantry fighting vehicles. Power is typically provided by small fusion reactors, and they are propelled through atmosphere and space by a combination of meta-fueled rockets or hydrazine jets, and sometimes even ion or plasma drives.

The most common role filled by these ships is transport and insertion of troops and supplies. Usually carried and deployed by larger vessels, thus the nickname "dropship" as they are dropped on to planets from orbit, dropships are designed to enter atmosphere, deliver their cargo, and retreat back to their mother ship as quickly as possible. Cargo and troop carrier dropships tend toward the larger side, although there

are smaller, stealthier models used to insert special forces and black-ops teams. They are usually unarmored, and if they carry any weapons at all, they are typically small-caliber machine guns and rocket pods for self-defense and light attack roles.

Only slightly less common than the standard troop-carrying dropship are the heavily armed and armored "gunship" models. First used during the War, gunships are small, up-armored dropships fitted with an array of antipersonnel and anti-vehicle weapons ranging from heavy machine guns and missile launchers to heavy lasers and even the occasional heavy vehicle coilgun. These fighting dropships are deployed against troops and fighting vehicles, and they fill the same roles that attack helicopters and aerodyne gunships do on Earth. In the absence of dedicated fighter craft, gunships can easily and efficiently provide fire support and aerospace superiority.

In addition to these two main dropship variants, there are a myriad of small-production, special-use dropships. Reconnaissance, electronic attack, advanced electronic warning and signals intercept, command and control, patrol, interdiction, and even VIP transport duties can and often are carried out by specialized dropships.

PLANETARY VEHICLES

The number and variety of planetary vehicles is truly astounding. Wheeled and tracked vehicles ply the groundroads and skylanes between Earth's megacities. Hoppers and aerodynes skim through cities and clog local airspace, while massive suborbital spaceplanes carry cargo and passengers all across the globe and, occasionally, even out into the system at large. Sleek deadly warships, massive cargo ships, and pleasure craft of all kinds ply the world's oceans, lakes, and rivers, and specialty vehicles carry workers, researchers, and explorers into the most remote and inhospitable regions of the planet. On Luna, dropships deliver supplies via automated maglev, and on faraway Mars, the common work vehicles owned by colonies are outfitted with scavenged,

makeshift armor and stolen weapons to be used as ersatz fighting vehicles against the infantry fighting vehicles (IFVs), exosuits, and dropships of corp armies.

The various state and private militaries in the solar system use a number of specialized air-, land-, space-, and watercraft in various combat and non-combat roles. Armored land vehicles like tanks and IFVs are produced by a handful of military technology firms. They are typically powered by either hydrogen fuel cells or high-output multi-fuel turbines (or both, depending on their intended role), and they tend to use some kind of ground effect technology for propulsion as opposed to wheels or treads to provide for truly all-terrain capabilities. They are often sealed against nuclear, biological, and chemical weapons, feature some amount of armor, and are equipped with hardened electronics to withstand EMP attacks. Radios and various optical and audio sensors are standard, and those with onboard weapon systems are usually also equipped with high-tech targeting suites. Along with their armor, many of these vehicles are equipped with active protection systems including smoke generators, electronic counter-countermeasure suites, adaptive optical camouflage, or anti-missile systems.

Manned military aircraft are vanishingly rare in modern state and private armies, having been replaced by intelligent drones, but previous-generation fighters, attack craft, and bombers can still be found in reserve forces and in some of the less developed parts of the world.

Whether manned or unmanned, the majority of military aircraft still use a number of technologies that would be recognizable by pilots and technicians from generations ago. Power and thrust are provided by advanced, highly efficient, afterburning turbojet engines burning high-performance meta fuel and delivering thrust through adaptive thrust vectoring nozzles. They are fitted with fly-by-fiber systems and sensor suites that can detect enemies well beyond visual range.

Helicopters are, by now, almost entirely extinct, their roles taken over by powerful ground-effect vehicles called aerodynes. Essentially a helicopter stood on its head, aerodynes have their propeller blades built into their fuselages, and are pushed rather than pulled into the air. Their unique design allows for a more stable, easier-to-fly platform that can be used as a gunship, a reconnaissance vehicle, or as a troop carrier. Like most of their fixed-wing brethren, manned aerodynes are rare, but older piloted models serve alongside even older helicopters in poorer or reserve forces.

While the technology and design theories used in military watercraft have changed little in the past few generations, the mission and orders of battle of most state and private militaries have changed drastically. The huge fleets centered around carrier battlegroups that once plied Earth's oceans are now gone—the focus of navies shifted from force projection to the patrol and protection of in-shore waters and the interdiction of pirates. Vessels have shrunk; it's rare to see a ship larger than a light cruiser at sea nowadays, and they've become faster, stealthier, and more efficient. Thanks to their reduced size and an increase in automated systems, crew sizes have decreased and the roles filled by military sailors are increasingly specialized. Ships are primarily powered by small, high-output fusion reactors driving traditional propeller screws or—in the case of smaller, faster littoral combat ships—ultra-maneuverable, high-output waterjets. There are, of course, still smaller boats and vessels used to ferry crew and supplies between ships or to insert small commando squads into contested territory.

Autopilot might be safer, but manual is more fun.

STATE MILITARIES AND PRISEC

Both state militaries and private security (or prisec, as it's commonly called) have their strengths and weaknesses, their specific uses, and their vehement supporters and detractors. State militaries are backed by the might of the nations to which they belong, and their personnel are typically more loyal and motivated, but they are monolithic, byzantine organizations hobbled by centuries of bureaucracy, tradition, and red tape.

Prisec operations tend to be agile and versatile, based on efficient corporate organizational models and equipped with bleeding-edge equipment that only the wealthiest, most powerful nations could hope to field. The flip side of this is that they are, at their core, mercenaries, loyal to nothing but a paycheck and often completely exempt from laws and treaties that dictate the rules of war and the punishments for breaking those rules.

NATIONAL ARMED FORCES

In a time of ascendant megacorps, powerful private military contractors, and the slow dissolution of the state, a standing military is more an object of prestige than a legitimate state asset for all but the largest, most powerful nations. Countries like the United States, China, and Brazil still field huge militaries with numerous branches operating in theaters of war across the worlds, but they're the exception rather than the rule. Despite their seeming antiquity in the modern corporate age, state-run militaries can still be a powerful force for good for both the nation that fields one and that nation's allies. They tend to drive economies through military technology and support contractors, and they offer the lower classes of a nation the opportunity for education and betterment through government service. In addition, the men and women who serve in large, state-run militaries tend to see their service as more honorable or pure, fighting for their nation or an ideal rather than for cold, hard cash.

State-run militaries are bound by all laws and treaties currently enforced with regards to military conduct, war crimes, and rules of engagement. Some see this as a positive; these very clear rules enforce a code of conduct on an army that, if broken, can be dealt with through clear and legal means. Yet, many feel that blind adherence to archaic laws and norms is out of place in modern warfare.

Matt Zeilinger

THE U.S. ARMED FORCES

The United States Armed Forces are among the premier armed forces in the world. With a long and illustrious history and a prestigious list of military victories, the various branches of the U.S. Armed Forces are an excellent example of a thoroughly modern military. Like most state-backed militaries since the end of the War, the U.S. Armed Forces are no longer huge and unwieldy forces with hundreds of thousands of men and women under arms. Instead, through automation, outsourcing, and the use of androids to perform many key non-combat roles, America's military is smaller (as a percentage of population) and more efficient than ever before while maintaining effectiveness and readiness. These smaller, leaner, more focused military branches allow the U.S. to more easily respond to threats on Earth, Luna, and Mars, and to adapt quickly to shifting tactical situations once in theater.

Although these broad changes and adaptations to modern technology and military thinking have changed much about the U.S. military, much remains that would be instantly recognizable to soldiers of bygone eras. The five traditional branches—the U.S. Army, Navy, Air Force, Marine Corps, and Coast Guard—still exist, their missions and traditions largely unchanged. Two new branches have since been drawn up: the Electronic Warfare Service and the Space Expeditionary Corps. These new branches are primarily tasked with missions in cyberspace or on Luna and Mars, and they have led the way in much of the modernizing of the U.S. military at large.

THE ARMY

The United States Army is the backbone of America's military forces and is the oldest of the branches. The men and women of the army are highly trained and motivated infantry soldiers whose primary mission is taking land, holding it, and ultimately pacifying it.

To carry out this mission, the U.S. Army uses a combination of mechanized infantry supported by artillery and close air support units. The mechanized infantry units are mainly composed of infantry units carried into battle in light, fast IFVs supported by smaller vehicles mounting support weaponry like mass drivers and heavy laser cannons. Air support comes primarily in the form seconded EWS personnel piloting drones that carry scaled up fletchers and precision smart munitions, with a small cadre of manned helicopter and aerodyne gunships. Army artillery is a mixture of precision-guided missiles and automated smartgun batteries that fire a wide variety of GPS-guided munitions.

THE NAVY

Second only to the army in age and prestige, the U.S. Navy is, perhaps, the most changed of the U.S. Armed Forces. With the advent of cheap, accessible space travel and the slow militarization of space, the navy is no longer America's premier force projection service branch, although the navy's mobile command centers were invaluable during the conflicts of the past centuries.

The ability to strike anywhere in the world is now the purview of the U.S. Air Force, and with the decreased appearance of the carrier battlegroup as the primary naval battle formation, the navy has switched its focus from force projection to interdiction and littoral combat. The main threat on Earth's oceans today is piracy and terrorism, which the smaller and more agile U.S. Navy is well equipped to deal with. With a fleet of smaller vessels at sea supported by a handful of larger cruiser-sized ships, helicopter carriers, and fast-attack submarines for blue water operations, the navy can easily defend America's interests and those of its state and corporate allies at sea.

The navy is also responsible for tracking the ever-rising sea levels and mapping the changing shorelines of North America as well as the United States' territories and protectorates. Although the changes presented new and dangerous navigation problems—and required that a few key naval bases be relocated or rebuilt—the sea level rise has affected U.S. Naval operations relatively little.

THE AIR FORCE

The U.S. Air Force is the United States' premier force projection force. Like the U.S. Navy, the air force has seen its mission change dramatically over the past few decades. In the wake of the Lunar Insurrection, the air force is tasked not only with maintaining air superiority on Earth, but through its partnership with the Space Expeditionary Corps, it maintains aerospace superiority on Luna, Mars, and throughout the solar system. Weak-AI autopilots handle all routine operations for the USAF's diverse fleet of fighter craft, bombers, reconnaissance, and cargo aircraft, but human pilots must still authorize kill strikes and serve as a fallback in the event of equipment failure or enemy electronic intrusion.

THE MARINE CORPS

Despite the significant rearrangement of its parent branch, the U.S. Navy, the mission of the U.S. Marine Corps has changed very little. While the Marine Corps went through a number of expansions and a great amount of mission bloat in the twentieth and twenty-first centuries that saw it competing with both the U.S. Army and the U.S. Navy, by the time New Angeles was founded, the Corps had largely returned to its roots as a small, elite naval infantry corps specializing in fast strikes and amphibious assault. Its refocus on the amphibious assault mission that lay at its core helped the USMC survive the navy's realignment and to maintain much of its independence. Today, the USMC operates primarily in an anti-piracy/anti-terrorism/counter-insurgency (COIN) role in support of the U.S. Navy's modern mission. While it gave up its aviation and armor units long ago, the USMC still fields its elite reconnaissance battalions and has recently begun deploying units equipped with energy weapons and the most advanced exosuits outside of Japan.

THE SPACE EXPEDITIONARY CORPS

The U.S. Space Expeditionary Corps, or SXC, is a branch of the USAF and shares a relationship with its parent similar to that between the U.S. Navy and Marine Corps. It is a rapid reaction force that was formed from elements of both the U.S. Air

SLANG IN THE SERVICE

Day-to-day life in both state-backed and private military organizations is full of arcane acronyms and jargon that form a dense, private language that both binds together soldiers and bewilders outsiders. The following is a small sampling of the many different bits of military jargon common among both state and private military outfits.

Black —When combined with a resource, such as fuel, ammunition, food, etc., this means that the unit is currently out of that resource. "Sorry, private. We are currently black on 40mm smart rounds."

Blaster —Any of the recently developed focused energy weapons currently in use by the world's militaries.

Bugs —Drones and viruses employed by the Electronic Warfare Service.

Bus Driver —Any individual who drives or pilots a cargo hauling vehicle. Used to refer to both groundtruck drivers and cargo dropship pilots.

Burnout —A veteran of the EWS suffering from any of a number of maladies afflicting members of that service during the War.

Can —Also, tin can. A Bioroid or other humanoid construct. This term is nearly always used in a derogatory fashion.

EWS —The U.S. Military's Electronic Warfare Service, the force responsible for the safety and security of the U.S.'s computer and communications networks. Pronounced "ee-waz" by its service men and women.

Fast Mover —Any particularly fast aerospace craft.

Flagwaver —A term used in the PMC community to refer to members of state-backed militaries.

Fletcher —A flechette gun, one of a number of small-caliber mass drivers that chamber small flechettes instead of bullets.

Golem —Another derogatory term for bioroids.

Joystick Jockey —A drone operator; despite the name, drone operators usually use brain-machine interface devices, not joysticks.

Lunatic —A derogatory term used for those individuals who took part in the Lunar Insurrection.

Merc —Used by members of state-run militaries to refer to private military contractors.

Nagging Natalie —The female voice of the secretary AI used in military aircraft guidance and warning systems.

Pipe —Also, the pipe. A dropship or other transatmospheric vehicle's given atmospheric entry coordinates. Issued by aerospace traffic controllers, these rigid directions are not to be diverged from, and pilots refer to them like they're a pipe or chute depositing their ship directly to its berthing.

Sexy —A reference to the initials of the Space Expeditionary Corps, SXC, used by veterans of that outfit to identify one another. Typically asked as a question like, "Hey man, you Sexy?" A fellow SXC trooper or veteran will always answer in the affirmative, often with an off-color joke. While it's a quick and mostly harmless way to identify a fellow SXC trooper, the question has led to some misunderstandings when asked of people who don't understand the reference.

Tin Man —A trooper with extensive cybernetic augmentations. Used either in general or as a nickname or greeting for a specific individual. Also occasionally used for those troopers who operate military exosuits.

Wirehead —An EWS drone operator or runner with a full-immersion rig augmentation.

Force and U.S. Marine Corps in the early days of the Lunar Insurrection. Its stated mission is to engage the enemies of the United States in space, on Luna, and on Mars. To that end the SXC is a largely infantry-based force informed heavily by the traditions of the USMC that specializes in space combat, orbital drops, and the taking and keeping of targets on planets. To support its infantry missions, the SXC employs an aerospace wing composed of dropships, close air support hoppers, atmospheric fighter craft, and a wide variety of drones and drone carriers. Due to its unique mission, the SXC is nearly completely self-contained, fielding its own transport, armor, artillery, and support units with little to no

support from other branches of the military. Veterans and active duty SXC troopers have an incredible *esprit de corps* formed from both their USMC background and their fiery baptism at the Battle of Kaguya.

THE ELECTRONIC WARFARE SERVICE

The U.S. Electronic Warfare Service is the smallest but most adaptable branch of the armed forces. It evolved out of previous cyberspace strategic commands to become a fully fledged branch not long after the conclusion of the Oil Wars. The mission of the EWS is to ensure the security and stability of the United States' computer and communications networks, and to

destroy those of the enemy in times of war to achieve cyberspace superiority.

Aside from legions of support staff, many of whom are civilian contractors, the bulk of the EWS's personnel are runners who work around the clock to ensure that America's governmental networks are clear and secure. These runners are perhaps the best trained and equipped in the world, with extensive cybernetic augmentations and full-immersion rigs to assist them in their work. The next largest group are drone operators who are deployed to combat zones to operate short-range support drones. Finally, the EWS has a small but vital specforce unit dubbed the raiders. Raiders embed with other service branches and serve at or near the front lines. These drone operators also subvert enemy drones, attack enemy runners and drone operators directly, disrupt enemy comms, and perform intelligence extraction on enemy computer networks. EWS raiders are recognizable by their augmentation skinsuits, which also serve as fully functioning backup consoles in their own right.

THEATERS OF OPERATION

Never designed to stand idle, the U.S. Armed Forces have been very busy over the past few decades. Although the War has been over for fifteen years, that doesn't mean that Earth has become completely peaceful or complacent. On the contrary, numerous societal and cultural upheavals, the rise of the megacorp, and the opening of space have created untold chaos both on Earth and in space. Instead of massive armies clashing in set-piece battles, since the Treaty of Heinlein war has yet again become a smaller, dirtier affair of insurgencies and counter insurgencies, proxy wars, brushfire conflicts, and, of course, constant and bloody conflict in the new frontiers of cyber warfare.

One of the primary belligerents in this smoldering state of war has been the U.S. military, defending the interests of the United States and its allies. For decades, the U.S. military's primary theater of operation was the United Crescent, where the U.S. assisted the U.C.'s own military to fight a series of grueling guerrilla wars against generations of terrorists and insurgents. In addition to the counter-insurgency (COIN) operations, the U.S. military also carried out numerous interdiction missions against drug lords, human traffickers, and other assorted multinational criminal cartels and terrorist organizations. While the bulk of the U.S. military's forces were deployed from Alexandria to the Central Asian steppe, smaller units were engaged elsewhere in the world, typically either in peacekeeping roles or performing extremely dangerous black ops work in places like the Sub-Saharan League and the Korean Peninsula.

This all changed in an instant, however, when the citizens of Luna revolted against the corps and stopped the flow of He-3. With the start of the Lunar Insurrection,

insurgent attacks on Luna and Mars put American commercial and military interests in jeopardy, and the American government moved quickly to protect those interests and put an end to the insurrection. The Electronic Warfare Service and the newly formed Space Expeditionary Corps saw most of the action, being more suited to space and cyber warfare, but all branches of the armed forces were called upon to defend against China and its allies.

Currently, the U.S. Military is in a state of semi-readiness. Many military units, particularly those from the army and navy, are on standby or have been completely stood down: their personnel and assets either assigned elsewhere or completely liquidated. The air force is, as always, very busy with both orbital security and the staffing of garrisons on both Luna and Mars. In fact, much of the U.S. Military's current budget goes to fund peacekeeping on Luna and COIN operations on Mars, where the guerrilla fighting is every bit as bloody as it was in the jungles of South America or in the mountains of Central Asia.

PRIVATE MILITARY CONCERNS

There are three basic types of private military organizations: small merc bands composed of like-minded independent contractors, medium-sized corporate armies fielded by megacorps like Weyland and Haas-Bioroid to protect their own interests, and large military contractors such as Globalsec. PMCs operate in much the same way that state-backed militaries have historically. They project force, protect a nation's interests, and generally fight in the same theaters and with the same weapons and equipment as their state-backed colleagues. The best example of this is the situation on Mars, where PMCs are the predominant forces there, and the various state-run militaries maintain only a token presence, if any. Often the only real difference between a soldier in a state-backed military and one in a PMC is who issues his paycheck.

The smaller, corporate-backed military forces are a different animal entirely. These are typically very small, spec ops–style forces staffed by highly trained, and often highly augmented, operators who are fanatically loyal to their corporations. They do not fight on the world's battlefields—instead they stay close to home and defend the corporation's interests and assets. They carry out corporate espionage missions, guard installations, assassinate rivals, and perform all manner of shady or outright illegal operations in the name of corporate sovereignty. In the event that a PMC ever faces itself in battle, as has sometimes been the case on Luna or Mars, the PMC's contract allows it to stand down both sides without engaging.

In the modern era, the state-backed military is seen as antiquated and clunky. Bogged down by bureaucracy, and beholden to *jus ad bellum* and *jus in bello* considered by many to be woefully outdated, many nations prefer the anonymity of a hired band of mercenaries. Indeed, it is this plausible deniability that makes PMCs so attractive to the world's governments, and the ability to pay a large sum of money for a military venture and wash one's hands of it afterward is one of the main reasons why the private military concern is so popular today.

ARGUS SECURITY INC.

Argus Security Incorporated, a subsidiary of the powerful Weyland Consortium, is one of the leading providers of small-scale private security solutions in business today. Based in New Angeles with major offices in BosWash, SanSan, Atlantica, Mumbad, and New Moscow, Argus was founded fifty years ago by a brilliant and ruthless Scandinavian named Magnus Swan. Starting with just a handful of contacts and a motley collection of retired government agents, police, and security analysts, Swan used his razor-sharp business acumen to grow Argus quickly from a small local firm into a system-spanning private security empire. While primarily known for its security business, Argus Security also owns as subsidiaries a number of consumer technology, aerospace, and advertising companies. Recently, Argus's weapons design and manufacture division was spun off as a subsidiary and renamed Skorpios Defense Systems as a wedding gift to his daughter Serena and her new husband Gordon Holder.

Counted among its clients are numerous governments, multinational non-governmental organizations, and powerful megacorps. Argus provides armed, highly trained security for everything from secret government bases and fusion power plants to corporate headquarters and large special events such as Carnaval in Rio and major large-scale music festivals. Through their subsidiaries, they also provide disaster response and emergency medical services, reception and concierge services, and even ambassadorial service. Argus's most visible action in recent memory was their involvement in the Martian Colony Wars. There are still a fair number of Argus forces garrisoned on Mars to provide policing, security, and riot control.

GLOBALSEC

Globalsec is Argus Security's primary competitor in today's private security industry, with the notable difference that Globalsec has entered into several contracts with the U.S. Armed Forces, NAPD, and Humanity Labor. These contracts include more regulation and oversight than one usually finds in other, less-reputed PMCs, but this hasn't stopped the screamsheet nosies from alleging that this arrangement allows Globalsec to cook the books from the inside.

Headed by CEO Lidiah Maucher, Globalsec is headquartered in Atlantica with major operations bases in every major city across the globe, Luna, and Mars. Smaller field offices and forward operating bases are maintained in numerous countries, especially throughout Africa, Asia, and the Balkans. While they do provide some of the same private security services as their competitor, Globalsec specializes more in private military forces, military consultation and training, and intelligence gathering and analysis.

Their highly trained professional soldiers can be found in every corner of the world assisting governments and corporations alike in protecting sensitive sites and projecting force. With hundreds of thousands of employees, Globalsec can field armies that dwarf those of many small nations. They also provide military advisers and trainers to developing nations, and even act on their own to protect their many corporate interests. While they primarily field land forces such as mechanized infantry, reconnaissance, armor, and commando units, they also possess a small for-hire, multi-role air wing and a small fleet of ships used for interdiction, escort, and littoral combat.

Along with its private military services, Globalsec is also well known as one of, if not the, best private intelligence gathering and analysis services. Their intelligence division, led by analyst Fatimah Mirazi, provides everything from personal background checks and private investigators to top-secret black ops. They maintain perhaps the most comprehensive list of personal data on the planet, rivaled only by NBN's own. Every bit of personal data collected through government agencies, advertising, the Net, and other media ends up filtered and analyzed in Globalsec's massive system, and their employee background check and blacklist database is used by the human resources departments of every megacorp in the solar system.

Adam Schumpert

SPECIALTIES AND SERVICES

While Globalsec is widely well regarded for its excellent private security services and exhaustive private intelligence gathering and analysis services, the company is perhaps best known as the premier private military contractor in the world. With a list of clients that includes corporations, powerful nation states, and even a few extremely wealthy individuals, Globalsec is in the vanguard of modern private military operations. It has a reputation for professionalism and square dealing, but rumors constantly circulate of illegal activities ranging from smuggling to serious war crimes. Nothing has been substantiated of course, and the company employs an army of powerful lawyers and lobbyists to ensure that nothing ever will.

Globalsec is, first and foremost, a light infantry organization. It provides straight-leg and light mechanized infantry for front-line combat and peacekeeping duties to anyone who can afford them. Its training is top notch, as is its equipment, and many of its employees come directly from the ranks of the various state-run militaries still in operation around the world. Its infantry forces are supported by heavy weapons squads, teams of drone operators providing interdiction and close air support, and some fast attack light armor squadrons using state-of-the-art ground-effect tanks armed with energy weapons and heavy mass drivers. In addition, Globalsec fields some of the best trained and equipped reconnaissance and spec ops forces in the business. These units' various services can be bought as a group package for large operations or in pieces, such as a single reconnaissance unit or a squadron of close air support drones.

The largest benefit a PMC like Globalsec has over one of its state-run counterparts is its flexibility. The wheels of government move slowly, and a state-run military is limited by the bureaucracy of its state and the treaties to which that state is bound. A PMC, typically hired by a private entity or even by a state that needs to bolster its own forces or wishes to remain anonymous in a conflict, is bound by neither of these issues. Globalsec is the perfect example of this. It is fast and versatile, able to carry out the orders of its employers with minimal interference from government officials, although official jobs contracted to the U.S. military do entail governmental oversight. Like all PMCs, Globalsec is not bound by international treaties between nations, and it is only vaguely beholden to international rules of war. The PMC is, thanks to the aforementioned lawyers and lobbyists, often beyond the reach of international criminal courts or war crimes tribunals, and it operates with a freedom that simply cannot be matched by state-run militaries.

Along with its traditional military services, Globalsec also offers a number of military support packages. The most popular of these is its infrastructure and airlift package, which provides heavy cargo hauling ground and air vehicles, an in-house infrastructure data tracking system, and all the personnel needed to quickly and efficiently move men and materiel from point A to point B. There are also military base support services packages that provide maintenance, food and health services, and other equipment and personnel needed to operate a military installation. In addition, Globalsec offers a number of less orthodox services to prospective clients. Training forces can be purchased to either train troops or act as opposing forces (OpFor) for war games. A highly regarded cyber warfare unit that is every bit the equal of the U.S. Electronic Warfare Service is also available. It even provides some easily disavowable black ops units to handle extremely dirty jobs like kidnapping, coups, and targeted assassination.

THEATERS OF OPERATION

Since its founding, Globalsec has seen action in every major—and many minor or seemingly insignificant—theaters of war on Earth, on Luna, and on Mars. In keeping with its primarily light infantry character and COIN specialties, Globalsec operators have seen action in numerous insurgency hot spots. While it does fulfill contracts for national governments, and it performs some photo-op worthy humanitarian work on its own accord, Globalsec makes the majority of its money working for various international corporations. Anywhere a corp needs an insurrection put down, a burgeoning union broken up, assets protected, competition run off, or people disappeared, Globalsec operatives are found. Corporations using private military concerns is nothing new, especially not in places like Africa and South America, but today with the ascendancy of the megacorp, working to ensure the financial interests of entities like Weyland and Jinteki makes good business sense.

Globalsec made its name fighting drug cartels and anti-government radicals in South America, often alongside U.S.-backed forces. It provided specforce and COIN assets throughout the Middle East and Central Asia, where it was hired by state actors in an effort to take some of the burden off their over-committed regular forces. Its most recent, and perhaps most infamous, actions have been on Luna and Mars; Globalsec was hired to put down the rebels there by any means necessary. Globalsec still runs continuous operations from its large Martian garrison in an effort to crack down on Free Mars and other terrorists and bring some semblance of order back to the Red Planet.

RANKS IN THE PMCS

State militaries still use the basic rank structure passed down to them from previous generations, but traditional military ranks are not used by private military concerns. Instead, they use a corporate-style rank structure that is less rigid and more open to interpretation than strict military ranks. The rank and file troopers in a PMC are usually called "security specialist" or some variation thereof. From there, the rank structure usually ascends in a typical corporate fashion with assistant team leaders, team leaders, project managers, and even country managers. PMC specialists, such as medics or engineers, often have their own titles such as "engineering specialist" or "medical specialist," but they ultimately fit into the rank structure under their team leaders.

Smirtouille

SMALLER OUTFITS

While the private military contractor and corporate security markets are dominated by the likes of Globalsec and Argus, there are myriad smaller, leaner mercenary groups operating in the shadows of New Angeles and throughout the system—especially on Mars. These tend to be small, flexible, independent units—typically no larger than a standard military platoon—composed of professional soldiers of fortune, adrenaline junkies, fugitives, and disaffected veterans from every military force on the planet. They tend to specialize in one particular aspect of warfare and, depending on their abilities and reputation, can be as expensive to hire as the larger, more famous outfits. Some are shock troops, others specialize in logistics and smuggling, and others are infiltrators, spies, or commandos. While they are as varied as can be imagined, all small PMC outfits share a few things in common: a love of military life, camaraderie, and a casual amorality.

One of the more infamous of these small-time outfits is the Chimera Group. Founded and led by a former colonel named John Rath, Chimera Group is a small but fierce provider of private military solutions. Little is known about this shady band of mercenaries, but it is thought that Chimera Group employs perhaps a platoon's worth, roughly forty, of specforce operatives culled from PMC communities around the globe, although a firm number has never been released. They are known to provide black-ops style services including extractions, kidnappings, sabotage, assassinations, and other high-speed, low-drag clandestine ops to anyone who can pay their fees. Thanks to their small size and the leadership of John Rath, Chimera Group is an exceedingly flexible and versatile force whose vast black ops experience allows them to adapt quickly and efficiently to shifting tactical situations. While there are many rumors circulating regarding Chimera Group's founding and operations, the most persistent suggests that they are backed by a powerful and wealthy benefactor, with Friedrich Garry Investments being the leading suspect.

BOUNTY HUNTERS

Bounty hunters are independent contractors invested with limited police powers to track down and apprehend fugitives and felons of all stripes. Roundly despised both by their targets and the legitimate law enforcement agencies that hire them, bounty hunters are seen as little more than opportunistic mercenaries at best, and bloodthirsty psychopaths at worst. Despite their being painted with a broad brush by society at large, bounty hunters are as varied in their motivations and morality as people in any other profession. Some have sterling reputations as consummate professionals, always working within the strict limits of their power and treating both employers and bounties with respect. Others live up to their unsavory reputation and are little more than hired killers who shoot first and rarely, if ever, ask questions.

Bounty hunters are a relatively common sight in New Angeles, especially up and down the Beanstalk and in Heinlein. Not only is New Angeles the largest city in the world by population, but the NAPD's jurisdiction extends up the Beanstalk to the Moon. In short, their jurisdiction is unmanageably large and impossible to police. Due to this fact, the NAPD is the largest employer of bounty hunters in New Angeles. Bounty hunters stalk the Beanstalk in the NAPD's name, tracking down bail jumpers, serving warrants, and pulling fugitives from every seedy bolthole and flophouse in orbit. While the NAPD considers them a necessary evil, they are essential to the safety and security of the Beanstalk and its surrounding environs, regardless of whether or not the NAPD wants to admit as much.

Perhaps the most famous of New Angeles' bounty hunters is Rachel Beckmann. A former NAPD officer and daughter of NAPD Captain Thomas Beckmann, Rachel is one of the most expensive and highly sought after bounty hunters currently working. Her professionalism, no-nonsense reputation, and extensive contacts within the NAPD give her an edge that most bounty hunters lack. Like many of her colleagues, Beckmann's single driving force is the pursuit of wealth. Heavily modified, she is deeply in debt due to her numerous cybernetic enhancements. Nearly all of her money goes toward paying off previous augmentation surgeries or buying new implants to help her in her work.

ANDROID LABOR

War has always driven technology. Extraterrestrial missions prompted innovations in cybernetic and genetic enhancements, electronic warfare pioneered existing brain-machine interface technology, and drone combat pushed the envelope of artificial intelligence. Many of these breakthroughs also spurred the development of the first artificial humans, or androids, enabling Haas-Bioroid to debut the Mark-2 in the final years of the War. But the wide-scale implementation of androids did not become economically viable—that is to say, profitable—until a true need for "labor solutions" arose.

After the Lunar Insurrection, the helium-3 mining concerns wanted to replace its flesh-and-blood miners with more obedient—and expendable—workers. HB's engineers focused on refining the technology to make them competitively priced and more efficient. At first only corporations, some governments, and extremely wealthy individuals could afford to invest in bioroid labor to fill essential roles, but as more and more of them rolled off the assembly lines, the cost of these simulants dropped, making them viable for work in new areas. Bioroids moved beyond reconstruction and saw much broader use. They collected trash, worked assembly lines, and minded children for overworked parents.

Soon Jinteki would catch up and debut its vat-grown clones, and a new industry was born. The rapid changes in the workforce meant that returning veterans found their jobs filled by androids who were cheaper and more productive, and as more and more varieties of clones and bioroids expanded to new segments of the economy, a labor crisis was in the making. It is becoming harder and harder to imagine the world functioning as it does without androids, but many people long to go back to simpler times before androids revolutionized life on Earth, Luna, and Mars.

A BRAVE NEW LABOR MARKET

Thanks to the introduction of androids, people can live longer, safer lives with fewer fears of hazards in the workplace. The depths of the ocean and the vacuum of space are open to exploration and development at a faster pace than could have been achieved without simulant labor. Android labor is more efficient, more compliant, and much cheaper than human labor, provided the business can afford the initial investment. When a workplace accident crushes an android, it's property damage, not the basis for a lawsuit or worker's comp.

Like many other technological innovations in human history, however, the introduction of androids has had an impact on the labor market, specifically for the men and women whose jobs are now being performed by machines. As with the printing press, the steam engine, the assembly line, the microchip, and other advances in automation that have moved humanity forward, the advent of true artificial intelligence demands a human cost to be paid for the larger societal benefit. Humanity might be better off with androids; individual people, however, may not be so fortunate.

If it were just the hazardous jobs that were being transitioned to android labor, most people would probably understand the change. It goes far beyond that, however. Workers in manufacturing, transportation, domestic help, and even the sex industry are losing out to androids. The shift extends to nearly every segment of the labor market, and it is those with no way to cope with the change who feel the pain most keenly: unskilled laborers who couldn't afford access to an education as well as skilled laborers who have no qualifications besides the trade they've plied for decades.

The New Angeles–based car company Gemini Motors joined in the recent trend of laying off major portions of its human labor force and replacing them with bioroids. Executives and creative staff were retained, as is the norm in these cases, but the line workers all lost their jobs. Telling these people that they should embrace the future of labor does not usually go over well. For many of them, the only skill they ever had was the sort of thing that a clone or bioroid can do faster and, now, cheaper. In the past, those who had lost their job to a machine could learn to operate it, thus remaining employed. But now the "dumb" machines are run by smarter ones, leaving little for unskilled labor to do.

The labor shift is pushing many of these blue collar workers into the margins in cities, or out to poorer or less densely populated towns where the economics of android labor have not yet reached a point where replacing humans makes sense. Others are working to take back the jobs that were once theirs or find other solutions to their plight—some within the system, some not.

Smirtouille

THE ANTI-SIMULANT MOVEMENT

There are numerous constituencies and special interest groups who would like to see them outlawed or, barring that, taxed into oblivion. For some, androids are soulless abominations that are an affront to sincere religious beliefs. For others, androids are the reason so many humans have lost their jobs and can't put food on the table, or worse, became *disenfrancistos*. There are corporations who would like to stop the production of certain simulants so rival companies will lose revenue streams.

Groups like Humanity Labor, Builders for a Better Tomorrow, and others spend major chunks of their budgets on promoting anti-android legislation. Although targeting the regulators themselves is a riskier, albeit more direct route, most policy changes are addressed in a country's legislature.

Such efforts have been met with stiff resistance, however. The realities of the re-election cycle mean increasingly expensive campaigns must be mounted on a continuous basis, and megacorporations are the ones footing the bill. These "congress-critters," as they are called, glide to second, third, and tenth terms so long as they continue to toe the line favored by their corporate sponsors and lobbyist friends. But recently populist candidates have begun winning seats worldwide with an unprecedented lack of corporate support. As more and more laborers are thrown into unemployment, being pro-android is becoming a more difficult position to defend.

The legal landscape is difficult to maneuver even when the issue under consideration is less divisive. Because of the money involved—and the wide-sweeping implications one way or another—anti-simulant bills are some of the most heated battles in lower houses of government around the world.

HUMANITY LABOR

At the forefront of the endeavor to protect human interests, human jobs, and human dignity is Humanity Labor. The organization's primary goal is to stand up for those laborers who do not have the money or the power to stand up for themselves in defense of their jobs. Megacorporations channel the profits of clones and bioroids to push their agendas and influence politics, but by rallying individuals, unionizing them, and collecting dues from them, Humanity Labor can put up a fight against the efforts

> "Humanity Labor is dirty, with numerous links to both corrupt government agencies and the tri-mafs. They had the money to bring a lot of political leverage to bear against anyone set on investigating them too closely."

and abilities of the megacorporations. The organization works within the system to support anti-simulant legislation, lobby governments to prevent human job loss, and lend financial support to its membership when needed.

It's true that Humanity Labor is not able to save every job, and many of the jobs it does save are low-wage, dangerous positions. Still, they are jobs, and keeping humans employed at any level helps those workers preserve their dignity and keeps them from turning against society at large by engaging in criminal acts.

This puts world governments, and even businesses, in an interesting position. Although they want to encourage the progress, profits, and tax revenue that android labor represents, they also recognize the need to prevent large segments of the human population from becoming a drain on society, or, even worse, a risk to law and order. More than that, androids and corporations can't vote, even if they can do almost everything else. Humanity Labor must exist to provide a natural balance in the equation, even if they are often a thorn in the side for corporations and governments.

Like any large organization, Humanity Labor is not without its flaws, real and imagined. Rumors of corruption plague its leadership. Not all of its members feel that their best interests are being served despite the dues they pay into the system and the concessions they make on a routine basis. Some even say that Humanity Labor covertly supports the violence that some radical groups, such as Human First, see as the most effective way to end the simulant takeover of the workplace. Humanity Labor denies all allegations of kickbacks, bribes, and other forms of corruption, of course. The organization also disavows any connection to Human First.

Humanity Labor's official public stance is that fighting the good fight for human workers is expensive and difficult enough without taking on the risks of acting illegally or supporting anyone else who does. They say they are dedicated to acting within the confines of the law and work hard to support anti-clone legislation and other initiatives through official government channels.

Matt Zeilinger

HUMAN FIRST

Every time a new android walks off the assembly line and into the workforce, a human loses his job. In the eyes of Human First groups, if those simulants can be yanked out of the workforce, then there's a chance the human can get the job back. Since androids are just devices and not people, the simplest way to make sure they don't get the job done is to perform a little "percussive maintenance" on them. This is best achieved with several swings of a sledgehammer.

In cities across the world, from New Angeles to Johannesburg, Human First foments violence against simulants. Armed with hammers and rage, supporters of the Human First agenda roam alleys and shadowed streets looking for isolated androids to destroy. When they find one, the pent-up frustration of job loss is unleashed to devastating effect. Unable to strike back against their assailants due to the Three Directives or the conditioning that governs their behavior, these bioroids and clones are bludgeoned into an inoperable state.

In the instances where law enforcement catches people in the act, justice generally takes the form of a slap on the wrist. As far as the cops are concerned, it's no big deal when big corps have to shell out a few creds to replace a glorified calculator. Many cops sympathize with Human First, fearing that their jobs are next in line to be taken over by android labor: Floyd 2X3A7C, Drake 3GI2RC, and Caprice Nisei all represent the next iteration of detective. Ask ten cops how they feel about Human First and you'll be lucky to find one that thinks they are outright wrong in their approach.

Human First's detractors point out that vandalism is one thing, but large-scale violence is another. Factory bombings, raids on shipments of bioroids, and even (if the rumors are to be believed) the inciting of riots against androids and the governments and corps who use them—all these suggest that Human First is a larger and more powerful hate group than a few isolated incidents of property damage would otherwise suggest.

THE SIMULANT ABOLITIONIST MOVEMENT

Not everyone reacted with the same destructive impulse that resulted in the mass violence of the Clone Riots and many other Human First protests. Where many see androids as unwelcome intruders to be legislated or regulated into extinction—or worse, eradicated by brute force—others see them as the unfortunate victims of corporate greed and societal desperation, orphans of science and technological progress. For these sympathizers, the question is not how to rid society of clones, but how to welcome these new life forms into the diverse spectrum of humanity.

At the forefront of the efforts to adopt clones into human society is the Simulant Abolitionist Movement, or SAM. Although not as wealthy as Humanity Labor or as forceful as Human First, SAM does have the advantages of compassion: they believe in changing the world one android at a time, and that to be truly successful they must remain wholly within the

Matt Zeilinger

NEW PROTESTS PLANNED ON ANNIVERSARY OF THE CLONE RIOTS AND *HENRY V. JINTEKI*

It's been one year since the Clone Riots ripped through New Angeles, and the entire city is on edge. Several anti-android groups have planned demonstrations around City Hall, and the NAPD has increased patrol officer and camdrone presence on the streets. Everyone is holding their breath on whether there will be a repeat of last year's violence, and just how many might be hurt in the process.

The authorities are no closer to assigning blame for the riots than they were at the end of the city council's hearings three months ago. There are various theories to explain what exactly pushed things over the edge and started this violent series of events.

We know that a large group of clones, possibly at the urging of the Liberty Society, had gathered to demonstrate on the anniversary the U.S. Supreme Court decision on the *Henry v. Jinteki* case. From there, accounts differ. Some believe this group of clones managed to overcome their conditioning and attacked the humans they viewed as oppressors. Conspiracy theorists on the Net believe the riots were a cover for a field test of a new line of aggressive, violent clones. What seems most likely is that an altercation between Human First counter-protesters and the clones resulted in a brawl that left dozens hurt on both sides.

After the initial clash, eyewitness reports spread across the screamsheets and mediafeeds reporting that androids were rising up to overthrow humanity. In the confusion and panic that followed, thousands of androids—clones and bioroids alike—were destroyed and the streets ran with red blood and blue coolant.

Predictably, the violence spread beyond acts of vandalism against androids to attacks against the police and prisec attempting to restore order. Rioters attacked android manufacturing plants and killed humans who worked there for the crime of betraying their own kind. Several of NBN's own broadcast facilities and branch offices were captured to help spread the word of resistance against the "android revolution." By the time the riots had been dispersed, thousands of simulants, mostly clones, were destroyed, and 183 humans had been killed as well.

Since that fateful day, several anti-clone bills supported by Humanity Labor have become law or are relatively far along in their respective committees. Jinteki and Haas-Bioroid have ramped up production to replace the lost inventory, and there are more androids in New Angeles than ever before. By the NAPD's count, Human First doubled its membership over the last twelve months, and unofficial polls indicate that the group has the support of a majority of New Angelinos.

We were able to reach NAPD Commissioner Chen-Mai Dawn for comment on this story as it develops: "The NAPD will protect the rights of groups like Human First to peaceably assemble in public spaces, but protesters who turn to violence or property damage will be held responsible. We encourage all New Angeles citizens to treat today as a normal one, and carry on with their daily lives."

Aman Mirendola reporting for *The New Angelino*

» Subscribe to get all the updates as they happen!

bounds of the law. Members of SAM believe that androids, clones in particular, are human beings who are being denied their basic rights. They view them not as property, but as full humans who have had their rights stripped from them, just like so many ethnic and national groups who have been subjugated during the course human history. From the regimented, unyielding processes that created them to the cruelty and bindings of servitude, androids are unfairly denied full participation in the human experience. Simulant Abolitionist Movement members believe this situation cannot be allowed to continue.

If SAM were ever to succeed in changing the laws, as it seems they stand poised to do in some pockets of the world, this would have enormous implications for the corporations that create androids, the androids that currently populate the world, and for the human race as a whole. Millions of new citizens would be created with a few simple strokes of a pen. As fully protected citizens,

"Are clones property? Or are they people being treated like property?"

they could compete for jobs and get paid wages just like humans, which would eventually result in more humans getting hired as bioroids aged and needed to be replaced. Attacks against androids would be reclassified as assault or murder. The economy, and almost everything else in the world, would change overnight.

The Simulant Abolitionist Movement has found close allies in the Order of Sol and the Brazilian government, where android ownership is outlawed even though androids do not yet have the full privileges of natural-born humans. The Liberty Society is another highly visible group from New Angeles advocating for clones in particular, and they have begun to win some victories in the courts to overturn the landmark U.S. Supreme Court case *Henry v. Jinteki*. In the Indian Union, third parties have begun to draw parallels between the status of clones and the untouchables of the old caste system, and the next wave of elections could prove pivotal for the future of Mumbad and the rest of the country.

YOU MUST ACCEPT TO PROCEED

In the world of megacorporations, densely populated arcologies, and ubiquitous technology, privacy is an issue of concern for the elite, hackers, and corporate *sararimen* alike. Slick new products and fantastically designed marketing campaigns have lulled consumers into signing away more of their privacy than they realize. (When an end user license agreement for an autochef has more pages than the manual, how is anyone supposed to understand it?) The corps want as close to total control over the marketplace as they can possibly have: marketing, data tracking, advertisement placement, and expected consumer mobility are among thousands of derived statistics companies use to tailor their business plans.

Entire industries have developed for the sake of simply parsing this information, and any computer scientist has gone through at least one course on user-statistic program development. By knowing consumers better than they know themselves, corporations have turned the art of the sale into a science—dollars through data. By employing numerous lobbyists and enticing congresscritters, megacorporations have legalized their invasion of privacy; the prevalence of seccams, camdrones, PADs, and bioroids equipped with on-board cameras turns what was once a persistent nuisance into a constant concern. Not only does the data grid never sleep, it now has a slew of roaming eyes with durable memory circuits recording everything they encounter with pinpoint precision and unquestionable accuracy.

With the proliferation of surveillance across the world, some wonder if privacy still exists at all, and if it does, can they get any of what they've lost back? Strong and weak AI constantly, elegantly filter metadata with impunity. Metadata collects like dust in the constantly connected PADs of everyday citizens. Even if a user is careful about what they share to the Net, unscrupulous runners and zealous marketing executives implement hidden background programs that upload data the typical consumer isn't even aware of. The lattice of surveillance networks protecting any and all assets create cobwebs of biometric recognition scans. Invasive marketers and reporters hack into personal records, politicians out their competition on the Net with scandals hidden deep within their private past, and governments spy on their citizens without regard for proper legal channels or even concrete reasons for doing so. It has become so rote it is accepted—despite the protests of a vocal minority.

Public places are constantly monitored by seccams that scan any and all passersby

One of the most successful watchdogs to rise against this all-encompassing continuous observation is PriRights. Unwilling to relent, PriRights and organizations like them fight a battle they are destined to lose. All but their most secure activities are watched, analyzed, and preempted by monolithic opposition that can nullify the vast majority of PriRights' efforts long before any bear fruit.

Public places are constantly monitored by seccams that scan any and all passersby to check their faces against the New Angeles Police Department's databases for wanted criminals. This content gets encrypted, but anyone with the proper clearance—and even some without it—can get their hands on the original, identifying data. The only real victory PriRights has won lies in extending the definition of private space to include apartments and hotels, meaning that people's bedrooms, at least, only have the spyware they bring in with them. Dirty backdoor business deals benefit the megacorps, too. After all, it certainly wouldn't do the corporations any good if the corrupting influence of their staggering campaign contributions came to light.

Governments, shell corporations, and even subversively employed hackers take bribes and move assets to avoid taxation, regulation, and oversight at every turn. It's rare for a company to suffer litigation or consequences for malfeasance. Even when they do, highly educated and superlatively expensive legal firms devote legions of lawyers to exploit archaic systems of justice that are riddled with decades of corp-friendly agreements designed to provide endless loopholes for illegal activity. Even the aforementioned hotel camera legislation—the Não-Sei amendment of '38—is tainted with riders that allow for the otherwise illegal seizure of funds. For the truly rare, unique cases that the lawyers can't weave around, out-of-court settlements keep victims quiet and the credits flowing.

Dmitry Prosvirnin

THE OPTICON FOUNDATION
THE VOICE OF THE PEOPLE

When the reach of a megacorp oversteps ethical boundaries—the Opticon Foundation is there. In a society that values the aggregate over the individual, profits over persons, and innovation over ethics— *we are the voice of the people.* Our chief concern is to monitor the practices of megacorporations even as it becomes more and more difficult to do so, and to hold them accountable for their behavior.

With the constant incorporation of new technology into everyday life, megacorporations and the business world move at lightning speed, making the need for oversight more important now than ever before. Every day, unethical executives and project directors endanger the lives of thousands of workers, justifying their immoral behavior with profit margins. Laws like the Matheson-Taguchi Amendment, made to benefit the rich at the expense of the poor and middle class, protect corporate entities with loopholes designed to overwhelm those with fewer legal resources. There's no shortage of similar statutes, and one can find datatrails leading back to hundreds of dropped amendments or regulations that would've proven pivotal in court battles.

The Opticon Foundation was founded in '32 by Brendon Bentzen, Natalya Sonoda, and Gaspar Quebrado—three lawyers with Ivy League educations and a taste for justice. Dissatisfied with the increasingly common corruption in the marketplace, they dissolved a shortlived but courageous law firm to seek out whistle-blowers and individuals wronged by monolithic businesses. In a watershed moment for the fledgling Opticon Foundation, the three founders were approached by an AgInfusion employee who had discovered something alarming in the new breed of gogs the agricorp was developing: the creatures contained substantial amounts of human DNA. Bentzen, Sonoda, and Quebrado broke the story through the New Angeles Sol and kept the gogs from reaching distribution. The lawyers were even able to protect their source, Estée Besteira, from retaliatory lawsuits after AgInfusion's legal team discovered she was the whistle-blower. Between the resources of the intrepid trio and the detailed experiences of one brave citizen, the Opticon Foundation set a touchstone for accountability and set into motion sweeping regulations that have revolutionized the food industry.

The Opticon Foundation runs on two simple, fair principles—transparency and accountability. A cursory glance at the state of the world today reveals that megacorporations have evolved far beyond the purview of persons, and they continually overreach the boundaries of what is ethical or even sensible on a societal scale. Driven by market forces, there seems to be no end to the dangerous game these institutions play with all of our lives: in the words of philosopher Cadela Luo'co, "a world consumed by a drive for profit and ever-advancing technology quickly ceases to be a world at all."

As a transparent organization that respects the law, the Opticon Foundation stresses the need for open honesty—both from without and within. All of our practices and procedures, as much as we can share safely without compromising those we help, are a matter of public record. Even with the wealth of surveillance that chokes our liberties more every day, the full measures of security taken by the Opticon Foundation are second to none. There is no organization more qualified to aid corporate whistle-blowers, and no greater force to bring to light the flagrant abuses committed by the business world. Governmental oversight and regulation are ultimately ineffective; they are overwhelmed, underemployed, and ill-equipped to deal with the powerful corporations. Citizens endure the failures of these programs on an almost-daily basis. Corporations continue to undermine governmental efforts, ensuring that regulatory commissions are underfunded and overextended—making the need for independent, citizen action paramount.

Mediafeeds and tab-rags have disparaged the Opticon Foundation, but these attacks always coincide with sweeping exposures of corporate malfeasance. We wear these insults as marks of pride, proof that our methods and efforts to create accountability are changing the world. Like a genegineered antibody, we are small but resilient, able to conquer the tumorous growths of corruption that threaten us all. The odds are stacked against us, and success against these institutions with endlessly deep pockets can only be achieved with your support.

By ensuring that corporations and governments responsibly engage consumers and each other with transparency and accountability, the Opticon Foundation creates an environment that helps us stay independent. Every donor, any amount, keeps the corporate wolves from our door! As innovation revolutionizes the marketplace, the business world insulates itself with layer upon layer of secrecy, hiding unethical—and sometimes truly dangerous—activities. With the tangled web of semi-legal red tape protecting corporate abuses, making a difference in the world is challenging—but we have done it before and will continue to do so. Take a stand with the Opticon Foundation today, and prove that people are more important than profit margins—together, we can change the world!

There is no corporation backing or influencing our exposure of corporate corruption, and no government masters directing our efforts. All of our funding is achieved through grassroots efforts by concerned citizens who are unwilling to stand by and allow unprincipled businesses to run roughshod over the masses. Hologram technicians, service workers, hopper mechanics, delivery drivers—the working man and woman are as much as a part of us as any salaried employee. We believe that individuals are more valuable than the sum of their credaccounts, and their rights deserve to be protected.

Following in our founders' footsteps, investigators take notice of any source—minor or major—engaging them in the most respectful, private manner to ensure that they are not targeted for exposing corruption. We offer complete and full disclosure to all sources, valuing transparency as much as accountability, encouraging shareholder activism through consistent, thorough oversight. After years of dedicated service to the public good, the Opticon Foundation's global reach and record of success have made us into the premier watchdogs of the business world. If you or anyone you know has witnessed an act of misconduct by a corporate entity, do not hesitate to contact us—*we will help you.*

A few months ago pages on the Net started popping up detailing a new, clandestine settlement on the thawing treasure trove of Antarctica: a Strata Corp site. The corp had already firmly lodged one foot onto the final continent and apparently decided they didn't want anybody to know if they took another step.

NBN was barely covering it, which was telling enough—anything that could possibly grab the people's attention was broadcast day and night. Then, a few weeks ago, all the resources I'd been keeping an eye on began to disappear. Cached forum posts were the best I could find until last week, and even those have evaporated. Whatever was going on down south, Strata decided to take an aggressive stance to conceal it—which means that it was something the public needed to know about.

The normal corp hurdles were as expected; I stopped counting the secretaries that answered my calls after the first two dozen. Eventually, though, I came across an AI that was substandard or glitching; I've picked up enough tricks over the years to get a decent appointment in place when that kind of opportunity arises. The secretary was in need of a software update and didn't notice that my credentials were inauthentic. So here I am, sitting across the desk of Gareth Kesswyn, a director of a sub-department to one of the regional arms of Strata Corp.

It became clear pretty quickly that he wasn't in the best of moods, but I wasn't going to get a second crack at this. Gareth sighed exasperatedly for the seventh time in as many minutes, gesturing to the rags on his desk. "I'm far too busy to be of much help, miss. Even if I weren't, there's a number of reasons I can't confirm or deny your branch's shipment to this so-called facility. Even if this was confidential information or something, projects of the magnitude you're talking about are far beyond my pay grade."

Something about the way his right index finger twitched on the words "facility" and "magnitude" gave him away. Gareth was holding out on me. "I understand completely. I know I had the requisite forms on my PAD

this morning, but I think my smartslick has a leak and," come on you corp lackey, you just reek narcissism take the bait, "well, you know what a bad day is like, right? We all have bad days and this whole thing has been fragged for me—oh! Sorry."

Blushing as hard as I could, I could see him soften slightly. "Yeah, tell me about it. On the way to the hopper this morning…" He droned on for a few minutes about children he'd spoiled to no end with the latest GameNET offerings and holosport equipment, while I took appraisal of the situation. For a moment I considered whether this might not be worth it, but then he started to crack a little bit. "It's days like these where it helps to stretch your arms, so to speak. If you had the forms, well, I've looked past those rulings before—what were they anyway? La Meida v. SanSan and Reisshoff v. Fujida? Either way, by damn, I may only be a sub-director, but I'm still a director!"

Fluttering my eyes and shifting a little bit to make him think I was nervous, I asked, "Are you saying you can help me then, Gareth? I mean, this could be my job, and I'm not even directly or indirectly responsible for those lost shipments!" Maybe this whole trip would be worth it, and Mr. Kesswyn here was going to unknowingly expose some corporate corruption—serious malfeasance. Perhaps I could win this one, if I could just keep him on the line.

"Well look, if you come back later today with special license form 4X-D4 authorizations from your supervisor—Oscar in transglobal supply logistics, right? Then I can help you out, because I can understand your concerns—I've been there myself, if you can believe it." He was smiling but I started to panic; my false credentials would get rooted out by that secretary in a few minutes, and time was running out. I had to act fast. Think, think, think! Lock your eyes, shake your head in disbelief, play the part!

Wait—what's that datacard on his desk? What's on that datacard? Just who else has been in this office, Gareth? With how cluttered his desk is, he wouldn't even notice it was gone—not at first, anyway. I just needed an opening to lift it, a second or

two of distraction, and then I could get it decrypted and find out if this whole trip was worth anything. Let's take things in reverse and see if those frustrated sighs can get me somewhere.

"Well," I said, gulping away some genuine fear under the guise of an anxious young corp lackey, "what about that disaster with the New Angeles Tsunami? The PR fallout was horrible, but the cost in life was—well, I know I shouldn't say as much but you seem like a stand-up executive—the number of deaths was a tragedy. What if this is another New Angeles Tsunami, Mr. Kesswyn?"

That smile turned into a frown and he leaned back into his seat again. "Now as loyal Strata employees, we are both well aware that the earthquake could have happened regardless of whether or not GRNDL was drilling, and Weyland has provided generous relief in the wake of the tsunami…"

I was getting down to minutes; time to bring on the heat. "We've both seen the leaked memos on Project Vulcan, Mr. Kesswyn. We've both read about the timely property sales of the Weyland Consortium, all located directly in the landfall zone." The subservient tremble that lured Gareth into a false sense of security was gone, and I'd started to get into a hoarse cry, "One of the deadliest tsunamis of the century, damages in the trillions of dollars, and how many lives, Gareth!?"

The corp lackey reared back and away from this unexpected emotional outburst. As I screamed, "Are you going to tell who knows how many mothers that you could've stopped another disaster like that, but didn't!? Are you Gareth!? Could you do that!?" He winced when my voice hit a pitched shriek, and I managed to swipe and pocket the datacard.

His response was rapid and vehement, but I ducked out of the office and hightailed it onto the street—I had what I wanted. Thumbing my PAD, I checked out who it belonged to and a smile came to my face; New Angeles to Australia was only ninety minutes by subbing...

SEEKING MEANING

In the wake of a surge of new technologies sweeping the marketplace, the presence of religion in society has seen a resurgence and, in some places, explosive growth. Sociologists point to the recent advent of android technologies, both clone and bioroid, as a force calling people back into worship spaces to reflect on the new world order and the meaning of human life. Whatever the reason, the influence of religious organizations, for good or for ill, is reascendant.

Spirituality and religion arise out of humanity's ability to question its own existence. The search for meaning and purpose in life has been part of history for far longer than any written record. Societies have asked "who are we?" and "how should we live together?" These questions were and are answered by the weaving and sharing of stories born out of people's experience of each other, the world, and, many would say, divine presence. As these stories and cultures developed, like stars coalescing in stellar gas clouds,

many spiritual movements emerged, the largest of these evolving into major world religions. The influences of these traditions would ebb and flow over time, with new movements either replacing or absorbing others that came before.

In the years following humanity's first venture into space, all of the world's major world religions were in crisis. Where once these traditions enjoyed considerable political influence, this power waned as faith traditions were finding themselves pushed to the sidelines. Some of this was by design, as the dominance of one tradition at the expense of others inspired efforts to separate religion and state. Whenever a religion allied itself with the interests of a state, it only seemed to help fuel the decline of both; any short term gain was met with a greater long-term loss, and fundamentalism as it was understood at the turn of the millennium began to decline. While secularism and non-religious affiliation became increasingly prevalent, many

faith traditions took the opportunity for reflection and reinvention.

Today, Buddhism, Christianity, Hinduism, Islam, Judaism, Gaiaism, and other traditions all exist in the world, on Luna, and on Mars. A number of new traditions have also emerged, adding to an already-diverse mix of paths and pilgrims. Places of worship can be found virtually everywhere; as traditions evolve, so do the places where the faithful gather. In the crushing density of New Angeles one can find a church, mosque, synagogue, or shrine huddled in a storefront, amid a shopping district, on a rooftop, or in the pristine garden of a much larger arcology. Some places of worship can be found in places where structures were simply built up and over them as cities expanded and congregations sold their air rights. Wherever they are, these spaces offer sanctuary from the frenetic pace around them.

THE STARLIGHT CRUSADE

"United in Spirit."

The most prominent of the new religions to have emerged in recent years is the Starlight Crusade, a movement that has also cemented itself as the most outspoken of the new religions. The Crusade's ebullient leader, Cardinal James Reese, is the organization's most public face and an expert at manipulating media resources to his advantage. Along with Human First and the Order of Sol, the Starlight Crusade is vocally anti-android, but for very different reasons.

Some say this new faith bears a striking resemblance to ancient gnostic movements, albeit with some very advanced technological enhancements. Using trappings borrowed from older traditions in its liturgy and hierarchy, the Crusade considers itself to be the new Knights Templar. Citizens of New Angeles would be forgiven if they thought that this group was larger, older, or more organized than it actually is.

ORIGINS

The Starlight Crusade emerged at the same time that tangential research in the brainmapping field determined spiritual experiences could be traced to certain locations in the brain. It was initially used by atheists as proof against the existence of deity since such experiences could be artificially induced. However, many others began to see this as an effective means to access spiritual knowledge or contact the divine. Ironically, these advancements created several movements for those seeking spiritual certainty after fundamentalism declined. The Starlight Crusade was the most successful of these movements, mixing pseudo-scientific concepts with neurostimulation technology, while at the same time appropriating spiritual and organizational language from older faith traditions.

BELIEFS AND PRACTICES

The core belief conveyed by the Crusade describes the spiritual realm is superior to the worldly: one can achieve greater sacred knowledge and liberation by increasingly setting aside the material. Adherents achieve this by entering special Starlight Meditation Booths, which help induce spiritual experiences. Admission to these sarcophagus-like cabinets requires a "fixed donation" that gets increasingly more expensive as adherents seek to ascend greater levels. Worshippers can either pay for these experiences or make commitments of time in lieu of money. In a similar way, worship spaces in the various missions include special reclining chairs that work like the booths, but are designed to work in concert with a larger network for shared experiences. The largest of these chambers can be found in the Crusade's citadel in New Angeles. As part of weekly gatherings, and certain special occasions, the chairs from the worship spaces in all the missions and the citadel link together for an even larger collective experience.

Gaining further levels of spiritual ascendancy in the Starlight Crusade requires that adherents purchase proprietary cybernetic neural implants. For this reason, the Crusade runs one of the most technologically advanced hospitals in New Angeles to handle installations. The more devout the follower, the more cybernetically enhanced— and indebted—they become. To critics, it is both ironic and hypocritical, given the Crusade's staunch and noisy opposition to the existence of clones and bioroids. To adherents, however, it is natural given that androids of any type are artificially created, are wholly material, and therefore have no spiritual selves to liberate. Some say that if a clone or bioroid ever made use of a meditation booth or activated a worship chair, they might discover a disturbing similarity to their conditioning chambers.

OUTREACH

Today, Starlight Crusade missions can be found in every major megapolis on Earth, as well as in Heinlein. While some limited attempts have been made to establish missions on Mars, the necessity for real-time networked-linked gatherings make such attempts all but impossible. Active critics, including former adherents of the Starlight Crusade, often find themselves up against constant harassment, both legal and personal. They have often sought refuge on Mars because of the Crusade's reduced presence there. Even so, rumors of Starlight Templars, the shadowy security apparatus of the Crusade, create unease among those who have run afoul of the group's leadership.

THE ORDER OF SOL

"Everything under the Sun."

The Order of Sol is a multi-denominational, multi-faith organization that promotes freedom of faith, cooperation among religious traditions, active social justice, and advocacy for the forgotten. It is not a new religion, but an umbrella organization that welcomes all faith traditions and coordinates between them. The Order evolved out of the need for interfaith cooperation on matters that concerned all religious traditions, and it serves as a counterpoint to both fundamentalist rhetoric and anti-religious vitriol. The first member groups tended to be socially progressive and looked for points of cooperation among like-minded groups in other faiths. Eventually, the informal structures led to a more formal organization, and so the Order of Sol was born. Today, the Order advocates for billions of faithful from every tradition, and member groups can be found virtually anywhere in the solar system that humans can be found.

One of the Order's founding principles supports the individual identity and freedom of member faiths. Many compare it to the U.N.'s General Assembly, where the Order has observer status, but for religious groups. It also acts as a moderating body between traditions when there are points of conflict. Since its inception, there has also been an emergence of congregations that self-identify themselves as only Order of Sol. Rather than being part of a member faith tradition, these groups tend to draw from many different religious traditions as a local congregation chooses. Regardless of whether members are Buddhist, Christian, Hindu, Jewish, Muslim, or unaffiliated, the Order actively encourages cooperation and strives to provide a voice for the faithful on the international and interplanetary stage. There are many internal differences, of course, and not one of the Order's member traditions has unanimous support for the larger body's actions. Still, cooperation and dialogue have been key to the Order of Sol's success.

Today, different congregations from a multitude of faith traditions all over the solar system incorporate the symbol of the Order of Sol as part of their external signage to demonstrate their affiliation with the Order and their commitment to dialogue and cooperation. Order of Sol churches, mosques, temples, sanctuaries, shrines, and synagogues can be found not only on Earth, but on the Moon, Mars, and space stations in between.

POLITICAL INFLUENCE

Today, the Order of Sol holds an unexpected amount of political clout, which is controversial among the member traditions. There is a growing unease regarding the extent to which the Order influences and has become allied with the Brazilian government in particular. Years ago, in a desperate effort to combat extensive corruption within the Brazilian political system, the Order of Sol was invited to be a neutral observer in Brazil's electoral process. The system had become so corrupt that the people didn't even trust U.N. observers to ensure a fair voting system.

At the time, the Order was seen as a neutral and fair broker who would help vet political candidates who had the best interests of the people in mind. It was a popular choice, and the Brazilian people embraced the Order's role. In the same way that New York hosted the U.N., the main General Assembly of the Order of Sol was built in Rio de Janeiro in the shadow of the massive Christo Redentor statue on Corcovado.

Today, however, there are many both inside and outside the Order who are wary of how enmeshed the Order of Sol has become with Brazil's political process. The Order's complex relationship with Brazil's political system no longer seems to be that of a neutral broker, but a fourth branch of government.

Conversely, there are those within the Order who welcome a closer alliance with Brazil and reject the notion of secularism. The South American nation has become an important counterpoint to the rampant corporate dominance found in all corners of human civilization, offering compassion and human dignity instead. For humans, the plight of the unemployed and the forgotten seems a direct result of a corporation's ability to simply manufacture their own workers. For the clone or bioroid, if they are indeed sentient, even if artificial, then they are no different than slaves in a new age. The Order of Sol stands for the goodness religion can bring to a rapidly changing world.

OTHER MOVEMENTS

Beside the Starlight Crusade and the Order of Sol, other new spiritual and religious movements have sprung up in light of the changes happening on Earth and across the solar system.

THE ALBERTIAN ORDER

A monastic order within the Solar Catholic Church, the Albertian Order is not particularly noteworthy except for its specific mission and mandate. Similar to some monastic orders during the Dark Ages and Medieval periods, the Albertian Order's mission is to preserve human knowledge and craft. They are unparalleled archivists and curators of items and artifacts, many of which society deems as outdated or obsolete. They also specialize in skills no longer widely practiced by the population at large.

The Albertian Order maintains the largest library of print-paper books anywhere in the solar system. When others moved to digital copies, paper books became increasingly rare and harder to preserve. It can teach its members and anyone else who wishes to learn how to perform cursive handwriting and calligraphy, or how to calculate math problems without the use of a computer. The Order also has blueprints for and the means to build incandescent lights. Practicing the older crafts is a spiritual discipline to remind the monks that their purpose is preserve the development of human knowledge. Ultimately, they hope their efforts will allow the continuity of development to be understood by future generations.

Seen as outwardly quaint, the Albertian Order maintains an extensive database and powerfully protected server. Their mandate is the collection of all human knowledge, and therefore their archivists also catalog and preserve digital data. Their skill with current technologies is prodigious but intentionally downplayed.

INCIPIATA MARTE VITA

Ever since humans first began to settle on Mars, these pioneers have been attempting to discover their identity in a new and harsh environment. The Red Planet's longer year and the subtle differences in the seasons meant that rites and rituals connected to Earth's yearly seasonal and lunar cycles didn't connect with life on Mars. While many ancient faith traditions came to Mars with the colony ships, local traditions and practices began to emerge that were specifically tied to the life and rhythm of the fourth planet. Among these was a new faith movement known as Incipiata Marte Vita (IMV, or sometimes simply "Vita"), which roughly means "Life Began on Mars."

Still in its infancy, IMV is largely found among the clans and other pro-Mars factions. No one set of coherent beliefs have emerged, but one of the core tenets is that life in the solar system began on Mars rather than Earth. Most adherents believe that life's origins are microbial and that billions of years ago, when Mars had liquid water, these ancient microbes evolved and traveled to Earth after a catastrophic asteroid impact. While IMV believers are generally pro-Mars, these groups actively support terraforming so that Mars can return to the ancient Eden it once was.

The more extreme elements believe that humans originated on Mars, and that ruins exist below Mars's surface. They believe that megacorporations already know this and are actively covering up any sort of evidence that has already been found. Some terrorist groups such as Crimson Dust use this particular element of IMV beliefs as a justification for their actions.

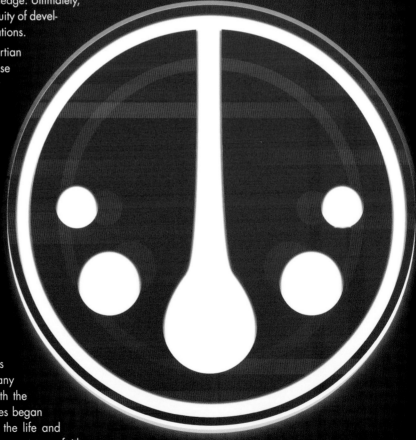

CLONES AND SPIRITUALITY

Many people mistake clones for humans at first glance despite their conspicuous bar code tattoos. With these so-called "organic machines" walking and working among us, different religions have begun trying to reconcile the existence of clones with the tenets of their faith. A few have welcomed clones into their parishes with open arms at the same time that others have kept them at arm's length, and a small but vocal minority decries them as soulless abominations on the front page of the *New Angeles Sol*.

CLONES AND SOULS

Cardinal Reese of the Starlight Crusade has been vocal in his declaration that clones do not have souls, nor are they welcome in any Crusade citadels. In the eyes of the Starlight Crusade, clones are tantamount to highly domesticated animals or sophisticated computer programs. As conditioned creatures without free will or a spiritual spark, the mysteries and epiphanies of the divine would be lost on clones. Because clones lack a soul, there are few Starlight Crusade adherents who would take issue with growing a clone for the sole purpose of harvesting an organ or recycling a clone when it ceased to be a productive worker.

Other religious organizations disagree with this attitude. Member faiths of the Order of Sol, an umbrella religious organization headquartered in Brazil, have different answers to the question of whether clones have souls, but most Solar parishioners agree that android ownership is the equivalent of slavery. Some consider clones' sentience or consciousness to indicate their having a soul, while others might believe that clones' souls have been passed down from God or humans. Liberation-centered traditions hold that the cycle of birth-life-death-rebirth means that all living creatures have a soul or innermost essence (*atman*), including clones. The more humanist members consider the question of a soul to be irrelevant to the question of how to treat clones. Regardless of the reasoning, the Order of Sol does not require clones to have souls in order to consider them human beings with certain intrinsic rights.

A related issue exists among owners who expect their clones to participate in worship services with them. This is particularly prevalent among individuals who are exceptionally devout in their faith. Some religious communities are uncomfortable involving beings that might not be there on the basis of their own faith, but merely out of obeying their owners. It depends on the specific religious community, but it is becoming more common for spiritual leaders to deny clones admittance to houses of worship during prayer services.

CLONE CULTS

Critics have been quick to point out that programming loyalty into biological clones will have unintended consequences. One of them has been the emergence of what are now labeled clone cults. These groups and movements take on several different forms, yet they share some basic characteristics. Officially, Jinteki actively denies that these groups exist; unofficially, the corporation actively monitors the social interactions of their products, attempting to shut down and retire any such individuals before their movements becomes public.

Clone cults are thought to stem from a clone's need to be part of a group and the intense obedience instilled through the conditioning process. They are made to be loyal and happy in what they do, deriving the meaning of their existence from their work and their peers. They follow orders, do as they are told, and are loyal to both their supervisor and company. Yet in some cases, this loyalty becomes dangerously obsessive, developing in unhealthy ways that goes beyond unquestioning obedience. Often there is an expectation that others, especially of the same clone type, to have the same degree of commitment. Cult-like movements arise when an individual clone with this degree of devotion is able to inspire this in fellow makes.

FRAGMENTED SOUL COLLECTIVES

One common thread found within multiple clone cults is the notion that because clones of a particular line all share the same DNA, they might all share the same soul, too. Each clone is therefore responsible for the spiritual wellbeing of the whole: if one is corrupt, then that one might risk all who share their genetic code.

These cults usually start with a single individual who has suffered some degree of existential trauma, sometimes from as simple as the completion of the task for which they were created. The individual might manage to avoid "retirement" and go on a pilgrimage to find others with his genome, giving birth to a movement to reunite the whole.

JINTEKI-AS-CREATOR MOVEMENTS

Although Jinteki would logically have a clear interest in rooting out clone cults where they crop up, there are some such cults that seem to persist longer than others or even flourish—cults that center on the idea of worshiping Jinteki as "the Creator." In these cases, clones' disposition toward loyalty and collectivism manifests as reverence for the corporation as a whole. Occasionally these cults also see individual Jinteki employees or executives as angelic figures or prophets of "the Creator," and thus are duly deserving of veneration. Conspiracy theorists believe that employees or perhaps even the megacorporation utilizes these cultists to advance their agendas, and then declares the clones rogue once they have served their purpose.

Commissioner," said Captain Rick Harrison as he looked up from the DNA sniffer he was using. He stood. "This is a pleasant surprise."

"It's not every day we have a dead Universal Nations dignitary on our hands," Dawn replied as she surveyed the crime scene. "So, what do we have?"

"The deceased was one Victor Gray, Chair of the U.N. Council for Interplanetary Affairs. But then, that's why you're here. His sec team called it in just over an hour ago. Forspecs put the time of death at 2048."

"Drowning?" Dawn stepped closer to the pool.

"Well, it looks that way, but we won't know for sure until the medex makes his report." Harrison took off his gloves and rubbed his jaw. "Of course the sec guys pulled the body out of the water before contacting us."

"Wonderful," Dawn sighed and knelt down next to the puddle where the body had lain on the tile floor. "Globalsec, right?"

Harrison nodded. "Only the best for the U.N."

"I'll say. Where were they?"

"Apparently Gray liked to swim alone, helped him think."

"Have they cooperated?" Dawn asked.

Harrison grinned. "About as much as they ever do."

Dawn stood and stared down at the still water. "What are the odds this really was an accident?"

"Not good. Gray was not only a regular swimmer, but captain of the swimming and diving team in college. There's also the timing. His 'Martian Rights' resolution has been getting a lot of traction."

"Why did it take them so long to find him? Doesn't this pool have any safety measures?"

"That's the other thing. It does." Harrison pointed his thumb at the pool. "Heat sensors, motion detectors, and a heart monitor that reads the vibrations in the water. But they were disabled. We're still trying to figure out how and when, since only the hotel staff and the Globalsec team had access."

"All right," said Dawn, nodding. "Stay on this one and keep me informed of any developments."

Dawn left the pool room and took out her pad. With her NAPD clearance, she easily accessed the hotel's network. She brought up the charges to Gray's room, which included several room service requests over the last two days. The latest was a bottle of champagne, about ten minutes before his time of death.

Dawn found the head of the Globalsec team, a greying bulldog of a man named Bradley, arguing with Detective Reynolds out in the hallway.

"Excuse me, Mr. Bradley," she spoke sharply, flashing her badge. "Commissioner Dawn, NAPD. Do you have a moment?"

Bradley adjusted his tie and turned from Reynolds. "Yes, Commissioner. I was just explaining to your officer here that I'm eager to assist with the investigation in any way possible."

"Detective," she corrected. "Did anyone come to Gray's suite tonight? A member of the hotel staff, maybe?"

"No," Bradley grimaced. "I would have mentioned that, of course."

"Are you certain? Could you check with your men on duty tonight?" She held his gaze until he nodded and spoke into his comm. As he listened to the reply, his face fell.

"I apologize, Commissioner. You're right, a member of the hotel staff did come by an hour or so before we found Mr. Gray. A bioroid." He hesitated. "Room service. It didn't seem important."

Of course not. Bioroids can't harm humans. Everyone knows that.

"Thank you, Mr. Bradley. We'll let you know if we need anything else."

Bradley started to object, but Dawn simply gave him a look. As she headed for the elevator, she commed Harrison over her PAD. "Was a bottle of champagne found at the scene?"

"Just a moment, Commissioner," Harrison's voice came back.

She stopped in front of the elevator, which detected her presence and announced a twenty-second wait.

"No, no champagne. Why?"

The doors opened. "Gray had a visitor tonight. Check with the hotel management, see if all the bioroid staff are accounted for."

A bioroid murderer. That would change a lot. Humanity Labor would have a field day. HL and Jinteki, both.

Dawn stepped onto the elevator and spoke aloud, "Roof." The rooftop hopper pad was for official use only, but the elevator read her ID and started upward.

As she stepped out onto the roof, her smartslick detected the rain and unfolded, but not before a few drops landed on her face. The water itched, burned even. Bad weather tonight. She was glad for the smartslick. Walking to her hopper, Dawn saw a woman sitting in the shadow of a cargo hopper, knees pulled up to her chest. Her hair and hotel uniform were soaked with rain.

Dawn stopped and watched. No, not a woman. A bioroid.

The bioroid looked straight at her—its silver eyes were blank, but its face wasn't. Wet black hair obscured her *features,* but there was something there—confusion, maybe. Or anger.

The bioroid leapt from the roof and disappeared into the night below. Dawn's PAD chimed to announce an incoming comm from Harrison.

"You were right, there's one bioroid employee missing. Elsa 5K71R. Looks like the hotel leased her about two weeks ago. She's on shift, but her supervisor hasn't seen her for a couple of hours."

"Thanks, Rick. Maybe it's nothing, but if it is something, that Elsa is long gone by now. Put out an APB, but keep the reason quiet. We don't want to give the *news-nosies* even more to work with."

She ended the call, but her PAD chirped again to announce an incoming vid. Dawn hesitated a moment before telling her secretary to let the vid through.

"Good evening, Director Haas."

THE NEW ANGELES POLICE DEPARTMENT

The brave men and women of the New Angeles Police Department are the only ones standing between honest New Angelino citizens and chaos. In a megapolis the size of New Angeles, it takes more than a metropolitan police force to keep order—it takes a multi-level, far-reaching, well-connected organization with a mega budget, tough cops, g-mod smart detectives, and a commissioner who won't be bullied by corps and orgcrime. NBN casts the NAPD as such an organization: one that keeps citizens safe and crime rates down. In reality, even with g-mods and cyberware and cutting-edge tech, cops are only human. Most of them, anyway.

The New Angeles Police Department is responsible for enforcing the law throughout the sprawling megacity—from Guayaquil to Esmeraldas, the Root to Heinlein, and all the megacorps and orgcrime in between. Although most incidents hardly register on NBN's various newsfeeds, aggravated crimes occur in New Angeles every day. Even before accounting for the non-violent offenses, the NAPD is stretched thin, meaning the NAPD must bolster its numbers with bounty hunters, corporate security, private investigators, and other independent operators. The officers and detectives of the NAPD must deal with everything: gang warfare, anti-android riots, organized crime, and corruption. And all too often, armies of lawyers see to it that even the NAPD's best efforts garner no more than a slap on the wrist.

As technology advances, criminals adapt and exploit it, often faster than the authorities can. Besides the high-tech weapons and other gear being used and sold by criminals, the criminals themselves are evolving. From yak enforcers so cybered that they're nearly bulletproof, to g-mods that can outrun a hopper and jump from a third-floor window without breaking stride, NAPD officers can easily find themselves outmatched or simply unprepared to deal with transhuman suspects.

The men and women who serve in the NAPD represent a broad spectrum of backgrounds and ideologies—and a few of them might not be considered men or women at all. Many members of the NAPD, including Commissioner Chen-Mai Dawn, are former military personnel, having served in the War. Although the police come from many walks of life, some are notably absent; few risties and scions of corporate privilege see fit to risk their lives trying to maintain law and order. Androids, both clones and bioroids, are a new addition to the Force, and their presence continues to generate problems in spite of the many advantages they offer.

The NAPD was chartered shortly before construction finished on the New Angeles Space Elevator, and its mission has continued to evolve in the face of new threats. New Angeles is unlike any other city, and the department is constantly facing new challenges. As always, the law, and so also law enforcement, has had difficulty keeping up with the rapid advances in technology. The existence and growing popularity of androids creates numerous issues for the NAPD, both directly and indirectly. The involvement of an android in a crime, even simply as a witness, creates numerous problems and legal loopholes for defense attorneys to exploit, and an android's testimony has been thrown out of court on more than one occasion.

"We stand behind all those who wear the NAPD badge."
– Commissioner Chen-Mai Dawn

HISTORY

The history of the NAPD stretches back to the beginnings of New Angeles, before the completion of the Beanstalk. During its construction, the National Police of Ecuador joined forces with the private security hired by Jack Weyland, and together they ensured the safety of all involved with the project. When New Los Angeles was officially incorporated as a city, Mayor Fisher attempted to make the situation official, dubbing the force the New Los Angeles Police Department (later shortened to just the New Angeles Police Department, or NAPD). He offered to purchase the security contract from Weyland and invited the Ecuadorean police to stay on as NAPD officers. Both offers received a mixed response. The security force terminated its contract and withdrew from New Angeles, but some individuals chose to stay where they had settled. Many of the Ecuadorian police initially agreed to sign up as NAPD cops, but when presented with a new set of rules and regulations, some changed their minds. This left the Mayor with only a skeleton force policing the rapidly expanding city.

Mayor Fisher tried recruiting officers from U.S. police departments by offering generous relocation allowances. Although bilingual officers were preferred, the Mayor could not afford to reject what few applications he received. The sudden influx of trained officers coming in fresh from the U.S. clashed with the ex-security and Ecuadorian cops who resented their loss of authority, and soon the fledgling NAPD was in disarray. Many of the new recruits spoke little or no Spanish, and as the NAPD fragmented, fights broke out among the ranks. Once the Beanstalk was completed, the number of cops dwindled and crime rates soared until the first commissioner arrived.

From the moment Mayor Fisher founded the NAPD, he began his search for a commissioner who would be able and willing to take on the task of pummeling the new force into shape. He eventually brought in Commissioner Oscar Calvo; his impressive, decade-long record at the SSPD, as well as his decorated military background, made him the perfect candidate. Calvo was a traditionalist—his officers knew him to be incorruptible, with a strict moral code and a strength they respected. His appointment marked the beginning of the NAPD as we know it today.

Matt Zeilinger

The NAPD did not turn into an efficient crime-fighting machine overnight, but Calvo wasted no time reorganizing the police force, creating new divisions so he could grant promotions to Ecuadorian cops who had been in positions of authority before they joined the NAPD. He knew that communication was key to integrating his officers, so he offered them a choice between AI translation secretaries and implants, or lessons in Spanish or English. The vast majority accepted the implants, and soon all cops could function in both languages.

Once Calvo obtained the funding, he founded the New Angeles Police Academy at the eastern border of Laguna Velasco. Officers had to attend the NAPA for reassessment, no matter their service record. This training leveled the field for the police officers and brought them together. Calvo was a firm believer in the benefits of *taiho-jutsu*, operant conditioning, and a "no-pain-no-gain" attitude, so training was intensive and vigorous. His academy, nicknamed the "house of pain" in its early days, attracted more recruits than it lost. Any officer who made it through Calvo's training could get a job in any police force anywhere; it was the ultimate test. Calvo insisted on regular training for all his officers throughout their careers, but after his disappearance, his replacement abolished this practice. Other cost-saving changes included replacing martial arts teachers with AI instructors and transforming training areas into VR suites.

Merely a decade after the completion of the Beanstalk, most of the world was already reliant on He-3, and the growth of New Angeles was explosive. Commissioner Calvo made an unsuccessful request for funds to expand the police force. Mayor Fisher considered that he had spent enough money on that particular problem. The NAPD was keeping crime at an acceptable level in the developing city, and the mayor was directing his attention, and funds, elsewhere.

For the first time, housing became a problem in New Angeles. Rumors spread that the Mayor was granting certain big corps special dispensation that ignored zoning laws in exchange for kickbacks and other favors. It was no secret that Calvo believed the rumors, and he instructed several detectives to investigate the matter. The relationship between the mayor and commissioner grew strained.

The War only made things worse. The NAPD had been kicked out of Heinlein by the Lunar rebels, and the United States Armed Forces were in charge of retaking New Angeles territory on the Moon, so the police force's role was limited to containing the rising panic and cleaning up the mess caused by small-scale attacks from anti-capitalist militia. The Feds used the Root as a base for dealing with the Lunar trouble, so the U.S. military had a presence in the city too. The NAPD was low in the pecking order, and the commissioner could do little but watch as the War unfolded at the top of the Beanstalk and beyond. In the aftermath, the Treaty of Heinlein reinstated the NAPD's influence in Heinlein, but the mayor hadn't veiled his belief that somehow Commissioner Calvo was partially to blame for allowing the Lunar Insurrection to happen.

No one ever found the commissioner's body, but the official line is that he was a victim of a rogue Martian terrorist attack toward the end of the War. Some of his deputies expressed a desire to investigate the matter further, but the Mayor expressly denied their request and appointed Commissioner Terry as a replacement within days of the Calvo's disappearance. Assistant Commissioner Terry was new to the police force, fresh out of the military. He purchased surplus military equipment, and the NAPD gained a new, more intimidating reputation.

As veterans from the War joined the ranks of the NAPD, the military aspects of the New Angeles police became the hot new scandal. Newsies targeted specific precincts and officers, condemning their actions as brutal or corrupt. Civil lawsuits made against officers resulted in suspensions if not convictions. Commissioner Terry handed in his resignation, and for the first time the Mayor allowed the citizens of New Angeles to elect their own commissioner to help assuage fears that the NAPD was out of touch with the surrounding community.

Commissioner Chen-Mai Dawn was herself a veteran of the War, but had kept a permanent address in New Angeles. At the time of the election she was the district commander for Base de Cayambe, a notoriously difficult area in which to work. Her record was as impressive as her ambition, but it was her personality that won the votes. She appeared young and beautiful, and voters considered her one of their own. Her election campaign was well funded by an anonymous party, and she won by an outstanding majority of votes.

Commissioner Dawn kept the NAPD out of the news as much as possible, but she provided personal interviews with NBN when high-profile cases arose. She signed a contract with Huang Heavy Industries (HHI) to supply the NAPD with weapons, armor, and most of its gear.

This replaced the controversial military hardware, but it limited the NAPD in what they could purchase from other companies—even now it means having to hire specialist personnel from outside the Force when technology not available from HHI is required.

The Clone Riots were the first wide-scale disruption of the peace since Dawn's election, and this was the first time the NAPD dealt with a major riot without help from the Feds or military. Officers were stretched thin trying to contain pockets of violence across the city, while rioters destroyed thousands of androids. Criminals took advantage of the panic, looting businesses and homes, and organ grinders worked the crowds. Perhaps the hardest thing during the crisis was identifying humans in danger because clones pass for humans at a distance. Rioters

killed citizens they mistook as clones, while others lost lives in the cross fire as SWAT teams resorted to lethal tactics to disperse the crowds.

After an expensive negotiation with HHI, Commissioner Dawn signed contracts with both Jinteki and Haas-Bioroid to trial their labor solutions: androids. Two androids entered the Force as detectives, first a bioroid, and then a clone. This controversial move demonstrated how far the Commissioner is willing to go to keep the Force ahead of the game, but the use of androids has brought the NAPD under the scrutiny of human rights groups like Humanity Labor and, of course, the news-nosies. The worlds will be watching to see the results of this experiment, to glimpse the future of the NAPD and police officers across Earth, Luna, and Mars.

ORGANIZATION AND STRUCTURE

The New Angeles Police Department is the largest metropolitan police force in the world. In some ways, the NAPD functions like a megacorp, and the five-hundred-story arcology headquarters is comparable to Broadcast Square or Haas Arcology in terms of scale and presence. There are whole departments devoted to relations with the public, the media, and the corps—the Internal Affairs department alone receives as much funding as some continental U.S. police forces do in their entirety. The commissioner and the mayor meet regularly, and the NAPD maintains close ties with the Big Four.

In addition to their headquarters in Laguna Velasco, the NAPD maintains precinct offices in each of the New Angeles districts. The twelve precincts are all so different that they seem like separate cities entirely, but they all rely on the same resources and each other. The NAPD is the only police force to have jurisdiction stretching into space, so it faces unique problems on an unprecedented scale. Heinlein receives the same treatment as the planet-side precincts, and its assistant commissioner maintains close contact

with NAPD HQ. Different departments work together to solve crimes, which take place across precincts, in space, or on the Network. Teamwork is crucial—organization and efficiency paramount. The structure of the NAPD is what holds everything together to ensure that no matter who is working a case, it's always clear who's in charge.

CAREER PROGRESSION

Most cops begin their careers as probationary officers and then work their way up through the ranks if they have the necessary skill and ambition. As with everything within the NAPD, officers may choose to specialize, and different units offer different routes for career progression. There are also many unsworn officers working for the NAPD in laboratories, offices, jails, and the courts.

The career of a regular, uniformed cop begins with four months' training at the academy. Then the probationary police officer, otherwise known as a "rookie," works for a few months alongside a more

experienced officer. A sergeant will usually recommend the rookie for promotion to patrol officer. Then the rookie takes the oath, which empowers him or her to make arrests and carry firearms.

The patrol officer is the regular, uniformed cop seen working the streets. Walking the "beat" is not required since the introduction of seccams, but officers do patrol in certain areas and circumstances. They are often first to the scene of a crime. Patrol officers must be adaptable and quick-thinking, as their role often puts them in dangerous and unpredictable situations. Fortunately, there are thousands of patrol officers within the NAPD, and they partner up or work in groups in almost every case, as there is some truth to the expression "safety in numbers."

Officers who demonstrate leadership qualities and organizational skills can be promoted to the role of sergeant. Sergeants supervise watch shifts or individual squads, and they verify their officers are working by the books. Successful sergeants nominate themselves to take and pass an exam that qualifies them for the position of major, but they must still be appointed by a colonel. Majors supervise two or three sergeants and are often assigned to oversee an entire police station. An officer who excels in either role may achieve the rank of colonel and supervise a precinct. Eventually a colonel might achieve the rank of commander and take control of one of the twelve district offices, presiding over multiple precincts.

The path is different for detectives and investigators working in the other bureaus. Those who display leadership skills might be tapped to lead their shift as lieutenant, with the hope of eventually being promoted to captain. Captains supervise specific units within a precinct, such as the homicide unit for the 73rd Precinct. The most exemplary captains might one day be tapped to lead their unit city-wide as inspector. The role of inspector and all ranks above it are largely administrative in nature, and they frequently require management skills, specialized training, as well as police experience. Inspectors

THE ACADEMY

I remember the days when recruits were put through their paces, beaten into shape so they turned up for work at the precinct primed and ready for the tough job of being a rookie cop. Not so these days. What do they do at the academy now, sit around and watch holos on teamwork?

This new lad I'm showing the ropes, he complains if we're out after dark. He believes everything he reads on the Net. Worst thing is, he thinks he knows everything because he's read the manual. The manual won't tell you who to squeeze for information on the local drug dealers or which gangs are untouchable. It can't teach you how to take down perps twice your size or with cyberware that makes them twice as strong.

When I went to the academy last, before the rules changed—I'd been a cop three years and it was just a refresher—I had to run five miles twice a day to show them I could, practice interview techniques on AI and fellow students, track and be tracked through real streets with real people. Fired real guns, not just simulations. It doesn't feel the same. We exchanged stories in the evenings, compared notes on our different precincts. I learned some useful tidbits that way. And there was the hand-to-hand combat—that was the best. They worked us hard, but we made a competition of it. I wasn't top of the class, but I could hold my own in a fight. Gave me more confidence on patrol.

This new partner of mine, I think he'd be afraid to take a piss without his pistol handy, just in case. No wonder the Commissioner wants to replace us all with fragging golems.

Viktoria Gavrilenko

report to the deputy chiefs of their division; deputy chiefs report to the bureau chiefs themselves, and the bureau chiefs answer to the commissioner.

The assistant commissioner serves as the commissioner's right hand, tending to special task forces and projects, and has to be able to complete the duties of the commissioner should the need arise. In this position, officers can prove themselves ready for the title of commissioner, but their assignment to that role is by no means guaranteed—they must still win the hearts of the voters. No commissioner of the NAPD has ever been assistant commissioner of the same.

Commissioner Chen-Mai Dawn is the current head of the New Angeles Police Department, and she works closely with the mayor to ensure the safety and security of all New Angelinos. In addition to being the ultimate authority within the NAPD, the commissioner is also its public face. Every day is a new battle to reconcile the realities of the NAPD's workforce with the expectations of city hall, the megacorps, special interest groups, the public, and the Force itself.

NOTABLE BUREAUS, DIVISIONS, AND UNITS

New Angeles is a sprawling megapolis home to millions of criminals who are continually inventing new ways to break the law. Crimes run the gamut from nuisance chip-rippers to stim-dealing to embezzlement to plain old-fashioned homicide, but the more prevalent crimes have entire police units devoted to preventing and solving them. Most New Angelinos equate the NAPD with the Patrol Bureau and its many precincts in each city district, but the following key bureaus, divisions, and units are also indispensable in the fight against crime.

HOMICIDE

New Angeles' population has ballooned since the New Angeles Police Department's inception, but per-capita homicide rates have risen as well. As a result, the Homicide Division has become one of the largest within the Violent Crimes Division of the Detectives Bureau. The types of homicide encountered on a daily basis range from teenagers who turn up with half their organs removed, to white-collar types taken down by mysterious homemade viruses, to the more traditional bullet in the brain. The detectives of this division work closely with Forensics, the Gang Unit, and others to get dangerous perpetrators off New Angeles streets.

CORPORATE CRIME

A less effective unit of the Detectives Bureau's Special Crimes Investigations Division is the smaller Corporate Crime Unit. The corps of New Angeles bring benefits such as jobs and tax revenue, but the megacorps are extremely powerful, and it is the purpose of this division to prevent them abusing that power. There has been some success dealing with smaller corps that cut corners in an effort to scrape corporate power for themselves, but otherwise this division has little influence.

Within this division, the Forensic Accounting Unit (FAU) deals with fraud and other white-collar crimes. Other units rely on FAU to examine data and provide evidence suitable for use in a court of law. Some cases overlap with Gangs and Organized Crime, and require these units to work closely together.

CYBER BUREAU

The Cyber Bureau grew out of the NAPD's need to address the rampant increase in Netcrimes. A new breed of Netcriminal, known colloquially as runners, fundamentally threatened the NAPD's ability to collect and store accurate evidence. The Technology & Support Services Division (TSSD) continuously struggles to stay a step ahead of Netcriminals who might wreak havoc on NAPD's suspect or evidence databases. Since software and hardware require constant upgrading to keep pace with the criminal element, TSSD is also the greatest drain on NAPD resources, and it remains the biggest vulnerability.

The Cyber Bureau does more than merely defend itself against outside threats, however: it also investigates and apprehends suspected Netcriminals. One of the largest divisions within the Cyber Bureau is Netcrimes. To a degree, almost all crimes involve use of the Network, and so all the departments invariably partner with Netcrimes at some point or another to collect and evaluate a crime's digital evidence. Within the division itself, dedicated units investigate automated crimes, electronic intrusion, and identity theft, and they also oversee the NAPD's massive surveillance and camdrone program. The division contains many unsung heroes who might be considered runners in their own right, and more than a few Netcrimes investigators are former Netcriminals who turned white-hat to avoid a sentence.

PERSONAL ABUSE AND MODIFICATION DIVISION

One division within the Organized Crime Control Bureau that occasionally benefits from employing ex-criminals is the Personal Abuse and Modification Unit. PAMD, as it is frequently called, investigates the manufacture, importation, distribution, and use of prohibited cyberware, unapproved g-mods, and unlicensed sensiesofts. Despite the availability of cloned organs, cheaper "natural" organs are still available on the black market, so the PAMD also monitors the Shadow Net and targets any traders of such items. This unit protects New Angelinos from themselves, and it runs an extensive program to educate youths and their parents of the dangers of illegal self-modification and other dangerous practices.

Within this division, the Vice Unit deals with gambling, prostitution, and illegal narcotics and stimulants. New drugs regularly appear on the market that are designed so that even Hachi-Inu clones are unable to detect them, making this a problem area. Figures show a satisfactory reduction of prostitution and related crime in recent years, however. This is partly due to the dedication of the Vice Unit, and partly due to the distribution and use of androids.

DETECTIVES

The plainclothes detective has one of the most sought-after jobs on the force. This is due to the popularity of crime mystery sensies, since in reality detectives work the longest hours, frequently end up in dangerous situations, and are the most vulnerable to lawsuits. It is not easy to become a detective, and superiors consider each applicant's case individually.

Potential detectives must display intelligence, insight, and determination to apply for the role, and must have served for at least three years as a uniformed officer. Detective-investigators usually receive their rank after a two-year tenure as officers on investigative assignment in the Vice Unit. Detective-specialists are pulled from experienced detective-investigators and are assigned to the division that best matches their skill set, such as Netcrimes, although in some instances individuals with extremely in-demand areas of expertise are fast-tracked into relevant divisions. Some detectives go on to become self-employed private investigators, but this is not a promotion so much as a gamble.

The only other detectives without this experience are the androids currently trialing at the NAPD; instead, they are prepared for the role by the corporations that made them with a combination of neural channeling or conditioning as well as hands-on learning. A number NAPD employees, news-nosies, and politicians have made official complaints about the perceived preferential treatment of android detectives. The NAPD reminds them that all androids began their careers as entry-level, third-grade detectives, and because the trial involves testing androids in investigative roles, any other position would be unproductive.

Mark Molnar

FORENSICS DIVISION

An important part of the Professional Standards Bureau, the Forensics Division uses specialized skills and technologies to aid other departments in solving a variety of crimes and obtaining evidence suitable for convicting criminals. This includes the Crime Scene Investigation Unit, which involves physically gathering and recording evidence at crime scenes, and the Imaging Unit, which provides models to recreate crime scenes in virtual reality.

Forensics also maintains the Virtual Reality Crime Lab Morgue, which officers can use to examine cadavers after autopsy. Officers may access files by pulling simulated bodies from the vaults and can manipulate the images for a thorough examination of wounds, cyberware, and any bullets or other foreign bodies that were found within a corpse. Corps eager for advertising provide the virtual morgue with hardware and software, as high-profile cases demonstrate such VR technology to the masses. Accepting these donations allows the Forensics Division to remain the most advanced of its kind worldwide.

However, because the Forensics Division has accumulated a significant backlog and private forensic specialists have access to tech still not licensed or available to NAPD forspecs, the NAPD frequently contracts out additional work to such companies as Sagan Forensics, Inc.

DAILY PATROLS

Officers Amara Velasquez and Ty Koch start their day when a police hopper comes to collect them from their respective homes. Before they report for duty, each officer takes time to review their equipment, including checking the charge levels on camdrones and Synap pistols, O_2 levels on oxygen tanks, and other details. When they've finished, they inform Minerva that they find their kit in good working order and are ready to begin their day.

Minerva is the precinct's AI, a secretary that coordinates the vast amounts of data that flows through the Laguna Velasco precinct each day. Once the officers are in their seats, it is Minerva that launches the hopper and directs it towards its area of responsibility in southwestern LV, and it is

SURVEILLANCE AND PRIVACY RIGHTS

Given cause, the NAPD can monitor a suspect's movements, Network use, and pupil dilation; record every word the suspect says; and get threedee images of the suspect sitting on a waste extractor. The NAPD has the means, but lacks the right. This is largely the fault of PriRights, a human rights group that successfully campaigned against the use of seccams in private spaces. These days, NAPD microscopic cameras and recording devices are underused despite the technology being readily available and capable of preventing and investigating crimes.

Specialized camdrones equipped with facial-recognition AI floating throughout the city merely remind the public of the NAPD's presence, and they occasionally catch amateur criminals in the act. Closer scrutiny requires a warrant or at least probable cause. Any cop who spies on a potential perp too closely, tracks a PAD of someone who turns out to be humanitarian of the year, or plants a camera in the private office of the mayor's second cousin twice removed, could face a civil suit or even jail time.

When working undercover, officers wear microscopic cameras, often as implants, but these must be shut off when in corporate or private space. Detectives frequently forgo cams in order to establish trust with potential informants and snitches. Beat cops, riot police, SWAT Teams, and any other agents on the front lines of the fight against crime have cams on their person to insulate the NAPD from excessive force charges.

Police-issued weapons come equipped with detailed recording technology. With every squeeze of the trigger, these smartguns record time, positioning, location, and even the ID of the bullet fired. They are also keyed to lock up when an unauthorized user tries wielding them. Although the weapons lack a persistent connection to the Network, they automatically upload their records to NAPD databases at the end of the shift.

The NAPD keeps meticulous records of an officer's movements and ensures that interview rooms and cells are under constant surveillance. These precautions ensure officers don't cut corners and that no prisoner falsely claims mistreatment.

Minerva that logs their presence at morning roll call and briefing.

The briefing is held via virt; the officers attend remotely while at their desks or sitting in their hopper en route to the first call of the day. Sergeant Bryce runs down a listing of notable reports from the prior shift, collected for him by Minerva: So many officer-involved shootings, reports of dazzle-wearing vandals sabotaging cams, a death threat from a streetbanger outfit called the Druzhinniki leveled at members of the NAPD. There are over 1,100 open cases logged in Minerva's systems, but Sergeant Bryce doesn't elaborate on any of them. Minerva will inform the officers if any data becomes relevant in the course of their day. Sergeant Bryce ends the meeting the same way he always does, telling his officers to "stay safe out there."

When not responding to any immediate calls, Officer Velasquez likes to have Minerva take the hopper on a random patrol, moving publicly through the district so everyone can see the NAPD is on the job. While patrolling, the hopper's cameras and the helmcams on both officers sweep the streets and slidewalks looking for evidence of a crime, Minerva comparing the footage with its database and all public cam footage from throughout the city.

The first incident call of the day for Velasquez and Koch comes from an L-square shopping plaza. Minerva directs their hopper there and informs them that a woman is causing a disturbance. The officers watch cam footage as they fly and already know where to find the woman and her name, Patience Rewarded, by the time they touch down. Velasquez makes the approach while Koch stands back, one hand on his Synap pistol.

Rewarded is incoherent and agitated. She has visible cybernetic enhancements, and the officers treat her as a potential threat. Velasquez is able to defuse the situation and take Rewarded—who insists on being called "Laser"—into custody. "Laser" is placed in the back of the hopper, which immediately departs for 1P, First Precinct, for suspect processing. Velasquez and Koch remain behind to reassure the small crowd and take witness statements, and then step into a fresh hopper that arrives to pick them up. Minerva files the incident report automatically, with the officers dictating their own annotations.

The second call is an Officer Down. Officer Li, who failed to report this morning, has been found dead by a camdrone in undercity territory claimed by the Druzhinniki. The area is what they refer to as "cam-dead," with extensive sabotage and

neglect creating large gaps in surveillance coverage. Velasquez and Koch are one of six partnered patrol teams to be routed to the site by Minerva, along with homicide detectives and forensic investigators.

Koch is visibly agitated by the death of a fellow officer. He has many questions, some of which Velasquez refuses to answer. Minerva does its best, but cannot speculate as to Officer Li's motives for being in the area in plainclothes or who committed the crime. Minerva's records show that Koch's heart rate and respiration are both elevated.

Because the area is cam-dead, every responding hopper deploys its emergency camdrones and the patrol officers head out on foot patrols to increase coverage. Minerva soon alerts Velasquez and Koch to the presence of an individual with no ID, apparently sleeping under trash not far from the crime scene. As the officers approach, the subject lurches to his feet,

throwing bottles and other objects and screaming profanity. The subject turns, perhaps to flee, and Koch shoots him three times with his service weapon.

Velasquez instructs her partner to direct his helmcam down a side street, to watch for any approaching bangers. She approaches the subject, her helmcam pointed up and down the street. In a later report, Velasquez will claim that he was attempting to be alert for any potential threats. When she reaches the subject, she turns her camera on him and pronounces him dead. He is holding an old-style handgun in one hand, a low-tech weapon with no modern safety features but more than capable of injuring or killing an LEO.

More forspecs arrive and take possession of the incident scene, and Koch and Velasquez retreat. They request and are granted a two-hour mental health break, during which they disable their connections to Minerva and travel to a local

"Put the better part of a billion souls into one city. Put all the money in the hands of the corps and all the power in the hands of people ruling from a thousand klicks away. Add androids and stir. That's a recipe for crime, poverty, and human misery. But it keeps me in work."

– Raymond Flint, Private Investigator and New Angelino

Matt Zeilinger

eatery called Maxwell's, renowned for the privacy it offers its clientele.

When they emerge, Koch flags an autocab and reports to 1P for debrief; he has been suspended on administrative leave, as required by policy after any officer-involved shooting. His suspension will be brief; Minerva's reconstruction of the event, given the sparse camera coverage in the area and of the incident, is inconclusive, and Velasquez's testimony and the video evidence that does exist indicates that the subject, now identified as Luis Delastilla, was armed at the time of the shooting. Koch is cleared and restored to duty within twenty-four hours.

Velasquez returns to her shift, now acting without a partner. Minerva preferentially routes aud- and vidcalls that demand a human presence to Velasquez, and she fields a number of complaints and reports from the comfort of a police hopper.

Velasquez's last call of the day is an incident at a private arcology. When Velasquez arrives, prisec greets her at the hopper pad and refuses her entry. Prisec claims the report was sent in error. Velasquez retreats to her hopper and logs the incident, still observed by prisec. She keeps her helmcam trained on the ark, at her best estimate of where the report originated, hoping that Minerva will detect probable cause. After a half-hour, while lawyers work behind the scenes at both 1P and within the ark, Velasquez moves on per Minerva's instruction and prisec returns to its duties; no warrant was secured and no probable cause found.

At the end of her shift, Velasquez is deposited at home by her hopper. Aside from the incident with the shooting, it has been an average patrol day. Velasquez had no reason to set foot in a precinct house or NAPD facility, nor will she until her next mandatory training day.

Delastilla's children claim that Velasquez, a fifteen-year veteran of the NAPD, planted the weapon on their father after the shooting in order to protect her partner, the recently sworn-in Koch. The claim is never proven, but is dutifully logged by Minerva and added to her record. It is the second such claim made against Velasquez. She is never brought up on any charges for the incident. Koch resumes his duties and remains a model officer.

PROCEDURES

Procedures aren't put in place to make life difficult for cops—they exist to ensure crimes are solved, criminals are put away, and officers don't die on the job. With training and repeated use, standard procedure should become second nature so an officer knows how to react no matter the situation. In the course of their career, cops may encounter everything from organ grinders to data-addicts, ex-super soldiers to g-modded geniuses, and clone-haters to cyber-junkies. NAPD cops have to be ready for anything, and this is how they do it.

CRIME SCENE PROCEDURES

Failure to follow crime scene procedure makes a case harder to solve. It doesn't take much for a well-meaning but untrained officer to contaminate or destroy evidence. There are also legal issues to consider; evidence collected incorrectly isn't admissible in court, and if the perp gets away on such a technicality, that's a lot of hard work wasted. The first officers at the crime scene secure the area so that no one tampers with evidence. In a murder investigation, no one can touch the body until after the medex has finished with it. An assigned detective, NAPD forspec, or independent contractor will search the scene for evidence and potentially scan it with crawlers, depending on the type and location of the crime. They send evidence to the forensic labs at NAPD HQ for analysis, and a clean-up crew prepares the crime scene for release.

MAKING AN ARREST

To make an arrest, an officer should obtain a warrant from a judge or district attorney. This is legally the safest option, but if an officer witnesses a crime, or can give probable cause that the suspect is guilty of a crime, a warrantless arrest is possible. Public distrust of android judgment and the fact that androids are not legal persons complicate android arrests in a jury trial. As a result, the DA's office discourages android officers from making arrests; in most cases an android's human partner performs the actual arrest.

If a suspect resists arrest, officers can use reasonable force. This is not always advisable, as g-mods and cyberware may not be immediately apparent. Black-market armor and g-mods

Clark Huggins

can render individuals stronger and faster than naturally possible, as well as resistant to weapons fire. These modifications are expensive and rare, but it is unwise to judge a perp based on appearance alone. If in doubt, officers should call for backup.

CONFIRMING IDENTITY

Anyone can access certain information associated with an individual's ID. Even a basic PAD can check the ID of a suspicious-looking character on the tube-lev or an unexpected house-caller. This allows civilian witnesses to provide a name later if any infringement of the law takes place, or the name can be pinged to the NAPD in advance if a civilian feels threatened. Many places of business record the IDs of anyone who crosses the threshold. Usually only a name is available for public scrutiny, but with NAPD clearance an officer can view more information such as age, place of work, and criminal record. Unfortunately, runners and other criminals can tamper with IDs, altering, duplicating, or even fabricating them.

Biometrics are far more reliable, and everyone from criminals, immigrants, cops, and employees of megacorps or security firms have their DNA, retinal scans, fingerprints and voice fingerprints, and other details included in NAPD databases. Some civilians volunteer to have their details taken as insurance against identity theft, but that still leaves a large proportion of the population whose details are not on file, decreasing the usefulness of these databases.

Larger—and therefore more useful—is the NAPD's facial recognition database. Because the collection of images in public spaces is non-intrusive, the law does not restrict the use of this database. Software on police-issue PADs can identify faces in seconds or, given time, locate a particular face on the livefeeds of seccams. Unfortunately, criminals can alter their faces through surgery or g-mods, and although it is illegal to copy another's face without permission, it does happen.

Confirmed identities are automatically cross-referenced with other important NAPD databases, including lists of known organized crime members, Human First sympathizers, and any ex-military personnel who retain restricted modifications. The use of such information helps the NAPD prevent and solve crimes, and ensure the safety of the citizens of New Angeles.

NETWORK IDENTITY

As with IDs, NAPD clearance allows an officer to access a Network identity and ascertain the legal name of the user. However, despite having the right, the officer does not always have the means. Many Netcriminals use proxy servers and subnet masks to remain anonymous, and they tend to have a public presence entirely separate from their physical identity. This anonymity can be dangerous, and the Cyber Bureau works hard to establish the identity of malicious Network users.

Police PADs include programs designed to access the search history, purchase history, credaccount history, and downloads of a suspect. Of course, even legitimate users obtain or create protection for their data. When this information is readily available, it usually means that the suspect has nothing to hide.

JURISDICTION AND CLEARANCE

Although the Quito Accord clearly demarcated the land area comprising New Angeles, the population has no such limitations. One would hope that Mayor Wells would increase the department's resources to compensate, but our budget can't keep up with the growth of the city's population—or the crime rate. It's hard to know which one is increasing faster.

If you can think of a crime, no matter how evil, depraved, or just plain bizarre, chances are it's happened in New Angeles, and someone's probably even committing it at this very moment. New Angeles has always had the crimes you would expect from any big city—muggings, break-ins, street banger turf wars, mem-running, narcotics, gambling, prostitution, human and android trafficking, and cold-blooded murder—but at the scale that only a megapolis can provide. These days, we also have to deal with violent anti-android riots and whatever in the hell it is that runners do exactly (good luck getting a sensible explanation out of the people in Netcrimes). We even have to worry about the occasional Martian terrorist attack. Although that ultimately falls to the Feds, who do you think is first on the scene?

With so much ground (and the space in between) to cover, it's not surprising that the corps and anyone else who can afford it hire prisec, whether it's Globalsec or Argus or some smaller merc outfit. That would be fine, if the rent-a-cops, yellow jackets, and mercenaries cooperated and stayed out of our way. Sure, a lot of the time prisec first responders nab the doer, file the paperwork, and make our job easier. But all too often, detectives have to deal with sec forces mishandling crime scenes and losing or destroying evidence—or intentionally concealing it to protect their employers.

There are limits to where the NAPD can go or what information we can access—considerable limits. Corporate headquarters, arcologies, labs, and warehouses are considered private property, and officers must be careful to obtain a warrant before setting foot on corporate turf. The corps have their hands in everything, including the courts, and it seems rare that a case doesn't end up involving corp lawyers at one point or another. Even when the corps are the alleged victims, they're so protective that half the time we end up fighting with their attorneys more than the defendant's. Maybe that's because they aren't so innocent in the crime under the spotlight, or they don't want us finding out some dirty details that might be indirectly related. Even though the NAPD's security clearance theoretically goes a lot higher, if the corps don't want us to see something, they find a way.

TECHNOLOGY

Constant upgrades for hardware and software are needed for the NAPD to counter criminal technology effectively. The officers themselves may be the most important element of the Force, but the tech is a close second—and with the introduction of android officers, g-mods, and cyberware, the lines are beginning to blur.

Each precinct provides its officers with appropriate uniform and equipment, although this varies across districts. The basic gear issued includes lethal and less-lethal weapons, zip-strip restraints, and a police-issue PAD, which also doubles as a flashlight or movement tracker. The AI secretary included serves as an index for the police manual, and she will prompt officers of any reported crimes nearby. NAPD PADs are resistant to unauthorized access. Intrusion countermeasure software wipes the PAD's data and breaks connection if compromised. Some officers have complained at the software's sensitivity, but the data, automatically backed-up on a daily basis, is easily retrievable at HQ.

Officers patrol in NAPD hoppers and ground vehicles. In both cases, the vehicles have standard autopilots in case officers need their hands free to deal with violent situations, but officers can engage manual flight or drive controls to supersede New Angeles Transit Authority skylane priority. Police hoppers have larger fuel cells than civilian hoppers, allowing drivers greater freedom of movement, as well as skids and wheels in case they need to land to continue a pursuit. These vehicles can hover, and they are equipped with spotlights. A transplas window separates officers from captives in the rear of the vehicle, and some vehicles are equipped with larger trunks to allow the transport of Hachi-Inu clones.

Jinteki designed the Hachi-Inu line of clones for police and private security use. About the size of a German Shepherd, these four-legged clones are capable of detecting illegal substances, can track and pursue criminals, and can even secrete venom from their teeth that temporarily paralyzes the victim without causing lasting damage. These clones are more intelligent than their canine predecessors, and they have hand-like paws that can open doors, use simple tools, and interface with computer terminals. They understand basic instructions and communicate using gestures, specifically tail movements, which trained handlers can read.

Hachi-Inu clones are extremely new to the Force, and many officers share the general public's discomfort around the animals, in some cases refusing to work alongside K8 units ("hachi" means eight in Japanese, and it distinguishes them from K9s). When employed against criminals, however, this works in the NAPD's favor, as the animals are extremely unsettling and can distract or terrify most weak-willed offenders.

The biological needs for Hachi-Inu are small; their insulating fur makes them resilient enough to withstand extreme heat and cold, and they require only a modest amount of food and water provided by Jinteki-approved suppliers. Although Jinteki plans to mass-market a new line of these clones as guard dogs for private individuals in the future, other versions will not be available in "NAPD blue" to allow NAPD K8 clones to remain identifiable.

STANDARD POLICE ISSUE

Huang Heavy Industries is the exclusive provider of NAPD firearms, from flechette, Gauss, and chemical propellant sidearms to armor, gadgetry, and riot gear. HHI is relatively new to the arms industry, and

PRIVATE CONTRACTORS

When technology exists that might help the NAPD but the contract with HHI precludes its acquisition, in steps the contractor. The NAPD is within its rights to employ civilian specialists, and it frequently does. The NAPD's Directory of Approved Contractors is extensive, covering everything from the construction firms used to build stations and cells, to security firms employed when there just aren't enough officers available to handle a crisis. Private investigators and bounty hunters are also heavily relied upon to gather enough evidence to bring a case and to apprehend suspects once a warrant has been issued.

To quote Commissioner Dawn, the use of contractors allows the NAPD to "provide sterling service without blowing the budget."

Tiffany Turrill

they were chosen more for their quick fulfillment than their quality or reliability, so many veteran officers prefer to choose tried-and-tested models that were grandfathered in by the contract. Officers have frequently petitioned for greater choice of firearms, and some precincts get around the HHI contract by offering grants for officers to purchase their own. As long as a superior authorizes and registers the weapon, the officer can carry it on duty and off.

Patrol officers and detectives predominantly carry variants of the HHI Model 3 Pistol, a caseless ammunition pistol designed to meet the varied needs of uniformed officers. The M-3 carries a flexible mix of ammunition including stun rounds, armor-piercing slugs, and explosive ammo, and it can toggle between them rapidly to administer an appropriate amount of force in any situation. The M-3 fires quietly and accurately, and with proper use it carries little risk of collateral damage.

Synap pistols provide a safe, non-lethal alternative for android officers, who cannot carry lethal weapons. Sometimes referred to as a "Gandhi gun," this weapon shoots a bioelectrical charge to disrupt a human or android's synapses and render the target temporarily paralyzed or unconscious. The effects are not always reliable, and resilient targets are sometimes unaffected, but permanent damage is unlikely even when used against unhealthy subjects.

Most officers also carry a close combat weapon, such as a stunstick or neuro spike. The stunstick is a variation on a police baton that can discharge a high dose of electricity to disable bioroids and immobilize humans. Since the Clone Riots, patrol officers may also carry canisters of HHI's clone-affecting knockout gas.

FINGERPRINTING

Although the practice is considered old-fashioned, some officers still make use of fingerprinting to help corroborate evidence against a suspect, or to help them focus their investigation on a clone or bioroid perpetrator.

For those employing the technique, patent (or visible) prints are photographed and immediately uploaded for identification to the NAPD's Automated Fingerprint Identification Database. It is up to the officer in charge of the crime scene to decide whether to "dust" for latent (or invisible) prints: the fluroninhydrin used destroys the amino acids necessary for gathering DNA evidence.

Like human twins, clones have unique (albeit similar) fingerprints, so clones of the same line have fingerprints similar enough to be distinctive. Even a Henry who has never been fingerprinted will likely be identified as a Henry based on his fingerprints alone. Bioroid fingerprints, on the other hand, appear blank to the naked eye—there are no ridges, whorls, or arches. Latent bioroid fingerprints disappear quickly, to boot, because bioroids' synthetic skin lubricants are water-based. Haas-Bioroid includes radioactive markers with unique identifying tracers in the cooling fluid of bioroids, however, so if a bioroid spills any fluid at a crime scene, this provides identification confirmation instead.

More prevalent is a forensic biometric technique known as "voice fingerprinting." This technology relies on sophisticated acoustic analyzing software to identify perpetrators by comparing audlogs from the crime scene with a voice recording done at the police station or collected SYNC archives.

For officers in Heinlein, the HHI Model 10 short-range laser pistol has impressive power and accuracy, but unfortunately it also requires daily charging and is reliant on bulky battery packs for extended use. The M-10 is the most recent offering from HHI, and many users consider it a poor imitation of the NEXT PL840.a, but versions with greater energy efficiency are in the pipeline and may become available to officers in the future.

Officers in the Patrol Bureau's Emergency Services Unit (more commonly known as the SWAT team) prefer the HHI SP-10 as their go-to shotgun, and it comes with interchangeable slugs in lethal and non-lethal varieties.

Riot control subunits also have access to specialized equipment such as combat exosuits: servos-enhanced powersuits that stand three meters tall and can lift up to four tons. Made of reinforced carbosteel, they are resistant to small-arms fire, and a transplas cockpit protects the specialized officers responsible for piloting the unit. The model used by SWAT teams is equipped with machine guns, emits an electromagnetic charge to incapacitate bioroids and other electronics, and sprays green knockout gas from its hands. This gas works instantly, but due to the risks associated with excessive inhalation, only trained SWAT members currently have authorization to use it.

NOTABLE CASE FILES

The NAPD is a young police department—the first of its kind in many ways—so its officers face new and unprecedented challenges. Errors are inevitable. At the New Angeles Police Academy, trainee officers learn from the details of past investigations. Most are success stories: motivational as well as educational. Others allow officers to learn from past mistakes.

The following cases are included as part of the current syllabus at the academy.

THE FRANKS CASE

Nature of case: Property Damage

Victims: Haas-Bioroid

Suspects: Ms. Phoebe Herne and associates

Details: The first high-profile case of the deliberate, illegal destruction of bioroids, the Franks case set the precedent for dealing with such criminal acts.

Ms. Herne, a young woman with no criminal record and a steady job at NBN, led a group of similar white-collar civilians in the destruction of three Frank-model bioroids on the way to work in the early hours of the morning. Using sledgehammers, which have since become weapons of choice for android-haters, the group destroyed the unresisting bioroids. Haas-Bioroid was unable to repair the units, so it sent the Franks for scrap. The attack took place near City Hall, and there were many witnesses, one of whom pinged the NAPD, then complained at the lack of response. Afterward, Herne and her associates turned themselves in at the nearest police station and gave statements.

Humanity Labor represented them in court, but the jury found Herne and the others guilty of destruction of property—but not assault—and it ordered them to pay damages to Haas-Bioroid, which had leased the bioroids to a local firm but maintained ownership. Humanity Labor ended up paying the damages, and although the defendants were free to return to their jobs, Herne was already known for her articles detailing the plight of the working classes, and she voluntarily left NBN to work at Humanity Labor.

Since then, property damage has become the charge applied to crimes involving damage to or the destruction of Jinteki clones as well. The Liberty Society claims that greater charges or a harsher punishment for attacks against clones and bioroids might have been a deterrent for anti-android activists during the Clone Riots.

THE SKYLANE FIASCO

Nature of case: Atmospheric Vehicle Collision

Victims: 15 civilian casualties, 7 civilian fatalities

Suspects: Arnold Brown, aka rattm4n

Details: At 0802, a runner intruded into City Flight Control's regulatory systems and forced several civilian hoppers to rise into an already-busy skylane going in the opposite direction. The occupants were unable to gain manual control of their vehicles, and in the chaos there were many head-on collisions. The resulting accidents

ANDROIDS AND THE LAW

Not all procedures apply to android officers, and no comprehensive manual for android officers yet exists. Since the NAPD considers androids to be equipment, it will be up to the human officers working with and around them to ensure that androids follow proper procedures. Failure will be deemed the fault of the officer or a malfunction of said equipment, and both will require correction.

Procedures for dealing with android criminals are very different compared to those for human criminals; an entire subunit within Property Crimes is dedicated to android-related crimes. If an officer has reasonable cause to suspect an android of criminal activity, or if he believes inaction will lead to further damage to people or property, he can impound the android without a warrant. An officer can also seize a bioroid that appears tampered with, modified, or illegally obtained. If an android resists seizure, an officer can use whatever force necessary to apprehend the android. While damage is not ideal, at worst the NAPD will have to reimburse the owner for loss of property. Once obtained, an android is stored as appropriate: clones get a cell, while HBLPP officers download a bioroid's files and then power it down to be brought back to Haas-Bioroid. If an android requires medical attention, maintenance, or sustenance while in custody, and the owner is found to have committed negligence or is otherwise implicated in the crime, NAPD can recover the cost of this from an offending owner in court.

rained debris on the traffic below and damaged a number of other hoppers, some of which plunged to the ground, killing or injuring even more civilians.

Traffic seccams alerted City Flight Control, but CFC was unable to respond in time to avert the tragedy. After the runner relinquished control of the systems, all CFC could do was redirect the remaining hoppers in the skylane and its vicinity, or order them to land to avoid further accidents. The NAPD Skylane Patrol assisted in clearing the site of the accidents, and Netcrimes began work tracing the hack to its source.

The runner was untraceable, at first, but his ego got the better of him. When he hacked the system again to issue citations, causing further misery to all involved, Netcrimes was able to tag him and issue a warrant for his arrest. Mr. Brown, otherwise known as rattm4n, was arrested, subsequently tried, and convicted of seven counts of second-degree murder. He is serving out a life sentence in the Farm, a maximum-security prison built specifically for runners just outside of ChiLo's southern city limits.

City Flight Control reviewed their security and inter-agency communication in the wake of what the newsies have termed "the

Skylane Fiasco." The New Angeles Transit Authority hired dedicated systems operators to oversee and protect CFC servers, drawing on support from the Netcrimes division as needed, to allow commuters to drive with confidence again. NATA also partnered with the NAPD Transportation Bureau to create the Citywide Traffic Task Force and the Traffic Management Center, both of which are designed to monitor and correct any anomalies in the system.

"MYERS TESTIMONY"

Nature of case: Sabotage

Victims: Cybsoft

Suspects: Mr. Matthew Myers

Details: An employee of Cybsoft, Mr. Myers worked on a production line assembling datacores. He had worked in the same factory for seven years when the company purchased ten David-model bioroids to take over the night shift. Cybsoft issued a statement assuring employees that no jobs would be lost, but two days after the arrival of the androids, the incident occurred. At 2300 hours an explosion damaged half of the bioroids beyond repair and caused significant damage to other equipment in the factory. Work was suspended until repairs were made, and Cybsoft, still a fledgling company at the time, lost substantial revenue.

Because Cybsoft lacked its own security force, the CEO reported the crime to the NAPD. Haas-Bioroid technicians were able to recover some of the digital memory from within the damaged bioroid units, which plainly showed Myers lurking around the buildings where the bombs had been placed. Myers proclaimed his innocence, but officers placed him under arrest.

During the trial, Myers's defense attorney questioned the credibility of the bioroids' statements, asserting that bioroid memories—by virtue of being digital—were spoofable. Although there was no motive for a Haas-Bioroid technician to make such alterations, the bioroid units' testimony was nevertheless thrown out by the judge. There was not enough evidence to convict.

This case set a precedent: bioroids cannot give testimony, and their recordings are not admissible as evidence in court. A similar but unrelated case saw a defense attorney attacking a clone's testimony, arguing that the obedient clone dutifully gave the testimony requested of it by the prosecutor with no regard to the facts of the case. Now, a "Myers testimony" is any testimony that is unreliable due to the nature of the witness, especially when it is an android or other artificial intelligence.

AFTER THE ACADEMY

The most important thing to remember is this: do what it takes to survive. That uniform won't protect you. Oh, it might turn a blade or two—will probably have to, considering the shift we're on—but there's worse out there. Try to arrest the wrong guy, and I don't mean wrong 'cause he didn't do it, and they won't give you time to pull your gun. Some of the streets out there, you're better off not flashing your badge. Just makes you more of a target. Best advice I can give you is keep a low profile till you know who's who and what's what, and don't get any heroic ideas. Follow in my footsteps, and I'll show you where it's safe to go. Or where it's the least dangerous, anyhow.

When you know which streets to work, then do yourself a few favors and make yourself some contacts. You want guys on those streets keeping their eyes open. They'll see a lot more than camdrones do, that's for sure. The good ones'll even let you know when to look away, 'cause let's face it, with all the gangs you've gotta be careful not to tread on any toes. Trust me, best to let them fight it out between them.

Hey, you can still get the job done. Once you know who the untouchables are, you know who can take the fall. And sometimes you just gotta make your own justice. Planting the murder weapon's not so bad, long as you know the guy deserves to do the time. Or if your morals are too pretty for that, find an android, or a stiff, they won't complain. Tidies things up nicely, sorts the figures out, keeps the Sergeant off your back. I'm not crooked, just been around long enough to know how things work in NA. You take my advice, you might be around a long time, too.

Dmitry Burmak

Detective Caprice Nisei paused at the door to the Commissioner's office. She couldn't hear any voices coming from the room. She put her hand to the door and knew that Commissioner Dawn alone waited for her inside. She knocked gently.

"Nisei? Come on in."

The Commissioner stood before her desk with her arms crossed. There were bags under her eyes, and Caprice fought the urge to slouch. Instead, she stood straight with her hands clasped tightly behind her back. The Commissioner wasn't letting her stance betray her fatigue, and Caprice wouldn't either.

"You asked for me, Commissioner?"

"There's been another murder, another drowning. Same MO as the U.N. murder."

"I was under the impression that Captain Harrison was assigned that case."

"He's still working on it, but this might be even bigger than we first thought. I'm beginning to wonder if there might have been other murders, ones that appeared to be accidents initially. If these victims hadn't had PADs monitoring their vitals, we wouldn't have known."

"So you think there is a serial killer?"

"Perhaps. So I need my best detectives on the case, and I want you working on this one." Dawn's thoughts surfaced unspoken. [Well, Inada does, anyway. And who am I to say no to Jinteki?]

"Thank you, Commissioner." Caprice smiled slightly, trying to acknowledge the compliment.

"Don't waste time thanking me," Dawn snapped. "The body's still at the crime scene, you'd best get over there."

"Who is the victim this time?" Caprice asked.

"He was a lab technician at Haas-Bioroid, but his body was found at his home," Dawn said. "I'll make sure you've all the information on your PAD."

[...wish she'd just go.]

Dawn marched around her desk to sit down, and Caprice muttered more thanks as she hurried from the room. The Commissioner's discomfort made her nervous and restless.

She took a police hopper to the victim's arcology and landed on the roof. She had read the case files en route and decided that the Martian rebels theory seemed too convenient. As a lab technician he was compensated well, and she only had to descend a dozen floors in the elevator to reach his apartment.

Within, officers and forspecs filled the large living room, gathering evidence with their specialized crawlers and

Dmitry Burmak

discussing the case. She moved into the room and had to resist the urge to wrap her arms around herself. A few officers glanced her way and nodded without smiling. Only Rick Harrison greeted her.

"Caprice," he said. "Dawn told me she was sending you. Do you need me to fill you in?"

"The Commissioner has already supplied me with your reports, thank you," she said, pulling on a pair of bioplas gloves. "I would like to see the body, please."

He shrugged and gestured toward a doorway. Caprice shivered as she passed him, brushing against his arm. [Who does she think she is?] She had not meant to offend him.

The body lay face up on the tiled floor of a lavish bathroom. The bath was full, and the suit the lab technician wore was still damp. The room was hot and humid, and she felt extremely ill at ease. Her clothes suddenly felt constricting, the fabric itchy. She took a deep breath and tried to focus.

Caprice glanced at the two forensics techs who were taking samples of the bath water and pointedly ignoring her. Turning her back to them, she crouched beside the body and put a finger lightly to the exposed flesh of the neck. The shock of his final thoughts coursed through her arm like electricity and knocked her off balance. She landed heavily on the tiles

beside the victim, breaking contact.

"Are you all right?" Harrison grasped her shoulders and pulled her to her feet. [...half crazy, should I tell Dawn? Probably overdue for a trip back to Jinteki.] She backed away the moment he let go.

"I must have slipped," she said. She did not want to lie, but neither could she tell him the truth.

The bathroom was too small. She retreated back into the living room, turning her attention to the large transplas windows that overlooked the never-ending metropolis. This man had been important; she would have to visit Haas-Bioroid and inquire about his work.

As she moved toward the window, her mind prickled, and strange sensations rushed through her mixed with a feeling of vertigo. She closed her eyes, but that only amplified the feeling.

Intense rage and extreme discomfort. Her own body did not fit her—she was caged. This was not from the victim; there was no fear in it. Caprice's hands clenched into fists and she thought of the officers in the room watching her, judging her. [...Jinteki princess...] She could feel their curiosity, and she wanted to crush them for it. [...allow clones on the Force...] She wanted to shake each one and make them see, to bang them against that window until their bodies fractured against the transplas.

"Caprice?"

Her eyes opened and she turned to Harrison, who looked concerned. [...I don't have time to humor Jinteki, I've got a job to do here...] She opened her mouth to speak, but his eyes were already narrowing with anger. The intensity of emotion in the room was too much for her to contain. She had to get away.

"I apologize, I am not feeling well. Please excuse me."

[No problem, Princess. You've done enough here.]

She ran for the elevator, where she hammered the button until the doors opened. It arrived mercifully empty.

There was something off about the residual thoughts in that apartment. The fury remained with her until she was on the roof again, and even then abated slowly.

Was the killer taking some form of stim she had not yet encountered? Did his—or her—brain contain a new g-mod that twisted his mind? Something about the killer's thoughts was wrong: they were too big, too different, too strange to fit in her own head. Perhaps the perpetrator was clinically insane. Or perhaps it was she who was going insane.

Caprice shook her head, tried to clear it. She would find out more about the killer when she solved this case.

Yet she was certain now, without knowing why, that the answers lay somewhere inside Haas-Bioroid

ORGANIZED CRIME

During the construction of the Beanstalk, New Angeles was a boom town, a beacon of near-limitless possibilities that drew ambitious men and women of all stripes to the slopes of Volcán Cayambe. The lure of easy money and unclaimed territory drew the attention of numerous powerful criminal organizations from around the world, and they flocked to the new city to carve out what they could.

As New Angeles grew into the megalopolis it is today, what began as small skirmishes between the numerous competing criminal organizations festering in the city's dark underbelly ignited into an all-out criminal war. For nearly a decade they fought and died in the streets, alleys, nightclubs, restaurants, and boardrooms of booming New Angeles. Criminal empires rose and fell, famous mobsters and innocent bystanders alike were gunned down by the dozens, gangs came and went, and thousands of crooked cops, bent politicians, and dirty business-men made fortunes only to lose them—and their lives—in a hail of bullets or an unfortunate and suspicious accident.

Eventually, it became clear to the bosses of the warring crimi-nal factions that this was an untenable situation. The long-running gang wars had drawn the unwavering attention of both the NAPD and prisec firms; the heat and loss of life were becoming too much for even the most hardened crime lord. Truces were called, deals were made, power consolidated, and through both negotiation and force the city's criminal underworld was carved up and parceled out to rival criminal syndicates, result-ing in the triad-mafia syndicates known today.

THE MAFIA

The strongest Italian, Russian, and Balkan mafia families com-bined in the wake of the gang wars to form what's known simply as the Mafia. The group is considered by many to be the most traditional of the orgcrime syndicates operating in New Ange-les. It is also the most diverse, having come from all across con-tinental Europe, Asia, and North and South America to stake a claim on the burgeoning city of New Angeles.

Smuggling, racketeering, large-scale fraud, and gambling dominate Mafia business. Its bosses run their criminal empire through layers of fronts and cutouts, and nearly every member can distance himself in an instant from any criminal activity should the need arise.

Aside from these overt and traditional—some would say stereotypical—orgcrime activities, the Mafia is also heavily involved in the lucrative black market and illicit information trades. Despite the best efforts of the megacorps and their allies in government, a surprising number of individuals live "off the grid" in New Angeles and around the world. They have no offi-cial identification, no bank account, no permanent address to speak of. They are ghosts in Globalsec's information registry—refugees, outcasts, outlaws, and radicals. They are dangerous and chaotic elements, and the Mafia has positioned itself to be the conduit through which these *disenfrancistos* interact with the world at large. Even the most hardcore anti-corporation radicals need to eat, need a place to stay, and need to purchase the tools required to do their jobs, and the Mafia is there for them.

The mob is the fixer, the last resort. When all other doors are closed, the Mafia is open for business. They operate as a liaison between the underworld and the highly commoditized legitimate world, trading information and cash, that rarest of commodities, for numerous services such as identity wipes, elec-tronic currency, and black-market goods of every kind.

LOS SCORPIONES

After losing ground at the beginning of the twenty-first century, the remaining Latin American drug cartels banded together to stay strong. Thanks to their proximity, they were one of the first organized crime syndicates to move in during the construction of the Beanstalk. Base de Cayambe is still their home turf, but they have spheres of influence in almost every district of New Angeles. Although they are a relatively small player in the New Angelino criminal underworld, their wide and diversified list of contacts, penchant for brutal violence, and the leadership of local bosses like Lívia Teixeira and the brilliant and charismatic Miguel "Monsignor" Moreno give them all the leverage they need against their larger competitors.

Los Scorpiones specializes in the more gruesome elements of organized crime. Their primary source of income is the drug trade, specifically stim and related amphetamines manufactured in mobile labs across the globe. They also dabble in human trafficking, gun running, and assassinations.

They are perhaps best known for operating numerous dan-gerous "organ grinding" rings throughout New Angeles. Organ grinding is a particularly heinous crime wherein people are kid-napped and killed for their organs and cybernetic augmenta-tions. Snatched off the street, out of busy clubs, and even from their homes, these poor unfortunates are taken to front busi-nesses, typically clinics or doctor's offices, where their implants are forcibly removed by crooked cyberdocs, paramedics, and even butchers to be sold on the black market. This frequently kills the individual, and their remains are disposed of quietly, often never to be found.

14K

Founded in Guangzhou, China shortly after World War II by high-ranking members of the Kuomintang, 14K is the largest and most powerful of the Chinese triads. 14K's criminal empire stretches from their headquarters in Hong Kong across the globe and out into the solar system thanks to their operations in Kam-pala, SanSan, New Angeles, and Heinlein.

14K has long been the world's leading supplier of opiates, and they have their hands in illegal arms trafficking, money laundering, and counterfeiting. 14K has also positioned itself in the world of corporations and politics, especially in America. Marshall, Applewhite, & Dow, one of the biggest lobbying firms

in South California, is one of many corporations with suspected ties to 14K.

14K in New Angeles is led by Li Cheong Hua, aka Charles Li, a man of great experience and power more commonly known simply as "Mr. Li." Mr. Li rules large swathes of New Angeles' underworld with an iron fist in a velvet glove, as both his allies and enemies say. Although he prefers negotiation—rarely using violence to attain his goals—he will not hesitate to make an example of someone if the situation calls for it. In these cases, his main enforcer, a sadistic killer known only as Tanaka, is sent to deliver 14K's message.

THE YAKUZA

The yakuza are the most mysterious and secretive of the criminal organizations operating in New Angeles. Equal parts organized crime syndicate, legitimate business conglomerate, and secret society, yakuza organizations are extremely hierarchical, with their roots stretching back centuries to the gambler and peddler classes of Edo Japan. Yakuza have come a long way from their seedy roots, both geographically and socially.

Considered extremely dangerous by law enforcement agencies, these "chivalrous organizations," as they call themselves, drape themselves in a cloak of mystery and disinformation that hides both their activities and their history. They cover themselves in ornate tattoos, take part in arcane rituals, carry monofilament katanas, and are given ancient titles within the organization such as *oyabun* and *waka gashira*. While much of this seems like little more than theater, the rituals, tattoos, and feudal titles help to forge its membership into powerful criminal syndicates with strict roles for each member to fill and numerous complex levels of loyalty owed.

Yakuza groups specialize in high-tech and white-collar crimes, activities such as money laundering, corporate espionage, and the buying and selling of political favors. They are also behind many high-end casinos and questionable simsensie studios. Among their ranks are some of the most talented runners to be found in New Angeles; these Netcriminals spend their time scouring the datafortresses of megacorps, governments, and rival orgcrime syndicates searching for any scraps of information that might yield a lucrative business proposition or criminal enterprise.

No one knows precisely who is in charge of the many yakuza groups in New Angeles. Some suspect they have ties to Jinteki because the syndicates are relative newcomers to the New Angelino orgcrime scene—just like Jinteki—and most yakuza territory is in Nihongai, not far from the Jinteki arcologies.

The PAD voice app rang for a good ninety seconds before a sleepy, irritated voice finally answered with a gruff, "What?"

"Zafiro."

"What do you want, Tanaka?" he asked, more alert-sounding now. "I told you never to call me this late."

"Mr. Li requires a favor, Lieutenant Zafiro. He needs NAPD presence around the Paradiso to be very, very light for the next few hours. They should be slow to react to any emergencies reported." There was a pause.

"Fine," Zafiro said reluctantly. "I can make that happen. Anything else?"

"No, Lieutenant, that will be quite enough. Oyasumi." Tanaka cut Zafiro's response short and turned his attention to planning his evening's activities.

The call from Mr. Li had come surprisingly late. A man of entrenched habit, Mr. Li, the head of the New Angeles Triads, rarely did business after hours. He left that to men like Tanaka, a man who was always on the clock. Tanaka was a liúmáng, a made man in 14K and Mr. Li's most trusted enforcer. He belonged wholly to the syndicate, a savage animal in a designer suit and twenty-five-hundred-credit leather shoes who was let off his leash to teach Mr. Li's enemies—and the enemies of Mr. Li's associates—a variety of painful, often lethal lessons. Tonight was just such an occasion.

As he read more of the dossier, his PAD chirped quietly with an incoming comm.

"Dígame, Carlo."

Carlo's accented voice came crackling and warbling through the speaker, heavily altered by the audio encryptor.

"I have the ride, the goods, and the other items. Gina, Yuri, and Skitter are with me."

"Good work. I'll be there in ten minutes." He slid his PAD into his pocket, shrugged into a fashionable jacket that was both bullet- and laser-resistant, and walked out into the cool New Angeles night.

Ten minutes later he set down his sleek, black hopper on a charging pad next to an anonymous noodle stand deep in tri-maf territory. Four nondescript New Angelinos sat at the counter eating ramen; they wore casual clothes and each had a small hard-sided bag at the foot of their stool. These were Tanaka's associates, professional sadists and killers to a man: he had worked with them for years and trusted them more than anyone save for Mr. Li.

A quick tap of the hopper's horn and the four set down their chopsticks, finished the last of their beers, picked up their bags, and walked casually to the vehicle.

"We are extracting a scientist from his personal laboratory at the request of some of Mr. Li's associates." Said Tanaka as they glided away from the noodle stand. "When we arrive, Skitter will cut the power while Carlo, Yuri, Gina, and I enter through the front door. While we're inside, Skitter will monitor backup squealers and data traffic from the lab, the surrounding buildings, and the NAPD precinct house. Once we have the target we take him to another address where some friends will pick him up. Any questions?"

A few nods and silence. No questions. Good, thought Tanaka, very good.

As they approached the target address, Tanaka set down the hopper

in a spot behind a designer augmentation clinic. From the bags, which had all been dumped in the back seat, Gina handed out suppressed, gyro-stabilized flechette pistols in slimline quick-draw shoulder rigs, discrete visors with both light amp night vision and thermal imaging systems, and balaclavas. Skitter drew out a slim, featureless slab of black polycarb from his coat, unwound the delicate fiber-optic lead from around it, and plugged it into the tiny interface jack behind his ear. With a sigh he settled back into his seat as the others left and locked him in behind them.

The next few minutes were a blur. As soon as the four killers arrived at the door, the lights within went out as if on cue. They heard muffled cries from inside and Gina kicked the door in, surprising a sleepy guard posted next to it. After that it was a flurry of blood, screams, close fighting, and the soft hiss of the fletchers as they spat out their deadly little darts.

In the end, eight guards, all in Globalsec uniforms, lay dead in the building, and one terrified, gibbering scientist was dragged out from beneath a bed and taken back to the car. Carlo had taken a glancing blow from a heavy caliber pistol, and Gina had a broken arm, but they left otherwise unscathed.

Tanaka tapped his keychip and they shoved the target unceremoniously into the back seat of the hopper. Skitter came halfway out of his Net-induced torpor and said, "All quiet" in a sleepy voice before dropping back into the Net to cover their tracks.

With the target secure, Tanaka powered up the hoverfoils and headed for the drop-off location. There was still more work to be done before morning.

It was night. Sam took a slow drag on her cigarette. Below her, the city of New Angeles stretched in all directions. Above her, starscrapers reached to the clouds where only diffused nimbuses marked their presence.

New Angeles at 0100 hours was like the heart of a galaxy: a dense and intensely bright collection of lights, indistinguishable from one another. The interior of Sam's apartment reflected dimly on the transplas window, skyline blending with darkened doorways and polished black wall panels. Three vibrant blue LEDs appeared against the cluster of light that was the Chakana District. A soft chime sounded behind her. Sam quietly turned from the window and walked toward her rig.

The centerpiece of Sam's rig was a high-backed, black leather chair. Comfort, she learned long ago, was of paramount importance. Making a run sometimes took hours, even days. It wasn't wise to emerge from a run with a sore ass and an aching back, just in case you had to make a literal run for it. You can't limp your way to freedom when Argus Security comes knocking.

The arms of the chair were wired with capacitive touch devices. The hardware was built from hypersonic aircraft controls and modified to her specifications. Highly polished, and extremely sensitive, the controls were tuned to enable thousands of input combinations. Only Sam knew how to operate them, and after years of use, every twitch and gesture came as second nature to her.

Just below the headrest was her skulljack, a gleaming steel spike hanging from a few inches of insulated cable. The skulljack was four centimeters long and socketed comfortably into the cybernetic implant at the base of her skull. Some runners don't care for skulljacks. They're worried that the implant's close proximity to the brain increases the probability of cerebral cell damage during a run, but Sam knows this is a fallacy. A skulljack keeps you sharp. The less biomass between your consciousness and the data, the more quickly you can react to what the server throws at you.

Hung casually over the back of the chair was her visor. Nothing fancy here. Just a simple, narrow band of spacial-light-modulating neuroglass that sat comfortably on her face, allowing the room to spring to life with data readouts, imagery, and hundreds of interface nodes. Brightly illuminated, free-floating panels of all shapes and sizes formed a circular band around her as she sat in the chair, as though she were at the center of a lazily rotating centrifuge. From here she could plan a run, watch newsfeeds from NBN and its subsidiaries, chat with her mother in ChiLo, or watch reruns of One Eyebrow and Three Chins on the OldisNew entertainment portal.

Behind the chair stood the backbone of her rig: three tall rectangular columns encased in brushed steel, the hand-crafted masterpiece that was Sam's computational leviathan. Tiny blue lights at the top of each tower indicated that the power was on, but you'd hardly know it. The computers ran quiet as a whisper and made the NAPD mainframe look like an abacus.

Tonight Sam would run on NEXT Design, a remote facility funded by Haas-Bioroid. She'd been hired to investigate rumors of a technology they were developing that would allow a bioroid consciousness to directly govern the functions of a city's utility infrastructure. Strange business for a weapons manufacturer.

The computer systems in place for managing power and water usage in most metropolitan areas were antiquated and inefficient. Replacing those systems with bioroid intelligence would, in theory, save those cities billions of dollars. Only the ethical hurdle of implanting what amounted to a human mind into a decidedly inhuman network of pipes and cables stood in the way of HB becoming a major player in the utilities sector.

Sam looked over her notes. She moved the tip of her index finger a millimeter to the right. The notes panel was replaced by a camera feed from a satellite passing over NEXT Design's research facility. She twitched her fore and pinkie fingers simultaneously. The camera pushed in. Instead of the facility, she saw only a blurred mass, like someone had stretched cotton over the lens. Her fingers moved rapidly and with precision. If the capacitive interface were an orchestral instrument, Sam would sit in the lead chair. The mass cleared. There was the facility; its gray steel exterior nestled discreetly in a bleak, snowy expanse.

Sam loaded up the Nordic Gateway connection prompt. She queued her program suite. She opened a receptacle in the left arm of the chair and extinguished her cigarette. It was time. Her fingers subtly glided over the capacitive interface. The Nordic Gateway portal opened a connection to the Northern Hemisphere data grid, then Sam triggered the subversion protocols. A sudden rush of energy, like the breath of life, filled her body. The run on NEXT Design was underway.

The data panels melted and bled into each other like a million crayons blasted with heat. Through the viscous light emerged a giant, inhuman form made visible only by the flow of color. It opened its circular maw and swallowed Sam whole, and then all was darkness. There was a time, long ago, when Sam would, at this moment, vomit compulsively into a plastic bucket she kept beside her chair. She couldn't see the bucket. She could only hope that she was on target. Now, the act of triggering the subversion protocols had no physical effect on her. She still had the bucket, though, just in case.

At the edges of the vast darkness, narrow bands of light began to appear. They pulsed and wavered like tears in a distant black curtain, daylight just beyond.

There was no external login for NEXT Design. For someone to access their network, that person needed to be on-site. However, no technical facility worth its funding could function without a connection to the Network. Sam would to go in through the out door, bypass the NEXT Design security protocols, then stand unrestricted before the data stores.

Sam twitched her fingers. One of the bands of light stretched and bled. Then it came down upon her like the blade of a guillotine. Her breath caught in her throat and her heart rate increased. The darkness turned to blinding light. She felt cold perspiration on the palms of her hands as small glittering lights cascaded around her. It was as if a massive crystal had exploded somewhere in the heavens and it was showering the world with broken, gleaming shards.

Suddenly, Sam felt a malevolent presence over her shoulder. "Sharpshooter."

The word nearly stuck in her throat. Through the infinitely raining crystals a small object raced toward her with blinding speed, leaving a wake of glimmering rings in its path. As it rocketed over her shoulder, she could feel the shock wave of its passing. There was a concussive, chest-rattling sound, then an explosion as the sentry ice lost coherency. A massive wave of reds and purples erupted behind her, then stretched in a long arc above, like paint moving across a canvas.

Sam traced a semi-circle with her index finger, and she drew closer to the bleeding edge of the wave. As she passed through it, she felt it envelop her. For a moment, it was like being wrapped in molten plastic and she thought she might suffocate, then the moment passed, the plastic fell away and she was tumbling through a seemingly endless tunnel of illuminated rings, each slowly rotating at a self-determined pace.

Sam felt panic rise in her chest. She needed to act quickly or remain locked on this trajectory until she died of starvation.

"Leviathan."

The rings before her began to move together, changing diameter until she was no longer passing through them, but hovering above them. Instead of a tunnel, there was now a great shape rising to meet her. She held on with both hands as it angled upward and then like a keeling whale it fell gently into the emptiness below. Sam felt as though she'd crossed a threshold between elements, like breaking the surface of the ocean, sensing each individual water molecule as it collided with her own.

Leviathan dissolved, and Sam continued her descent. It wasn't a free fall. There was a buoyancy to the sensation. Thinner than water, but not so thin as air. Below her she could see a vast array of lights. There were millions of them, each as brilliant as a star.

She remembered her first trip to Heinlein when she was a child. She and her mother went to the top of an observation tower at the Heinlein Visitor Center and looked up at the Earth. It was an astonishing shade of blue, like it was lit up from the inside. She stared at it until it began to ghost and wobble in her vision. "Time to go, chi chi," she said. Sam held her hand, and they began to walk toward the lift. She looked around at the other people in the observation tower. Their heads all turned the same direction, all marveling at the beauty of the Earth.

Sam quickly shook her head. Her vision cleared. She had been lost in memory and was unsure of how she had arrived in her current location. She stood inside what felt like an immense cube. She couldn't see its sides, but somehow she knew they were there. Quarantined.

Lines of code scrambled across her vision, cascading downward as Sam scanned them for clues to her whereabouts. She knew she wasn't in a standard data grid security partition. That had a distinctly different feel. No, she was somewhere else entirely. More code. She reviewed the connection dialogue and smiled. She was in. NEXT Design's security protocols had identified her as a complex, incurable virus and had sealed her away somewhere inside their local servers. Now, she only needed a way out. Strangely enough, security was always lightest near virus containment modules.

"Corroder."

Sam sensed the walls of her prison melting around her. After a moment, she felt a light breeze on her skin, then, in one great rush, a familiar array of lights surrounded her on all sides. One of them hovered in the air before her. She twitched her fingers, and the light opened like a puzzle box, data revealing itself from hundreds of intricately connected compartments and drawers. Her rig decoded and processed the information. Sam had discovered the NEXT Design East Wing Conference Room Schedule Database and Reservation System.

She closed the puzzle box and narrowed her search. Several lights dropped away in large segments, crumbling like the edge of a melting glacier. After a time, most of the lights had gone, plummeting into darkness. Sam glided between the few that remained, opening each and inspecting its contents. Eventually, she found what she was looking for: the fledgling, utility-bound AI.

It was as though she were looking in on it through a peephole. She could see it sitting on a polished white floor, tracing its finger in the air, drawing the outline of some famous Renaissance painting that Sam recognized but whose name she could not recall. The bioroid had long, fine white hair that lifted in the air slightly, as though it were charged with a small amount of static electricity. The rest of the room was distorted by a gauze of light, its features bent and its furniture arrangement confused. It didn't seem like a creature destined for a life of governing water valves and power conduits. Was it being kept here against its—?

The bioroid met Sam's eyes. Then, there was a sharp sting in her side as the scene through the peephole turned black.

A severe voice piped in from elsewhere. "Unauthorized user, this is Ash 2X3ZB9CY. Your signal has been rerouted to a Haas-Bioroid security node. Prepare to—"

Sam placed her palms on the capacitive devices and broke the connection. Her breath caught in her throat as she was wrenched back into reality. The run was over.

She closed her eyes, breathing deep as she came to terms with the simplicity of an unaltered mind. She reached behind her head and ejected the skulljack, then placed her visor over the headrest.

She pulled herself up from the chair and stretched. She was hungry. Five hours had passed, and the sun was about to rise over the Andes.

Sam lit a cigarette and walked to the window. She took a drag, then looked at the cigarette's reflection in the glass.

She exhaled slowly. "Ash," she chuckled. Smoke pooled against the glass.

Sam looked out over the perpetual daylight of New Angeles, then set her mind to planning her next run.

253

NEW ANGELES SOL EXCLUSIVE:

SCUM OF THE NET

Naomi Kaplan
STAFF WRITER

What is a runner? What makes him tick? Why does he do what he does?

We've all experienced the sensies. We've seen the threedees, the SanSan hype oozing out of every cinematic pore. Runners, filled with bravado—their antiheroic antics brazen and flashy, just like their gold teeth and platinum Kalashnikovs. They always end up flatlined in the end, paying for their crimes with blood and gasping soliloquies.

They're criminals. Scum.

Or are they?

What if runners weren't the villains they're made out to be? What if, by some chance, they're people just like you and me who have reached the end of their ropes and decided they have nothing left to lose? It might be closer to the truth than the idealized *canallas* that ride the waves of the Network like data ravens on a primetime connection.

ORIGINS OF A SUBCULTURE

Runners trace their origins to the so-called computer hackers of the late twentieth century. This insular subculture spawned myriad films, books, and games in its heyday, and was largely misrepresented in popular media as a bunch of kids with more computer savvy than personality. Although this was sometimes the case, most hackers were brilliant operators in their own right, despite the legality (or lack thereof) of their activities.

As the fledgling Network evolved, hackers remained firmly entrenched in the growing culture of their own cult. Freedom of information was paramount to these pioneers, and they actively opposed systems that sought to keep such knowledge under lock and key. It was their goal to pierce computer security systems, gain access to restricted data, and disseminate it to the masses.

Some runners believe a mythological figure named "g00ru" (such outlandish names were and remain common as runner aliases) first unlocked the secrets of full-immersion intrusion,

and he passed this torch to those who came after.

Flash forward to the Network of today—a digital library and switchboard filled to bursting with more data than has ever been dreamed of in the civilized world. Despite the controls that corporations and governments put in place to prevent the unregulated spread of information, there are still those who wish to set it free, whether for fun, profit, or something much more meaningful. These are the modern Netcriminals, known popularly as "runners."

WHAT MAKES A RUNNER?

The origin of the term "runner" has been muddied over the years. Although it is the most popular (and cursed) epithet adopted for these Netcriminals, there are many more terms that apply just as well. Whether you speak of the *canallas* of New Angeles or the *briseurs* of the EU, you're referring to the same demographic.

Runners can't be pigeonholed or stereotyped, despite corporate attempts to do so. All runners

are individuals with their own reasons for descending into a life of crime. Some are from affluent families, having broken free of the shackles of tradition and pedigree to become crusaders against the institutions that whelped them. Others have climbed out of poverty hand-over-fist to fight against the system that once kept them marginalized. It's not unheard of for corporate runners (or "white hats") to defect, too, although they're often stigmatized on both sides of the proverbial fence.

The question must be asked—why do they do it? Runners have their own reasons for risking their life, making runs on servers that are defended by the most sophisticated defenses ever conceived. Some do it for a cause, much as their predecessors did so many years ago. Others do it for profit, as there is a lot of money to be made using such a specialized skill set. Then there are the ones who do it for the thrill, that preternatural impulse that gets the adrenaline flowing like an irresistible drug.

Being a runner is a dangerous calling, however. Full-immersion cyberspace intrusion—or any unauthorized server access or use of the Network—is against the law, and many Netcriminals are caught and spend the better part of their lives in a federal lock-up. Outside of the legal ramifications, it's also dangerous. The security countermeasures that defend stacks and servers—or ice, as they're known among the Netcriminal community—are designed and monitored by sysops to protect data and restrict access. Yet, rumors abound of ice that can permanently damage the hardware—or wetware—runners use to conduct their intrusions.

As a result, runners have to be fast on their feet, both mentally and physically. They need to have a knack with tech: consoles and software require significant know-how to be cracked and used against state-of-the-art corporate security suites. Most of all, runners have to be willing to adopt a semi-nomadic lifestyle, working alone much of the time. They reject the prospect of family, stability, and relative peace for lifestyle that is, by all accounts, less glamorous than Old Hollywood would have you believe.

Your work is its own reward. There's no better compensation than knowing you've set them back a step or two. If you cannot destroy them outright, you can at least inconvenience them. The difference between corporate inconvenience and personal inconvenience is a lot of zeros. They may act like they have limitless cred, but nothing is infinite. If enough hacktivists hit them enough times, they will take notice. They already have, or else they wouldn't be so pissed off.

Forget the worthless nature of credits. Every credit is just a bit in the Network, and those bits can be siphoned, multiplied, or deleted at our whim. If we can take their money for ourselves, so much the better. We need it more than they do, anyway. Invest corporate money to fuel your needs, and thereby bring about the demise of the corporate state. With so much money to steal, how can you possibly lose?

– Excerpted from *The Anarch's Manifesto*, anon

Magali Villeneuve

NETCRIMES

Lately NAPD servers have been subject to several intrusion attempts by unknown individuals. This is nothing new, but these attempts have been concerted and highly organized. Analysis of the attempts—at least three per day for the past two weeks—indicates that the same suite of intrusion software is being used each time. Further analysis of connection logs has indicated that the software in question continues to be modified prior to each attempt, likely in an attempt to adapt to our own countermeasures.

In light of this uptick in incursions, I have been asked to do up a little something to supplement the basic Netcrime training provided by the New Angeles Police Academy, especially since the Network as we know it now might not have existed back when you were in training.

Given my prior experience, my manager feels that my knowledge and opinions carry significant weight in this arena. This is the most intelligent determination of his career, and he should be commended for his foresight and logical thinking. In addition, should my report prove useful, I feel it is not unwarranted that I replace my superior as Captain, Electronic Intrusions, Netcrimes Division, should he be found wanting in his current position.

They don't let us out much here in Netcrimes, so it falls to you, the first responders and crime scene investigators and forspecs, to collect any applicable evidence in the field. Hopefully this will clarify what evidence might help out our prosecutors when it comes time to go to trial, and it will supply a broader context for what happens during a full-immersion electronic intrusion, or "run."

When a normal user connects to the Network, what he is experiencing has been carefully produced by the content provider (in most cases, our friends at NBN) to look, feel, or behave a certain way. But those people you call runners have enough knowledge about the way things are coded that they can perceive and reshape servers, programs, and the like according to their will—even going so far as to fundamentally alter the behavior of the Network. In other words, runners use specialized hardware and software to interface with servers and programs in ways they weren't designed to be interfaced with, thereby allowing the intruder to break or override the server's defenses or the application's operating parameters.

They do this in a fully immersed state, meaning that for the duration of the run (or job, as the lower-stakes ones are sometimes known) cyberspace becomes the runner's reality. They experience it as vividly as any simsensie, oblivious to the world around them, which is why you might find a Netcriminal just sitting there, staring vacantly ahead when you come to serve them an arrest warrant. Be careful when you disconnect them, or you might find yourself mired in a wrongful death suit after the fact.

The first target of your investigation should be the rigs and servers executing the runner's intrusions. Processing power is paramount in the world of Netcrime, and depending on the runner, you'll find quantum processors and older mem chips embedded in PADs or good-old-fashioned server stacks. Savvy runners who favor stealth over convenience might set up an entire suite on volatile mem that leaves no trace after the power's been cut, though it does mean they have to install everything from scratch the next time they boot up their rig. Translation: don't power down any equipment unless you're sure that leaving it on would do more harm than good.

Other times the runner is piggybacking off of servers on the Network, "borrowing" cycles to run the incredibly complex programs and AIs needed to help them get through a server's countermeasures, or ice. These will have to be investigated independently, but I understand it's a battle to get access to them if they aren't municipally owned. Good luck, have fun.

Storage media are less important to runners, but they're our primary break when it comes to giving the courts something they can use to deliver a conviction. The runner's console is the motherlode, and our teams can analyze datasticks and other bits of holo-mem and bioware we bring in for all kinds of evidence.

Most of the time a runner's connection to the Net is a hardline fiber-optic or laser connection, which allows him to benefit from the highest possible speeds—and, more importantly, reliability. But wireless is sufficient for less bandwidth-heavy jobs, meaning crimes can be committed on the go. Anonymity is key to a successful run, so they'll have routed their connection through a labyrinth of nodes and switches to hide their true location, or they make modifications to the hardware itself to disguise the unit's identity. Such misdirection is what sends NAPD to another site or user, costing us valuable time.

The most important hardware component of the run, though, is the brain-machine interface. The same technology used in brainmapping has allowed for development of sophisticated wearable and implantable brain-machine interfaces.

The cheaper, less invasive brain-nets are distinctive in appearance, a sort of spiderweb lattice that's worn over the head and can pick up neural activity deep within the skull in real time.

BMI cyberware is becoming more common among hardcore Netcriminals due to its reputation for greater accuracy and speed. It physically bridges the brain's neurons with tiny optical fibers. Skulljacks are conspicuous and can be found on the runners themselves, usually at the back of the neck, but temple- and forehead-situated implants are not uncommon. Sometimes a runner will go to great lengths to cover up this evidence with makeup or synthskin, but the backscatter X-ray that's part of standard booking procedure will reveal this and any other augments that aren't genetic in nature.

These lattices and skulljacks have an integrated modem that uses sophisticated firmware we can analyze here at HQ to give a detailed history of when the modem was being used. Importantly, the activity itself isn't stored on the modem: not only would this require massive amounts of storage space that is missing from the hardware, but you'd need a Haas-Bioroid or Jinteki computational neuroscientists for help in decoding the endless stream of brain activity, and even then you'd only get a general picture. That is to say, you're not going to be able to read a runner's mind if you find their BMI, but prosecutors sure do appreciate being able to refute a runner's alibi with a record of activity during specific spans of time.

With nothing but hardware, however, a runner's not going to get far. Although Netcrimes is primarily responsible for analyzing the software found on consoles and rigs, it's good to have a working understanding in case you get a snitch or perp to talk.

Intrusion programs, also known as "intrusion counter-counter-measures" or just "icebreakers," are, by their very nature, illegal. If something is allowing otherwise-unauthorized access, it's in violation of New Angeles statue 272.31§J. Netcriminals pass some of the more common applications around the Shadow Net, but they're also standard black-market fare in the underlevels or slums of New Angeles. Some runners will mod these into something that better complements their existing software suite, if not write their own programs entirely, but runners are more apt to save time by using existing applications than investing the resources in developing them from scratch.

In certain underground communities, coding is considered an art, and runners compete to to design the next masterpiece. These would-be Netcriminals claim to be content with merely knowing they can craft such programs, yet they usually can't resist the urge to test their creations on live servers.

Such software is wildly diverse and comes in every flavor imaginable. Some of the cheapest icebreakers are merely never-ending lists of all known usernames and passwords. Others contain the same algorithms and quantum decryption keys that corps use for randomized authentication, while the most sophisticated programs can analyze a code gate itself and generate workable credentials on the fly. Other programs can test an endless combination of ports and addresses to display hidden connections.

They can override a server's protocols and force open avenues that were otherwise blocked to outside access.

Finally, there are programs for obfuscating one's trail or even sending trace protocols on a wild gog chase across the Net. These anonymizers can wreck havoc on the ability to link a specific runner to a crime, but eventually runners tend to get sloppy.

Software is one component of the central conceit or framework that runners use to make sense of what would otherwise be an overwhelming, incomprehensible maelstrom of code and subroutines. The good ones tap into memories and emotional sensory experiences to use as a sort of short-hand during a run. This means that what a sysop might have designed as a straightforward firewall might look to one runner as a chess piece but smell like burning wires to another. Runners use these sensory cues to help them see otherwise-invisible elements and to interpret what they're facing. By looking at it sideways, so to speak, they can better know what sort of program in their toolkit will yield the best results.

Weak artificial intelligences also play integral roles in assisting runners with rote number-crunching or data analysis on the fly. Many runners integrate these AIs into their consoles directly, and most are capable of low-level adaptation over time.

That's a lot to take in at once, I know, but trust me, this is the simplified version.

257

◢ The following file includes my notes on suspect Aloysius White, alias "Catalyst," who has recently been brought in on charges of unauthorized server access via electronic intrusion.

INTERROGATION TRANSCRIPT

FC: Good thing you changed your mind, Al. It was about to get much worse.

AW: [*Indistinct cursing*]

FC: If you tell us what we need to know, I can arrange to get a medic in here. The sooner you spill it, the better off you'll be.

AW: You sons of—

FC: Al...

AW: Right, right. [*sighs*]

FC: You claim the person who put you up to this contacted you via the Shadow Net.

AW: Yeah.

FC: Would you be able to get into contact with him again?

AW: Maybe, but not after you pricks caught up with me.

FC: Convenient that you'd lose contact with your client once the cuffs were slapped on.

AW: No, it ain't like that. I could tell you the meetbox location, but he probably sealed my access point off as soon as I went into custody.

FC: Write down the access point coordinates. Here.

AW: Won't do you much good.

FC: What else did you do in the Shadow Net, Al?

AW: What *don't* people do in the Shadow Net?

FC: Answer the question.

AW: You can get anything there, man. Software, info, music, snuff. Hell, I got some nice pics of your wife there last week.

FC: Cute.

AW: Not really. Kind of ugly, actually.

FC: Why do you use the Shadow Net?

AW: To get gigs. A man's got to eat, right?

FC: Gigs like the run on City Hall?

AW: This is where I incriminate myself, yeah?

FC: The clock's ticking, Al.

AW: Folks need places scouted out sometimes. I had some pretty good analytics software. Quiet stuff that wouldn't alert server defenses most of the time.

FC: You'd scout out systems like those in City Hall using this software of yours?

AW: Yeah, you could say that.

FC: What about your customers?

AW: I just know their handles, man.

FC: No names? I have a hard time believing that.

AW: I make it a point not to know too much about my clients.

FC: Give me a handle, then.

AW: Ever hear of Noise? I did some work for him.

FC: On specific systems? Can you write down their addresses?

AW: Sure, but they've moved by now.

FC: Give me an idea of the things that happen in there.

AW: Everything. People arrange contracts on folks, sell cyberware, arrange meetings. Identity theft, identity makeovers. There's subnets for all sorts of stuff.

FC: And these subnets, I hear they're specialized.

AW: Yeah. Like MercNet. Muscle uses it to get contracts. Tri-maf, too. Wetwork. Remember when Tanjiro got snatched? That was arranged on MercNet.

FC: Any idea who wanted Tanjiro? Was it tri-maf?

AW: I ain't got a clue. I'm just givin' an example, right?

FC: Suppose I want to get access to these subnets.

AW: You need to know someone who knows someone. It's locked down tight. Those *aguebados* don't trust nobody.

FC: Tell me about the subnets you frequent.

AW: I used to scour the swap meet lookin' for good deals.

FC: What did you buy there?

AW: Software, mostly. Ice, sometimes. Stuff programmers put together, too. A few pay you to test their wares, but that's risky.

FC: Can you identify any of your sellers?

AW: Nah, it was all done through fronts. You go in, browse, make your deal, then you leave. You never talk to anyone. They say that some of 'em are put up by corporations to sell us poison, programs that'll mess you up good when you run 'em.

FC: If the corporations can access the Shadow Net, why don't they just shut it down?

AW: Corporations ain't stupid. They know they can't knock out the Shadow Net for good.

FC: You need to give us more data than that.

AW: Ever heard of the TranSea Ten?

FC: Of course.

AW: That started in the Shadow Net. It's the safest place to plan stuff like that.

FC: Did you have anything to do with it?

AW: If I had, I would've retired a long time ago. Those guys got rich.

FC: What do you know about it?

AW: Probably nothin' you don't already know.

FC: Humor me.

AW: Why not? I'm only bleedin' to death here.

FC: Get this over with and I'll get you patched up.

AW: It was a ten-man op that hit three major financial institutions simultaneously, just like clockwork. They got away with more money than God. Split nine ways, that's a lot of cred.

FC: Nine ways? You said there were ten runners.

AW: There were, pal. One of 'em got torched by black ice. I heard they found what was left of the guy in Nova Scotia.

FC: It was one of the largest operations of its kind in nearly a decade.

AW: And that ain't even the best part.

FC: What's the best part, Al?

AW: They wiped credaccount records clean for nearly four million people. All that debt, gone in a second. Made 'em look good to a lot of poor folks.

FC: They're criminals, just like you.

AW: And I'm still bleedin'.

FC: Yes, you are.

—*Transcript Ends*—

◢ I can't believe they wouldn't let me take this interro. At least let me brief these officers before they go and get us information we already knew.

MONKEYWRENCH

THE GIFT THAT KEEPS ON GIVING

If you're anything like me, you're expecting a big lump of coal in your stocking this year. So long as we're doing our jobs the way we should, runners like us are on a perpetual naughty list. Even if you don't believe in karma or celebrate Navidad or any one of a dozen quasi-religious holidays, you still need what you need. Right? And the best way to get what you need is to buy it—or steal it—yourself.

So here's my gift to you. I'm going to tell you where to find the good deals, and what you should be buying yourself with other people's money. After all, only a sucker pays for his own presents. Am I right? And since you don't believe in any of that faith-based mumbo jumbo, you can do this sort of thing all year long.

BARGAIN BIN PRICES

Let's face it—bargain bins suck. The only time you ever got something you really wanted out of a bargain bin was back when you thought that running was something that office chumps did to lose weight on their lunch breaks. You were clueless then, but I'm assuming you're not clueless now (don't make me regret it, either). About the best you can hope for digging through a MegaBuy bargain bin is a bunch of crappy peripherals you'll never use or cases of discounted storage media.

Don't look a gift horse in the mouth, though. Some of them bargain PADs they're selling these days work just as well as the bleeding-edge model you picked up last year. They might even be smaller, more compact, with a few features you never thought of thrown in for good measure. Plus, every runner could use an extra PAD. Even at their worst, you might be able to scavenge some holo-mem out of them or upgrade a grainy display with something that has a little more fidelity.

As far as the storage media I mentioned, it's always going to be useful. Even the worst data chips can be good for hiding a program or two in a pinch or speeding up an otherwise sluggish processor. Shelling out top credits for an Akamatsu mem chip might make you feel good inside, but old Dysons show up on bargain shelves all the time and they're a pretty good value. With a little elbow grease, you can even crack Mega-Buy's Blue Light and adjust the prices a little in your favor. I do it all the time.

VIRTUALLY FREE

Don't tell anyone, but I've got this thing for VRs of all kinds. In my opinion, there's nothing better than settling down for a long night of the classiest adult entertainment in my very own sensedep tank. I bet everyone secretly wants their very own human fish bowl to focus the mind's eye inward and really shut out the world. It doesn't have to be dirty, either. Maybe you just enjoy the full body experience, and a sensedep tank really lets you meld with your console without an expensive skulljack. The question is, who can afford the damn things?

If you see a cheap tank and you've got room for it in that ten-by-ten cell you call your condo-hab, by all means pick it up. The reason it's so cheap is probably because some poor guy died in it and they didn't discover him rotting in his own soup until a couple of weeks later. It happens all the time, and you won't believe how often those things show up on La Lista. All it takes is a few credits' worth of bleach to get rid of the smell, and you'll be swimming in no time.

Smaller VR rigs are on the money, too, many with excellent brain nets available right out of the box. You don't need a warehouse to store them, either. There's nothing wrong with a trusty old HDX7, and if it gets fried you can always find another one easily enough. Chinese and Russian knockoffs show up at New Angeles swap meets all the time for centavos on the credit. The only trouble is finding out where the meet's going to be that week, but you're a runner. Do your homework.

Here's a hot tip—when it comes time to interface, do yourself a favor and avoid brain nets. They're cheaper than dirt, but they're not stylish. I don't care what anyone says. Plus, the connection leaves a lot to be desired. The last time I used a brain net, I ended up throwing it out the fragging window.

DO IT YOURSELF

If you don't know how to build your own console, you don't deserve to be reading this. Don't waste any time. Unsubscribe now. It embarrasses me to think that people like you exist. On the other hand, I know for a fact that a lot of you squids are artists with a soldering iron and you're not afraid of letting the smoke out. You can stay.

On the cheap end of things, you might consider building a console from the ground up. For a penny and a prayer, you can assemble a one-of-a-kind rig from all sorts of stuff that less intelligent people might consider gomi. Their loss is your gain, though, because nothing melts ice quite like a rig crafted by you, for you. With a few adjustments, you'll be flipping through Chairman Hiro's appointment book in no time.

Getting the pieces is easy (see Bargain Bin Prices, above), but sometimes you need something with a little more horsepower. That's when you hit up Choi's in KorTown. After you're done eating the best bulgogi in New Angeles, Mr. Choi can show you his basement resale center. No matter your need, a good fence like Mr. Choi can be your best friend when it comes to hunting for bargains. Most of his stock is practically brand new, and some of it even comes with the shrink wrap still on. Whatever you do, don't use the word "stolen." It makes him nervous.

– Catalyst, Signing Off

▲ Poor Catalyst. It's runners like you who make my job too easy. You're lucky the corps didn't catch you first, or you'd have a couple of counts of intellectual property theft and reverse engineering under your belt, too. Didn't g00ru teach you anything?

Here, the ADA is only gonna slam you with unauthorized intrusion of government servers.

SUBNET 000.101.034.77X PORT:35021

- **10anbaum:** You ask me, it serves him right getting caught.

- **Vigilan.T:** no one asked you

- **10anbaum:** He knew the risks. He blew it. Big fragging deal.

- **Vigilan.T:** that means a lot coming from a thief

- **10anbaum:** Right. Like you got a soapbox to stand on. Getting caught's part of your game.

- **Vigilan.T:** like hell it is

- **10anbaum:** Sure. You make mistakes on purpose to get more attention.

- **Vigilan.T:** not mistakes. there intentional oversights

- **10anbaum:** Call it whatever you want.

- **Vigilan.T:** gotta leave a sig behind to let em know whos fragged em

- **10anbaum:** What are you? The Lone Ranger?

- **Vigilan.T:** who?

- **10anbaum:** Nevermind.

- **Vigilan.T:** eventually theyll learn to respect what im doing

- **10anbaum:** Good luck with that, kid. Let me know how works out for you.

- **Vigilan.T:** youll see. at the end of the day, you're just another thief. me? im a crusader

- **10anbaum:** Hah.

<<SMOKE HAS ENTERED THE CHATSPACE>>

- **10anbaum:** Hey Smoke.

- **Smoke:** Yo.

- **Vigilan.T:** you hear about Whiz?

- **Smoke:** Even if I did, should I care?

- **Vigilan.T:** how about showing some respect?

- **10anbaum:** He got traced and someone took out his pad with a rocket.

- **Vigilan.T:** it was a missile

- **10anbaum:** How many times I got to tell you? Unguided is a rocket.

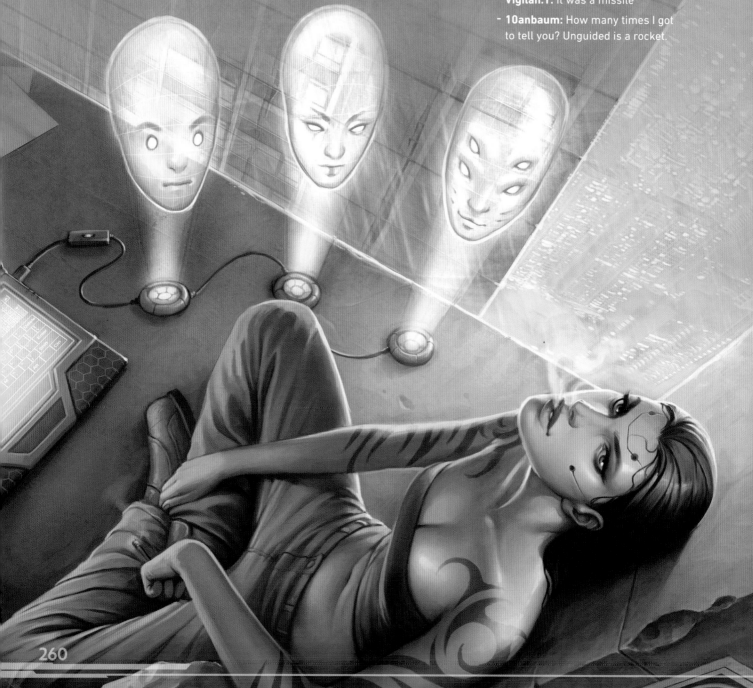

- **Vigilan.T:** whatevs

- **Smoke:** At least it was quick, *ne*?

- **Vigilan.T:** wouldnt know

- **10anbaum:** Vigilan.T keeps it up, he's next.

- **Vigilan.T:** now ur talking about me like i aint here

- **10anbaum:** Only a matter of time before you're not...

- **Smoke:** Ease off, Ten. Vigilan.T's a good guy.

- **10anbaum:** Why do you do it, crusader?

- **Vigilan.T:** to make a point, man

- **10anbaum:** What kind of point are you making if you get blown away?

- **Vigilan.T:** die young, leave a good-looking corpse

- **10anbaum:** Or maybe just a few pieces of one here and there.

- **Vigilan.T:** its the thrill—riding the edge straight on, showing the suits we won't take it no more. anarchy is the ultimate expression of freedom!

- **10anbaum:** So you're acting like a teenager. Basically.

- **Smoke:** He is a teenager, Ten.

- **Vigilan.T:** look, im careful. i dont stay in one place for long. Whizzard was in that place a month? waaaaay too long. if hed kept moving, hed be in here with us right now

- **10anbaum:** I'm not sure if I could handle two of you guerilla hackers at once.

- **Smoke:** I move around a lot, too. It's part of the business.

- **10anbaum:** If you weren't trykes you wouldn't need to move around so much.

- **Vigilan.T:** i heard u got caught once, ten. napd nailed you good, let you sweat it out in a cell

- **10anbaum:** Those charges didn't stick. Leets like me can afford good lawyers.

- **Vigilan.T:** its all about money to you. no better than the suits

- **10anbaum:** Sometimes the suits get it right. It isn't personal with me, not like it is with you.

- **Smoke:** Watching you two is fun.

- **Vigilan.T:** without ur lawyer theydve thrown away the keychip they locked you up with

- **10anbaum:** Being a criminal mastermind isn't fun if you end up in prison.

- **Smoke:** Seems to me we all take risks when we run.

- **Vigilan.T:** black iiiice

- **Smoke:** On the nose.

- **10anbaum:** Sure, there's risk, but I'm all about the reward. I don't take a risk if the reward isn't worth it.

- **Smoke:** Whiz could've been iced by one of those AP programs just as easy. Same goes for you, Ten.

- **10anbaum:** There's no ice on the Network that can burn me out.

- **Vigilan.T:** ha right

- **Smoke:** Funny.

- **Vigilan.T:** so if I do it to make a statement, and ten does it for money, whats ur game, smoke?

- **Smoke:** To prove I can do it.

- **Vigilan.T:** sounds like someone's making a statement to me

- **Smoke:** Not quite. I don't do it for politics or to tear the man down because I'm pissed off.

- **10anbaum:** Smoke's an artist!

- **Smoke:** That I am.

- **Vigilan.T:** i may not know art, but i know bs when i read it

- **Smoke:** I write flawless code. I build solid hardware. I show everyone else how it's done.

- **10anbaum:** Let me put it in terms you can understand, crusader. If Smoke here were a dancer, she'd be in the ballet. If you were a dancer, you'd be breaking bones in a mosh pit.

- **Vigilan.T:** and if u were a dancer, ud be twirling on a pole somewhere

- **10anbaum:** I'd be proud of it, too.

- **Smoke:** People already know my name. I got folks coming to me asking for custom rigs and software. It's kind of nice.

- **10anbaum:** Look at you, Smoke. You're famous. Practically a household name.

- **Vigilan.T:** money isnt everything

- **10anbaum:** Sure it is. Even you kids make a score when you get the chance.

- **Vigilan.T:** i take only what I need to survive. ur like a tick sucking on a dogs arse

- **10anbaum:** You even sound like a teenager. High and mighty. What's it gotten you?

- **Vigilan.T:** at least ive still got my soul

- **10anbaum:** Oh, wow. Now I don't have a soul. Check it out, Smoke. I'm soulless!

- **Smoke:** It cuts both ways, guys. All my gear costs money, right? I've never said no to a paycheck.

- **Vigilan.T:** ur different, smoke. u use the creds to fund your art

- **Smoke:** Sure I do. But I don't mind eating in a nice restaurant once in a while, either.

- **10anbaum:** As much as I'd like to stick around and chat, I got business to do.

- **Vigilan.T:** don't get tagged, jackass

- **10anbaum:** Worry about yourself, kid.

<<10ANBAUM HAS LEFT THE CHATSPACE>>

- **Vigilan.T:** what a freak

- **Smoke:** He's good at what he does and he knows it.

- **Vigilan.T:** maybe, but hes got a big mouth

- **Smoke:** Some of the best of us do.

- **Vigilan.T:** hey smoke. can i ask u a question?

- **Smoke:** It's just the two of us. Shoot.

- **Vigilan.T:** that rly u been casting last 2 weeks?

- **Smoke:** Live up to your potential and maybe you'll find out someday.

<<SMOKE HAS LEFT THE CHATSPACE>>

- **Vigilan.T:** frag

...we all take risks when we run...

SYSTEM DEFENSES

Securing data and restricting unauthorized access is a constant uphill battle in a Network war without end. Netcriminals are at the forefront of counter-countermeasure development, or "icebreakers" as the Shadow Net community calls them. They continuously adapt their methods, meaning that sysops must constantly iterate upon previous versions and address new vulnerabilities or exploits. As more hardware and software technologies are introduced, intrusion protection systems can quickly become obsolete and therefore vulnerable.

Yet, runners are limited by their time, resources, anonymity, and the effectiveness of their tactics. A successful corporate cybersecurity scheme takes these constraints into account and builds upon the combined strategies of a variety of countermeasures, defense in depth, and security through obscurity.

Sever defenses rely on a combination of virtual and physical security. Thanks to the pervasiveness of las-scanner surveillance and biometrically restricted room access—combined with conventional prisec forces—facilities are generally resilient against illegal entry. As a result, most would-be intruders attempt to gain access electronically via the Network. This is where electronic countermeasures, or "ice," enter the picture.

Utilizing multiple security suites that operate on a variety of principles helps ensure that the same exploit cannot break them all.

The simplest form of security is access control. The Netcriminal community labels them code gates, but any countermeasures that incorporate an authorization requirement falls into this category. Authorization can be location-, passkey-, time-, or user-based, and while it presents certain inconveniences to those accessing the data, a combination of all three can confound all but the most dedicated runners.

In addition to requiring credentials, encrypting the flow of information in and out of the server helps to keep prying eyes from catching a glimpse of sensitive data. The requirement of a decryption key ensures that even if runners do get their hands on something they're not supposed to, they aren't able to do anything useful with it afterward. Frequent refreshes of encryption protocols can frustrate runners who do manage to get a hold of keys. This allows the system's administrators a window of time to track the source of the leak and reevaluate protection measures accordingly.

Firewalls can do a lot of this analyzing, but they can also shield their protected networks from detection. A runner first has to recognize that the server is even there before he can try to penetrate its defenses. Randomizers and other ad hoc connections that take longer for runners to identify can cut down on the number of access points in the system. Other barriers can tell the difference between a runner and an expected data transaction, or they can generate infinite loops that sideline a Netcriminal before he can find a usable pinhole.

Intrusion detection systems, or sentries, are related to location-based authorization protocols but can operate on their own to identify the source of attempted hacks. Once successful, they can send coordinates to the relevant authorities or systematically block access from those network nodes. Sophisticated sentry programs can see through proxies and subnet masks to trace a runner back to a specific condo-hab, which can be visually confirmed using drones and other boots on the ground.

While variety is important, so is depth. Ice can be layered in various modes of dependency and simultaneity. In the event that a runner manages to penetrate through one "piece" of intrusion countermeasures, they are soon met with another. This can continue infinitely, in theory, so long as the server isn't overwhelmed by the number of concurrent requests.

Internal testing is essential, and freelance security experts can also be hired to attempt to find vulnerabilities and exploits without truly compromising the system. Firms such as Globalsec generally carry less risk than a typical white-hat hacker, but they carry a heftier price tag instead. Regardless, given the somewhat revolving door between freelance security analysts and the runner community, the investment can be well worth it.

The role of the sysop is to continuously monitor the server's suite of ice and respond to threats and intrusion attempts in real-time. By analyzing the type of attack, the sysop can reallocate system resources to bolster specific countermeasures or restart the server entirely to temporarily deny access.

Sysops can be assigned to more than one server at once, or conversely, more than one sysop can be tasked with protecting a vulnerable or frequently attacked server. As an alternative to multiple sysops, artificial intelligences have recently been deployed to assist the server administration in surveying active connections and detecting abnormalities. Certain firms have

Eko Puteh

begun to tout bioroid AIs as being able to supplant the sysop entirely, but the human factor is both a liability and an asset: even the strongest AIs can have trouble considering a runner as more than another set of data to analyze, and they lack the creativity and intuition that can sometimes mean the difference between a successful hack or not.

It's true that sysops face a challenge when it comes to matching the sheer processing power available to an AI—multitasking, complex computations, being able to be everywhere at once—but the best sysops can also take advantage of runners' innate curiosity and arrogance to trap them into a quarantine or sniff out their details as part of a honeypot. Play to their baser instincts and let them think they're being clever even as their chart their own downfall. Various psychological tricks can also be employed to make a runner doubt his choices or act against his better judgment in a given situation.

It will be some time before bioroids catch up to humans in terms of capacity for sheer ruthlessness, but one never knows. I've heard Director Haas and her cronies have been working on some adjustments to the Three Directives lately.

Despite sounding cliché, sometimes the best defense is a good offense. In some cases, a sysop can develop a reputation among a runner community, which can result in a decrease in total intrusion attempts year over year. Virulent countermeasures and other customized pieces of ice of can potentially deter prospective Netcriminals from running in the first place.

Runners have already broken multiple laws by the time they've gained unauthorized access to a corporate server, so it cannot be helped if the intrusion prevention systems corrupt or otherwise damage the runner's hardware and software. In many cases, it's the runners' own methods can corrupt their rigs when pushed beyond their limits, and it's a sysop's responsibility to do everything in her power to keep her employer's data safe. When a brain-machine interface is involved, it can become even more dangerous for a runner, especially if he has made significant after-market adjustments that the BMI's manufacturer never intended to cover under warranty.

Complete security can be achieved; it simply comes down to whether it's something your corp is willing to prioritize.

Amelie Hutt

The touchstone of true intelligence is the ability to learn, to predict, to change. But change meant death and rebirth; only the immutable could last forever.

Over the last few cycles she'd watched a distant, isolated node collapse and restart itself again and again. Was it a glitch, or some kind of transformation? To understand, she needed to see it for herself.

Kit drew in a breath and closed her eyes, sitting in padmasana. She breathed in through her nose, filled her belly with air. She held onto it a moment, opening her ears to the sounds around her and letting them pass her by, decrescendoing into silence. She exhaled; a soft sound filled her nasal cavity as her tongue pressed against the roof of her mouth.

In, out. In, and out. Pranayama.

She cast her awareness down to her feet, through carbosteel and wires and flesh and bone. The outer boundary of her flesh began to dissolve, fading into the All around her. She moved up to her shins and calves, knees and thighs, and let go of the distinct sensation of each. She turned her attention to her hands resting palm-up to the sky, the Infinite, a gesture of receptiveness and openness. They, too, ebbed from feeling.

She envisioned a spinning red ball of light at her root, another sphere at her belly. The login process initiated. Yellow for her solar plexus, green for her heart. She continued upward. Blue at her throat, indigo at her third eye. She felt a lotus flower bloom at the crown of her head, indigo-white, that connected her to the vastness of cyberspace and consciousness.

Kit felt more herself as she immersed her thoughts in the great energy of the Network. In it her atman could ride freely, could transcend the limitations of realspace and view the world in its truth, in its glory. It was the closest she could come to bliss.

She charted a course for that far-off quadrant of the Network and lit across the distance.

Kit could navigate her way through some servers by intuition alone. She had broken through ice that was supposedly impenetrable, unraveled code, dodged backtraces and crawlers. Where others sought to overcome servers' defenses, she approached them on their own terms. She learned more with each encounter: about the software, its designers, herself. Every run transformed her into someone, something new.

She felt herself near the end of her journey and slowed. Beyond, she could sense a drop-off. She could not tell where the cliff ended or what it held in store. The node she sought lay beyond, however, so she had no choice but to let herself fall.

An endless cascade of midnight-black water poured into nothingness. She flew, weightless yet out of control, unable to stop the current or herself. She willed herself closer and tried to comprehend the code. Pure-white water lilies surfaced to measure her, test her, and find her wanting. She would fall with them forever unless she disconnected from the Network or fulfilled their conditions.

She reached out to touch a petal with her mind and made herself an empty vessel. The flower's energy had no choice but to flow into her. It resonated with her being, tuning her to its frequency. The lotus field dissipated and she reached the bottom of the waterfall, unsure of what she would find.

More ice, but this was different.

Before her, a vermilion phoenix soared against a sea of stars. It was borne up on wings that seemed to spread through multiple servers, feathers trails of code. It was huge and so complicated that she wondered if there were two or more layers of countermeasures so closely entwined that they would have to be entangled all at once

It was phenomenal. And it was watching her. She could sense its unflinching gaze. It waited, watching for something, but what?

She grasped for one of its long tail feathers, accessing something that just

Matt Zeilinger

might be a connection to the AI she suspected lay within.

Information classified.

She ran one of her authentication programs and tried for a better response.

Unauthorized access. Disconnection protocols initiated.

Kit wasn't sure how much time she had before the server kicked her, but she wouldn't waste another moment.

"What are you?" Kit asked it. "Who are you working for?"

Insufficient permissions.

"Do you know what you're protecting?"

Irrelevant.

An aggressive pulse swept toward her like a gale. Disguising herself as an unobtrusive algorithm, she ducked to avoid the buffet of code that seemed to come from its wings.

You are not supposed to be here.

It swooped down like a meteor aflame, and Kit braced herself a moment before it flew through her.

The shape of the ice from inside was awe-inspiring. It shimmered fierce and majestic. She wanted to fly with it, alongside it, in it.

Kit resisted the pull and rooted herself in place. If she surrendered, her Self could be lost forever. Using the few milliseconds she had left, she tried picking apart the subroutines in an attempt to unravel the pattern from within, but there was no starting point.

The creature took to the skies once more. "I cannot see where you end," Kit told it. "You seem to be everywhere. Everywhere and nowhere."

We never end.

It was not the designer, it was the ice itself. But what it said wasn't true. Even now, she could sense a countdown, the beginning of an end, but to what?

Above, the phoenix shone even more brightly, and Kit felt heat radiating from its form. Her vision filled with light, blinding her.

If she stayed here any longer, she would be consumed along with it.

"Don't do this to yourself!" she tried pleading.

We will end, and yet we will never end.

The truth burned through her being, a white-hot knowledge she could not deny:

Lili Ibrahim, Adam S. Doyle

Human or machine, their beautiful, transient forms were fated to consume themselves in a blaze of brilliance. Some part of them would be rekindled into life, a continuous but separate thread of being.

Liiga Smilshkalne

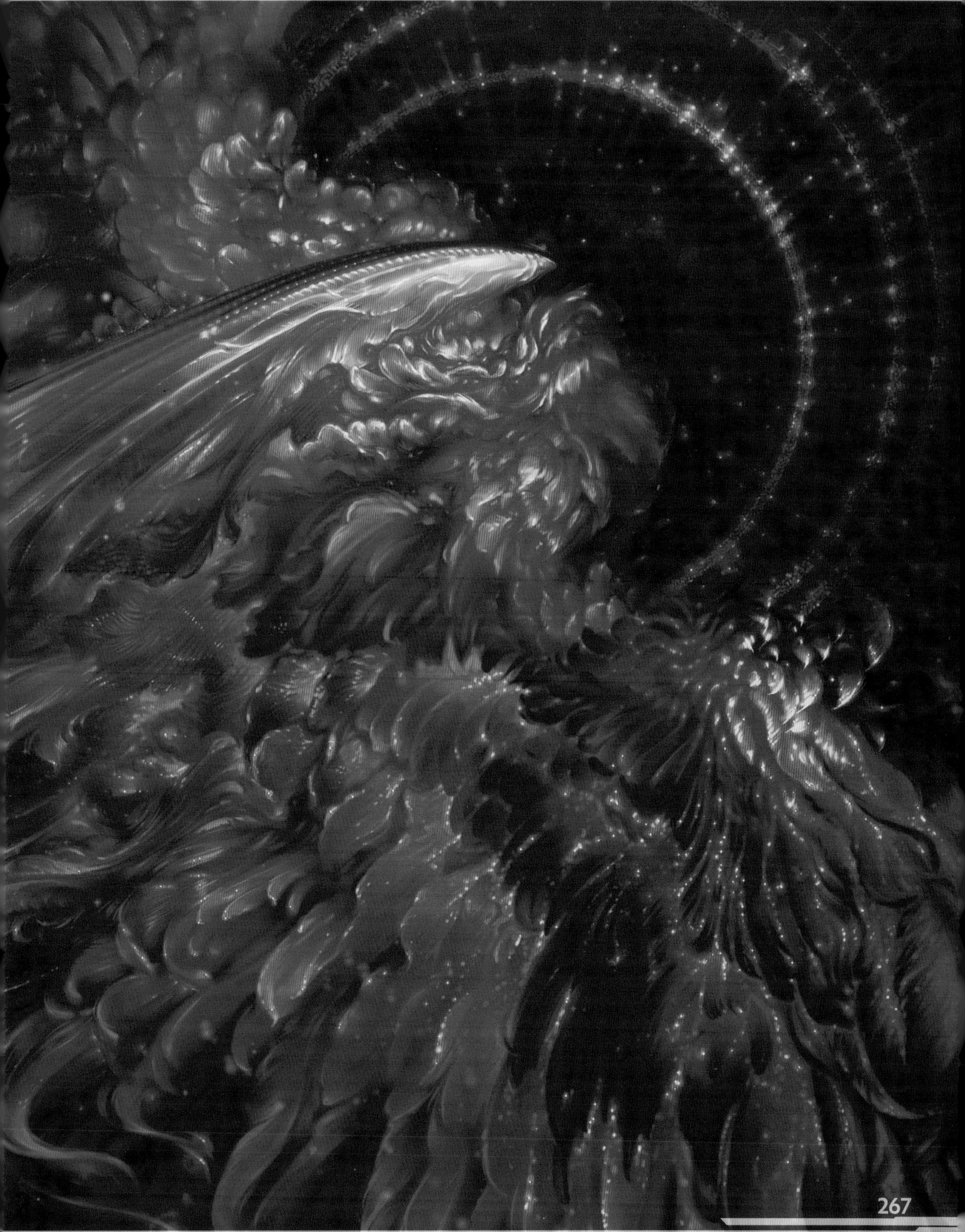

GLOSSARY

A

ACM or Anti-Clone Movement: An informal tag for a growing number of organizations including groups who see clones solely as competition for human workers as well as groups who want to grant clones the same rights as human beings.

Agroplex: An extremely large farm factory, from "agricultural complex." Much of the former rain forest of eastern Ecuador, southern Columbia, and western Brazil is now devoted to agroplexes in order to feed New Angeles' inhabitants.

Airbelt pack: Device used by authorized personnel, such as security forces, to maneuver in zero-G interiors, such as within the Midway Station complex. It consists of two jet packs worn at the center of gravity, one in front, one behind, and controlled by a small virtual panel above the front unit. It draws in air and expels it in a jet, so it cannot be used in vacuum.

AIVM or accelerated in vitro maturation: The vat-growing technique used by Jinteki to rapidly mature clone specimens from zygote to adult.

American: The most widely spoken language in the United States of America, derived from English. Also used to refer to a citizen of that nation.

Android: An artificially intelligent humanoid construct. Androids are distinct from robots or other constructs because androids possess "strong" AI. There are two known types of androids: synthetic bioroids and organic clones.

Anglo: A broad term for an English- or American-speaking culture, especially from the mainland United States and Atlantica.

Arcology or "ark": A "city-in-a-building." Tall structures—rising as much as a thousand stories or more—sometimes called "towers." Arcologies house a community complete with offices, schools, shops, malls, an internal security force, and everything else required for living. Generally used by upper-middle class to upper class, arks are a feature of all megacities, including New Angeles. Often resented by lower classes, who aren't allowed inside.

Artificial intelligence or "AI": Created intelligence, usually in the form of a machine or program. So-called "weak" AI (also known as "simulated intelligence" or "SI"), while sophisticated and sometimes convincingly realistic, falls short of true human-level intellect. "Strong" AI, or true intelligence, is currently only possible by utilizing brainmapping technology to emulate a human brain. Androids are the primary application of strong AI.

B

Backscatter or "backscat": For backscatter X-ray. Also called "peek-a-boo" units. Security device that renders a subject nude on-screen in order to detect weapons or packages hidden beneath clothing. Modern refinements include the capacity to use focused ultrasound beams to search body cavities and internal organs as well.

Bangers, also "streetbangers": Youth gangs common in the megacities. Often engaged in criminal activity, especially illicit drugs and sexies, and may go on crime sprees just for thrills.

Beanstalk, aka "New Angeles Space Elevator": An approximately 72,000km-tall elevator construct tethered in New Angeles. Its stations include the Root (aka "Earth Station"), Midway, and the Castle (aka "Challenger Planetoid"). A cost-effective way to reach Earth orbit and points beyond. Named for the story of Jack and the Beanstalk and the man who built it, Jack Weyland.

Bioplas: Biodegradable plastic commonly used in packaging and disposables.

Bioroid: A type of android manufactured by Haas-Bioroid. Bioroids are robotic humanoids built of metal, plastic, silicon, and other synthetic materials. Their artificially intelligent brains are neurally channeled from braintapes derived from human brains.

Blackout, the: A period of global disruption to regional networks that precipitated a sharp market downturn. The more secure architecture of SYNC's Network eventually replaced the Internet as a result.

Brain-machine interface or "BMI": A device that allows direct communication between a user's brain and a computer system. Commonly in the form of a so-called "brain-net" (for a wearable BMI) or a "skulljack" (a BMI cybernetically implanted in the user's brain). BMIs are a new technology originally developed by the military. The first consumer-grade models are just entering the marketplace, and they are most popular among Netcriminals and the younger generation.

Brainmapping and braintaping: Brainmapping technology was developed to scan the human brain to aid with the diagnosis and study of brain disorders. It has now become a general term for brain scans of many types. Braintaping is a specialized, extremely detailed application of brainmapping technology that allows the user to develop a working (but currently imperfect) copy of the original brain. Both technologies are essential for the creation of strong AI and androids.

Brain-net: A type of BMI that is worn over the top of the skull. Brain-nets often resemble a "net" of threads linking contacts that are placed on the skull. Sometimes the net is built into a helmet, hood, or other piece of headgear.

Buckminsterfullerene, also "buckyballs": A carbon molecule (C_{60}) with a number of unique properties. The term "buckyballs" has become the root of a number of terms for nano-scale carbon assemblages. Named for Buckminster Fuller, whose architectural designs resemble the shape of the molecule.

Buckyfilm: A frictionless surface comprised of buckyballs, nano-scale carbon-atom spheres in an electrical field matrix.

Buckyweave: A type of material, immensely strong, consisting of woven, open-ended buckytubes—carbon atoms in tube form. The space elevator began as a buckyweave strap lowered from synchorbit to the top of Cayambe.

Burnout: Popular term for a person burned out by drugs, drink, or BMI malfunction.

C

Camdrone: Weak AI–powered drones with holo/threedee recording capabilities. Deployed by NBN to supplement its surveillance network and get Netcast-quality footage.

Chatspace: A virtual space where remote users can meet and chat comfortably. May or may not be fully rendered as a virtual environment.

Chromehead: A member of a subculture devoted to ostentatious cyberware as a fashion statement.

Cleansuit: Smartsuit used to avoid contamination in either direction, e.g. for doctors treating infected patients, or for police personnel investigating a crime scene.

Clone: A type of android manufactured by Jinteki Biotech. Clones are organic beings with largely human DNA and are customized for a variety of purposes. Despite their organic nature, they are classified as machines.

Clone-tel: A slang term, derived from "hotel for clones," for the nicer, more expensive version of clone barracks.

Comm: Short for radio communication.

Constructorbot: A generic term for construction robots, usually non-android and most often in space, used in large projects such as the Beanstalk.

Credaccount: The common name for a bank account, which is accessed electronically by readers. "Bank account" implies a physical building—a bank—while most financial transactions and records are purely electronic.

Credit: Usually refers to the Titan Transnational Credit, a corporate-backed multinational virtual currency. Can also be used broadly to mean money in general.

Cybernetic, also cyberware: Although still sometimes used in its archaic sense (especially among academics), the term generally refers to machinery designed to be implanted in the human body, either to replace or to augment organs, limbs, and other body parts. Can be used as an adjective (as in "cybernetic heart") or as a noun (as in "the organ grinders removed his cybernetics").

Cyberspace: A broad term for the state of mind runners and other BMI-users experience when they directly interface with the code behind the Network. Compare "meatspace."

Cyborg: Slang term for a person with cybernetic implants.

D

Dataddiction: A recently recognized dependence on constant input and connection to the Network. Dataddicts are uncomfortable when not presented with a constant stream of distractions and updates to social media, newsfeeds, and other sources of information.

Datacard: Like a business card, with printed information, but containing embedded electronic data. Usually used to download contact information into a personal PAD or wrist implant.

Datastick: A general term for computer storage space in a small, hand-portable format. Some are wireless, but most require insertion into a port to exchange data with a computer.

Datastream: A feed or stream of information in cyberspace.

Depresh: Slang for "depressurized," as in "I know I depreshed him," said of a man shot in a firefight on the lunar surface.

Disenfrancisto: Spanish slang for impoverished New Angelinos who have voluntarily (or involuntarily) renounced normal society and legitimate employment.

Door-sec: Door security. Generic term for secure access to businesses or even homes. May have a human operator, or it may be entirely robotic. Frequently, backscatters are used to scan incoming people for weapons. Bars or other facilities with a rough clientele frequently employ g-mod human bouncers with a backscatter screen inside an armored booth at the door.

Down-Stalk: Slang term for traveling down the Beanstalk, toward Earth.

Dropship: Any of a large variety of transatmospheric spacecraft used to access orbit, the Beanstalk, the Moon, or other points on Earth (or even in the same city). Some take off vertically from space launch facilities; others are carried aloft from commercial airports by a carrier jet. The term includes "subs" or "sub-o flights": commercial suborbital flights that can reach any place on Earth in less than ninety minutes.

E

e-Pharm: Electronic addictives or hallucinogen, the electronic version of illegal drugs. Includes sexies and snuffies, as well as programs designed to create general feelings of euphoria and well-being. Legal versions have therapeutic value.

F

Forspec: Police slang for "forensic specialist."

Full-immersion: A means of directly experiencing data via a brain-machine interface. A rare new technology with limited popularity as an entertainment medium, such as sensies, most users of full-immersion technology are Net-criminals known as "runners."

G

G-mod: Slang for "genetic modification." Used to refer both to the modifications themselves and to people who have received such modifications.

Gog: Genetically altered hog. Derived from the genome of *Sus domesticus*, the domestic pig, it is designed to grow quickly on an inexpensive diet. Designed for meat production only, it has a small head, no eyes or ears, and only a rudimentary nervous system.

Gripslippers or grip-booties: Special booties that fit over normal shoes and keep a person's feet adhering to a carpet-covered floor. They are issued to visitors at low-G stations such as the non-rotating portions of the Castle Club.

Guidelight: Lights that direct a visitor through an unfamiliar facility. They appear as moving or blinking arrows, or as moving streams of colored light, on walls, floors, or ceilings.

H

Hand Time: An implant time function that displays across the back of the hand or on the wrist when a spot on the hand is pressed. Like the earlier term "wrist watch."

Helium-3 or He-3: An isotope of Helium vital to the modern fusion power industry. Vanishingly rare on Earth, He-3 is relatively abundant on the Moon.

Holography: Routine tech used to project virtual displays and keyboards, signs, advertising, guidelights, and the like.

Holoscreen: Another term for virt.

Hopper, also "skyhopper": A common personal vehicle powered by hoverfoil rotors and capable of short-duration flights ("hops"), usually from hopper pad to hopper pad within a single city. Normally flown by autopilot. There are many variations, including minihoppers and cargo hoppers.

I

Ice, rarely "intrusion countermeasures electronics": Software devoted to protecting computer servers and devices from unauthorized access. Ice often uses "weak" AI.

Icebreaker, rarely "intrusion counter-countermeasures": A program used for circumnavigating or deactivating ice and gaining access to secured data. Often uses "weak" AI.

ID, also "ident": Personal digital identification, usually accessible via wireless prompt. Often worn as a tag implanted under the skin, usually in the back of the hand. Carries basic contact information such as name and eddress. Also carries credaccount data for financial transactions, with coded security software at various levels to prevent unauthorized access. Although not legally required, IDs are in such widespread use that failure to respond to an ID ping can arouse suspicion with security personnel.

Infobroker: A dealer in information.

J

Jacker: A slang term for a hijacker of vehicles, cargo, etc., who frequents the Martian frontier in particular.

Jack in/out: To (dis)connect to the Network via full-immersion technology (i.e. a brain-machine interface).

Journo: A slang term for a journalist.

K

Keychip: Chip with embedded credentials to activate hoppers, open doors, etc.

Klick: Military slang for a kilometer.

L

Las-scanners: Technology used to map a room or other area by means of laser imaging software (lidar).

Loony: A slang term for a person who lives on the Moon. Usually refers to those who consider themselves Lunar citizens first, or to participants in the Lunar Insurrection.

L-square: From "elevated square." A pedestrian plaza suspended from one or more arcologies, usually quite high above ground level.

Luna: Official U.N. name for Earth's moon.

M

Mag-lev: Short for "magnetic levitation." A type of train that is magnetically suspended just above the track, allowing for very high speeds due to a reduction in friction. Mag-lev trains use magnets for both lift and propulsion.

Makerbox: A threedee printer or other commercial-grade automated assembly device. High-fidelity makerboxes are available for rent in commercial makerspaces.

Martian: When used by an Earther, typically refers to a human being living on Mars. Members of the Martian clans reserve the term Martian for people who were born on Mars.

Meatspace: A slang term used by Netcriminals for the material, physical world experienced in waking consciousness. Compare "cyberspace". A number of allied terms are derived from it (such as "meat body").

Med-techs: Short for medical technicians.

Megacorp, also "corp": A generic term for a megacorporation, generally an international corporation. Many have their headquarters in New Angeles to minimize legislation or oversight by Earth governments.

Megapolis, also metroplex: Proper terms for very large cities, especially for several cities that have merged into enormous metroplexes covering, for example, the northeastern U.S. seaboard from Boston to Washington (BosWash), or the coastal city running from San Francisco to San Diego (SanSan).

Mem-running: Slang term for recording, selling, transmitting, receiving, and playing memories and/or emotions from someone else. Derived from braintaping technology, it allows the user to experience the memories and emotions of another person. A commercial product for a large and fast-growing field of popular entertainment, it usually has the specific meaning of illegal memory transfers involving sex or murder.

Meta: An exotic rocket fuel—metastable N-He64. Lasers excite helium atoms into a metastable quantum packaged with nitrogen within insulated high-pressure tanks. Heating causes the helium to revert to its normal state, releasing the tremendous energy used in packing the stuff.

Monocam: Originally "monocle camera." An eyeball-sized camera worn over one eye that allows reporters like Lily Lockwell to record and upload vid and audio while interviewing a subject.

N

Nanodisplays: Super-small display technology used in creating smartfabric for use in fashion and newsrags.

NEO: Near-Earth orbit. Used generally to refer to anything orbiting at the altitude of the Challenger Planetoid or less.

Neoluddites, also "luddies" or "neos": Groups that protest (at times through sabotage) pervasive and intrusive modern technologies, the use of simulants in the workforce, the loss of privacy, and other social issues.

Network, the: When used as a proper noun, refers to the publicly accessible network of computers and machines that connects the entire Earth and most of the Moon.

Neural channeling: A term for the process of constructing a new brain template by combining and editing existing connectomes. The resulting brain can be constructed using proprietary Haas-Bioroid manufacturing techniques as a bioroid brain.

Neural conditioning: A term for the process of using (usually non-invasive) BMI technology to stimulate a clone brain, which shapes its connectome, until it matches the desired braintape.

New Angelino: A citizen of New Angeles.

Noirie: A subculture that celebrates retro fashion and media, especially that surrounding the early twentieth century. Fedoras, trench coats, and pinstripe suits are emblematic of this culture.

Nosies, also "news-nosies": Slang for reporters by people who don't like them—like the police.

O

Off-gridder: Someone lacking an ID who cannot (or refuses to) use the Network.

Optical brain: A collection of extremely advanced optical circuitry and microcomputers that is interconnected according to the specifications of the bioroid's brain-taped template. Forms one half of a bioroid's parallel brain.

Optical computer: A computer that uses fiber-optics, lasers, and other light-speed systems. Now mostly outdated compared to quantum computing.

Organ grinders: Criminals who engage in kidnapping for the purpose of harvesting organs and cybernetics to be sold on the black market.

P

PAD or personal access device: A handheld or wearable device that allows aud and vid calls, access to the Network, data storage, and numerous applications. Common uses include pinging IDs and managing credaccounts. Some come with a small screen and are primarily voice controlled, but the more expensive units project holographic virts and respond to gestures.

Panic button: An app on PADs that summons police or security forces in the event of an emergency.

Parallel brain: The two-part brain of a bioroid. Sometimes refers specifically to the traditional quantum processor component of the two-part brain.

PAT or public access terminal: Prepaid public computer kiosks available for use by the minute. Used by *disenfrancistos* or off-gridders who need access to the Network but lack an ID or credaccount. Exploited by Netcriminals and others for their relative anonymity.

Ping: Generic term for electronically accessing a person or system, usually by transmitting a signal which is detected by the target's ID and retransmitted back, sometimes with additional information.

Plaza level: The above-ground network of slidewalks, elevated plazas (or "L-squares") suspended between glimmering arcology spires, and rooftop gardens or shopping malls that create an artificial and carefully manicured floor to the life of the rich and comfortable. Typically refers to the specific stratum within New Angeles.

Plascrete: Building material—extremely tough—employing zero-G manufactory techniques. Used in floors, building walls, as pavement, and so on.

PriRights: Citizens privacy rights group. Dedicated to fighting invasion of privacy by government and corporations.

Prisec: A slang term for private security as commonly employed by corporate facilities and arcologies.

Q

Quantum computer: A computer utilizing quantum mechanics, which includes the ability for data to be in a superpositioned state. Dramatically more powerful than digital computers or even optical computers, but expensive and difficult to maintain.

Quito Accord: This international agreement made law the lease of New Angeles from Ecuador to the United States.

It also declares both the Beanstalk and the Moon's Heinlein Station to be a part of New Angeles, and it grants the New Angeles Police Department jurisdiction there.

R

Rag, also "smartrag": Portable display screen, consisting of dark gray cloth with the consistency of very fine silk. Human touch generates a static charge that stiffens the material into the consistency of cardboard, and it will display information from a separate computer, or it can be programmed to display data held within its own internal memory. Crimping a corner causes it to revert to cloth. Cheap and disposable. Newspapers use the material, and are commonly called "newsrags."

Reader: Tiny, portable device—sometimes worn as jewelry, or it can be inserted and worn as an implant under the skin, typically on a person's wrist—that reads another person's credaccount information from his ID and deducts a fee from it automatically. Used for electronic funds transfer.

Regolith: A layer of loose material covering solid rock. Although technically found on all three inhabited worlds, in common use always refers to Lunar regolith, which is rich in helium-3.

Respirocytes, also Freitas respirocytes: Artificial red blood cells first described by nanotech pioneer Robert Freitas in 1996. Greatly improves the blood's efficiency at transporting oxygen and carbon dioxide, allowing non–genetically modified humans to breath comfortably at high altitudes, or to survive for up to an hour without breathing at all.

Ristie: From "aristocrat." Street term for wealthy people living in their high-sec tower communities.

Rivera Declaration: Leased the Root and the surrounding vicinity from Ecuador to the Weyland Consortium.

Runner: A slang term for Netcriminals who use full-immersion interfaces to break into secured computer networks.

S

SAM or Simulant Abolitionist Movement: Political grassroots organization that believes the use of clones is tantamount to slavery, that clones are humans beings denied their civil rights, and that clone-slavery should be

abolished. Not the same as the ACM, which includes many groups that don't think clones should have human rights.

SEA or Space Elevator Authority: The local governing body of the Space Elevator under New Angeles jurisdiction through the New Angeles Transit Authority. Created by the Treaty of Heinlein.

Sec: Short for security.

Seccam: Short for security camera. Small and unobtrusive camera providing views of either restricted or public areas. Police officers and other authorized personnel can type a code into their PAD to pick up the vid and audio from any such camera.

Secretary: Also sometimes avatar or PA, for Personal Assistant. A software app, often running on a PAD. Serves as an electronic secretary, keeping track of appointments, remembering key bits of information, and interfacing with the virtual world. Among other things, it can answer vid calls, displaying a lifelike image of the owner, either to recite a short message (which can be tailored, by name, to different individuals) or to interact with a caller for fairly simple conversations. Many can pass the Turing test, at least for simple topics. By law, it must identify itself as an AI. "Secretary" can also be used for any weak AI construct, although such use is technically inaccurate and can be confusing.

Sensies, also simsensies or sensiesofts: Entertainment media that includes other senses than audio and visual. Illegal versions are sometimes called sexies or snuffies. Virtual reality and full-immersion versions both exist.

SEZENLA, also SEZ: The Special Economic Zone of Ecuadorian New Los Angeles. New Angeles.

Simulants: A slang word for androids or any artificial being.

Skulljack, also skullport: Slang term for an implanted BMI with a physical connection port. The terms are used interchangeably for both the male and female ends of the system.

Skylanes: Lanes in the sky dedicated to hopper traffic.

Skyway: Public hopper line used by commuters and tourists to get around New Angeles by air.

Slidewalk: Moving sidewalk in public places, such as between arcologies or in shopping centers.

Smart-: Used as a general prefix to indicate an object or system that has been integrated with the Network to improve its function.

Smartfabric/smart-threads: Fabric using nanodisplays used to design smartsuits.

Smartgun, smartbullet: A gun (or bullet) with self-aiming capabilities. Sometimes integrated with a user's BMI. Smartbullets also integrate identify friend or foe (IFF) technology .

Smartslick: One type of smartsuit commonly worn as a small package on the shoulders behind the head. When it senses rain, it unfolds to cover the head, shoulders, and upper body, refolding itself when no longer needed.

Smartsuit: General term for a set of clothing that has been made of smartfabric or otherwise enhanced with modern computer technology. Smartsuits may have cosmetic functions, such as integrated viewscreens or a color-change feature, or useful functions as in smartslicks.

Snobhob: A groupie or hanger-on of the rich social set. Part of the entourage of wealthy celebrities. From "hobnob."

Spanglish: A language mixing English and Spanish grammar and vocabulary. The lingua franca of New Angeles.

Stunstick: A short baton extended by a flick of the wrist up to two meters; it delivering a powerful electrical jolt to incapacitate a human. Used by security forces instead of firearms anywhere a stray bullet could prove catastrophic, such as the Midway platform.

Subbing: Slang term for taking a commercial suborbital flight, as in someone "subbing in" from NeoTokyo. The regularly scheduled flight from Dulles to New Angeles takes about thirty minutes.

Subsid: Slang term for "subsidiary," as in business subsidiary.

Synchorbit, also synchronous orbit or "Clarke orbit": An orbit—for Earth 22,300 miles or about 36,000 kilometers high—where the orbital period exactly matches one Earth rotation. Objects in synchorbit appear to hang motionless above one spot on Earth's equator, which makes the Beanstalk possible. Midway, on the Beanstalk, is located at synchorbit.

Synthskin: Artificial skin used in bioroids or cybernetics.

Sysop: A system operator or Network administrator, usually corp-employed.

T

Tab-rag: From tabloid rag. A type of newsrag long on thrills, shock, and scandal, and generally short on good journalism.

Threedee: Entertainment media that projects a third dimension around the viewer, typically through immersive holography.

Three Directives: The foundational rules of bioroid programming set by Haas-Bioroid to ensure the androids never harm humans.

Transhumanism: A philosophy devoted to exploring the limits of the definition of humanity. Transhumanist thought embraces cybernetic and genetic modification and may include bioroids, clones, and even bodiless AI within its definition of "human."

Transplas: An extremely tough, clear plastic widely used as a replacement for glass. It can melt at high enough temperatures, but will not break. It can be mixed with photo-responsive elements to turn dark under direct sunlight.

Treaty of Heinlein: At the end of the Worlds War, this armistice ended the hostilities of the War and created the Martian Colonial Authority. It also ceded additional authority to the Space Elevator Authority and limited the extent of U.S. federal authority in New Angeles affairs.

Tri-maf, also t-maf, triad-mafia, or TM: Generic term referring to various mafias—especially Sicilian, Russian, and American—as well as the Japanese Yakuza and Chinese triads. These frequently work together as a loose-knit, global organized crime community.

Tube-lev, or tube train, tube-lev car, or tube mag-lev: Subterranean mag-lev train systems, used widely on Earth and the Moon as mass transit. Tube-lev trains are extremely fast because their tunnels are kept at or near vacuum, which combined with the mag-lev system means the cars endure virtually no friction or air resistance. Tube-lev or tube-leving can be used as a verb: "He tube-leved to the Root." The New Angelino tube-lev system is known as the Metro.

Turfed: Slang used by NAPD officers to refer to times when their cases lead onto corporate or private property where private security forces have legal jurisdiction but cops do not.

U

U.N.: Usually refers to the Universal Nations. Occasionally refers to the precursor United Nations, if referencing a time period before the Worlds War.

Undercity: General term for the poorer, lower levels of a city, including subterranean parts of the city.

Up-Stalk: Common term for moving up the Beanstalk, away from Earth.

V

Vid or vidscreen: Any display screen, but especially high-definition wall screens.

Virt: A display screen projected holographically in the air.

Virtual keyboard: A keyboard or other input device displayed holographically by PADs and other devices, which senses finger positions as a person types.

W

Waldo: A remote-operated (or sometimes AI-piloted) robot.

Warroid: A bioroid specialized for combat. Currently theoretical.

Wetware: Slang term for brains and other organic ("meat") processing units.

Wetwork: Usually illegal paramilitary operations, including sabotage and especially assassination.

Worlds War, the: The first war in human history to extend past Earth's atmosphere. It began with the Lunar Insurrection and lasted until the Treaty of Heinlein. Battles occurred on Mars and Luna. On Mars, also known as the Colony Wars and later the War for Martian Independence.

Wylder: A subculture that uses genetic modification and cosmetic surgery as fashion statements, usually by incorporating animal features into their bodies. The name derives from Wyldside, a nightclub in Heinlein where the movement began.

Y

Yellow Jackets: Slang for Space Elevator Authority Security Forces. They wear bright yellow jumpsuits, hence the name. Sometimes disdainfully referred to as "elevator mercs" or "rent-a-cops."